The Rise of Milwaukee Baseball

The Rise of Milwaukee Baseball

The Cream City from Midwestern Outpost to the Major Leagues, 1859–1901

Dennis Pajot

McFarland & Company, Inc., Publishers
Jefferson, North Carolina, and London

LIBRARY OF CONGRESS CATALOGUING-IN-PUBLICATION DATA

Pajot, Dennis.
The rise of Milwaukee baseball : the Cream City
from midwestern outpost to the Major Leagues,
1859–1901 / Dennis Pajot.
p.   cm.

Includes bibliographical references and index.

ISBN 978-0-7864-3951-5
softcover : 50# alkaline paper ∞

1. Baseball — Wisconsin — Milwaukee — History — 19th century.
I. Title.
GV863.W52M557   2009   796.35709775'9509034 — dc22   2009023167

British Library cataloguing data are available

©2009 Dennis Pajot. All rights reserved

*No part of this book may be reproduced or transmitted in any form
or by any means, electronic or mechanical, including photocopying
or recording, or by any information storage and retrieval system,
without permission in writing from the publisher.*

On the cover: Bay View Club; antique border ©2009 Shutterstock

Manufactured in the United States of America

*McFarland & Company, Inc., Publishers
Box 611, Jefferson, North Carolina 28640
www.mcfarlandpub.com*

Acknowledgments

Naming people always leads to leaving someone out, so I will try my best to avoid this. My first and most appreciated acknowledgment must go to my wife, Angie, who was very patient while I spent time at libraries and in front of the computer, leaving too many household chores to her.

I cannot thank and praise enough the staff of the Milwaukee Public Library for their assistance with everything I asked for and needed during this project. From the small assistance with copiers, to the larger help of digging for misplaced microfilm and locating obscure material, the staff never fell short of excellence.

I also thank the SABR members who spent time looking up small details and proofreading chapters for me; these include Priscilla Astifan, David Black, Bob Buege, Mark Dugo, Dennis Dagenhardt, Marc Fink, Jack Little, Mark Pestana, Denis Repp, Bob Tholkes, and Jim Wagner.

And finally, I need to acknowledge the baseball players of the era. The great, the not nearly great, and everyone in between. Those players who set fine examples, and those who led troubled lives. All the players, named and unnamed, who played in Milwaukee in the nineteenth century set the stage for what we play and watch today. This book is dedicated to them.

Table of Contents

Acknowledgments	v
Preface	1
1. Organization and War (1859–1864)	3
2. The Cream City Club (1865–1868)	8
3. Many Changes (1869–1874)	23
4. The West Enders (1875–1877)	34
5. Milwaukee: A National League City (1878)	53
6. Amateur Era (1879–1883)	72
7. A Tale of Two Dead Leagues (1884)	92
8. Setting the Foundation (1885–1887)	111
9. Western Association (1888–1890)	140
10. A Baseball War and Merger (1891)	175
11. Allotment and Bicycles Deaden Interest (1892–1893)	192
12. Picking Up the Pieces (1894–1896)	205
13. The Mack Years (1897–1900)	244
14. The Final Step (1901)	288
Appendices:	
I: Results of Cream City Match Games with Top Clubs	309
II: Results of West End Games with Top Clubs, 1876–1877	310
III: Batting and Pitching Statistics	312
IV: Players on Milwaukee's Minor League Teams, 1884–1900	314
V: Amateur Clubs Organized in Milwaukee, 1860–1899	317
Chapter Notes	333
Bibliography	341
Index	343

Preface

This is an exploration of the early history of baseball in Milwaukee, beginning around the time that Milwaukee received the nickname the Cream City due to the distinctive cream-colored bricks produced by its brick companies. Milwaukee's part in the early history of baseball is not well known even to the city's many baseball buffs, of which I am one. Many baseball history books give a very brief account of Milwaukee's nineteenth century forays in the National and American leagues, as well as the city's partial seasons in the Union Association and American Association. However, very seldom are any details given on the specifics of how Milwaukee received a franchise in these major leagues, or any details on why a franchise was lost. The scope of the present work includes the entirety of Milwaukee's early baseball history, from its amateur beginnings through the 1901 season, when the Brewers were part of the American League's inaugural lineup of self-declared major league teams.

Although Milwaukee had four brief tours in the major leagues, the majority of the city's time in organized baseball in the nineteenth century was in the minor leagues. It must be remembered that throughout much of the second half of the nineteenth century, the differences between minor leagues and major leagues could be subtle, in regard to both talent and pay. Although the struggles of independent and minor league clubs were unique to each city, these struggles were not often categorically different. Frequently, in fact, they were intertwined, the loss of a team having to be absorbed by its league rivals, whose success at the gate relied in no small extent on league stability. Having explored the baseball past in a city that straddled the line between major and minor league, we're better prepared to consider the experiences of other cities—Midwestern cities in particular—and the development of urban baseball scenes in general.

It should be pointed out, too, that in the second half of the nineteenth century, Milwaukee was already a large, prominent city. In terms of population, it occupied roughly the same position as it does today in relation to other U.S. cities. (According to the U.S. Census Bureau, Milwaukee was in 2000 the 19th largest city in the county; its ranking in the last half of the nineteenth century rose steadily from 20th in 1860 to 14th in 1900.) And like Cincinnati, Chicago, and St. Louis, the city had a large population of German immigrants, a group heavily represented in baseball during the last part of the nineteenth and the first part of the twentieth centuries. Adding to Milwaukee's baseball significance is the major role it played in the Western League's evolution into the American League.

Much of the information in this book was mined from the local newspapers of the day, a rich repository of game accounts and commentary. The papers do present certain challenges, however. Reporters attended the games infrequently, working instead from secondhand accounts. Predictably, these early reports were sometimes directly contradicted by one or more reports published in rival papers, and for the historian it can be difficult to disentangle fact from fiction. Where I was unable to resolve inconsistencies, mention has been made in either the text or the endnotes. As the sport grew in popularity, newspaper reporting improved, and papers seldom contradicted each other factually, though continued efforts to "scoop" the competition occasionally led to the publishing of incomplete or inaccurate stories. By the 1890s nearly every rumor was put into print, complete with splashing headlines. It has to be remembered that loyalty for the home team ran very high, a fact familiar to anyone who has read widely in the sporting papers of the period.

In the pages ahead, amateur and semiprofessional clubs are given significant attention, perhaps more than some readers might expect. These clubs and the players on them were at times as popular as their modern major league equivalents, and certainly they formed the foundation of baseball in Milwaukee. Some of the men on these teams went on to prominence in the big leagues, and these individuals—the Abner Dalrymples, Clark Griffiths, and Connie Macks—are discussed in many books that cover this period. A few more can be found in the batting or pitching registers of baseball encyclopedias. Others never made the big leagues, however, and are long forgotten to the baseball world. I hope this work will bring them back for at least a fleeting moment, for they did a lot in their way, to help baseball in general and Milwaukee in particular.

1

Organization and War (1859–1864)

Milwaukee's roots in baseball can be traced back to 1836. In an article in the *Milwaukee Sentinel* of April 19, 1892, it was reported E.W. Edgerton of Milwaukee had presented to the Old Settler's club a baseball that young fellows of Milwaukee had used to play a ball game in 1836 on a flat field about where the present southeast corner of North Milwaukee and East Mason Streets is located. It was reported the ball (now in the possession of the Milwaukee County Historical Society) was made by Mr. Edgerton himself, and the cover had been sewn on by Mrs. Edward Wiesner, wife of the first shoemaker of Milwaukee. Many years later, in an article in the *Milwaukee Journal* of March 3, 1946, Franklyn Baltes, secretary of the Settler's Club of Wisconsin, told a reporter the ball was made of yarn wound around a rubber center, the cover being cut in quarters. Among Edgerton's companions on the playing field in 1836 were Talbot Dousman, Enoch Darling, James Patterson, Morgan L. Burdick, Paul Vieau, George C. Tiffany, George Hosmer, Henry Hosmer, Thomas Homes, William Sivyer and Charles James—many familiar Milwaukee pioneer names. According to the 1946 *Journal* article the primitive game played in 1836 was probably "one, two, three or four old cat." Franklyn Baltes also told the reporter there was a legend from pioneer days that the city's founder, Solomon Juneau, once umpired a primitive ball game.

The first report of baseball being played in Milwaukee played under a set of rules more recognizable to the modern eye is found in the Thursday, December 1, 1859, *Milwaukee Daily Sentinel*. The paper wrote:

BASE BALL — This game, now so popular at the East, is about to be introduced in our own city. A very spirited impromptu match was played on the Fair Ground, Spring Street Avenue, yesterday afternoon six on a side, with the following result:

	1st innings	2ddo.	3rddo.	Total
J.L. Hathaway	0	2	3	5
F.J. Bosworth	4	0	0	4
C. Steele	4	0	3	7
F. Clarke	3	2	3	8
L. Sexton	3	2	3	8
H. Sands	1	1	3	5
F.J. Hill	1	2	0	3
	16	9	15	40
R. King	2	2	3	7
Cap. Coate	3	0	3	6
H. Barclay	1	2	0	3
J.P.C. Cottrill	2	1	1	5[sic]
C.B. Allen	2	2	3	7
J. Ledyard	2	1	3	6
F.H. Hill	1	0	1	2
	13	8	14	35

Should the weather be fair, the return match will be played on the same ground, at 2 o'clock this afternoon.

There is no record of this Thursday match, but we have scores for matches on December 10 (33 to 23 in favor of Hathaway's club in 5 innings, with 9 on a side) and December 17 (54 to 33, again in favor of Hathaway's club in 5 innings, with 10 men on each side listed in the box score). The last match was played in weather that "was blustering and patches of snow on the ground made it slippery and rather too damp for sharp play."[1]

Organized baseball began in Milwaukee on April 3, 1860, when "a lively game of Base Ball came off"[2] between a group of gentlemen at the old Fair Grounds on Spring Street (Wisconsin Avenue at North 13th Street) in the afternoon. That night the first baseball club in the city was founded, the Milwaukee Base Ball Club.

One reason for the new interest in the sport was a "new code" of playing rules. Milwaukee was beginning to play under the same rules the eastern clubs, ruled by the National Association of Base Ball Players, were using. The new game was "altogether ahead of the old fashioned game, both in point of skill and interest."[3] Of course, the eastern playing rules were not accepted by all. The Janesville club still played under the old set of rules. "Waiting for a ball to bound, instead of catching it on the fly ... and various other methods of play adopted by this new fangled game, looks to us altogether too great a display of laziness and inactivity to suit our notions of a genuine, well and skillfully conducted game of Base Ball." The cry of some was, "Give us the old fashioned game or none at all." [4]

The Milwaukee Base Ball Club organized under the new rules of play. After a few more practice sessions, the club met at C.B. Allen's on Main Street (now North Broadway Street) on April 20 "to elect members, complete their organization, and choose sides for the first regular match of the season"[5] to be played the following afternoon.

The club met for their practice and matches on Wednesday and Saturday afternoon at the Fair Grounds. An omnibus left the corner of Main and Wisconsin streets ten minutes beforehand to take members and spectators to the grounds. The public, especially ladies, were invited to watch these games. The club also held monthly meetings, at C.B. Allen's, to discuss the sport.

For at least a month, the Milwaukee Base Ball Club was the only show in town, prompting the *Sentinel* on May 9, 1860, to write an editorial on the subject, asking, "How soon are we to have other clubs formed in this city? The game is a manly one, and deserves all encouragement. There ought to be three or four Base Ball Clubs organized in our city this season. Who will follow the lead [of] the Milwaukee Base Ball Club." On the heels of the editorial, the Wisconsin Base Ball Club was organized in the city. Very little is known about Milwaukee's second club. The secretary of the club, George L. Gransberry, ran an article in the local papers, but nothing else is known.

In May of 1860 Abraham Lincoln was nominated as the Republican candidate for president, and the Republican-minded editor of the *Sentinel*, Rufus King, sadly neglected baseball in the paper. Likewise, the Democrat-backed *Daily News* ran articles promoting Stephen Douglas. But the sport continued to grow in popularity. It should be noted here that the ball players of this age were not the youth of the city, but middle-aged men, and usually of some means. It was strictly amateur in those days, played more for social fun than all-out winning. A check of the City of Milwaukee directories from the period reveals the occupations of some of the known members of Milwaukee's baseball club. The two outstanding names are Rufus King, editor of the *Milwaukee Daily Sentinel* and later a general in the U.S. Army; and William Beck, the chief of police. There were also eight lawyers, four men in produce, two clerks, a land agent, a salesman, a book store owner, a cattle broker, a grocer, a music store operator, a U.S. marshall, a soldier, a newspaper man, a travel agent, a policeman, and a laborer. The members of the club would pick up sides and play a match. The first known score of one of these match games is from June 7, 1860. The match was first scheduled for Wednesday, June 6, but postponed by rain until the next afternoon. The nine-inning affair ended in a score of 33 to 27, played "lively and well contested."[6] Unfortunately, newspaper space in those days was scarce. Papers usually consisted of only four pages, with the first page having local and political articles, along with advertising. The second usually ran all advertising and the final pages were dedicated to the commercial activities of the day. Baseball was lucky to receive three or four lines a couple of times a week, so the results of most match games went unpublished.

The match game of Saturday, June 16, was reported nicely in the local newspapers. The *Sentinel* of June 18, 1860, reported "an excellent match ... contested with great spirit and some capital play shown." The June 17 *Daily News* went one better. It reported "a close and well played" game with "much interest manifested, not only by the players, but spectators." Most important, it gave a box score of the game, the first known of the Milwaukee Base Ball Club.

		HL	R			HL	R
J.L. Hathaway	3b	4	3	R. Chandler	p	3	4
J. Sexton	c	4	2	W. Beck	c	3	4
J.P.C. Cotterell	1b	3	3	H. West	cf	2	5
W.G. Tisdale	cf	4	2	G.W. Adams	1b	2	4
J. Davis	2b	3	3	G.C. Ledyard	lf	0	4
R. King	p	2	3	N.H. Hempsted	rf	1	2
W.A. Prestiss	rf	3	3	D.G. Hooker	3b	6	4
Jno. Pierson	ss	2	4	T.B. Elliot	2b	4	2
C. Caverno	lf	2	4	F. Vanvalkenburg	ss	6	0
			27				26

J. L. Hathaway, Capt. 0 6 4 0 6 0 0 8 3–27
R. Chandler, Capt.   3 0 3 1 6 3 4 5 1–26
C.B. Allen–Umpire   C.P. Hewitt–Scorer

The Milwaukee Base Ball Club was "improving rapidly" and "beginning to play in first rate style."[7] In short, the club was "well worth seeing."[8] It received a boost in June when one of its members, J.W. Ledyard, visiting New York, sent back six bats and twelve baseballs made to the specifications of the National Association.

To celebrate the Fourth of July the club played a match of baseball, beginning at ten o'clock in the morning and lasting until the mid-afternoon, stopping only for lunch. The club continued to practice and play match games after the holidays, but these contests were only between members of the team. It is known that early in the season the Janesville club wanted to play one of the Milwaukee teams. In early August a special meeting was called by the secretary of the Milwaukee Club, C.B. Allen, to act on a challenge sent by the Chicago Base Ball Club. Apparently neither game was played. The first known match with an outside club was on September 1, with the newly formed Excelsior Base Ball Club of Milwaukee at the Fair Grounds. The Excelsiors stomped all over the Milwaukees, winning 48 to 13. "The first 2 or 3 innings were well played and closely contested. After that, the play of the Milwaukee nine fell off while that of the Excelsiors improved."[9]

The return match was to be played September 8. The match went unreported, however. The tragic sinking of the *Lady Elgin* in Lake Michigan, which resulted in the loss of 300 lives, took the lion's share of newspaper coverage for the next few weeks. Little else is known of the remainder of the 1860 season other than the Excelsior and Milwaukee Base Ball Clubs continued to play match games well into October.

Unfortunately, the Civil War was not good for organized baseball in Milwaukee, or anywhere for that matter. We know the old Milwaukee Base Ball Club existed in 1861, after the outbreak of conflict. On May 25 the club had a game at the Camp Grounds on the lakefront. This is the only mention of baseball found the entire year. It could have been that newspapers did not consider baseball coverage essential or proper in the midst of a war. Or it could be that the teams disbanded.

Rufus King — newspaper editor, army general, and organizer of the first baseball team in Milwaukee.

However the game did not roll over and die. The National Association of Base Ball Players, formed in 1857, had 62 clubs in membership in 1860. Although attendance did drop through the war years (34, 32, 28 and 30 in respective years) it did not stop functioning.[10]

The game of baseball was played differently in the 1860s in some ways than we know it today. Nine players had been on each side since the rules were put into place in 1842. Only since 1857 was a game set at 9 innings — originally the game lasted until a team scored 21 runs.

The diamond had base paths 90 feet long, but the pitcher only stood 45 feet from home plate, throwing the ball underhand from within a box — on flat ground. In 1863 strikes and balls were called. Three bad pitches — after warnings from the umpire — gave the batter first base.[11] To the batter's advantage, foul balls were not counted as strikes. Until 1864 a fair ball could be caught on the first bounce for an out; however, foul balls continued to be ruled an out if caught on the bounce.

No equipment was used by the players; fielders did not wear gloves and the catcher had no protective gear to wear. Playing without equipment caused more injuries than today, as this fictitious conversation from the *Buffalo Commercial* between a ball player and a gentleman implies.

"What is the matter with your finger?"
"Struck by a ball and drove up," was the reply, "but it is a noble game."
"Precisely, and your thumb, it is useless is it not?"
"Yes, struck with a ball and broken."
"That finger joint?"
"A ball struck it; no better game to improve a man's physical condition, strengthens one's sinews."
"You walk lame, that foot, isn't it?"
"No, it's the — the — well, a bat flew out of a players' hand, and hit my knee pan. He had the innings."
"One of your front teeth is gone?"

"Knocked out by a ball; an accident though."
"Your right hand and your nose have been peeled, how's that?"
"Slipped down at second base, a mere scratch."
"And you like this kind of fun?"
"Glory in it, sir. It is a healthful game, sir."[12]

Then, as now, baseball did not have the sporting field to itself. Horse racing was probably the most popular spectator sport of the period, and was reported heavily in the newspapers. Prize fighting was also very popular. The 42-round bout between Sagers and Heenan was reported round by round in the *Daily News*. Boxing, however, did not meet with the approval of everyone: "They had a prize fight at Grand Rapids.... Two citizens of Wisconsin anxious to show the world that this state had just as big fools in it as any other, stood up and pounded each other before an admiring crowd."[13]

People of the 1860s were also happy to part with their money to watch billiards. Maybe the amusement sign of the times was the shooting gallery at Phillip Lawrence's, where one could "enjoy a pleasant hour popping at Jefferson Davis."[14]

Baseball was not yet a major spectator event. It was still a social event, the only spectators being friends and wives of the participants. At least in Milwaukee this was the case. Back in summer of 1858 the *New York Times* reported on a game at the Fashion Race Course on Long Island, between selected players from the Brooklyn and New York clubs, at which "a nominal charge of ten cents for each person entering the grounds, and an additional fee of twenty cents for each one horse, and forty cents for each two horse vehicle, to defray expenses"[15] would be charged. The surplus funds of this match were to go to the widows and orphans of the fire departments of the two cities. It was estimated 8,000 people witnessed the match.

Probably the most popular participant sport of the day was cricket. It received a good share of newspaper space and teams even played opponents as far away as Illinois. But ball players made their intentions clear that they would make baseball a very popular sport in the near future. They did not "intend to let cricket bear off the honors and amusement alone."[16] Clearly it was time for baseball to bloom here. Anyone could find an open field and play. One of the local papers hit the nail on the head: "Only favored localities can enjoy certain sports, as rowing. Many require expensive apparatus. Our ball games can be played everywhere, and cost nothing; while the exercises they give are among the best than could be invented and every way interesting and delightful."[17]

In 1862 baseball again attempted to organize itself in the Milwaukee area. A movement was started to organize a baseball club and a quoit club (a game similar to horseshoes) on the route of the Horse Railroad (Lake Shore) and play two games a week. The plan met with favor, but no evidence can be found that it ever came about. With the war continuing, baseball became non-existent in the press for three long years.

2

The Cream City Club (1865–1868)

The war finally came to an end with General Lee surrendering to General Grant in 1865. It was time to rebuild in the South. In the North it was a time to live a normal life again. This meant the revival of baseball. The resumption of the sport began in Milwaukee on August 10, at Camp Scott, with a number of members of the Old Milwaukee Base Ball Club on hand and a sprinkling of "green hands" thrown in. Two of the members from the old club were chosen captains and made the sides. Chief Beck's side scored 20 runs and "swung their hats in token of triumph," as H.H. West's team could only tally 19 runs.[1] Everyone wanted to see a new ball club organized in the city and hoped to see it challenge some of the clubs already formed throughout the state.

Hope became reality when on August 17, 1865, a baseball club again was organized in Milwaukee. H.H. West (co-owner of S.C. West & Co, bookseller and stationer at Water and Michigan) was elected the president; James G. Jenkins (an attorney for the City of Milwaukee), secretary; and Samuel Howard (a lawyer and notary public), treasurer. This club continued to practice at Camp Scott, but never met the expectation of playing outside clubs. And it had the opportunity to do so. As mentioned above, other clubs were being formed in Wisconsin. In late September, the Dubuque County Agricultural Society offered "a heavy silver ball of regulation size, a prize to the club declared to be the champion Base Ball Club of the northwest." The second prize was a silver mounted rosewood bat.[2] The Milwaukee club was urged to go, but declined, content to stay home.

In October this ball club either reorganized or disbanded and was replaced by a new club. About 30 players met at H. Bentley's (a local tavern on Michigan Street) on Friday, October 6, "for the purpose of permanently organizing a club." H.H. West, president of the first club, was selected chairman of the meeting and J.B. Brown chosen secretary. A committee of four, consisting of Chairman West, J.A. Bryden, Morgan Furlong and J.B. Brown, was appointed "to draft a constitution and by-laws for the government of the club."[3] After discussing the organization, the players adjourned to meet again the following Tuesday. At the second meeting permanent officers were elected. West continued on as president, and James Jenkins became vice president. Richard Allen was elected treasurer and O.G. Leach was made secretary of the club. Martin Larkin, J.A. Bryden, and Frank Smith became directors of the club. Thus on October 10, 1865, the Cream City Base Ball Club of Milwaukee was formed. The new club met with great favor in the press.

During the formation of the Cream City Club, rumors were spreading that the team was to play a match game against the Chicago Base Ball Club. The contest was to be held in Chicago on October 19, but never was played for reasons unknown. Once again the club only practiced among its own members. In the November 7, 1865, *Sentinel*, nine members of the Cream City Club published the following notice:

We, the undersigned nine players, will play any other nine players of Base Ball in the City of Milwaukee, on Wednesday next at Camp Scott, at 2:00 P.M. sharp. J.B. Brown, A. McFadyen, M. Larkin, J.A. Bryden, R. Rickerson, Riordon, T.L. Mitchell, Chandler, Wood.

This challenge had not been published twelve hours when it was met.

We, the undersigned, hereby accept the challenge offered by J.B. Brown & Co., and will play them a match game on the day proposed. O. Gilbert Leach, Frank A. Smith, G.P. Kelly, Geo. O. Sweet, Morgan Furlong, James B. Jenkins, A. Jackson, H.H. West, E.M. Moore.[4]

If one looks closely at the reply, one will find these men are also from the Cream City Club. In accepting the challenge they "had little thought of vanquishing their opponent as they merely accepted for the purpose of having a match game before the season should become so far advanced as to prevent any more play."[5]

The match came off, almost as scheduled. Two of the Jackson party did not show up, and two men from the crowd were picked to play for that side. One of these was old reliable Chief of Police Beck. Only seven innings were completed before darkness set in, and the score stood 36 to 30 in favor of the challengers. Only one complaint was made regarding the affair; the *Daily News* thought it was much too noisy a contest.[6] Here is the box score of the Cream City's first match game.

CHALLENGED (JACKSON)		O	R	CHALLENGERS (BROWN)		O	R
Jenkins	p	2	4	McFadyen	p	4	4
Jackson	c	3	4	Brown	c	2	6
West	1b	2	4	Riordon	1b	1	4
Kelly	2b	1	4	Wood	2b	1	3
Whitcomb	rf	3	1	Mitchell	3b	3	4
Leach	ss	3	2	Larkin	ss	2	5
Beck	3b	5	1	Bryden	rf	3	3
Smith	cf	1	5	Chandler	cf	3	3
Sweet	lf	1	5	Rickerson	lf	2	4
			30				36

Runs Per Inning: 1 2 3 4 5 6 7 Total
Brown, Capt.   4 2 4 11 4 10 1   36
Jackson, Capt. 3 4 7 2 9 4 1   30
Fly Catches—Jenkins 1, Jackson 4, Kelly 1, Brown 1, Larkin 2, Chandler 2
Umpire—Ed. M. Moore of Fond du Lac City Base Ball Club.

The city was blessed with lovely weather that year and a few more challenge match games were played between Cream City members. As the scores of these games are read, it is apparent baseball was beginning to change. The younger members of Cream City Club continued to beat its older members. This change is important, because soon winning would become more and more important to the team members.

❊ ❊ ❊

Before the next season even started, fans were calling on the Cream City Club to secure decent playing grounds. It was noted that other cities had suitable grounds, so why should "Milwaukee strip herself of her urban character and confess that she is not in advance of any country village or four corners ... [Cream City] will not be put to the humiliating ordeal of inviting their adversaries to play a match at ball on a corner lot or some wretched place cut up by ravines and ditches, and obstructed by fences and trees."[7] Nevertheless, the club opened the season at old Camp Scott in April 1866.

The Cream City Club held its first meeting of the new season at the city attorney's office on April 6. Ten members were present and the only business transacted was the admitting of nine new members. Further action was postponed until the next month's meeting when new club officials were elected. Two of the new elected officials were H.R. Hayden, president, and Frank S. Smith, secretary. Unfortunately, the names of the other officials are lost to time. The actual playing season began on Saturday, April 14, with a fine practice on moist grounds.

As practice games continued, it was hoped the club would play outside competition. A step was taken in that direction in May when the club "directed the secretary to send a challenge to the Capitol City Club (Madison) for a match, to be played as soon as convenient."[8] Within a few days the Capitol City Club accepted and a match game was set for May 30, at Camp Randall in Madison. The nine players selected to go to Madison practiced with the rest of the club and most were confident of a Cream City win. But not the *Daily News*:

> We doubt whether Milwaukee will ever take a prominent position in the field sports, from the fact that it is an impossibility to get any good practice out of those who participate in these sports.... The Cream City Base Ball Club seems destined to learn in the same way, (as the Milwaukee Cricket Club) in defeat. Having sent a challenge to the Capitol City Club, the nine selected to play the match have never had an afternoon's play together, and some of them are not at all up in the rules of the game, having played it but two or three innings.... By the time our club is beaten in two or three matches they will get better practice, no doubt.[9]

The first nine tuned up for the big game with the second nine, who "proposed to give them a tussle for the mustering," winning 45 to 23 in seven innings, as George Redington hit three home runs for the victors.[10] Clearly, the Cream Citys were as ready as they would ever be.

The club left the day before the match for Madison "in high spirits." One reason may have been news that the young ladies of Madison were "preparing to crown the victors after the manner of the ancient Grecians."[11] The game itself was no contest. McFadyen's pitching "completely demoralized the Capitol City nine."[12] Cream City had consistent scoring, topped with 15 runs in the eighth inning to win 48 to 15 in the two hour and thirty-five minute game. We are fortunate enough to have a box score of the first outside match of the Cream City Club.

CREAM CITY CLUB		HL	R	CREAM CITY CLUB		HL	R
Redington	c	4	7	Fuller	c	4	2
McFadyen	p	4	6	Bates	p	3	2
Sweet	cf	3	7	Dorn	sf	1	2
C. Smith	1b	0	5	Hopkins	1b	4	1
Kelly	3b	1	4	Fisher	2b	3	2
West	lf	5	4	Curtis	3b	3	1
Jackson	sf	5	4	Reynolds	lf	4	1
F. Smith	rf	3	5	Dickson	cf	3	1
Larkin	2b	2	6	McCormick	rf	2	3
			48				15

Passed Balls: Fuller 8, Redington 5. Fly Catches: Fuller 4, Reynolds 1, Bates 3, Dorn 6, Hopkins 2, Curtis 1, Redington 5, C. Smith 1, Larkin 2, McFadyen 1. Missed Balls: McCormick 2, Reynolds 1, Kelly 1[13]

Shortly after the victory Cream City was invited to a tournament in Rockford "to contend for the championship of the Northwest," and prizes including "a magnificent gold ball, regulation size, a gold mounted rosewood bat, silver pitcher, silver mounted belt, goblet, tea set, and a number of other beautiful and costly presents."[14] Ball players were still amateurs, so prizes such as these were given at the various tournaments. But amateurism around the country was being pushed to the limit; Milwaukee was no exception. What the *Milwaukee Daily News* of June 19, 1866, suggested might have been within the technical rules of the Association, but it was not in the pure amateur spirit:

> We suggest to such of our citizens as desire to see a champion club in Milwaukee, the proprietary of assisting the fund of the Cream City Club. It will be impossible for the players to pay the entire necessary expenses and devote their time to play, as many of them are dependant upon salaries for their support. We have the material for the championship nine of the West if those interested in manly sports will but lend a little material aid.

It is not known if the Cream City Club supported this view, but nothing was published to counteract it. The club must have accepted the aid given, for it was reported "the Cream City Club has been pitted against first class players, and their backers will look with much interest for the result." It was clear the club had "obligations to our citizens who have so liberally assisted them financially."[15] At this monthly meeting the club decided to attend the tournament and change its practice site from Camp Scott to Camp Reno (on North Cambridge near North Farwell Avenue, north of Brady), which was considered a better site because the street car ran near by.

The nine selected to make the trip to Rockford were A. McFadyen, Redington, Chandler, Sweet, Kelly, Larkin, N. McFadyen, C. Smith and Frank Smith. It was the biggest event that had happened in Milwaukee's baseball existence. Even the trip to Rockford was reported in the press. Readers were informed how the players stayed in Kenosha, waiting for train connections to Rockford. They were "bent on having a good time" and toured the city. Their first stop, as could be expected, was "at a lager beer establishment, where they satisfied their voracious appetite for that much sought for commodity in short metre."[16] Once in Rockford, the team captains met at the Holland House and a playing schedule for the ten clubs was arranged by lots, as follows:

FIRST DAY (June 27)
Detroit vs. Pecatonicin   Atlantic of Chicago vs. Bloomington

SECOND DAY (June 28)
Julian of Dubuque vs. Cream City   Forest City of Rockford vs. Shaffer of Freeport
Empire of Freeport vs. Excelsior of Chicago

The first day's action saw Detroit and Bloomington emerge victorious. The following morning Cream City took the field in its new uniforms. A bright crimson shirt with a silk breast plate "richly embroidered" bearing their name, blue pants and a white cap trimmed in blue made the boys dressed in the "prettiest uniform upon the ground."[17] Julian hit first and scored a run, but Cream City came back with five in its half inning. By the end of four innings, Julian had closed the gap to 9 to 8. But in the 5th inning Archibald McFadyen hit a triple and scored on a long drive by Kelly, and by the time Cream City was retired from the inning, the score stood 15 to 8. Dubuque never recovered and lost 23 to 15 in an interesting game, though "there was a lack of excitement, and of nerve so necessary to good playing."[18] It was also a slow game, occupying three hours five minutes. Forest City and Excelsior won that afternoon to complete first-round play.[19]

The next morning Cream City met Rockford to begin the second round of play. Fifteen-year-old Albert Spalding, later to make baseball's Hall of Fame, pitched for the Forest City Club, as it jumped to an 11 to 6 lead after the first three innings. In the fourth, Redington — the star of the game, not having a passed ball in an era when passed balls were numerous — took three foul balls at his catching position to turn things around for Milwaukee. Cream City slowly chipped away at Rockford's lead, scoring three times in the ninth to win 14 to 13. The loss knocked Forest City from the tournament and gave Milwaukee at least a third-place finish. The two crack teams of the tournament, Chicago and Detroit, finished in the afternoon; Chicago won 16 to 10 in the "best game perhaps ever played in the west."[19]

Controversy started the third round of play. Detroit, whose conduct was "marked by an ungentlemanly assumption of superiority" throughout the tournament, thought it should be in the game even though the team had lost a game. The Detroit protest was disallowed and play was finally called. Cream City came into the game with Bloomington (which beat the favored Atlantic) in rough shape. Catcher Redington's hand was "almost totally disabled." The short fielder's right arm was hurt, and McFadyen's pitching arm was so stiff he could not complete the game. After dropping behind 2 to 1, Cream City roared back in the second inning. Larkin beat a throw home when the Bloomington catcher dropped the ball, but the umpire declared him out. In the same inning the umpire called what appeared to be a home run a foul ball. These decisions cost Cream City four runs. "Larkin bore the unjust decision against himself with perfect equanimity," but Cream City called for a new umpire and Bloomington agreed to it. Milwaukee scored seven runs in the fourth and five in the fifth to take a 13 to 3 lead. "Five to one was offered on Cream City with no takers" because it was obvious to the crowd the team was beginning to tire. Bloomington scored seven runs in the fifth inning, "stealing bases one after another" on the tired and disabled crew, and pulled ahead of Cream City going into the ninth inning. Cream City scored three in the ninth to tie, but Bloomington made three tallies in their final try to win 23 to 20.

Bloomington went on to play the Excelsiors and lost, giving the Chicago team the gold ball. Cream City had won as many games as either opponent, but the loss gave them the third place silver ball and silver mounted bat award. Redington took home one of the individual play prizes, a silver goblet, for the second best thrower. The club returned from its first tournament "with an assured position as Base Ball players of which Milwaukee need not be ashamed."[20]

Shortly after their return, Cream City received another tournament invitation. This tournament, in Bloomington, had various team prizes, as in Rockford, but had an added unusual feature. The captains of the worst-beaten club and tournament champion team picked nine players apiece, worst-beaten club's captain to choose first, and played for a sweepstake prize valued at $50. The tournament was held in September, but Cream City did not attend. However, the club received two challenges for return games with Capitol City of Madison and the Forest City Club of Rockford.

Baseball was again gaining popularity fast, and many fans, including "the fair sex, of which Milwaukee has her share,"[21] were expected for the matches. Camp Reno, where both games were to be played, was prepared for a large crowd and room was even made near the grounds for those who wanted to watch the game from their carriages. The *Daily News* of August 22, 1866, with its flair for excitement, gave a reason for the surge in popularity of the game:

> The days of the knightly tournaments, when clad rider met and vanquished his opponent in lethal conflict, have passed away forever, but the spirit which moved men to such contests still remains, and in this more advanced age manifests itself in a more mitigated and peaceful form.

2—The Cream City Club (1865–1868)

Cream City Club—Milwaukee's first powerhouse club, three-time state champions. Standing: Archie McFadyen, E. Clinton Welles, Martin Larkin, W.L. Dodsworth, Clarence Smith, Geo. Redington. Seated: James Wood, Frank Smith, Chas. Norris (courtesy of Milwaukee County Historical Society).

The Forest City game was played first, on Wednesday, August 22. A large crowd gathered and saw Cream City win the toss and take the field. Rockford drew first blood in the opening inning and Cream City did not score in the first two innings. With the score 1 to 0 in the third, Rockford exploded for 12 runs. Milwaukee never recovered and lost 24 to 10. After the game the Cream City players gave three cheers to the victors and the Forest Cities returned to Rockford even with Cream City for the 1866 season.

The following day the Madison club visited Milwaukee for its match. An improved club since the two teams' first meeting, it was still no match for Cream City. The Capitols held their own through the first three innings, leading 9 to 5, but things turned around in the fourth as Milwaukee scored eleven runs in "handsome manner" to put the game out of reach. The final score was 44 to 15, Plummer of Cream City scoring seven runs and all others scoring at least four times. An interesting note to the game was the umpiring. No person could be found unconnected with either team qualified to umpire, so Frank Smith of Cream City was chosen by lot. After the match both clubs "adjourned to the Newhall House, where they dined together."[22]

For more than two months the club was idle of match games. In October a challenge was sent to the Forest City Club to play a match game in Chicago, but arrangements were never made. Finally, in November, a match game was set up with the Whitewater Club to end the season. Fans (who could obtain half-fare tickets if going to the match) and players took the train to Whitewater, where Cream City won 29 to 11. Cream City had ended its first full season "without a doubt the champion club of the state."[23]

Readers should not get the impression that the Cream City Club was the only team in existence in Milwaukee at the time. All around the state clubs were forming, and Wisconsin's largest city had its share. Cream City was the best and naturally received the most publicity. A club was to be organized early in the spring of 1866 on Milwaukee's south side to compete with Cream City for the championship of the city, but no mention was ever made of it during the season. Cream City had a second nine that not only practiced with the first nine, but played outside clubs. In its games with the first nine, it received odds of five outs to three. On one occasion the second nine beat the first nine so badly it was wondered if those odds were too much and should be changed. However, the odds were continued in further matches. Plans were then made for the second nine to play in Columbus in the fall. The southsiders, who were "never very far behind the rest of mankind in anything,"[24] organized a club in July, calling themselves the Badger State Club, and practiced once a week. In August they played the Cream City's second nine at Camp Reno. In the fall, two more clubs were organized: the Actives and the Badger Boys Club, composed of the junior ball players of the city.

New clubs joined the field in 1867. A club composed mostly of Germans organized and called themselves the Teutonia. Two of the better junior clubs were still the Badger Boys Club and the Cream City second nine, with the teams frequently playing each other. The Badgers were a colorful crew, uniformed in blue pants "tastefully trimmed with white," a white shirt with blue trim, and a white "skull cap, scored with blue."[25] They even challenged the Madison Junior Club and the Columbus team. In July the Badgers Boys Club changed its name to the Independence Club and continued its match games. Cream City's second nine improved, playing match games with the first nine, until they were good enough to beat the Independence Club 106 to 56, hitting 19 home runs; "in several instances the ball was sent a distance of two or three blocks."[26]

Other clubs began to form that summer. In June the Union Base Ball Club played the South Side Badger Boys Club, losing 34 to 27. The South Side Badgers even thought they might be able to beat Cream City after a little more practice. In July they too changed their name, to the Excelsiors. The Stars and Atlantic Club, composed mostly of young men, formed in July, along with the Arctic Club. The west side lads also formed a club, calling themselves the Alert Club, and even beat the Excelsiors. On July 29, 1867, the Independence Club (formerly Badger Boys) again changed its name to the Cream City Juniors, and became affiliated with the senior club.

In August new clubs made their entrance. A new club, the Muffins, beat the old Active Club 46 to 45, in a game played after dark. Even a match was planned between some men in the city whose only qualifications were that they knew nothing of the game. The Monitor Base Ball Club was organized and played on Monday, Wednesday and Friday evenings at the Second Ward Park. Another new club, the Nationals, popped up. Even in the fall new clubs were organized and played the game. The Juneaus, from the First Ward, and the Inmans also established themselves. In October the Washington Club played the Monitors at Quentas Park (Seventh and Walnut), losing 49 to 16. But the Cream City Club was clearly the class of the field and the darling of the press.

✳ ✳ ✳

The Cream City Club opened the 1867 season as usual at Camp Reno near the lakefront. Practices were light because snow fell until late April. Again new officers were elected to run the club for the coming season. E.H. Chandler was elected president and the stars of the previous year, George Redington and Archibald McFadyen, were elected vice president and secretary. Richard Allen became the treasurer, and Martin Larkin, James Wood and James Bryden were the directors of the club. The first order of business of the new season was a challenge by the Atlantic Club of Chicago, but it was turned down at that time. Practice continued through May, to "brush up from the effects of the winter's inaction."[27]

In June the Beloit Olympians were challenged by Cream City, and they accepted immediately. The match was set in Beloit for June 19. The new edition of the Cream City first nine—consisting of Redington and McFadyen as the battery, James Wood, Clarence Smith, C.G. Holister and R.H. Chandler in the infield and E. Clinton Welles, Martin Larkin and Rickerson in the outfield—left confident for Beloit. The Olympians soon stuck a pin in the champion's balloon. Cream City fell behind 12 to 3 after three innings, and Beloit scored eleven tallies to ice the cake in the fourth. At the end of nine innings the score stood 43 to 25, and Cream City was advised to "stop blowing and go to work."[28] The papers came down hard on the team now that they thought Cream City had lost the championship of the state. However, McFadyen set the record straight. In his letter to the editor printed in the June 22, 1867, *Sentinel*, he rightly pointed out that the loss meant "nothing but the possession of the ball" because under National Association rules it took two wins out of three match games to decide the championship. He thought the boys did their best and had "expected at least fair treatment at the hands of the press of their own city."

Soon Cream City received another challenge from the Atlantics of Chicago for a game on July 4 in Milwaukee. This time Cream City accepted the Chicago challenge. The game was promised to be the best of the season, the two clubs being "nearly evenly matched."[29] Newspaper coverage of the game was by far the best to date. An inning by inning description was given, as two entire columns of page one were dedicated to the game. The Atlantic Club wasted little time, jumping on Cream City for ten runs in the first inning, and the score stood 23 to 2 after Chicago batted in the third. Cream City roared back with eleven tallies in the third, and crossed home 13 more times in the fourth to close the score to 29 to 26. At that point the Atlantics changed pitchers and again built a comfortable lead. By the final inning the hometown boys were "getting the hang" of the change pitcher, but fell short, losing the match 48 to 45. Some modern-day fans who complain about the length of today's ball games can take some comfort in knowing the 2,000 people who went to the match watched a five-hour game, the late innings played in rain and heavy winds.[30]

Cream City had made a very good showing against the strong Chicago club and decided to play the Beloit team again in an attempt to decide the state championship. A challenge was sent, but the Olympians refused to come to Milwaukee, offering to play the match in Janesville. Cream City "properly" refused. They were still the champions and would remain so until "that title is wrestled from them by manly generous rivalry, and when that is done none will offer to the victors warmer congratulations than the Cream City Club."[31]

By now Cream City was considered one of the four best clubs in the Northwest, along with Excelsior and Atlantic of Chicago, and Forest City of Rockford. This qualified them to play in the big tournament in Chicago, in late July. The famous Washington Nationals were in Chicago and the tournament was centered on that fact. Local fans were encouraged to go to the tournament, and Goodrich's Steamboat Line issued round-trip tickets, including meals and state rooms, for $3.00. The Chicago and Northwestern Railroad also issued tickets at excursion rates. It was hoped Cream City would have a chance to show its strength to the Nationals in Chicago, as the Nationals could not come to Milwaukee, having to be back in Washington by the end of the month. Unfortunately, Cream City did not have a chance, for on the second day of the tournament the Atlantic Club flexed its muscles and defeated Cream City 71 to 20, knocking them from the tournament. A few weeks after the tournament, the Atlantic Club sent Cream City some silk flags with the inscription:

CREAM CITY CLUB
FROM ATLANTIC CLUB
CHICAGO, AUGUST 10, 1867

Also sent were a number of fine bats and balls "as a testimonial of their respect for the members of the Cream City Club."[32] The flags were then put on exhibition at the chamber of commerce for a day.

The club was definitely in a lull after the Chicago tournament. They had not won a match with an outside club all year and were so demoralized they did not honor a challenge already sent out. However, they were brought around by the prospect of the announced State Base Ball Tournament in Beloit, scheduled for the first week in September. A tournament had been in the wings all summer. In July Cream City had considered holding one in Milwaukee. At a meeting of the State Convention of Base Ball Players at the Myers House in Janesville on July 23, W.S. Wescott, president of the association, discussed plans for the tournament to be held in that city during the county fair, the second week in September. At least 13 clubs intended to attend, but plans apparently fell through. In late July the *Fond du Lac Reporter* wrote the tournament would be held if its citizens could produce $500 worth of prizes.[33]

Beloit succeeded in gaining the state tournament by offering a guarantee of $1,300 for prizes. Driving Park, which had a large grounds enclosed by an eight-foot fence, was selected for the games. Fifteen hundred people could be placed in the enclosed seats, with tents and tables set up for the reporters and scorers. Some thought Fond du Lac would have been a better site, but sentiment was still high against Beloit because of the earlier refusal of the Olympians to return to Milwaukee. The tournament was open to all clubs in the state belonging to the association before September 3 (the beginning date of the tournament). The clubs were divided into four different classes. Senior clubs were placed into first and second classes. The first class senior club winning the tournament received $100 in "greenbacks" and a gold mounted bat, total value about $200; second and third place prizes were also awarded, valued at $150 and $125. Similar but less expensive prizes were awarded in the second class senior division, junior division (players under 18 years old) and pony clubs (under 15 years old). Out of state clubs were invited and allowed to compete for prizes among themselves.[34]

Cream City increased its practices to every day except Sunday, and officially notified the state secretary that it would attend the tournament, and also would send its junior club. More than twenty clubs were entered, and the tournament opened with the pony and junior clubs. The Cream City Juniors lost to Beloit's Juniors 41 to 40, in a game called after seven innings because of darkness. The juniors appealed to play a full game, but were turned down. Whitewater then defeated Beloit to start senior division play.

The senior Cream City Club had changed a few faces for the Wisconsin tournament. The backbone of the club remained the same, but Lawe was the new pitcher, and McFadyen moved to shortstop. Two new players, Otis and Middleman, were inserted at second base and right field. This team met the Madison Capitols, winning 32 to 13 in six innings. The next day Cream City beat Whitewater 44 to 19 in five innings to take first place in the first class senior division. Clarence Smith pitched a good game for Cream City, as "our country cousins could not believe that a ball could be pitched with such velocity."[35] Redington won an individual prize for best catcher of the tournament for his all-around play and by throwing a ball 340 feet and one inch. The outside competitor prize went to the Belvidre Club of Illinois. For the second year in a row Cream City held the championship of the state.

The state tournament closed Cream City's play with outside clubs. Although the club did receive an invitation from the North Star Base Ball Club of St. Paul to attend their tournament, Cream City declined to go because of the young men's business commitments during "the busy season."[36] The only action Cream City saw the rest of the 1867 season were match games between the first and second nines through October.

✳ ✳ ✳

As a prelude to its third full season, Cream City displayed the various trophies it had won during the previous two years, with promises of more to come. Shortly, an announcement was made that in April the State Base Ball Association would hold its annual meeting in Milwaukee. Four of Milwaukee's ball clubs would attend the convention — the Monitor and Juneau clubs, Cream City and the Cream City Junior Club. As a rule was in effect that a member club of the Association could not play a club that was not a member, these four clubs became the major powers of Milwaukee baseball in 1868.

The Monitor Club became the first to elect its new officers. George Abert became president of the club and his brothers, H.W. and Byron, were elected as secretary and a director of the club. Andrew Hoffer was chosen vice president, with David Knab named treasurer. Adam Schnure and Johan Mathias became the other club directors. The club was composed mostly of Germans, and records can be found for only two games played that year. In June the Monitors were beaten by the Juneau Club 32 to 19, and they defeated the Diamond Club of Waukesha by a score of 75 to 8 in August.

The Cream City Juniors soon followed suit, electing H.T. Griffin and Charles Norris as president and vice president. The secretary duties were given to D.C. Green, and J.G. Steever became the treasurer. Steever was also a director, along with J.A. Whaling, R.K. Smythe, Joseph Hooley and R.W. Dunlap. Griffin and Dunlap were appointed delegates to the state convention, and Smythe the captain of the team. Shortly after the convention the Juniors changed their name to the Atlantic Club and continued play under that name. The Atlantics were still a junior club (players all under 18 years old) and played other junior clubs of Milwaukee. In July they also traveled to Waukesha, losing to the Diamond Club 51 to 31.

The Juneau and Cream City clubs did not elect permanent officers until after the convention. In late April Juneau members elected J.T. Dunn as their president and Martin Bray to the second highest office. T.C. Tinker held the post of secretary and C. Trapshuh was elected as treasurer. Directors of the club were J. Conney, E. Moran, M.H. Seery and E. Phillips. The Juneaus were a promising young club. They played Cream City's second nine several times, winning by eight runs on one occasion. The club became good enough to be challenged by the Capitol City Club of Madison in June and again in September.

The defending state champion Cream City Club held its annual election of officers on May 5, at the Library Building (corner of East Wisconsin Avenue and Broadway). M.A. Boardman became Cream City's fourth president, while H.R. Hayden and Frank Smith were elected vice president and secretary. Richard Allen continued as club treasurer. The new club directors were J.H. Wood, E.C. Welles and A. Middleman. Allen and R.H. Chandler were made the delegates to the state meetings. Cream City underwent minor reconstruction, adopted a new constitution, and hoped to "win fresh laurels"[37] in the new season.

The city still had many other clubs that did not wish to attend the upcoming convention. These clubs existed "merely for the purpose of affording their members healthful exercise and not with a view of entering the field to contend for the mastery against other clubs,"[38] and will be discussed shortly.

Twenty clubs were expected to attend the convention, but when roll call of the clubs ended, only nine had shown up for the convention at the Kirby House (North Water and East Mason streets) on April 1. Besides the four Milwaukee clubs, the Bower City and Western Star clubs of Janesville, Capitol City of Madison, Everett Club of Oshkosh and the Whitewater Club were in attendance. A committee on credentials was appointed in the afternoon, after which the delegates adjourned to play a game of ball at Camp Reno. The convention convened again at 7:30 that night and elected the following officers for the ensuing year:

President	H.R. Hayden, Milwaukee
Vice President	B.K. Otis, Oshkosh
Secretary	M. Treadway, Madison
Treasurer	C.E. Church, Janesville
Directors	C.W. Kimball, Green Bay; C.C. Danforth, Whitewater; F.M. Dorn, Madison

The most important rule to come out of the convention was aimed at Cream City. It stated the club holding the gold ball, symbolizing the state championship, must accept all challenges for the championship within 30 days of receipt, and must give ten days notice as to where and when the match would take place. A club still had to win two out of three match games to decide the championship. The delegates also let it be known that any club could join the association by notifying the state secretary and paying the customary fee. The National Association had also adopted a new rule for 1868 stating that the size and weight must be stamped on the ball before a game to avoid confusion.

Cream City opened its season in May by playing the field at Camp Reno in a few practice games and practicing with its second nine. The club played its first outside match of the season on Monday, June 22, against the famous Atlantic Base Ball Club of Brooklyn. The Atlantics were the defending national champions and were making a western tour. When Cream City officials learned the Atlantics would stop in Chicago for a match, they sent an invitation for a game in Milwaukee, which was accepted. Of course, Cream City did not entertain any visions of upsetting the mighty Atlantics, but wanted to give the people of Milwaukee a chance to see "the best base ball playing in the United States."[39]

The Atlantics were no ordinary ball club. Their players were astoundingly good. Seven of them were good enough to eventually play in the major leagues. Twenty-seven-year-old Charley Smith, who captained the team, also played third base. Three years later he was to play 14 games for the New York Mutuals of the National Association of Professional Base Ball Players. Dickey Pearce, the senior player at age 32, later played seven years in the big leagues. Joe Start, the Brooklyn first baseman, starred in major league baseball for 16 years, batting higher than .300 seven times and gaining the nickname "Old Reliable." George Zettlein was credited with 129 victories in his six seasons in two leagues. Three of the Atlantics became managers as well as players in the big time. John Chapman managed for ten seasons and would return to Milwaukee in a decade. Tom Pratt had the dubious honor of managing the Philadelphia Union club to last place. Robert Ferguson managed 16 years and became an outstanding third baseman. Little wonder they were the champions of 1867.

About eight acres of Camp Reno were graded perfectly level and enclosed with a high fence for the game. Seats were fitted for the large crowd that was expected, including club directors from all over the state. The big day turned out to be beautiful, the type of day only a long-forgotten sports writer could write about:

> The sun had been showering its sultry rays on the hot street since noon, but as the time approached for the beginning of the contest, clouds began to rise in the sky, and at 3:00 the sun was partially obscured with great banks of vapor, throwing shadows which covered the grounds at intervals throughout the playing ... all seemed in perfect condition for the combat; the pure lake breezes acted like wine in its exhilarating influence on the athletes.[40]

The local boys did not fare as well as the weather. Cream City failed to score in the first inning, and the first six Atlantics scored before Cream City settled down. Brooklyn continued to pad its lead and exploded in the eighth inning, scoring 24 runs, winning the contest 67 to 13. After the game Redington won a throwing match with a 336-foot throw to pocket the $25 prize. Cream City was surely not humbled, for people realized the Atlantics were professionals who made their living playing baseball, while Cream City were amateurs "who spend only the leisure they can borrow from their businesses to indulge in this recreation."[41]

CREAM CITY CLUB				ATLANTIC CLUB			
		O	R			O	R
Wood	1b	3	1	Pearce	ss	5	5
Larkin	cf	2	2	Smith	3b	6	5
Redington	c	4	1	Start	1b	2	8
Norris	lf	3	1	Chapman	lf	3	6
Smih	p	0	4	Crane	2b	5	8
McFadyen	ss	2	2	McDonald	cf	0	11
Hooley	3b	3	1	Ferguson	c	1	10
Welles	rf	5	0	Pratt	p	2	7
Sweet	2b	3	1	Zettlein	rf	3	7
		27	13			27	67

Runs made per inning 1 2 3 4 5 6 7 8 9
Cream City Club   0 1 3 0 2 0 3 0 4 — 13
Atlantic Club   6 1 2 7 5 11 6 24 5 — 67

Cream City's next challenge was set for July 4 in Milwaukee against Chicago's Garden City Club, which claimed to be as good as the great Excelsior team.[42] About 500 spectators attended despite the great heat, and saw Chicago win 52 to 20. Cream City was horrified by the "outrageous violence" used by the Garden City players. A Milwaukee player was injured by one of Garden City's "enfans terribles," causing Cream City to declare it would play a rematch only if they could "procure a uniform that will make them ironclad." Worse yet, it was rumored the umpire of the match had a bet on the Garden City Club, held by the scorer.[43]

After its second loss of the new season, Cream City decided to play some Wisconsin competition. The club's secretary sent challenges to the Ripon and Janesville clubs but neither match was played. Cream City had to be satisfied with practice between its first and second nines until the Capitol City Club challenged her for the gold ball in mid–July. The first game of the challenge was set for August 1, and Cream City tuned up with practice games and a match with the second class Juneau Club to improve what had been their chief weakness—hitting. Camp Reno was even renamed Cream City Park before the contest, and extra streetcars were put on the line for this championship game.

Cream City did not enter the match overconfident, for the Capitols were an improved ball club. As it turned out, Cream City need not have worried. Their practice paid off. They scored five runs in their first inning and held Madison scoreless. Cream City led 17 to 2 after 4 innings, and coasted to a 41 to 15 victory.

On August 7, 1868, Milwaukee fans got their last chance of the season to see "professional" ball players in the persons of the Union Club of Morrisana, New York, billed as "the present champions of the United States."[44] The Unions were also making a western tour and proposed making a scheduled stop in Milwaukee. Cream City was delighted to accept. The Unions had made a large tour in the East the previous year, beating all comers except for a small New York Club in Lansingburgh. Their success was slightly suspect, however. They had their own umpire and would not accept any other. One source reported that they should "secure the services of an intelligent blind man" as an umpire.[45]

As with the Brooklyn Atlantics, Cream City did not "indulge in the hope" of beating the Unions, but to achieve the best possible score. Because of the certain loss, local interest was low, but still 1,000 people attended the game. Cream City did not fare that badly. They lost 43 to 16, but the score was the second best to date against the Unions on their tour. One reason for the score could have been the high winds of the day, causing numerous errors on both sides. The Unions complained that they "had played ball before, but never in a hurricane."[46] Charles Pabor was the star of the game, hitting two home runs to complement his fine pitching. The shortstop listed in the Union box score is George Wright, later elected to baseball's Hall of Fame.

CREAM CITY CLUB		O	R	UNION CLUB		O	R
Wood	1b	5	1	Goldie	1b	4	4
McFadyen	ss	3	3	Austin	cf	3	5
Redington	c	1	3	Martin	2b	5	3
Clark	2b	4	1	Pabor	p	0	8
Larkin	cf	4	0	Wright	ss	2	5
Dodsworth	rf	3	2	Birdsell	c	3	5
Smith	p	0	3	Shelley	3b	3	4
Welles	lf	3	2	Smith	lf	4	4
Norris	3b	4	1	Dellan	rf	3	5
		27	16			27	43

Runs made per inning 1 2 3 4 5 6 7 8 9
Cream City Club   2 2 0 0 2 2 3 3 2 — 16
Union Club   3 2 3 5 4 2 11 7 6 — 43
Umpire — Mr. J.A. Tabor of Endeavor BBC of New York

Cream City's two defeats at the hands of professional clubs did not sour the spirit. They still tried to induce the Union Club of St. Louis and the Central City Club of Syracuse to stop in Milwaukee, but failed to do so.

Cream City started to warm up for the second game for the gold ball with Madison's Capitols by playing a friendly match with the Racine College team, which Cream City won 45 to 16, in a no contest game at Racine. After a few practices they were ready to meet for the championship. Capitol City was ready too. The Madison club had obtained a new pitcher, "Sawyer, of Rockford, noted for his swift delivery of the ball, since the first game, and have hopes of making a close play this time, if they do not win."[47]

All of this pre-game publicity did not mean much, as Cream City won 45 to 18. Although the score had stood 67 to 22 in the sixth inning, the game was called because of darkness and reverted back to the fifth inning score. Cream City had easily retained the state championship. An interesting note to the contest was the pre-game notice that ladies would be admitted to the game free of charge. This was the first reference to the fact that admission had been charged at games. A junior club that will be discussed later, the Stars, charged 10 cents admission to its games at Cream City Park that year to help pay for their rent at the park. Nevertheless, August 27, 1868, was the first Ladies Day in Milwaukee's baseball history.

Cream City ended its season with out-of-state competition by scheduling a home-and-home match with the Chicago Atlantic Club in October, the first game to be played at Cream City Park. Cream City won the first game 20 to 17 in seven innings, but no evidence can be found that the second game was played. Later that month the Muscles of Randolph challenged Cream City and lost 67 to 16. The victory ended Cream City's third championship year.

The city of Milwaukee was growing by leaps and bounds. In 1860 the population was around 45,000. It was up to 56,641 in 1865, and stood at 76,498 in 1867. Beer was already becoming a major business in the city. From July of 1867 to July of 1868, local brewers sold 101,086 barrels of beer. At $12 a barrel, the brewers brought in $1,213,032. According to the April 29, 1868, *Sentinel*, baseball was becoming "a passion with our people." Baseball was to Americans as cricket was to the English. It was even thought to be a remedy "for many of the evils resulting from the immoral association of boys and young men."[48] Books and articles were written about the sport. The best was *Beadle's Dime Base Ball Player*, which gave pointers on the game, rules and regulations, and information on club constitutions. Copies of the *Beadle's Dime* book were sold at Tunis & Company (Wisconsin and Water). And it was advertised that Charles F. Gray & Co. sold baseball supplies to all the clubs in the Northwest.

Along with the existing clubs of the city from the last two years, new ones were formed. A group of the city's editors formed a team and played a club made up of compositors, the typos winning 39 to 24. In a rematch, the editors lost again, this time 43 to 39. The typos later formally grouped, calling themselves the Nonparallel Club. A group also formed of legal men and had some fun playing the editors. The Stars, a junior club formed the previous year, began to cut its name into Milwaukee baseball. They beat numerous local junior clubs, including a split in two games with the Atlantics (Cream City's former junior club). In July the Stars traveled to Kenosha and beat their Athletics 14 to 8. At the end of the season the Stars presented their pitcher, Ted Sullivan, with "an elegant silver medal, as a slight testimonial of their appreciation of his general good playing."[49] The Stars were soon to be a club to be reckoned with.

At the peak of baseball excitement, the game began to take a different course. Baseball legend says that professional baseball started the next year with the formation of the first all-salaried team, the Cincinnati Red Stockings. However, there were professionals and even professional teams long before that. As we have seen, local papers made no bones that the Unions of Morrisana and Atlantics from Brooklyn were professionals. Professionalism was coming even closer to home when Madison's Capitol City Club admitted a professional pitcher to its ranks. As far back as 1867 National Association rules defined professional players, but stated they could not play in a game with an association club.

As far as can be determined, Milwaukee had no professional players yet, but money was in the workings. Papers were asking citizens of the city to help support certain clubs. Admission was being charged to games, and prizes—including cash—were being given at tournaments. Money was being made, but the United States Department of Treasury had decided that baseball clubs were not taxable.

Even though professionals were not prominent in Milwaukee, players wanted recognition. An "anonymous correspondent" complained that after winning the state championship, Cream City received "no escort, no speeches were made, and no public welcome given."[50] Some thought the Cream City Club was not appreciated enough. Strange ideas for gentlemen just enjoying some of their leisure time.

As the time began to lean toward a new era in baseball, a writer in the June 18, 1868, *Milwaukee Daily News* put down his thoughts on what baseball had been to him:

> All of this we did and filled ourselves full of real enjoyment, toughening our muscle and while deepening our breath, and taxing our presence of mind, and there was an end; and we were content, and thought; poor ignorant chaps, that we had played base and that our scores—kept on a tally stick, chalk on the fence, or mayhap, only scratched on a smooth piece of ground—were a sufficient record of our skill and our endurance. But it seem that we were woefully ignorant and unsophisticated. We should have had umpires and uniforms. The fellows that were out catching should have been severally designated as long stop, short stop, center field, pitcher and so forth; we should have had printed rules and regulations, and above all, reporters to have given an account of our games in the newspapers. For what satisfaction is there—although we used to think there was sure fun in a few lads or young men playing a few games at Base Ball, if their doings cannot be recorded in print for the benefit of an admiring world.

Those days were coming to an end.

3

Many Changes (1869–1874)

Just when the Cream City Club should have been riding high after winning three straight state championships, things seemed to turn sour. The club's star player, George Redington, left Milwaukee, moving to New York. His heir at the catching position, Martin Larkin, also decided not to play with the team a bit later. As a goodwill gesture the team decided to allow clergymen the free use of Cream City Park, but charged all other clubs $10 a season, forcing many teams to use other fields. Something was changing in the organization.

Cream City started the 1869 season with the annual election of officers in April. M.A. Boardman continued as club president, with Clarence Smith becoming the new vice president. Frank Smith, who a week earlier had been elected president of the State Association, took over the combined post of secretary and treasurer. These three, along with E.C. Welles and James Wood, became the Cream City Club's Board of Directors. Richard Allen was now the official club scorer. It was hoped Milwaukee's citizens would "lend their aid in maintaining its [Cream City] high standard and name."[1] The meeting then adjourned with a vote of thanks to the proprietors of the Kirby House for the use of their parlors.

Actual play began in late April with practices at Cream City Park, which continued into May. Cream City's trouble began when in late May the Capitol City Club of Madison challenged every club belonging to the State Association to a match. Cream City soon accepted the challenge and stepped up its practices to every day. The match was set for June 17 in Madison, and things were running smooth right up to that day. On the morning before the match, Cream City members were given half-fare rates on the train to Madison. All of a sudden "business engagements of several of the nine"[2] prevented the club from making the trip and Cream City asked for the game to be postponed. As could be expected, the Madison papers came down hard on Cream City. They pointed out the Milwaukee club had a recent history of not leaving its home grounds. Could they not get two substitute players to fill the vacancies? After all, every first class team had extra players. Cream City was afraid to leave home, it was reasoned. Capitol City considered the match a forfeit and was satisfied it had won the game and the championship ball. Cream City took the position that the rules stated the challenge must be for the ball and the Madison challenge did not include this, thus would not surrender the ball.[3] The dispute was never settled and the two teams never met again.

There was enough truth in the Madison claims. Cream City had played all of its match games with first class teams at Milwaukee in 1868, leaving its home ground only to play the lowly Racine College team. As already noted, late in the 1868 season Cream City was to play the Atlantics of Chicago on a home-and-home basis, but the game in Milwaukee is the only one on record. Earlier in the 1869 season Cream City received a challenge from the Forest City Club to play in Rockford, which it did not accept. Surely Cream City had more than nine players, substitutes could have been found for Larkin and McFadyen—the two players unable to attend — and Larkin was soon to leave the team. These two men must have known of their business commitments earlier than one day before the match. If Cream City had a valid excuse, it did not disclose it. The *Milwaukee Sentinel* on June 28, 1869, reported:

> The cloud of uncertainty which has for a time obscured the movements of this Organization [Cream City] has at last been dispelled by the formation of the following nine — Captain and shortstop — A. McFadyen; Pitcher–Clarence Smith; Catcher–Martin Larkin; First Base–James Wood; Second Base–Charles Norris; Third Base–C.J. West; Left Field–Clinton Welles; Center Field–J. Taintor; Right Field–A. Harrock.

The following day Larkin's resignation was announced, and Clarke became the new catcher. Only four players were left from the nine that played the Morrisana Unions the previous summer. Clearly things were changing in the organization.

Cream City played its first match of the season on July 5, with the Chicago Athletic Club — at Cream City Park — when they accepted a challenge sent by the Athletics in May. Again Cream City Park was prepared for the crowd, this time with a large refreshment stand. Again admission was charged, continuing the previous year's pattern. The Athletics batted first but could not score, and Cream City scored four in their half inning. Milwaukee led 11 to 1 after the second inning and coasted to a 34 to 20 win. The new catcher did not play, so McFayden caught, a position he had never played, yet did quite well. The visitors left Milwaukee after making a favorable impression, especially with the ladies, for their gentlemanly conduct. It seemed Cream City was coming out of its lull.

Cream City's next challenge was one that is overlooked by most historians of local baseball. It started in July when Cream City sent an invitation to the mighty Cincinnati Red Stockings, who were in the midst of their famous tour, to play in Milwaukee. Cincinnati contacted the local club by telegram, stating they could not play here at that time due to another commitment. Cream City continued its attempt until the Red Stockings agreed to play in Milwaukee on July 30, giving local fans "an opportunity of witnessing the superb playing of these celebrated players and probably will be the only chance this season of seeing the national game played as it should be played."[4] It was reported the Red Stockings were guaranteed $400.

The Cincinnati Red Stockings of 1869 are a fascinating story. Captained by Harry Wright, the first all-salaried baseball team won 57 games and lost none the entire year.[5] In the month of June the Red Stockings won 20 games, scoring 649 runs to 215 by their opponents. Of course, many of these teams consisted a locally picked nine, but against first class clubs the Red Stockings scored 203 runs while giving up only 90. What made the Red Stockings different than other professional teams was the fact they were all under contract — in the open — to the backer, Aaron B. Champion. Sources vary, but the salaries ranged from team star George Wright's pay of $1,400 for the season to the substitute player's salary of $600.[6]

The Red Stockings arrived the night before the game and stayed at the Plankinton House, guests of the Cream City Club. The morning of the game the Red Stockings visited places of interest in the city, highlighted by the National Military Asylum (now known as the Woods VA Hospital). The large crowd at Cream City Park started early. One source reported "there scarcely could be found an available spot on the grounds for the accommodation of spectators, as dense was the mass of human beings, horses and carriages"[7] outside the area roped around for play. The *Sentinel*, putting the figure in perspective, estimated that about 2,000 people were in attendance.[8] Tickets could be purchased at the City Railway Company, which showed baseball had started its long marriage with transportation companies in Milwaukee.

Cream City had practiced hard to play a creditable game, attempting to keep Cincinnati's score as low as possible. But it was all in vain, as the Red Stockings scored 15 runs in the first inning and whipped Cream City for their worst loss, 85 to 7. The game was called after seven innings. The *Cincinnati Gazette* of July 31, 1869, wrote: "The grounds were poor, and the play was thus considerably interfered with. The game was too one sided to be very interesting."

CINCINNATI		O	R	H	CREAM CITY		O	R	H
G. Wright	ss	2	11	10	Wood	1b	3	0	0
Gould	1b	3	10	8	Clark	ss	4	0	0
Waterman	3b	5	7	7	McFadyen	c	2	1	1
Allison	c	2	9	9	Norris	2b	2	2	2
H. Wright	cf	3	10	8	Larkin	cf	2	1	2
Leonard	lf	0	11	8	Warrock	rf	3	1	1
Brainard	p	0	10	11	West	3b	0	2	2
Sweasy	2b	4	8	8	Smith	p	2	0	1
McVey	rf	2	9	8	Welles	lf	3	0	0
		21	85	77			21	7	9

Innings	1	2	3	4	5	6	7	
Cincinnati	15	8	7	16	6	19	14	— 85
Cream City	0	0	1	3	0	3	0	— 7

After the Red Stockings game, the top club of Milwaukee went into a long period of inactivity, and it is hard to reason why. It had been expected for some time that the Forest City Club of Rockford would play Cream City, which had sent the Illinois club a challenge, but no game was ever played. Racine College sent a challenge to Cream City, but it decided not to accept. They also received a challenge from the Aenas Club of Chicago, but did not accept this one either. Cream City claimed to have sent a challenge to the Athletics of Chicago for a rematch, but the Athletics denied they received one, extending an invitation for the Milwaukee nine to visit Chicago. Apparently Cream City was not interested in traveling to Chicago. Later Cream City was to play the Amateur Club, also from Chicago, but again did not. The *Sentinel* rightly pointed out that if it were not for the junior clubs, one might think "all love for the practice of this noble game had died out in our community."[9]

The inactivity of Cream City gave these junior clubs some encouraging new spirit. More and more new clubs were being formed in Milwaukee. As far back as April the Monitors and a new club, the Pacifics, had attended the State Convention in Madison with Cream City. After the convention two established clubs, the Juneau and Star clubs, elected officials. In late May a new club, the Athletic Club, was formed. The old Actives beat the new Eureka Club, 33 to 23, at Camp Scott in June. In July the Haymakers, Resolutes and Roanokes were formed. The city's policemen formed a club and even had the idea of challenging Cream City. The typos and editors continued their friendly match games. During one of these games an eclipse "kindly consented to put in an appearance"[10] during a twenty-minute intermission. The Merrimac Club was formed and played the Monitors; this time the Monitors won. Another new club organized using the name of the hated Chicago club, Garden City, and still another called themselves the Solomon Juneaus, after the city's founding father. Junior clubs took names like the Milwaukee Boys and Italian Boys. They also took the nicknames of other famous organizations, such as the Mutuals and White Stockings. A picked nine from the chamber of commerce, including a few Cream City players, even played a picked nine from the Chicago Chamber of Commerce.

Of all these clubs the Stars made the biggest impression. At the club's elections in May, Douglas Van Dyke and Robert Waldo were elected president and vice president. Charles Simonds was chosen for the secretary-treasurer post. The board of directors consisted of Ted Sullivan, the team's star pitcher, E. Davis and W. Jennings. Chosen for captain was Alfred Brimer. At the meeting they also selected their first nine, consisting of E. Davis—catcher; T. Sullivan — pitcher; A. Brimer —first base; G. Ball — second base; W. Love — third base; W. Longmore — shortstop; D. Van Dyke, R. Waldo and C. Simonds—outfield, left to right. This nine played the Athletic Club for the championship of the city and won in June, 44 to 30, after scoring 16 runs in the first inning. The Stars then moved on to Waukesha to play their Excelsior Club, winning 37 to 7. Fans now knew their Stars would "never grow dim."[11]

The next stop for the junior club was Racine, with its two top junior teams, the Actives and Eckfords. The Stars won both games, beating the Actives 43 to 21, and the Eckfords 28 to 27, nearly losing the game in the last inning when the Racine club scored nine runs. "Baseballically and astronomically, [the Racine Clubs] were not a cure enough to see our Stars."[12] In August the Stars again beat the Athletics for the city championship.

The undefeated Stars were challenged by the Alert Club of Burlington for the junior championship of the state at Cream City Park. The Alerts had won the tournament at Union Grove and were possibly the best junior club in the state. They proved this by beating the Stars 25 to 14. After beating the Pacifics, the Stars left for Burlington for the rematch. Before the game could start, a hitch arose. The Alerts claimed Sullivan was actually from the Cream City Club. With this dispute finally settled, another arose "in the shape of hay ricks promiscuously scattered through the Base Ball grounds."[13] The Stars finally moved the hay and the game played. They then proceeded to lose 22 to 12.

After the loss, the captain of the Stars received this letter.

Spring Prairie, August 19, 1869
   Captain of the Star Base Ball Club: Dear Sir — As a friend of your club, I wish to inform you that the Alert nine that defeated your club last week are members of four different clubs; two from Geneva, one from Kenosha and one from Spring Prairie. Another is a railroad hand and lives in Chicago. If you lose the championship, you will do it through foul play.
   Yours respectfully,
   ONE INTERESTED[14]

Due to the information in the letter, the Stars still claimed the state championship under association rules that stated a player must be a member of the club for 60 days before he could participate in a match for that club. The Alerts denied the accusation, saying they had sent the Stars a list of their players beforehand and they all were from Burlington. "The motto of the Alerts is fair play, and when they cannot uphold it, the club will disband."[15] The Stars then lost to the Racine Eckfords, 36 to 18, to end their trip, with a letter of thanks to the Western Union Railroad for the excursion rates they received. The club ended its season against the Wide Awakes of Menomonee Falls, winning 76 to 26, to complete an eight-win and three-loss season, scoring 355 runs to their opponents' 191. The Stars were now the new darling of Milwaukee. Their game with the Alerts had received twice the newspaper space as the Cream City game against the Red Stockings.

Cream City ended its long period of inactivity in September by playing the Mutuals of Janesville, again in Milwaukee. The Mutuals were a very good club, having beaten both the Capitol City Club and Whitewater Club in two out of three matches. A win in Milwaukee could give the Mutuals the gold ball. Cream City had never played so poorly. Several of their players played out of position, and Cream City was out of practice, as they lost

55 to 46. The *Daily News* gave some sound advice to the club: "Get your positions well filled, boys, and indulge freely in practice, and take our word for it, you will find no trouble in gaining laurels."[16] The advice was too late, for Cream City had played its last match of the season.

Signs were starting to show that Cream City had plans of becoming a professional or at least a semi-professional team. Soon after the loss to the Mutuals, it was announced that the club would undergo a complete reorganization in an attempt to make it "one of the leading clubs in the northwest."[17] Cream City was a bit more open when in January it stated they were adding "several experts"[18] to their club. The local newspapers also gave indications. On December 4, 1869, the *Sentinel* asked its readers if Milwaukee players intended to form a good amateur club, apparently disregarding that the city had one in Cream City. In early spring the *Sentinel* compared Cream City to a number of other clubs that were known professional teams. In the same article it reported that the cost of running baseball clubs throughout the country was more than two million dollars because "many players, both in professional and amateur clubs, received for their services political and other preferment."[19] Again at the Cream City annual meeting in spring the club planned a complete reorganization.

Cream City's first match of the new season was with the professional team of Chicago, the White Stockings, at Cream City Park on May 28, 1870. After shutting out Chicago in the first inning and scoring four runs themselves, things looked good for the Milwaukee nine. From there it became a disaster, as the White Stockings stopped the Cream City attack and scored with ease themselves. Cream City lost 71 to 19 in the one-sided affair, lacking the "discipline to mechanical readiness that comes from practice."[20] The box score of this game reveals that four of the members of the Cream City team were from the Star Club. This touched off some excitement.

The *Wisconsin State Journal* called Cream City a muffin club, referring to the fact that several of its members had left the club and the Star players filled the vacancies. The *Sentinel* replied for the Cream City Club, stating it always encouraged other clubs, knowing they would train players for Cream City.[21] The Stars rallied immediately, saying they were an independent club and "not intended as a reserve for any other club." They were not likely to lose themselves to "a club whose record is all in the past, and who have not shown a firm front in two years." The Stars then sent this challenge to Cream City:

> In view of the thoughts and rumors set afloat through the White Stocking's game last Saturday—in which our identity as a club is almost lost in connection with that of the C.C.s—we hereby challenge you to a match game for the golden ball and title of champions of the state.
> For the club,
> C.D. Simonds, Secretary

It was wondered if Cream City had the courage "to pick up the gauntlet."[22]

Cream City did not answer. In fact, they could not answer for they were again reorganizing their club. This time they had a merger with the Stars in mind. Cream City wanted to form a nine so strong it could challenge any team in the union. The Stars refused the suggestion, so Cream City changed its tactics. It invited members of all clubs in the city, presumably including the Stars, to meet with them at Cream City Park in a practice game. An unknown gentleman even offered each of the winners a prize as an incentive to come. A few days later Cream City finally announced it had completed its reorganization.

The next match for Cream City was set for July 4, against the Athletics of Chicago. The Athletics were considered the best amateur club in Chicago, having added new faces since last coming to Milwaukee, and thought they could beat Cream City. McFadyen did not take the team lightly and called for his club to practice every day until the match. Before the game Cream City officials announced they had paid all bills for enclosing Cream City Park and all proceeds from then on were to be "devoted to promote the efficiency of the club, except such share of it as may equitably be paid to visiting clubs."[23] The grounds, however, needed more work. The White Stockings complained after their match here that it was the worst they ever saw, having ditches, pitfalls and ridges on the playing field. Admission was 50 cents to the games that year.

For the game Cream City presented basically the same nine, with only a couple new faces. The score stood 7 to 2 in favor of the Milwaukee boys after four innings, but after the Athletics scored nine in the fifth, this lead was cut to 12 to 11. When the Athletics scored seven in the next innings, "the brigade of Chicago loudmouths near the lager beer stand yelled vociferously and drank freely."[24] Only two years earlier Cream City bragged that "Milwaukee had not degenerated as they had in Eastern cities"[25] by allowing intoxicating drinks to be sold on the grounds. The Chicago crowd was silenced, however, in the seventh inning when Cream City scored eleven runs and ended up winning 36 to 26. Cream City wore new uniforms for the occasion, consisting of a white shirt with C. C. on the front, blue pants that buttoned at the knee, cream colored stockings and a blue cap with a cream star in the crown.

Cream City began to receive numerous challenges. The first came from the Harvards of Boston, then the Lone Star Club from New Orleans. These were accepted, but one from the Muscles of Randolph was turned down because of the club's busy schedule. Before these games could be played, Cream City had to travel to Chicago for the rematch with the Athletics and a game with the Amateur Club. Since the first Athletics game, the Chicago papers had been berating Cream City, calling the Athletics a fifth rate amateur club that should have beaten Cream City had it not been for the umpires. But this was the "favorite excuse of the Chicago clubs when they are beaten."[26]

Those two games were the first Cream City had played with first class teams outside of Milwaukee in more than two years. Only 200 people attended the Athletic game, played in 90 degree weather. The *Chicago Journal* reported "the grounds were rather better adopted for aquatic sport than for Base Ball" as "the once famous but now degenerated Cream City"[27] lost 32 to 21. The following day the Amateur Club also beat Cream City, 35 to 22. The Chicago papers rejoiced. They had been led to believe Cream City was a team that "strictly amateur clubs" could not beat—again giving a hint that Cream City was a semi-professional club—but they were really a poor club, with only Wood at first base playing his position superbly. It was claimed Cream City could be beaten by at least a dozen junior clubs in Chicago.[28] This bragging led the *Daily News* to reply that "if Milwaukee grieved as much at her defeats as Chicago rejoices, the affair would be tragic indeed."[29]

While in Chicago, Cream City received another challenge, from the Palmer Potter Club of that city, to play in Milwaukee. However, the Palmers did not come, one rumor suggesting "they got into a squabble at Janesville over their defeat by the champion muffs of that city and 'threw up' their engagements."[30] The Olympics of Washington started their western tour about this time and Cream City sent them an invitation, which unfortunately could not be accepted. Cream City was to play the Harvard boys next. They were an amateur club that played good ball and excelled in their classes too. It was reported they were all gentlemen, a contrast from the Chicago clubs that Cream City had just played. The Harvards beat Cream City 41 to 13.

The proposed match with the Lone Stars of New Orleans on August 1 did not come off due to the sickness of two of their members and was set for the next day. But the Lone

Stars were in Chicago the next day and the two sick players were well enough to play there. No doubt the Lone Stars wanted more money. The agreement to play was for half the gate money, but the Lone Stars wanted a guarantee of $80. Cream City agreed, but New Orleans decided to break the engagement. Instead, Cream City played the Occidentals of Quincy, Illinois, which was in town to play the Stars for the junior championship of the Northwest. Cream City won two games from the junior club on successive days.

Cream City next received challenges from the Shabbanas of Ottawa, Illinois, and the Janesville Mutuals. The match with the Shabbanas was postponed indefinitely when the Illinois club telegrammed Cream City, informing it could not attend. The Mutuals' challenge was to be a three-game affair, the first in Milwaukee, the second at Janesville, and the third, if necessary, at a neutral site. This was the first challenge for the gold ball Cream City had received that year. Janesville, however, claimed the gold ball should be theirs because of their win the year before over the Milwaukee nine. Cream City claimed that challenge was not for the ball. They also claimed to be shorthanded when the Mutuals beat them, and when they were all ready to play, the Mutuals refused to meet them. It was felt it was the Mutuals' place to challenge Cream City if they wanted the gold ball. The Mutuals did and the first game of the match was set for August 18, at Cream City Park. Cream City scored 15 runs in the second inning to pull away 21 to 4, and Janesville never came close. Smith and McFayden each scored ten runs and Cream City won 64 to 20, as the game was called after seven innings due to darkness.

Cream City's next game was with the vastly improved Racine College team, with which Cream City had failed to keep an engagement earlier in the year. Cream City went into the match slightly shorthanded and overconfident, and lost 33 to 27.

The rematch between the Mutuals and Cream City was to take place in Janesville on August 30. The Mutuals had promised Cream City half the gate receipts for an added incentive to travel to Janesville. The day of the match Cream City found not the Mutuals, but a make-shift team from different clubs. In addition, many of them were professionals. Two of them were from Forest City of Rockford, who returned home after the game, and one from Cleveland. Another, Dennis Collins, was only three days before with Cream City. He had been promised "a lucrative situation in Janesville"[31] if he joined the Mutuals. A game was played and Cream City lost 19 to 17. However, a disagreement lays in the game. Janesville claimed Cream City decided to play the match for the championship and the winning team would be declared champions of the state, but as they lost, Cream City decided to call the game only an exhibition. Cream City took the position that National Association rules stated players must be on a club at least 60 days and that beforehand both clubs had decided the match would be an exhibition so as to not disappoint the fans that had come to see a game. "The idea of bringing men from other states to play one day and return the same night or the next day is simply ridiculous,"[32] so Cream City considered the match a forfeit and the championship of the state still theirs. To make the entire day ludicrous for the Milwaukee club, there was a big crowd on hand and the Mutuals claimed Cream City's share was only $15.

Cream City returned home and faced the champion club of the Northwest, Forest City of Rockford, now a professional club. The Rockford club had played Cincinnati's Red Stockings twice, losing by one run once and tying them in a second game. Forest City had also beaten the White Stockings twice and the Brooklyn Atlantics. Albert Spalding still pitched for Forest City. Spalding was now 20 years old (in fact the game was played on his birthday) and he had become one of the outstanding pitchers in the country. He was to win 253 games in the first six years of the professional leagues. Others from Forest City made the professional leagues, including Roscoe Barnes (who topped the .400 mark four times before the fair-foul hit was made illegal), Bob Addy, Fred Cone, Will Foley, Winfield Hastings and Garrett Stires. Rockford had built itself a very fine team.

Rockford showed its superiority by jumping to a quick lead. But for the first six innings, Cream City did well, considering the Forest City strength, falling behind 21 to 3. Then Rockford blew the lid off the game, scoring 20 runs in the seventh inning, and won 52 to 3. Local fans could not see why Cream City fell apart in its professional games. "A few bad plays seem to demoralize them."[33] Cream City was now through with professional clubs — forever as it turned out.

A strictly local nine from Elkhorn next entered the lion's den to challenge the state champions, for this is what Cream City was, amidst all the controversy over that golden ball. The Mutuals from Janesville had beaten Cream City late in 1869, but the Milwaukee team claimed this was not for the championship. Even if it had been, rules required two wins to take the ball away. Their decisive win over Janesville earlier showed Cream City was still the champ. Cream City did not take the Centrals seriously. Only three or four of the regulars bothered to show up, and the remainder were taken from the retired list. Elkhorn won 33 to 25 in six innings, and only Cream City could be blamed for not having its regulars on hand. After leaving Milwaukee, the Centrals proved they were for real by traveling to Janesville and beating the Mutuals. Cream City was eager to play Elkhorn again, but the opportunity never arose.

The Elkhorn game proved to be the last for the Cream City Club. That winter the *Sentinel* reminded its readers that Cream City, "with its usual enterprise, inspirited by a desire to create an interest in the game," had brought numerous professional clubs to Milwaukee for local fans to see and had been champions of the state again, for the fifth straight year. The paper continued with an editorial that should have been written two or three years earlier. It turned out to be the Cream City obituary.

> It is suggested that a meeting be called to form a State Association, so that the Clubs playing in this state may have some rules governing them. The extraordinary performances of playing men from all parts of the country is too ridiculous a proceeding for clubs who wish to gain victories on their merits and maintain a high standard among the clubs in the country.[34]

As already noted, the Star Base Ball Club had a trying year, almost losing its identity in a merger with Cream City. Even late in the 1869 season rumors were spreading that the club was disbanding. The Stars immediately denied this and challenged any junior club or picked nine to a match. For the new season, the Stars started meetings early and chose to wear new uniforms, "to keep up and even to increase the wide reputation which they now bear in this city and state."[35] As the playing season neared, they chose their first nine and thought they might be able to challenge Cream City, "not with the hope of demoralizing them, but with the hope of instilling renewed energy in their ranks."[36]

In late May the Stars played their first game of the season, defeating the newly formed Eckfords 51 to 19 at Cream City Park in a free admission game. A week later they beat the Eckfords again in a rematch to win the junior championship of the city. Before the Stars could play another game, the dispute with Cream City arose. The dispute was costly to the Stars, as they lost their catcher and two infielders to Cream City.

The Stars were forced to regroup fast, for their next game was with the Actives of Racine, a club selected from the Active and Eckford clubs of that city. Due to an "unusually elastic ball"[37] and some heavy hitting, the Stars won in a high scoring game, 81 to 72. A very unusual aspect of this game was a triple play made by the Stars. Shortly after this victory the Stars beat the Wide Awakes of Menomonee Falls, a senior nine, 36 to 13. The

Stars had challenged the Actives of Chicago, the champion junior club of the Northwest, to a game on the Fourth of July at Cream City Park, but could not procure the grounds; they instead played the Red Jackets of Sheboygan in that city. To encourage the club, Goodrich's Line issued half-fair tickets to the players on the steamers for the trip to Sheboygan. Reminiscing about this game twenty-seven years later, Charles Simonds told a *Milwaukee Journal* reporter the Milwaukee players "feasted upon strawberries and cream during our stay at that town. The strawberries were elegant, and the cream — of which we had a sufficient quantity to swim in — was rich. The reason why they fed us so well was probably to put us in a condition in which they could easily defeat us...."[38] The local fans advised the Red Jackets to study the Stars' playing, "as they will thereby discover many points in the game of ball which have never occurred to them before."[39]

The Sheboyganers watched, almost too closely, as they jumped to a 14 to 6 lead after four innings; but the Stars then scored ten tallies in the next inning to tie the score. After eight innings the score stood 31 to 29 in favor of the hometown boys. The Stars then used their final inning to cross home three times to win 32 to 31. After beating the Diamond Club of Waukesha, the Stars prepared for the Occidentals of Quincy, Illinois, which along with the Actives of Chicago claimed the junior championship of the Northwest. The Quincy team proved their claim by not only beating the Stars, 30 to 22, but playing two good games with the Cream City Club.

The State Fair was approaching and the State Agricultural Society decided to offer prizes to the two best clubs entering the competition. The entrance fee was set at $5, which admitted twelve members of each club. Competition was open to all clubs in the state that had a notice of intention to play filed by September 1. Most of the baseball clubs in the city practiced for the tournament, including the Stars and Cream City. The Stars prepared to put their best nine on the field to keep all the prizes in Milwaukee. Cream City, however, did not attend. The tournament was played on September 29, at the Fair Grounds, located two miles in a straight line northwest from the Spring Street bridge (Wisconsin Avenue bridge between Plankinton and Water Streets) on Vliet Street (around today's North 35 Street). The Stars met at the Plankinton House, in full uniform, ready to play. When they arrived at the grounds only one other club was entered, the Alerts of Milwaukee. The Stars won 46 to 24, to win the silver pitcher, waiter, and goblets that were the first prize. The Alerts won the second prize silver pitcher by simply losing the game.

This was the beginning of the end for the popularity of baseball in Milwaukee, at least for a while, for 1871 brought more changes.

✻ ✻ ✻

The biggest news to hit baseball in some time occurred on March 17, 1871, when a professional league was started. The National Association of Professional Base Ball Players did not affect Milwaukee, for the city had no entry. The cities represented in this initial year were Philadelphia, Boston, Chicago, Brooklyn, Cleveland, Rockford, New York, Washington, D.C., Fort Wayne and Troy. The association, plagued with a heavy turnover rate, lasted five years prior to being replaced by a new league.

How would Cream City have fared in the new association if the club had continued to play? This is a difficult question. We have no idea how many professionals, if any, the Cream City Club had. In its match games with professional clubs, Cream City never fared well, losing all five by lopsided scores. Chicago, with about the same club that had beat

Cream City 71 to 19 in 1870, took third place in the association's first year. Second-place Boston had many of the players from the 1869 Red Stockings of Cincinnati. Rockford, which had beaten Cream City by 49 runs, placed last in the association, but this is misleading because they were without their stars, Spalding and Barnes. Because of Cream City's lack of top-flight players, no one from the club ever appeared in the association, and with their dismal record against professional clubs, one would seriously doubt if they were of the caliber to play in this league. Of course, if Cream City had made the move to join the National Association, it would have undoubtedly imported players, as all the other clubs did, so the club's success would have been told by the caliber of play these men would have brought to the city.

As interesting as it is to speculate, the fact remains that the Cream City Club did not exist. Cream City Park did not even exist anymore. That winter it had been broken up and divided into city lots. Ball games could still be played at the site, but later it was said to be "desecrated by the snouts of pigs owned by the independent First Warders and the herds of enterprising and frugal milkmen of the city."[40] New grounds were found, but if any of these were to be able to support a first-class team, they would have to be enclosed so money could be made. New officers would have to run the club and they would have to be "gentlemen"[41] in order to bring other first-class clubs to Milwaukee.

Milwaukee had enough good players and it was still hoped a first-class club could be organized. Players were eager, but they knew the problem — they needed financial help. Professional clubs expressed an interest to come to Milwaukee, but there was no team to play here. All other parts of the state still had their teams, but baseball enthusiasm was "sickly."

> It is rather singular that Milwaukee has not a Base Ball club while Janesville, Elkhorn and Fond du Lac and other interior cities and towns support clubs, several of them claiming the championship of the State. The city now holds the emblem of the championship of the State and must support a club if it wishes to hold it. But the truth is that in this matter, as in everything else, our city is behind the times. Young men are leaving daily because of the solidity and dullness of the place.[42]

There were still some clubs left in the city. The Alerts took up the grounds opposite the First Ward School, on Cass Street, and invited others to join in. Two more clubs, the Monitors and Excelsiors, remained and also played that season. However, the Monitors' 33 to 0 win could mean the Excelsiors had completely reorganized themselves with less proficient players. Because Milwaukee "afforded no amusements to our baseballist,"[43] the Monitors and Alerts left the city for the Fourth of July festivities. The Monitors beat the Pioneers of Oak Creek, a club the Alerts had previously defeated, while the Alerts were beating the Diamond Club of Waukesha. The Alert Club was considered to be the best in the city and arranged a match game in September with some of the members of the old Star Club. Unfortunately, baseball was not as popular in the press as it had been, and the old darlings of Milwaukee could not get their results in the newspaper. Baseball coverage was so bad, the *Daily News* only had one article the entire year on the sport. The turf was the popular press item now, and racing results filled the papers as baseball scores once had.

So that interest in baseball would not die entirely, a group of amateur players and some members of the old Cream City Club met for a few practices at what was left of Cream City Park. But these practices were only "scattered regiments of past warfare," as a "kind of remembrance of the by-gone."[44]

Although two new clubs, the Orientals and the Academy Club, were formed in the fall of 1871, they were short-lived. By spring baseball was said to be "obsolete"[45] in Wisconsin except for clubs in Fond du Lac and Monroe. An effort was made in Milwaukee to organize an amateur club, with several of the former Cream City members on hand. It was hoped the fans of Milwaukee would see a baseball club as good as the 1868 Cream City Club be formed. Nothing came about at this early date, but in mid-summer baseballists met on Saturdays at old Cream City Park and played. They had their fun, but no organized teams came out of it.

A few clubs organized in 1873, but fans were hoping for a strong nine that could bring the professional teams to town. Because Chicago was still crippled due to the great fire, it was thought professional clubs would probably come to Milwaukee if only the city had a strong enough club. Again, only a few clubs were in operation the following year. Of these the Mutuals appeared to be the best. They attempted to challenge the Diamonds of Waukesha in August:

> The Mutuals desire to be informed, at your earliest convenience, whether your club dare meet them for a trial of skill. As to the garbled letters which you have caused to be published in a Waukesha paper, we have only to say that we are inviting you to a game of baseball and not a spelling match.[46]

The coarseness of the challenge apparently did not please the Diamonds, and the match never came about.

It seems ironic that just as national interest was growing in professional baseball, interest in Milwaukee hit rock bottom. Just as strange, when national interest in the professional National Association was declining due to gambling, alleged throwing of games and the league's overall instability, Milwaukee would again find the baseball spirit. As one looks back on the Cream City era in Milwaukee, a very interesting six-year period is found. Although Cream City never beat a professional club, it did bring this exciting brand of first-class play to Milwaukee. Even though it claimed to be the champion club of the state five straight years, only in 1868 did it score a clean-cut victory over all other state teams. Overall Cream City won 18 games and lost 17, if we count the disputed 1870 game with Janesville a forfeit, and thus a Cream City victory. With Wisconsin teams the Cream City Club fared quite well, winning eleven and losing only four. In the end, a lack of strong financial backing ended this era.

A new era was ahead and baseball fans of Milwaukee were ready and waiting for it.

4

The West Enders (1875–1877)

Baseball was again becoming popular in Milwaukee. The *Milwaukee Sentinel* of May 11, 1875, reported that "every ward seems to have half a dozen baseball clubs, but they are in almost every instance organized by lads from 11 to 16 years of age." Only the seventh ward (the east side of town) had a "private club,"[1] which we might assume was an older club, not unlike the Cream City Club's organization. The first clubs that can be found playing were the Westerns and Unions, which played a three-game series, with the Westerns coming out victorious. The Oxford Club beat the Rockford Club 70 to 38; it is not known if this club was from Milwaukee or Rockford, Illinois, as this is the only mention of the club all year. Meanwhile, the Actives beat a picked nine and baseball was again off and running.

The Stars again formed a club and beat the Alerts 24 to 23, but there were no familiar names in the box score. After beating the Young Chicago Club, the Stars prepared to play the Unions, but unfortunately the outcome of the game is lost to time. Later the Stars again beat the Young Chicagos and were ready to receive challenges from any club whose members were under sixteen years old. They then played the Unions again, this time winning after the Unions refused to play after the seventh inning.

More clubs came into existence. The Modocs lost to the Oxfords, while the Monitors beat the Milwaukee Boys. It was reported that the Oxfords were highly indignant because the Lone Stars failed to show up for a scheduled game. The Ironhands, a group of 18-year-old players, beat the 14-year-old Humbolt Boys, 60 to 23. The Academy Club, Chippewa Club and Riversides played along with the Irvings; even the old Cream City members played together. The Excelsiors and the Rolling Mill nine of Bay View played a match, with the winner taking $10 from the loser. The compositors and editors of the *Sentinel* again planned a match, but it did not take place because the editors backed off. The police and sheriff departments picked their best nines and played each other. Even the city and county officials picked players and got into the fun. Bankers, hardware and grocery men also formed similar teams.

Numerous clubs believed they were the best in the city. The Atlantic Club reported they were open to challenges from any club in Milwaukee, and the Yankee Champions team claimed to be the "crack nine" of the city.[2] Clubs again played teams from other locales. The Academy club traveled to Pewaukee and beat its crack club. A picked nine of local ball players played the champions of Delafield on July 4. The Oxfords lost to Racine College 55 to 9, and the Westerns of Racine beat the Atlantics 52 to 13 in July. The Hair-Rakers of Kinnickinnick beat the Atlantics, now considered the champion club of Milwaukee, twice to become the "champion of the Flats."[3] Later the Alerts beat the Hair-Rakers for the championship title.

As this increased interest in baseball hit Milwaukee, it brought new problems. All these clubs needed somewhere to play. As mentioned, Cream City Park had been torn down and progressively fewer games were played at that site until it was converted into grounds "for elegant residences"[4] in August. New grounds were found, the best at 19th and Sycamore (Michigan Avenue).

Problems, however, arose elsewhere. The *Milwaukee Herald* called on the police to stop ball playing in the streets due to injuries to bystanders. The *Daily News* reported that in one of these street games, a woman was knocked down. Another time it was said the players waited for a pedestrian and then "knocked his head off with a hot ball." In another incident ball players were taken to municipal court for "scoring their runs on the windows of Mr. Fuches' residence." Only five unbroken windows could be found on a North Jackson Street block because of ball players. The Gas Company became so frustrated it did not replace the broken glass for five years on the corner of Division (East Juneau) and Jackson. It was even said burglars employed ball players by having the unsuspecting boys distract the family by playing in the street while they went through the home. Clearly, baseball was becoming a "nuisance to the general puplic [sic]." The police discontinued games at the Northwestern depot, and when the Oxfords announced they would play Forest City on a Sunday, a reader sent a letter to the *Sentinel* demanding their arrest and signing it "PURITAN." Probably the worst publicity came when the Lone Stars gave a ball at Eimermann's Park and a fight started, causing seven of the Lone Star players to be arrested.[5]

Not all baseball players were chastised for their actions, though. One group brought praise, as read in the *Sentinel* of May 31, 1875:

> Time was when the East and West Siders would listen to nothing short of a bridge war, but the civilizing influence of the age have reduced local prejudices to an extent really wonderful to contemplate, and instead of arming themselves with axes and sledges, as of old, the young people arm themselves with bat and ball, and take issue in a friendly game on the green.

The first of these new East-West wars was fought on May 29, 1875. The East Side Club and West Side Club met and played a lively seven-inning game, the Eastsiders winning 45 to 10.

EASTSIDERS		O	R	WESTSIDERS		O	R
Simonds	3b	3	4	E.K. West	c	1	3
Austin	cf	5	4	Bradford	1b	1	2
Traverse	1b	4	4	W.P. Rogers	rf	2	2
"Robert"	2b	0	6	Sam Green	p	3	0
Hooley	ss	3	4	Cole	3b	2	2
Chandler	p	2	5	W. Taintor	cf	3	0
Van Dyke	rf	2	6	L.C. Rogers	lf	3	0
E. Oliver	lf	1	6	H. West	ss	4	0
Waldo	c	1	6	J. Taintor	2b	2	1
		21	45			21	10

As the box score indicates, many of the players were from the old Cream City and Star clubs. Even though the Eastsiders were triumphant, it was the Westsiders who stuck together and gained fame.

The Westsiders took the grounds at Nineteenth and Sycamore for their home and called on west side ball players to join their organization. After more than a month the West End Club was organized enough to play a match with the Atlantic Club, but the winner of the match is unknown. A week later the West Enders beat the Oxfords to begin their season. They then played the Oak Creek Baseball Club, losing 20 to 10, but came back to again best the Oxfords 22 to 18 in a game the Oxfords refused to give up the ball, symbolizing victory. The West Enders then played the Pewaukee Club two games. The victors of the first game are lost to time, but the Milwaukee team won the second game 32 to 20. As a true amateur club, the West Enders charged no admission to their games this first year. The club then ended the season by playing the Alerts for the city championship, with the game ending in a tie. Another date was set to decide the championship, and after bad weather postponed this attempt, the Alerts won the title with a 16 to 8 victory in the final try.

✳ ✳ ✳

For the 1876 season, the West End Club made a decision to go semi-professional. In the late summer of 1875 it was announced the capital stock for the club was to be set at $20,000, with shares in the club costing $100 apiece. In May the club held its first meeting, picking a playing nine and explaining its purpose to the public. By playing exhibition games with the leading professional clubs and playing match games with amateur clubs of the country and state, their dream was to bring baseball back into the limelight here. To do this the organization badly needed a new place to play. Grounds were found at Twenty-eight and West Wells, at the time on the outskirts of the city. The club went to "great expense, and have secured one of the most convenient and excellent baseball parks in the country," which included enclosing the park with an eight-foot fence and putting up seats to accommodate 500 people.[6] These grounds, known as the West End Park, were also convenient, because they were on the line of the West Side Street Railway. Admission was set at 25 cents for amateur games and 50 cents when professional clubs appeared. This fixed price sometimes varied, and the *Sentinel* once complained that advance notice should be given when admission fees were raised. Season tickets were sold at the Wisconsin News Company, but occasionally these were declared invalid just before game time. In a late season game with the St. Paul Red Caps, season ticket holders were requested not to use these passes and instead pay for their admission due to the "unusually heavy expense involved in securing the Red Caps."[7] The passes were discontinued, also in a game with the Chicago White Stockings and 50 cents was required for all who attended the match. In September the club found that unauthorized persons were using these passes and called them all back and issued new ones.

These occasional problems with admission and the other factors of baseball — mainly weather and the quality of the team in town — resulted in a wide variation in attendance at West End Park. Figures are unreliable because there were no turnstiles, leaving only reporter's estimates. For example, in an early season game with Evanston, the *Sentinel* reported a crowd of 800 to 1000 spectators, while the *Daily News* reported that 1200 to 1500 people witnessed the game. Attendance ranged anywhere from 500 to 2,000 people a game. Advertising became a new tool for attracting crowds to the West End Club's games. Before this time, baseball had relied only on articles in local papers to secure attendance for upcoming games. Now the West Enders bought newspaper space on page one of the *Sentinel*, advertising the game of the day.

Another gimmick was a club flag that was flown from the main staff of the Plankinton House (North Water Street and Grand Avenue, today's North Plankinton and West Wisconsin Avenues) on game day, which was lowered if the weather became "unfavorable" and the game was called off. This method was not foolproof, however. On at least one occasion, no one inspected the grounds on a rainy day. The flag was still up at 3:00 and many fans went to the park, only to find the grounds unplayable and the contest postponed. It was also discovered that more money could be made by canceling games against lesser competition and playing a first-rate club instead. After promising to play the Oshkosh Amateurs in September, manager Rogers wrote to the club that the West Enders could not go to Oshkosh due to some of the players' business commitments. Instead, he booked the Chicago White Stockings. The club also rented West End Park for an exhibition between the White Stockings and St. Louis Brown Stockings of the National League in October for revenue, and management charged local clubs $25 per game to rent the park.

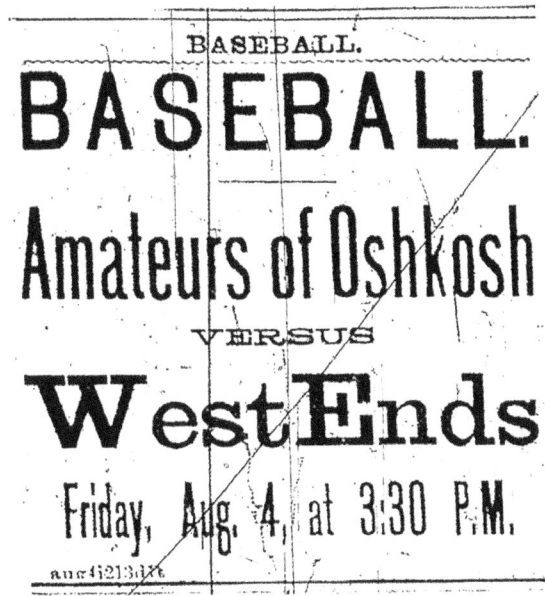

Early advertisement for a West End game in the *Milwaukee Sentinel*, 1876.

At first, prominent real estate dealer William P. Rogers was the sole manager of the West Enders and all business went through him. However, others had control of the club, primarily the stockholders. Because of poor attendance as the season continued, it was soon urged that the club find new management. After a big loss to the National League's Hartford Dark Blues, a local paper thought "it is simple suicide on their part to bring the strongest professional clubs in the country in order to make the home club appear ridiculous in the eyes of everyone who visits the grounds."[8] On August 2, new management was found. At a well-attended meeting of the stockholders, John M. Ewing (an insurance agent with offices on Wisconsin Avenue) became president and Harry Chandler was chosen as vice president. W.P. Rogers and S.H. Cole were elected to the posts of secretary and treasurer. The board of managers consisted of Charles D. Rogers and B.C. Meadows, president and secretary ex-officio. W.P. Rogers became the manager.

Of course, fans did not pay a quarter or half dollar to see the management. What they cared about were the players. The original West End Club of 1876 included: Frank T. Bliss, catcher; Harry E. Chandler, pitcher; George Hooley, shortstop; Edward Gault, first base; Edwin Oliver, second base; E.K. West, third base; C.W. "Chan" Simonds, right field; Percy Stone, center field; and William P. Rogers, right field. The reserve players were Hugh McDonald, E. Elmore, Frank Travers and Louis Rogers. The club was a rather promising one. Bliss was a fine catcher "with great skill and nerve and throws to the bases with notable accuracy," while Chandler was the finest pitcher in Milwaukee. Gault played his position "with remarkable efficiency" and Hooley was "the best baserunner ever seen in this city." McDonald became "one of the best general players outside of professional organizations."[9]

The West Enders started play in May by beating a picked nine 47 to 6, then defeated the local Atlantic Club 53 to 13. The club then set up a date with the powerful Chicago

West End Team of 1876 — *Standing, left to right:* Hamilton Vose, Edward Gault, Harry Chandler; Seated: Hugh McDonald, Billy Furlong, Joe Lawler, C.W. "Chan" Simonds, Frank Bliss; *Reclining:* Percy Stone (courtesy of Milwaukee County Historical Society).

White Stockings of the National League, but a rained out league game in St. Louis forced the White Stockings to stay there and postpone the exhibition in Milwaukee. The West Enders then beat the Markham Academy 21 to 1 before it started to play first-class competition.

Evanston College was the college champion of the Northwest. They had held the White Stockings to only 9 runs, a fine feat for a college team composed of boys 18 to 20 years old. The players were gentlemen, proving it in the third inning of the West End game when the umpire ruled a West Ender out at first in a bad decision. Evanston, "observing that the decision was incorrect, refused to take advantage of it, and the umpire reversed his ruling."[10] After four innings the score was tied 3 to 3, but from then on it was all Milwaukee's game. The West Enders won by a score of 14 to 5; but it was a costly victory as Hooley broke his nose in the game.

West End Club		O	R	Evanston		O	R
Gault	1b	3	2	Wheeler	lf	4	0
Oliver	rf	4	0	Adams	1b	4	0
Hooley	ss	3	2	Theirs	c	3	1
Bliss	c	3	1	Knapper	2b	4	0
McDonald	2b	4	1	Meyers	cf	2	2
Chandler	p	4	0	Horton	rf	2	1
Simonds	lf	3	2	Hamilton	3b	2	1

		O	R			O	R
West	3b	3	2	Evans	p	4	0
Stone	cf	0	4	Brainard	ss	2	0
		27	14			27	5

The West Enders shortly thereafter played a rematch with the college nine, winning again 11 to 5. Hooley took another shot in the nose.

Sandwiched between the two Evanston games, the West Enders played the Alerts for the city championship on May 30. The next day's local papers reported the game attracted a large crowd and no one went home disappointed about the quality of the game. West End scored two runs in the second inning, but the Alerts held them scoreless and scored two of their own in the fourth to tie the score. In the fifth inning a throwing error by the West Enders allowed two unearned runs, producing the oldest excuse in baseball, "the fact that Gault stood facing the bright sun will perhaps account for this." A bit later Stone dropped a high fly "as if his hands were greased." After seven innings the underdog Alerts were ahead 13 to 10. At this point Captain Bliss said something to the team. "It must have been something very inspiring," for the West Enders rallied to win 22 to 15. Neither side displayed superior fielding, as the West Enders committed 20 errors and the Alerts 19 — a high amount, even in a time when fielders did not wear gloves. The umpire for this big inter-city match was Ted Sullivan, the old pitcher from the Star Club.[11]

The West Enders tasted defeat in June at the hands of the Racine College Club. The Milwaukee club led 2 to 1 after three innings, but the college boys played a better game the rest of the way to win 11 to 4. Two weeks later the same teams met again, only to have a disputed ending. With West End winning 5 to 1, a foul-tip hit the Racine catcher in the nose, breaking it. After an hour's delay, the college club forfeited the game, claiming they had no other catcher. The Milwaukee papers saw this action as Racine's way of escaping a legitimate defeat by calling the forfeiture. Racine claimed all its players played in only one position and did not know how to play elsewhere. Thus, the score stood 9 to 0, West End.

On June 21, 1876, the West Enders played their first game against one of the National League clubs. In all they would play seven, losing every game. This first exhibition was with the Chicago White Stockings, the eventual pennant winner of the National League's inaugural year. The professional club started slowly, leading only 3 to 1 after four innings, but they pulled away to win 11 to 1. Albert Spalding, who Milwaukeeans had seen in several different uniforms, pitched the first five innings before Ross Barnes took over. The *Daily News* of June 22, reported the "Chicago's were lenient enough to give them [West End] a chance once in a while, thus making the game close and interesting."

Chicago		O	R	West End		O	R
Barnes	2b	3	2	Hooley	ss	4	0
Hines	cf	2	2	Gault	1b	4	0
McVey	1b	3	2	Chandler	p	3	0
Anson	3b	3	2	McDonald	3b	3	0
Spalding	p	5	0	Bliss	c	3	0
Belaski	rf	3	0	Stone	cf	4	0
White	c	1	1	Simonds	rf	2	1
Peters	ss	4	1	Theirs	2b	2	0
Glenn	lf	3	1	Vose	lf	2	0
		27	11			27	1

Runs per inning	1	2	3	4	5	6	7	8	9	
Chicago	1	0	2	0	3	1	4	0	0	—11
Milwaukee	0	0	1	0	0	0	0	0	0	—1

A week later the Philadelphia Athletics visited town and won an exhibition 14 to 4. Again it seemed the National Leaguers did not play their best game, "seeing they had an easy thing, played a weak game in the field, muffing balls that would have been held by a kindergarten nine."[12] In July the Hartford Dark Blues also visited Milwaukee and scored an easy victory. These sound defeats caused a stir and the exhibitions were discontinued until later in the season, when the West Enders were a stronger club.

Observers of West End believed the club needed a third baseman because the two they had, Hamilton Vose and Waldo, did not "fill the bill."[13] The outfield was also "lamentably weak."[14] In June the club attempted to solve the problem by picking up McCarthy, an infielder, and Ball, an outfielder, from the Princeton College club.

A dispute then arose over the status of the West Enders. The *Spirit of the Times*, a popular sporting journal of the day, claimed the bulk of the Milwaukee club was paid salaries to play. One member was reportedly paid $75 per month, others $50. "Two or three members have no other occupation, one being imported from a neighboring state" to play. The journal concluded the West Enders were a professional club and should not advertise that they were "purely an amateur club and it must be understood that the game to be played today is an exhibition, etc."[15] The club responded in a strange way, denying yet almost admitting the accusation. While saying no players received salary at the time of the article, the club admitted one had been added since that time. "One other receives something, but is supported mainly by a situation in a business house." Another was paid "during the brief time that he has been waiting for a business situation." However, a letter to the *Sentinel* claimed its author had talked to the White Stockings and they had said the West Enders were professionals. And one of the "leading umpires" of Milwaukee also claimed the team was comprised of professionals.[16]

Soon the club filled its infield gap by adding two new players, Joe Lawler and Billy Furlong, a shortstop and a third sacker. The *Sentinel*, who had in the past defended the club's amateur status, almost brought the club's paying players into the open by writing, "The *Sentinel* is entitled to thanks for securing so good a player for third base as Furlong, who is the man it advertised for."[17] These player deals had been common for some time. The practice was called revolving, and it was as old as professionalism in the sport. It was simple—a player would leave one team while still under contract for another offering more money. It had been going on for some time in the big cities, but it was new to Milwaukee. Team jumping had already been seen in Milwaukee when Theirs played for Evanston College and shortly thereafter appeared with the West Enders. It was seen again within a few weeks when the Philadelphia Athletics played Kershaw at third base; only the day before he had played against the West End for the Racine College team.

Team rosters often changed radically. In a period of two weeks between the two Evanston games, the college club had six new men. In a three-week period, the Chicago Fairbanks club had five new members. When the St. Paul Red Caps came to Milwaukee, they had five professionals in their lineup who were not with the club when West End played in Minnesota. Probably the most outstanding attempt was by the Mutuals of Janesville. After losing the first game to West End, they attempted to get two professionals, Quinn and O'Rourke, from the Chicago Franklins. Unfortunately for the Mutuals, they did not arrive, and Noah Edwards from the West End Club was signed to play with them.

The West Enders were furious and claimed Edwards had been signed by Janesville before he left Chicago for Milwaukee, and only wanted free train fare. The Mutuals denied this, saying they signed Edwards when Milwaukee could not come to terms with him. The West Enders also lost Ed Gault in a similar manner. In late August the St. Paul Red Caps came to Milwaukee and when they left, Gault left with them.

After the loss of Gault, the West Enders captured their biggest prize, "Cherokee" Fisher. William Fisher was considered one of the best non-league first basemen in the country. The Cincinnati National League club released Fisher in July 1876, where he had a disastrous season as a pitcher. Some of this may be attributed to the fact his young son, Charles, was dying in a Philadelphia hospital. Some may have been due to his being "too much of a beer pitcher."[18] However, he had played five years in the National Association, not an outstanding player but the first first-class professional to play on a Milwaukee team. Fisher soon proved himself to be a "Moses" in Milwaukee.[19] The West Enders went on a signing spree. The club snared Sam Hay from the Oshkosh Amateurs. Then came Farrell, a crack shortstop from the Detroit Aetnas. Then another National Leaguer, John Carbine, who had played briefly with Louisville, was brought into the fold. By season's end, five of the nine — Lawler, McDonald, Fisher, Carbine and Farrell — were crack professionals. In late October a sixth, Fred Andrus, was secured. The *Beadle's Dime Base Ball Player* wrote this about the West End Club: "This club was organized in the spring of 1876, and was then composed strictly of amateur players; afterward two hired players were added, and in a large portion of the games no other hired ones took part. Subsequently, to be better able to cope with the class of clubs visiting that section, three more professionals were added, making five in all, the remaining four — Chandler, Furlong, Vose and Stone — being amateurs."[20]

With these additions the West Enders were said to be "one of the strongest non-league clubs in the country."[21] They proved this by again playing National League clubs. In late September the West Enders took on the White Stockings again. Chicago scored one run in the first, but West End held them scoreless through the next four innings, scoring three themselves in the third. In the sixth inning the league champions tied the score, but Milwaukee scored three more to take a 6 to 3 lead that held through seven innings. By the end of regulation play, the score stood tied at 6 to 6. Only in the tenth inning could the White Stockings win, 10 to 7. The West Enders had given Spalding and his club a scare indeed. The following month West End lost to the St. Louis Browns 17 to 3, but bounced back and played a very good game against the White Stockings, losing by only one run.

While this transition from an average club to a powerful non-league club was being made, the West Enders played a heavy schedule of games. The Fairbanks Club of Chicago was beaten 10 to 6 in eleven innings after the loss to the Philadelphia Athletics. Then a club called the Pacific Slope Champions of San Francisco played at West End Park. This club beat West End 8 to 4, but the local boys believed the defeat "was more directly due to the partial rulings of the umpire than to the superior playing of their opponents."[22] The umpire was a Mr. Taylor, who was the left fielder for the California club. A second game was played, using Dunphy of the Alert Club as umpire, and the West Enders won 12 to 3. The West End Club then "started for scalps in Minnesota,"[23] as they took their first out-of-state trip. The trip was a total success, as West End won both their games in that state, beating the Clippers of Winona and the St. Paul Red Caps. They then returned home to beat the Alerts, split two games with the Fairbanks of Chicago in a home-and-home series, and lost to the Oshkosh Amateurs in a very poor defensive showing, committing 21 errors.

The stage was set for the long-awaited match with the Mutuals of Janesville. The two cities had not met on the field since August 1870. The Mutuals were claiming the championship of the state and were acting like it. In a letter to the *Sentinel* they showed their confidence:

> Will you be kind enough to inform the Mutual Baseball Club if the West End Club still exists? A letter received here in June promised our boys a game shortly after the fourth. A letter mailed last Saturday and one Monday following, remained unanswered or acknowledged. Are we mistaken in the name of the Association? Please look this business up some cool day, and favor us with the result of the inquest.[24]

The West Enders were now ready, and it was reported "there is blood in the face of the moon"[25] when they thought about the Mutuals. West End won the game in Milwaukee 20 to 4, taking advantage of 20 errors by the Mutuals, as well as the rematch in Janesville.

The St. Paul Red Caps made their trip to Milwaukee next. West End won the first game, but the second match turned into a fiasco. West End scored 12 runs in the first two innings to begin a rout. The weather looked like rain, and the Red Caps began to stall.

> So the Red Caps catcher would throw the ball at the pitcher's feet, who could not possibly stop it, and it would roll out to center field. Center field would trot along after it lazily, and toss it to second base; second base would muff it, and after several fruitless attempts to pick it up, would toss it to the pitcher, as if it were a cannon ball; pitcher would wipe it off for several minutes; roll it in his hands for several minutes, and finally put it through with such surprising rapidity that it would bound past the catcher into the crowd.[26]

West End countered by striking out and not running out hits. "It was the worst bit of nonsense ever exhibited on the grounds."[27] The umpire would have no part of it and left after the five innings constituting a legal game. A full game was finally played, West End winning 18 to 3.

The West Enders won their next six games, extending their winning streak to 10 games. A game with the Detroit Aetnas then drew fire. After winning three close, well-played games, West End lost 18 to 0. Throughout the series betting had been even and there was a great deal of gambling on the fourth game. The talk was after the loss that the game had been fixed. The *Sentinel* investigated and reported, "The *Sentinel* can hold up its right hand and swear they [the players] would quit the club if they believed one of its games had been sold." The excuse given centered on Harry Chandler's sore arm. Others thought the Aetnas, the semi-professional champions of Michigan, had not played their best in the earlier games to secure better bets for the fourth game.[28]

West End management continued an investigation into the sell-out. On January 6, 1877, Milwaukee newspapers reported that Fisher confessed to selling out the September 18 game to a local businessman, the *Evening Wisconsin* reporting Fisher obtained $100. In a detailed report the *Daily News* stated Fisher "has confessed that he helped to throw the game at the instigation of a well known man in this city who holds an important position." The paper withheld this man's name "because The News will not be a party to the injury of any person upon the statement of a man like Fisher." According to Fisher the fix was set up in one of the side rooms of the Newhall House, which included at least one other West End player and two Detroit players. Fisher was to get "a liberal percentage of the money won" on betting, but claimed he only received $15. Of course, Fisher was dismissed from the club, and the management was praised for "their untiring efforts and final success in ferreting out the bad scheme."

These numerous games played at West End Park were part of state fair week. West End management had decided to conduct a tournament during fair week with cash prizes amounting to $800. The club later found there were not enough clubs interested to ensure the success of a tournament and decided to stage numerous games between the Alerts, Detroit Aetnas, Janesville Mutuals and themselves that week. Bad weather prevailed and many games were postponed. It was beginning to cost the Janesville and Detroit clubs money to stay in Milwaukee with no income from games. With at least a game every day, sometimes one in the morning and another in the afternoon, it was possible for ends to meet. The bad weather and loss of game revenue gives power to the claim the Aetnas let up in their first three games with the West Enders to pick up on the bets. To end the week, the West Enders beat the Alerts twice to win the city championship.

After the fair week West End traveled to Racine to play that city's Athletics and were dubbed the Waxed Ends by the Racine press after losing 6 to 5. They later redeemed themselves by beating the Athletics at West End Park. The West Enders' schedule for 1876 was rounded out with wins over the Liberties and West Ends, both of Chicago. After the formal season concluded, the club played three match games among themselves to benefit the West End Baseball Association. On October 25, 1876, the *Milwaukee Sentinel* commented, "When it is considered how largely that organization has contributed to the entertainment of our citizens during the past season, the propriety of taking advantage of this occasion to show their appreciation will be recognized by all lovers of the noble game."

The second biggest club in terms of newspaper space in the city in 1876 was the Alert Club. In early May the club elected Martin J. Bray (owner of Bray Brothers printing company on East Water Street) as its president, Paul C. Rindfleisch and Fred C. Millard as treasurer and secretary, and Edward T. Lay as captain of the playing nine. Shortly after, the Alerts played their first game and won, beating the Prairie Boys 26 to 9. The Alerts were reported to have a good, "promising club."[29] In June the club issued a statement that it was open to challenges for the state championship. In a direct swipe at West End, who had beaten the Alerts once, the statement contained a clause stating they would not play any club for the championship if the nine was composed of professionals, although a challenge had been received from the Janesville Mutuals. Oshkosh and Berlin were also expected to compete for the title. The Mutuals beat the Alerts 12 to 10 in their first meeting.

Before the loss to the Mutuals, the Alerts played the Atlantics of Milwaukee. It was said to be "the worst game of baseball that has taken place in Milwaukee for many a day.... The most ardent lover of the game can hardly stand riding two miles in a crowded street car and paying money to see a scant game."[30] Those fans that enjoy high scoring games might have liked to witness the 32 to 22 win for the Alerts at West End Park. Next the Alerts were to travel to Beaver Dam for a contest but did not, "owing to the inability of several of the players to absent themselves from the city."[31] The next week it was revealed the Alerts had sent a letter to Beaver Dam asking, "What guarantee can you give us? Whatever you give us, when we play in Beaver Dam, we will reciprocate when you come to Milwaukee."[32] Remember, the Alerts were supposedly a pure amateur nine! The Alerts next known game was with the Amateur Club of Oshkosh. West End had just lost to Oshkosh, and the Alerts were given little hope for victory. However, they "saved Milwaukee's reputation"[33] by winning 22 to 15 in a game in which the Amateurs made 35 errors and the Alerts 22.

In August the Alerts reorganized the management end of their organization. They felt there was room for two first-rate clubs in the city and wanted to compete with any amateur club in the country. William Stapleton and Fred Millard were chosen to head a committee to draft a constitution. Under the constitution the club was to be directed by a president, three vice presidents and a board of directors. This board would elect a secretary and treasurer and a business manager, which would constitute the board of managers.

This board of managers would have the power to mail contracts, engage and discharge players, and control all aspects of the business of the club. A $3 annual fee was charged to members.[34] Because of the $25 fee charged for the use of West End Park, the club decided to build a new park. The Cream City Railway Company agreed to aid the club, which meant construction would only cost the Alert Club about $100. The park was to fence in an area of 600 x 400 feet in Kane's Addition, just south of Siloam Spring, in the First Ward. The work began immediately on the 2,500-spectator capacity park.

These new grounds were ready in early September, but the opening game with the Chicago Fairbanks was postponed due to rain. On September 15, the grounds were opened officially when the Alerts beat the Mutuals of Janesville 9 to 0. The Mutuals refused to play the entire game, using darkness as the cause. "The umpire thought otherwise and called play. But the boys were mad and bundled their bats off the grounds."[35] The score had stood 18 to 16 in favor of the Alerts at the time. Admission to this opening game at the park was 25 cents and carriages were admitted free. However, this rosy picture and new park were all for nothing. As an obituary to the Alert Club, the *Sentinel* wrote on February 21, 1877, "An indebtness of $800 is all that remains of the Alert Baseball Club."

The 100th anniversary of the United States was a banner year for the amateur baseball clubs of the city. In addition to West End and the Alerts, twenty-nine amateur clubs were known to be in existence. The Mutuals held the honor of club longevity, having been around since 1873, even though only one game can be found that they played in 1876. They were also around for the 1877 season. The Atlantics started off their second season with a social ball in May before playing baseball, which included a grand tour of central Wisconsin in July. Other clubs continued into the '76 season with spirit, the Western Boys, Actives and Excelsiors among these.

Many new clubs were formed. In early April a group of young men organized themselves under the name of Prairie Boys. Later that month two groups of boys played a match to determine who should wear the name Centennials. The Turner's Society formed baseball clubs on each side of town and played for the Turner's championship. Companies formed groups and played each other in great numbers, showing a new direction in employee relations and entertainment. Western Union, Atlantic & Pacific Telegraph, the Electric Company and Storm Hill & Company were a few such companies. The newspapers formed clubs to play each other in friendly competition. The *Evening Wisconsin* was the first, and the *Sentinel* soon formed its own club to "pound the conceit out of the Wisconsin nine."[36] Unfortunately for the pride of Milwaukee's oldest newspaper, the *Evening Wisconsin* nine won the contest 16 to 4. Organizations comprised of barbers and bankers formed clubs, the bankers even playing a group of tellers from Michigan.

Games were played for charities during this era. A group calling themselves the Fat Men and another using Lean Men played a game with the profits going to the Industrial School, which amounted to $198.19. The following year a benefit game was played between the Milwaukee Chamber of Commerce and a team called O. Kanchee, proceeds going to the Protestant's Orphan Asylum. The Maple Leafs played the Athletics to help "defray the expenses of the improvements at the library rooms."[37] As the summer rolled on, more clubs were formed. The Aucklands, South Ends, Molly Maguires, Lone Stars, Barney Hard Knocks, Lakesides, Maple Leafs, Clippers, Starlights, Hazel Boys and Wide Awakes were a few of the teams—often with players under 14 years old—to sprinkle the newspapers that summer.

In mid-summer the *Evening Wisconsin* reported there were no hard feelings between the baseball players and cricketeers of the city. There was some discord, however, between some citizens and the baseballists of the streets. In early spring these citizen groups started their drive to stop the game from being played in the streets, citing the numerous accidents that had occurred the year before. Throughout the summer articles could be found, such as the occurrence on Cass and Biddle (East Kilbourn) where a man was hit by a ball "whizzing recklessly through the air, striking this gentlemen on the head, rendering him for a moment quite senseless." By August an ordinance was passed in the Common Council to prohibit ball playing and other sports in the streets, and soon the police were enforcing it.[38]

Even though street ball was being curtailed, organized baseball was going strong in 1877. Even more clubs existed than the previous year, totaling at least 33. It began early that year, with an invitation in February for all to play at West End Park during the season. By April numerous clubs were in operation. One such group in the 9th Ward called themselves the Jim Ludingtons "in honor of a distinguished citizen [also the governor of Wisconsin] and as a slight testimonial of the gratitude they feel for financial encouragement."[39] Some of the old groups, such as the Academys, Lone Stars, Excelsior, Hard Knocks, Aucklands and Athletics, were still around. Another wave of fresh teams hit the scene — the Nationals, Comicals, Our Boys, Oak Leaves, Arctics, Custers, Aetnas, Live Oaks and Emeralds to name some.

One group, the Maple Leafs, made one of the best showings in its second year. With all of its players under 18 years old, and some as young as ten, they beat the Amateur Club for the city junior championship, 38 to 2. The Maple Leafs also beat out-of-town clubs, such as the Oconomowoc Browns in August. In September a crowd of 2,000 saw them beat the Actives 15 to 10 to highlight their season. Another club to win a championship was the Athletics, which won the city championship and a prize of $100 in September by beating the Aucklands 15 to 12.

Again men with something in common grouped into clubs. In May the Fat Men of the East Side played a friendly game with the Overweights from the West Side. The grocers lost to the hardware men, and the East Side barbers beat the hairtrimmers of the West Side 34 to 14. The Milwaukee Chamber of Commerce snuck a win by the Chicago Board of Trade in August, 25 to 23. And of course, the newspapers continued their friendly battles. This year the *Sentinel* won 25 to 1 when the *Evening Wisconsin* club committed 63 errors, mostly by the shortstop, J.C. Keefe, leading the *Sentinel* to comment that "he seemed a little off."[40]

✳ ✳ ✳

West End began its new season with an all-out professional approach. At the club's first meeting of the season, held on March 12, 1877, at the Plankinton House, it was decided to form a joint stock company. The club's plan required $5,000. Two hundred shares of stock in the club, at $25 a share, were to be issued. Although bad weather held the attendance down at this initial meeting, twenty shares were sold. Two days later at another meeting attended by more people, the plans were completely unfolded and discussed. The goal was obvious—the Milwaukee Baseball Association, as it was now being called, was out to make money. C.W. Norris was chosen chairman of the meeting, which became a fiery one. It was suggested that young men who could not afford to buy individual shares be allowed to "club together" in order to double up to buy one share. The proposition was immediately voted down, its opponents claiming this practice would necessitate issuing two season tickets instead of one. Mr. Simonds pointed out ladies were admitted free and to start a clubbing together policy would "reduce the income materially." W.P. Rogers added to this point by observing that clubs in other cities made ladies pay admission. In a related proposal, admission was dropped to 25 cents.[41]

A committee of eight was appointed to promote the sale of stock. This job proved to be a most difficult one. Shares in the club sold very slowly, but the *Sentinel* was sure "fine weather would stir people up."[42] By early May only 50 to 75 shares had been sold, so the club decided to only sell 100 shares, probably realizing even this goal might be quite impossible. The *Daily News* rightly pointed out that "the old interest which attached to the West End Club because it was home talent, is lost; and now people don't pay their money for any other purpose than that of seeing a skillful game."[43] In mid–September William P. Rogers, then the club manager, reported 40 shares were out, amounting to $1,000. In light of these facts, the drive to sell stock in the association was a failure. Some blamed the businessmen of the community, claiming they had not "come up to the mark in the matter of taking stock in the Association. Out in little Janesville there was no trouble in getting whole barrels of money."[44]

In April West End met for its formal elections of officers and board of directors. The *Daily News* of April 11, 1877, was very impressed with the West End officials who were chosen to posts of importance:

> The Milwaukees cannot be too warmly congratulated upon the election of officers of the club. The president, Mr. E.H. Chandler, is of the well-known firm of Chandler, Brown & Co. The vice-president, Mr. Rufus Allen Jr., is of the great leather firm, the Wisconsin Leather Co., the treasurer, Mr. C.W. Norris, is of the prominent ship chandlers firm of G.D. Norris & Co. Mr. W.P. Rogers, the secretary, is one of our prominent and respected real estate dealers. Right here we wish to say that Milwaukee owes its possession of a first class baseball club very largely to the unceasing efforts of Mr. Rogers. As secretary of the club he will have most of the work to do, but he is energetic enough to perform the arduous duties in the best possible manner.

Fred Andrus was chosen as captain of the 1877 West End Club. Andrus was a 26-year-old Michiganer who had played eight games with the Chicago White Stockings in 1876, hitting .306. He inherited a club of semi-professionals, with the key players having already deserted. Players were hard to control in those days, "as a general thing players are but little more than boys, and however well disposed, they are at times wild and unruly."[45] They were also hard to keep. Farrell, Fisher and Carbine were gone. Frank Bliss was gone too, now with the Mutuals of Janesville. He was also suing the West End Club for "a considerable amount of money." Bliss claimed that West End engaged him the previous year for $1,300. He received his salary for August, September and October, but the club failed to pay him the rest of the year. With interest, he claimed he was entitled to more than $1,000.[46] Unfortunately, no evidence can be found if he won his lawsuit. Fred Anson, cousin of the famous Cap Anson, was signed by West End, but he could not play because of a crippled leg from the previous year.

Andrus still had Bill Furlong, Joe Lawler, Hugh McDonald and Harry Chandler, but this was not a first-class organization able to compete with any club in the country. The first break came in late March when the West Enders secured the services of Charlie Bennett. Bennett was born in New Castle, Pennsylvania, in 1854, and played his early ball there, being "a slugger of the sluggers on the old Neshannocks" in the seasons of 1874 through 1876. It was said he "broke the directors because of the number of balls knocked into the river."[47] Initially breaking into professional ball with the Aetnas of New York, he played with the Philadelphia Athletics, a league Alliance club, just as Milwaukee was for this year. Bennett was a disputed player, and the League favored Milwaukee in its decision. Charlie, at this stage in his career, was a catcher and the *Sentinel* of April 25, 1877, wrote he "takes everything near him with wonderful ease and his throws are remarkably fine." The *Lawrenceburg* (Mass.) *Guardian* quoted Bennett's salary at $1,700 for six months, "and a private purse, made up by the citizens of Milwaukee of $300."[48]

Another newcomer to the club was Everett Mills, a first baseman who had played regularly with the Hartford Dark Blues the previous year. Yet another newcomer was W.J. Turner. Chandler, the heralded pitcher of 1876, had lost his value as a pitcher by the new season, as indicated by the club's willingness to sign Valentine from the Nameless Club of Brooklyn, yet the attempt failed. Later the club attempted to sign future Hall of Famer Candy Cummings, but again failed. On May 5, West End opened its 1877 season with the following lineup: Lawler, ss; Mills, 1b; Bennett, c; Turner, 2b; McDonald, p; Andrus, lf; Furlong, 3b; Chandler, cf; Vose, rf.

This nine did not suit anyone. Observers thought three new players would make West End a club "stronger than a majority of the league clubs."[49] Of course, three new men would cost money, so Milwaukee remained a strong semi-professional club. Some, however, contended West End had the money to build. After a game with the Janesville Mutuals, which drew a good crowd, the *Sentinel* reported "the claim on behalf of the managers that they haven't the financial support to justify them in procuring nine strong players is answered by the attendance on Saturday. They should understand that there is no economy in keeping weak players."[50]

West End soon starting picking up new players. Daniel Morgan and Abner Dalrymple were signed first. Morgan became the club's much-needed pitcher, while Dalrymple — who had played with the Freeport Reds in 1876 — played the outfield. How Dalrymple came to play in Milwaukee was told by an unnamed former West End player to the *Milwaukee Sentinel* years later:

> You remember the fierce rivalry that existed then between the Janesvilles and the West Ends. Well, we were booked to play in Janesville, and on the day of the game ran an excursion train out. Dalrymple was at that time a semi-professional player in Beloit, and the Janesvilles had wired him to go there and play with them against us. He went, but had neglected to notify them, and they had engaged somebody else under the impression that he would not show up. After the game he came to me, and he was dead broke, and requested permission to ride into Milwaukee on the excursion train. I agreed to let him ride with us. On the way in he offered to play with us for his board, and if his playing should prove satisfactory to receive $10 a week. We told him we would give him a trial, and paid a week's board for him at a hotel. Well, he played such good ball that we hired him at $10 a week. He became a great favorite, and at the close of the season I collected $300 for him from the chamber of commerce boys.[51]

Abner did not do a great job in his initial appearance, but in one of Milwaukee's biggest newsprint understatements, the *Sentinel* of May 19, 1877, wrote, "He may do better in the future." West End's next acquisition was Davy Rowe from Chicago to shore up the weak pitching. Rowe came to Milwaukee injured and could not pitch for about two weeks. West End almost got a brother combination when Albert Spalding, owner of the White Stockings, offered Jack Rowe in exchange for Charlie Bennett. Bennett objected to the deal and it fell through.

The club was beginning to look improved and Morgan was named its new captain in June. It next landed a first-rate pitcher, Sam Weaver. Weaver was born in 1855 in Philadelphia, and pitched for local amateur clubs until joining the professional club there in 1875. When that club disbanded in July 1876, Weaver joined the Neshannock club of New Castle (Pennsylvania), and started 1877 with the Philadelphia Athletics. Weaver made an amazing debut in Milwaukee. He complained of sickness and a "physician was summoned during the progress of the game, who prescribed for him, and advised his retirement, but he stayed" and won the game.[52] It was now thought in Milwaukee that West End was "the peer of any in the country—League, Alliance or International."[53]

In July the Memphis Reds disbanded and Billy Redmond, the captain of the club, was signed by Milwaukee.[54] In September Joe Ellick of the St. Paul Red Caps was signed to complete an organization. Of course, by this time many of the old names were gone. Joe Lawler, the shortstop who refused to wear spikes, resulting in his frequent slipping on the field, was at Bloomington, Illinois, along with "Cherokee" Fisher. Davy Rowe ended up with Springfield, and even Frank Bliss finished in Buffalo. The West End claim to being the best club in the country was nowhere near the truth, but the final League Alliance standings show Milwaukee had a first-rate club.

	W	L		W	L
St. Paul Red Caps	23	21	Memphis Reds	7	8
Indianapolis Blues	20	23	Cricket	5	7
Minneapolis Blue Stockings	20	23	Philadelphia Athletics	3	2
Milwaukee West End	19	13	Fall River	2	12
Syracuse Stars	17	16	Chicago Fairbanks	2	16
Lowell	12	3	Chelsea	0	3
Janesville Mutuals	12	15			

Charlie Bennett would become one of the best catchers in the country, and a "prime favorite" in Milwaukee.

As a side note, C.G. Yohn, secretary of the Indianapolis Blues, said the Red Caps won 19 games from Minneapolis, so the Blues should be the champions. On October 29, West End disbanded for the season.

As can be seen by the League Alliance final standings and the quality of players on the 1877 West End Club, Milwaukee had by far its best ball club ever assembled to date. This club was fortunate enough to play in a new park, which also was the best built in Milwaukee. These new grounds were at North Thirty-fourth and West State streets. It was larger than old West End Park, being about 500 x 400 feet. The grounds began to resemble later parks by having such features as a 90-foot space between home plate and the backstop, and a body of seats in a semicircle behind this backstop. However, without any type of protective device in front of the seats, the spectators were in danger of being injured by a foul ball. The grandstand had cost in excess of $800, and more than $300 was put into the park for various improvements. The new park, with a three-year lease, was completed in time for the opening game with Fairbanks of Chicago in May. Before the opening, the club practiced at the old grounds on Wells Street, the Nineteenth Street and Sycamore (Michigan Street) grounds, and the grounds on 10th and Clybourn. In July the management built a new tier of seats on the right side of the park, "adding materially to the accommodations for visitors."[55] At the Fourth of July game, 3,000 spectators jammed into the park.

Three thousand was an exceptional crowd and a big money maker, but this was not the rule. The receipts of West End's first four games of 1877 were $123, $130, $125 and $160. As it cost $125 to secure the Stars, and $75 for the Mutuals, it can be seen that good crowds were needed to make any amount of profit. On top of the guarantees, it was estimated that player salaries totaled about $720 a month. Later in the season, with more professionals in tow, salaries were around $1,000 per month. Even with these numbers, in September W.P. Rogers claimed the Association had $250 in the treasury and that the club had made money on every game except one, which came within $5 of breaking even. He claimed the average attendance to be about 500, although newspaper coverage estimates would make that a bit low at that point. Later in the season, with colder weather setting in, crowds were smaller and management lost money on more games. To compensate for this, management had a bargain sale for its final games. Although admission had been set at a quarter at the beginning of the season, it was changed to 50 cents at some point during the season; during this bargain period, three tickets could be bought for $1.00. To give incentive to the players, the West End Board of Directors offered a prize to the player selling the most tickets. A friend of the club also offered a ring to the player who sold $150 worth of tickets. Another new gimmick used that year was a system of dispatches that were sent from the field to Harry K. Phillips Cigar and Tobacco store at 106 Wisconsin Avenue (later address 306 East Wisconsin Avenue) immediately after the third, sixth and ninth innings of the game. These were the first known direct communications from the baseball field in Milwaukee. Later the score was posted after every inning.

On the field, the West End Club won some, lost some, and even tied some. Practice for the season began in March, with those members of the club in town working out at a gymnasium on Grand Avenue. For a warm-up game, West End clubbed the local Athletic team 20 to 2, before meeting first-class competition. On May 5, West End opened its season with an 8 to 5 win over the Fairbanks Club at the new West End Park. A few days later they met the Syracuse Stars and became involved in their first dispute of the infant season. With the score tied 4 to 4 in the ninth inning, Higham, the captain of the Stars, "raised a rumpus"[56] over a call by the umpire and pulled his team off the field. The score remained a tie in the club records. The Stars settled the score the following day by beating the Milwaukee club 8 to 0.

After West End was defeated by Janesville in its next two games, the cry began for new and better players. "The people of Milwaukee cannot be expected to find much pleasure in sitting on a hard bench to see the home club beaten, especially by an amateur nine from the interior."[57] Two new players arrived in the persons of Morgan and Dalrymple, but this was not enough to save West End from a loss to the National League's St. Louis Browns. The club then played a home-and-home series with Fairbanks, winning in Chicago and losing the match here. West End then traveled to Minnesota, first stopping in Minneapolis and losing to the local club there 13 to 11. After having a game in St. Paul rained out, they returned to beat the Minneapolis club. West End then played the Red Caps of St. Paul, losing 1 to 0 in a well-played ten-inning game.

West End returned to Milwaukee, only to be beaten by the Cincinnati Red Stockings of the National League, 7 to 5. The team was not playing well together. At one point in this game with the Red Stockings, West End made four straight base hits, but could not score a run. The club's record was now 3 wins, 8 losses and a tie. Following modern baseball strategy, a new captain was chosen; Daniel Morgan replaced Fred Andrus. Under this new leadership the club won its next two games, beating Racine and whipping Evanston. The club's weak spot was still at the pitching box. Even though the management had recently acquired Davy Rowe, his injury prevented him from playing, which meant Andrus and Morgan shared the pitching duties. In mid–June Rowe pitched for the first time, but may not have been totally recovered, as Memphis beat him 4 to 0. The next day West End won with Andrus in the box. The pitching problem was soon solved with the arrival of Sam Weaver; he beat the St. Paul Red Caps twice, allowing them a total of only one run. The fielding also began to jell, as West End backed Weaver with no errors in the first game, marking the first time the feat of an errorless game could be recalled here. The club then traveled to Racine and beat their local nine 8 to 2 before whitewashing Minneapolis. The West Enders had won 7 of their last 8 games.

"We might play until morning and no one get a run."[58] These were the words of Albert Spalding at the close of West End's best-played game of the season. The game occurred on June 27, with the White Stockings making their first visit of the season to Milwaukee. West End was to host the Racine nine, but cancelled them in order to draw a better crowd by playing the National League club. Each team scored two runs in the first inning, and not another player managed to cross home plate for the next ten innings. The game ended in the 2–2 deadlock because Chicago had to catch the 7:00 P.M. boat from Milwaukee. The tie marked the first time West End had not lost to a National League club; to do this against the mighty White Stockings made it that much better. West End then honored its commitment with Racine and took a beating.

Minneapolis was in town next and committed 27 errors, helping West End to a 16 to 2 win. After beating Janesville twice, West End played the White Stockings again. Although hopes were high for a win this time, the local club made 13 errors en route to a 16 to 2 beating. After defeating the Syracuse Stars, Milwaukee baseball fans received their first look at the then-famous Edward Nolan of the Indianapolis Blues. Because of his great pitching skills, this 19-year-old had acquired the nickname "The Only." He showed his skill at West End Park by beating West End 1 to 0. West End then downed Manchester of New Hampshire and lost again to the White Stockings before its shining moment.

The date was Friday, July 27, 1877, and the Hartford Dark Blues were in town. After nine innings the West Enders had finally posted their first win over a National League club. Milwaukee totally outplayed Hartford, collecting 15 hits to the Dark Blues' 4. The 6 to 1 win was refreshing indeed.

WEST END		AB	R	H	E	HARTFORD		AB	R	H	E
Morgan	3b	5	1	3	0	Burdock	2b	4	0	0	1
Andrus	rf	5	0	2	1	Holdsworth	3b	4	0	0	0
Redmond	ss	4	0	2	0	Start	1b	4	0	1	2
Mills	1b	4	0	0	0	Carey	ss	4	0	0	1
Dalrymple	lf	5	1	2	0	Harbidge	cf	4	0	1	0
Turner	cf	5	0	1	1	York	lf	3	0	0	0
MacDonald	2b	5	1	1	2	Cassidy	rf	3	0	0	0
Bennett	c	4	2	2	0	Allison	c	3	0	2	0
Weaver	p	3	1	2	1	Larkin	p	4	1	0	2
		40	6	15	7			33	1	4	6

	1	2	3	4	5	6	7	8	9	
Hartford	0	0	0	0	0	0	0	1	0	—1
West End	1	0	0	0	2	0	0	0	3	—6

After this historic win, West End beat Manchester again before trouble started to brew once more. When Indianapolis failed to show up for a scheduled match, West End booked a game with Janesville "to avoid disappointing the public, which has a weakness for Saturday games."[59] The Mutuals won the contest and a rematch was set up a few days later in Janesville. With no score in the ninth inning, Janesville scored five runs, but West End players began to argue the play as well as a previous play. West End claimed a ball was thrown into the crowd during the previous inning and "a boy in the crowd picked up the ball, threw it into the diamond and it was fielded to third where Redmond was declared out."[60] Milwaukee then left the field and the game was forfeited to the Mutuals. West End then lost three straight games to National League clubs before beating Indianapolis, which had won more games against National League clubs than any other Alliance club.

By mid–August, even though West End was third among National Alliance clubs with a 12-win and 11-loss record, disappointment had set in. After a loss to St. Louis, the *Sentinel* on August 17, 1877, voiced its opinion: "The Browns were beaten the other day by a country club in Illinois and of course, they hunted up another club which they could beat in order to redeem themselves. The puzzle is, what club can the Milwaukees find to beat. Janesville? Probably not."

Time was at hand to see if West End could beat the Mutuals. A best-of-five series was set up between the two clubs to determine the state championship. Local comment was that "unless there is a change in the management, the Milwaukees may be expected to win one game of the series."[61] The Mutuals had played West End six times during the season and won four, so there was some basis for the opinion. In the opening game the Mutuals outscored Milwaukee 4 to 3. About two weeks later game two was played in Janesville. Betting on the game was about even, but West End won decisively. Back in Milwaukee the following day, West End won by an even bigger score. And in game four West End won the championship with a 6 to 0 victory; Sam Weaver did not allow the Mutuals a hit.

WEST END		AB	R	H	E	MUTUALS		AB	R	H	E
Morgan	3b	5	1	1	1	James	rf	4	0	0	0
Redmond	ss	5	1	3	0	Bliss	ss	4	0	0	0
Andrus	rf	5	1	0	0	Ward	p	4	0	0	2
Dalrymple	lf	5	0	2	0	Shoupe	2b	3	0	0	0
McDonald	2b	4	0	2	0	Phillips	1b	3	0	0	1
Mills	1b	4	0	0	0	Bushong	c	3	0	0	4
Weaver	p	4	1	1	1	Arundel	cf	3	0	0	0
Rowe	c	4	1	1	5	Cantillon	lf	3	0	0	0
Turner	cf	4	1	1	1	Morrissey	3b	3	0	0	0
		40	6	11	8			30	0	0	7

	1	2	3	4	5	6	7	8	9	
West End	1	0	1	2	0	2	0	0	0	—6
Mutuals	0	0	0	0	0	0	0	0	0	—0

The turnabout from game one was amazing. West End completely dominated the series, outscoring the Mutuals 38 to 7, collecting 42 hits to their 16, and committing 23 errors compared to Janesville's 48. The Mutuals could see the change as well, and tried to have the games cancelled. Claiming that the second and third games were only played because of cancellations from clubs, the Mutuals did not think these games should count toward the championship. West End disagreed, and the games counted.

Between the first and second championship games, West End played three games with the Alleghany Club of Pittsburgh, taking abuse from all sides. After West End lost the first game of the series in eleven innings, the *Sentinel* reported on August 24, 1877, "the club showed the good effects of better management." But not better security. Instead of playing in their usually sharp uniform, which included a variegated cap, white flannel shirt with a dark navy blue belt, white pants and dark blue stockings under white shoes, West End was forced to take the field in "borrowed pants and cheap and gaudy blue shirts."[62] Burglars had broken into the clubhouse and taken five uniforms, for which the management was offering a $25 reward for recovery. In the second game a dispute arose before play began. West End offered the game ball to the manager of the Alleghany club, who refused to accept it because it was not enclosed in a sealed box, as according to the rules. The game was delayed an hour as a new ball had to be brought in from town, causing the *Sentinel* to sarcastically state "if the Milwaukee Baseball Association hasn't money enough to buy more than one ball at a time, they should take up a collection."[63] Speculation was the Pittsburgh club was upset with West End signing Bill Holbert and George Creamer to contracts for the 1878 season, a practice outlawed the next year. Once the game was underway, Milwaukee scored an easy 8 to 4 victory. After losing game three 1 to 0 in 12 innings, it was suggested in the press that West End was getting a little lazy. "One would think to see some of them bat and neglect to run that they are in training for positions in the police force."[64]

West End, now with the state championship under its navy blue belt, won its next six games, beating the Springfield Reds, Syracuse Stars and Janesville Mutuals twice, before losing to the Alleghanys. West End had now won nine of its last ten games and departed for an eastern tour that would take the club further away from home than any Milwaukee club had ever gone. The first stop was Detroit, where West End beat the Cass Club 11 to 1. The club then crossed the border into Canada to play the London Tescumsehs. After losing the first game, West End won an 11 to 1 contest. Back in the States West End beat the Buffalo club twice and tied the Indianapolis Blues before returning home in early October. West End then closed the season in late October with two games against the White Stockings, who had finished a poor fifth in the National League standings; West End won the first and lost the second.

At the final meeting of the board of directors in November, the club decided to build a new stadium in the Fourth Ward and announced "the prospect is flattering that Milwaukee will have one of the strongest clubs in the country."[65] With a strong nine lined up for 1878, the prospect was bright. West End had compiled a 33–25–3 record for all games played in 1877. As noted, its League Alliance record was 19 and 13. Against National League clubs, West End won 2 and lost 9 and tied one. Against all non-league clubs, their record stood 31–16–2. In their final 20 contests, Milwaukee won 15, lost 4 and tied one.

However, certain events changed the entire picture in 1878.

5

Milwaukee: A National League City (1878)

The year 1877 did not turn out well for the National League of Professional Baseball Clubs. The six teams in the two-year-old-year league lost money. A report shows even the pennant-winning Boston Red Stockings, with Harry Wright at the helm, lost $2,230.85.[1] In financial trouble, the Cincinnati Reds disbanded in June, but days later reorganized. Later the National League would take the Cincinnati games out of the final 1877 standings because first, the club did not pay the regular entry fee, and second, it had not been in the league all season. In Louisville three players were expelled for "conspiring to sell games and tampering with players" and a fourth "because of disobedience of positive orders of general misconduct and suspicious play."[2] On December 4, Louisville and Cincinnati were cut from the league, although Cincinnati was reinstated. St. Louis resigned from the league the next day. Hartford was also now vacant, and it was decided a new Hartford team could not enter the league on the basis of the former club's membership. When all this is sorted out, the National League stood with three clubs under its banner—the Chicago White Stockings, Boston Red Stockings and Cincinnati Red Stockings.

Back in Milwaukee a decision was in the making. *The Sentinel* stated, "With no clubs at St. Paul, Minneapolis, Janesville, and when the League clubs include all the best clubs in the West and East, the Milwaukee Club will literally have nothing to do." Answer—"It is to the financial interest of the club to unite with the League."[3] Two National League constitutional provisions no doubt were seen as a great help to the club. The National League gave every club "exclusive control of the city in which it is located, and of the territory surrounding such city to the extent of five miles in every direction."[4] Another league condition required a member club to be from a city with a population of 75,000 or more, unless approved by a unanimous vote of the league. Two other provisions would hurt Milwaukee. There was no Sunday ball, with a National League team or any other club. A National League club could not even permit a game to be played upon its grounds on Sunday. No National League club could "play a game with any organized club prior to the commencement of the League season, nor can any club play on its own grounds a game with an club outside of the League during the League season."[5] This rule would hurt Milwaukee's profitable games with local rivals. However, for any exhibition games played with a non-league club, the National League club demanded "a surety of $100"[6] and $50 if the game was postponed for any reason.

The Milwaukee Board of Directors weighed the facts and on November 30 decided to unite with the National League. Of course, the league was not the only way to go. Aside from remaining independent, the Milwaukee club could have joined the International Baseball Association. The IBA was looking for new members and sent out this flowery circular with the Baseball Fraternity of the United States and Canada, which read in part:

All know its objects and aims are to preserve, foster and purify the game, and to throw out bad features and bad men from the profession: to establish uniform rules and usage, and preserve harmony. It assures the stronger and protects the weaker clubs, and compels clubs and players alike to deal honestly with each other.

W.A. Cummings-President[7]

At the National League winter meeting, held at the Kennard House in Cleveland, the Milwaukee Baseball Club presented the names of the members of its 1878 club:

Fred Andrus	Jacob Goodman
Charlie Bennett	Bill Holbert
George Creamer	Daniel Morgan
Abner Dalrymple	Billy Redmond
Joe Ellick	Sam Weaver
Bill Foley	

Milwaukee was admitted to the National League on December 5, 1877. With the admission of Indianapolis, the National League now consisted of Boston, Chicago, Cincinnati, Indianapolis and Milwaukee. Providence was eventually named as the sixth member. William A. Hulbert and Nicholas E. Young were re-elected to their positions of president and secretary of the National League. The NL Board of Directors consisted of Hulbert, J.W. Neff of Cincinnati, W.P. Rogers of Milwaukee, W.B. Pettit of Indianapolis and A.H. Soden of Boston.

League officials met again in April, this time in Buffalo. Representatives from each club were present, Milwaukee represented by its new manager, John Chapman. The most important decision to come out of these spring meetings was an agreement between the National League and International Baseball Association. Surprisingly, the agreement favored the International. Teams from the two leagues were given permission to play against each other, charging admission of 25 cents and splitting the gross receipts after the guaranteed $75 was met. The National League even promised to honor International's player contracts and territorial rights. Internally the National League ruled that any game between its member clubs would count toward the championship, even if played in a neutral city. The final results of the meeting were the unveiling of the National League schedule, with Milwaukee opening its 60-game schedule on May 1 in Cincinnati.

Milwaukee was now officially in the National League, and back home preparations for the big season were underway. Stockholders and management appeared to be essentially the same as in the 1877 Milwaukee Baseball Association. If this is true, it can be assumed the new Association had the previous year's acting capital to work with. In March all stockholders were assessed $15 for season tickets, good for 40 admissions and a reserved seat; such reserved tickets were $25 in Indianapolis. The season tickets were placed on sale to the public a little later at George Morton's Cigar Store in the Plankinton House, as well as Harry Phillips' on Wisconsin Avenue. Phillips was the club's official scorer. "The tickets were being rapidly disposed of, but the sale could be increased. The stockholders were subsequently supplied with tickets and will make a personal effort to sell them."[8]

Admission to games in Milwaukee in 1878 was to be 50 cents, and another quarter for reserved seats. Any complaints about the high admission fees was countered by the *Milwaukee Sentinel* of March 12, 1878: "This may seem to some too much, but we think that when you come to take into consideration that it is League games, the very best talent that the country produces, the expense will be enormous to carry out the season successfully, and it seems to settle right down to this: You cannot carry on a first class club or entertainment of any kind on a second class basis."

The plant where these admissions were gathered was at 10th and Clybourn, which in November of 1877 the Milwaukee Baseball Club Board of Directors had decided to secure. There was a playing field at this location the previous year, and the work referred to on this park could have been renovation or the complete rebuilding of a new park. W.P. Rogers was reported to have undertaken the removal of the stands and buildings. The park was completed in mid–April. The seating capacity of the park was about 4,000 with 500 grandstand seats, and was said to be the equal of any other in the country. It was 400-feet square, and spectators were "protected from the rays of the sun by a double row of shade trees"[9] on the north side of the grounds. The *Milwaukee Sentinel* of April 6, 1878, reported, "The diamond is one of the finest in the country, although grounds are not as deep as at some other points. Ground rules, similar to those in force in Chicago, will be established," which meant the right field fence was close enough to home plate that balls hit over it on the fly were ground-rule doubles. However, the field was not perfect. It was not level in all spots, and other improvements were needed. "The backstop ought to be fixed so that balls will not skew over towards the south" and "the facing of the grandstand, that ornamental board arrangement, ought to be shortened, as it intercepts the view of the high flies by persons on the top seats."[10] As the grounds were only a 15-minute walk from the center of town, it was hoped the savings of horse cars or bus fare would bring in more fans. The 3:30 P.M. starting time also helped businessmen come to the park after work.

In the March 16, 1878, *Milwaukee Sentinel*, one read, "The only object of the management is to make the nine pay expenses. It is not expected that any money will be made out of the games and all charges are as low as possible in order to run a first-class club." Even in the old days this must have been hard to believe. Milwaukee's timing in entering the league was poor. David Quentin Voigt wrote in his first volume of *American Baseball:* "With severe business depressions racking the land, many potential fans were out of work. The nadir of the depression was reached in 1878, and a slow upturn followed."[11] The Milwaukee Baseball Association did find some ways to bring in extra money. Bids were received early by the club for advertising space on the fences. In addition, the Cricket Club paid more than $50 to the baseball club for use of the grounds.

Of course, expenses were high, too. Total expenses were estimated to be from $25,000 to $30,000 a year per club. The majority of this expense was in player salaries. What the Milwaukee salaries were is not known, but Voigt reports the Boston Red Stockings' payroll was $18,814 for 1878.[12]

To pay these expenses, most revenue came from attendance, of which visiting National League clubs received 15 cents per capita of the gate receipts. In April the Milwaukee club hosted a contest with two pick nines of "notable strength" at the park. Admission to this exhibition was set at a quarter, with a dime extra charge to occupy a grandstand seat. Stockholders were to be admitted free "so that the advantage to be gained by purchasing season tickets will be at once recognized."[13] An estimated 600 to 800 attended the game that Saturday. For opening day on May 14, an estimated crowd of 1,500 attended, and the editor of the *Sentinel* noted that seats should be reserved in advance to avoid the rush for the next day's contest. At this point, game attendance was up to about 2,000.[3] As the club continued to lose games throughout the season, the *Sentinel* reported, "Milwaukee is nearly as bad as Indianapolis for pouting. Because the Grays have lost games, and notwithstanding they have played some good ones, only about 600 people went out to see yesterday's contest with the Chicagos."[14]

The small crowds may have been losing money for the club, but it was reported in late June that despite rumors to the contrary, the club was in excellent financial condition. A week later, it was reported that a proposal was made to turn over control of the club to William P. Rogers, who had "retired from all official connections" with the club, "on condition that he assumes all the liabilities of the club and bind himself to fill out the rest of the league schedule."[15] This report probably stemmed from an earlier report that Rogers claimed the club owed him $1,192.93 from the previous year, and he planned to have the grounds attached. The directors of the club claimed that the expenditures Rogers made were not authorized, and it was thought Rogers wanted control of the club. In a turnabout from the previous year's praise, Rogers drew fire from the press, "as he is not a conspicuous success as a manager, he will fail in his effort."[16] Unfortunately, the Milwaukee Baseball Association never revealed its true financial situation, or the papers never reported the situation, until the end.

As today, players were greatly appreciated by the press at times and run into the ground on other occasions. The *Sentinel* wrote on April 15, 1878, "Professionally, the baseball player is to be looked upon very much as a horse, to be put through his paces for practice, dieted, rubbed down and treated altogether as a pitcher, catcher, shortstop, or whatever be, without any regard to his individuality." In reality, the truth was, as still is—"once more the church-choir tenor, who has been the winter idol of the public, is returned to indifference and the baseball player becomes the hero."[17]

As every athlete knows, the press has many moods, usually depending on winning performances. In pre-season and early-season comment, the press was high on the Milwaukee club, with a "well grounded belief that the home club will stand at the top at the close of the season."[18] However, as the season continued, and the Grays continued to lose, the press came down on the club. On June 4 the *Sentinel* sports headline read: AT THE TAILEND—THE MILWAUKEE'S AT LAST REACH A NOTABLE PLACE IN THE LEAGUE. By late July the paper's headline read: AMATEUR BASEBALL—IT SEEMS TO BE MUCH BETTER THAN THE PROFESSIONAL PLAY.[19] Other headlines read, "The Milwaukee Muffers" and "Dropped a Game, as Usual."[20] By the end of July the paper was so down on the club it only gave the score of the Milwaukee-Providence game, but gave a full account of the Chicago-Indianapolis contest.

Salaries of ball players were not terrible. There is no record of the salaries paid to the 1878 Milwaukee players. We know that Charlie Bennett's salary in 1877 was $1,700, but he was probably one of the highest paid players on that club. In any instance, baseball players were paid better than the other workers of the city and state. Wages for lumbermen in Wisconsin were $15 to $25 a month that winter. City laborers received from $1.25 to $1.50 per day. Assuming the workers toiled at their jobs six days a week, their yearly salary would be $470, which is likely considerably less than the worst-paid ball players.

The Milwaukee Board of Directors in April issued a set of 14 rules for the "government of players"; if a player disobeyed he would be fined not less than $10 or more than $20 "for each offense." These dozen-plus-two rules included several rules still enforced and a few that might seem strange. As today, players in uniform could not converse or mingle with friends in the stands, smoking in uniform was outlawed and, of course, players were to obey the captain. The players had to "deport themselves in a gentlemanly manner at all times, to dress neatly, to avoid association with gamblers ... conduct themselves in a quiet and gentlemanly manner and guard against practices which will injure their own reputation or that of the club." In addition to keeping his uniform clean, the player had to make sure that "the spikes in his shoes were securely fastened." No player, except for the captain or his assistant, was allowed to dispute a decision by the umpire, and players had to play as quietly as possible — no "kicking" was allowed. At home games players could not appear on the grounds in uniform earlier than 30 minutes before game time. When on the road, they had to enter the field together and once on the field, fungo batting was prohibited in front of the crowd. Players could not invite friends to ride in the "conveyances" to or from the park without the manager's permission. Last, but not least, the players were required to be in the hotel no later than 10:00 P.M. when on the road.[21]

Referring to players as only contracts with clubs is not exactly what baseball is all about. Players have names and personalities. The Milwaukee Grays, the team fell heir to the nickname when John Chapman was hired as manager (Fred Andrus having decided "to retire permanently from the business"[22]), had names and personalities, as well. John Curtis Chapman, 35 years old that year, took over control of the team. Chapman had been playing organized ball since 1858, and in the 1860s played with the famous Atlantic Club of Brooklyn. He first assumed charge of a club in 1871 by managing the Eckford Club of the National Association. He then retired from baseball until 1874. He played with the Louisville club in 1876 and managed the team in 1877, the year of the scandal, and took the nickname Grays to Milwaukee with him. Chapman was considered a good manager, well "posted as to players."[23]

Chapman had a better team to work with than Rogers did the year before with the West Enders. The December 1, 1877, *Sentinel* was quick to point out "it was shown last year that the choice, high priced players were not necessarily the best." Rogers said of the team, "We feel proud of our new nine, as their reputations are all above reproach — that's the kind of men to win with — and their integrity beyond question."[24] By mid–March the Grays took this appearance:

Name	Position	Last Year's Club
Charlie Bennett	Catcher & Change Pitcher	Milwaukee
Bill Holbert	Pitcher	Allegheny
Sam Weaver	Pitcher	Milwaukee
George Bradley	Pitcher	Chicago
Jacob Goodman	First Base	Allegheny
Billy Redmond	Shortstop	Milwaukee
John Peters	Second Base	Chicago
Bill Foley	Third Base	Cincinnati
George Creamer	Left Field	Allegheny
Abner Dalrymple	Center Field	Milwaukee
Joe Ellick	Substitute	St. Paul/Milwaukee

As can be seen, some played for Milwaukee the year before. Charlie Bennett was a "prime favorite in this city."[25] He continued his baseball career for 15 years, catching 954 games, remarkable for those days. From 1881 until going to Boston in 1888, he was the backbone of the Detroit club, which won the National League championship in 1887. The *Sporting News* later wrote of Bennett: "He was as pretty a catcher as ever shot the leather down to second. He was perfect in his position. He was a model.... As a backstop he was the same as a bulletin board, and his throws to second were marvels for bounty and accuracy. He is an easy and graceful catcher."[26] In January of 1894, while on a hunting trip, Bennett slipped while attempting to board a moving train and fell under the wheels, losing his legs. When Detroit opened a new ballpark in 1896, it was named Bennett Park in Charlie's honor. Sam Weaver was back to handle the pitching chores, with Billy Redmond at shortstop and utility infielder Joe Ellick. All had a few games' experience in the professional leagues. The fifth returning player was Abner Dalrymple. Abner, at 20, was the youngest player on the club and one of the youngest in the National League. Born in Wisconsin and raised in Warren, Illinois, he was considered to have one of the best arms in the country along with a fine bat. The *Sentinel* prediction that he was "very promising"[27] was true. The left-handed outfielder starred in Chicago under Cap Anson for eight years, hitting over .290 six straight years and leading the league in hits, total bases and runs scored in 1880, total bases again in 1884, and home runs in 1885. Dalrymple, much like Bennett, became one of the league's established players, but today is one of the forgotten stars of the era.

New faces included Holbert, Goodman and Creamer from the Pittsburgh Alleghenys. Bill Holbert was a fine outfielder in Pittsburgh and could also help out at the catching position. Not much of a hitter, he played 12 years in the big leagues, finishing with a .208 lifetime batting average. Jacob Goodman became the steady first baseman the club needed. George Creamer, whose real name was George W. Triebel, brought some good fielding to Milwaukee. Two established starters also were in the fold. John Peters, a heavy hitting shortstop, had played the previous two years in Chicago, hitting .351 and .317 for the White Stockings. Bill Foley, at third base, a "position he has probably no superior and few equals,"[28] was a weak hitter from the Cincinnati Red Stockings.

The Grays soon were involved in a controversy over pitcher George Bradley. Bradley had won 45 games for St. Louis in 1876, including the first no-hitter in National League history, and 18 games for Chicago in 1877. Bradley sent a telegram to Milwaukee stating, "Send on the contract at once.... I can secure my release (from the New Bedford Club) by returning $50."[29] The Grays supposedly sent Bradley a contract and $100. Bradley, on advice from Harry Wright, decided not to obtain his release. For days the controversy continued in the papers, with Milwaukee pitted against Boston, who also appeared to want the pitcher. Bradley did not play baseball in the National League in 1878, but won 138 games before ending his big league career in 1884.

Milwaukee secured Michael Golden after this loss. Golden, who had pitched for Indianapolis in 1877, was seen as a good pitcher, "his incurve and drop are said to be entirely phenomenal,"[30] and was thought by the *New York Mercury* to be better than Bradley. However, the *New York Clipper* of May 4, 1878, wrote, "Golden is a hard working, earnest player, and has gained the confidence and respect of Milwaukeeans by his willingness to work, but his pitching is not up to the League standard...."

On April 3, the *Sentinel* compiled a list of the previous year's averages to show how the Grays stood with the other league entries, excluding for an unknown reason Providence:

	B.A.	F.A		B.A.	F.A
Peters	.299	.888	Creamer	.246	.391
Dalrymple	.298	.807	Redmond	.233	.888
Golden	.298	.821	Foley	.206	.849
Bennett	.264	.879	Weaver	.179	.896
Goodman	.256	.942	TOTAL	2,529	8,702
Holbert	.250	.821			
Boston	2,729	8,663	Cincinnati	2,716	8,551
Chicago	2,749	8,503	Indianapolis	2,631	8,414

As shown, Milwaukee's batting average for the ten-man squad was the lowest, but their combined fielding average was the best.

With the season approaching, predictions followed in the newspapers. In late March the *Sentinel* made the prediction that because of Milwaukee's batting record, "it is safe to wager something that the pennant will come to the Cream City."[31] More experienced, and less prejudiced, papers looked at it differently. The *New York Sunday Mercury* was sober in its evaluation:

> The Milwaukee Club is an unknown quantity as yet. They are young men, however, and ambitious, and as they have nothing to lose and everything to gain by winning, there is no doubt they will give a favorable account of themselves when the time comes. The Milwaukees will mark and astonish some of the old clubs before the season is over.[32]

The *Mercury* picked Boston, primarily on its experience, to be on top at the end, with Cincinnati giving them a battle because of its batting strength. Chicago was given the second or third nod, followed by Indianapolis, Providence and Milwaukee, which was expected to bring up the rear. Boston papers conceded that the Grays had probably the best fielders, but were weak at the plate, which would agree with the above statistics.

In the *Sentinel's* full analysis of the league, it was thought "anyone familiar with the record of the League players will look over the list of men who comprise the nines without prejudice, will find that Milwaukee stands a fine chance to win the championship." Boston was thought to have an outstanding club and "their chances of victory were as good as those of any club." Chicago had a powerful club, "but whether the members will play together is the perplexing question." Cincinnati, "puffed higher than any other ball organization in the land," had a good club, but was poor on the bases, the *Sentinel* concluded. Indianapolis' chances were said to be hurt by Nolen's bad temper, while Providence "may do great things and is just as likely to fall short of what its friends hope."[33]

In reading the local papers' pre-season predictions, one must remember local prejudices were high. The *New York Clipper* had little hope for the Milwaukee club: "If they do nothing more, they will at least be able to keep their Chicago neighbors from occupying last-place position in the race in the place of the Cincinnatis, who considerately helped the Whites in this respect in 1877."[34] The *Clipper* thought the Providence club would land higher than Milwaukee in the final standings, prompting the *Sentinel* to write that the *Clipper* "doesn't know a foul-tip from a third base."[35]

On April 3, John Chapman returned from Buffalo and practice began with a few of the players on hand. By mid–April all the players, except John Peters, who had just become a father, were in town. Chapman put the men "through a severe course of drill,"[36] including a 3-to-8 mile walk in the morning and three hours in the afternoon devoted to practicing the basics of the game. He also added "the pleasant amusement of manipulating the 500 pound roller on the grounds."[37] On April 13 the first exhibition game was played at the Tenth and Clybourn grounds. The Grays, along with some familiar names, joined to play the contest.

Player	Position	Player
Weaver	Pitcher	Golden
Bennett	Catcher	Holbert
Goodman	First Base	Chapman
Creamer	Second Base	Ellick
Foley	Third Base	Andrus
Redmond	Shortstop	Peters
Dalrymple	Left Field	Gault
Chandler	Center Field	Stone
Kershaw	Right Field	Furlong

For the record, the team, behind pitcher Michael Golden, won 5 to 3. Although the team was rusty, it was fairly impressive, especially in hitting. On April 17 the Milwaukee regulars played a picked nine of locals. With Golden pitching for the picked nine, the Grays collected 32 hits en route to a 26–0 win. Three days later the regulars again played the picked nine, winning 7 to 3. After having a game in Racine rained out, the Grays played the Racine College team, allowing the collegiate ten players, winning 14 to 9, largely due to the college boys' 33 errors, and Weaver's pitching — only allowing one hit. Milwaukee was now ready for the National League schedule.

✳ ✳ ✳

To play any game, authority must be on the field. Baseball has umpires to keep the peace. According to the National League rules in 1878, umpires were selected in a number of ways. The two clubs could agree (in writing) on any man to umpire a game. The National League also had an umpire pool, consisting of names submitted and approved by member clubs who were "persons of good repute, and who are considered competent to act as umpires." The visiting club could also submit to the home club five names from this umpire pool, "none of whom shall reside in the city of the visiting club." The home club then chose from these five. If the visiting club did not furnish five umpire candidates, the home club selected the umpire. The visiting club paid the fees and expenses of the umpire.[38] The umpires selected from Milwaukee were three former ball players from the area: Billy Furlong, W.J. Turner and Chan Simmonds.

Abner Dalrymple — the batting star of Milwaukee's National League Grays, going on to win the 1878 batting championship.

Umpires attempted to keep things running, but drew fire from the press on several occasions. "There was considerable dissatisfaction with the umpire, whose ... decisions seemed to favor the visitors (Cincinnati) in every instance" and "...as the umpiring was decidedly against the Milwaukee."[39] The *Chicago Tribune* of July 30, 1882, summed up public opinion of the umpire:

> For the most part the umpires of today are played out ball tossers, fellows who are driven by necessity to accept the pittance of $5 per game which is allotted as their compensation. Instead of being, as he should be, far above the level of the ballplayers, the umpire of today is far below that level, and properly belongs to the "bum" category. He travels, sleeps, eats, associates with the players,

and frequently joins them in tossing the ball about before the game begins. It is quite likely he is, when at home, the associate of thieves and gamblers ... and when on his travels naturally spends his leisure hours in the same company. His intimacy with players off the ball field renders it impossible for him to be strict and impartial during a game, and a desire to curry favor with the club management which chooses him will inevitably cause him to show favor to one side or the other. Granting that he is not dishonest — which is granting a great deal in the light of developments and appearances — the average League umpire is a worthless loafer, easily tempted and swayed by improper considerations, and is a very unsafe and eminently unworthy person in whose hands to place the arbitration of a game of ball played in the presence of great crowds of ladies and gentlemen.

✳ ✳ ✳

From the "Official Playing Rules for 1878," published in Beadle's *Dime Base-Ball Player* of that year, one can catch a glimpse of how the game was played in Milwaukee's season in the National League. The bases were "30 yards" apart, as today. However, the pitcher's position was a space of ground six feet square, the front line of which was 45 feet from the center of home base. The corners of this area were marked by four six-inch square flat irons or stones. The batter took his position and called for either a "high ball" (between the belt and shoulders), "low ball" (between the belt and knees) or a "fair ball" (between shoulders and knees). The pitcher then delivered the ball with his "arm swinging nearly perpendicular at the side of the body, and the hand in swinging forward must pass below the waist." If the batter failed to swing at a ball he called for, or swung and missed the ball, a strike was called. If the batter did not swing at a good pitch after two strikes, he received one warning from the umpire. Finally when the third strike was made (either swinging or called), the catcher had to catch the ball before it hit the ground, or "after touching the ground but once." If the catcher failed to catch the ball in this fashion, a put-out at first base had to be made. However, if the pitcher did not deliver the ball over home base in the area called for, it was considered "an unfair" pitch. Every third "unfair" pitch was called a "ball" and after three "balls" the batter would take first base.

If the batter hit the ball directly to the ground in foul territory, it could go into fair territory before first or third base and be considered a fair ball. As now, a fair ball had to be caught on a fly for an out. However, a foul ball could be caught after hitting the ground once for an out.

Most other major rules were the same or similar to those in effect today. However, of those differing, three are of interest. The previous year the home club batted first. "This removed one of the elements of expectancy in the game, and thereby detracted from its interest to that extent. The old method of flipping a coin by the captains has been returned to" for 1878. There was no substituting of players after the first inning "except for the reason of illness or injury." If a base runner needed to be substituted for — again due to illness or "injury incurred in the game then being played" — the opposing captain selected the man to run. The Rule First, section 4, read in full: "When the ball becomes out of shape, or cut or ripped so as to expose the yarn or in any way so injured as to be unfit for fair use, a new ball shall be called for by the umpire at the end of an even inning, at the request of either captain. Should the ball be lost during a game, the umpire shall, at the expiration of five minutes, call for a new ball."[40]

✳ ✳ ✳

The Milwaukee Grays opened the 1878 regular season on May 1 in Cincinnati. Chapman submitted the five names for umpiring duty for the contest and George Bradburg was selected. Bradburg could not attend the game, so Robert Crandell umpired the Milwaukee maiden voyage in the National League. Though the Grays were strong at the plate, weak fielding caused a 6 to 4 loss to the Red Stockings. Sam Weaver, who had just recovered from a hand injury from pre-season practice, was "plainly out of kilter."[41] He had nine balls called on him, giving two men bases on balls, and let a Red Stocking score on a wild pitch in the early innings. Weaver's lack of control led to the loss of his temper, of course directed at the umpire, and finally the crowd was heard to yell, "Fire him!" The Grays—clad in their light gray pants, shirts and caps, trimmed in red with a German text M on the breast, along with cardinal stockings and belts, made by A.G. Spalding and Brothers of Chicago—committed ten errors to Cincinnati's two, but out-hit the Reds 12 to 11.

MILWAUKEE		AB	R	H	E	CINCINNATI		AB	R	H	E
Peters	2b	4	0	3	0	Pike	cf	5	1	1	0
Holbert	rf	5	1	0	1	McVey	3b	5	2	4	0
Bennett	c	4	1	2	2	Geer	2b	4	1	1	1
Dalrymple	lf	5	0	1	0	J. White	c	5	1	2	0
Creamer	cf	5	1	2	0	Mitchell	ss	4	0	0	0
Redmond	ss	5	0	1	0	Jones	lf	4	0	1	1
Foley	3b	5	1	2	1	Sullivan	1b	4	0	0	0
Golden	1b	4	0	1	2	Kelly	rf	3	1	1	0
Weaver	p	3	0	0	4	W. White	p	4	0	1	0
		40	4	12	10			38	6	11	2

```
Milwaukee   3 0 0 0 0 0 1 0 0—4
Cincinnati  4 0 1 0 0 0 0 0 1—6
```

In commenting on the game, the *Cincinnati Gazette* observed the Grays could not "retain their coolness of self-possession in a close game." The *Cincinnati Commercial* believed "the playing of the Milwaukee Club was individually strong, but the individual strength was in want of united action and harmony."[42]

The following day the Reds beat Milwaukee again, 6 to 2, and the Grays' problems behind the plate started, a problem that would last the entire season. In the fourth inning Charlie Bennett's hands gave out and he went to center field, Bill Holbert replacing him at the catching position. Two days later the Grays lost the final game of the series 4 to 1. John Peters and Abner Dalrymple were bright spots, both hitting safely in each of the three games, collecting five and four hits, respectively.

After scouting the Blues for a day, the Grays invaded Indianapolis for their next set. The first game lasted ten innings, ending in a 2 to 2 tie, called by darkness. On May 9 Milwaukee scored its first victory of the season with a 2 to 1 win over the Blues. "The playing of the victors was steady and careful throughout the entire game, while the playing of Holbert behind the bat was a beautiful exhibition of catching. Weaver's pitching was the finest ever displayed on a Hoosier diamond."[43] Dalrymple collected two hits to run his string to four games. Defensively, the Grays committed only three errors, the team's lowest total of the new season. The Grays then replayed the tie contest and the final game of the series, losing both. Dalrymple continued to bat well, having a hit in all six games of the season.

Milwaukee hosted its first National League game on Tuesday, May 14, 1878. The gates to the park opened at 2:00 in the afternoon for the 3:45 contest. The home opener was a success against the Cincinnati Red Stockings, giving the Reds their first defeat of the season, 8 to 5. The Grays scored single runs in the fourth and fifth innings and two more in the sixth, before Cincinnati scored its first run. The roof fell in on McVey's team in the eighth when Milwaukee scored four runs, giving the home crowd something to cheer wildly over. Manager Chapman had changed his batting order to find success with a 13-hit attack. The press immediately jumped on the Grays' bandwagon, with the *Sentinel's* May 15 headline reading, THE COMING CHAMPIONS." The *Sentinel* again had high hopes and declared, "Yesterday's game demonstrates why there should be no good reason to doubt that they are the heaviest hitters in the league and this is the reason why they should win the pennant, unless ... luck overruns the boys."[44] The paper then boldly predicted that the Grays would win their next five games. The *Cincinnati Enquirer* cried, "Jerusalem! Our brave bantams have been beaten at last, and by a club that the public looked upon as weak. The *Enquirer* has frequently warned its readers not to underrate the Milwaukee Club."[45]

Sam Weaver — Milwaukee's ace pitcher, who holds honor of pitching the first known no-hitter for a Milwaukee team in the major leagues.

MILWAUKEE		AB	R	H	E	CINCINNATI		AB	R	H	E
Dalrymple	lf	4	2	3	0	Pike	cf	4	0	1	0
Peters	2b	4	3	3	0	McVey	3b	5	1	2	0
Goodman	1b	4	0	1	0	Geer	ss	5	1	1	0
Foley	3b	4	1	2	0	J. White	c	5	1	0	1
Bennett	cf	4	0	0	0	Gerhardt	2b	5	0	0	1
Holbert	c	4	1	2	1	Jones	lf	3	1	1	0
Redmond	ss	4	0	0	3	Sullivan	1b	3	0	0	0
Golden	rf	4	0	1	1	Kelly	rf	3	1	1	2
Weaver	p	5	1	1	2	W. White	p	3	0	0	2
		37	8	13	7			36	5	6	6

Milwaukee   0 0 0 1 1 2 0 4 0—8
Cincinnati   0 0 0 0 0 1 3 1 0—5

On Thursday the Grays were again victorious over the Cincinnati club. "Milwaukee stock went away up booming in the first inning when the big hitting commenced and the fellows who had bet the boys couldn't do it again to the man in specs were glum."[46] The Grays opened for five runs in the first inning. Two of these came when Redmond struck out and Jim (Deacon) White, the Reds catcher, intentionally dropped the ball. Hoping for a double play, he threw to first base to put out Redmond, but Sullivan threw wild to home, scoring Foley and Bennett. The Grays collected 19 hits en route to the 12 to 8 win. "The man in specs" was Will White, Cincinnati pitcher, the first known player to wear glasses on the field. The *Sentinel* was now sure that "evidence easily furnishes that the Grays should win the pennant by reason of spectacular batting strength."[47] To end the three-game series, the Grays lost to Cincinnati 10 to 2. Mike Golden's slow delivery hurt the Grays, the Reds even stealing third base twice. Also hurting was the team's sloppy fielding, Milwaukee committing 14 errors. Dalrymple continued to be hot, running his hitting streak to all nine games.

The Grays next took on Indianapolis again, facing "The Only Nolan," a pitcher they usually had no difficulty hitting. "Nolan vindicated his right to have his picture in every window in the city ... as he won the game by his magnificent curves,"[48] 6 to 5. Before the game Daniel Morgan had joined the Grays. "Pidge" had been released by the club the previous winter (he had played with the West End club) and had been with the St. Louis cooperative club. For the second Indianapolis game Chapman inserted him at second base, and put Charlie Bennett back behind the plate. The change did little good, as Nolan struck out eight men en route to a 9 to 3 win. Chapman, still trying to find the right combination, again changed his lineup for the final game of this series. He put Peters back at second and moved Morgan to right field. Golden was the starting pitcher, because he was slower and easier for Bennett to catch; Charlie was still hurt, and Holbert had a split hand. The lineup appeared to click, as the Grays went ahead 9 to 0. Indianapolis then exploded for seven runs in the eighth inning, all unearned because of Morgan's "fearful muff on Shaffer's easy fly,"[49] after Peters erred on a grounder. Dalrymple again collected hits in all the games, extending his streak to 12 games; but Jacob Goodman was the best hitter of the day, going four-for-six, as Milwaukee held on to win 10 to 7.

As of May 27, the standings looked like this:

Clubs	Cin	Ind	Bos	Chi	Mil	Pro	WON
Cincinnati		–	–	6	4	–	10
Indianapolis	–		–	2	4	–	6
Boston	–	–		–	–	5	5
Chicago	–	4	–		–	–	4
Milwaukee	2	2	–	–		–	4
Providence	–	–	3	–	–		3
LOST	2	6	3	8	8	5	32

Milwaukee had scored 50 runs, 11 of them earned, compared to their opponents' 69 runs, also eleven earned. The Grays had 101 hits, two fewer than their opponents, and had committed 99 errors to 81 for their opponents. "The showing is by no means a bad one when it is considered that six of the games were with the Cincinnatis and that crippled men saved Indianapolis last week," reported the May 27 *Sentinel*.

The Grays then left for their eastern trip, leaving the injured Bennett behind. Providence fell easily to the Grays' hitting, with 17 hits in all, and Sam Weaver's pitching, the score being 12 to 4. After an exhibition game in Springfield and a Decoration Day rain out in Providence, the Grays' two-game winning streak came to an end. Bill Holbert's hand was still sore, and Bennett had not accompanied the club, so Joe Ellick caught. Ellick had caught an exceptional game for Weaver at Springfield, but committed eleven errors, eight of them passed balls, in this Providence game. Milwaukee was ahead 7 to 0 after four innings, but the Down Easters came up with four runs in the fourth and six in the sixth to coast to a 14 to 7 win. The Grays as a club committed 21 errors. Dalrymple collected three hits to run his hitting streak to 14 games. Another loss the following day put the Grays in the cellar. Dalrymple went hitless in four trips to the plate to end his steak at 14 games. In this game Goodman drew the first known fine for a Milwaukee player, when he was fined $15 for insulting the umpire.

The cellar-dwelling Grays then traveled into Massachusetts to meet the powerful Red Stockings of Boston. On June 4 they lost their first encounter with Harry Wright's team, 9 to 3. Holbert started behind the plate, but was replaced after the third inning by Bill Foley, who did quite well. The Grays almost upset Boston in the next game by scoring nine times in the last two innings to tie the score at 15. Golden had pitched the first six innings, allowing the 15 runs, but Ellick then came on from third base to shut the door until the ninth, when Boston scored a run to win the contest.[50] The third game in this Boston series was postponed due to rain.

The Grays' record had fallen to 5 wins and 12 losses. The club was weak at a few positions, most notably catcher. "There are a number of persons who are cursing the Milwaukees because they don't win games and suggest bad management, sell-outs, and all that sort of nonsense. The simple fact is that the Milwaukees are playing without a catcher."[51]

Bill Holbert's hand was injured, rendering him unable to play, much like Charlie Bennett, who had hurt his arm. The two last minute replacements, Joe Ellick and Bill Foley, were not catchers but infielders and could not do the job. Because of the lack in the catching position, manager Chapman was forced to use Mike Golden as his pitcher more often. The slow pitching style of Golden allowed other teams to steal bases and score more runs. In mid–June Bennett was temporarily released from his engagement with the Grays, as it was thought his injured arm would not heal that season. Although Bennett was re-engaged later, sporting a broken nose sustained in a pick-up game, the only hope at this time was in Holbert recovering soon.

John Chapman tried frantically to obtain a catcher, but players at that position were scarce. In late June the club signed Frank Bliss, who left his law studies at the University of Michigan, and had played for the 1876 West End Club. Bliss caught Golden, committing seven errors, and the Grays again turned to Foley. Days later, Jacob Knowdell, from the Alleghenys, was signed but did not last long. When Charlie Bennett returned, his weak arm allowed runners to steal almost at will. Late in the season the club tried Al Jennings, but with little success. "Zip came the ball from Golden's hand, bang it went against the backstop."[52] In all, the Grays used no less than eight catchers during the season.

On June 12 the Grays entered Chicago and played the White Stockings for the first time in a National League contest. The first game was acclaimed as the best played in Chicago since the National Association era. The game went scoreless for the regulation nine innings, with both sides playing very fine defensive ball, capped by Dalrymple's fine throw to the plate, catching Larkin. Chicago then scored a run in the tenth to win the contest. The following day Milwaukee rebounded with a 2 to 0 win, again playing good defensively, although Bennett had seven errors. Injuries finally caught up with the Grays in the rubber game of the series. Weaver, who had been sick for two days, started but "should have stayed in bed,"[53] and was replaced by Golden in the second inning. Bennett's hand could take no more punishment and he also left the game. In all, Milwaukee committed 18 errors in the 12 to 2 loss. After the game, Charlie Bennett was released.

With a third of the season gone, the Grays were firmly entrenched in last place. The *Cincinnati Enquirer* put up some interesting statistics regarding National League clubs, in order of standings.

Team	Games	Runs	Hits	Errors
Cincinnati	20	129	187	131
Boston	16	110	166	111
Chicago	20	83	185	145
Indianapolis	21	92	163	177
Providence	16	102	174	142
Milwaukee	21	95	203	212

STATISTICS PER GAME

Team	Errors	Hits	Runs	Hits Per Run
Cincinnati	6.55	9.35	6.45	1.47
Boston	6.94	10.38	6.88	1.51
Chicago	7.75	9.25	4.15	2.30
Indianapolis	8.43	7.78	4.38	1.66
Providence	8.89	10.88	6.38	1.71
Milwaukee	10.09	9.67	4,48	2.14

One of the reasons why the Cincinnatis have 34 more runs than the Milwaukees, although the latter lead them in base hits by 16, is because the Cincinnatis have done better base-running and done more sacrifice batting when it is necessary to work around runs. It is mainly the Cincinnatis and Bostons working together; their good judgment in running bases and their right field batting when men are on bases that has won them so many games.[54]

About this time a rumor started that the Indianapolis Blues were about to disband and Milwaukee would sign pitcher Nolan and Silver Flint, his catcher. The rumor was squelched when Chapman received a telegram saying "it will be many moons before this club disbands."[55] About this time the rumor that W.P. Rogers would assume control of the Grays was also around town.

On June 18 the Grays made their first appearance at home following the road trip, and only a small crowd was on hand to watch the home nine beat Chicago, 7 to 5. On June 20 the Milwaukee weather played its part and the umpire played his part, letting the game continue in the rain. The Grays were ahead 7 to 3 when the rain started, but Chicago went on to win 9 to 7. "Every one of the 500 persons who dared the rain ... came away cross and ugly.... The crowd prayed for rain enough to float the umpire off."[56] Milwaukee concluded the series by losing the next game 14 to 3.

Providence next came to town to wax the Grays in the opening game, in which Goodman hit the Grays' first home run. The Grays again lost to Providence in the next game, 7 to 6, and the third game was rained out. Before the Boston series in Milwaukee, Charlie Bennett was re-engaged. It helped little, as the Grays lost 4 to 1 in the first of the set. On Independence Day, another fine defensive show was put on by Boston in winning 3 to 2. Boston then made a clean sweep of the series with an eleven-inning win.

Bill Holbert — Weak hitting catcher/outfielder for 1878 Grays, who attempted to organized a professional club in Milwaukee the next year.

✳ ✳ ✳

On July 5, an off-day for baseball, the Red Stockings played the Milwaukee Cricket Club in a game of cricket. The Red Stockings must have pleased their manager, Harry Wright, himself a former professional cricket player and instructor, as they beat the home club, with Schaffer and O'Rourke leading the way. When Boston returned to Milwaukee in late August, the Red Stocking players again played, and beat, the Milwaukee cricketers.

While on the road and on occasion at home, the Grays spent their baseball off-days in sport — not cricket, as the Red Stockings did here — but in exhibition baseball games. Because of the National League rule, these games could not be played in league cities, so they were played in International Association cities, League Alliance towns, or just against independent clubs. The Grays' first exhibition was in Springfield, Massachusetts, where they beat that local club 7 to 0 in May. On June 7 the Grays beat the Manchesters in New Hampshire, 3 to 0. While returning home from their first eastern trip, the Grays stopped in Cleveland to beat the Forest Cities 4 to 2, before 1200 spectators. On June 21 an all-star team of sorts — consisting of players from the Grays and Chicago White Stockings — traveled to Waukesha, Wisconsin, to beat a picked nine from Milwaukee 7 to 0. In July the Grays beat the Davenport, Iowa, club, Peoria club and Cleveland Forest Cities twice. Early August saw Chapman's team beat Lowell 5 to 2 in six innings, called short by rain; and on August 5 the Grays suffered a loss to the Buffalos of Buffalo, New York, but rebounded to beat the Washington Nationals twice in successive days. Another loss to the Peoria club a few weeks later caused John Chapman to say, "It was the worst give away on the part of the umpire he ever saw."[57]

On August 26 the Grays and Boston played an exhibition game for the benefit of the yellow fever sufferers in the South. The *Sentinel* believed it a worthy cause and hoped for a large attendance. The players agreed to purchase tickets for the cause. The Red Stockings won the game 15 to 4, and $110 was raised for the sufferers.

When the regular playing season ended, the Grays played two games at Milwaukee Park with the Peoria Reds, winning both games by shutouts: one game only attracted 50 people. The Grays then left for a western trip, with schedule stops in Davenport, Dubuque and Chicago. The exhibition season finally ended in mid–October with a win over a picked nine.

✳ ✳ ✳

It was early July and the Grays record stood at 7 wins and 21 losses. The Grays entered Chicago, only to lose three more games. With new caps and stockings, the Grays returned home hoping for better luck, but again took a beating from Chicago, losing 14 to 8. After the next contest, a 17 to 10 loss to Chicago called after 8 innings because of 115-degree heat, the *Sentinel* voiced an opinion that "If there was any possible excuse for the apparently inexcusable errors of yesterday's game, the small audience in the grandstand failed to comprehend it and loudly vented their displeasure at the carelessness of the home nine. Weaver merely tossed the ball in and was pounded all over the field."[58] The *Daily News* predicted the Grays would lose their next game in Chicago, and was correct.

The Grays next traveled to Providence, where they lost 6 to 4. In the second game of the series, the Grays ended their 14-game losing streak, with a 7 to 1 win. The Grays and Providence then went to New York for a make-up game, Providence winning 4 to 1. Milwaukee won the fourth game back in Rhode Island. It was now late July and Boston was leading the pennant race, with Chicago a close second, followed by Cincinnati, Providence, Indianapolis and Milwaukee. Though Milwaukee was still in last place, the *Sentinel* thought the team was playing better baseball.

The last-place Grays entered first-place Boston's territory and both firmly help their grip on those positions, as Boston won all four games played. A six-game series in Cincinnati produced only two wins for the Grays before they returned to Milwaukee to play Boston again. The *Sentinel* had by now long given up on the club. "If one goes to these games to see fine play, he will enjoy it, but he should harbor no wild hope that the Milwaukees will win. They may win, but it will be because the Fates are asleep."[59]

After losing 4 to 3 due to some bad base running, the Grays finally beat Harry Wright's club. About 1,500 witnessed the contest, in which Chapman's heroes collected 12 hits and Sam Weaver held Boston to only six. The 5 to 2 victory would be the Grays' only victory over the Red Stockings, as they lost 5 to 3 in the final contest. Indianapolis followed Boston to town and won two out of three before Milwaukee returned to Indiana to win only one. This series in Indianapolis was to have been moved to St. Louis, at the request of Indianapolis club president Pettit. However, the *St. Louis Globe-Democrat* reported Pettit cancelled because of "fever and the prevailing hot weather." The *Globe-Democrat* called this a "flimsy excuse" and concluded it was a good thing the games were not played in St. Louis because "the two worst clubs in America" would only hurt baseball interest in St. Louis.[60]

To end the playing season, Providence came to Milwaukee to win the first two games, and the Grays won 4 to 3 on September 16, 1878, to finish the season. It would be the last National League regular season game played in Milwaukee until April 15, 1953.

✳ ✳ ✳

Although the game on September 16 was the end of National League baseball in Milwaukee, the end had started earlier and came later. Not only Milwaukee, but all National League cities were in financial distress. On August 9 and 10, an emergency session of the clubs was called in Providence. After the all-night meeting, it was reported because "the expenses of the League would exceed the receipts this year, that the aggregate salaries to be paid in 1879 must not exceed the sum which the experience of this year indicated each club would be likely to earn."[61] The National League decided that no advance money would be given out. Fixed salaries were also discussed, and the Milwaukee club had devised its schedule. Pitchers were to receive $1,200; catchers $1,000; shortstops, second and third basemen $800; first sackers and outfielders $1,000; substitutes $500. In an obscure and overlooked sentence, the reserve clause was announced. "A uniform contract for the engagement of players was adopted."[62] Milwaukee was not present at this Providence meeting.

Management problems had begun in June when William P. Rogers attempted to gain control of the club. A few days later H.M. Northrop resigned as treasurer of the club and John Chapman was elected to the position (in addition to being the club's manager). President John L. Kaine (incidentally, editor-in-chief of the *Milwaukee Sentinel*) also intended to resign, but soon withdrew his resignation. Rumors began to spread that the club was to move to St. Louis. The *Daily News* on June 29, 1878, reported that "some informal negotiations to this effect have been made, but the terms offered have not been accepted, as yet." On July 1 the board of directors unanimously voted Rogers the manager of the Milwaukee Baseball Association. Rogers immediately denied the club had any intention of moving to St. Louis. However, the Indianapolis club temporarily transferred its home games to St. Louis in mid–July and the *New York Clipper* urged the Milwaukee directors to transfer their franchise to Brooklyn for the remainder of the 1878 season and beyond. Rogers must have entertained some idea like this, as Milwaukee's correspondent to the *New York Clipper* wrote in the August 24, 1878, edition that Roger's plan to schedule home games in other cities made season ticket holders "much dissatisfied." The correspondent went on: "The manager claims that the average attendance he receives from this city will not pay expenses, and he proposes to play his club where he can make the most money. This may be eminently satisfactory to Mr. Rogers, and it may be a fine financial system, but it is questionable whether it is the square thing for the stockholders and season ticket holders.... They paid for the full quota of games, but because some other people refuse to pay for the privilege of witnessing the defeat of the home team they are deprived of what rightfully belongs to them." It was concluded that the general feeling was there would be no National League club in Milwaukee the next year.

As early as June trouble also had started with the players. Bill Holbert offered the directors of the Grays $100 to cancel his engagement in order to take a better offer with Chicago. His offer was refused. Trouble again surfaced on August 31 when the game was delayed a half-hour because the players claimed they had not been paid and "refused to put on their uniforms until satisfaction was given." Rogers "secured two gentlemen to back him up and assure the boys they would get their pay if they would don their uniforms and play the game." Sam Weaver still refused to play, "it seems he had not a very high opinion of Rogers' promises."[63] The September 2, 1878, *Sentinel* wrote, "It is difficult to understand why the Milwaukees have not been paid. They have drawn good crowds everywhere except here, especially in Boston, Cincinnati and Chicago, to say nothing of the games in non–League cities." As an interesting side note, only 200 people (150 according to the *New York Clipper*) were in attendance at this particular game in Milwaukee.

A week later the players (except one) still had not been paid. The September 14 *Clipper* reported the ensuing fiasco.

> The club was advertised to play in Indianapolis Thursday, Friday and Saturday, and were to leave here on the 4 P.M. train Wednesday. They made all arrangements and left the hotel in a body, with the exception of Peters, who absolutely refused to stir a step until Rogers had made good his promises. When the depot was reached, Foley, Holbert and Golden concluded that they would not go; the train started with Jack Chapman and the remnant of the team, but before it had gone a quarter of a mile they jumped off, and left the portly "Jack" to continue the journey alone; he managed to get off, however, when he saw the men meant business. The men are all here, and emphatically refused to budge an inch. The Indianapolis games have been advertised, but the Milwaukees will not be there. The sympathy of the people is with the men; they have been living on promises for two months, and have discovered that promises won't pay board-bills.

In the end, the club did make the trip to Indianapolis. The players' troubles were noticed in other cities. During their second eastern trip, a Washington, D.C., paper reported that the Milwaukee players had stated they wished their releases, for the club owed them "more money than they could afford to lose,"[64] but they could not obtain a release. If players left without this release, they would be expelled from the league. The *Evening Wisconsin* of August 16, 1878, had this to say about the Grays: "And this is the immaculate League. The Milwaukee nine are good looking, gentlemanly fellows, but their uniforms are perfectly horrible, and make the players resemble canvasmen in a circus. Peters, in his suit, looks like the driver of a beer wagon — and a driver, too, who wouldn't see any beer wasted without a desperate attempt to guzzle it."

It was reported that on September 25 the players were paid in full, except for John Peters. Rogers claimed that Peters had forfeited his contract by leaving the club during the season to play for St. Louis and Chicago. Peters had earlier claimed to be sick of baseball and reportedly wanted to go back to St Louis to work again. Shortly before the season ended, Rogers reported Peters was released, although Peters claimed to be suspended and the club owed him $350.

Although management admitted the season was not a financial success, they claimed they were ready for the 1879 season, and that some players had already been engaged, including John Remson of the White Stockings, for the captaincy. Others included Charlie Bennett, Sam Weaver, George Creamer, Bill Holbert, John Sullivan from Cincinnati, Russell McKelvey from Indianapolis, Wilber Coons and Ferguson Malone from the Philadelphia Athletics, and Moynahan from Davenport.

As late as November 23, 1878, the *New York Clipper* was reporting the 1879 National League would include Chicago, Cincinnati, Boston and Providence, and "Milwaukee, too, will probably join, as also Buffalo," and printed the likely rosters of the 1879 teams, including Milwaukee. On November 28, the stockholders of the Milwaukee club met and elected the following directors for the ensuing season: W. P. Rogers, A.W. Hill, C.J. Kershaw, R.L. Jenning, Rufus Allen Jr. and C.H.M. Tobey. Rogers was elected president, David Vance the vice president, Tobey the secretary and A.W. Hill the treasurer. "The howl of a certain class that Milwaukee will be expelled from the League is the rankest nonsense,"[65] reported the club, as rumor continued that the Grays were to be expelled. Still disbelieving, Rogers and the newly elected board of directors raised the diamond 18 to 20 inches and re-sodded the playing field. They also claimed to have $15,000 in working capital.

The National League met for its winter meeting in Cleveland. On December 4, the Milwaukee club had three charges brought against it. There was the matter of an unpaid fine imposed on Goodman in a game at Providence; the claims of Peters and Ellick of not being paid; and the club owing two hotel keepers in Cincinnati $260. These charges not being satisfactorily explained by W.P. Rogers, the National League adopted the following:

> Resolved, that if within twenty days from date thereof, the Milwaukee Baseball Club shall have paid all just claims against said organization, it shall be allowed to withdraw honorably from the League. But if said claims are not paid at the expiration of said time, and satisfactory evidence furnished to the Secretary of the League of the liquidation of the same in full, then, and in that case, said organization shall be declared expelled under this resolution.[66]

To the end Rogers claimed the club should not have been expelled and that Chicago was behind the plot. Indianapolis, also a financial failure, left the National League "with a clear and honorable record."[67] The National League admitted Syracuse, Buffalo, Cleveland and Troy to form an eight-club circuit for 1879.

How much the Grays lost is anyone's guess. Boston, the pennant winner of 1878, lost $1,433.31.[68] According to the *New York Clipper*, only the Cincinnati club made money on the season, having a surplus of nearly $3,500 in its fund.

The 1878 Milwaukee story perhaps ends with a short note under the Brevities in the February 14, 1879, *Milwaukee Sentinel*. "Sheriff Van Vechten sold the grand stand, fences, seats, etc. of the Milwaukee Base Ball Club yesterday afternoon to satisfy a judgment in favor of Giles H. Spear for $135.61. Mr. Spear bid in the 'farm' and the Sheriff issued a certificate of transfer to Mr. Kneeland's lease of the grounds."

Baseball was back in the amateur's hands in Milwaukee for a while.

✻ ✻ ✻

The season of 1878 was a banner year for the National League in one way, for it was the first year all clubs had completed their schedule. The Grays had the most difficulty with Boston. The Red Stockings beat Milwaukee eleven out of their twelve games played. Chicago beat the Grays ten out of twelve. Against Providence, Cincinnati and Indianapolis, the Grays managed four wins against each club.

	Wins	Losses	PCT.	GB
Boston	41	19	.683	—
Cincinnati	37	23	.617	4
Providence	33	27	.550	8
Chicago	30	30	.500	11
Indianapolis	24	36	.400	17
Milwaukee	15	45	.250	26

As can be seen, the early-season predictions of the local press were anything but correct. The descriptions of the Grays' "heavy hitting" did not come true, as they ended the season with a .250 team batting average, fourth in the six-club circuit, ahead of only Boston and Indianapolis. The only bright spot was Abner Dalrymple's league leading average.[69]

The Grays' fielding was rock bottom with 376 errors for a .865 average. Their pitching was also the National League's worst, with the fewest complete games (54), strikeouts (147), and shutouts (1) and highest earned run average (2.60). Only in bases on balls did they not record the highest (55), placing third. In the most important category—runs—the Grays scored the fewest (256) and had the most runs scored against them (386).

In addition to Paul Hines and Dalrymple, three other players hit higher than .340 in 1878: Bob Ferguson, Joe Start and Cap Anson from Chicago. Hines also led the league in home runs (4), runs batted in (50) and total bases (125). Joe Start led in hits (100), with Dalrymple second (96). Tommy Bond of Boston was the year's best pitcher, winning 40 games against 19 losses. He pitched 533 innings, striking out 182, while completing 57 of 59 games and recording 9 shutouts. Sam Weaver allowed the fewest walks per nine innings (.49) to go with his 1.95 earned run average (4th).

Several players among the five other clubs in the National League of 1878 went on to be great stars. Adrian Anson and Alfred Spalding from Chicago, Jim O'Rourke and the Wright Brothers from Boston, John Montgomery Ward from Providence and Mike "King" Kelly from Cincinnati became Hall of Famers.

6

Amateur Era (1879–1883)

Milwaukee was out of the National League, but potential backers still claimed to be interested in reorganizing the team. About two weeks after the expulsion of the Grays, a meeting was called for this purpose at the Plankinton House. However, "the gentlemen who were reported to have interested themselves in next year's Milwaukees failed to show themselves.... There were not enough present to fill the positions of chairman and secretary." Several businessmen decided to reorganize under new management and apply for admittance to the National League in March. Even if not admitted, "small importance would be attached to the fact, as there are a large number of outside teams, and many of them as good as the League nines."[1] Unfortunately, nothing was to come of this talk.

In late February word came that Charlie Bennett and Bill Holbert were to organize a professional club. The *Evening Wisconsin* rejoiced in its editorial, writing that "the average citizen of Milwaukee feels a deep interest in baseball," and after the failure of the Grays, the new organizers should be congratulated "upon the prospect that we are not to be left entirely out of the baseball records of the coming season."[2] It was first reported the proposed club would play in the minor league Northwestern circuit. Bennett disclaimed this, saying it would be a good semi-professional club, playing all its games at home so the people of Milwaukee could see more baseball. Capital stock of $1,000 was needed to set the club up, and Bennett hoped to bring "the people of Milwaukee baseball as it was given in the days of the West End Club; i.e., baseball for pure enjoyment and at a cheap price."[3] In addition to Bennett and Holbert, Weaver, Sullivan, Creamer, Coons and McKelvey were reportedly signed. Some of these players said they had offers from other clubs and would take those offers if the club was not organized soon.

More than $250 was quickly obtained for the Sanderson Baseball Club, as it was to be called, and within a week Bennett claimed to have enough money to start the club. E.T. Durand was named treasurer of the club. It was announced the club would play at Athletic Park on the east side, charging 25-cent general admission and a dime to sit in the grandstand. The *Evening Wisconsin* thought this price reduction in itself would raise attendance, as the 50-cent National League admission was thought to be too high. However, the editor quickly pointed out "if the effort to raise the necessary sum of $1,000 should fall through now, let no one grumble hence because of the failure."[4]

Within two weeks the club fell through and the money was returned to the backers. Bennett dropped the attempt, concluding the baseball business in Milwaukee was a thankless job. "If you ever catch me undertaking such a task again here, you can just lift my head from my shoulders and use it for a football."[5]

The Milwaukee Grays of 1878 were now completely in the past. John Chapman would manage 1879 at Holyoke, Massachusetts. All the players were engaged with other clubs. Sam Weaver and Charlie Bennett went to Worcester of the International League, although Weaver was soon "retired in favor of Richmond, the phenomenal pitcher of that city."[6]

Weaver was then engaged in business in Philadelphia and pitched there for a few more years. He finished his big league pitching career with 70 wins and 80 losses, and died in Philadelphia at the age of 58. Charlie Bennett went on to have a great career in Detroit and Boston. He lost his legs in 1894 and passed away in 1927 in Detroit at the age of 72. Bill Holbert played with the Syracuse Stars of the National League. Holbert would play ten more years in the major leagues, finishing with a modest .208 batting average. In 1893 the *Sporting News* reported he had "a good position in the government secret service in New York City."[7] Bill lived to be 80 years old, passing in Laurel, Maryland, in 1935. Others also signed with National League clubs. Abner Dalrymple and John Peters signed with the Chicago White Stockings and Bill Foley with Cincinnati. The Rockford club engaged five others— George Creamer, Michael Golden, Billy Redmond, Jacob Goodman and Joe Ellick. Baseball was back in the amateur's hands in Milwaukee.

Of course, amateur ball had never departed the city. The year of 1878 had many clubs, although overshadowed by the Grays. Early April brought out the young amateurs. Many established clubs and some new ones dotted the city's diamonds. Clubs such as the Live Oaks, Aucklands and the Comicals continued to play, along with newcomers like the Houstons, Franklins and Alleghanys. A group even started playing under the Cream City Club, and the Star Club re-organized.

Ball playing in the street became hazardous again. "The supposition that there is an ordinance prohibiting baseball playing on the streets is incorrect. If a leather covered rock collides with your best hat, why pick it up. Thus you will contribute your quota to the urchin's fun. It is good for boys to laugh."[8] In June an ordinance was passed that brought to a halt baseball in the streets, and Police Chief Kennedy warned boys to quit playing in the streets.

Members of local firms and stores challenged each other, such as the challenge from the clerks of Dixon and Berry to T.A. Chapman's clerks for "a box of the best cigars the market affords."[9] Picked nines, many times with members of the Grays, played in contests. In September nine doctors got together and played nine dentists, making more than $100 for the yellow fever fund for the South.

The year 1879 brought more baseball action. More games were being played on Sunday by now. Sunday baseball, however, was not approved by all yet. Residents living around old Milwaukee Park were making complaints of ball playing on the Sabbath to the police chief. Still, the opening game of the season was on Sunday, April 27.

Jacob Knowdell, who had played briefly with the Grays, formed a club under the name of the long-forgotten first club in the city, the Milwaukee Baseball Club. The club was soon reported to be the strongest in the city. Another strong club, the Pastime Club, was formed. They later played the Milwaukees, losing 9 to 2. The Milwaukee Baseball Club, said to be a semi-professional nine, lost to the Janesville Mutuals, 11 to 9, in June. The club also lost its press space to another club.

"Even though Milwaukee will not support a professional club, amateurs are doing well," the *Sentinel* reported on May 28, 1879. A club called the Maple Leafs was doing the best. Organized in 1876, the club was the most popular amateur club in town by 1878. Claiming to be the champion amateur team of the state for that year, the Maple Leafs secured the grounds at Tenth and Clybourn for their home, sharing it with the Grays. Not everyone considered the Maple Leafs the champions, however. The *Janesville Gazette* thought the "claim seems slightly conceited" for an unknown club. "If they will only come to Janesville, they can get up a game almost any afternoon, as the primary schools let out about 3:00."[10]

The Maple Leafs' first known game of the 1878 season was an 8 to 7 loss to the White Stockings of Waukesha. A week later they beat the Chicago Athletics at Milwaukee Park before 1,500 spectators, more people than the Grays were drawing by then. Although popular, the Maple Leafs were probably not the strongest amateur club in the state. They beat the local Aucklands and Alerts, but lost to the Comicals in June. In July the Maple Leafs avenged their defeat to the Comicals and also beat the Chicago Crooks. They then beat the Waukesha club, but maybe not under fair play. "Considerable indignation is expressed by our citizens [Waukesha] because Knowdell, of the Milwaukees [Grays] was imposed upon them by the Maple Leafs in Saturday's game of baseball, under a fictitious name."[11] After losing to the Dreadnaughts of Chicago, the Maple Leafs beat the Aucklands for the city championship. In early August the club beat the Dreadnaughts, but then lost to the Alerts, the new West End Club and the Aucklands. In the last known game of the '78 season, the Maple Leafs beat the Alerts 9 to 4.

For 1879 the Maple Leafs reorganized. The Leafs opened the season in late April with a mixed nine from their club and the Stars against the Aucklands. Fully organized, the Maple Leafs beat the Aucklands 12 to 7 the following week, and then defeated the Live Oaks. The first game of the new season with an out-of-town club drew between 800 and 1,500 spectators, depending on whether one believed the *Sentinel* or the *Daily News*. The Maple Leafs managed to win this game 9 to 8 over the Dreadnaughts of Chicago. The Maple Leafs sent the Racine College boys home "draped in mourning"[12] and crushed the Waukeshas 20 to 5. The Maple Leafs then played two Chicago clubs. On June 1 they played the Uniques, an all-black nine, and lost 2 to 0. A week later the local club beat the Athletics of Chicago.

After losing to the Janesville Mutuals, the Maple Leafs beat the Milwaukee Baseball Club 4 to 2, and then the Atlantics of Chicago by the same score. The Maple Leafs went into a tail-spin, losing to the Dreadnaughts 6 to 0, as "in 27 times at bat [the Maple Leafs] failed to reach first base once,"[13] to start a month-long drought. After losing to the Chicago club again, the Dubuque club "ran around the bases until exhausted, while the hosts didn't get so much as one run."[14] The Detroit club won two games in successive days, scoring 28 runs in the two games. The Maple Leafs finally ended the losing streak by beating the Oconomowoc Brown Stockings 15 to 5. Two weeks later they tied the Uniques in twelve innings.

Opinion on Sunday ball was rapidly changing, and the Maple Leafs played almost all their first-rate games on Sunday at Milwaukee Park. This not only enabled fans to watch the games, but caused less of a problem with the players. The first nine of the Maple Leafs took this appearance in July: Clayton-pitcher, Straub-catcher, Reynolds-first base, Sullivan-shortstop, Young-second base, Parker-third base, Mead-left field, Dever-center field, Delaney-right field.

The Maple Leaf Club in ways resembled the amateur clubs of the 1860s. Like olden days, the club set up a junior club, called the Young Maple Leafs. The season ended in September, with two games between the "New" Maple Leafs and the "Old" Leafs, splitting the mini-series. This new and old reorganization consisted of a split of the junior and senior clubs:

Sullivan	Catcher	Straub
Hanrahan	Pitcher	Clayton
Sexton	Shortstop	Morris
O'Connell	First Base	Wolf
Young	Second Base	Lee
Shean	Third Base	Parker

Mead	Left Field	Delaney
Timblin	Center Field	Dever
Lynch	Right Field	Mellon

The final game between these two clubs was postponed because of Sullivan's hand coming up lame.

Others continued into the '79 season. The Aucklands, formed in 1876, were still around. So were the Live Oaks, established a year after the Aucklands. More new clubs hit the scene. The Centennials beat the Young Maple Leafs early in the season, 22 to 12. The Roankes managed to beat the Red Stockings in early June. The Fairbanks Club, "hitherto unknown to fame, had a ball at the Milwaukee Garden ... during the progress of which several of the members became both intoxicated and demonstrative. The police undertook to put them out, and succeeded in doing so only after some pretty sharp batting and fielding."[15]

Occupational groups still played each other. In July the bakers and carpenters of the Fourth Ward played for three boxes of cigars. The bakers eventually lost 22 to 11. "For a little while it looked as though the umpire would find himself reduced to sausage meat by the defeated knights of the cleaver, but the latter being rather exhausted from following the ball, finally cooled down and took the defeat with the best grace they could assume."[16] In 1879 baseball could still be fun.

Unfortunately, 1880 showed a tremendous loss in popularity for baseball in Milwaukee. The baseball men started with an effort to organize a club in late February. This effort never materialized. All was quiet on the baseball front until late May when "several well-known baseballists of the west side talked of organizing a semi-professional team."[17] Again nothing happened, unless these ball players organized the Milwaukee Base Ball Club (noted below), but there is nothing to connect these two groups.

Only two organized clubs can be found to have played in 1880 — and only one game was played. The two clubs were the "newly organized"[18] Milwaukee Club and the old Maple Leafs. This game was played on June 8 at Athletic Park on Farwell Avenue, "a plant provided with an amphitheater that will seat several thousand people."[19] Only 300 people showed up, as the Maple Leafs won 5 to 3 in an interesting game, "although the pitchers had everything on their side."[20]

This game was played during Milwaukee's Reunion, a four-day affair with thousands of soldiers, parades, camps and celebrities such as Ulysses S. Grant and General Sherman in town. The Milwaukee Club announced a series of games at Athletic Park during the reunion, with two games against the Manitowac nine, two against the Maple Leafs and one against the Dubuque, Iowa, club. The game with Dubuque was rained out and all the others were either not played or went unrecorded in the local papers. One June 12, 1880, the *Daily News* commented, "The Reunion is now over, thank goodness, and the neglected local events of the city again have the proper attention paid that they deserve." Apparently baseball was not one of these, as baseball was not mentioned again in the paper, as it expired on January 1, 1881. Baseball coverage in the other papers disappeared also.

Baseball, at least in Milwaukee, had fallen victim to other sports. Cricket became the most popular sport in town. Full accounts and scores of the Young America Cricket Club appeared in the press. The Bay View Cricket Club challenged "any sixteen baseball or cricket players to play a match."[21] The new craze of bicycling also hit Milwaukee. In May there were about twenty in the city. By mid–July "the straddlers of the steel steed were stealing all the honors away from fast trotters and racers of every description"[22] and had formed a club. Along with this, a tournament was formed in August. The *Sentinel* of August

15, 1880, had this warning: "Polite athletics do not appear to flourish any better than ordinary sporting. Bicycling has not proved remunerative, and archery is not the rage so much as it was."

✳ ✳ ✳

The 1880s did produce bring a faster and exciting brand of baseball. In no other decade did the rules change in this direction so much. Of course, these changes mainly involved the batter and the pitcher.

Major changes came forth in the pitching department. In 1881 the pitcher's box was moved back five feet, to 50 feet. Throughout the decade the area of the pitcher's box would be altered, until it became 4 × 5½ feet in 1887. Probably the biggest change in the pitching rules was allowing the pitcher a free motion with only one step before delivery in 1884. Thus, overhand pitching first entered the rules. In reality, it had been going on for some time. As far back as 1877 the West End Club complained that McCormick's pitching, for the Syracuse Stars, was illegal, "in many instances being clearly above the waist — a clean throw,"[23] but nothing was called.

Since 1863 the base on balls was part of the game. Going into the eighties it took nine bad pitches to walk a batter. This was gradually reduced to four by 1889.

For the 1887 season, the rule allowing the hitter to call for a high or low ball, established back in 1878, was abolished. Also a strike zone from between the shoulder and bottom of the knee was defined. The batter was also given a fourth strike if he had not swung at the third strike (but only for this season). Also to the batter's advantage, in 1883 it had been ruled a foul ball caught on a bounce was no longer an out. Back in 1880, a rule stipulated a third strike had to be caught without hitting the ground for an out.

With these and many other rule changes, many umpires and scorers throughout the nineteenth century were not up to date, especially those out of the major leagues. So on occasion "the score books kept by the two sides differed materially."[24] To the fans, the game was becoming faster and better.

✳ ✳ ✳

The amateurs again kept "up the interest in the great American game"[25] in 1881. The first club to organize was the Arctic Club in late April; however, no record can be found of a contest until the first of June, when the Maple Leafs beat the newly formed Newhall House Mutuals. On the following two weekends the Milwaukees and Excelsiors clashed, splitting the two games, while baseball interest slowly increased.

The *Sentinel* reported on June 27, 1881, that "Milwaukee will not have a club of any particular prominence this season," but a few clubs vied for the local honors. In July the Phoenix Baseball Club of the south side appeared and "shyed their castors into the ring,"[26] challenging any amateur club in the city to a game. Manager Beiner of the Arctic Club accepted the Phoenix challenge.

The first game of this challenge came off Sunday, August 21, at the Arctic's grounds on Twentieth and Vliet. The Phoenix club won the contest 9 to 2. Three weeks later the same clubs met again for a rematch. In an hour and 30-minute game, the Arctics won 4 to 1. The *Daily Republican and News* credited R.W. Schierz, the Arctic pitcher, with a no-hitter, while his club committed a total of six errors. The Phoenix players immediately claimed this scoring was wrong, stating they had made four hits. The Arctics never replied and the box score was never redone.

Before this challenge came about, the Phoenix Club twice defeated the Excelsiors of the Third Ward, 19 to 8 and 10 to 7. They then lost to the Cream City Club and Maple Leafs before playing the Arctics. The only game that can be found of the Arctics before the challenge is a 22 to 16 victory over the Cream City Club on August 14. Between the two challenge matches the Arctics lost to the same Cream City Club, while the Phoenix beat the Excelsiors again and then the Unknown nine.

Another club to play in the ball field was the Quicksteps. In July Captain Cary challenged any other club whose members were under age 17 to a contest. This challenge was soon met by the Westerns at Athletic Park. On July 31 the Quicksteps lost to the Red Stockings, who were "supposed to be the champions of the city under 17 years of age,"[27] even though the only game found up to then involving the Reds is a victory over the Westerns in July. The Red Stockings beat the Green Leaves in August before the Quicksteps avenged their defeat in September by winning 18 to 7. Another club, the luckless Excelsiors, after splitting an early-season series with the Milwaukees, lost to Phoenix twice and again to the Alerts. Another team the Bengel Baseball Club, challenged any nine in the city. Some clubs showed interest, but no record of the club playing any games can be found.

In 1881, a new dimension for Milwaukee baseball was found in the press, the Milwaukee High School baseball team. In late June the high school club (located at North Cass and East Knapp streets) went to Racine, playing the college nine and losing 7 to 5. The press had now covered baseball from the amateur and local high school level to the professional level. However, the biggest dimension of ball that year was the business nines of the city.

These games began on July 3 with an interesting contest between the "upstairs" and "downstairs" nines of the M. Heimann & Company, a millinery establishment on North Broadway (modern address system 731–739 North Broadway). A young man called Kleiner Klein proved to be the star of the game, in a 7 to 5 victory for the downstairs team. On a Saturday later that month players from J. Ferneke's and G. Zielger's candy stores met, with Ferneke's winning 22 to 10. The following day Heimann's nine took on their next-door neighbors, the Ramien Brothers nine, losing 20 to 8. In a rematch the following Saturday, the Heimanns evened the series. By August the Heimann team was being called the champions of the city. They beat the Ball and Goodrich team 18 to 14 at Athletic Park on August 6, only to lose 30 to 15 the following week. In the second match, played "before a considerable number of spectators, the grocerymen won a handsome victory ... and deserve the laurels they so well tried to win."[28] The following week Heimanns beat the Ramiens 25 to 9, or lost, if you read the *Evening Wisconsin*.

As the summer continued, good amateur games were played at Athletic Park and throughout the city, mostly on weekends. However, youths still played the game in the streets and complaints rolled into the police. A stabbing that took place in a street game in the spring marred play that year. Though Heimann became the best of the business teams, they were not the only business team. The employees of Landauer & Company played match games with the Ranniers Brother's workers, who called themselves the Red Caps. The General Office and South Milwaukee nines of the Chicago, Milwaukee and St. Paul Railroad squared off at the Stock Yard in July. A team from David Adler and Sons beat the Sharkman & Company nine, 11 to 2, in late August. The following month the Adler team took a 20 to 6 beating from Heimanns. The Reliance Foundry nine took on the Railroad nine one Sunday. Two German newspaper rivals, the *Freie Presse* and the *Harold*, put their compositors to war on the diamond. In the Ziegler-Ferneke rematch, the Z's won 18 to 7.

The season ended on a sad note, with the assassination of President Garfield. On the day of his funeral "in every city and village all over the land business was suspended, stores closed and draped in mourning, and places of amusements remained with unopened doors."[29] A sad day in American history, indeed. The Phoenix and Arctic clubs were to play two games that week, with 25-cent admission to the grounds, but the games were postponed and never played.

By 1882 baseball was rebounding in popularity. Many of the established clubs entered the season reorganized, including the Phoenix, Excelsior and Quickstep clubs. Others entered the diamond battles again or made their debuts. The Arctic club kicked the season open with a Saturday evening ball at the Milwaukee Gardens on April 15; the proceeds were to go for new uniforms for the club. Actual play began that Saturday afternoon with a practice game between members of the Heimann & Company team.

The first club that can be found to have organized in 1882 was a group of men in the First Ward. They gathered at the Drake House on April 14 and 15, elected officials and decided to call themselves the Drake House Baseball Club. The next day they played their first and only recorded game, losing 15 to 8 to a picked nine.

The first match game of the season was played on May 1, when the Milwaukee High School nine traveled to Racine to play that city's college — the college champions of Wisconsin in 1881. With basically the same team as the year before, the high schoolers won 18 to 17 before some 300 spectators, including 30 Milwaukee boys who "shared the glory of victory."[30] The Milwaukee boys were actually ahead 23 to 17 when they found out that a new league rule stopped the game when the winning run was scored in the ninth inning. Later that month Racine evened the series with a 13 to 11 victory in "the incessant drizzling rain."[31] Throughout the season this became a regular rivalry, with the college boys winning three out of the five games played. The high schoolers also scheduled contests with the State University nine from Madison. As Racine College, Madison belonged to the College League, which also included Evanston and Ann Arbor. In addition to the college contests, the high school played some of the local amateur clubs. To practice for these matches, the club rented the First Ward Park for the season in May. Two games with the strong Milwaukee Club resulted in a split, though three of the regular Milwaukee players failed to show for the second game, tainting the lads' win. The high schoolers also managed to beat the Morgan Club 4 to 3, then were whipped 23 to 3 by the same club, after losing to the Phoenix.

Although the Milwaukee High School Club was by far the best high school team in the area, it was not the only squad of high schoolers to dot the local diamonds. In September two teams of high school boys calling themselves the Insuperabeles and the Unanklagbarens clashed, the former winning 12 to 6. A few days later a picked nine of high school scholars defeated the local chamber of commerce nine 7 to 5. In a six-game series the High School Blues and the High School Reds ran off with three victories apiece.

In early May the powerful Arctic Club held its annual meeting and elected officers. The manager again was to be Lorenz Berner. The club's first recorded game was played later that month when it beat the Phoenix Club 17 to 6. After beating the Milwaukees, Berner's men beat the Excelsiors 10 to 8 "in the best game of ball played in the state this season."[32] The next day the Arctics repeated the victory over the Excelsiors. Disaster soon struck, as the "hitherto invincible Arctics"[33] lost to the Welcome Club 16 to 6, before 1,000 spectators. The Arctics bounced back by beating the Manitowac nine on July 4, only to lose to the Phoenix the following week. The club then became involved in challenges with the Maple Leafs, which will be discussed later.

The second powerhouse of Milwaukee baseball in 1882 was the Milwaukee Baseball Club. Originally the Mutuals, the club changed its name in early June to the Milwaukees. "Composed of the best amateur baseball talent in the city,"[34] the club showed its strength with a decisive win over the Manitowac Club after the loss to the Arctics. In July the Arctics fell to the Milwaukees 8 to 6, as did the high school nine. In mid–July the Milwaukees beat the Maple Leafs at Athletic Park, 10 to 9, in an exciting game before 2,000 people. The Milwaukee Club scored three runs in the top of the ninth, but the Maple Leafs crossed home four times in their last turn to nearly pull the game out.

Next came the embarrassing defeat to the High Schoolers and a disputed win over the Maple Leafs. The score stood 11 to 9 in the sixth inning in favor of the Maple Leafs. At this point the Leafs protested against Lee's overhand pitching for the Milwaukees, and refused to bat when overruled. A disturbance occurred and the umpired forfeited the game to the Milwaukee Club. "The decision created much feeling and the spectators were divided in their opinions as to its justice."[35] The Milwaukees next lost to the Chicago Greens at First Ward Park, and then suffered their first defeat at the hands of the Maple Leafs. In September the club set sail for Green Bay. Although no record of a game can be found, one was played. It was mentioned later when the Maple Leafs and Milwaukees were to play. The press reported that the proceeds of the game would go to Thomas Lee, the Milwaukee pitcher who broke his arm in a game in Green Bay. The Milwaukee Club closed its season on October 15, losing to the Maple Leafs.

The third major amateur club in the city was the Maple Leafs. Reorganizing itself in mid–June, the club was ready to play local amateurs, the winner taking all money brought in at the gate, which was 25 cents per admission. For their first game the Leafs reached for the stars. On June 30 the club announced it was negotiating with the Troy Club of the National League. The Trojans were to play in Chicago on the Fourth of July and would come here the next day. The Leafs were expected to at least entertain the visiting club. Their manager, T.H. "True" Rice, put the Maple Leafs' intentions into words: "When only parative boys they held the state championship and now propose to see whether they have their grip on the sphere."[36]

On July 5 one thousand people witnessed the return of a National League team. Troy had such stars as Buck Ewing, a future Hall of Fame catcher who would have his great years as a New York Giant; Roger Conner, another great Giant who would hit 136 lifetime home runs, a record until broken by Babe Ruth; Bob Ferguson, whom Milwaukeeans had already seen; Fred Pfeffer, one of the better second sackers of the nineteenth century; and Tim Keefe, another future Hall of Famer with great years as a Giant ahead of him. Neither team scored until Troy crossed the plate three times in the third. Troy loaded the bases in the fourth inning, but the Leafs would not allow the Trojans to score. Troy scored two more in the sixth, and added single runs in the seventh and eighth. Behind 7 to 0 in the bottom of the ninth, the Maple Leafs finally scored on a passed ball. The Leafs had played a good game in limiting Troy to seven runs.

The Maple Leafs' next move was to challenge the Arctics to a match for a stake of $50, plus the winning team to take home half the gate receipts. The Leafs asked a week's notice, but the Arctics were in no hurry to reply. While waiting for the reply, the Maple Leafs brought out a new white uniform with gray cap and red belt and stockings. The Leafs then lost to the Milwaukee 10 to 9 in the previously mentioned exciting game. Next the Leafs beat the Excelsiors, forfeited to the Milwaukees, and whipped the Excelsiors again. After besting the Milwaukees for the first time in August, Manager Rice and Treasurer Delany presented the Maple Leaf players with gold badges.

Finally on August 30 the Arctics and Maple Leafs announced they would play for the championship of the city and a $50 stake per side at Cold Spring Driving Park on September 3. Manager Berner of the Arctics announced the following day that he would present a gold medal to the best player on his club in the game. The game was played before 3,000 that Sunday, with the Maple Leafs taking the $100 by winning 7 to 6. Sullivan and Young starred for the Leafs, and Otto Schomberg, the Arctics first baseman, was presented with the gold medal. Immediately after the loss, the Arctics again challenged the Maple Leafs, and Rice accepted. The game was set for the following Sunday at Athletic Park. The stakes were increased to $125 a side. Attendance dipped to 800, and the Arctics scored three tallies in the ninth inning to win 8 to 7.

The following Sunday the deciding game was set and a total of $300 was put up. Confusion reigned the afternoon of the game. Circulars had been out all week advertising the Arctic-Maple Leaf game, but circulars were also being distributed announcing the Arctics would play the Dreadnaughts of Chicago. The manager of the Arctics could see trouble coming and notified the chief of police. Chief Wasson also believed there might be trouble, and shortly after 2 o'clock a police squad was at the grounds in a patrol wagon. Delany, treasurer of the Maple Leafs, was the first on the grounds and took possession of the ticket office, barring the door. The Maple Leaf treasurer sold quite a few tickets before the clubs arrived. After some arguing, it was agreed to let the Dreadnaughts and Arctics play. The 2,000 people in attendance saw the Chicago club emerge victorious, 11 to 3. The Arctics and Maple Leafs played each other into October. After a 17 to 11 Maple Leaf win, the *Sentinel* reported that "judging by the season's work, the Maple Leafs are the best nine in the state."[37] The Maple Leafs not only captured city championship honors, but led the state in average.

Of course, other clubs entertained themselves and spectators in 1882. Although industrial teams still played, these clubs did not thrive as they had in the previous years. The mighty Heimann nine still existed, as did the Ball & Goodrich Club. The Heimann club played the Merchants Club three times in three weeks, losing twice. The Merchants introduced doubleheaders, of a sort, to Milwaukee on July 9 with a 10 to 8 victory over Heimann in the morning and a 5 to 4 victory over the Newport Club in the afternoon. In August they duplicated the twin killing by defeating the Cream City Club and the Western Club. Business nines from establishments such as Shadbolt, Boyd & Co., Suelflohn & Seefeldtod, Clarence Shepard & Co., William Steinmeyer's, F.J. Dixon and J.C. Iverson played each other in the local parks.

Other business nines took fancy names, such as the Quilldrivers from the Northwestern Mutual Life Insurance Company, and the Uncle Sam's Stampstickers from the post office. In September the Greens and Buttons beat H. Bosworth's team to become the champion druggists of the city. Bosworth came back to beat the Greens the following week. However, things were not all that rosy for the business groups, as the Chicago, Milwaukee & St. Paul nine discovered. In June they were forced to disband "owing to its inability to secure acceptances in response to challenges."[38] The business clubs were giving way to formal organized amateur clubs.

In addition to the big three amateur clubs, numerous others existed. The Phoenix Club had reorganized in April and came on strong. They scheduled their first game of the 1882 season with the also reorganized Excelsiors in late May. The Phoenix then beat the newly formed James Morgan (a clothing and dry goods establishment on East Water — present address would be 628 North Water Street) nine, 27 to 4, in June. Later that month the club traveled to Janesville to play the Mutuals, but had only played four innings and led 4 to 1 when the rains came. By July the Phoenix were strong enough to play the Arctics and win. In mid–July the Phoenix clubbed the Morgans again 27 to 3. Janesville returned its visit on July 23 and beat the Phoenix 9 to 3 (the *Evening Wisconsin* reported the loser's score as 2), even though they had borrowed the Maple Leafs' catcher for the game. The *Evening Wisconsin* was confident the Phoenix only needed to get better players at one or two positions to be one of the strongest clubs in the state.

Another club to reorganize was the Quicksteps. In May the club was ready to accept challenges from teams whose members were under 20 years old. In June a challenge arrived, and the Quicksteps lost to the Welcomes 42 to 15. In July the Quicksteps were defeated by the

Otto Schomberg — Popular local player who a decade later almost became president of the Brewers.

Welcomes again, this time by a respectable score of 5 to 3. Finally, on July 31 the Quicksteps appeared not to lose to the Welcomes, tying them in a rain-interrupted game, 14 to 14. But alas, the August 1 *Sentinel* rectified the mistake: Welcomes 14, Quicksteps 13. The Quicks had an easier time with the Pastime Club, besting them for the third time back on July 23. The Welcomes, meanwhile, found they were not "invincible,"[39] losing to the Merchants 19 to 15. Another club, the Clippers from Bay View, beat the Quicksteps in August for their fifth win without a loss. Two weeks later the Quicks beat the Clippers 20 to 0 to hand the Clippers their first defeat. By September the Q's were in high gear, beating the Nationals 11 to 1 and the Merchants twice, finishing the season on winning notes.

Other clubs not to be overlooked were the Excelsiors, James Morgans and Welcomes. These nines rounded out competition with the bigger-named clubs and the numerous other amateur clubs of the city. Perhaps the most exciting team would have been one that was never formed. In late August the *Sentinel* reported that a picked nine from the Maple Leafs, Excelsiors and Milwaukees were to travel to Grand Rapids, Michigan, to play the Co-operative Club of that city. Immediately Manager Rice of the Maple Leafs denied that his team was in on this, and nothing was ever heard of the trip.

Another interesting aspect of the 1882 season was the attempt to get National League clubs to play in Milwaukee. Except for the Troy-Maple Leaf game, no other contest was played, but numerous attempts were made. The first attempt began in late June when Albert Spalding, now president of the Chicago White Stockings, offered to come to Milwaukee on July 6 or 7 for a guarantee of $100 and 50 percent of the gross receipts in excess of the $100 guarantee. Milwaukee promoters immediately accepted. The deal fell through, but as seen, Troy did come on July 5. The local group then tried to promote a game between the Detroit Wolverines of the National League and either the St. Louis or Cincinnati nines. Above the guarantees, "as an additional incentive to good playing, the movers of the project propose to offer a stake of $25 to be given as cigar money to the winning nine."[40] Neither St. Louis nor Cincinnati was able to come, so the game was called off.

Promoters were still confident that National League or Alliance clubs would come to Milwaukee, as the teams playing in Chicago could make it here on their off-days. Most National League clubs were demanding $500, with a $250 guarantee if rained out. Promoters offered the clubs a $300 guarantee to come, play or not, but were rejected. Local promoters continued to wait, believing that in the fall, when crowds were smaller at National League games, the clubs would be more willing to listen. It was then announced there was a plan to have the Boston Red Stockings play either Detroit or Chicago in September, but soon this was modified to locals playing National League clubs for a $500 prize. Spalding became interested and proposed bringing his White Stockings to Milwaukee for $500, but insisted on a $300 guarantee, even if there was no game because of rain. Promoters balked at the $300 guarantee, "especially as September is one of those uncertain, county fair months."[41]

Interest was high in the local amateurs, and thoughts of bringing in National League clubs diminished. In late July the manager of the Star Club of Chicago requested the amateur nines of Milwaukee contact him in regard to setting up a series of games, but no local clubs were interested. Again in mid–September talk surfaced of Chicago and Providence playing a game in Milwaukee, but no game occurred. By then talk of a new club in a new league was in the paper, and the amateur era appeared to be fading away.

✳ ✳ ✳

Talk of putting Milwaukee back into the world of organized baseball began in June of 1882 with a movement to place a National League club in the city. The principal organizer, Harry D. Quin (son of the president of Quin Blank Book & Stationery Co.), along with Archie McFadyen (the old Cream City star) and Robert Nunnemacher (secretary and treasurer of the Nunnemacher flour mill), claimed to have $5,000 on hand with more on the way. It was also reported the England and German merchants of the city, plus the chamber of commerce people, would support this. A group of enthusiasts had talked to Albert G. Spalding, now a strong man in National League politics, about Milwaukee entering the league for the 1883 season, and reported him interested.

Of course, Milwaukee had had a chance in the National League and failed. That failure had been due to "lavish and unnecessary expenditure of receipts of the city by one of the managers and bad management generally."[42] Because of the 1878 Grays' bad management, Milwaukee had a "bad odor"[43] in league circles. Even if not admitted to the National League, the Milwaukee backers would put a club somewhere in the League Alliance. As for players, to go with good local talent the backers had contacted several outside players, including Charlie Bennett, now playing in Detroit, who expressed an interest in playing in Milwaukee for the right amount of money.

Reality soon came to town in the form of a letter from Spalding. Quin had sent a letter to Spalding to find out Milwaukee's chances of obtaining a National League franchise. Spalding forwarded the letter to the National League president, but thought Milwaukee's chances were slim. The National League limited itself to eight clubs, with east-west balance, but with the arrival of a new major league — the American Association — the National League was considering expanding to ten clubs. Spalding reminded Quin that any club making application to the National League must have paid capital of $7,500.

Harry Quin was confident Milwaukee would be represented in the National League for 1883. However, the *Sentinel* felt Spalding would be one who would vote against Milwaukee's admission, only two needed as Milwaukee's 114,702 population was over the required 75,000. It turned out after the season the National League put franchises in New York and Philadelphia, with Troy and Worcester leaving the league.

James Morgan's company advertisement — His nine became one of the best of the many amateur clubs formed in the 1880s.

By late July 1882 Quin and his associates gave up on the idea of landing a National League club, and planned to form a Milwaukee Baseball Club "composed of the very best ball players in the country."[44] This club was to be set up like the Metropolitans of New York. The idea was not to join the National League or League Alliance, but to play these clubs once or twice a week in Milwaukee. Playing in this manner, the Metropolitans were doing just fine. Organized in September 1880, the Mets played 151 games in 1881, including 60 with National League clubs, with gate receipts estimated to be more than $30,000.[45]

The Milwaukee backers were sure they could secure first-class talent for the operation. Bill Holbert, now playing in Troy, was the son-in-law of a local police officer, and it was reported he wanted to make Milwaukee his home. Holbert showed interest in the organization, believing there was enough talent in Milwaukee to have a good nine. It was soon reported that Holbert and Sam Weaver, another former Gray, had received "positions of business"[46] in Milwaukee. Abner Dalrymple, still with Spalding's White Stockings, also expressed interest in playing in Milwaukee if an off-season job could be obtained for him. On July 16 the *Sentinel* believed that a team "can and will be found."

However, all this planning was for the future. Harry Quin wanted a club in 1882. On July 22 Quin traveled to Chicago to investigate moving an existing League Alliance club to Milwaukee to finish the schedule. It was reported that $5,000 had been subscribed to bring a team here. His efforts failed, and all energy went toward the 1883 season. The enthusiasts began looking into playing fields and had several locations as prospects. But, by the end of July the *Sentinel* expressed doubt if Quin's club would come about.

In August Quin's hopes came alive again with plans to form the Northwestern Baseball Alliance. It was reported clubs were to come from Minneapolis, St. Paul, Dubuque, Janesville, Milwaukee and Grand Rapids. On October 27, 1882, at the Palmer House in Chicago, this new league was formed. Present were representatives from Peoria, Springfield, Quincy (all Illinois cities); Bay City, East Saginaw, Grand Rapids (Michigan cities); Toledo, Ohio, and Fort Wayne, Indiana. Calling the new league the Northwestern Baseball League, the clubs had pledges from $3,000 to $10,000 in support. Milwaukee? "Local players not having been notified,"[47] Milwaukee was not present. It was rather apparent Milwaukee was not wanted in the new league, and Quin's dreams were put aside again.

✳ ✳ ✳

As winter turned into the spring of 1883, baseball matters in Milwaukee remained motionless. There was talk of organizing a strong club, but this was only talk. Baseball was in "too dim and uncertain shape to refer to in any definite way."[48] By April Milwaukee was "still dumb on baseball matters."[49] Not one club had stood up and organized yet. "While many surrounding cities are associated actively with some league, either in an amateur or professional way, Milwaukee has no representation in that direction, so will have to go it alone."[50] The 1883 season began to look like a washout.

In mid–April the Merchants became the first club to organize. The Merchants were ready to accept challenges from first-class teams, but showed the shape of things in Milwaukee by corresponding with several out-of-town clubs. The Maple Leafs were next to organize in late April, but will be discussed later with the Arctics. Not until mid–May did more clubs begin to form. On the south side the Our Boys Club was ready to play other teenagers, as were the Unknowns. The first game of the 1883 season was played on May 20 at 20th and State Streets, the Welcomes defeating the Live Oaks 13 to 12.

The Quicksteps were ready later that month, on June 10, to play the Maple Leafs. The Quicksteps lost their chance at the Leafs when the game was rained out. The following week the Quicks, clad in their new uniforms from Spalding of Chicago—white flannel with green stockings, belt, cap and tie—lost to the Leafs 8 to 4. The Quicksteps followed the loss by beating the Athletics at Athletic Park, 13 to 1 and 18 to 3 in two successive weeks. In the following weeks the Welcomes fell three times to the Q's. The Quicksteps were next to play the Arctics.

Before the Quicksteps could meet the Arctics, they became involved in a minor misunderstanding with the newly organized Phoenix Club. The Phoenix, a power in recent years but off to a slow start in '83, had apparently been talking big. The Quicks were quick to answer. "The Phoenix Baseball Club claims to be able to beat the Maple Leafs. They know they cannot do it, and they also know they cannot beat the Quicksteps. To show that we believe that we can give them the little end of the score, we challenge them to a game for from $25 to $100, and deposit $25 as forfeit."[51] The Phoenix immediately claimed to be

1883 Quicksteps. *Top row, left to right:* Cornelius Corcoran, ss; James Keyes, cf; Hugh O'Conners, 3b; Dan Driscoll, lf; David Andrews, rf. *Middle row:* William Daley, 2b; William Cary, manager; Jack Haggerty, manager; Jack Shea, 1b. *Bottom row:* Willy Lee, c; Dennis Moran, pitcher (courtesy Milwaukee County Historical Society).

misquoted, but would be willing to play the Q's for $25 in about three weeks' time. Unfortunately, the match never came about.

The Quicksteps met the Arctics on July 29 at Cold Spring Driving Park and came ever so close to a major upset. Through the first seven innings the Q's had the game all their way, but the Arctics scored seven times in the eighth to tie the score and won it in the ninth, 9 to 8. A few weeks later the Quicksteps were again defeated, this time by the Greens, in a one-run game. There was a rematch, for $50, again won by the Greens. Finally in September the Quicksteps ended the losing streak by besting the Live Oaks, 19 to 5. With a win under their belts, the Quicks traveled to Portage, first losing to the Cambria Whites. This loss prompted the *Cambria Journal* to brag that before Milwaukee organized a professional nine, they should get up an amateur club that could beat their Whites. The Quicksteps stayed in Portage and beat the Phoenix Club of that city, 11 to 7, in a $40 match game. The Quicksteps returned home, and in October again lost to the Greens to end their season.

Meanwhile, having started off as a slow baseball year, 1883 turned into the biggest year for the game in Milwaukee. More clubs—well over 100—were organized throughout the summer than in any other year. In late May the Lacawannas organized. They will probably never be remembered—only two games can be found in which they played, losing them both—except as maybe having the most nicknames on one club. Only the catcher, Lou Robinson, was not tagged with a nickname. The other members took these:

Jack Rowan "No. 1"–ss
"Pugilist" Gunning–3b
"Coal Tosser" O'Neil–rf
"Dutchie" Sexton–1b
"Painter" Mitchell–lf

Jack Rowan "No. 2"–p
"Salty" Brennan–2b
"Painter" Dwyer–cf
"Original" O'Neill–sub

The Welcomes organized and whipped the North Milwaukees, 21 to 12. The High School again organized a nine. In July the Greens, from the south side, who would beat the Quicksteps three times, organized and played the Palmyra Reds, winning 14 to 8 on July 4. On the last weekend of July, four games were played that Saturday and eight games were played on Sunday. By September thirteen different games were being reported on a single Sunday.

Ballparks sprang up all over town. A portion of Cold Spring Driving Park — Thirty-fourth and McKinley — was converted into a ball field (from a race track) in late April. The ballpark was 400-feet square, and gave "Milwaukee for the first time a really desirable place to contest and witness the national game."[52] The name of the park was changed to Maple Leaf Baseball Association Park, but continued to be referred to as Cold Spring Driving Park. Bad weather delayed the opening of the new park, and the Maple Leafs' opener was scheduled for the park at Nineteenth and Clybourn. The press found fault with the new park, specifically the "rights of reporters in their working quarters."[53] The *Sentinel* felt "the [reporters'] stand is for their convenience and not for the benefit of the crowd that seems to take it for granted that they can crowd in everywhere."[54] Manager Rice of the Maple Leafs explained that he kept the stand open to all so as not to hurt anyone's feelings. The *Sentinel* thought "if he had a thought of this kind for the newspaper men, he would forever live in grateful remembrance."[55] The *Sentinel* also felt the clubs continually starting the games half an hour late was annoying, at the least. The old park at Tenth and Clybourn as well as Athletic Park and First Ward Park were still around. Playing fields were found at places like Twentieth and State Street, Fifth and North Avenue, National Avenue, Twenty-third and West Cherry Street, First and North Avenue, Thirty-second and West State, and East North Avenue at North Richards. In all, at least fifteen different parks hosted baseball in Milwaukee in 1883.

In the past year the business clubs of the city appeared to be dying. However, in 1883, like all of baseball in Milwaukee, it was booming. Combinations joined to become the Grocers and the Druggists. Employees of the newspapers again played each other. The railroad employees all over the city started a league of sorts, composed of the Lake Shores, Wisconsin Centrals, the St. Paul nine and the Western Railway Fast Freights. When the Lake Shores beat the St. Pauls, the St. Pauls claimed the Shores beat a scrub nine, not the office nine. A challenge was sent out and the *Sentinel* summed up the railroad baseball situation: "There is blood on the face of the moon, and the universe holds its breath in painful suspense until this vital question of supremacy is decided."[56] The big game was finally played and the St. Pauls won 9 to 1. However, the Wisconsin Centrals, a club that would not play Sunday games, claimed the railroad championship with a 13 and 2 record.

Business groups from almost all types of establishments played in 1883. Heimann's team was still on the field and the Northwestern Mutual Life Insurance Company also fielded a team. Matthews Brothers represented the furniture industry. "Being in daily practice with watermelons and other vegetable products,"[57] the West Water Street Commission team was an easy victor over Shadbolt & Boyd. Remember Ball & Goodrich and the Zieglers? They were still around. The Milwaukee Mattress Company sprang onto the diamond, as well as the P.V.s of H. Roff cigarmakers; many, many more played baseball, as well.

Without a doubt the most interesting clubs were again the Maple Leafs and Arctics. Both went their separate ways through most of the season, but in the end the two clubs together created the excitement. The Maple Leafs organized in late April, securing a portion of Cold Spring Driving Park for its games, and as mentioned changed the name of the park. The original squad consisted of Thomas Delany, left field and pitcher; Douglas Young, catcher; Thomas Sexton, shortstop; Otto Schomberg (from the previous year's Arctics), first base; John Lee, second base; Frank Parker, third base; Zach Clayton, pitcher; Denny Sullivan, right field; John Hanrahan, center field; and Thomas Drew (from the previous year's Milwaukee Club) as change third baseman. Almost immediately Manager Thurman Rice (his regular job was a bookkeeper for Hibbard & Vance on North Broadway Street) had trouble holding his players. He had already lost one star, Pat Sullivan, to the Quincy Club of the Northwestern League, and it was rumored Clayton and Sexton were on their way, although he denied this. Two weeks after this denial, Sexton and Denny Sullivan were gone. Peter Morris had "signed articles"[58] to play shortstop for the Maple Leafs, and Tommy Lee took over for Sexton in the captain's role. Lee played right field and pitched for the season. (In 1884 Tommy Lee would sign with Chicago of the National League and pitch for both the White Stockings and its reserve team. Later in the season, he went to the Baltimore Unions. He won a total of six games and lost twelve in the big leagues in 1884 and batted .245. Tommy would die in Milwaukee on March 4, 1886, at the age of 23.) In July Rice almost lost his catcher to the Columbus club of the American Association, but Young decided to stay in Milwaukee. In September Johnny Lee decided to resign from the club due to out-of-town business engagements, but apparently changed his mind and remained with the club. Late in the season Rice recovered the services of Sullivan and Sexton from Quincy, just in time for the fateful final game.

The status of the Maple Leafs—professional or amateur—is in doubt. In late April it was reported that manager Rice had received a request from the Quincy club to send them four players. The *Sentinel* then reported "as all are under contract and prefer to remain at home and win a record for Milwaukee, the invitation could not be accepted."[59] As already noted, two players were lost and Morris "signed articles" to play for the Leafs. However, when the Leafs lost to Muskego later in the year, the September 3, 1883, Sentinel stated, "... and when it is remembered that the Maples are only amateurs, the wonder is that they did so well" against the salaried team. In light of the newspaper's statements early in the season and Schomberg jumping over from the strong Arctic club, we must believe the Maple Leafs were at least a semi-professional club. When Sullivan and Sexton returned after the Northwestern League season, the supposition becomes even stronger.

The Maple Leafs' playing season was to begin on Sunday, May 20, at Tenth and Clybourn; Cold Spring Driving Park was not finished for baseball. However, the game with the Merchants was postponed due to unfavorable weather. The season opener thus was played at Cold Spring Driving Park the following Sunday against the Chicago Greens before 500 spectators. The game was close for five innings, in favor of the home club 4 to 3, but then the Leafs "seemed to gauge the Chicago pitcher's delivery"[60] and ran away with a 13 to 3 win. A few days later, the *Evening Wisconsin* broke a story that the Greens were actually the Star Club of Chicago, the amateur champions of Illinois. The loss sent them "back to the City of Sin feeling much greener than when they arrived."[61]

The Maple Leafs' second match of the season was a $100 match game with the Arctics in the first test of local dominance. Rice, in a stunt one would think worthy of such later promoters as Bill Veeck, engaged a Professor Donaldson and a Captain Dalton "to appear in a friendly sparring exhibition with gloves, in connection with the game."[62] Something must have told Rice he was ahead of his time and he cancelled that part of the show. The game was show enough. The teams played to an 8 to 8 tie in regulation time, and both teams scored three runs in the tenth inning. In the next inning the Maple Leafs scored two runs and blanked the Arctics to secure their second win of the season, pinning the Arctics

1883 Maple Leafs. The inscription at top reads, "Presented to Old Settlers Club by Otto Schomberg. Maple Leaves Base Ball Club 1882 [*sic*]. Champions of Middle West." **Back row, left to right:** Johnny Lee, 2b; Otto Schomberg, 1b; Jack Clayton, p; Tom Drew, 3b; Tommy Lee, c; Dennis Sullivan, rf. **Seated:** J. Rice, asst. manager; Doug Young, cf; Bill Delaney, secretary; Thurman Rice, manager; unidentified (possibly Tom Delaney, lf). **On ground:** Peter Morris, ss; Jack Hanrahan, pitcher and outfield (courtesy Milwaukee County Historical Society).

with the loss in their season opener. The following Sunday the Quickstep match was rained out, but the Leafs took them the following week.

The Maple Leafs tasted their first defeat the following week with a 4 to 2 decision to the Chicago Brown Stockings, one of that city's best amateur clubs. The Leafs then sent Chicago's Blues home thinking about a 27 to 7 loss. The difference in these two games appeared to be the coaching. In the loss, the club "showed a want of coaching, they hesitated at times when delays were costly, when good captaining would have helped them through the advantage."[63] Then in the win, Tommy Lee, the field captain, "looked after his men in the best way, their excellent work at the bases being done in a great measure to his coaching."[64] That week the Maple Leafs traveled to Chicago and played their first weekday games, beating the Browns twice, 17 to 7 and 17 to 2 — the home nine collecting only two hits off Tommy Lee in the second loss.

The Maple Leafs were now ready to play the Arctics again. The Arctics also had just returned home from a northern trip, where they had beaten De Pere and Green Bay. A big crowd was on hand to see the Leafs win 12 to 7. Where Lee had recently earned the praise of the *Sentinel*, Burner of the Arctics found the paper's disapproval with his arguing with the umpire. The Picketts of Chicago visited Milwaukee on July 15, with their catcher, Jackson, "who is said to be immense,"[65] the only black man with a white club in the west. "A better battle with ash and leather has not been seen this season,"[66] as the Leafs made their four hits good for a 5 to 4 victory.

By mid–July the Maple Leafs' record was 8 and 1, but they had problems in two directions. First was local support:

> ...there is not a city of Milwaukee's size and pretensions in the United States where less support is paid to local clubs. The Maple Leafs are a fine organization and have the stuff to make a high mark, but Manager Rice and his indefatigable secretary [Tift] have almost carried the club on their own shoulders to the present point of perfection.[67]

The second problem was finding contests with strong Wisconsin clubs. Six of their nine games had been with Chicago clubs, while the other three were with local Milwaukee clubs. Rice set out to solve this by announcing the club was ready to play any Wisconsin club for $200 to $300, provided $100 was put up in advance. A rumor was also around that Rice was going to retire, but he stayed on to the bitter end.

The strong Wisconsin club appeared in the form of the Beloit nine, which had just beaten the Milwaukee Greens twice by big scores. In this game Beloit had disagreements with the umpire, who was removed in the sixth inning. The Maple Leafs were victorious, 6 to 1— Tommy Lee striking out 14. With nine victories in ten tries, the *Sentinel* on July 23 asked, "Who says Milwaukee has no ball club?" The Leafs had some of the wind taken from their sails in Chicago the following Sunday with an 11 to 4 loss to that city's Union Club.

Rice accepted a challenge for $100 a side to play the Arctics on August 5. The Arctics had just beaten the Quicksteps in a close game and were geared up to beat the Maple Leafs. Five Arctics games can be found previous to this match, with the A's winning three. The Arctics put a team on the field that consisted of Schierz pitching and Anton Falch catching. Falch had caught for the Peoria Reds earlier that season for $125 a month and all expenses paid, and was the only player around to still catch without the aid of gloves or a mask. The remainder of the nine consisted of Drew, 1b; Straub, 2b; Furcell, ss; Himmerstein, 3b; Francis, lf; Ebbitts, cf; and McCormack, rf. More than 2,000 people witnessed the Arctics take their first victory over the Maple Leafs, "sending them to the zenith of supreme satisfaction."[68] The 4 to 1 victory convinced the Arctics they had settled the question of supremacy.

The Maple Leafs soon became entangled in a gate money controversy, among other things. Back on July 23, the Leafs announced they would play the Green Bay Club in Milwaukee. It was reported at this time the Green Bays had four salaried men. Green Bay denied that they had any salaried players, claiming the men in question were "merely visitors to this city, and being good players and fond of the game, are taking a hand in with the boys for pastime."[69] Green Bay, which had won five of its last six games, without further ado lost to the Maple Leafs 11 to 4 on August 12 at Cold Spring Driving Park. Immediately following the game, Rice complained that Green Bay's charge of $18.75 for the umpire was too much. Green Bay claimed this charge was just as fair as the Maple Leafs' charges of $27.70 for advertising, watchman's fee, etc. They also believed that the Maple Leafs cheated them on the ticket count. F.K. Joannes of the Green Bay Club explained that the tickets were as follows:

495 whole or 25 cent tickets	$123.75
53 tickets @ 15 cents	7.95
39 tickets @ 10 cents	3.90
TOTAL IN BOX	$135.60

They did not have enough 25 cent tickets to hold out on sales, cashier asked me for some out of box during sale of tickets. Gave him 100, he sold 67, put 33 back. Total of whole tickets was 495 which did not include 67 resold, should have been added to total. After expenses there was $105.49 to divide equally.[70]

Joannes' figures tend to prove the Maple Leafs had not done him wrong. After the game the *Sentinel* reported that Green Bay had taken home about $55. If the 67 disputed tickets are added to the $135.60, the total becomes $152.35. Deduct the umpire's expenses and the Maple Leafs' charges, totaling $46.45, the total would be $105.80 — only 40 cents off of Joannes' figure. Thus the Green Bay share would be $52.90. The Maple Leafs sent a challenge up to Green Bay for a rematch money game in September and Green Bay accepted. The *Evening Wisconsin* believed all this warfare between the two clubs "looks like a good advertising scheme for the benefit of the respective clubs,"[71] but Rice later withdrew from the contest, saying he "prefer[red] to match his club against men."[72] The Leafs next beat the Dreadnaughts of Chicago, 8 to 7, by scoring three runs in the ninth inning.

The Maple Leafs again went after the Arctics, challenging them to another money game. The Arctics balked until Rice put up his $100. Once he did, the match was set. The game was indeed a money game — not only on the field, but in the stands, where it was reported "big money changed hands."[73] Lee was again marvelous for the Leafs, pitching a three-hitter. The offense produced single runs in the seventh and ninth, as the Maple Leafs won 2 to 0. On the first Sunday in September, 2,000 attended the game at Cold Spring Driving Park to see the all-salaried Muskegons beat the Leafs 9 to 8. The Leafs bounced back with a win over the local Milwaukee Club the following week.

Thurman Rice secured the Elgin Club, the champion amateur club of Illinois, thought to be as good as some of the National League clubs, for the Maple Leafs' next challenge. The game took place on September 23, and the Milwaukee boys "did themselves proud."[74] Down 2 to 0, the Maple Leafs scored three in the sixth and beat the Elgins by that score. Again it was a big money game in the stands, "there being more money upon the game, with the odds all in favor of the visitors, than any game this summer."[75] The following week a nine composed of the best Chicago amateurs, calling themselves the Alaska Blues, took on the Maple Leafs. The Leafs entered the game without Clayton, Lee or Delany, replacing them with a player from the Arctics and another from the Quicksteps, along with their regular umpire Timlin. The Maple Leafs lost 10 to 9.

Meanwhile, the Arctics were playing a few games, ready to take another shot at the Maple Leafs. On September 23, at National Park, the Arctics defeated the Greens of Milwaukee, 13 to 11. At the end of the month the Arctics traveled to Green Bay to meet that club at the Brown County Fair. The first game ended after only five innings in a 7 to 5 Green Bay victory. The Arctics complained about the umpire, a Milwaukeean, and had him replaced by a Fort Howard man. They liked him no better, and left the field. The Greens, who had come with the Arctics, lost to Green Bay the following day. The Arctics were to play again on Saturday. This game almost did not come off. The original agreement for the games had been the Arctics would receive 70 percent of the gate receipts. Green Bay, probably looking back on the A's actions two days previous, thought this a little high. The Arctics refused to play unless the original division of the purse was reinstated. It finally was agreed upon, and the Arctics won the game, 11 to 6. The series was concluded the next day with a Green Bay win. The Arctics then came home and lost to the Milwaukees.

The table was set for the game of the year. The Maple Leafs had beaten the Arctics three of four times, but supremacy would be decided here. As already mentioned, the Leafs again had the services of Sullivan and Sexton. In a good, close game, the Arctics won 9 to 8.

The great controversy now began. The Arctics were claiming the championship of the state and disbanded after the game. The Maple Leafs had won three of the five games played between the teams, but the Arctics won two of the last three. The *Sentinel* was sure the Leafs would dispute the championship. The Arctic players were presented badges symbolizing the championship. "The badges are quite elaborate and handsome. The design is a scroll at the top bearing the individual name of the wearer and the club, with crossed bats, a miniature ball and other emblems of the diamond filed underneath, the whole being pendant by a red ribbon."[76] Badges meant nothing to Rice, and he deposited $100 to play the Arctics, the conditions being both clubs play exactly the same men as in the deciding game. The winning club would take all the money and be recognized champions.

The Arctics answered by reminding everyone that they had disbanded and were not obliged to play another game. They claimed that Rice and Frank Schwind, the two managers, had agreed upon the two out of three championship games. No doubt the Leafs figured with the two returning professionals that they should have won. Rice's counterclaim was that the Maple Leafs had the best record in the state and should be champions. Although the *Milwaukee Journal* believed another game would be played, that game marked the end of the 1883 season. In November the Arctic Club gave a ball at the West Side Turner Hall and were presented with the championship flag. Upon one side of the flag, on a blue background, were the traditional crossed bats and ball, with the wording: Arctic Baseball Club, Milwaukee, Wisconsin. On the reverse side: CHAMPIONS OF WISCONSIN.

7

A Tale of Two Dead Leagues (1884)

In September 1883 the idea of putting a professional club in Milwaukee was again seriously considered. "The formation of a Milwaukee nine would bring the city into prominence in sporting circles the country over, as the club would find matches in plenty all through the West and all wished for the remote East."[1] Local players were interested, as were promoters. In December James F. McKee, of Rockford, came to Milwaukee to organize a club and place it in the Northwestern League. The *Dubuque Herald* described McKee as "a live, pushy and energetic manager."[2] Back in 1879 McKee had been president of the old Northwestern League and manager of the Rockford Club. McKee figured that a stock company with $10,000 should be formed, and on December 27, it was unanimously resolved to organize an incorporated joint stock company, with the $10,000 divided into shares of $125. Stock worth $5,000 was immediately subscribed and the *Milwaukee Sentinel* on December 28, 1883, felt "there is no reason why baseball in this city should not receive a boom sufficient to insure the permanency of a strong nine." An election was then held for the officers of the club: John C. Iverson (co-owner of J.C. Iverson & Co., makers of frames, looking glasses and cabinet hardware)—president; Louis Auer (owner of Louis Auer & Sons, European Steamship & Railway agent)—vice president; George Ziegler Jr. (of the Ziegler Candy Company)—secretary; Charles M. Kipp (co-owner of J.C. Iverson & Co.)—treasurer; Harry D. Quin (future president of Quin Blank Book & Stationery Co.)—corresponding secretary; and McKee—manager.

The annual meeting of the Northwestern League was set for January 9, in Chicago. Prospects for the 1884 season were discouraging for the Northwestern. There was little chance Springfield would again field a club and Toledo, the league's strongest club, had joined the expanded American Association. Few thought Peoria or Quincy would stay. Secretary Samuel Morton of the Northwestern assured McKee there would be a place in the league for his club. The Northwestern, as of then, consisted of Fort Wayne, Peoria, Grand Rapids, Saginaw, Bay City and Quincy. It was figured St. Paul would join Milwaukee to make eight clubs. Other outside contenders for the openings were Evansville, Terre Haute, Dayton and Rockford. Milwaukee made its formal application and sent a delegation of Iverson, C.M. Kipp, Auer, A.F. Tanner, B. A. Kipp and Quin to Chicago for the league's meeting. As expected, Toledo and Springfield withdrew, but in a surprise move the Northwestern admitted St. Paul, Minneapolis, Stillwater, Milwaukee, Muskegon and Terre Haute to form a twelve-club circuit on January 10, 1884. J.J. Rust of the Saginaw club was elected president and Samuel Morton secretary of the league, which joined the National Agreement. The incorporation papers of the Milwaukee club were signed in Madison on January 10, with Iverson, Kipp, Tanner and Auer being the incorporators.

The Northwestern League had positioned its 12 franchises in five states. Wisconsin's only entry was Milwaukee. Michigan had four clubs: Grand Rapids, Muskegon, Saginaw and Bay City. Minnesota had clubs in St. Paul, Minneapolis and Stillwater. Peoria and

Quincy were the Illinois cities, while Indiana had Terre Haute and Fort Wayne. Quin explained that in order to secure some privileges, Milwaukee had to pull in St. Paul, Stillwater and Minneapolis. However, this turned out to be a problem, as the clubs in Minnesota, Indiana and Michigan united in preventing Milwaukee from placing a representative on the scheduling committee. This committee split up the holidays. Milwaukee, being the largest city in the league, wanted and got July 4, but lost Decoration Day to Grand Rapids. McKee explained Muskegon was picked over Evansville because it had six millionaires backing it. Sunday ball was a different story, though. To Milwaukee the Sunday games issue was of "paramount consideration."[3] "It will be remembered that on account of the large foreign element in Milwaukee, the league at its recent meeting voted to allow the question of Sunday games and beer selling on the grounds to each club."[4]

Tom Loftus — captain, field manger, and then full manager of Milwaukee's 1884 club.

Elais Matter, the outgoing president of the Northwestern, said games would technically be allowed, but not scheduled. Only the year before, Fort Wayne was almost expelled, in part for playing Sunday games. Milwaukee lost the Sunday issue when the schedule was made out in March. The tables were turned on Grand Rapids, however, when Milwaukee refused to give the team 50 percent of the receipts on Sunday exhibitions.

As a member of the Northwestern League, the new franchise needed players. Not much was known of local players, but it was expected some of the powerful amateur Maple Leafs would be contacted. Before the club was even formally admitted to the Northwestern League, money had been advanced to seven players. Soon afterward it was reported the club had signed Steve Behel (recently released by Fort Wayne), Ed Hogan (from Peoria), Tom Morrissey (from Janesville), Pat Dealy, Tom and Michael McDermott, James Burke and Steve Dunn (from London, Canada). Salaries ranged from $100 to $175 a month per player. By the end of January, the club had 18 men under contract, and in February McKee announced his players. He had decided to go into the season with four pitchers. Morrissey was his main pitcher, but would alternate with Dennis McGinley at third base, both from Janesville. The other two were Tom McDermott from Fall River, Massachusetts, and R.W. Schierz from the local Arctics. McKee also went into the season with four catchers. Joe Straub, a former Maple Leaf who had played with Columbus of the American Association the previous year, teamed with Mike McDermott, Dealy from Connecticut, and James Purvis from Canada. Tom Griffin from Rockford, who "covers the first base with great dexterity and it is a wild ball that passes him,"[5] was pegged for first base. For second McKee choose Thomas J. Loftus. Loftus, 27 years old, had nine games experience in the big leagues. In 1877 he played three games for the St. Louis National League club and in 1883 played six games with the St. Louis Browns of the American Association. His lifetime average in those two years was .182, but he was considered a good all-around player, and was made the field captain. Tom Sexton, the graduate of the Maple Leafs who played with Quincy of the Northwestern League in 1883, became the shortstop. Steve Behel was selected for left field. How he came to Milwaukee is an interesting story. In 1883 Behel played for the Chicago Union team and when that club disbanded in August, he was reserved by Fort Wayne. When the Union Association formed in 1884, the Baltimore club signed him. But he soon found out that if he played for the Union club, he would be expelled from the National Agreement (to which the Northwestern was a member). He gave Baltimore his advance money back, and ended up in Milwaukee when McKee purchased his release from Fort Wayne.

"Loose Jointed" Steve Dunn went to center field and was alternated with Tom Griffin at first base. It was said Behel was better than Abner Dalrymple, his "striding between the bases is not to be equaled."[6] Ed Hogan, who played for Peoria and St. Paul the previous year, finished the outfield. Burke, one of the originals, had been released in February.

In early March Charles B. Baldwin, a lefty from Hastings, Michigan, who would become a 42-game winner with Detroit's National League club two years later, was signed. The club now had 22 men under contract, of which nine were local talent. A week later McKee again attempted to strengthen the club by signing catcher Cal Broughton, a 23-year-old "big free-hearted granger boy"[7] from Albany, Wisconsin. He had caught a total of 12 games the previous year in the National League and American Association. More important, he had caught for McGinley in the old Beloit-Janesville combination and together would be called "the Wisconsin Battery."[8] In early April another pitcher, Edgar Cushman, was signed. Cushman, a 22-year-old Buckeye, had a 3 and 3 record with Buffalo in 1883, and was slated to be the team's star pitcher. Earlier a Cleveland paper reported that Anton Falch, a former Arctic, jumped his Chicago Union contract and signed with Milwaukee.

With the new players, McKee again announced a lineup for opening day.

PITCHERS	CATCHERS
Ed Cushman	Joe Straub
Dennis McGinley	Cal Broughton
Tom McDermott	Mike McDermott

INFIELDERS	OUTFIELDERS
Tom Griffin (1b)	Steve Behel
Tom Loftus (2b)	Steve Dunn
Tom Sexton (ss)	Ed Hogan
Tom Morrissey (3b)	

The other players under contract were on the reserve team; these were teams formed by National Association clubs, in part to keep players from the newly formed Union Association. Milwaukee's directors agreed to form a reserve club in January, composed of professionals and players from the better local amateur teams. The directors also stated that these players could be brought up to the regular team if a player was disabled. The reserves were to be paid monthly while playing clubs in the state and other reserve teams at home when the regulars were on the road, charging 25 cents admission. Unfortunately, these reserve clubs killed the good local amateur clubs. For example, the Maple Leafs lost five of their best players to the Milwaukee and Chicago reserves. In March the managers of Milwaukee, Chicago, Pittsburgh, St. Louis, Cincinnati and Cleveland set up a season schedule for their reserve clubs. The season would last from May 1 through October 1 and a championship flag valued at $60 was to be presented to the first-place club.

Entering the season the reserves had twelve players signed. The pitchers numbered three—Baldwin, Zach Clayton from the Maple Leafs, and Schierz. Three catchers were also under contract—Falch, the 6' 6", 220-pound local boy—Dealy and Purvis. From first to third the infield was Otto Schomberg [real name Otto H. Shambrick], the former Arctic-turned-Maple Leaf; James Toole, the captain, at second; Phillip Himmelstein, from the Arctics, at third; and another Maple Leaf, Peter Morris, at shortstop. T.F. Delaney, an all-around utility man who played ten years with the Maple Leafs, played the outfield along with Roberts, newly acquired, who had played in Philadelphia the previous year, and other players when not in their usual positions.

Of course, these clubs needed a place to play and seat the people who would be willing to pay to see them. As far back as September of 1883 the press was suggesting the old Catholic cemetery grounds on Grand (West Wisconsin) Avenue. The *Sentinel* was sure "a few years use of the lot as a ball ground would do away with the cemetery memory that now haunts it."[9] But others were to have a say. The south side capitalists wanted the park on National Avenue and were willing to fix up the grounds, and erect fences and grandstands. Other locations considered were near Mitchell

Cal Broughton — Albany, Wisconsin, native and the catching portion of the "Wisconsin Battery."

Heights (approximate area bounded by North Oakland to Maryland Avenues, East Bradford to Park Place), the Lake Front, Cold Spring Driving Park (Thirty-fourth and McKinley) and Wright Street. Another group to have a say was the streetcar companies. The *Sentinel* thought it was likely the West Side Railway Company would be liberal, as it would surely benefit from a park close to its lines. It was pointed out that in Peoria, Illinois, a streetcar company had subscribed $200 to that club when they selected grounds near their line. The Northwestern Railroad Company and the Cream City Railway Company proposed to furnish a park free on the east side. The Milwaukee City and West Side Companies promised the same on the west side. The manager of the new baseball club, James F. McKee, assured the companies that with an average attendance of 800, they would get their money back in the first year. However, the directors of the baseball club were in favor of purchasing the grounds outright in order to have exclusive control and place the park on centrally located grounds.

In February, the club announced the new grounds would be on Wright Street, between Eleventh and Twelfth, with the entrance on Twelfth Street. The ticket office would stand immediately inside the gate. From there, the customer would pass through the turnstiles and enter the 26-foot-high grandstand, which was situated 90 feet behind home plate and was divided into three sections with stationary chairs. To the right of the grandstand would be large, open stands. The capacity of the park would be 5,300. Dressing rooms for the players were beneath the grandstand, along with "commodious toilet rooms for ladies and gentlemen."[10] From home plate to center field was 326 feet.[11] The distance to the fences was so short balls hit over them were a ground-rule double. The plans for the park were drawn up by Bradley Brothers of Rockford, Illinois. The park would be only a 25-minute ride from the center of town. The job was given to local carpenter William Klocksin, and the estimated cost was $3,500. Work began in late March on the project. Nearly 800 loads of soil were dumped to level the grounds. Between 75,000 and 90,000 feet of lumber were used to erect the stadium. Then bad weather hit Milwaukee and work slowed down. By late April the diamond was finally laid out and 20,000 yards of sod were laid, with workers staying until after dark to complete the job by opening day. A new feature to the park was a four-foot-wide base path, made of layers of broken stone, gravel and ashes to assist players working around the bases. An artesian well was also dug, along with a windmill and pump to supply water to the grounds. The *St. Louis Globe* claimed the final cost was $11,000. Nicholas Lutz was engaged to look after the refreshment stands and Welcome Kirby was given the scorecard rights. The *Evening Wisconsin* reported the club was the only one in the United States owning its own stadium.

With the season underway, the directors began to find flaws in the new park. To curb nonpaying visitors and stop youngsters from entering the park via this route, management decided to put up a barbwire guard around the fence. To accommodate expected large crowds, 300 additional chairs were added to the grandstand in late May and 100 more in June, bringing the total grandstand seating to 1,200. But when an estimated 5,000 fans showed up for the Fourth of July afternoon game, the management was criticized for the overflow and the Grand Rapids manager pulled his players off the field "until the intruders were driven back."[12] The conduct of the Milwaukee fans gave the city the reputation of a "hard-kicking town."[13] The *Grand Rapids Times* called the Milwaukee fans the worst in the Northwestern League. The *Evening Wisconsin* thought putting police officers in the stands was the only way to control the hoodlums. To improve the playing surface, the club filled the field with large quantities of gravel and rolled it until it was perfectly level. A Western Union wire was installed at the park and an operator reported results of all league games. Reporters soon complained that the management should keep the fans out of the reporters' stand, a seemingly common complaint of the press. The management estimated that the park, improvements to it, and player salaries cost more than $53,000. Iverson broke down the projected cost for the press (these numbers include the Northwestern League club and its reserve team):

24 players and manager	$19,200
Printing and advertising	2,000
Suits, bats, balls, etc.	650
Janitor and help on grounds	900
Grandstand, seats and diamond	3,500
Estimated pay to visiting clubs	9,000
Tax, interest, repairs, etc. on grounds	900
Charter, plans, seal, etc.	150
Cost of grounds	11,500

Traveling expenses of two nines and managers	5,000
Special expenses not yet accounted for	*700*
TOTAL	$53,500

Getting paying customers into this park was another problem. As of one week before the season opened, none of the west side railway companies had begun extending their lines to the park. The closest line stopped at Garfield Avenue, three blocks from the park. Iverson told the *Evening Wisconsin* on April 18, 1884, "those horse-railroad are more bother and trouble than the entire club put together." Within a few days, however, the Becker Street Railway Company began extending its track to the grounds. Soon the Milwaukee City and West Side Street Railway followed suit. Cars were to run every ten minutes to the park. If necessary, the management was going to add a line of omnibuses to transport fans for a nickel. For customers who wished their own transportation, the club added 20 feet across the lower end of the park to secure carriages with 100 hitching posts and even provided hostlers. Because games started in the late afternoon, getting paying customers to the park from their jobs was a problem. The directors of the club made a proposition to the Merchants Association to give clerks half-holidays on Saturday or at least be released at 2 o'clock. The club also took out advertising space in the *Milwaukee Journal and Milwaukee Sentinel*.

As is the case with any business, the Milwaukee Baseball Association needed capital to work with. As already noted, half of the $10,000 needed was subscribed at their original meeting, and Jim McKee sought out businessmen to get up the additional $5,000 in January and February, with unknown success. With any business venture, customers are the road to lasting success. In March the club began its season ticket drive. Fifty-five games were scheduled for Milwaukee, and season tickets went for $15, or 27 cents a game, almost half price. The club announced only 300 season tickets would be issued and would be on sale only until May 1. The club explained honestly that after the season opened, the club made more money selling single tickets. As the Northwestern League policy was a 50–50 gate split, the Milwaukee club would have to hope for both good attendance at home as well as on the road. Manager McKee saved the club some money by getting special rates from the railroads on trips in and out of Milwaukee.

Even though the Northwestern used turnstiles, attendance figures in the papers still were estimates and varied greatly. For example, at the first home exhibition between the regulars and reserves, the *Sentinel* placed attendance at 800. The *Evening Wisconsin* reported a crowd of 1,200 for the game, while later in the same article placed 1,500 at the contest. Opening day, usually a big gate attraction, drew only between 500 and 700 in threatening weather. Between 500 and 900 fans attended the following day (all three local newspapers giving different estimates) and 1,000 on the final game of the St. Paul series, for an estimated total of 2,100 for the opening series; that was well below McKee's prediction of an average of 800 a game. Minneapolis came in next and after a rainout, only 400 attended. After that, crowds of about 1,000 began to attend games. Non-championship Sunday games were a big attraction. More than four thousand came out on May 11 to see the Gordons of Chicago lose to Milwaukee. After coming back from a long road trip of almost a month, playing 21 games in seven cities in June, the club reported that it was not "a financial triumph,"[14] but was doing better than most clubs. Playing under .500 ball, the club was still drawing well at home. The club drew 1,500 to a Thursday game, 600 the following day and again 1,500 on Saturday, all against Peoria in championship games. On Sunday, in an exhibition game with the same club, 3,000 turned out, showing how popular Sunday ball was.

Attendance on the road was even more erratic. On a Sunday exhibition game in

Muskegon, 1,200 showed up. On the Monday and Wednesday games, only 300 attended. On Decoration Day in Grand Rapids, 629 showed up for the morning game and 2,577 passed through the turnstile in the afternoon game, bolstered by the Detroit, Grand Haven & Milwaukee Railroad's $3.00 round trip from Milwaukee to Grand Rapids for fans. It was rumored that after this series, Secretary Ziegler of the Grays had to "negotiate for a small loan"[15] to purchase a ticket back home, which he denied. In a Sunday exhibition game in Fort Wayne, only 500 fans came, amid rumors that Fort Wayne may disband. The total series in Fort Wayne drew only 1,000, with the Milwaukee club receiving only $325. Attendance in Minneapolis was above average, as 3,000 attended a Tuesday game there. But on one occasion the Minneapolis management pulled a fast one. With the clubs on the field and 500 people in the stands, the Minneapolis manager asked for the game to be postponed, even though the rain had stopped. In reality, he was waiting for a new pitcher and won his battle when the game was called off. In Quincy, a Saturday game drew 1,200, but a Monday game drew 600 and only 400 showed the next day. On this long road trip McKee made the unbelievable claim that the club made $1,800 above expenses.

Home from the road trip, the Milwaukee management instituted two attendance helpers. The club put up a two-inch mesh wire screen in front of the grandstand to protect fans from foul balls. They next re-instituted Ladies Day on Thursday, when ladies were admitted free. On the first Thursday a total of 1,500 fans attended, but how many free admissions were granted to ladies is unknown. On July 18, the *Sentinel* claimed that the special day was a success "as far as the attendance of the fair sex is concerned, but the home clubs always loses on that day." Further concessions to women were made later when "no smoking" signs were posted in the ladies area. On July 4, the club made off big. In the early game, between 2,000 and 3,000 attended, and an overflow crowd of 5,000 witnessed the afternoon game, including 500 Grand Rapids fans, accompanied by a band and two military companies. Later in the season the management began renting out cushions to spectators, but had trouble with youths throwing the cushions on the field.

One sad note to the club's money difficulties was the fate of the reserve team. Because of the bad weather in Milwaukee, the reserves went to Rockford with the regulars to practice. For their first game, the reserves beat the Rockford club 11 to 9 on April 24. Before returning to Milwaukee, the reserves lost to the regulars 6 to 5. Once back home, the regulars whipped the reserves before a good crowd. These reserves, known as the Cream Cities, wore two uniforms. One was of white flannel with red stockings, belts and caps; the other a chocolate colored mixture with white flannel and cream stockings, belt and caps. They then traveled to Rock Island, Illinois, to play their first real contest. On May 2 Rock Island beat the Cream Cities 5 to 1 before a large crowd of 1,000. The following day they again lost to Rock Island. The Cream Cities returned home and lost to the Cincinnati reserves 1 to 0 in five innings. Even though this was a Sunday, only a small crowd attended the game, played in fog and chilly rain. The following week, the reserves traveled to Green Bay and beat the local club twice. They then traveled south to Chicago and beat the Chicago reserve club 5 to 4, before losing 13 to 6 because of very bad pitching, and then again 4 to 3.

On May 15 the directors of the Milwaukee Baseball Association announced because of the financial losses of the club, the players on the Cream Cities were being released. The reserves were in Chicago on their way to Akron at the time, but were ordered to return home. The players were still under contract to the club for twenty days and the directors still figured to play them in some games. That Sunday the Cream Cities played the Chicago Blues. The Blues were the amateur champions of Chicago, but lost to the reserves 16 to 0, as Will Murphy, a newly acquired pitcher from Rockford, pitched a no-hitter in the seven-inning game witnessed by 1,000. In their final game, the reserves lost to the Chicago Whitings in a game that at times "was a veritable circus."[16] The Cream Cities' short-lived record was four wins and five losses.

With the reserve club aborted, the players were given their releases. Of the 13 under contract at the time, five—Baldwin, Clayton, Falch, Roberts and Murphy—were signed with the regulars. Schierz and Himmelstein went back to the Arctics and Toole stayed in Milwaukee to play with the Maple Leafs. Dealy signed with the Washington Unions but never played there, appearing with St. Paul later. Otto Schomberg was offered $150 a month to play with Rock Island, but signed with Stillwater because he wanted to stay in the Northwestern League. Morris and Delany also signed with Stillwater, but Delany was soon on the Wausau club. Purvis faded into oblivion back in Canada.

For the Northwestern League's second year, first with 12 clubs, it divided itself into two divisions: the Eastern, composed of the four clubs from Michigan and the two from Indiana; the Western, composed of the two Illinois clubs, three from Minnesota, and Milwaukee. The *Sentinel* of January 28, 1884, gave each club's designated colors:

Milwaukee	Cream	Fort Wayne	Olive Green
Bay City	Red and Black	Grand Rapids	Gray
Minneapolis	Black	Muskegon	Red and White
Peoria	Red	Stillwater	Blue
Quincy	Brown	St. Paul	White
Saginaw	Old Gold	Terre Haute	Dark Green

With the teams shaping up, a Muskegon paper predicted Grand Rapids would finish first. Without any argument, the *Milwaukee Sentinel* pegged Milwaukee for third place, with president John Iverson adding no worse than that. Waiting for the season to arrive, the players were in practice. Tom Loftus, the captain, was in St. Louis practicing with future Hall of Famer Charles Comiskey. By mid–April most of the players had reported to Milwaukee. Because of the bad weather in Milwaukee, the club practiced in the Milwaukee Athletic Society rooms (in the Plankinton Hotel) with dumb bells and Indian clubs as well as running. As the weather did not break, the club continued indoor training while other teams were already playing exhibition games. The bad weather forced the team to go to Rockford to practice. For its first exhibition, the team beat the Rockford club 14 to 7 and narrowly beat the reserves the following day. When the team arrived in Milwaukee, the club again beat the reserves twice. Two days before opening day, the club received a setback when Tom Morrissey traveled to Janesville for the funeral of his brother, John, a professional ball player who had played in the National League briefly in 1881 and 1882. Hogan took his place at third base and McGinley went to right field. A local enthusiast, Louis Henry, donated a $50 gold medal to the Milwaukee player scoring the most runs, and Iverson would present $50 to the player credited with the most hits.

On May 1 the Grays, as the regulars had been nicknamed by the press, opened at home against St. Paul. Threatening weather kept the Ladies Day crowd down to between 500 to 700, but a game was played. The Grays in their uniforms of electric blue trimmed with cream colored flannel and cream colored stockings and mixed caps went to bat. For windy and wet days like this, the players were also provided with old-gold jerseys. Ed Hogan led off by grounding out and then Steve Behel doubled for the club's first hit in regular competition. Tom Sexton then singled, scoring Behel. After six innings, the umpire called the game on account of rain with the Grays ahead 13 to 1, Ed Cushman striking out 13 batters.

	MILWAUKEE							ST. PAUL				
		R	H	PO	A	E			R	H	PO	A	E
Hogan	3b	1	1	0	1	0	Hunter	p & 2b	0	0	1	7	3
Behel	lf	2	1	0	0	0	Olen	rf	0	1	0	0	1
Sexton	ss	2	1	0	0	0	O'Brien	3b	0	0	1	2	2
Griffin	cf	2	2	0	0	0	Foster	2b & p	1	1	2	3	0
Dunn	1b	0	0	6	0	1	Barnes	c	0	0	7	2	3
Loftus	2b	1	0	0	0	0	Clapp	lf	0	1	1	0	0
Straub	c	2	1	11	3	0	Ganzel	1b	0	0	6	1	2
McGinley	rf	2	1	0	0	0	Galvin	cf	0	0	0	0	1
Cushman	p	1	1	1	14	1	Merrick	ss	0	0	0	0	1
		13	8	18	18	2			1	3	18	15	13

```
                       1  2  3  4  5  6
           Milwaukee   2  0  3  2  5  1 — 13
           St. Paul    0  1  0  0  0  0 —  1
```

The Grays finished their first series in the Northwestern League by winning 11 to 5 behind McGinley and then losing 11 to 6.

Cushman, who had developed a sore arm, got help from the weather when the opening game of the Minneapolis series was rained out. He used the extra day off to strike out 13 again in a 2 to 1 win the next day, but came down with a lame arm. The following day Zach Clayton pitched a two-hitter, and Morrissey then pitched a four-hit shutout as Milwaukee swept the series. Stillwater then came to town and Milwaukee whipped them three times. The Grays left town with an 8 and 1 record, scoring 88 runs to their opponents' 33.

The Grays moved on to Saginaw, and the sporting headline of the May 16 *Milwaukee Sentinel* showed the results of game one: THE MILWAUKEES TEACH THE SAGINAW HOW TO WIN A GAME. The other two games of the series showed Morrissey's erratic pitching, winning the first on a four-hitter and dropping the second with him giving up 21 hits. The club was strong in the field and at the plate, but had a problem in the pitcher's box. Cushman had pitched well but had a sore arm. Morrissey was erratic and McGinley had been called back to Milwaukee, suspended for 30 days and put under the care of a physician. It was at this time the reserves were disbanded. To make room for the players brought up to the Grays, the club released the McDermott brothers, who went to Oconto to play.

Milwaukee continued on to Bay City. Cushman's shutout gave Bay City its first loss, but Morrissey and Murphy lost the next two. The Grays took their 11 and 4 record into Muskegon, which had a 4 and 10 record, and Milwaukee lost all three games. The Grays next entered second-place Grand Rapids territory and Cushman was again excellent, pitching a four-hit, 6 to 0 shutout, striking out 12. The following day Grand Rapids won two games from the Grays. The occasion being Decoration Day, the Grays lost the morning game 5 to 4, making 12 errors. In the afternoon game the Grays played "the poorest game of ball ever seen on any ground."[17] Ed Cushman started, but his sore arm would allow him to pitch only thee innings. Ed Hogan relieved and allowed 12 runs in the fourth inning. Morrissey, Sexton and Dunn finished up, as the Grays lost 30 to 4, committing 23 errors. This performance caused a "former enthusiastic admirer of the team" to suggest "they had better disband and walk home."[18] The Grays then traveled to Fort Wayne, losing two of three.

The Grays' record had now fallen to 13 and 11, and the directors were concerned. For one, they believed Cushman should pitch more than once a week. Although McKee was ordered to pitch him in the third Bay City game, he did not find Cushman in good enough shape. It was also rumored McKee was saving him until later in the season when he could win a championship. The directors figured Cushman was making about $150 a game (with his salary at $2,100) and "appears to be too expensive a luxury to be long sustained."[19] The *Sentinel* of June 1 was to the point on the subject.

> If the management chooses to pay him his present salary for pitching once a week it is their own business, but if they want people to patronize the games they must secure a couple of strong pitchers to play in the other four or five games that must be played during the week. Winning a game once a week will not do for the Milwaukee baseball public either, and it is time that the players understood that they must win games if they wish to earn enough to pay their salaries. It is all very well for Muskegon, Terre Haute or Stillwater to be satisfied with a place in the rear, but a club representing a city like Milwaukee in the Northwestern League must either head the list or be very close to it, or else withdraw altogether.

The *Journal* reported an "old sport" saying the club had "demonstrated that it can not earn a standing in the Northwestern League series."[20] To be fair, the players were hurt. Along with Cushman's sore arm, two of the catchers were disabled. Joe Straub hurt his finger in an exhibition game on May 25 and was expected to be out for two weeks. Cal Broughton dislocated his thumb on a foul-tip. Anton Falch was forced to take their place behind the plate, although Broughton caught some time with the sore hand. Tom Morrissey had developed a sore arm, and Ed Hogan, Steve Dunn, Tom Sexton and Steve Behel were suffering from sprains and injuries.

The club continued on into Terre Haute and the *Sentinel* commented that if the club would win there and in Peoria "there will be no necessity to return home in the night or by the back streets."[21] Charles Baldwin lost the opener in Terre Haute and McKee "read the riot act"[22] to seven of his players and fined them for late hours and indifferent play. It worked, for one game, as the Grays collected 22 hits in an 18 to 1 victory, but then lost the third game of the Terre Haute series. Milwaukee went into a six-game series with Peoria next, three in the Illinois city and three at home. The Grays were fighting Peoria for fifth place — Peoria 16 and 10 and Milwaukee 14 and 13 — but came into the series in trouble. Cushman took a short vacation, at his own request, to heal his arm; Sexton had been hurt in Terre Haute, being replaced by Roberts. Some wanted Sexton's head, but the *Sentinel* came to his defense, saying he was the best shortstop in the league and used the time-worn excuse that most of his errors were balls that other shortstops would not have reached. Then the *Sentinel* used some old-fashioned logic: "Even if Sexton was an indifferent fielder, the fact that he is a native Milwaukeean should cause him to be viewed with greater leniency than the imported players."[23] Morrissey also had a sore arm and could throw only three balls in the series opener before he was forced to leave. Falch also came up lame and Joe Straub had to be recalled. Tom Loftus split his finger to add to the injuries, as the Grays lost all three in Peoria.

The Grays returned home with 30 games under their belts and a 14 and 16 record. Worse yet, they had lost 15 of the 21 games on the road trip. President Iverson held a team meeting and organized "a sort of court martial."[24] He did not take too much stock in the injuries story and held the outside thought that crookedness or hippodroming might be sneaking in and insisted he would not tolerate that. The press expected several releases by the club. When the Grays won the home opener from Peoria, the *Sentinel* proclaimed that there is "NO PLACE LIKE HOME,"[25] as Baldwin pitched a superb two-hitter. However, as the Grays lost the next two games, the same paper told readers how the "Milwaukees sustained their usual defeat."[26] Some light moments were found in the losing stretch. The club's mascot, a young boy, brought some smiles to readers when the *Evening Wisconsin* gave this account of him: "The youngster proved himself a Jonah while in Bay City, wasting too much time hanging over a billiard table and flirting with the waiter girls."[27] The mascot was soon changed to a dog.

Before Peoria left town, the Grays were to engage in a Sunday exhibition. The *Sentinel* threw a little sarcasm at the club by editorializing that "the Milwaukees will probably put in their strongest battery and strain every nerve to secure the victory."[28] Although the Grays went with an untried pitcher—Winters, from Kalamazoo, who failed to finish the first inning and eventually lost the game—there was some truth to the paper's statement. To date the club had played four exhibition games and had won them all. Their first exhibition was on May 11 against the Gordons of Chicago, the champion all-black nine of the country, which the Grays won 11 to 9. Later in an exhibition at Muskegon, Zach Clayton pitched a 3 to 2 victory. In Fort Wayne, Murphy tossed a three-hitter en route to a 16 to 1 win. The following week the Grays edged out Evansville, an independent club that received protection from the Northwestern and had been guaranteed placement into the league if a club should leave. One exhibition that did not come off was with an all-girls club from Philadelphia that had disbanded before arriving in Milwaukee. Because of these Sunday exhibition wins, the Grays were called the "Sunday club."[29]

As the club traveled to Minneapolis and Quincy, Jim McKee's job became more insecure. Losing three of five did not help much. Before leaving, the directors announced that Tom Loftus would have complete control of the players, on and off the field. McKee was only to be in charge of the business affairs of the club. Loftus announced he planned to experiment more with his pitchers, but in his first game at the helm, Baldwin and Morrissey were hit hard by Minneapolis. The directors immediately began to send letters all over the country to secure players. McGinley was permanently released. Ed Cushman was ready to come back and pitched a strong five-hitter, striking out 11. Pat Sullivan, a former local Maple Leaf, was reportedly signed from Quincy, but he could not get his release. Zack Clayton was then released. McKee had been saying for some time he was about to sign a pitcher, "a dark horse, but full of promise,"[30] but would not mention names. The directors went so far as to place an advertisement in a Chicago sporting journal for players. The *Sentinel* really came down hard on the club for this, stating, "This is another of the many stupid moves that have been the cause of so much dissension in the club."[31]

Loftus tried out numerous players. James Harmon, released by Fort Wayne, applied to the club, as did Joe Connors, formerly of the Altoona Unions. Harmon got his try, but no contract. Mike Moynahan, a four-year veteran second baseman with four different clubs—most recently Cleveland—was given a try and signed, but before he arrived Joe Straub was tried at second, mainly to get his bat into the lineup. Steve Dunn sprained an ankle to go along with his lame shoulder and was released on his own request on June 27. Loftus contacted Grant Brown, from Rochester University; Coty and Parker, released from Cleveland; Sullivan, a catcher from Amherst College; and Charles North, a pitcher from Chicago who had "the quadruplix quiver, the triple tremor"[32] and all the other pitches. All these produced no signatures on contracts. Another, Joe Knight, was a different story. The club really wanted him, and when Harry Wright in Philadelphia released him, the Grays telegraphed Wright to find his whereabouts. The directors contacted Knight, but his terms were too steep, as one put it he wanted "the earth and a place to put it."[33] Actually, he wanted $150 in advance money and $350 a month, and the Grays were only willing to advance him $100. Tommy Bond, the former Boston star, was negotiated with after being released from the Boston Unions. The Grays had a chance to sign a player named Lotz, but he signed with Terre Haute because the directors thought they could sign Bond. Bond, in turn, signed with Providence. Denny Driscoll was released by Louisville and Milwaukee attempted, but failed, to sign him.

Meanwhile, the managerial aspect of the Grays made news. Jim McKee was never a hit with the press. Even before the season began, the editors of the *Sentinel* believed the players should have their pictures taken like other clubs, but McKee ignored them. Michigan papers called McKee a hard loser. McKee's wife became very sick after the first game of the season and he left for Rockford to be with her. When he returned, the press was again on him.

Advertisement in *Milwaukee Journal* for both a Northwestern League games and the game against Chicago Gordons on May 11, 1884.

"Manager McKee's loud denunciation of a decision of the umpire ... caused considerable adverse comment. It was said that if the umpire made a wrong decision, which is very doubtful, Manager McKee should have selected some other place than the grandstand to express his disapprobation."[34] McKee often roasted players in public and the *Evening Wisconsin* was sure the Grays would never do well under him.

When the rumor began that McKee was to get the axe, the press was quick to print it, even though the club denied it. Incidentally, a rumor was around at the same time that the Grand Rapids club would be transferred to Milwaukee, and Evansville would fill the gap. Before the transfer got off the ground, the citizens of Grand Rapids got up $2,760 to help the club through. In late June the president of the Milwaukee club, John Iverson, asked McKee to resign. Iverson told a *Journal* reporter that the club was run in too loose a manner. "When a manager finds it necessary to consult the directors before imposing a fine upon a player, and will allow himself to be openly insulted by his subordinates, it is time a change was made."[35] It was reported that several directors wanted McKee out, but some others wanted him to stay. Even though the club would have to pay him until November, the *Sentinel* believed the money was of little matter. Phillips from Grand Rapids was the choice of the *Evening Wisconsin* to replace McKee, but the *Sentinel* wanted Bill Furlong, the former local West End player from 1876. Furlong was not anxious for the job and Phillips could not get his release, so Tom Loftus became the heir apparent. But McKee insisted he was still in charge until requested to retire by all the stockholders. He claimed Iverson had made the statements without the knowledge of three or four stockholders. The next day McKee resigned and Loftus became the manager. McKee was still under his player contract, meaning he could be released with a 20-day notice. Joe Straub became the field captain. Director Harry Quin soon claimed the club had no manager, Loftus was still the captain, and he [Quin] and Iverson were the management; but Loftus was indeed the manager. On August 1, Steve Behel was named field captain, and on September 1 Ed Hogan took over the position.

On June 25 the Grays returned home to play Quincy, and after a rainout, during which the Quincy club attended the performance at the Opera House, split the two-game series. The team then traveled to Stillwater, where they lost, and the June 29 *Sentinel* wrote the team was "succeeding well in their efforts to reach the foot of the list, but before another month the Milwaukees will doubtless oust them of the place." Milwaukee's 18 and 23 record was nine wins better than last-place Terre Haute's. The Grays then lost a Sunday exhibition to St. Paul in White Bear Lake, Minnesota, before posting two championship wins in St. Paul, slightly improving their position. Returning home, the Grays split a Fourth of July doubleheader and lost the rubber match to Grand Rapids to fall 14½ games behind that first-place club. On their Sunday day off, 3,000 fans saw the Grays beat the Gordons, the Grays trying out a few new players. Terre Haute came to town and Murphy beat them 9 to 5, with Mike Moynahan playing in his first game. Charles Baldwin then pitched a four-hitter over the same club, before Murphy was bombed in the final game of the series.

The press and the fans were dissatisfied with the Grays. After the final bad outing against Terre Haute, the *Sentinel* declared "that near midnight on Wednesday [the night before the game] five of the Milwaukees were holding up the bar in a saloon on Grand Avenue."[36] A week later the Grays "played as though they were recovering from a drunken spree, which in reality, some of the members were."[37] Between these two incidents Milwaukee played well, winning five of six — excluding the two hangover dates — on some fine pitching. Included were a four-hit shutout by Ed Cushman, a 9 to 1 victory by Tom Morrissey, and another four-hitter by Cushman to even the Grays' record at 26 and 26. The management then tried out a former Janesville Mutual, Harry Arundel, who had signed with Cleveland of the National League but never played. Arundel beat Saginaw. Cushman came back with a three-hitter before the hangover incident. Sandwiched between these wins was a one-hit loss to Saginaw. Moynahan, who had been given a day off to return home to Chicago, failed to report and was fined $100. After Cushman struck out ten to beat Muskegon, club president Iverson gave the team a lecture on drinking, and got this reaction: "The boys seemed very much affected, so much so that Straub wiped his eyes with Morrissey's stocking by mistake, while Hogan, who was engaged in his usual pastime of tossing up pebbles, paused to listen."[38] So fines replaced lectures. Straub, Morrissey, Behel, Sexton, Hogan and Arundel were fined $50 apiece. If caught again, they would be released, Iverson warned. At the same time Iverson released Murphy and Roberts, the cause given was an excess of players. The excess may have been Henry Porter and George Bignall, who were signed a few days later for $2,800 and $600 in advance money.

Meanwhile, the Northwestern League was in trouble. On July 23 Bay City disbanded and shortly Fort Wayne quit. Evansville was to replace Bay City, which was to come to Milwaukee next, but were in Omaha and could not make it to Wisconsin. This was costing the Milwaukee management money. They attempted to make some money by playing the Chicago reserves, but they wanted too much, and the Grays played the local amateur Quicksteps and won 12 to 0. The Northwestern delegates met at the Kirby House in downtown Milwaukee on July 30 and revised their schedule. There was talk of dropping two of the weaker clubs, but there were no complaints from players on back salaries, so the subject was dropped. The next day St. Paul came to town and Foster pitched a no-hitter against the Grays, who also lost Harry Arundel to that club for a $200 a month contract. The Grays then won their next five games.

Then another bombshell for the Northwestern occurred — Stillwater, $3,500 in the red, disbanded. The *Sentinel* was convinced "when baseball players ask salaries equal to those paid to ministers, towns like Muskegon, Fort Wayne and Stillwater ought not to meddle with them."[39] The league decided Evansville would not be allowed to compete for the championship. On August 5 Terre Haute and Peoria, $700 behind in salaries and $300 to $400 behind to debtors, disbanded. The little cities were falling apart. With the exception of Milwaukee, Minneapolis and St. Paul, there was not a club in the Northwestern that could get enough attendance to pay the $75 guarantee. The Northwestern delegates met again and dropped Grand Rapids and Muskegon. It was further required that clubs put up $500 to assure they would not disband. Milwaukee then played its ace in the hole. The club demanded Sunday games on the schedule or threatened to quit. The demand was granted.

The Northwestern now consisted of Quincy, Saginaw, Minneapolis, St. Paul and Milwaukee. President Rust resigned and Whitmore of Quincy took his place. Two days later Quincy withdrew from the league and made application to the Union Association. Omaha applied to fill the vacancy but was turned down. The Northwestern directors met again in Milwaukee and expelled Saginaw for refusing to play a game. The directors admitted Winona, Minnesota, to the league and elected Welcome Kirby of Milwaukee league president. In another move, Milwaukee was voted the champion, having won the most games against incumbent members. However, Milwaukee declined, wanting to play a new schedule. This schedule consisted of 24 games, eight against each club.

On August 19 the Grays beat Winona 2 to 1 in the first game of the new schedule. Tom Morrissey and Joe Straub had been released to reduce expenses, and Myers, formerly of Muskegon, was contacted but not signed. Morrissey was a popular player, but his $250-a-month contract was too high. The directors asked him to drop that to $150, but he refused. Morrissey did not go on the Minnesota trip and was suspended, but was later reinstated. Milwaukee breezed through the schedule by winning its first six games, but on September 3 Minneapolis, $1,800 in debt, withdrew from the league. Omaha again applied for admittance, but the Northwestern expired on September 7. The Grays beat Winona in an exhibition before returning home, but Winona refused to pay the guarantee in full, promising to send it within a week. Milwaukee finished the revamped schedule with an 11 and 4 record. St. Paul was 7 and 6; Minneapolis 5 and 4; and Winona 0 and 11. In all, Milwaukee was 53 and 34 in the total Northwestern League, having won 24 of its last 28 games.

The downfall of the Northwestern League was apparent. Of the original 12 clubs only Milwaukee, Minneapolis, St. Paul and Grand Rapids were over 35,000 in population. By late June the *Evening Wisconsin* could see there were too many clubs in the league and suggested only Milwaukee, Minneapolis, St. Paul, Peoria, Saginaw and Quincy should have made up the Northwestern. In mid–August the *Grand Rapids Times* finished off the Northwestern like this:

> The glory of the original and only Northwestern League, however, has departed. It got a black eye when Bay City disbanded, and a foul-tip when Fort Wayne went out. Stillwater's death gave it a sprained ankle, and the withdrawal of Terre Haute took a leg off. There was an attempt to plaster up the unfortunate, but the construction of a circuit of 2,000 miles was too much for the victim and it died a violent death. Grand Rapids and Muskegon omitted from this portent long distance arrangement, have also disband and separated. St. Paul's club went to Milwaukee yesterday, and will probably go on home and give up the ghost also.[40]

The Northwestern was gone, but there was still a month to go in the season and baseball was not dead here yet.

On September 12, 1883, representatives from eight cities met at the Monongahela House in Pittsburgh and organized the Union Association of Base-ball Clubs. The following resolution was unanimously adopted: "That, while we recognize the validity of all contracts made by the League and American Association, we cannot recognize any agreement whereby any number of ball payers may be reserved for any club for any time beyond the terms of their contracts with such club."[41] At this first meeting, H.B. Bennett of Washington was elected president of the Union Association, but soon Henry V. Lucas, a St. Louis millionaire said to be the "leading spirit of the new Union,"[42] was elected its president.

Annual dues were set at $100, and the rules and regulations of the AA were adopted. The Union secretary, Warren White, expressed confidence the new association would succeed, citing a cash capital of $100,000 and the excepted goodwill of the players for enabling them to make the money they were worth. The Unions did not anticipate any trouble from the two established major leagues.

However, the new Union Association was causing "much consternation"[43] to the other two major leagues by signing reserved players and offering large salaries. In early November the St. Louis Union club signed Tony Mullane and Jack Gleason, the former for $2,500 — $500 more than the St. Louis AA club was offering. It was soon reported others were signing with Union clubs for a lot of money. The *New York Times* of December 3, 1884, reported with some sarcasm, "Professional base-ball players are very modest in their demands. Corcoran, of the Chicago club, nearly distracted the President of his club by informing him that his services for next season would be worth $4,500. After some time he came down to $4,000, but refused to consider the offer of $2,500 made by President Spalding...."

To combat this new league, the American Association added four franchises to become a 12-club circuit. The two older major leagues passed a resolution that players who played a game with a club other than that which had reserved them would be banned from these established leagues.

As it became apparent that the Union Association would not be recognized by the National League or American Association, it became more difficult for the Unions. The *New York Times* reported many of the proposed clubs had no grounds or players and "one by one the clubs are dropping out of the new enterprise."[44]

Finally in March the Union Association met in Cincinnati and a Boston franchise was admitted to form an eight-club circuit of Philadelphia, Washington, Baltimore, Chicago, St. Louis, Cincinnati, Altoona and Boston. A 112-game schedule was decided upon, with a percentage system of games won/lost adopted for the championship. A resolution "was adopted to adhere closely to the principle of observing all contracts in a spirit of fairness," but the UA wanted to use "every legal means to obtain redress" in the matter of players who broke their contracts.[45] By July 1 the Union Association directors decided not to respect any American Association or National League contracts with players "since the manager of those associations seemed determined to do everything in their power to injure the union clubs by seeking to get their best players."[46]

The 1884 Union Association had numerous franchise changes. On May 31 the Altoona franchise disbanded and was replaced by a Kansas City club. On August 7 the Philadelphia Keystones disbanded and were replaced by Wilmington. Later in August the Chicago club was transferred to Pittsburgh.

Milwaukee came into the Union picture in August when it was reported Henry Lucas was extremely anxious to have the Grays in his association. The *Milwaukee Sentinel*, which in March quoted James McKee as saying the outlook for the Unions was "dark and unpromising,"[47] thought this unlikely. Lucas continued to send telegrams to Milwaukee. When it was apparent that the Northwestern would fold, the Milwaukee directors pondered what to do with their club. Arrangements could possibly be made to play exhibition games with National League clubs, but if the club disbanded it would lose its players. The club was a moneymaker in the beginning of the season, "but of late the stockholders have been compelled to go down into their pockets."[48] Businessmen helped, but the slim crowds discouraged them. President John Iverson estimated the salaries at $3,000 a month and by October additional expenses would probably be $5,000 or $6,000. Iverson figured the club lost about $1,000 to $1,500 on the Northwestern season.

Mike Moynahan was released and other clubs were anxious to get some of the other players. Ed Cushman had received letters from a half-dozen clubs. Henry Porter had been contacted by Cleveland, Cincinnati and St. Louis. Tom Sexton, Cal Broughton and Steve Behel were wanted by Indianapolis. Cleveland wanted Ed Hogan. To keep the club in tact, the directors decided to join the Union Association or the American Association. Tom Loftus went to St. Louis, where both associations had their key owners. When Milwaukee decided on the Unions, Lucas pegged them to fill the Wilmington slot, a club that was expected to die on its next road trip. But Wilmington, on the verge of bankruptcy, denied to withdraw and continued on its trip.

As it appeared the Grays might not get into the Union Association, the press came down on the directors. The stockholders had wanted the protection of the National Agreement, but on September 14 the *Sentinel* expressed the opinion they should have taken a chance. "If the Milwaukee management had heeded the emissary of the Union Association who requested the club to join that organization early last spring, there would be money in the club treasury today, and the season would have closed with a comfortable balance on the right side of the books."

The *Evening Wisconsin* thought it was better to join the Union Association than the American Association, as the Unions did not recognize the reserve rule and obtaining better players would be easier. Others thought the Grays were not good enough to play in the Union. The *Mirror of American Sports*, a paper published in Chicago, claimed Lucas had "the success of playing upon the vanity of the Milwaukee club officers." The paper thought the Grays could not compete with other Union teams and believed "Milwaukee was doing the cats paw act for some clever monkeys."[49] Loftus replied, saying he would see if his team could compete. If not, he would have to secure better players. Lucas was sure the Union Association would survive with Milwaukee in it, and the *Sentinel* believed that except for Boston, the Unions had better teams than the National League. With the Northwestern League gone, the Milwaukee club might lose its protection under the National Agreement, and joining the Unions seemed logical.

On September 15 Wilmington finally disbanded, and on September 19 in Washington, Milwaukee was formally admitted to the Union Association. Lucas told the directors the city would have its first Union game on Saturday, September 20, but did not know with which club. The expected opener was delayed a week because of the unexpected disbanding of Pittsburgh. In the meantime, the Grays received copies of the official Union baseball guides and balls, and played three games with the local Maple Leafs. The Leafs had reorganized into a semi-professional club, using many of the released reserves.

Enthusiasm was high for the opening Union Association game, to be played against the Washington Nationals. The day before the game the Grays finally succeeded in signing Al Myers for $150 a month. On Saturday, September 27, major league baseball again was played in Milwaukee. Fifteen hundred came out to Wright Street Park to see the Grays win 3 to 0. All Milwaukee's runs were scored in the seventh inning when with one out Morrissey lifted "the 5½ ounce double cover"[50] for a double and Broughton doubled him home.

Broughton then went to third on a wild throw and scored on Porter's sacrifice. Bignall walked, stole second and scored on Sexton's hit. Porter pitched a one-hitter, striking out 13.

MILWAUKEE		R	H	PO	A	E	WASHINGTON		R	H	PO	A	E
Sexton	ss	0	1	0	1	0	Moore	lf	0	0	5	0	0
Hogan	rf	0	0	0	0	0	Powell	rf	0	0	0	0	0
Behel	lf	0	0	1	0	0	Fulmer	1b	0	0	12	1	0
Griffin	1b	0	1	10	0	0	Halpin	ss	0	0	0	2	0
Myers'	2b	0	1	3	3	1	McCormick	3b	0	0	0	2	0
Morrissey	3b	1	1	0	0	0	Gagus	p	0	1	1	5	4
Broughton	cf	1	2	0	0	0	Evers	2b	0	0	0	3	1
Porter	p	0	1	0	14	0	Gunson	c	0	0	4	0	1
Bignall	c	*1*	*0*	*13*	*1*	*0*	Franklin	1b	*0*	*0*	*12*	*1*	*0*
		3	7	27	19	2			0	1	24	14	7

Milwaukee   0 0 0 0 0 0 3 0 x—3
Washington   0 0 0 0 0 0 0 0 0—0

The following day, 32-year-old Edgar Leander Cushman put his name in the record books by pitching major league baseball's 17th no-hit game. With dark clouds overhead, Cushman struck out 12 and Morrissey made two fine plays on ground balls to help etch Cushman's name into history.

MILWAUKEE		R	H	PO	A	E	WASHINGTON		R	H	PO	A	E
Sexton	ss	1	1	0	2	0	Moore	lf	0	0	1	1	0
Hogan	rf	1	1	1	1	1	Powell	p	0	0	1	3	0
Behel	lf	0	0	1	0	0	Fulmer	c	0	0	2	1	1
Griffin	1b	1	0	12	0	0	Halpin	ss	0	0	1	2	1
Myers	2b	0	1	1	2	1	McCormick	3b	0	0	1	3	1
Morrissey	3b	0	1	0	3	0	Gagus	rf	0	0	2	0	0
Porter	cf	0	1	0	0	0	Evers	2b	0	0	4	3	2
Broughton	c	1	0	12	0	0	Gunson	cf	0	0	0	0	2
Cushman	p	*1*	*0*	*0*	*13*	*1*	Hughes	1b	*0*	*0*	*12*	*1*	*0*
		5	5	27	21	3			0	0	24	14	7

Milwaukee   0 0 0 0 0 5 0 0 x—5
Washington   0 0 0 0 0 0 0 0 0—0

The next day the Grays won their third game without a loss by jumping to an early lead and hanging on to win 7 to 5 behind Porter. Finally the Grays lost, as Washington scored two in the eighth and three in the ninth to beat Baldwin 5 to 3.

On October 3 Boston came to town and 1,500 saw Henry Porter strike out 18 but lose when the Beaneaters scored three in the ninth to win 5 to 4. Cushman then faced Boston and almost accomplished a feat Johnny Vander Meer would complete 54 years later. The Beaneaters "were like so many infants in front of his left handed lightening."[51] The lead-off batter in the ninth, Ed Callahan, hit a little pop fly over first to break up his no-hitter. In the next game 2,500, witnessed Boston win 3 to 1 in George Bignall's last game as a Gray. Bignall—the catcher—took himself out of the game as a protest to Porter's wildness and was released a few days later. Cushman wrapped up the series with a 6 to 2 win. Baltimore next came to town and Porter beat the Union's biggest winner, 40-game winner Bill

Sweeney, 7 to 4. Baldwin then pitched a three-hitter before a controversial loss. The Grays went into the seventh inning ahead by three runs and everyone thought it was too dark to continue play. The Marylanders "bulldozed"[52] the umpire to continue and in the semi-darkness scored six times to win 8 to 5. Between 4,000 and 5,000 then saw Cushman win 5 to 2.

St. Paul, who had been admitted to the Union Association shortly after Milwaukee to replace Pittsburgh, was to come into town but failed to show. The 1884 Union Association season was over. Milwaukee's 8 and 4 record clearly showed their critics who claimed they did not belong in the Union wrong.[53] Financially it was reported the 12 games netted about $3,000 for the Grays, even though they were the second-highest salaried club in the Union, behind Lucas' Maroons. Tom Loftus claimed the Union games averaged 1,800 on the weekdays and 5,000 on Sundays.

As the management settled for the season and the players returned to their homes, Loftus looked forward to the 1885 season. Although he had no definite plans, he was sure he would keep six or seven players. Only two players had actually signed — Henry Porter and Anton Falch. While the season was still in progress, Adrian Anson of Chicago was in town, reportedly to sign Cal Broughton, but the *Mirror of American Sports* denied this. Al Myers was to sign, but the management's policy of no advance money held it up. He soon signed with the Philadelphia Phillies, and Loftus said he was a good ball player "but the woods are full of them."[54] Steve Behel, who ran a tavern in Milwaukee in the off season, was reportedly unhappy and wanted to leave. An eastern sporting journal reported Cincinnati of the American Association had signed Porter, but the club denied it. Cincinnati had tried to sign Porter for $500 a month during the Northwestern-Union lull, without success. Now they were offering $750 a month. Another problem was Ed Cushman. It was estimated he received about $70 for every game he pitched in 1884, not bad for those times, and was in big demand. The Athletics wanted him and the Philadelphia papers reported him signed for $3,500 in December, but the Grays honestly did not know if he was. The snag was that Cushman wanted Broughton to come along.

Meanwhile, Loftus was in town to negotiate with players. The policy of no advance money was hurting, but it was a necessity because of the uncertainty of the players jumping to other leagues. The club managed to sign Kid Baldwin from Kansas City in November. They also tried for Art Whitney, who had hit .398 for Pittsburgh. "As his terms include about half the real estate within the city limits, and Mitchell's bank for an advance fee, he will be allowed time to get over an attack of a swelled head."[55] Soon Tom Sexton was reported signed, and then John McSorley agreed to play third and captain the club. Before the new year "Stooping Jack" Gorman, Tom Forster from Pittsburgh and Lewis "Jumbo" Schoeneck were under contract.

The Union Association itself was in trouble, however. In late November it was announced the Unions would probably add Toledo and Columbus, which withdrew from the American Association, and maybe even Detroit, who was rumored out of the National League. It was rumored Lucas' St. Louis club was to join the National League. The rumor was denied, but it was felt even if St. Louis did defect, the Unions would still survive. At a December Union Association meeting in St. Louis, only Cincinnati, Milwaukee, Kansas City and St. Louis showed. Baltimore resigned and five clubs applied to the Unions. Lucas again denied the rumor he was joining the National League and a meeting was set for January 15 in Milwaukee. Before the Milwaukee meeting, rumors flew that Cincinnati, in addition to St. Louis, was to join the National League. On January 6 Lucas purchased the Cleveland National League franchise, and within days formally applied to the league. The

National League directors voted for admittance, but three American Association clubs turned Lucas down. Later in the month the differences were settled and Lucas was admitted to the National League.

While all this was happening, Milwaukee baseball men thought Lucas and the National League were "utterly devoid of principle."[56] It was felt the Union Association still had Kansas City, Cincinnati, Indianapolis and Milwaukee, with a good chance of getting the Ohio cities of Cleveland and Columbus. At the January 15 meeting at the Plankinton House in Milwaukee, only Kansas City and Milwaukee showed up. The Union Association was disbanded and the representatives planned to form a new league.

Ed Cushman — Almost pitched back-to-back no-hitters in 1884 Union Association.

8

Setting the Foundation (1885–1887)

Immediately on the disbanding of the Union Association, Milwaukee and Kansas City—the only clubs represented—put forth plans to organize a new minor league. Indianapolis men had already telegraphed the delegates with their interest in joining a new league. Milwaukee, Kansas City, Indianapolis, St. Paul, Cleveland and Toledo were named for the circuit, with possibly Columbus and Detroit, if the latter could be lured from the National League, as an eight-club circuit. This preliminary league was not firm and others had differing thoughts. A Cleveland paper thought a league setup with the following eight clubs would be ideal: Milwaukee (population 165,000), Cleveland (220,000), Indianapolis (120,000), Toledo (70,000), Columbus (65,000), Dayton (65,000), Evansville (25,000), and a combination of East Saginaw, Saginaw and Bay City (65,000). Others wanted Minneapolis to form a club and join or merge with St. Paul; the two cities had about a 180,000 combined population. Local management in Milwaukee was sure a strong and profitable Western League could be formed. Others were not so sure of success. In October the St. Paul papers had doubted if the league could get enough clubs on solid ground.

The Western League was not by any means a reality in January of 1885, and Milwaukee directors still looked toward the American Association with one eye. The National League was taking steps to admit Henry Lucas' St. Louis club into their fold and some American Association clubs were threatening to leave the National Agreement if he was admitted. Another rumor was spreading that the National League wanted to buy out the Cincinnati club and transfer it from the American Association. Milwaukee was ready to make application to the American Association if this occurred. Lucas entered the National League, replacing Cleveland, and no changes came about in the American Association. The Lucas situation looked like it might start an inter-league war, and the Western League declared it would side with the American Association if this occurred. However, things were smoothed before any outbreaks.

Representatives of the new league now began to round up clubs. Charles Kipp was Milwaukee's traveling secretary and Ted Sullivan was Kansas City's. Sullivan was born in Milwaukee and lived there until about seven or eight years prior to 1885. He was the great pitcher of the old Star club in Milwaukee and had managed the local Alerts. Kipp and Sullivan set out to establish a solid league. Sullivan soon reported Indianapolis would join their league, and then traveled on to Columbus. Kipp was in St. Paul. By the end of January, Milwaukee, Kansas City, Indianapolis and Toledo were in for sure and Sullivan reported Columbus, Cleveland, St. Paul and Minneapolis were favorable prospects. Kipp then reported that St. Paul looked good and the grounds would probably be somewhere between St. Paul and Minneapolis, excluding the latter city from league plans. The *Cleveland Herald* believed that Ohio city's chances looked good for a strong club and a six-city circuit looked like a certainty, with Columbus out of the running. Four of these six cities had populations over 100,000, with only Kansas City (75,000) and Toledo (70,000) under.

Lucas' Union Association crony, Justice Thorner, made a last-minute bid on behalf of his Cincinnati club, but "the chances were decidedly against Thorner."[1]

The league set up a meeting in Indianapolis to establish itself. The *Milwaukee Sentinel* felt Kipp should be elected president of the new league, as Milwaukee had always sat in the back in the past, and those associations (Northwestern and Union) crumbled. Kipp and Harry Quin left for the February 11 meeting, but a heavy snow hit the Midwest, delaying the meeting a day. Once called, the meeting was well attended with delegates from Kansas City, Cleveland, Toledo, Indianapolis, St. Paul and Milwaukee. An unexpected visitor, Nashville, showed up and was voted in as a seventh member. Omaha or Columbus was eyed to fill an eight-club circuit. The Western League showed its favoritism to the American Association by adopting its rules, with minor changes, and using the Reach ball instead of the Spalding. Quarter baseball was adopted, as in the association; the National League still charged its original 50-cent admission. The only dispute came on how to split profits. Milwaukee was in favor of the $75 guarantee, but as Indianapolis, Cleveland and Toledo were unable to play Sunday ball at home, a percentage system was instituted, with the guarantee at 30 percent to the visitors. Elected officials of the Western League were A.N. McKim of Kansas City, president; Charles Kipp of Milwaukee, vice president; and Phillip Igoe of Indianapolis, secretary and treasurer at a salary of $400 a year.

Now established, the Western League paid the necessary money and became part of the National Agreement. But this brought on two new problems. First, the Western was forced to drop Nashville, as that city already had an agreement club in the Southern League. St. Paul was happy to see Nashville gone because of the long trip to Tennessee and had threatened to withdraw if Nashville stayed. Next was the question of blacklisted players. All reserve and contract jumpers to the Union Association had been blacklisted. Many of the Western League clubs had signed these players, including Milwaukee, which had one — Kid Baldwin. Baldwin had been blacklisted for jumping his contract with the Quincy club in 1884. He claimed he was not being paid and jumped only "after trying in vain"[2] to get his pay. The directors of the Quincy club made out a petition to reinstate Baldwin, which he finally was, but not in Milwaukee's favor.

Established, but by no means entrenched, the Western League started toward its season. By late February only Milwaukee, Kansas City and Indianapolis had their teams made up, while the others reportedly had "the nucleus for strong clubs."[3] Nothing was known about the Cleveland club, but the *Cleveland Herald* assured everyone there was one being formed. St. Paul had not paid its initiation fees until the end of that month. Western League officials publicly stated they wished to remain a six-club circuit, but left the door open by saying if two good cities made application, they would probably be admitted. Minneapolis, Keokuk, Columbus and Omaha were willing to join, but they were not what the league was looking for. Milwaukee would have liked to see Minneapolis admitted so they could play eight games on a Minnesota trip instead of only four in St. Paul. Kansas City wanted Lucas' St. Louis club, which was threatening to quit the National League over the disputed blacklisted players and Sunday ball, but then the Western would be forced to drop out of the National Agreement. In late March a vacancy occurred when St. Paul, unable to find suitable grounds, withdrew. Minneapolis, Keokuk and Omaha applied. Omaha was admitted, with Keokuk made an alliance club. Peoria soon got into the act by trying to transfer the Keokuk club to that city and joining the Western.

The Western League was formally admitted to the National Agreement on April 3, but found out what type of protection was in store. In March Detroit signed Frank Ringo, under contract to Kansas City, and Joe Quest from Cleveland. Agreement clubs were prohibited from signing reserve or contracted players from other Agreement clubs, but Brooklyn signed Henry Porter from Milwaukee after he had signed with the Wisconsin club for $2,400. Porter signed with Brooklyn for $100 more, saying he wished to return to the East to be close to his Massachusetts home. As mentioned, Kid Baldwin was on the blacklist and in the process of being reinstated. On April 3, the same day the Western League was formally admitted to the National Agreement, Baldwin was reinstated by the Arbitration Committee. That day he signed with Cincinnati. It was found that Cincinnati manager O.P. Caylor had used his influence to get the Kid off the blacklist, and Baldwin promised if he got off he would sign with Cincinnati. Milwaukee's baseball president, John Iverson, told the *Sentinel* he was "about sick of the baseball business. The players seem to have no sense of honor, while most of the professional managers are positively dishonest. It's about time the honest men left the baseball business to the disreputable sharks who are fast destroying it."[4] Harry Quin wrote Denny McKnight, the president of the American Association, about Milwaukee's dissatisfaction with the situation. McKnight wrote back saying Baldwin was on the blacklist when signed by Milwaukee, therefore his contract with the Grays was void and he was up for grabs. The Milwaukee directors wanted to start proceedings in the United States court system to secure an injunction preventing Baldwin, whom Milwaukee had advanced $300, from playing anywhere but with the Grays. When Baldwin explained his position and promised to pay back the $300, the Milwaukee club let the matter drop. Later, when newly acquired Dick Phelan landed on the blacklist and was lost to Cleveland, the *Mirror of American Sports* commented that "[Milwaukee's] local management does not seem to understand the trick of securing the reinstatement of blacklisted players."[5]

In early March Ted Sullivan, Tom Loftus and William Watkins of Indianapolis formed the committee that set up the Western League playing schedule. Western clubs were to play 90 games, beginning on April 18, in four-and five-game series, until the end of September. When St. Paul was replaced by Omaha, the dates were slightly changed.

The directors of the Milwaukee club were heading for the new season a little wiser with one year's experience. The stockholders' meeting was held on March 3 at the Kirby House to set up the financial planning for 1885. The stockholders in the club were F. Falk ($750), C.M. Kipp ($750), B.A. Kipp ($750), H.D. Quin ($750), G. Ziegler ($750), T.J. Loftus ($750), J.C. Iverson ($500), F. Brosius ($500), A.F. Tanner ($500), G.W. Kipp ($250), C. Pfister ($250), W. Kirby ($250), totaling $6,750. Expenses of 1884, exclusive of the grounds that three of the directors personally owned, were broken down.

RECEIPTS OF 1884

Stock	$ 6,750.00
Donations	$ 2,075.00
Gate Receipts	$26,401.40
	$35,226.40

DISBURSEMENTS

Salaries	$17,260.84
Running Expenses	$13,395.09
Building Grandstands	$ 4,303.57
	$34,959.50

RECAPITATION

Total Receipts	$35,226.40
Expenditures	$34,959.50
Balance end of season	$266.90[6]

The actual value of stock shares was only $85 on each original $100. Expenses in 1885 would be lowered. For immediate working capital, stockholders were assessed 10 percent of their stock paid in. This money was necessary to raise money for fares for the players to travel to Milwaukee for training by April 1. Later that month officers were elected, with John C. Iverson remaining as president, Albert F. Tanner the vice president, George Ziegler corresponding secretary, Harry D. Quin the recording secretary, and Charles M. Kipp the treasurer.

The Grays of 1884 were almost all gone. As we have already seen, Al Myers, unhappy with the no advance money policy, went to Philadelphia. Kid Baldwin was lost on the blacklist reinstatement (he had never played here), and Henry Porter jumped to Brooklyn. Ed Cushman finally signed with Philadelphia. Cushman's catcher, Cal Broughton, was signed by St. Louis of the American Association. Ed Hogan signed with St. Paul for the coming season, and then with Cleveland when St. Paul disbanded. Tom Griffin was working as a fireman in Rockford. The club's shortstop, Tom Sexton, was not signing because of the advance money policy. Because Loftus would not give him $100 in advance money and he had given Kid Baldwin — still on the blacklist at the time — $300, Sexton looked around and finally landed a job in Toledo. Tom Morrissey went to the Washington Nationals. George Bignall played with Brockton, Massachusetts, in 1885.

Only Steve Behel, Charley Baldwin and Anton Falch remained from the 1884 club. Before the collapse of the Union Association, Tom Loftus had signed John McSorley, Jack Gorman, Lewis Schoeneck and Tom Forster. In January Dick Phelan was signed, but he was on the blacklist and eventually lost to Cleveland. In February Loftus added John Arundel, a catcher with a fine fielding average who could only manage an .085 batting average for Toledo of the American Association in 1884. After talking to but failing to engage Foley, a pitcher from Quincy, and Walker, a catcher from Minneapolis, Loftus signed Dick Burns, who had won 23 games for the Cincinnati Unions, for $2,500 and $200 in advance money. With Kid Baldwin on the blacklist, Loftus tried to fill his catching vacancy by negotiating with Burns' battery mate, Bill Harbidge, but could not sign him. George Bignall was then contacted, but again no contract. Loftus then signed John Meister, a utility infielder who had played in Toledo the previous year, but he was released two days later to go to another club. Infielder Art Whitney, who was contacted in late 1884 but wanted too much, was again contacted. However, his stance had not softened to the point where the Milwaukee directors would be willing to sign him. "He was offered the courthouse and the Plankinton House, but he desired the Exposition building thrown in, and the local management ceased bidding for his services."[7] Whitney remained in Pittsburgh for the 1885 season. Once Baldwin jumped to Cincinnati, George Mappis, a catcher from the previous year's Terre Hautes, was signed. To replace Sexton at shortstop, Tommy Lee was signed. Lee was a local boy and another former Maple Leaf. In 1884 he had signed with Chicago of the National League and pitched for both its reserve team and the White Stockings. Later in the season he played with the Baltimore Unions. He won a total of six games and lost twelve in the big leagues in 1884, in addition to hitting .245. Tommy would die in Milwaukee on March 4, 1886, at the age of 23.

Milwaukee had a fine club, but not the caliber to win the Western League pennant. The *Sporting Life* thought Indianapolis would finish on top, and the *Cincinnati Enquirer* believed Kansas City and Indianapolis would finish on top. Even the *Milwaukee Sentinel* did not believe the Grays could win it all. The club was weak at shortstop and catcher. Tommy Lee was not as good as Sexton had been. Arundel was a fine catcher but a very poor hitter. Falch was not doing well at all. Mappis was only an experiment and was released two games into the season, not being big enough to take the punishment behind the plate. Loftus then shored up the club by signing Joe Brown, who had been released by the Chicago White Stockings after reporting late for spring practice, for mound duty. Len Stockwell, formerly of Grand Rapids, was signed to catch him. Still looking to strengthen his catching, Loftus considered paying the $500 fine to get the veteran Emil Gross off the blacklist, but only if he stopped "looking on the wine when it is red in the cup, or toying with the foam crest schooner."[8] The directors decided Gross was not worth the risk. A *Sporting Life* correspondent now thought "Milwaukee is decidedly the strongest club that has been here [Kansas City] this season."[9]

Instead of reporting to Milwaukee in April, the players were directed to report to St. Louis, where Loftus had scheduled some exhibition games. Assembled in St. Louis, the team played its first exhibition game on April 4, losing to Chris Von der Ahe's St. Louis Browns (American Association) 4 to 2 with "Lady" Baldwin pitching. The next day Burns pitched in a 6 to 1 loss, again to the Browns. The following week the Browns were again victorious in St. Louis. As a final tune-up, the Grays beat the Keokuk club, in Keokuk, 9 to 5.

The Western League season began for Milwaukee on April 18 at Indianapolis. A fair attendance saw Indianapolis score first on a wild pitch, but the Grays immediately tied it when Burns doubled in Behel. In the eighth inning Arundel singled up the middle to score two runs for the Milwaukee victory.

MILWAUKEE		R	H	PO	A	E	INDIANAPOLIS		A	H	PO	A	E
Gorman	rf	0	1	4	0	1	Donnelly	3b	1	2	0	0	0
Behel	lf	1	0	0	0	0	Poorman	rf	0	0	1	0	1
Burns	cf	0	2	0	0	0	Thompson	cf	0	0	0	0	0
Schoeneck	1b	0	0	0	0	0	Collins	ss	0	2	2	3	1
Forster	2b	0	0	5	3	1	Moriarity	lf	0	0	2	1	1
McSorley	3b	1	0	0	1	1	McQuery	1b	0	0	12	0	0
Lee	ss	1	0	1	3	0	Crane	2b	0	0	5	2	1
Baldwin	p	0	0	3	0	1	McGuire	c	0	1	5	3	2
Arundel	c	0	1	6	1	2	Casey	p	0	0	0	2	1
		3	4	27	8	5			1	5	27	11	7

	1	2	3	4	5	6	7	8	9
Indianapolis	1	0	0	0	0	0	0	0	0—1
Milwaukee	1	0	0	0	0	0	0	2	0—3

The Grays lost the next three games to Indianapolis, the only noteworthy feat being Arundel's $25 fine for "ruffianly conduct."[10] Before entering Kansas City the Grays again stopped in St. Louis, this time to lose to Lucas' National League team 13 to 0. In Kansas City the Grays dropped two games to the Cowboys before breaking the five-game losing streak with Baldwin's 13 to 4 win, giving K.C. its first loss. Brown pitched his first game in Milwaukee's uniform (red cap, belt and stockings and white knickerbockers pants and shirts with the name MILWAUKEE in red silk across the front) and won on a three-hitter.

Tom Loftus tried to explain that the club's 3 and 5 record was not that bad since they had been playing in rain and mud. Some were accusing the directors of being "niggardly and of securing cheap players."[11] The *Sentinel* came to the club's defense, reminding its readers that it was not the club's fault key players jumped. Only a few games had been played and all on the road. "The local public should, at least, wait until it sees the present team at work before condemning the players. The team is a good one and when it strikes its gait, will capture victories enough to satisfy the local enthusiasts."[12]

The club made its first appearance at home on May 2 and 1,000 attended on a unseasonably cold day. Down 4 to 3, the Grays scored four runs in the eighth inning for a 7 to 4 victory. The Grays then went on to sweep the three-game set over Dan O'Leary's Irish Agitators from Toledo. After the series Milwaukee split exhibition games with Toledo—first on the ball field and next on roller skates. A huge crowd went to the Exposition Rink and watched a baseball game on roller skates, Toledo winning 7 to 3. A softball was used and it was reported "several players have become so expert in the use of the rollers that they can stand up alone."[13] A week later they played the same roller game with Cleveland.

In this early season the club had a few key injuries. First, Behel hurt his eye in the Indianapolis series and returned home wearing a pair of blue goggles. He missed eight games before his eye improved satisfactorily. Then Brown came down with a severe cold, combined with malaria, and was out. Once back, he came down with a sore arm. Soon Baldwin was disabled. For bench strength Loftus hired Bill Alvord, a reserve infielder.

The club won five of its next eight games and was battling Kansas City for second place when the Grays came to Milwaukee. The Tame Rabbits, as Ted Sullivan called the Grays, won three of the four, and their 14 to 9 record put them in second place, behind Indianapolis. The team left for a 12-game road trip and O. Kirby [Oak A. Kirby listed in 1885 City of Milwaukee Directory as a clerk at the Kirby House] promised each man a new hat if they won all twelve games, and a new necktie if they won 8 of the 12. The Grays won two of three in Toledo, but troubles hit the league.

The trouble began in Omaha. Because of poor local support, mainly due to the grounds being too far from the central population for public transportation, the club was looking to move. Two weeks later the club secured new grounds and decided to continue. Paying audiences were still very slight, owing to the team's 4 and 19 record, so the club decided to switch its home series with the Grays to Milwaukee. In early June Omaha disbanded and Keokuk, originally thought to be too small, joined the Western. This move was thought to help the league by cutting traveling costs. Travel estimates at the beginning of the year were 39,691 miles for the entire Western, with Milwaukee's to be 6,931. This was compared to the eight-club circuits of the National League (51,903), American Association (51,903), Southern League (47,079) and Eastern League (27,733).

Cleveland was next to leave the Western League. First, some of its players were convicted in local court of playing Sunday ball. Talk then centered on transferring to Minneapolis, but it was doubtful Minneapolis wanted the franchise's troubles. Within a week the Cleveland club, $2,500 behind, was disbanded. The *Toledo Commercial-Telegram* reported the Toledo club was $300 in arrears, and its players had not been paid since the season opened. Toledo went under two days after Cleveland.

To plug these gaps the Western League looked for new cities. Youngstown and Springfield, Ohio, and St. Joseph, Missouri, along with Evansville expressed interest, but were considered too small. Milwaukee, along with Kansas City, was ready to give up the fight. Some thought was given that maybe the American Association would take these two franchises in. Cincinnati was rumored to be jumping the association and entering the National League. The local press thought "if Milwaukee can obtain Cincinnati's place, local ball enthusiasts will be satisfied, and the white winged dove will roost perpetually on the grandstand at the Wright Street grounds."[14]

If the Western folded, Milwaukee's club directors were to make no great effort to keep the club alive, "as they seem to feel that their efforts in the direction have not been appreciated by a portion of the local public."[15] Low attendance and the public's objection of paying for scorecards dimmed the directors' enthusiasm. The scorecard issue came up in late May. Local fans were accustomed to receiving free scorecards when attending the games, but the policy was changed this year and 5 cents was charged. Manager Loftus defended the nickel charge, saying it cost a lot to run a club, and the $20 to $30 profit from this sale each game helped. All clubs in the American Association and National League were charging. The *Milwaukee Journal* came out against the practice, and the Wisconsin Central Railroad began supplying scorecards. They were of better quality than those of management and more people used these.

Several directors were willing to sell the franchise at half price. However, Harry Quin said the club would last through the year and took out a refreshment license for the Wright Street Park for $50, good until November 1.

Indianapolis ownership was ready to leave the Western League and offered Detroit $5,000 to withdraw from the National League in order to get in. The deal fell through. The Indianapolis club was expelled from the Western for failure to continue its schedule, and was sold to Detroit for $5,000. The *Evening Wisconsin* thought $5,000 was too high, as Brooklyn had bought a better Cleveland club in 1884 for only $2,500. It was soon reported Detroit only paid $2,000 and held out the remaining $3,000 because two players did not transfer. Local Milwaukee enthusiasts proposed a plan, having the four remaining clubs put $500 into a kitty and the winner of the most games would receive $1,500, with second place receiving $500. This plan was not accepted.

Milwaukee finished off its Western League stay for 1885 by winning five of eight from Keokuk to end with a 22 and 13 record. On June 22 the Milwaukee club disbanded.

The fall of the Western League was simple economics. Higher salaries, bad weather, low crowds, 25-cent admission equaled financial failure. The Grays had a payroll of $13,875. Burns led with a reported $1,700. Baldwin, Gorman, Stockwell, Forster and Brown received $1,200; McSorley $1,100; Arundel and Schoeneck $1,000. Under $1,000 were Lee ($975), Behel ($900), Alvord and Falch ($600). The early season was plagued with terrible weather. On the Grays' first road trip, almost every game was played in rain or on muddy fields. Once home, it was even worse. For some unexplained reason, the club did not sell season tickets this year. The opener was played before only 1,000 in winter-like conditions. At the first Sunday game, 3,000 to 4,000 attended in very threatening weather. Cold weather continued through the homestand, and once only 200 people attended a game. The first Ladies Day game in May was snowed out. A Saturday game with Cleveland drew only 400. A new experiment was tried to please the fans. A bulletin board was erected in center field to give fans scores of all Western League, American Association and National League games. One problem was fans were unable to decipher the writing on Milwaukee's first scoreboard. Throughout the abbreviated season, Sunday home games drew between three to five thousand, while weekday games were almost always under the thousand mark. On the road, attendance was erratic. Indianapolis drew only fair crowds. During the franchise problems, five exhibition games were played in Indianapolis, with the Grays receiving only about $200. A Sunday game in Kansas City drew 8,000, but two days later only 600 paid their way in to the 11,000-seat stadium. A Sunday game in Toledo drew only 1,000. Small Keokuk, once in the Western, drew 1,000 on weekday games.

Once again Milwaukee dismantled a team. In late May Anton Falch was fined $100 and suspended for 30 days for missing a train. Ten days before the club disbanded, Dick Burns was asked to take a $175 cut per month and was then released to cut expenses. Len

Stockwell was released two days later after refusing to accept a 50 percent cut in salary. The day the club disbanded, an exhibition was played against the Chicago White Stockings in Milwaukee, the Grays losing 2 to 1 before only 1,381. Cash receipts were $726 (with a 50-cent admission), with Chicago receiving 50 percent of that. In its last game together, the team played the local Whites, with the proceeds going to the players. Only 350 to 400 Milwaukeeans attended, so the Grays received only $58 to split up. Charley Baldwin then signed with Detroit for $550 a month. Stockwell and Jack Gorman went to the New Britain (Connecticut) club. John McSorley and John Arundel went down to Memphis to play. Tom Forster signed with the New York Metropolitans and Joe Brown joined the Baltimore American Association club for $200 a month. Bill Alvord went to Waterby (Connecticut). Tommy Lee, Anton Falch and Lewis Schoeneck stayed and played for the local semi-professional Whites.

As a last fling, readers opened the July 18 *Milwaukee Sentinel* to read: "A NEW BALL CLUB: Milwaukee Ready to Join the National League." The story explained how the Buffalo franchise was in financial trouble, ready to withdraw from the National League, and Milwaukee had asked for the opening. The next day Buffalo announced it would stay and the 1885 professional season in Milwaukee was dead. In late September Harry Quin again attempted to have the Buffalo club transferred to Milwaukee. Buffalo owners went so far as to ask Quin on what terms they could transfer the club to Milwaukee for the balance of the season. The hang-up was that Detroit had bought the entire Buffalo club to acquire its Big Four — Dan Brouthers, Hardy Richardson, Rowe and Deacon White. Buffalo continued on through the season after National League president Nick Young ruled the four must finish the season with Buffalo. It was apparent they would go to Detroit in 1886. Without the Big Four, Quin would not make a deal.

❋ ❋ ❋

Although the professional Grays dominated baseball space in the newspapers during the 1884 and 1885 seasons, amateurs continued to play. Around 200 clubs reportedly played in Milwaukee during the 1884 season. Of course, because of the vast number they cannot be covered in detail, but some made interesting reading.

First to organize were the 1883 champion Arctics. Having lost many of their former stars to the Grays or Cream Citys, the club took on a new appearance, and lost their first recorded game to the Welcomes. After beating their archrivals, the Maple Leafs, now only a picked nine, the Arctics vanquished the Welcomes to hold the amateur championship to that point. A few days later they again beat the Leafs, but then fell on hard times. Another old name was the Quicksteps, who claimed the amateur championship in the spring because of the downfall of the Arctics and Maple Leafs. As the season drew near, they received challenges from Wisconsin clubs for a state championship. The Quicksteps opened this series in Berlin with a loss. They also lost to Oshkosh and Green Bay before returning home. The series then fell through, however, as Oshkosh disbanded, Green Bay players were likely to be arrested for a Sunday exhibition that will be discussed later, and Berlin had a local umpire who bet on the games. After beating the Bay Views, the Q's boldly announced they would present a solid gold medal to any local club that beat them two of three games. They backed this arrogance up by whipping the Arctics 22 to 10 before 2,000 at Cold Spring Driving Park. Manager Hagerty said the medal would be played for between the Bay Views and Welcomes, the only local clubs to beat the Quicksteps the entire 1884 season.

The popular Maple Leafs had a trying season. At first they were only a pick nine, losing to the Arctics and Jolly Muffers, and then beating the Regulators and Green Bay. The Maple Leafs became semi-professional in July on a co-operative plan by picking up many of the disbanded Cream Citys, such as Clayton, Schomberg, Morris, Schierz and Himmelstein. On August 10 this club beat the Dreadnaughts of Chicago when they scored seven times in the ninth inning. Soon the manager of the Dreads made the incredible statement that the club the Maple Leafs beat had not been the Dreadnaughts, but the Gordons, an all-black nine. Two weeks later, shored up with the acquisition of the released Tom Morrissey of the Grays, the Leafs beat the real Gordons 10 to 4. At the end of their season, the Leafs played the Grays a few times while using some of the opposing players to make a close game, yet being shut out in all of them. The Maple Leafs and Arctics finished the season on October 19, with the Leafs winning 18 to 10.

Sunday ball was big in Milwaukee, and with the Northwestern Grays unable to compete in championship contests on Sundays, local amateur clubs had fine attendances. Four hundred witnessed a May contest between the Arctics and Welcomes at Cold Spring Driving Park, not bad considering the Cream Citys were also playing in town and drawing 800. The good amateurs usually drew between 200 and 400, although big attractions like the Arctics-Quicksteps game drew 2,000, and the Maple Leaf-Gordon contest 1,000. Other cities were not as welcoming to Sunday ball. In Fort Wayne, Indiana, a grand jury investigated Sunday ball, but failed to bring back an indictment. Closer to home the issue was worse. The Milwaukee Greens played in Green Bay on Sunday, June 1, and three players from each side (A. Halloway, P. Conley and J. Ley from the Greens) were arrested after the fifth inning. The local court commissioner discharged them on $25 bail and then bound them over for trial, but no record of a disposition has been found.

Amateur clubs of all sorts were playing in Milwaukee, ranging in age and occupation. Old standbys like the Heimann "Ups" and "Downs," "P.V.'s" of the H. Rolf Company and "Mark Twains" of the Segnitz Company were on the field. New interest groups, like the Schlitz Park Ushers—all under 18—and even entertainment people, such as the Bijou Opera Bouffe Company, Fay Templeton Opera and Rice's Big Burleques, formed and played the Newspaper Terrors to big local print. Both the American Eagles and Gold Stars were all under 12 years old. With all these clubs, the press had difficulties; the *Sentinel* stated, "No baseball games will be published in the *Sentinel* hereafter unless the score is brought in by the captains of both clubs. So many games have been misrepresented that corrections cannot now be made."[16]

An interesting game was proposed, but unfortunately apparently never played, in late May. Some of the old-timers wanted to play a match using "the old-fashioned rules, the man behind the bat standing back and catching on the bound, while the umpire will be seated on a chair under the protecting cover of an umbrella."[17] Included were McFadyen, Dodsworth, Middleman, Bryden and Chandler from the old Cream City Club. The idea of old-timer's day is more than one hundred twenty years old in Milwaukee.

The spring of 1885 was dominated by talk of the Western League, but a group of local semi-professionals, many of them cut from the Grays, gathered to play primarily when the Western League club was on the road. Calling themselves the Whites, they were managed by Frank Schwind, formerly of the Arctics. The club was composed of Doug Young, Delany, Schierz, Purcell, Schomberg, Straub and Himmelstein. Wearing uniforms of ash gray with white caps, stockings and belts and regulation deer skin shoes, they planned their first game for Sunday, April 19, against the Chicago Blues at Wright Street Park, but the game was postponed when the grounds were not ready. Finally, on April 26, the Whites played, losing to the Chicago Blues 10 to 0 before 600, while the Grays played in Kansas City. The Whites beat the local Welcomes and the Phoenix before reorganizing in late May. Welcome Kirby became the club's new manager and a few new players were picked up. The reorganized club then beat the Acmes, a crack all-black nine from Chicago, before 400 to 500 people. A few weeks later the Whites lost to the Waukeshas 26 to 5 in Waukesha, and later traveled to Menominee and beat that city's club 14 to 7. After defeating the local Bay Views before 1,000 spectators (the Grays had now disbanded), the Whites traveled to Eau Claire and split two games. Back home the Whites beat the Quicksteps and faded away, only heard from in September when they lost to Port Washington.

Two local amateur clubs flourished. The Bay Views and James Morgans first met on May 3, with the Morgans winning 8 to 6. Three weeks later the Morgans beat the Welcomes at Cold Spring Driving Park before 500 people. The Bays Views then beat the Welcomes and were presented Hagerty's gold medal for the championship of the 1884 season. The Bay Views continued on by beating the Quicksteps 10 to 9, and again beating the Welcomes and then the Nationals. Both teams played through the summer in the City League, which consisted of the Morgans, Bay View, Golden Eagles and Welcomes. Bay View ended the City League season with a 14 and 6 record, while the Morgans had an 11 and 4 record. Joe Harper of the Morgans was the star pitcher of the city, having struck out 262 in the 19 games he pitched. The two clubs set out to decide the city championship with a three-game series, but rain cancelled the games.

Other local clubs had their ups and downs. The Union Boys and Young Arctics had the distinction of playing the first game of the 1885 season, with the Arctics losing 30 to 28. The once mighty Arctics were now just another club and in September even changed their name to the Badgers. In May some of the old West End players and former Maple Leafs — Young, Oliver, Delany, Dunn, Kershaw, Hooley, Furlong, Van Dyke, Knowles and Dailey — formed the Old Timers Club and had some fun. Another club, the Planets, won the city championship for clubs under 18 years old.

This year, more than ever before, local clubs traveled throughout the state. In late April it was suggested 8 or 10 clubs from throughout the state form a Wisconsin Baseball Association, scheduling about eight games in each city and giving the visiting club a guarantee and percentage. But these plans were quick to fall through because of insufficient financial backing. The plan was brought up again in mid-May, but with little interest. After the Western League folded, the *Sentinel* threw its support behind a state amateur league. "It would create a friendly rivalry that would lend great interest to the games, and while the playing might not be as brilliant as that of some professional games, it would certainly be well worth witnessing."[18] The *Sentinel* suggested a league of Wisconsin's bigger cities, including Milwaukee, and wished those interested to write the newspaper.

By August a league was formed and the Quicksteps of Milwaukee were to play Hartford in the first league game, but it was rained out. The following week the first game was played between the Q's and Berlin, with the Berlins winning 8 to 3 before 300 at Wright Street Park. Unfortunately, the State League had no organization and was on a helter-skelter basis. At one point, Eau Claire could find no one to play and offered $150 for two games or $200 for three games for a club from Berlin, Cambria or Milwaukee to play there. In early October Lake Mills defeated Cambria and was awarded the state championship.

Though not official state tournament games, Milwaukee clubs played state clubs many times in 1885. The first to travel out of the city was the Northwestern Mutual Life Insurance Company team, which lost to Racine College 23 to 17 on April 25. The next club, the Reds, ran into trouble in Kenosha. With Sunday ball illegal there, the sheriff put his hand on one of the Reds, telling him he was under arrest, when the player drew a revolver! Everyone concerned was taken to the sheriff's office and soon released. Most clubs stayed rather close to home, but some, like the Greens, traveled to Janesville and the Golden Eagles to Oshkosh and Eau Claire, a good distance in those days. The Morgans posted the best record with state clubs, winning four of seven, including three wins over Sheboygan. One contest in Waukesha drew 3,000 fans.

After the Western League disbanded, the Quicksteps took their turn as the top attraction in Milwaukee. Their first game, against the local Bay Views, was a 10 to 9 loss. Their next contest was with the semi-professional Whites, losing by the identical score. The Q's then lost in the first state league game to Berlin with the former Gray, Joe Brown, pitching. The following day they again played the Berlins, this time to a 13-inning tie. The Quicksteps then changed their name to the Milwaukees.

At the time a female club from the south, the Blonde and Brunette Club, visited Milwaukee and was engaged to play the Milwaukees. Hagerty discovered the gals' club was "not what it was represented to be [in terms of talent] and at once called off the engagement."[19] A crowd of 2,800 watched a picked nine beat the girls, 13 to 6, "demonstrating the fact that women never can play ball,"[20] at least according to the *Sentinel.*

The Milwaukees finally won a game, beating Bay View 18 to 9 for $25 at the annual picnic of the Sons of St. George. On August 28 the Milwaukees played the National League Detroit Wolverines. "The Milwaukees appeared to be in mortal terror of their opponents and permitted errors to pick up pretty liberally against them."[21] One thousand saw the Wolverines win 11 to 4. Two days later they whipped the Chicago Reds 6 to 0 before 2,000 at Wright Street Park. A week later Hagerty's boys beat the West Enders, and the game's proceeds went to Murphy, who broke his finger in the Detroit game. "The scorer tired of keeping the record of runs made,"[22] as the Milwaukees won 20 to 5. The following day the former Quicksteps defeated the local Nationals to end their brief moment of glory.

Another big attraction of '85 was the return of National League clubs. After Detroit played the Milwaukees, with good financial success, Harry Quin worked at getting two National League clubs to play each other in Milwaukee. He succeeded by getting first-place Chicago to play outgoing Buffalo on September 4, guaranteeing both $200 and expenses. Between 2,000 and 2,500 paid 50 cents, or 75 cents for grandstand seats, to watch Chicago win 12 to 4 at Wright Street Park. Quin managed to bring Chicago back on September 25, this time against outgoing Providence. Between 2,500 and 3,000 witnessed an awesome White Stocking club win 21 to 3. Quin attempted to get Chicago to play second-place New York here in October, but the clubs wanted a $1,000 guarantee and were left alone.

Of course, Quin's plan was to land a National League or American Association club. After failing with Buffalo, Quin looked in a different direction. Hope for a club in 1885 was gone and everyone was confident of a club in 1886. With Buffalo and Providence leaving the National League, and Pittsburgh rumored to be transferring from the American Association to the league, there would be openings in both circuits. Because of the National League's 50-cent admission and no Sunday ball, Quin and Loftus would rather join the American Association. The *Sporting Life* believed Milwaukee would be a better choice than Kansas City, because it was the best paying city in the Western League, and was more accessible for travel from St. Louis and Cincinnati. In an editorial the paper went on: "There will be no American Association club in Chicago next year. Milwaukee is ripe for such a club, and with Sunday games and beer privileges—neither of which would be tolerated in

Chicago—a club would do well in the Cream City."[23] The *Mirror of American Sports* wrote, "The liberal patronage bestowed upon the two league games played there this season shows conclusively that Milwaukee will support a good club under favorable conditions. There is no Western City whose admission would be so advantageous to the American Association."[24] The *Evening Wisconsin* had no doubts Milwaukee would be in the American Association because Chris Von der Ahe of St. Louis supported the franchise. The *New York Harold* was also sure Milwaukee would be admitted.

Others were not so confident. The Cincinnati correspondent to the *Sporting Life* thought Indianapolis would get the association spot over Milwaukee. Ed Cushman, formerly of the Grays, did not think Milwaukee would get in because it was not conveniently located for all the clubs. At the initial American Association meeting on October 17, 1885, Milwaukee was not admitted to that body. But neither was any other city, and another meeting was called in December. In November, action within the National League picked up. Washington applied for admittance and Detroit got the Big Four, leaving Buffalo definitely out of the league. Word spread that Cincinnati people would buy the Buffalo franchise and Washington men would purchase the Providence club, but nothing was definite. Milwaukee had a chance to obtain the Buffalo club, but 50-cent admission, no Sunday ball and awkward railroad connections made it look unattractive to local enthusiasts.

Little was definite in either league. It was certain the National League would lose two clubs, but which cities would replace them was anyone's guess. In the American Association no one knew if any clubs would be lost. On November 18 Harry Quin told an *Evening Wisconsin* reporter he had given up all hope of getting into the American Association, but maybe had a chance in the National League. The following day the *Milwaukee Journal* quoted Quin as saying there was every likelihood that Milwaukee would be in the American Association. Such were the state of things. On top of all this, the *Sporting Life* was predicting a new league because of the recent $2,000 ceiling on salaries set up by the National League and American Association. Washington, Cincinnati, Cleveland, Newark, Indianapolis, Milwaukee, Chicago and Boston were eyed, but the *Evening Wisconsin* was sure Milwaukee would not be so foolish to join a new league.

As it turned out the American Association made no changes. However, the National League, with only six clubs, gave Milwaukee a chance. At first it was reported the league would go with only those six clubs (Chicago, St. Louis, Detroit, Philadelphia, New York and Boston) for 1886. Soon it was decided that two clubs would be admitted. Washington had the inside track in the east, while Cincinnati, Milwaukee and Kansas City headed the western candidates. Quin asked the league for special inducements (presumably Sunday ball, beer and/or 25-cent ball) but was turned down. He was, however, guaranteed some players.

A meeting was held on January 12, 1886, at the Plankinton House in Milwaukee and enough money was pledged to enter a club in the National League. Although the names of the subscribers were not made public, $10,000 was pledged with $5,000 to be paid immediately upon entering the league. It is known that the horse car companies, whose cars went to the park, pledged money. However, this is where a falling out began. Two days after the meeting the companies pulled out. Washington Becker, president of the West Side Line, had volunteered to take $1,000 worth of stock, provided Peter McGeoch, owner of the rival line, would contribute $750. When McGeoch refused, Becker withdrew. Quin was sure each would make $2,000 by the end of the season. By the end of the month, the two company heads decided to meet the obligation and Milwaukee was again in the running. Quin went to the February 9 National League meeting in Chicago, making only one demand of the league: that Milwaukee receive 12 good players, without having to purchase their releases. Kansas City ended up the National League's eighth member. Quin explained that Kansas City had given a $5,000 bonus for six players, not even knowing who they would be. Milwaukee just would not bid any higher.

Numerous minor league plans were being made, but because Milwaukee had had bad experiences in the minors, the *Sentinel* believed "they will probably die a natural death."[25] Ted Sullivan came to town to talk of his new idea, the Northwestern League. "The famous hustler of the baseball world"[26] explained his idea well and local promoters indicated they would be for it if every club deposited a forfeiture bond of $800 to $1,000, as a guarantee to play the season. Milwaukee's real interest, though, was in playing exhibitions with National League and other strong clubs. A $1,000 deposit was set on for the Northwestern, and Minneapolis, Duluth, Milwaukee and Eau Claire were certain to join. St. Paul was favorably considering the matter, the problem was again a lack of suitable grounds. On March 5 a meeting was called in Eau Claire with Duluth, Minneapolis, La Crosse, Madison, Milwaukee, St. Paul and Oshkosh represented. The delegates decided on a six-club circuit with the original five mentioned (St. Paul had found grounds) and Oshkosh or La Crosse to be the sixth. Soon clubs from Janesville, Racine, Dubuque, St. Joseph and Omaha applied, and an eight-club circuit was proposed. Dubuque, St. Joseph and Omaha would make for long trips, but directors believed the bigger crowds would make up for that inconvenience.

Still uncertain what cities would constitute the Northwestern, the present delegates met in Minneapolis. They put up $1,000 to be in the National Agreement and adopted the constitution and by-laws of the American Association with only minor changes. Harry Quin, now secretary of the league, reported Oshkosh did not have enough interest to gain admittance, and St. Joseph was just too far away. It is more than 500 miles from St. Joe to St. Paul, and even though the Missouri club offered a guarantee of $5,000, it was turned down. Then in a surprise move, the Northwestern moved to place a club in Chicago. A club in the Windy City would make a nice 400-mile radius league, but Albert Spalding of the White Stockings refused to let the Northwestern settle there (his right under the National Agreement) on the "very thin excuse that Sunday ball was against the spirit of the National League."[27] Peoria and Grand Rapids then applied but were turned down. Finally, in late April, Oshkosh, Wisconsin, was admitted to the sixth spot. The Northwestern was ready for the season.

Ted Sullivan became the sole manager of the club, as the old Milwaukee Baseball Association had disbanded in January. The only control others had was with Wright Street Park, which had recently been purchased by Charles M. Kipp, Benjamin A. Kipp and Harry Quin. The park was then leased to Sullivan. He was expected to bring a winner to Milwaukee, as he had "a faculty of ferreting out good players without reputation and developing them."[28] As most of the Northwestern players would be "comparatively beginners in the pro arena,"[29] salaries were expected to be low.

Sullivan arrived from St. Louis in March with some players engaged, but as the Northwestern was not yet in the National Agreement, he would not name them. He continued correspondence with numerous players, including a "phenomenal pitcher from Minnesota who has spent the winter in breaking barn doors for practice."[30] Sullivan also expected to give the two best local pitchers, Harper of the James Morgans and Clough from Bay View, a trial. By early April Sullivan had a team set. At first base he had John Pickett, who had played in Stillwater in 1884 before returning to a Chicago business. At second was Crawford, the batting champion of the Iowa State League. Shortstop was pegged for Tom Sexton, and at third was Johnson. From left to right, his outfield was to be McCall from an eastern club, Tom McCullum, who played the previous year with Youngstown, and W. Holmes from the Haverhill club. At catcher Sullivan placed Duane from the previous year's Dubuque club. The bulk of the pitching was slated for Joe Masran, who pitched for Memphis in 1885. Sullivan also had his two local boys. In mid–April he took his team to Leavenworth, Kansas, to play that club and other Western League teams.

On April 13 the Milwaukees beat Leavenworth 19 to 10 to start the 1886 exhibitions. The following day Harper struck out ten St. Joe hitters in a losing cause, and then two days later St. Joseph was victorious again. The Milwaukee club then split two games with Omaha's Union Pacifics to end its brief spring training there. Though they lost more than they won on the diamond, the club came home the winners. Manager Sullivan signed Pat Sullivan, the graduate of the Maple Leafs, and William O'Donnell, the crack batter of St. Joseph. He also signed Duvbeck and Charles Isaacson, the third and first basemen of that same club. When Sullivan brought his club home, it took this appearance: Masran, O'Donnell, Harper — pitchers; Holmes and Pat Sullivan — catchers; Isaacson — 1b; Sexton — 2b; Pickett — 3b; T. Dougherty, from last year's Union Pacifics — ss; Charles Almin, formerly of Ann Arbor College and the Bay Views — lf; McCullum — cf; and the catchers alternating in right field. Unfortunately, these new players were all under contract to their former club in St. Joseph, and court injunctions were now upon them. However, they all got out of town, with the law looking for them. Once back in Milwaukee, the club beat Racine 17 to 3 before only 200 to 300 people on a Ladies Day. The following day, 1,000 witnessed the local Maple Leafs, with John Cusick pitching, beat the Northwestern League club 4 to 3. Before the regular season opened, the club scored a 10 to 2 victory again over Racine.

Prior to the start of the Northwestern League season, it was obvious the Milwaukee club was weak at third base, left and center fields, and pitching. To shore up the pitching, Sullivan took Cusick from the Maple Leafs, who pitched opening day, May 8, at Wright Street Park. Only 400 to 500 attended after the Milwaukees and Eau Claires were escorted to the grounds by a band of music. Milwaukee lost 12 to 8.

MILWAUKEE		AB	R	H	TB	EAU CLAIRE		AB	R	H	TB
Sexton	2b	5	1	1	2	Roberts	2b	5	2	1	2
Pickett	3b	5	1	2	4	Doan	3b	4	2	3	6
Cusick	p	5	1	1	4	Cantilion	cf	5	1	0	0
P. Sullivan	rf	5	0	1	1	Nagle	c	5	0	2	2
Dougherty	ss	5	1	1	1	Lynch	ss	5	3	3	4
Holmes	c	5	2	1	1	Murphy	rf	5	2	1	2
McCullum	cf	5	2	2	2	D. McGinley	p	5	0	1	1
Isaacson	1b	3	0	1	2	M. McGinley	1b	4	1	1	1
Almin	lf	*3*	*0*	*0*	*0*	Sheehan	lf	*4*	*1*	*0*	*0*
		41	8	10	17			42	12	12	18

	1	2	3	4	5	6	7	8	9
Milwaukee	4	0	2	0	1	0	0	1	0 — 8
Eau Claire	0	1	4	2	0	0	0	5	0 — 12

The next day Eau Claire beat Milwaukee again, 11 to 5, with O'Donnell losing. The club then traveled to Oshkosh, where Harper lost, before Cusick won the club's first game in Eau Claire, 9 to 2. To shore up his outfield, Sullivan acquired McQuaide, formerly of Quincy. Ted Sullivan pitched next, losing. Then a 20 to 6 whipping by Oshkosh dropped the club's record to 1 and 5.

8—Setting the Foundation (1885–1887)

Apparent that Milwaukee needed stronger pitching, Sullivan went to St. Louis to find help. Meanwhile, McQuaide and Holmes were released. Sullivan had his eye on Ed Silch, playing for St. Louis Peach Tree Nine, but signed Shortell and Ed Gastfield of Chicago. Shortell, a pitcher, was from the amateur Chicago Whitings, while Gastfield had caught in 1885 for the Detroit club. Sullivan also picked up John Lavin, a center fielder, and Sloccum, a catcher. His new pitcher had not arrived, so he pitched Grabe, a local, against Oshkosh and won. Another local pitcher, Fred Fass, again beat Oshkosh after O'Donnell, recovering from a lame arm, took a beating. Fass again beat Oshkosh on May 23 to become the club's first two-game winner. Fass was a local school teacher and could not go on road trips, hurting his chances for big success. Meanwhile, Shortell and Gastfield had not appeared. Shortell only had a verbal commitment, but Gastfield had signed a contract. He was soon playing with Oshkosh, denying he signed with Milwaukee. The *Sentinel* blasted this action: "It is necessary for the preservation of the Northwestern League that the underhand work of stealing players under contract to another club should be restricted at once, and as the association possesses the power to blacklist, it might be well to use it on Mr. Gastfield as an example."[31] But the league did not, and Gastfield continued to play for Oshkosh.

Milwaukee then traveled west, winning three and losing three to the three Minnesota clubs. The club's 7 and 9 record was good for fourth place, but Ted Sullivan now had more trouble. Grabe hurt his finger and Joe Harper jumped to Oshkosh, leaving Milwaukee short on pitching. As Harper had no contract with Milwaukee, no blacklist proceedings could be started. At an exhibition in Lake Mills, a local boy named George Bishop struck out 17, impressing Sullivan, who brought him to Milwaukee. Sullivan also purchased the release of pitcher William Kelley from Chattanooga for $300. Back home Bishop teamed with his catcher, Frank Mills, to beat St. Paul 8 to 2. The problem with Bishop was he was the editor and owner of the *Lake Mills Leader* and he did not want to leave Lake Mills, but promised to sign with Milwaukee if he decided to play professionally. The lone win put Milwaukee in second place, five wins behind Duluth. The home-only combination of Fass and Bishop then won three more, bringing about Cusick's release. The two were now 6 and 0. Kelley then teamed with his new catcher, James Banning, a promising youngster from St. Paul, for a win. The club's record was 12 and 9, having won five straight, and was only three wins out of first place. Fass then won his fifth before the roof fell in.

Fass lost his first game and then Kelley lost to Eau Clarie, 8 to 6, on a Pat Sullivan error. The *Sentinel* could not see the wisdom of playing Sullivan at shortstop. In the last 8 games he had 12 errors, for a fielding average of only .714. Sullivan was there because Tom Sexton had a sore shoulder, "but even in a crippled condition is preferable to Sullivan at short field."[32] Milwaukee then picked up Arthur Pope from Oshkosh to fill in at shortstop. Wessling, a local pitcher, took the loss, followed by Kelley losing. Ted Sullivan then signed two new pitchers, John "Kid" Hendricks and Williams. Williams won his first game, but was then injured while batting. Meanwhile, John Lavin was released.

The Milwaukees record was even at 14 and 14 now, still in second place, though they had lost five of its last six. The *Evening Wisconsin* could see one problem.

> Manager Sullivan should see that the members of the Milwaukee team keep better hours. Their stupid playing and inability to hit the ball show that there is a screw loose somewhere, as their fielding and hitting were decidedly better during the early part of the season than at present. Late hours and carousing are not conducive to good ball playing, and Milwaukee audiences are becoming thoroughly disgusted with the poor exhibitions given by some members of the team.[33]

Sullivan came up with a strange explanation. He stated his reason for not strengthening the club was that he did not desire to have a club that could "mop the diamond with the up-country clubs,"[34] and lead to the end of the Northwestern League. Fass pitched the next five games for the club, winning three. Kelley then lost three in a row, dropping Milwaukee to fourth place. On June 28 the *Evening Wisconsin* again blasted the club.

> Milwaukeeans pay a stipulated price to see ball playing by professionals, and in that they are disappointed, for the players, with, of course some exceptions, are the poorest that could be found.... It is high time the managers, Sullivan and Kipp, should rectify these matters. The public is becoming disgusted with the Milwaukee baseball club, and justly so, and if the management fails to appreciate that sentiment, the vacant chairs in the stands will soon testify as to their disapprobation.

Milwaukee lost three of the next five, capped by a 25 to 9 loss to Duluth, with Fass (now a full member and traveling with the team) taking the loss, to bring his record to 9 and 5 — still the best on the club. The club's 19 and 22 record was good for fourth place, only two games ahead of St. Paul.

Back home Ted Sullivan changed some faces. He released Arthur Pope and said a half a dozen more releases would follow in hope of bettering the team. He tried a Chicago pitcher named Princville, who "did not prove a sterling success,"[35] losing to last-place Minneapolis. He also signed Doug Young to catch. Next Sullivan signed Hugh Daily, a one-armed pitcher from Baltimore, at $200 a month and $100 in advance money. Though Daily had only his right arm, he had already won 69 and lost 69 in the major leagues before 1886. Sullivan then signed William Colgan, a catcher, and Louis Say, a shortstop. By July 25 Sullivan's club was 21 and 26, and fighting to keep fourth place.

Attendance was poor in Milwaukee, and Sullivan stated if it did not get better he would move the club. The *Evening Wisconsin* wrote that "wouldn't be a bad thing to do, if he could only leave it somewhere, and bring back a better one."[36] Now Sullivan was proposing to move his club to West St. Paul. No club could play within four miles of the St. Paul city limits without St. Paul's consent, and that club refused Sullivan. Sullivan denied this, saying a meeting had been held by the league managers, and they did vote him the privilege of moving to West St. Paul or any other city, if he could not meet expenses in Milwaukee. The *St. Paul Globe* wrote that this meeting was without the St. Paul club's knowledge. Sullivan then went to La Crosse to feel the baseball pulse of the western Wisconsin city. He denied rumors of transferring the Milwaukee club there, saying he wanted to move the Decatur club. Sullivan also said he wanted to secure four cities — Madison, La Crosse, Winona and Dubuque — to make the Northwestern a 10-club circuit in 1887.

Gus Krock, the young star pitcher from Bay View, beat Eau Claire on July 31, but Daily and Kelley dropped the next two games. Pat Sullivan was released, as was Williams, "for exhibiting a fondness for late hours and whiskey."[37] Sullivan had been fined $115, all of his salary, before being released. Soon Sexton retired, claiming he wanted to attend to his regular business on the railroad. He later revealed he quit because Manager Sullivan docked him a week's pay when he was laid up with an injury. William O'Donnell was also released. Fass, the club's winningest pitcher with 10 victories, and Sloccum were also gone. To fill these holes, Sullivan signed J.W. Walsh, a shortstop from the Macon club, and Billy Taylor from Nashville, whose arm gave out before he reached Milwaukee. Krock was then lost to Oshkosh. By early August the Milwaukee club had used 32 men. Thirteen pitchers and seven catchers had been given opportunities. The club's record was 26 and 29, good for fifth place.

The Milwaukees lost three of their next four and were now fighting to stay out of the cellar. Sullivan's pitching policy was now under attack by the *Sentinel*.

> Every time that the team plays away from home either Kelley [2 and 8] or Ted Sullivan [1 and 2], than whom it would be difficult to find worse pitchers, are trotted out and the result is invariably disastrous. Were it not for the utter lack of judgment on the part of the manager, the Milwaukees would occupy a far better position. The idea of securing cheap players seems to have been predominant in Sullivan's management of the team and has undoubtedly reacted against him financially, as Milwaukee people are more than willing to see good ball playing, and the attendance at the games this year would have been easily doubled had there been a good team. This has been most clearly demonstrated since the addition of Daily, Say and Colgan to the nine.[38]

Wissing, "another local amateur discovered by the indefatigable Ted Sullivan,"[39] took the next loss. James Sweeney, a newcomer from the Bay Views, took over at shortstop, and "the infusion of new blood worked like a charm"[40] as Daily won two over first-place Duluth. Dougherty, who played second base "like an Egyptian mummy,"[41] was released. On September 5 Milwaukee was only a half-game out of last place. About this time the Southern League was disbanding and it was thought Milwaukee might get some good pitchers from there. The *Sentinel* took a swipe at Sullivan's policy of pitching so many local boys by saying "of course while Bay View's stock of pitchers hold out, it is out of the question."[42] Sullivan did sign Billy O'Brien, a shortstop, and John "Tug" Arundel from the Southern League and released Colgan. In the first inning of the first game Tug played with the 1886 Milwaukees, he was fined $75 for abusing the umpire in Duluth. A warrant was issued for Arundel after the game, but he could not be found. Incidentally, Milwaukee won the game with its new players. Steve Behel was released by the New York Metropolitans of the American Association and signed by Milwaukee. Hugh Daily refused to pitch against St. Paul, pleading illness. Sullivan released his eight-game winner. Daily signed with St. Paul, along with Billy O'Brien. Sullivan quickly signed Dick Phelan and Tom Forster from the Mets, Leven Shreve from Savannah, and re-engaged Dougherty.

Milwaukee was fighting again for fourth place and only two wins out of second with the season drawing to a close. On September 20 more trouble began. Duluth was in town and arrived at Wright Street Park at 3:00 P.M., but was denied admittance, Sullivan claiming the grounds were unfit for play. Harry Quin, still secretary of the Northwestern, said that if Duluth was not admitted by 3:45 — game time — he would forfeit the game to Duluth and demand Milwaukee be expelled from the league. The *Sporting News* of October 4, 1886, provided this background on this forfeit:

> There are few St. Louisians but know Ted Sullivan; at one time the manager of the St. Louis Browns. Ted is a good fellow, but he never forgets an injury, and in consequence has led a very rocky life. Not long ago Ted, who is now the proprietor of the Milwaukee Club, was in Duluth and he tried to get the management of that club to play off a postponed game with him. The Duluth manager, for some reason or other, refused to play the game, and Ted in consequence was knocked out of considerable money. The other day the Duluth Club arrived in Milwaukee and Ted, itching to get even, told the Duluth manager that they would not play ball that day, as the grounds were too wet. As it had not rained the night before the Duluth man thought Ted was jesting, and when the time came drove his men out to the grounds. There they were refused admission, however, on the ground that the field was not fit to play on. The manager of the Duluth Club, who was furious, sent for Secretary Quin of the Northwestern League, and he instructed the umpire to give the game to Duluth. This was but little recompense for the loss of gate money, and Ted was able to laugh in his sleeve over his victory. But while Ted got his revenge on the Duluths, he has incurred the ill will of Milwaukee base ball patrons, a number of whom had assembled at the park, and he is likely to play to empty benches during the remainder of the season.

The following day a game was advertised, but neither Milwaukee nor Minneapolis showed. The next two days only 100 spectators were in Wright Street Park. On September 26 the Milwaukee club disbanded, even though it had three games left to play. The *Sentinel* looked at the end like this:

> The close of the Northwestern League season in this city yesterday is greeted with a universal sign of relief by admirers of the game. The season has been a dismal failure and the blame for it is to be laid at Manager Sullivan's door. Though the league itself was not a strong one, Milwaukee should have been represented by a good team, such as it has been accustomed to in the past, and should have taken the foremost position in the race for the pennant. There was money in the enterprise and it is only by the grossest kind of mismanagement that there has been loss instead. False economy in every direction has been the leading trait of this year's management, a policy which is sure to prove disastrous in baseball as well as in other business enterprises.[43]

The *Journal* of September 25, 1886, wrote this biting editorial:

> There has been a number of combinations formed in the disguises of ball clubs to filch the surplus in the pockets of the people in the northwest, but there never before has been such a daring robbery. Heretofore the managers have engaged some men who could play at ball and have given the public a pretense of show for their money. This season the legitimate amateurs have been prostituted to the uses of professionals. With a few accidental exceptions, there has not been a display of ball playing in Milwaukee this season, and the only return which patrons have had for their money has been newspaper promises that the managers were strengthening the club, when the veriest fool knew that they could not make a change and do anything else.

The paper went on to say that Milwaukee was a good baseball town and would support the best club that could be gathered, "as is evidenced by the fact that she has kept the worst alive.... But the present incompetents ought to be disbanded." The final standings of the 1886 Northwestern League were:

	Win	Loss		Win	Loss
Duluth	44	34	St. Paul	37	41
Eau Claire	43	36	Milwaukee	35	41
Oshkosh	41	36	Minneapolis	35	44

The Northwestern showed good balance, with last-place Minneapolis only nine wins behind pennant-winner Duluth.

With the season over the *St. Paul Pioneer Press* disclosed why Milwaukee had disbanded early. Ted Sullivan had sold Behel, Say, Arundel and Shreve to Eau Claire to strengthen that club to win that pennant. Harry Quin, who had done more than anyone else to help local baseball, got out by selling his interest in Wright Street Park to the Kipp brothers for $4,500. Ted Sullivan, as expected, severed his connections with the club. For the first time since 1878, as a member of the National League, Milwaukee was in a league that finished a season intact.

✻ ✻ ✻

The amateur season of 1886 had started with talk of a new State League in February. Although efforts to organize a league the year before were a failure, a league of Milwaukee, Green Bay, La Crosse, Eau Claire, Oshkosh and Racine were discussed. Though it was doubtful, it was more popular than the Northwestern League idea at the time. With proposed admission at 15 cents and 25 cents, the league never formed.

The only local amateur club to make a name for itself in 1886 was the Bay Views.

8—Setting the Foundation (1885–1887)

Manager Felix McIver (a Bay View saloon keeper) secured new grounds for the club in April on Kinnickinnic Avenue, one block south of the Russell Avenue streetcar terminus. McIver, Anton Stollenwerk (who owned a saloon and boarding house on South Bay Street), and Richard M. Moore (listed as a "heater" in the 1886 city directory) formed a partnership to run the park and club. The estimated cost of new Bay View Park was $4,500, and the park, with a grandstand and dressing rooms for both clubs, was completed in May. After losing a practice game to the local Dreadnaughts, the Bay Views were ready to open their season. The club's battery was Jim Sweeney and Frank Musgrove, formerly of Kewaunee, the champion amateur club of Illinois. At first base was A. Gardner from the Hamilton (Ontario) Clippers, Swinburne of the previous year's Golden Eagles played second, while Fred Fass and Gus Krock rounded out the infield. Dick McGraw, J. Parks and W. Keyes made up the outfield. Musgrove was offered a good contract from the Leavenworth (Kansas) club, but turned it down because he had steady employment at the Bay View Mills.

The Bay Views opened their 1886 season by beating the Welcomes 7 to 2 on May 16. The following week they beat the Quicksteps 11 to 9 before 1,200 in their new park. A week later they met Hagerty's Quicks for $300 a side. The Q's had lost Harper, their star pitcher, to the Northwestern League Milwaukees, and pitched Hobdy, with Bay View winning 14 to 9 before 1,500. Krock was credited with the win. The Views then beat the Unions, who were made up of many of last year's Golden Eagles, and the Badgers, who were the previous year's Maple Leafs and Quicksteps. The Bay Views then lost their first game, to this year's Maple Leafs. Bay View played the professional Milwaukees, losing to the Northwestern club 16 to 3 before 500 spectators at Bay View Park. The Bay Views then beat Kenosha, the Mystics, Welcomes and Lake Mills to run their record to 9 and 2.

On July 4, Bay View met the Maple Leafs for one-third of the gate receipts and $100 to the winner. The Leafs received an offer from Menomonie, Michigan, to play there for $75 and expenses, but decided to stay home. Bay View won 9 to 0. The Views then traveled to Lake Mills, losing a doubleheader, and split a two-game series at home with Hartford—the second game drawing 1,500. After whipping the Maple Leafs, the club traveled to Hartford. Krock struck out 16, but gave up 19 hits in a 16 to 2 loss.

Bay View picked up Doug Young to catch, and then beat the Golden Eagles on August 1. Later that week Gus Krock received a tempting offer from the Oshkosh club, but had trouble as his aging parents did not want him to leave his molding trade. He soon signed with Oshkosh for $200 a month. Before Young left, however, he pitched marvelously against Decatur, a team that had only lost two previous games, to Baltimore and the St. Louis Browns. Young struck out 11 on a three-hitter before 1,100 fans. Sweeney now took over on the mound and beat the Golden Eagles, with former Bay Viewer Fass pitching, 7 to 3 before 1,809 at Bay View Park. Fass came back to Bay View and beat Cambria twice.

The Bay View record was now 17 and 6. The team then lost the first game with the Silverstones for the city championship. After beating Lake Mills at the Jefferson County Fair 25 to 9, the Bay Views beat the Silverstones 13 to 3 for $75 to even the championship series. On September 19, Bay View won again to win the city championship. A week later the Bay View Club beat Hartford for the state championship. After beating the Welcomes, the Bay Views twice played a picked nine of professionals from Milwaukee and other Northwestern clubs, Gus Krock (back from Oshkosh) winning 6 to 3 before 800 at Bay View Park and then 7 to 6 before 600. The Bay Views ended 1886 with a 24 and 7 record.

Another club of interest was the Maple Leafs. In late March they organized the old club with these players: Young—c, Clayton—p, Drew—1b, Himmelstein—2b, Parker—3b, Hanrahan—ss, Delaney—lf, Bigler—cf, Murphy—rf. They arranged a game with the professional Milwaukees for May 2. For the game the Wisconsin Central provided scorecards that "were the neatest thing of the kind ever seen here."⁴⁴ After beating the professionals 4 to 3 before 1,000 spectators, the club did not amount to much.

Gus Krock — Local Bay View boy who would win 32 games in his big league career.

* * *

The minor league Milwaukee franchise waited through the 1886 winter without a manager. At the October meeting of the Northwestern League, Ted Sullivan was absent. He had been expelled from the league, presumably for disbanding his team before the season was over. It was then reported Charles Morton, ex-manager of Detroit and an organizer of the Southern League, would take over the Milwaukee club. At this meeting the Northwestern admitted La Crosse and Des Moines, expanding to an eight-club circuit. Harry Quin became acting president when H.H. Bell quit the post.

All things were not running smooth in Milwaukee. Although it had been reported Morton would take over the club, nothing was heard from him. No one was even sure what league the club would play in. As early as August the old rumor of going into the American Association began again. St. Louis of the National League was talking of disbanding, and Pittsburgh and St. Louis of the American Association were willing to join the National League. The *Sentinel* thought it was probable Milwaukee would get the opening. The *Journal* believed if this happened, the club would have to get better players, not the same Northwestern players.

If the association spot fell through, the *Sentinel* believed a new league composed of St. Louis, Chicago, Milwaukee, Kansas City, Indianapolis and St. Joseph would be formed without National Agreement protection. The *Evening Wisconsin* thought the proposal silly and was sure the Milwaukee club would be in the American Association. Some letters were received in Milwaukee assuring the club a spot in the association, and plans for a $10,000 stock company were started. However, by the time of the Northwestern League meeting, Milwaukee's chances of entering the American Association were reported to be slim. Yet another proposed league, including Milwaukee, came out of St. Joseph. This new Western League would have clubs in Kansas City, St. Joe, Omaha, Topeka or Lincoln (perhaps Des Moines and Davenport) for it southern portion and St. Paul, Milwaukee, Minneapolis and Eau Claire in the northern. A salary limit not to exceed $125 would be imposed, as it was to be "a young players' league, where they will go through the elementary branches of the National game preparatory to graduating to the National League or American Association, and it is universal throughout the world of trades and professions for new beginners to receive apprentices' salaries. They should learn also that if they desire to keep the 'school' going they will have to pay their 'tutor' by accepted moderate salaries."⁴⁵

Without a manager or a definite league, the Milwaukee club continued. In October John Barnes, manager of St. Paul, negotiated to sublet the Wright Street Park grounds in ensure the club would be in the Northwestern, but was turned down. Next Tom Loftus received a good proposition from the Kipp brothers to manage the club in 1887, with Bill Watkins, the manager of Detroit, as a partner. It was also reported Ted Sullivan had sold the Milwaukee club to Loftus for $1,000. At first it was thought the idea was to organize a new league with Cleveland, Toledo, Columbus, Indianapolis and the four best Northwestern towns included. It was later learned the intention was to secure the grounds to place an American Association team in Milwaukee. Loftus had assurances from the head of the association that a vacancy would occur, and that it would be offered to Milwaukee. All the association plans fell through, however, when it was learned the holders of the Northwestern franchise refused to permit an American Association club in Milwaukee. It was impossible to put another club in Milwaukee under the National Agreement unless the Northwestern franchise could be transferred to another city. At the American Association meeting on November 22, Milwaukee did not apply and Harry Quin stated the club would remain in the Northwestern. The *Milwaukee Journal* of December 8, 1886, had these feeling on the decision: "It looks now as though Milwaukee's unfortunate experience of past seasons in baseball is to be repeated in 1887. The best team that the city will have next year is a Northwestern league club."

Several prominent managers were after the Milwaukee Northwestern franchise and the *Sentinel* believed one should be secured immediately to sign some players before all the good ones were taken. W.R. Harrington, ex-manager of the Oshkosh club, was seeking the position but did not receive it. Meanwhile, directors of the club advertised extensively for players in the East and reportedly had five good men secured in November.

In late December James A. Hart finally secured the management of the club. Hart, 31 years old, had managed Louisville of the American Association to fifth- and fourth-place finishes the previous two years. He had absolute control of the club in every respect. That winter he was managing the Louisville club in California and Francis Richter of the *Sporting Life* called him "one of the best posted, as well as one of the most honest baseball managers in the country."[46] When Hart arrived in Milwaukee, he proved that statement by explaining he would not promise the city a pennant because of his late start, but promised a fine club with no drunks. He rented rooms at East Water and Mason Streets as his headquarters (the same building where Harry Quin had his office) and began to build his team.

Meanwhile, the Northwestern began its second season. At first Duluth and Eau Claire were not expected to be in the league. Appleton, Wisconsin, and Winona, Minnesota, were waiting to in wings. Eau Claire soon shaped up, but the other members believed Duluth was badly located and would much rather have had Winona. Duluth decided, however, to field a team. In January the Northwestern met in La Crosse. By a unanimous vote, a 10-club league was turned down. M.J. Roche of St. Paul was elected the president and continued the $1,500 bond decided upon in October. Quin remained as league secretary and treasurer. The Northwestern League for 1887 was Oshkosh, La Crosse, Milwaukee, Eau Claire, Des Moines, St. Paul, Minneapolis and Duluth. Winona, Marshalltown and Webster City (the later two in Iowa) were later made alliance clubs. The Spalding ball was chosen as the official ball. A reserve rule was devised that permitted each Northwestern club to place 14 men on its reserve list at the end of the season. Such a rule did not prevent clubs from other leagues signing Northwestern reserved players, but it was binding on all members of the Northwestern League. The league also adopted the percentage plan for the championship instead of most games won by a club. Samuel Morton, on behalf of A. G.

Spalding, offered a trophy to the champion of the Northwestern after the season, which cost $500. In order for a club to obtain permanent possession of the trophy, that club had to win three straight championships. With this new eight-club circuit, the teams would have to travel the following miles to complete their schedule:

Duluth	2,242	Minneapolis	4,726
St. Paul	5,266	Eau Claire	5,481
Oshkosh	6,008	Milwaukee	6,256
La Crosse	5,485	Des Moines	6,002

In Milwaukee Jim Hart appointed George Bailey his assistant manager. Bailey had been the official scorer in Louisville. The local club had capital stock of $25,000, divided into 250 shares. The incorporators were Hart, L.A. Hansen and H. Deffert. According to the articles of association filed, the purposes of the club were defined to be "for the development of the bodily powers by gymnastic exercises and by practice and competition in the game of baseball and other lawful games and sports."[47]

Jim Hart had to build his team from nothing, as all of the 1886 team was gone. The first player under contract was Cal Broughton, whom Milwaukeeans had already seen play, for $1,500—$200 of which was advance money. Hart next went after George Van Haltren, a 20-year-old West Coast player. All the leading clubs were attempting to sign him, but Hart thought he had a good chance. Unfortunately, he soon signed with Pittsburgh. Van Haltren would play 17 years in the big leagues, hitting .316 in addition to winning 40 games as a pitcher. By January's end, Hart almost had a set club. His catchers were Broughton, Joe Strauss, who had played in Louisville and Brooklyn of the association the year before, hitting only .219, and Jim McDonald from San Francisco, who played briefly in the American Association and National League in 1884 and '85. At first base was Tom Morrissey, who had played in Milwaukee in 1884 and with Oswego in '86. Second base was covered by Frank Reccius, a young but promising Louisville boy. Hart's shortstop and captain was Tom Forster, who had played in Milwaukee in 1885 and then went to the New York Metropolitans. Third base was doubtful with Henry Smith, a pitcher with his first professional club, temporarily covering. In left field Hart placed Leech Maskrey, a 31-year-old veteran who had been with Louisville since 1882 before going to the Western League late in the 1886 season. Hart's tentative center fielder was William Shenkle, another pitcher from Louisville who had also played third base in Decatur, Illinois, the previous year. If Hart could sign Hogan, who "places his services at an exorbitant figure,"[48] he would put him in right field. Five pitchers were under contract: Shenkle, Smith, Varney Anderson, who averaged 13 strikeouts a game at Rockford, Robert Hart, a 21-year-old from Leavenworth who ranked second in the Western League in 1886, and William Stellberger, a lefty from Adrian, Michigan. Anderson had an interesting financial set up. F.C. Lander had brought a suit against James McKee, the former Milwaukee manager, back in Rockford for $60. It seemed Anderson paid McKee and Lander $120 for securing his Milwaukee engagement. McKee and Lander had formed a combination, with Anderson agreeing to pay them 10 percent of his salary if they were successful. This was probably Milwaukee's first dealing with a player agent.

Hart soon began to strengthen the club at key positions. In early February he signed Hercules Burnett, a 22-year-old amateur from Louisville. Two weeks later he signed Arthur Hull, who previously played third base at Leadville of the Western League. Hart next signed Owen Williams, formerly of the Maple Leafs of Guelph, Ontario, for left field, moving Maskrey to right. McDonald would be moved to center field. Around the start of the season, Hart signed Henry Hines, a young Rockford catcher. Hart went into the 1887 season with these players, minus McDonald, who never showed up in Milwaukee, giving Hart 15 players.

Spring training began in mid–April with Leech Maskrey the first to arrive in Milwaukee. Practices were held at Wright Street Park. The park on Wright Street came close to not being the Northwestern grounds for 1887. As early as October of the previous year, it was rumored the club would move to more accessible grounds. Suggested sites were the State Agricultural Society grounds or Cold Spring Driving Park. However, Manager Hart soon signed a contract with the Kipp brothers for Wright Street Park, which was the best of the three sites. He began to improve the park by placing new benches in the grandstand, thus increasing the seating capacity, in addition to adding hitching posts in a vacant lot across from the grounds. Work on the grounds was completed for some exhibition games before the start of the season. Once the season started, the *Evening Wisconsin* found one fault with the park. "The management of the Milwaukees should provide at least one more ticket office at the Wright Street Park and another entrance. It was almost impossible to secure tickets ... owing to the immense crowd gathered at the entrance."[49]

Hart arranged for practice and exhibition games in Milwaukee because he considered going south, which was becoming more common, a useless expense. The players had all arrived by April 17, when they beat the Chicago Whitings 9 to 2 before 2,000 to 3,000 at Wright Street Park. Only Morrissey was out, due to an injured hand he had arrived with. After besting Kalamazoo of the Ohio State League twice, the Milwaukees lost to the Chicago White Stockings future Hall of Fame pitcher John Clarkson, 8 to 6. The exhibition season was concluded with a win over Madison University (University of Wisconsin) on April 28. In these six games, the team had a .326 batting average, with Maskrey hitting .483, Reccius .440 and Forster .400 (keeping in mind walks counted as hits for the 1887 season).

The season was at hand and Jim Hart had ideas to improve attendance. First he announced clergymen would be admitted free, prompting the *Sentinel* to report "such an announcement is likely to develop a large increase in the number of divines residing in the city."[50] To cut down on rowdiness, Hart admitted members of the police force free by showing their badges. As there was no great demand for season tickets, Hart decided not to sell them. Single game admission was set at 25 cents, with a grandstand seat an extra quarter. Nearly, 10,000 pocket schedules were distributed, and the Wisconsin Central Railroad's offer to furnish free scorecards to patrons was accepted. Ladies were admitted free every day except Saturday and Sunday, although free with a gentleman on Saturday. All persons "of questionable character"[51] were to be refused admission. The players were to look sharp on the field with two new uniforms. At home they wore white flannel shirts, caps and pants, with blue stockings and belts; on the road they donned white shirts, dark trousers and caps with red stockings and belts.

The season opened on April 30 and "The 9 of Hart's"[52]— as dubbed by a leading sporting paper — won their first six games, beating Eau Claire and Duluth three times each in Milwaukee. The club then turned around and lost three straight to St. Paul, dropping from first place. During these first two weeks the club had some difficulties. First, Robert Hart hurt his arm, unable to pitch until the last game of the St. Paul series. Anderson, Smith and Shenkle carried the staff, as Bill Stellberger was released to Duluth when that club was in town. Hull was soon injured and out for a while. Next Forster was hit in the face by a pitch, fracturing his jaw and breaking two teeth, forcing him out of the lineup for two weeks. Hart was forced to change his infield, putting Morrissey at third, Strauss at short and his utility players on the right side of the infield. Once Hull and Forster were back, Hercules

Burnett and Henry Hines were released. Milwaukee finished off the homestand by beating Minneapolis two of three. In third place with an 8 an 4 record, the club was first in the league in hitting with a .375 average and second to Duluth in runs scored.

1887 Milwaukee Club — *Rows left to right from top:* Tom Morrissey, Tom Forster, Arthur Hull, Joe Strauss, Frank Reccius, James A. Hart, William Stellberger, Henry Smith, Hercules Burnett, team mascot (Jim Hart's son), Robert Hart, Varney Anderson, Cal Broughton, Leach Maskrey, Owen Williams, Harry Hines (Historic Photograph Collection/Milwaukee Public Library).

The Milwaukee team then traveled to Des Moines and won all three games to recapture first place. The team returned home to be greeted by several hundred fans at the depot. After splitting two games with La Crosse, the Milwaukees beat Oshkosh five out of six to pull three games into first place. The homestand ended with two wins in three games with La Crosse, and on June 7 the *Sentinel* wrote of the club: "LESSONS IN BALL; The Home Team Gives Them to Outside Clubs."

Traveling to La Crosse, Jim Hart's men won their twentieth game before losing their first road game. Second-place St. Paul then pulled within one game of Milwaukee with a 7 to 3 victory; the rest of the series was rained out. The club again had to fight injuries. Reccuis hurt his ankle, to go along with Muskrey's lame leg and Broughton's sore eye. Hart signed Elmer Roussey, recently released by Eau Claire, to play second base. The bad weather followed the Milwaukee team to Duluth, where only one game could be played, with Smith winning it. The club then split two in Minneapolis to remain one game in front of St. Paul.

Back in Milwaukee the club played two exhibitions. First, there was a Sunday exhibition game with Oshkosh, Milwaukee winning 6 to 4 before 2,500 at Wright Street Park. The next day, June 20, the Philadelphia Phillies of the National League came to town. Only 1,200 attended as Anderson lost, 7 to 5, when the Phillies scored four runs in the eighth inning.

Milwaukee won two of its next three games at home, but it was apparent to everyone that the team needed a third baseman. Strauss and Hull were there for the time, but neither was making it. Hart expected to sign a third sacker, but wanted to wait until a first-class player was available. Meanwhile, he went with Strauss at third, Hull moving to center field, Forster to second and Roussey to shortstop. Frank Reccuis was released, followed by

Robert Hart, who was 0 and 3 on the season. The lineup now set, Hart's boys beat Des Moines two of three to stay in first place, with Strauss "accomplishing wonders"[53] at third. After losing two of three in La Crosse, the Milwaukees beat Oshkosh six straight and La Crosse four straight, but second-place St. Paul stayed close. Hart managed to get himself into trouble during this winning streak. In Oshkosh he was arrested for striking a lad who was insulting his son, who was the team mascot. Hart was fined $25 and costs after he pled guilty to assault. Hart again made a few changes in his team. First he signed Mills, the Lake Mills catcher. He then released Arthur Hull and signed Benny Stevens, who had hit .403 in 26 games at Eau Claire, to play first base for the injured Morrissey. When Morrissey returned, Stevens went to center field. The Milwaukees then went into Des Moines and lost all three games, but still held a slim half-game lead over St. Paul for first place.

Meanwhile, controversy arose in the Northwestern League. First players and managers began to complain about the quality of the Spalding balls. The complaint was that the balls were "soft, spongy and without vitality."[54] After a few innings they were unfit for play. A Northwestern League rule provided that the home club supply two new balls and when these were gone, three old ones. Clubs were having problems. The *St. Paul Globe* wrote the balls sounded like sausage when hit. Spalding claimed these balls were for amateur use and Harry Quin had ordered the wrong balls. Quin denied this, and finally things were settled. Then Quin decided to quit his post as secretary-treasurer of the league. Manager Bryon of Des Moines had accused Quin of owning the Milwaukee club "body and soul, while Jim Hart is only a figure head," and thought Quin should be removed as "he is far from being an impartial man and it is only natural that he should want the Milwaukee team to win when he is so largely interested in its financial welfare."[55] Quin stated his father made $10,000 a year in a stationery business in Milwaukee, and he did not care for his $500 salary. But others sided with Bryon. Later, when Roche resigned as president, he stated that while Quin was handling the umpires, it was common talk that no umpire dared to do the fair thing by teams visiting Milwaukee. In any event, Quin resigned on July 20 and Sam Morton took his place.

Milwaukee won 9 of 14 on its next homestand to be a comfortable three games ahead of Des Moines going into August. Two points of interest in this homestand were the July 19 and 26 games. On July 19 fans got their first real doubleheader, seeing two games for the price of one; attendance was 1,000 — good for a Tuesday. Then on July 26 the team hit hour home runs (Roussey two, Shenkle and Stevens one apiece), quite unusual for those days. The Milwaukees then traveled to Duluth and Eau Claire, two tail-enders, winning four of five. After splitting two in St. Paul, Hart's team lost two of three in Minneapolis. Milwaukee was now 4½ games in front of the field.

❋ ❋ ❋

Not enough is known of the local baseball scene in 1887. Unfortunately, information is sketchy. In early March a Milwaukee City Baseball League was formed with six clubs: the Bay Views, Nationals, Welcomes, North Milwaukees, Badgers and Gold Eagles. A week later another meeting was held and a constitution and by-laws were adopted. Five clubs formally entered the league — Bay View, Nationals, Welcomes, Silverstones and Regulators. Each club was to play five games against each other, with National Park, Bay View Park and Cold Spring Driving Park used as the league grounds. The uniform colors were to be as follows: Bay Views—brown, Nationals—grey, Welcomes—blue, Silverstones—light grey, and Regulators—dark blue. A local man put up a $100 medal for the champions. On March 30 it was reported the Badgers, not the Regulators, would be the fifth club. Then on April 11 the Cream City Club became that fifth club, with John Haggerty as its manager. On Sunday, April 24, the City League series began at Bay View Park, with 400 spectators watching Bay View beat the Welcomes 12 to 3.

Soon a second league, the Cream City League, was formed. Included were the Keystones, Bay View Stars, Metropolitans, Phoenix, Planets and Whites. Each team in this league was to play 18 games each for a "handsomely engraved silver cup."[56] Admission to Cream City championship games was 10 cents, and 15 cents for grandstand seats.

The City League soon ran into trouble. Carrier, the secretary of the league, resigned to take charge of the Bay Views; Eugene Casey replaced him. In June it was reported the league was tottering and would not hold out much longer. The action of the Silverstones quitting the league was said to be the cause. At the time Bay View was leading the league with a 5 and 0 record. Nothing else is known of the City League, and we must assume it folded. In late June manager Schloegel of the Welcomes accepted Bay View manager McIver's challenge for a $100-a-side game, provided the same players were on the field that the Welcomes beat a few days previous. This certainly does not sound like a league action. Incidentally, the Welcomes did win the game 4 to 2. James Sweeney, the star Bay View pitcher, signed with the Neillsville club for $100 a month, plus expenses. In July the Bay View Club and park were transferred to a new company.

Meanwhile, the Cream City League was still in operation. The Planets, Keystones, Phoenix and Bay View Stars were still in the league, but now the Silverstones and Fortunes also belonged. Then on August 12 the league expelled the Phoenix club. The Planets, the first-place club, resigned. These two clubs were replaced by the Maroons and Cream Cities. In September it was reported the Cream Cities had not lost a game since joining the league, but nothing else is known of the Cream City League.

The Maple Leafs again organized in 1887, making the twelfth straight year a club had organized under this name. They were considered the strongest local amateur club with the likes of Doug Young, Pat Sullivan, Pete Sexton, Tom Delaney, Zach Clayton and others. Unfortunately, no record of any games in which they played can be found.

Others organized and played out-of-town clubs. In April Bay View took it on the chin from Racine College. In July the Quicksteps beat the Watertown Mutuals 13 to 2. The Phoenix traveled to Watertown in August and lost, but later beat that club in a $50 game. Later that month the Welcomes traveled to Rock County and beat the Beloit Blues before losing to Janesville. In September the Keystones traveled to Columbus and lost 11 to 6. One Illinois club, the Posters of Chicago, traveled into Milwaukee and were defeated by the Jay Gould's, 20 to 19, at Wright Street Park. The first local game this season had been played on April 17, with Bay View defeating the Cream Cities 7 to 6. The same two clubs played the last game of 1887 on November 6, with Bay View again winning 9 to 4.

✻ ✻ ✻

Back home the Northwestern, Milwaukee club prepared to play Oshkosh, who had lost 12 of their last 13 games. Oshkosh won both games. After losing one and winning one from second-place Des Moines, the two teams played to a 6 to 6 tie, leaving Milwaukee four games in front of the Iowa team. Milwaukeeans were proud of the club's position and the *Evening Wisconsin* of August 20, 1887, pointed out one main reason:

> In spite of the fact that Des Moines, Oshkosh, St. Paul and in fact all the clubs in the Northwestern League have been expanding a great deal of money in securing new and valuable players, Manager Hart has pursued an even tenor, and made but two changes in the Milwaukee team, at the same time keeping up a lead.

After splitting an exhibition series in Rockford, Hart secured Lou Sylvester, an outfielder recently released by the St. Louis Browns, to shore up his infield. La Crosse then came to town and Milwaukee won three of the five games played. Varney Anderson failed to appear for the first game of the series and was fined $50, but the money was remitted when it was learned he stayed in Rockford because he was sick. Also Bishop, the Lake Mills pitcher, was signed to fill the gap created when Smith severely strained his ankle. Hart's team then traveled into Iowa and lost two of three to second-place Des Moines.

With a month to go in the season, Milwaukee held first place (57–33), Des Moines second (54–35), St. Paul third (57–37) and Oshkosh fourth (52–38). The Milwaukee club was in a bad way for a pitcher. Anderson was the only regular ready to go. Shenkle had a lame arm and Smith's ankle showed no signs of recovering. Bishop would be pressed into service more often. The *Daily Review* detected another problem. "The Milwaukees do not seem to be as well up in team work as they should be. One to watch their play must arrive at the conclusion that each individual player is striving to build up an individual record, spurred on probably by the hope that next season managers of the National League clubs will be attracted to them by the record when looking about for good material."[57]

Oshkosh came to town next and the Sawdust City team won all three games. During the first game the Milwaukees were "assailed by scoffing remarks from the hoodlum element present."[58] Hart claimed the criticism was undeserved and the *Oshkosh Northwestern* wrote the following:

> Manager Hart is of the opinion that Des Moines will take the championship. He intimates he is not anxious to have first place, for he claims that the Milwaukee people do not care anything about his club and he is sure the players are not particularly fascinated with Milwaukee. He says he does not know whether he will manage a team in the Northwestern League next year or not.[59]

When asked about this by a *Daily Review* reporter, Hart admitted saying this and further stated that in the previous day's game (a win over Duluth), a crowd of only 200 had attended. Receipts were $50, of which he had to pay Duluth $75, and his own expenses were $100 a day. On top of this, the *Sentinel* was after Roussey, believing his work at shortstop had demoralized the whole team. He was benched for one game, but was right back in the lineup as the team took four from Duluth. Milwaukee was still on top of the Northwestern with a 61 and 36 record, but Oshkosh (61–38) and St. Paul (61–39) were closing in. Henry Smith, with a 20 and 10 record, asked Hart for his release because of his injured foot and he went home. Hart replaced him with George Washington McGinnis. "Jumbo" had been in the American Association since its inception in 1882, pitching for St. Louis until going to Baltimore in the middle of the 1886 season. McGinnis had started 1887 with Cincinnati and had won 102 games in the association until his arm gave out. McGinnis claimed he was fit to pitch now. Hart then signed another pitcher, O.K. Fitzsimmons, from Omaha.

Shenkle lost to last-place Eau Claire before Anderson beat that team 17 to 7, before only 400 in Milwaukee. Fitzsimmons next gave up 7 runs in four innings, but Shenkle came in and finally won the game. McGinnis then lost the second game of the doubleheader to drop Milwaukee from first place. Fitzsimmons and Elmer Roussey were released. With Forster at short and Maskrey at second, the club beat Duluth in a one-game stay. Minneapolis came to town and lost three, putting Milwaukee back in first place. McGinnis came up with a lame arm, and Broughton became sick with a big series against St. Paul coming up, so Hart went out to sign Ed Cushman.

The first games of this crucial series were played in Milwaukee. Owing to an argument over the batting order of St. Paul in the first inning, the first game was late getting underway and Shenkle won a five-inning decision 8 to 3. After a rainout, Milwaukee lost 5 to 0 — the first time they were shut out in 1887. In what was supposed to be the last home game of the year, 2,000 fans saw Ed Cushman, who had been signed for $50 a game to replace McGinnis, win 4 to 3. Shenkle lost in St. Paul, as Milwaukee and Oshkosh were tied for first place with 69 and 40 records. Des Moines was in third place (67–42) and St. Paul in fourth (67–43). Anderson then lost to drop Milwaukee into second place. The teams then split the last two games of the series.

In Minneapolis the Milwaukees won two of three to stay in second place. The club unexpectedly finished at home when Hart made arrangements with Duluth and Eau Claire to come to Milwaukee. On Sunday, October 2, Oshkosh came into town and 4,500 jammed into Wright Street Park to see the battle for first place. But when Oshkosh learned Cushman would pitch, they refused to play a championship game, and the 13 to 3 victory for Milwaukee did not count in the standings. Oshkosh took home $350 for its share of the exhibition game. Milwaukee then beat Duluth three straight games to stay in second place, only .005 of a percentage point behind Oshkosh. Anderson then beat Eau Claire to pull even closer. The next game Cushman won to put the Milwaukees in first place (77–43) over Oshkosh (73–41) by .002 percent points. On October 10 Oshkosh won two from Minneapolis to regain first place over idle Milwaukee. The next day Milwaukee beat Eau Claire 9 to 3, but Oshkosh again beat Minneapolis to win the Northwestern pennant.

Jim Hart quickly announced there still was a chance Milwaukee could take the pennant. He had appealed to the league to have the game lost in Minneapolis on the last trip thrown out because Murphy, who played for Minneapolis, had not been released by Oshkosh. If upheld, Milwaukee would win the championship. Later that month the league refused to throw out the game on the rule that allowed a club to play a man in five games on trial before signing him. Oshkosh was formally given the championship. The official Northwestern League standings for 1887 were:

	W	L	Pct		W	L	Pct
Oshkosh	76	41	.649	Minneapolis	53	65	.449
Milwaukee	78	43	.644	La Crosse	45	77	.369
Des Moines	73	45	.619	Duluth	40	76	.345
St. Paul	75	48	.610	Eau Claire	39	84	.317

A banquet was held for the players the night after the last game at A.C. Schieldt's, 710 Twelfth Street (later address, 2040 North Twelfth Street). Joe Strauss, who had finished first in the Northwestern in fielding for third basemen, was presented a handsome gold medal. Afterward the club disbanded for the winter.

Jim Hart's team had played well. All three of the top-line pitchers had won 20 or more games. Shenkle ranked third in the Northwestern in earned runs per game (1.89), while Anderson was fifth (2.05) and Smith eleventh (2.65). The club hit for a .305 average (seventh in the league), led by Williams' .396 (fourth best in the Northwestern). Because of the inflated averages (due to walks counting as hits), eight players hit over .300 on the club.

The other regulars over the mark were Maskrey (.366), Strauss (.340), Morrissey (.308), Forster (.308) and Broughton (.303). The club was also fourth in team fielding and stolen bases.

The Northwestern's second season was to be its last. All the clubs were paying double the salaries of 1886, ranging from $1,200 to $1,800 a month. Oshkosh was paying about $2,500 a month. As early as July, Eau Claire thought of dropping out for financial reasons. In August La Crosse had only $16 in its treasury and thought of disbanding. At season's end first-place Oshkosh had lost $20,000 and La Crosse about $12,000. Des Moines cleared around $3,000 and St. Paul finished a couple hundred dollars ahead. Milwaukee's profit was between $6,000 and $8,000. For the most part, local crowds were good. On a Saturday and Sunday in late May the club took in $2,200. Unfavorable weather in June cost the club about $1,300, Hart estimated. A Saturday game in July drew 3,500 people, for the largest non–Sunday attendance that season. Crowds slimmed down toward season's end, but the profit was still there.

A new league was being formed, and the *Sentinel* on October 12, 1887, said good-bye to the Northwestern League.

> With the exception of a few incidents ... the Northwestern League has been a great success, and has opened up the way for a larger and better league next year. As it was a great improvement over the Northwestern League of the previous year, so it may be justly expected that the new Western Association projected for next year will be comparatively free from the evils that trouble this year's league.

Top: William Shenkle would pitch 3 seasons in Milwaukee, producing the Northwestern League's third-best ERA in l88 (Historic Photograph Collection/Milwaukee Public Library). *Bottom:* Leach Maskrey — solid player who would lead the 1887 team with a .366 batting average (Historic Photograph Collection/Milwaukee Public Library).

9

Western Association (1888–1890)

The Northwestern League's two-year stay had strengthened the foundations of minor league baseball in the West. It was time to organize a new and stronger league. Back in July of 1887, Jim Hart, in a letter to the *Sporting Life*, developed a plan for the formation of a new league for 1888 to include Milwaukee, Chicago, St. Louis, Omaha, Kansas City, St. Paul, Minneapolis and Des Moines. The plan seemed feasible. By late August word was in the press that a new league would be formed for 1888.

On September 27 representatives from nine cities met at the Tremont House in Chicago to set up this new league, the Western Association. Sam Morton, secretary of the Northwestern League, was elected chairman over delegates from the eight cities that Hart had mentioned in his letter, in addition to Lincoln, Nebraska. Chris Von der Ahe, owner of the St. Louis American Association team, also owned the St. Louis Western franchise, and wanted to use this new league as a training school for "der Browns."[1] The other clubs did not care for his idea and Lincoln was admitted instead of St. Louis to form the eight-club circuit. On October 26 the clubs met again and formally united. The delegates had a change of heart and admitted St. Louis into the league, cutting Lincoln. The constitution of the National League was adopted, with bonds of $1,500. The guarantee to visiting clubs was set at $100, with clubs receiving 30 percent of the receipts on all days except Decoration Day and the Fourth of July, when receipts would be divided equally. Samuel Morton was elected president, secretary and treasurer of the Western Association.

The new league had some detractors. Some thought it was a ploy by Albert Spalding to keep the American Association out of Chicago. Others wondered why Oshkosh was not in the Western. After all, it had won the Northwestern pennant. Rumor had been that the Oshkosh club would be transferred to Chicago. It was generally believed, however, the Western Association would be the strongest minor league in the country.

In Milwaukee a few issues were making news concerning the Western club. Back in August the *St. Louis Republican* announced that Jim Hart was anxious to secure the Louisville club of the American Association. In October Hart announced he was indeed attempting to buy the association club and transfer it to Milwaukee. Hart could then mix the two clubs and have players left to sell. If Milwaukee entered the American Association, it was believed Oshkosh would replace the franchise in the Western Association. Hart offered President Phelps of Louisville $15,000, but Phelps wanted $25,000, and the deal fell through. Then a rumor went about that Hart had been offered the manager's job of the Kansas City team, and would go there, before he announced he would remain in Milwaukee.

Before long there was trouble in Kansas City. From St. Louis came dispatches that Kansas City was withdrawing from the Western to take a place in the American Association. It was believed that K.C. would replace the outgoing New York Metropolitans and either Duluth or Oshkosh would enter the Western. Most expressed doubt, however. It was not believed the Kansas City people would pay the $15,000 demanded for the New York franchise. If they did, it would be doubtful that the other clubs would substitute a town like Oshkosh for Kansas City. Manager Manges of Kansas City decided to stay in the Western Association, saying that there was no assurance attendance would be better in the American Association. Milwaukee thus became the most desirable candidate for the American Association vacancy. The club would have jumped at the opportunity in the past, but was not tempted this time. For one, the association's long-standing 25-cent admission charge was changed to 50 cents for 1888. Hart also told the *Sentinel* that the club would probably end near the bottom in the American Association — at an increased price. He was confident in the Western Association.

War almost broke out when Kansas City was admitted to the American Association in January. This franchise was not awarded to the Western club, but to another group. Although the *Sentinel* believed the two K.C. clubs would merge, Menges stated he would remain in the Western and "they [the American Association] will starve, as I have the grounds, low price of admission, and the best team."[2] The American Association club then asked the arbitration committee of the two leagues to shut out the Western Association club on the grounds that it was a violation of the National Agreement's territorial rights. The American Association club held the franchise of the previous year's Western League club in Kansas City and made the claim on that point. If the arbitration committee ruled against the Western Association, it vowed to start war. The Western Association stated the Southern, Western, Southwestern and a half-dozen eastern leagues would be invited to join a compact and boycott the two major leagues, blacklisting any player who left a minor league for those circuits. As we shall see, the National League and American Association realized about $15,000 from the minor leagues for protection, and the boycott threat was apparently enough to settle the issue. As it turned out, both leagues would play in Kansas City in 1888.

The above-mentioned protection money was received because of a new rule agreed to by the major and minor leagues. In December of 1887 the arbitration committee had proposed that at the end of each season, the league and association be permitted to select two of the best players in all of the minor associations, throw them into a pot, and select them. The minor leagues would have the privilege of reserving all others. This proposal was unanimously rejected by the minors. The committee then granted the minor leagues proposal that each minor league of six or more clubs receive the privilege of reserving players by paying $50 annually for membership and not more than $2,000 annually for protection. The right of reservation had to be claimed before March 1 and each club could reserve 14 players, with notice given before October 10 of each year. The agreement saved the minors from extinction by major league player raids in the off-season.

Further changes were taking place in the Western Association. Manager Seeley of Omaha signed nine of the Oshkosh club's players in December, stopping all thought of Oshkosh joining the Western. Then the Minneapolis franchise was sold to W.E. Gooding, a former city ticket agent for the Burlington Road, for $7,000. It was soon discovered the Kansas City club was $9,000 in debt, including a deficit in the treasury of $7,871—the remaining being the mortgage on the grandstand — but vowed to stay in the Western. The Western Association was now ready for the 1888 season.

Manager Hart in Milwaukee began the process of assembling a team. Henry Smith's injury was worse than feared and he appeared to be permanently disabled. To fill this pitching gap, Hart attempted to sign the local boy, Gus Krock, who was offered $325 a month, but declined saying the Milwaukee fans were too hard on the home players. He soon signed with the Chicago White Stockings. To put Hart's $325 a month offer into the financial picture of the times, these average weekly wages were taken from the February 29, 1888, *Milwaukee Sentinel*: Bricklayer—$21.00; baker—$12.75; carpenter-$15.00; common laborer—$8.00; plumber—$18.00; railway fireman—$12.00. In addition to losing Smith to the injury, Hart lost more players to other clubs. Tom Morrissey and Varney Anderson signed with St. Paul. Cal Broughton signed with Detroit. Hart had offered Broughton a $50 a month increase, but the National League club offered more. Owen Williams was lost to Davenport and Ed Cushman to Des Moines.

Remaining from the 1887 club were Frank Mills, Bill Shenkle, Joe Strauss, Tom Forster and Leech Maskrey. To fill his gaps, Hart signed William Fuller, a good hitting catcher from the Kalamazoo club who also had played shortstop in the Southern League. To replace Morrissey at first base, Andy Cusick, who had played in Philadelphia since 1884 as a part-time player, was signed. Second base went to Pat Pettee, a high-priced player from Salem of the Eastern League. Holdovers Forster and Strauss finished the infield. For the outfield Hart selected Robert Lowe for left, who had played in Eau Claire in 1887, his first professional year. Lowe would go on to fame in the next decade with the Boston Beaneaters of the National League. In eighteen years in the big leagues, Bobby would hit for a .273 average with 70 home runs, including four consecutive home runs on May 30, 1894. In center field was David J. Davin from the Portland (Maine) club. Maskrey continued in right.

To strengthen the pitching, Alex Ferson was signed, formerly of Manchester of the New England League. The *San Francisco Call* said of Ferson, "He is a very rank twirler, as wild as an Apache, no judgment, and sure death to his catcher."[3] Hart still liked him. Next Hart signed Jack Horner and Edward Warner of Maryland. They were known as the Siamese twins, as they had grown up and played ball together on smaller clubs until 1886 when they signed with Rochester of the International League. In 1887 the two played with Hamilton (Canada). To complete the club Hart signed John Quincy Adams Struck, a Louisville boy who played his first professional ball in Little Rock of the Southwestern League the previous year. The *Evening Wisconsin* quoted Hart as saying, "I have exercised a great deal of care this season in selecting the players, and I think we have the best club in the northwest. My directors are liberal, and we will have good men for good money judiciously expanded. I know something about ball playing, and I know I have a good team."[4] Hart declared that the 1888 Milwaukees would cost about $5,000 more in salaries than 1887, or a 40 percent increase.

The Western Association began to make ready for the new season. The schedule committee released the schedule in March, with the northern clubs opening in the south. Each club was scheduled to play 126 games, from April 28 through October 9. Des Moines was the only city where Sunday games were not allowed; Milwaukee received 12 home Sunday games on the schedule. Milwaukee's home opener was slated for May 22. Clubs in the Western were to travel more than 60,700 miles—Minneapolis (6,404), St. Paul (6,696), Milwaukee (7,455), St. Louis (7,694), Kansas City (7,733), Omaha (8,190), Des Moines (8,287) and Chicago (8,256)—averaging 7,590 apiece. At an average of 3 cents per mile, this came to $227.70 per man, with 14 men per club. This made each club's traveling expenses about $3,187 or $25,500 for all eight clubs. Other trips would probably swell this total to about $30,000. Umpires were also appointed at an annual salary of $1,000, plus traveling expenses. They wore a neat light blue uniform while working the games. Newspapers began finding nicknames for the clubs. St. Paul had been known as the Apaches, but was called the Man Killers or Apostles this year. Omaha players were called Omahogs or Emigrants. The St. Louis Whites were also known as the Red Lions and Chicago as Apprentices. Milwaukee players were tagged Tame Rabbits, while Minneapolis men took Minnies. The Kansas City Blues were sometimes called the Cowboys or Duelists, and Des Moines players were known as the Prohibitionists.

Back in Milwaukee, a decision was being made on playing grounds. Wright Street Park was no longer acceptable. The grounds were inadequate both for ball playing and comfort of spectators. Besides this, the proprietors were demanding a higher rental. New sites were being considered. These grounds had to be more accessible, of more ample size, and arranged for large crowds. The baseball directors also wanted the new park to be suitable to any sport, such as lacrosse and football in the fall. A circular track of one-fifth of a mile was wanted inside. A shooting gallery and bowling alley were also proposed.

Four sites were proposed. John A. Hinsey, a cable car man, had two in mind. The first, between Twentieth and Twenty-first, Cedar (Kilbourn) and State streets, was a 600 x 300-foot plot of land. Of course, Hinsey's lines would be there. Another was between Sixteenth and Eighteenth on Lloyd. This site depended upon the city council passing an ordinance enabling Hinsey to run his West Side Cable Company lines past there. On October 24 the council passed the Hinsey cable ordinance, seeming to

Bobby Lowe would go on to have an 18-year career in the big leagues.

assure the park there, as Hinsey promised to defray some of the cost of the proposed 7,000-seat double-deck grandstand stadium, on the 800 x 465-foot tract of land. Peter McGeoch, of the Milwaukee Line, quickly offered to equal Hinsey's cost. A third was in Whitefish Bay, where the Whitefish Bay Railroad Company offered a 600-foot square tract of land rent-free for five years. It was accessible by rail over the Milwaukee, Lake Shore & Western and the Chicago & Northwestern Roads. Plans for a streetcar to take 2,000 people to the site were also proposed.

The club, however, wanted to buy the new site outright, so they favored the fourth site, between West Chambers and Burleigh and North Seventh and Eighth Streets. Ephraim Mariner, the owner of the Lloyd Street grounds, did not wish to sell, but would give a five-year lease on the grounds. The Chambers Street grounds were 588 x 366, smaller than those at Lloyd, but larger than Wright Street Park's dimensions. The Broadway, Third and Eighth Street branches of the McGeoch lines all ran to Chambers Street; Becker's Twelfth Street line was only five blocks away, and the Cream City Road was to build an extension. In February the club purchased the land on Chambers Street for $25,000 from A. L. Carey and Somers & Meagan.[5] After improvements the total cost was estimated at $35,000, and the *Journal* reported only the Polo Grounds in New York was bigger than Milwaukee's park. In accessibility it was no better than Wright Street Park, but centrally located grounds were impossible to find. The *Chicago Times* claimed the park was too far from the central city, although the *Sentinel* disagreed, writing it took only 35 minutes from the center of town, while Wright Street Park took 30 minutes to reach. It was noted that very few cities had grounds that could be reached in less than 30 minutes. The horse car companies guaranteed it would only take 25 minutes to go from the corner of Grand Avenue and West Water Street (North Plankinton) to the park. The *Sentinel* put forth another reason for abandoning Wright Street Park.

> The grounds just north of Wright Street Park will be broken shortly for the erection of a Catholic Church [St. Bonifactus—on 11th Street between Clarke and Center Streets]. This is the principal reason why the directors of the Milwaukee Baseball Club did not want to lease the old grounds, as this will eventually prevent the playing of Sunday games.[6]

Work on the park began in late March by Edward V. Koch & Co. and by contract had to be done by May 15, at a cost of $7,800. George Walthers was appointed groundskeeper of Athletic Park, as it was to be called. Walthers, a nephew of Solomon Juneau, had been in charge of the Wright Street Park grounds since they were first converted into a baseball park. The Chamber Street grounds were above the level of the street and fairly level, but still 8,600 yards of dirt were needed for fill. Total cost for the field was $2,600. The grounds were ready for opening day. Shortly after a scoreboard was erected, giving the inning-by-inning score of the game in progress and scores of the other Western games.

Seating capacity at Athletic Park was only 4,800—grandstand 1,000, pavilions 1,300 and bleaching boards 2,500. The ticket scale was 50 cents in the grandstand, 35 cents in the pavilions and 25 cents on the bleachers. Also 16 private boxes on top of the grandstand were erected, each with room for a dozen or more people. In charge of the ticket office was again George Bailey, who received a suggestion from the *Daily Review* to improve the facilities for selling tickets as in "the rush to get tickets numerous hats were smashed"[7] before opening day. The club decided there would again be no season tickets sold this year. Women were admitted free to Athletic Park every day except Sunday, Milwaukee being the only city in the country where women were admitted free. And this cost the ball club, for the manager of the home club had to pay 7 cents to the visiting team for each woman admitted free. The management also sold scorecards that gave the playing rules, averages of the home club from week to week, latest baseball news and several other features—all for only a nickel. In April Phil Lederer, a local businessman, issued 15,000 pocket schedules that gave the dates of the National League, American Association and Western Association games. On May 15, 1888, the *Evening Wisconsin* gave this suggestion: "There is one disgraceful evil which the directors of the Milwaukee club should wipe out this year, and that is the peddling of beer among the spectators in the grandstand."

Because of the Western schedule starting with the northern clubs opening in the south, Hart had his players report to Louisville on April 13, becoming the last Western club to start. The next day they played the Louisville Eclipse of the American Association and lost 8 to 5, as Shenkle gave up 13 hits. The following day Hart's men lost again, 9 to 4, before 3,500 Louisville fans. The team then practiced in Louisville for a week before traveling to New Albany (Indiana), where Struck won a game. The team then traveled to Lafayette

(Indiana), where Shenkle won 23 to 3. The Milwaukees then beat the Deppin club of Louisville before beating Peoria and Danville, then losing to Bloomington (Illinois) of the International League to finish the exhibition season. The *Evening Wisconsin* ran this editorial for the start of the 1888 season:

> The Western Association, though in its infancy, is strong, will be balanced and backed by wealth and enterprise. At no time in the history of the national game has there been as strong organization in the country outside of the National League and the American Association as the Western Association is.[8]

The regular season started on Saturday, April 28, at St. Louis. Shenkle started, but nine errors by his teammates—4 by Forster—caused his downfall and the Whites won 14 to 1, with no earned runs being scored.

ST. LOUIS		AB	R	H	SB	MILWAUKEE		AB	R	H	SB
Nicholson	2b	5	0	0	0	Forster	ss	4	0	0	0
Beckley	1b	4	2	2	0	Lowe	lf	3	0	0	0
Crooks	3b	5	2	3	0	Strauss	3b	4	1	2	2
Burch	lf	5	3	2	0	Davin	cf	3	0	0	0
Herr	ss	5	2	2	1	Maskrey	rf	4	0	1	0
Hines	rf	5	2	2	1	Pettee	2b	3	0	1	0
Kenyon	cf	5	1	1	0	Cusick	1b	3	0	1	1
Dolan	c	5	1	0	0	Shenkle	p	3	0	1	0
Staley	p	4	1	2	0	Mills	c	3	0	0	0
		43	14	14	2			30	1	6	3

```
              1 2 3 4 5 6 7 8 9
St. Louis     1 0 0 1 0 6 4 2 0—14
Milwaukee     0 0 0 1 0 0 0 0 0— 1
```

Afterward the *Journal* wrote "that game [was] a sad blow to the Milwaukee people who placed great confidence in the team after their tour among the little flick in the Inter-state League."[9] After two rain postponements, Horner lost to the Whites 8 to 3.

The Milwaukees then traveled to Kansas City where Ferson was whipped 18 to 2, causing the *Journal* to suggest the club write a book entitled "What We Don't Know About Baseball."[10] After a postponed rain game, Shenkle won the club's first game 13 to 7. On to Omaha, Horner won, giving Omaha its first defeat. Three games in a row were then rained out. The bad weather followed to Des Moines, where the first game was rained out. Shenkle lost a game, but then the city's levee gave way and Des Moines' ballpark was under three feet of water. The Milwaukees then traveled up to Minneapolis, where wet grounds postponed the first game there. Milwaukee then won two of the three games.

The club was to travel into St. Paul next, but the Mississippi River overflowed there, flooding the grounds. The St. Paul games were then transferred to Milwaukee. On Saturday, May 19, the Milwaukees should have opened at Athletic Park, but were rained out. The Milwaukee team had a 4 and 5 record, good for a tie for fourth in the Western Association. The club was strong in every department except pitching, so Hart signed a new pitcher, George Stephens, from the Hiawatha Club of Detroit. Alex Ferson was gone. The club had lost about $4,000 already due to the rainy weather. On this first road trip, three Sunday games were lost and one played, bringing in only $140.

The home opener in Milwaukee was played on Sunday, May 20, before 7,000 to 8,000 spectators. When Forster, the first Milwaukee player to appear for practice, came out, "no

Roman gladiator was ever received with more joyous applause."[11] Shenkle went on to beat St. Paul 9 to 5. The following day Horner lost to St. Paul 2 to 1, with a little less than 2,000 in attendance. Chicago then came to town and Milwaukee beat the Maroons three of four, Stephens winning two before good crowds.

During the Chicago series both Davin and Pettee were injured, so Hart put Shenkle in center field and Mills at second base. Davin's injury was slight and he soon returned, but Pettee, who made $100 a week, had a badly hurt ankle. Minneapolis then came into town and lost two of three. St. Paul was next, and after Shenkle's 13 to 4 loss, Hart decided Shenkle had been doing such poor work he would keep him out for a week or so. Shenkle's record was 4 and 4, and it was discovered he had a lame arm. Struck then got his first chance and beat St. Paul 3 to 1. Stephens and Horner lost the remaining two games to St. Paul, even though Pettee was back in the lineup. Omaha came next and after Stephens lost, Horner and Struck won to keep the club in fourth place with a 13 and 12 record.

Athletic Park from the February 15, 1888, *Milwaukee Sentinel.*

At this point Hart became the proud father of a baby girl and things changed within the club. After a one-game trip to Chicago, where Stephens won, David Davin was suspended and then released for "indulging too freely in the 'ardent.'"[12] He had been fined $25 twice before and now Hart was through with him. Frank Mills replaced him in center field. Back home, the Milwaukees took two of three games from third-place Kansas City to tighten up the race. Horner then beat St. Louis and the club moved into third place. Hart then signed Henry Heup, a pitcher from the local Welcomes, who beat the Whites again. The Milwaukees were now in second place, behind Des Moines. The next day 3,000 saw Stephens beat Des Moines 3 to 0 to take over first place. This will show how close the race for first place was as of June 16:

| Milwaukee | 19–13 | .593 | Des Moines | 18–13 | .580 |
| St. Paul | 20–14 | .588 | Kansas City | 20–16 | .555 |

When Heup lost to Des Moines before 4,500 to 6,000 the next day, Milwaukee dropped to third.

Bill Shenke's hand was improving, which was lucky for Hart, because Jack Horner hurt his. To strengthen the outfield Hart signed Jim McAleer, after paying $1,000 for his release from Memphis. (A Boston paper claimed only $500 was for the release.) McAleer had the highest batting average in the Southern League before his release.

In Chicago Stephens lost, and back in Milwaukee Shenkle lost to Des Moines, as Milwaukee stayed in third place. The next six games were played against Chicago, with Milwaukee winning two, losing three and tying one, dropping the club to fourth place.

Meanwhile, St. Louis dropped from the Western Association. Since mid–May it had been rumored Von der Ahe would disband the club or sell it, as he had lost $5,000 on the club. Denver, Davenport and Oshkosh wanted in. In early June it was decided the franchise would be transferred to Denver or Lincoln. But this fell through as neither would pay Von der Ahe's price of $10,000, or $7,000 for all the players except the pitcher Staley. Finally in late June the Whites were gone. St. Louis had "been a constant source an annoyance to other association clubs with its stories of early dissolution and prophecies of the inability of the association to keep together during the season."[13] Von der Ahe had sold several of his players and released the rest. He had forfeited the first two of a three-game series to Des Moines before selling out without notice. Davenport became the top candidate for the opening. But from nowhere Sioux City received the opening and a new schedule was set, with Sioux City finishing the St. Louis schedule. The Whites' record had been 14 and 27.

Hart engaged Clark Griffith, a pitcher from Bloomington, Illinois, for $1,000 and gave that club John Struck. The price may seem high, but Griffith was the Inter-state League's best pitcher, averaging 12 strikeouts a game. Griffith would go on to pitch 20 years in the big leagues, winning 239 games. "The Old Fox," as he is remembered, managed 20 years, bought the Washington Senators (the franchise later transferred to Minnesota) and was elected to the Baseball Hall of Fame in 1946. Around this time Hart received an offer of $1,000 from Indianapolis of the National League for Bill Shenkle's release, but he felt Shenkle was too good to let go. On a trip to St. Paul the Milwaukees lost all three, and the club dropped to fifth, with a 21 and 22 record. Traveling over to Minneapolis, Hart's men lost two of three. New standings were figured out, with the first four games each club played against St. Louis being dropped. During this disastrous nine-game road trip, the club hit only .188, scoring 32 runs and committing 35 errors. The club dropped to sixth place, its revised record being 20 and 22.

Future big league pitcher, manager, owner, and Hall of Famer Clark Griffith pitched in Milwaukee for three years.

Milwaukee then played a ten-game homestand, winning four, losing four and tying two before dwindling crowds. With Griffith on the team and Horner back in the lineup, Henry Heup (1 and 5 record) was released, along with Andy Cusick, with Fuller going to first base. The team then traveled back into the Twin Cities, losing two of three to Minneapolis and two of four to St. Paul.

The Western was having more problems. The Chicago Maroons were up for sale, but "it would be a long day when a club is again run in Chicago beside a league club."[14] The Western Association was in shaky condition. Hart claimed no clubs were making money, saying Kansas City was the only club that was even, only because of its exhibition games with the Kansas City American Association club. St. Paul was $2,000 behind, Chicago about $4,000, Minneapolis between $4,000 and $5,000 behind, Omaha and Des Moines about $2,000 in the red. (Menges claimed Des Moines was $3,000 ahead and Omaha $5,000 ahead, causing the *Evening Wisconsin* to state that the *Sentinel* was "the official stool pigeon of Jim Hart"[15] by saying all clubs were losing money.) Milwaukee was $2,000 short. Chicago then sold two of its better players to Kansas City, and talk was the franchise would be transferred to Davenport or Dubuque. The *Sentinel* was calling for Sam Morton, president of both the Maroons and the Western, to be ousted. Minneapolis, which had lost the privilege of playing Sunday games, looked to end its financial problems by having a benefit game with tickets going for $1 apiece. Three thousand attended the game against Chicago, clearing the club $900; the Western gave its directors a week to decide if they wanted to stay in the association. On August 2 it was announced Minneapolis had sold out to Davenport. The terms of the agreement provided for the holding of 7/15 of the stock by Manager Gooding, who was to be the financial secretary or assistant manager, and receive $125 a month. Davenport set up a stock company of $12,000 and the new company was to assume the debt to the players from July 15, which was $1,500. The Chicago Maroons were then to be transferred to Minneapolis for $5,000 in cash. But at the last hour the Davenport directors backed out, citing the loss of two players, who had gone to Milwaukee.

Milwaukee had departed on a southern trip after leaving Minnesota, winning three in Sioux City, before losing three of four to the Kansas City Blues. Hart cited Lowe's absence, due to the death of his mother, and injuries to McAleer and Mills for the downfall of the club in K.C. The bottom then fell out as the club lost three in Des Moines and four in Omaha, to run its losing streak to 10 games and drop the club to seventh place. The Brewers, as the *Sentinel* had first called the club on August 4 [usually called the Milwaukees, the *Journal* also referred to them as the Creams], could not get hits. After this road trip, McAleer was leading the club with a .322 average, but then dipped down to Mills' .280 and then Strauss' .251. The team batting average was only .230, and they had scored 304 runs (4.28 per game).

Jim Hart had to reorganize his team. Milwaukee's record had now fallen to 32 and 42. Hart signed William C. Crossley and John McCabe, the catcher and second baseman of the Davenport club. It had been expected that they would stay in Davenport, if that city received a Western Association club, but Hart offered them more money. Hart then signed Bert Wilson, a pitcher from the Fremont (Ohio) club and Albert Fisher, a shortstop from Crawfordsville. Hart released Pat Pettee. The high-priced second baseman was hitting only .203, although he led the Western in fielding. Before the 1888 season had started, Hart had been offered $1,000 for the player's release. McCabe was made the new team captain. The Milwaukee manager then secured G.G. Winkleman, a pitcher, William Hawes, a first baseman, and Joe Walsh, a shortstop. These three players from the Minneapolis club were signed for $650 in cash, with Hart paying the men their back salary due from Minneapolis, which amounted to $700 a month for several months. Hart cut Tom Forster and Edward Warner, along with two pitchers—George Stevens (9 and 13 record) and Jack Horner (8 and 7). During this transition period the Milwaukees had beat both Minneapolis and Des Moines two of three. The starting team was now: Hawes—1b, McCabe—2b, Walsh—ss, Strauss—3b, Lowe—lf, McAleer—cf, Maskrey—rf, Crossley—c, with Shenkle, Griffith, Winkleman and Wilson as pitchers. This club then lost to Sioux City before Winkleman beat the Iowa team in the first game of a doubleheader. The second game was forfeited to Milwaukee when the Sioux City manager refused to play, saying Andy Cusick, now a Western umpire, was "systematically robbing him of games."[16] Hart refused to pay Sioux City the guarantee and appealed to the association, which fined Bryan $300. The Milwaukees then beat Omaha two of three.

The entire Western Association was having money problems, especially Minneapolis. The problem was no secret. Wrote the August 13, 1888, *Sentinel:*

> It is small wonder that so many of the Western Association clubs are finding it difficult to make both ends meet this season. There is a hue and cry about bad weather and consequent small attendance work ruin to the clubs, but there is a factor more potent in its bad effects upon the finances than unpropitious weather; it is exorbitant salaries. Here in the Western Association there is hardly a club that is not paying League salaries and that in the face of the very evidence that the cities of which the association is composed do not justify it. It is the wildest sort of fallacy to think that Milwaukee, St. Paul, Minneapolis, Des Moines, or any of the rest of them can pay their ball players salaries as large as paid by Chicago, Pittsburgh, New York or other of the League cities.

Take Des Moines, as an example. Its salary was $24,000, guarantees $6,300, association dues $1,000, initiation fees $100, reserve privileges $250. In addition there were manager's salary, advertising, scorer's pay and other costs estimated at $2,500. All these totaled a little over $34,000. The price of admission in Des Moines was 25 cents and 50 cents, so the average per capita was about 35 cents. Figuring 63 home games, Des Moines would have to average 1,550 per game to break even. As clubs seldom realized more than traveling expenses on the road, only home games were counted. The Milwaukee club had a salary of two-thirds that of Des Moines, and Hart claimed it was higher than any salary list he had in the American Association. It was estimated 9 of 10 minor league clubs in the country would lose money in 1888.

Minneapolis was next to fall. Having a monthly payroll of $2,750, the club had lost $10,000. On August 16 Manager Gooding, who had predicted before the season started he would make about $20,000 on his club, could not raise the guarantee money and Kansas City refused to play. The club then turned into a co-operative club, and in the first game under this new system, the players netted $4.25 each. On August 20 the Western Association directors took the club from Gooding to give it to several Minneapolis businessmen. No one seemed to want the franchise, as only two local businessmen were willing to put up money. Finally on August 23, the franchise was sold to Davenport men for $500 — $250 for reserve privileges, $100 initiation fee and $150 for associations dues.

Milwaukee won three of its next six games against Kansas City. One face changed, as Albert Fisher was released to join Davenport. Milwaukee then split a four-game series in Sioux City. The club, buried in fifth place, went into first-place Des Moines and lost three of five. In Omaha Hart's team lost the first two games, as the *Sentinel* headed its game reports with "THE USUAL STORY" and "KEEP ON LOSING."[17] Griffith won the third game to end the four-game losing streak, but Wilson lost the last game, as Milwaukee could manage only one hit.

Back home, the Milwaukees finally turned it around. Winkleman beat second-place St. Paul, then the two teams battled eleven innings to a 4 to 4 tie. Davenport came to town, but "the people of Milwaukee did not express a remarkably keen desire to see the new team, as only 300 of them went to the park"[18] the first day. Milwaukee won both games of a rain-shortened series. St. Paul was back in town next and Griffith shut them out 3 to 0 on a three-hittter the first game. The next day a doubleheader was played, Skenkel winning the first 1 to 0 and Winkleman then losing to end a five-game winning streak. St. Paul also won the final game of the series. When the Milwaukees won three from Chicago, the *Sentinel* thought it was too bad the club had not filled its weak spots earlier.

After beating Appleton, Menasha and Janesville in out-of-town exhibitions, the Milwaukees came back home to lose three in a row to Kansas City before very small crowds. The local team then managed to beat first-place Des Moines two of three, and Omaha twice before a tie to end the regular season.

The final standings of the Western Association were a bit confusing, and were made worse when Davenport disbanded a week early. The club lost $5,000 and paid off its players at 30 cents on the dollar owed them.

	W	L	Pct.		W	L	.Pct
Des Moines	74	40	.649	Sioux City	27	49	.355
Kansas City	75	42	.641	Chicago	40	73	.354
St. Paul	72	46	.610	xMinneapolis	27	52	.342
Omaha	67	52	.563	xSt. Louis	14	27	.341
Milwaukee	61	63	.491	xDavenport	4	22	.154*

*Because of St. Louis dropping out and games subtracted, some games were apparently added in again, causing the win-loss total not to agree.
 x Did not finish season

Kansas City complained bitterly that Sioux City had forfeited games to Des Moines to save the guarantee, thus giving Des Moines first place without playing those games; Des Moines, however, was awarded the pennant.

The Milwaukees finished the season in batting ranking eighth among the nine clubs listed in the papers. (St. Louis listed, Davenport and Minneapolis put together.) Jim McAleer led the club with a .294 average before dropping to Bobby Lowe's .246. The club was fifth in fielding. After the season Milwaukee and Omaha played five games for the bulk of the gate receipts (75 percent to the winner), with Milwaukee winning four.

Milwaukee manager Jim Hart stated every club in the Western Association claimed to have lost money, with Des Moines leading the way, losing $12,000 to $15,000. Morton claimed to have lost $3,000 in Chicago. St. Paul did not lose much; its manager claimed to have made some money because he had cut the squad to ten men two months before the close of the season. Hart blamed high salaries for these losses, stating that Omaha had taken in $34,000 at the gate and lost money. If Milwaukee had to pay rent and a manager's salary, the club would have lost $10,000. Hart gave this statement for the losing financial year: "We had bad weather, we lost games, our players were crippled part of the time, and to cap this it's a presidential year."[19] The *Sentinel* had a better explanation for the Western losses.

> The causes for the failure of the association may be reasonably attributed to two things. The mistake of placing teams in cities where they had to compete with old associations, as in Chicago, St. Louis and Kansas City; and the utter incapacity of the head of the league, Sam Morton, whose actions seem to have been based on self-interest in every instance where he has appeared officially.[20]

Shortly after the close of the 1888 season, James Hart sold all his interest in the Milwaukee Baseball Association to the directors, giving Harry D. Quin and Robert W. Maguire (the cashier and paymaster of the Wisconsin Central Railway) the controlling interest in the club. It was first thought Hart would still manage the Milwaukees, as he had accepted a five-year offer from the club the previous year, but he would be dumped. The directors were looking for a player to run the team.

In early November Ezra Buttou Sutton was signed as captain, manager and third baseman. Sutton had started his baseball career with the Cleveland Forest City club in 1871, and in 1873 went to the Philadelphia Athletics. In 1877, when Philadelphia was expelled from the National League, Sutton went to Boston and excelled at third base and shortstop until June of 1888, leaving the National League with an overall big league batting average .294. Soon after Milwaukee signed Sutton, the *Syracuse Herald* revealed that the Rochester Club of the International League, where Sutton had been playing third base and captaining, would attempt to get him back, as that club had him reserved. Sutton claimed he had a special contract by which he was exempt from the reserve; Rochester denied this. The board of directors of the International then decided Rochester had the rights to Sutton. The entire controversy was settled in March when the Arbitration Committee declared Sutton did not belong to Rochester.

After the 1888 season rumors and talk of Milwaukee entering the American Association were around again. This had been the case even during the season. After McAleer and Griffith were signed, the *Milwaukee Journal* believed James Hart was going to put the club in the association for 1889, and even the *Sporting News* was sure after Milwaukee built its new park.

Ezra Sutton — Milwaukee's not-so-popular manager.

After it was learned Cleveland was jumping from the American Association to the National League, the *Milwaukee Sentinel* felt it was probable Milwaukee would fill that vacancy. When Worcester and Columbus applied for the vacancy, the paper felt Milwaukee would have a better chance than either of these cities if the directors applied. Both Sutton and Hart went to the American Association meeting in St. Louis in December to fight for a club in Milwaukee, but Columbus was admitted. It was thought by most that Milwaukee's location was going against her. But a St. Louis dispatch claimed "that Uncle Ezra Sutton did not attend the Association meeting as much for the Milwaukee club as he was in the interest of Uncle Ezra."[21] It was thought Sutton was only making sure he was legally out of the Rochester contract.

Changes in the Western Association were inevitable for the 1889 season. No one agreed on which cities would be represented, but Milwaukee, St. Paul and Omaha were sure bets to stay. Kansas City was first to make a noise. It was reported the Western and American Association clubs of that city would consolidate and play in the American Association at the Blues' park. Denver soon offered $8,000 to transfer the Kansas City franchise to that city, but K.C. announced it would stay in the Western. The *Evening Wisconsin* editorialized against admitting Denver because of the long distance, remembering "long distances and heavy traveling expenses, not high salaries, broke up the Northwestern League in 1884 and the Western League of 1885."[22] Denver still persisted and again in November offered $5,000 in cash for the Kansas City franchise and ten players. Ten days later Kansas City was sold to St. Joseph, Missouri, for $3,000, including seven players.

Sioux City raised its capital stock from $5,000 to $25,000 to ensure its place in the Western and announced the team would play its Sunday games on the Nebraska side of the river, as Sunday games were not allowed on the Iowa side. It was rumored the Des Moines club was to be sold to interests in Oshkosh, but stayed after all. Davenport, which had disbanded its team in the final week of 1888, was not allowed back in the Western Association. Sam Morton had assured its directors when they entered the Western that they would stay in for 1889, but a clause in the Western constitution doomed Davenport. It provided:

> That in case any club shall forfeit its membership during the championship season [which Minneapolis had done] the board of directors may elect a non-association club to temporary membership (which Davenport was) to play all games scheduled and remaining unplayed by the retired association club, and that such temporary membership shall terminate at the next annual meeting.[23]

As expected, Davenport was not invited back and Davey Rowe got his Denver franchise in. Thompson, of St. Paul, was chosen as a committee of one to go out to Denver and check it out. Within two weeks he made a favorable report. One hitch was that the new $100 guarantee that the other Western clubs were paying, instead of the percentage system, was $150 in Denver, even though they only received $100 when traveling. On Decoration Day and the Fourth of July all clubs split receipts 50–50. The $100 guarantee assured all clubs of losing money on the road, as $100 did not quite cover travel expenses. To fill out the changes, the Chicago franchise was transferred to Minneapolis. Minneapolis soon leased grounds for a new stadium in the center of the city and asked permission of the Common Council to erect a grandstand. When action was deferred, Morton threatened to drop out of the Western if not approved. Shortly he received the O.K.

Samuel Morton announced he would not seek the presidency of the Western Association. John T. Pope, who had managed the affairs of the Chicago City League for some years, became the top candidate. When it was learned Henry Lucas, formerly of the Union Association, was being proposed for the $1,000-a-year job, the *Cleveland Plain-Dealer* was to the point: "Keep him out."[24] At the December meeting, J.S. McCormick of Omaha was voted president and treasurer, while Morton was elected secretary. In other action the directors voted no club should pay its players more than $2,500 per month, with a fine of $1,000 attached for violations. The Western also put aside $3,500 for the season for four umpires, "individual salaries to be fixed according to the worth of the men."[25]

Following the 1888 season the Milwaukee club had reserved 13 men: Crossley, Fuller, Mills, Hawes, McCabe, Walsh, Strauss, Winkleman, Griffith, Shenkle, Lowe, McAleer and Maskrey. Wilson had been released. Later in October Joe Strauss was released. The same day Milwaukee signed a pitcher, Frank Wells. Wells had pitched for Des Moines in 1887, where he started 1888, but then went to Sioux City — where he had beaten Milwaukee every time he faced them, shutting them out twice. The club next signed Luke Schildknecht, Wells' catcher with Sioux City. Sutton next secured Tommy Poorman to play right field in place of Leech Maskrey, who would be released later. Poorman started his career in 1876 in his hometown of Lock Haven, Pennsylvania. After a few more years in the minors, he made it to Buffalo of the National League in 1880. Then he was back in the minors until 1884, when Toledo joined the American Association. In 1885 and '86 he played with Detroit before being sold to Philadelphia. His batting average in six big league seasons was .244.

The club was looking for a second baseman and went after Bobby Wheelock, who played for Worcester in 1888. Wheelock, the best second sacker in the New England League, said he would like to sign with Milwaukee, but was reserved by the Worcester club, which he figured would disband. His price was $1,500. Detroit eventually signed Wheelock and Milwaukee signed William Klusman, who had played with the Boston Beaneaters in 1888, hitting only .168, but had hit .302 in the New England League with Manchester. The Milwaukees then had a bit of trouble signing Bill Shenkle. The pitcher had won 18 and lost 14 the previous year and wanted $250 a month. He soon cut that to $225, and said he would not play for less. Shenkle was soon signed for that amount. The club then signed another catcher, George McVey, who had played with Columbus of the Tri-State League the previous year, hitting .301.

The Milwaukee club's first deal of 1889 involved Jim McAleer. Late in December Cleveland offered Milwaukee $1,000 and pitcher Ed Keas for McAleer, but Harry Quin reportedly wanted Keas and $2,000. Cleveland soon raised the money involved to $1,500, but on January 12 McAleer went to Cleveland for $1,000 and Keas, plus infielder Gus Alberts. It was planned to put Alberts at third base and Sutton at shortstop. A Chicago paper reported Alberts was refusing to play in Milwaukee, preferring to play in the International League, which would mean Milwaukee would receive another $500 from Cleveland. Soon it was reported he had signed with Washington, but in March the Milwaukee directors received a letter from Alberts saying he would play in Milwaukee. He stated he did not refuse to come to Milwaukee; he just wanted to go where the money was. McAleer would play the outfield for the Cleveland Spiders until 1898, and then manage in the American League until 1911. Milwaukee also signed a substitute, James Nash from the Eastern League, who was released before the season started.

After signing Bobby Lowe for a second season in left field, the Milwaukees traded William Hawes, with a $200 cash consideration, to St. Paul for Tom Morrissey, who had been in Milwaukee earlier, and had hit .290 with St. Paul in 1888. George Winkleman reported he would play in Milwaukee for $275 a month—he had made $400 a month in 1888—but management did not want him because of the new pitching regulations, reducing the number of bad pitches to four for a base on balls. Winkleman bought his release for $200 and signed with Hartford, as did John McCabe after his release. Frank Mills, who reportedly would remain in Lake Mills and tend to his father's lumber business, was signed in February. Joe Walsh was also signed, but was released in April. It was announced Fuller was to be released, but because of fan support he was sent a contract in late March. Two others players from the 1888 squad were signed: Clark Griffith and William Crossley. The Milwaukees bought Joe Herr from the St. Louis Browns in March for $500. Milwaukee had tried to buy Herr in January, but Von der Ahe was not selling then. The utility player had hit .267 in only 43 games in St. Louis the previous year. He was immediately made the Milwaukee assistant manager.

Milwaukee started its exhibition season on April 6, tying Louisville 8 to 8. Then in successive days the team lost to Louisville, Cincinnati, Columbus twice and Indianapolis twice. After a day's rest the team beat Columbus, Dayton twice and Springfield, Ohio, before losing to Cleveland on April 18. The Milwaukee management received a $100 guarantee for every game, in addition to taking a percentage of the receipts. Wells, Keas and

Shenkle were sent home with various ailments. Griffith also had a sore arm, and Sutton was looking for pitchers. In Dayton he pitched Clark, an amateur from Ohio whom he later signed. Shortly before the regular season started, Milwaukee bought Julius Freeman from Von der Ahe for $1,000. Freeman had had an 0 and 1 record with St. Louis in 1888.

The Milwaukee club now had eighteen men under contract:

Pitchers—Shenkle, Griffith, Keas, Wells, Clark and Freeman
Catchers—Mills, Crossley, McVey and Schildknecht
Infielders—Morrissey, Klusman, Alberts, Sutton and Herr
Outfielders—Poorman, Fuller and Lowe

Because Milwaukee had signed some high-priced players before the Western's salary limit was put through, it was reported the club would be allowed to go over the limit. However, it is unknown if they did exceed the limit. The salary limit was a takeoff of the National League's salary classification that put players in different classes and paid them that classification's limit, from $2,500 down to $1,500, in five classes. With the salary limit in force, the *Sentinel* was confident for the upcoming 1889 season. "In consequence of the salary limit the teams of the Western Association are more evenly matched than ever. A successful season can be looked for and patrons of the game may expect to get the worth of their money."[26]

Before the season could get underway, however, a problem arose over scheduling. In March the schedule committee of Hart, Morton and Rowe met in Sioux City and wrote up a schedule beginning on April 25; Milwaukee's first game of the 126-game schedule was at home. This schedule was very faulty, with some clubs scheduled to play in two cities on the same day and others making big jumps that would be extremely costly. Milwaukee wanted to open at home later in May. St. Paul, Omaha, Sioux City and Des Moines were also unhappy with the schedule. Hart, now manager of Des Moines, wrote to the directors of the Milwaukee club, stating he had advised the Des Moines directors to disband rather than play the schedule he himself helped write. In April a schedule committee of Rowe, Quin and Lord of Sioux City met in Des Moines and rewrote the schedule, beginning in the south on April 20 and closing in the north on September 30. Milwaukee's home opener would be May 12.

On Saturday, April 20, Milwaukee, in traveling uniforms of Providence gray with dark red caps and belts, red stockings and the word MILWAUKEE in red letters across the face of the shirt, opened in St. Joseph. Julius Freeman lost 19 to 7. The following day Shenkle lost before Griffith recorded the club's first victory. Sutton had hurt his arm in an exhibition and was out of the lineup, replaced by Herr at shortstop. The remainder of the lineup consisted of Poorman, Fuller and Lowe in the outfield, Morrissey at first, Klusman at second and Alberts at third base. Sutton alternated Mills and McVey behind the plate, hoping for fewer injuries at this position with a requirement for his catchers to wear a glove to protect their hands. The club then traveled into Denver, where the rarity of air seemed to hurt visiting clubs. Milwaukee lost two of three in Denver.

The Milwaukee club was heading nowhere and it was already time for a move. The three pitchers used had given up 58 runs in only six games. It was believed Wells would be released, as he reportedly was not popular with management, and was paid up to May 10. In late April it was reported the club was trying to sell Wells and Schildknecht to Sioux City. Luke Schildknecht was released, but Wells returned home injured, as did Freeman. The Brewers then went into Omaha, losing three straight, and more changes were in order. Bill Klusman, who had a sore shoulder, was released and Herr went to second. Shortly George McVey was released, reportedly for going on a spree in St. Joseph. The club then bought John Kirby, a shortstop from Philadelphia, with the understanding that he would be sold back to the Phillies in October for the same price paid for his release. Kirby had hit .369 in the Tri-State League in 1888.

After losing two of three in Sioux City, in which Sioux City scored 65 runs, Clark with his 0 and 3 record was released. The *Sentinel* sports headline of May 8, 1889, read "NEW MEN NEEDED," and was accurate. The May 10 *Evening Wisconsin* headline was blunt: "NEED BIBS AND RATTLES." The *Journal* even wrote a poem:

> Ere the ball season had begun,
>   We forward looked with pride,
> Upon the wagon's foremost seat,
>   To see the "Brewers" ride.
> Alas! Our pride has fall with
>   A dull and sickening thud,
> The wagon's tail-board has dropped out
>   And their name is "Mud."[27]

Griffith was the only pitcher to have won, the club being 3 and 9. The Brewers signed Bill Hassamaer, an outfielder who played with Kansas City the year before. Milwaukee then traveled into St. Paul with a new pitcher, O'Donnell, an amateur from Minneapolis. A plumber by trade, he would be helpful even if he did not win "should it become necessary to do any plumbing upon the time-worn joints of the club."[28] Griffith, Keas and Shenkle lost in St. Paul.

The Brewers returned to Milwaukee to play their first home series in trouble. Fuller had an injured thumb, Mills an injured finger and Herr a sore arm. Kirby had not arrived yet, so Sutton signed Charlie Newman, a catcher from Albany, Wisconsin, and Charles Riley, a local amateur pitcher. Ed Keas was released. In the home opener Shenkle beat Des Moines 12 to 9 for his first victory before 3,000 fans. Freeman then lost before a 5 to 5 tie ended the series. The home uniform consisted of a white shirt with MILWAUKEE in black letters across the front, white breeches, white caps, black stockings and black belts.

The Milwaukees were then on to Minneapolis to lose three games to the Millers. The club returned home and lost two games to St. Paul. With a 4 and 18 record the directors had a general shake-up of the team. A new catcher, Jeremiah Hurley, formerly of Boston, was signed. Frank Wells and Bill Hassamaer were released. Bill Shenkle was notified he would be laid off without pay until his arm was in condition. Shenkle's record was 1 and 5. Julie Freeman, with an 0 and 5 record, was also released, as was Fuller. New pitchers were tried. Fred Lunt, from the University of Wisconsin, was sought but decided to remain in Madison. The Milwaukee club signed George Davies, also from the university. Griffith beat Minneapolis, as did Davies the following day, to make the first time the 1889 edition had won two straight games.

Rumors and new movements were still circulating regarding the Western Association. One movement was afoot within the league to raise the salary limit. It was thought Omaha and another club were behind the push, both believed to be over the limit already. Milwaukee was probably under the limit, Sutton, being a player-manager, helping. Another movement was a campaign by the media to acquire the Louisville (American Association) franchise for Milwaukee. As soon as the season began some in the association were beginning to regret taking in Columbus, and it was felt Milwaukee could get the first vacancy, if she wanted it. In May the Louisville club was up for sale. The *Evening Wisconsin* urged the local directors to buy the franchise, citing games against American Association clubs would draw 2,000 instead of the 500 against Western clubs. Both associations had 25-cent admission. Of course, it was not to be, as two wealthy Louisville men purchased the club. In late May a report was circulated in St. Paul that the owners of the Milwaukee club had made an offer of $15,000 for the St. Paul team, with the intention of moving it to Milwaukee and putting it in the American Association. One reason for this rumor may have been an effort in St. Paul to stop Sunday ball. Milwaukee directors claimed to know nothing and it turned out to be a false rumor. For one reason, there was no opening in the American Association. The *Sentinel* commented "that Milwaukee will eventually get into the American Association, however, there is but little doubt. It is drifting near the association every year and it is not improbable that the next year will find it there."[29]

The Brewers, as they were commonly called now, moved into Des Moines and acquired two new pitchers—Charlie Brynan, released by Des Moines a few days earlier, and Quistow, a Chicago amateur. Brynan immediately lost his first game. Griffith then split a Decoration Day doubleheader to end the series. Back home Griffith again lost the only game in a rain-shortened series against Omaha, in which Hurley severely injured his hand. The club then dropped two to Denver.

William Fuller — A player not released due to his popularity with fans.

The Brewers then underwent "a process of rejuvenation which will enable it to meet other clubs with some chance of winning games."[30] Murphy, a catcher from the Franklins of Chicago, was signed to replace Jeremiah Hurley. Doyle of Boston, who had pitched in the New England League in 1888, was next. Then Nelson, from the Southern League, was secured. A trade involving Shenkle and $1,000 to Cleveland for a pitcher was discussed, but nothing happened. Joe Herr was suspended, charged $50 for indifferent play, and sent home until in condition. William Crossley was fined and released. The local amateur, Riley, was also released. Then an outfielder, McCullom, from the Dayton club was secured. Charlie Brynan was also released.

These transactions were a necessity to rejuvenate the team. After a doubleheader loss to Sioux City, which dropped the Brewers record to 7 and 25, the *Sentinel* blasted the club. "The public pays to see ball playing and not burlesquing and will not tolerate by their presence the sort of playing that some of the members of the local team have been doing of late."[31]

After beating the local Phoenix club 51 to 3, Davies won two and Griffith one from St. Joseph to pull the club out of last place. Davies and Griffith then lost to St. Joe to send the club back in the cellar. After Davies lost in Denver, Griffith and Shenkle beat that club in a twin bill before Davies lost the last game. Before moving on to Omaha, Milwaukee signed George Shoch, a shortstop-outfielder who had played the previous three years in Washington, plus 30 games in 1889. The Brewers lost three in Omaha and two of three in Sioux City before returning home.

The team was again changing. Milwaukee had secured the services of Edgar McNabb, the best pitcher in the Texas League, for $1,000 from the Waco club. The Waco directors soon received a $2,000 offer from Denver and sold him to that club. Milwaukee put its case before National League president Nick Young, but Denver got McNabb. McCullom was released. The Brewers then re-engaged Charlie Brynan and signed Ed Knouff, late of Philadelphia of the American Association. In five seasons with four clubs in the association, Knouff had a 20 and 20 record. Doyle was given his release. The *Sentinel* was getting tired of Sutton and called for George Shoch to be the field captain, which he was made in July.

Back home, Des Moines as the opponent, Brynan won. On July 4th, 3,000 attended a doubleheader, Davies winning the first game and Knouff losing the second to the Buckeyes. The Fourth of July standings were:

Omaha	38	15	.717	Denver	24	30	.444
St. Paul	37	16	.698	Des Moines	21	28	.429
Sioux City	29	24	.547	St. Joseph	16	33	.327
Minneapolis	26	28	.481	Milwaukee	15	35	.300

Griffith then lost to end the Des Moines series. Minneapolis came to town next and lost three of four, Lunt losing the only game. Lunt, studying to be a lawyer, still refused to sign a professional contract. Charlie Brynan was again released and Bill Shenkle went over to St. Paul after his release. In a home-and-home series with St. Paul, the Brewers won four of the seven from the Apostles. More changes had been made during this period. Joe Loehrbeck, a catcher from the Cleveland club, was secured with the understanding he would be returned to Cleveland when the team wanted him. Robert Emmerke, a pitcher from Des Moines, was then signed. Joe Herr was released. The Brewers went on to lose three in Minneapolis and win two in Des Moines.

Meanwhile, Sioux City was having problems. The club, in third place, held a meeting in mid-July and discussed selling out to Lincoln, Nebraska. The club expected to lose $4,000 on the year. Three days later the directors offered the club to Lincoln for free, if they would keep it on the field. Two men refused the offer before D.T. Hedges, a cable car man, offered to take the club. But the citizens of Sioux City subscribed sufficient funds to put the club on sound footing. The *Sentinel* told the Sioux City story this way:

> It was never really expected that Sioux City would be a profitable or money-making member of the association, and the cry of anguish which comes from there over bad business and lack of interest on the part of the public in their team fills nobody with surprise. The Sioux City fiasco is but another illustration of about the greatest financial evil that besets the national game, the inequality as to population in the various members of the leagues.... The trouble lies in the fact that the smaller places go in upon as big a scale as the larger and they must of necessity play a losing game in consequence. Sioux City is a striking instance of this. Its population is less than that of any other city in the Western Association, and its opportunities for baseball patronage correspondingly less.

But notwithstanding this fact the Sioux City club was as expensive as any other in association and more money was really spent in getting it together than was expected in organizing the clubs of the other cities. It was a case of biting off more than could be masticated.[32]

Before returning home the Brewers picked up a new pitcher, Daniel Alexander, late of Des Moines, with "the idea to develop him for next year along with several other twirlers who are not phenomena yet, but hope to be."[33] With the season half over, clearly the directors had thrown in the towel. The Brewers were in last place with a 24 and 43 record. After losing a doubleheader to seventh-place St. Joseph, Alexander lost to Denver 12 to 4, in a game in which the entire infield made at least one error — Morrissey (1b), Kirby (2b), Shoch (ss) and Alberts (3b) 2 — and each was fined $50 for poor work. Before the next day's game, Milwaukee traded John Kirby to Denver for Ed Silch. Kirby refused to report until the fine was rescinded. After Milwaukee refused, Rowe, the owner of the Denver club, gave Kirby $50 to cover it. Davies won that day's game from Denver. The Brewers then took three from Sioux City and two from first-place Omaha to run their win streak to six games before losing to Omaha to close the homestand. The *Daily News & Daily Review* wrote "now that the disease has been diagnosed ... the $50 pill is the remedy for the affection."[34]

As usual, Milwaukee was calling for Sam Morton to be ousted as secretary of the Western, but now Des Moines, Denver, St. Joseph and St. Paul were as well. It took these five clubs to have Morton bounced, but President McCormack refused to call a meeting, saying only Milwaukee and St. Paul called for a meeting. The *Sporting News*, which also called for Morton to go, quoted Brundell of Cleveland as describing Morton "as the late president of the Western Association, president of the Minneapolis club, hireling at all times, partner of Harrington, operator of baseball bureaus of scaly principles, Spalding's tool, sales agent for anybody, and general and clumsy trickster."[35] The five clubs agreed not to pay Morton. Morton soon announced he was thinking of taking Pittsburgh's place in the National League after the season. Pittsburgh was expected to lose $5,000, and Minneapolis was averaging about 4,000 people a game. Pittsburgh immediately announced the franchise was not for sale. Morton then announced he had resigned, and his resignation had been with McCormack for six weeks. Amazingly, at a meeting in Minneapolis, which only Denver, St. Paul, Sioux City, Minneapolis and Omaha attended, Morton was asked to stay on until the end of the season. When he did stay, the *Sentinel* reported, "It can be said without fear of contradiction that the men who make up the Western Association have got about as much backbone as an oyster, and their ideas of business are about one grade higher than those of the bivalves."[36]

Sioux City was slow paying back the $4,000 subscribed, only $500 so far, and considered quitting. James F. Peavy had advanced the club $3,000, and when the club could not meet the debt, the franchise and players were turned over to him. Des Moines, as well as Sioux City, was hurting financially. In early August the club dropped its "superfluous players"[37] to save money, realizing it would be a tail ender. Des Moines transferred its home games with the Brewers to Milwaukee. If Des Moines dropped, Grand Rapids was ready to fill in. Then President Truckenmiller of St. Joseph said he would sell his best men and transfer the franchise if the businessmen of the city did not subscribe enough money to compensate him for the light attendance. In September baseball enthusiasts of that town held a meeting and planned to raise $3,500 for the club, which was said to have lost $9,000.

Before the Brewers traveled to Omaha, both Emmerke and Loehrbeck were fined $50 for failing to return from Ashland, where they had been playing. Robert Emmerke was released. Soon Loehrbeck was suspended for the rest of the season and fined $200. The Brewers lost two of three games in Omaha and won two of three in Denver. The Brewers ended the road trip by sweeping a three-game series in St. Joseph, and losing three in Sioux City. On this trip the directors bought a new catcher, Billy Earle, from Chicago. Gus Krock, the local pitcher, had just been released by Indianapolis of the National League, and was signed by Milwaukee. Ed Knouff was then released, citing a sore arm and a 2 and 6 record. Krock was around for only two games, winning both, before he was released to Washington. He had been secured with the understanding the Senators could have him if they wanted him.

The club was home for Encampment Week (Army Review) in late August and large crowds saw the Brewers take three from Des Moines and two of three from St. Paul. The Brewers next lost two of three games to Minneapolis. The pitcher in one of the losses was Mike Morrison, a new pitcher from Minneapolis, who replaced the recently released Daniel Alexander. The Brewers suddenly began to make a move upward. Four in a row were won from Des Moines to put the club in fifth place.

During this homestand George Walthers, who had been in charge of Athletic Park, left his job. A director "upbraided George for letting the grass grow high enough in the park for the ball to be lost in. George advised [him] to take a trip to the North Pole, and then released himself."[38] Jeremiah Hurley also left to go to the Pacific Coast Stockton club for the winter, but signed a Milwaukee contract for 1890 before leaving. In Minnesota the club lost two of three to both St. Paul and Minneapolis, plus an embarrassing exhibition loss to Ashland, to drop the Brewers back to sixth.

Back home to finish the season, the Milwaukee directors made their final personnel changes. August Jantzen, a catcher from Minneapolis, was signed. (A report out of Chicago in the December 2, 1893, *Sporting News* stated "Long" was a star catcher in the indoor league, and at 6 feet 2 inches he was "too tall to let any high ones go over him, and his feet are large enough to stop all low deliveries.") Mike Morrison was released. The Brewers decided to finish the season with Griffith and Davies, but pitched Silch and Alexander one game each. After beating St. Joseph three straight, the Brewers split four with Denver. After a forfeit to Sioux City—following an argument in which the Brewers left the field, costing them $100 in guarantee money—the club took two from Sioux City and four from Omaha to finish the season. The final standings of the 1889 Western Association:

Omaha	84	37	.694	Milwaukee	59	63	.484
St. Paul	75	47	.615	Denver	51	70	.421
Minneapolis	66	57	.536	St. Joseph	41	67	.379
Sioux City	61	60	.504	Des Moines	41	77	.347

Billy Earle, in limited playing time, led the Brewers as well as the Western with a .380 average. Poorman, Sutton, Shoch, Morrissey and Silch also hit over .300. The club hit .287 and scored 921 runs, fourth in the Western. Clark Griffith won 23 games while losing 18, and Davies won 24 and lost 11.

The Western Association's second year ended with mixed results. St. Joseph was said to have lost $9,000. Des Moines lost about $4,000 and Sioux City between $4,000 and $6,000. Omaha cleared about $1,000, only because of the sale of John Crooks to Columbus for $1,750. St. Paul cleared about $5,000 or $6,000. Minneapolis and Denver made big money: $15,000 and $20,000, respectively.[39] Milwaukee made $2,000 to $4,000, having spent over $8,000 on players. In all, the Brewers signed 38 players. Early in the season there were five rainy Saturdays and four rainy Sundays, which cost the club an estimated $10,000. Over 75,000 attended games at Athletic Park, but 100,000 might have with better spring weather. While attendance was fairly good, the directors were unhappy, and shortly before the close of the season the *Sentinel* let their feelings be known. "While there will be no profits, there has been an abundance of trouble, worry and confusion attending the management of the club, and as a result of this the men who own the club are quite willing to sell out and get rid of an unproductive but troublesome investment."[40]

The *Daily News & Daily Review* of September 30, 1889, took a sober view of professional baseball.

> Baseball managers will regard the assertion that Milwaukee's club be pennant winners in order to keep interest alive here, as rather shortsighted. In the first place the pennant amounts to nothing. The Milwaukee team is not a Milwaukee team at all and the true enthusiast doesn't care a picayune which one of the hired aggregations wins the game as long as both play ball. Another thing ... should the local team show marked superiority they would gain little at home in attendance and the weaker clubs in the smaller cities would be disbanded before the season was half over for lack of support. It is a good deal for Sioux City to know that her club is ahead of the Milwaukee combination and it doesn't sour Milwaukee beer a little bit....It is time some people realize that baseball is no longer an amusement but a business.

✸ ✸ ✸

On June 25, 1888, the *Sentinel* wrote that "Milwaukee can claim about as many good amateur baseball clubs as any city of her size in the country." With the new Athletic Park built, many of these clubs began to play their games at Wright Street Park. The first story to break of Wright Street Park was in March when the *Sporting News* printed a story that Rockford of the Interstate League was to be moved to Milwaukee. It reported Charles Kipp, the proprietor of Wright Street Park, had offered to rent the park to them for $500 and pay a bonus of $2,500 for the transfer. The *Sentinel* did not like the idea, one reason being that the admission at Wright Street Park would surely be lower than that of the Western Association team at Athletic Park. Kipp claimed his only interest in the Rockford club was to rent his park. The transfer never materialized as the club received a large inducement to stay in Rockford.

Kipp then turned his attention to the proposed City League for rental of his park. In early April two clubs, the Welcomes and Golden Eagles, were ready to form the league with a $50 forfeiture bond. A league could not be formed at that time, but in late May another meeting was called to start the league. The Planets, Phoenix and North Milwaukees were interested, but again nothing occurred. Both the *Daily Review* and the *Journal* were calling for a league to be formed. The *Journal* pointed out that there were 23 different first-class amateur clubs in the city and the managers could surely arrange a City League. Tony Schloegel, manager of the Welcomes, agreed, but nothing was underway. Finally, in late June the *Journal* decided to take matters into its own hands, asking for those who wanted to enter an amateur league to contact the paper. After this failed, no more talk was heard of a City League.

The official opening game of the 1888 season was played at Wright Street Park on Sunday, April 23, when the Chicago Whitings beat the Welcomes 6 to 2. Though the day was cold, about 500 to 600 attended. The week before the Welcomes had drawn 2,000 at the park, beating a picked nine from the Fortunes and Nationals in an exhibition game. Others to play at Wright Street Park that year were the YMCA members and a game between the doctors and druggists of the city, netting more than $200 for the Emergency Hospital.

Milwaukee had a population of 200,587 and had more than 375 amateur ball clubs.

Team photograph of one of the strong Bay View clubs of the 1880s (Historic Photograph Collection/Milwaukee Public Library).

The *Daily Review* gave these amateur clubs fine coverage and offered them free scorecards. Even the city's Asians formed a club, called the Chinese, with the players using these names: Ah Poo—c, Sing Lee—p, One Lung—ss, Ah Sin—1b, Sam Ring Kee—2b, Pah Yoo—3b, Long Hing Wing—lf, Ching Fu—cf, and Lung Wing—rf. The Chinese grocery store at 208 Grand Avenue was their headquarters. The Phoenix club rented out old Bay View Park on South Bay Street for Sundays and drew good crowds—1,000 at a September game and 800 in an October game. The Phoenix also drew 3,500 in Racine on October 8. The Phoenix attitude, and that of many other clubs, was summed up in these lines in the *Daily Review* of August 20, 1888: "The Phoenix would like to play the Milwaukee Greens next at South Bay Street grounds for money. If the Greens want to play they must play for purse, as the Phoenix will not play for fun. Money talks."

Of all of these so-called amateur clubs in Milwaukee, three were the cream of the crop—the Welcomes, Bay Views and Maple Leafs.

Welcomes manager Tony Schloegel, when unsuccessful in his attempt to form a City League, decided to play other amateur clubs of the state and local area. As noted earlier, the Welcomes' season began with a loss to the Chicago Whitings. The Welcomes were to play the Maple Leafs next, but when the Leafs failed to put up money, the game was called off. The Welcomes then lost to the local Western Unions. The Welcomes, who wore blue pants and shirts, white caps, belts and stockings, again challenged the Maple Leafs for $100 a side and gate receipts to be divided 75 percent and 25 percent at Wright Street Park. On May 6 the Welcomes lost their third game before nearly 1,000, as the Maple Leafs won 9 to 8. Even though they had not won a game, the Welcomes were cocky enough to challenge Jim Hart's minor league club for $100 a side. They received no reply. A week later they finally won a game, beating Racine 10 to 1 before 500 fans. The Welcomes' next scheduled game was with the Chicago Lake Views, but Schloegel cancelled it because the date was the opening Sunday of the Western club, and he wanted Hart's opening weekend to be free from competition. The Welcomes next played on Decoration Day in Oshkosh, winning 4 to 1. After losing to Bay View, they beat Racine 14 to 7, with the Welcomes pitcher, Oberly, striking out 14. On the Fourth of July the club lost a doubleheader in Oshkosh, after beating the Lake Views of Chicago twice on July 3. No more was heard from the Welcomes.

Doug Young put together a strong club, called the Bay View Club, and leased Bay View Park. J.E. Parker managed the club. The Bay Views' first game was supposed to be against the Maple Leafs in May, but the Leafs did not show for this one either. On Decoration Day they finally played, beating Oak Creek 13 to 9. That Sunday the Bay Views beat the Maple Leafs before 500 at Bay View Park, 13 to 7. After besting the Welcomes, they again beat the Maple Leafs. On the first of July, 1,000 saw Bay View beat the Oconto Clippers 7 to 6 to start a state trip. The next day they beat Marinette. Then on July 3 the club lost 6 to 3 before 1,500 in Menasha. On July 4, Bay View lost to Marinette in the morning and Columbus in the afternoon. After beating the Planets, Keystones and Phoenix back home, one thousand saw Bay View beat the Keystones to end their season.

The Maple Leafs, once reorganized in early summer, contained many of their usual faces: Young and Wise — c, Clayton, Murphy, Hanrahan — p, Sullivan — ss, Casey — 1b, Sexton — 2b, Miller — 3b, Delaney — lf, with the pitchers alternating in the other fields when not pitching. At first the Leafs planned to use Wright Street Park for their Sunday contests, but turned to Athletic Park when the Western Association club was out of town, charging 25 cents for open seats and 35 cents in the pavilions and grandstands. The Maple Leafs' opener was a $100 a side game with the Welcomes, which the Leafs won. It was thought that fully $1,000 changed hands on the result through bets. The Leafs' next game should have been May 27, but they did not show for some reason to play Bay View. Clad in their blue flannel pants, white shirts, belts and stockings and white caps with blue stripes, their next contest was a loss to Bay View on June 3. Later that month the Leafs again lost to Bay View 7 to 5. Their first match with an out of city club occurred July 1 when they lost to the Chicago Whitings 8 to 6, before 300 to 500 at Athletic Park. On the Fourth of July the Maple Leafs again lost to the Illinois team 10 to 0. After this no more was heard from the club for years.

The Fourth of July was a busy day for local amateurs. While the Bay Views were in Marinette and Columbus, the Maple Leafs were at home and the Welcomes in Oshkosh. Meanwhile, the Planets were in Manistee, Michigan, splitting a doubleheader. The Keystones traveled to Beaver Dam, winning 18 to 4, and then went to Columbus, where they lost to the Blues 6 to 6. The Unions lost in Watertown, 17 to 9, to the Cadet Browns from that city. The Phoenix traveled to Beloit, where they won two games.

Before the start of the 1889 season, a bad slate was foreseen for the amateurs, or semi-professionals might be a better word. On February 18, 1889, the *Sentinel* wrote, "Amateur ball will probably not thrive to any extent. Most of the managers have given it up as there is no money in it. Wright Street Park has been demolished. When the Western Association is here the public sees them and when away they do others things. The number of amateur clubs playing in 1889 dropped to slightly more than 150 (from more than 375 in 1888), but some made news, especially during the Brewers' terrible start.

The first game of the 1889 season was played on March 24 with the Willows beating the Mutuals 14 to 2 in three innings. The first full contest was on April 14, with Phoenix beating the Meadows 21 to 6. The Phoenix club had purchased Bay View Park and changed the name to Phoenix Park in April. Sporting a uniform made of orange colored flannel with black belts and black stockings, with their name written across the shirt in black, the club next beat the Greens before losing to the Racine Association Club 6 to 5 in Racine. After a month of inactivity the Phoenix traveled to Sheboygan and lost 5 to 4. After losing to Racine on the last day of June, the club traveled to Ludington, Michigan, and beat the Bay City Club 17 to 4 on July 4. The Phoenix then beat the Young Ladies Ball Club of Chicago by a close score. The ladies' fling was short, as they were arrested in Manistee, Michigan, two weeks later for playing on Sunday. The *Evening Wisconsin* blasted Manistee officials: "Manistee can stand dog-fights and prize ring contests, but when it comes to letting girls play ball on the Sabbath, they won't have it there."[41] The Phoenix then lost in Manistee, Sheboygan and again in Manistee, before beating Racine and Watertown to end their season.

Another local club to make it was the Bay View Club. After selling its park, the club secured grounds on South Bay Street. Their first game, with the Planets, ended in a grand dispute. The *Sentinel* of April 29, 1889, reported the incident.

> The manager of the Bay Views states that the game was played in open grounds and no admission was charged. The hat was passed around and a collection of $2.15 taken up with which to buy a ball. The game then went on and continued smoothly until the third inning. Then the manager of the Planets inquired of the Bay Views whether they would pay the Planets bus fare. Upon a negative answer being given the Planets refused to play and rode off in their bus.

The Bay Views' first complete game was on April 30, a 6 to 5 loss to the Racine Association Club before 3,000 fans in Racine. On May 19 Beatty pitched a no-hit, 3–0 win in Kenosha, causing the *Sentinel* to comment, "It is gratifying to know that Milwaukee has one club that can win,"[42] blasting the Western Association Brewers. Later in May Beatty beat the Racine Association Club 9 to 8 in ten innings. After beating the Nationals the Bay Views lost to the new Cream Citys 10 to 2. On July 4, Bay View split in Kaukauna and then lost in Racine later that month. The club then beat Sheboygan in August and lost to Racine in September. This last contest was a Sunday game allowed by the mayor, as Sunday ball was no longer allowed in Racine. It had been agreed beforehand that no noise or demonstration of any kind would be allowed and police officers were present. "The agony of the spectators was pitiful at times, while trying to applaud the good plays of the home nine."[43]

The biggest semi-pro club was the newly formed Cream Citys. For some time Rudolph Giljohan had been working to organize a strong team to play strong independent clubs of other states. He leased Athletic Park and played in town when the Brewers were on the road. The players were to receive no salaries, but donate whatever money made above expenses to deserving charities. The club was Sexton — ss, Moriarity, who was with Chicago of the Western in 1888 — rf, Schomberg — 1b, Keyes — 2b, Wise — cf, Young — c, Parker — 3b, Fass — p, Himmelstein — lf. When it was announced the Cream Citys had signed Beatty, Bay View complained they were attempting to break up their club. Beatty stayed on the south side.

A crowd of 300 attended the Cream Citys' first game, and they beat the West Ends of Chicago 10 to 7. After securing Hobday and Jaffrey, both pitchers, the club beat Oshkosh 11 to 0 before 600 at Athletic Park, Jaffrey striking out 15 in the two-hitter. The club had a few new faces on the field. Hall substituted for Keyes on occasion, and Timlin and Holloway were new in the outfield. Before 750 at Athletic Park, the Cream Citys beat Bay View 10 to 2. On the Fourth of July the club traveled to Oshkosh and won a doubleheader. Ten days later they beat Manistee 6 to 2, Jaffrey striking out 17, before returning home to play Racine. After 5 innings, with the score tied 4 to 4, the game was called to allow a wrestling match to proceed. The Cream Citys then lost in Sheboygan. In August the Cream Citys managed to beat Racine 14 to 12 in Racine before 1,600. A week later they beat Manistee again. On September 1 the club issued a challenge to play any club in Wisconsin for $500, but had no takers. On October 20 a group of professionals from the Brewers and other clubs beat the Cream Citys 6 to 3 before 250 at Athletic Park. The Cream Citys' season ended on October 29, losing to St. John's Academy of Delafield, 1 to 0, in Nashotah.

One unfortunate note of 1889 was the lack of a Maple Leaf club, the first time a club failed to field a team under this name since 1876. The majority of the old Maple Leaf players were on the Cream Citys.

Interest in amateur ball picked up a little in 1890. As early as November of 1889, a City League among the commercial clubs of the city was formed. George H. Roundtree was elected president, with M.P. Addis, secretary, and Hugo Keissler, treasurer. The league hoped for six clubs and would play on Saturday afternoons at National Park with no admission charge. The Yewdales, Calumets (who changed their name to Athletics a month later), Chamber of Commerce and West Milwaukee Shops were ready by February. By March the league gave its four members team colors: West Milwaukee Shops—gray and brown, Athletics—navy blue and white, Yewdales—maroon and old gold, Chamber of Commerce—white and black. Two other clubs, one composed of bankers, the other from the Northwestern Mutual Life Insurance Company, fell through.

On Saturday May 3 the City League opened with the Chamber of Commerce beating the Athletics 12 to 10, and West Milwaukee defeating the Yewdales 8 to 5. After five weeks the league announced it would charge admission of 50 cents. Attendance was still good, as 400 came out for a late June game. The Athletics lost their first eight games, and dropped out in July, having a 2 and 9 record. The Frankfurths took their place and record, and immediately lost their first game. After only this one game, the club was replaced by the Monitors. By the end of August the City League was done, with the Chamber of Commerce's 12 and 5 record good for first place, the Yewdales and West Milwaukees tied for second, and the three-club combination winning only two games.

In the winter between '89 and '90 the *Sentinel* again urged that a Wisconsin State League of Amateur clubs should be organized. It was thought Milwaukee, Janesville, Oshkosh, Racine, Ashland, Hurley, Eau Claire and La Crosse would form a good circuit. The *Evening Wisconsin* agreed. Although two or three men in Milwaukee who had money were willing to organize, the *Sentinel's* dream died. At the same time the Baseball Committee of the Amateur Athletic Union issued circulars calling for a series of contests for the championship of the United States. Team entries were $50 and schedules would be made after four or more teams entered from every region. The Milwaukee region found no takers.

Except for the City Commercial League, no other leagues were organized. However, teams still played in the city. The first game of the 1890 season was on April 5, with the Young Alerts winning 11 to 0 over the Sunlights. Soon a dispute over a nickname arose. Both a south side and an east side club took the name Dewdrops, and a challenge match was set for the right to the name. But, alas, the big name game never materialized. Others formed teams. The Plankinton House Reds, the city's first known all-black team, organized in May. They soon played another all-black club, the Lime Kiln Club, winning 4 to 2. In June the Plankinton House Reds played the all-white Blue Stockings, winning 25 to 21. When the Singers played the Northwest Life Insurance Company, more than 1,000 fans showed up at Athletic Park. In August the first Fire-Police game was played, with the firemen winning 27 to 20. About $5,000 was made on the contest, going to the respective organizations.

Players' League (Brotherhood) baseball came to town. On September 23 the Chicago White Stockings beat the Boston Beacons 8 to 3 in an exhibition game at Athletic Park. The game was originally billed as a championship game and 2,000 Milwaukeeans attended. When it was discovered the teams had played each other the required number of times, the game was forced to be an exhibition. Stars such as James Ryan, Fred Pfeffer, Mike Kelley and Dan Brouthers played in the game.

The Cream Cities again organized, but without the success of 1889. Playing at Athletic Park when the Brewers were on the road, names like Otto Schomberg, Parker and Halloway were still on the club, but the club was no match for good teams. After playing some smaller clubs, the Cream Cities lost two of three to the H.W. Vogels of Watertown in a series billed as the amateur championship of Wisconsin. The darling of Milwaukee was once again the Bay View club. After losing its opener in Racine in April the club, which consisted of players like Sweeney, Krock, Gus and Phillips, then beat the Phoenix club, which was claiming the state championship, before 700 at Bay View Park. After losing in Racine, the Bay Views went to Sheboygan and won 7 to 4. In July they beat Racine, but lost to Burlington twice. After beating Whitewater, the club had a three-game series with the Vogels, winning the first contest 11 to 4, but then lost the next two. In October the Bay Views ended their season by losing to the Racines.

❋ ❋ ❋

In late September of 1889 the *Sentinel* informed its readers that the Brewers were for sale for $10,000 and $2,500 for the rental of Athletic Park. In November full terms of the deal were disclosed. The club had been incorporated with a capital stock of $25,000, which was still there since the club had always paid. A value of $4,000 was put on the players and franchise. At the sale each of the two directors (Harry D. Quin and Robert W. Maguire) were to receive $2,000—$1,000 in cash and $1,000 in stock. The balance of the stock would be sold at $100 a share. Quin and Maguire would carry between them about $8,000 of the $25,000 in stock. Stockholders would elect their officers and form a board of directors. Quin and Maguire would still own Athletic Park and would lease it to the new organization for three years, receiving $2,000 the first year, $2,500 the second and $3,000 the third. Apparently there were no takers, however.

In what league the Milwaukee club would play in 1890 was again in question. As usual, the American Association was mentioned. However, a new league entered the picture, the Players' League. As grievances piled up, the players found backers were planning their own league for 1890, stating their motives in a press release.

> The principles upon which the Players' League was formed do not recognize any of the arbitrary rules which seek to deprive the player of his natural rights, to restrict his ability to make a free contract, to impose upon him harsh and unconscionable conditions, to limit his personal liberty or transfer him without his consent for the club owner's monetary gain.[44]

The National League and Players' League were preparing for war, and the Western Association was right in the middle.

The Players' League was said to have an eye on Milwaukee and also opened negotiations for St. Paul and Minneapolis, offering $10,000 for St. Paul. However, in late October Quin said no further talks with the Players' League had occurred. He was sure "that all this stuff on the part of [John Montgomery] Ward [the Brotherhood leader] and his colleagues is a big bluff at the National League. They think they can scare them into rescinding the reserve rule and blocking the classification enactment."[45] Unfortunately, Quin was wrong. Although the Player's League did not invade any Western Association cities, they were a main force in the proceedings. The American Association did not bother the Western Association in its multi-franchise movements with the National League, and it was believed that the Western had better players and cities than that major league circuit. Just as the season began, another league was proposed, the Players' Western League. Cities named were Detroit, Milwaukee, Chicago, Indianapolis, St. Louis and Kansas City. A letter Harry Quin received stated the league would be similar to the Players' League, but each club would have control of local affairs, such as Sunday games, liquor and admission. No attention would be paid to other organizations' blacklists or the National Agreement. When asked by an *Evening Wisconsin* reporter of the scheme, Quin replied, "Preposterous. Nothing in it."[46] The players seemed to know nothing of it either. A little later the *Sporting Life* believed a Players' Western League could be formed, but the league died on the drawing board.

The Western Association was facing franchise problems. There was talk St. Joseph, Des Moines and Sioux City would drop. Des Moines issued 200 shares of $50 stock, which the directors thought sufficient backing to stay in the Western. At the close of the 1889 season it was rumored Boston had purchased the Omaha club and was interested in four other Western clubs, including Milwaukee. However, the *Omaha Bee* disclosed McCormack, president of the Omaha club, was determined to buy all the stock, which he did. At the Western's annual meeting in November, the St. Joseph franchise was forfeited for non-payment of $245 in dues. Shortly after, all the St. Joe players were released. McCormack was re-elected to the presidency of the Western Association, and Roche of St. Paul elected secretary. Samuel Morton was finally gone, and Roche got in when Denver, Omaha and Des Moines wanted the part of the constitution that stated a club may be dropped for business reasons removed. They could not get a fourth club to go with them and thought Roche would side with them. But after he was elected secretary with Denver's help, Roche voted to keep that part of the constitution in. Milwaukee also was looking to exit the Western Association, and apparently some plans were in the making for a baseball solution in Milwaukee. The *Sporting News* of November 9, 1889, reported:

> Milwaukee, the city of beer and pretzels, has always felt sore, first because the people would not patronize the games, and next because the representatives of the club never secured anything in the way of advantages at any of the meetings of the association. For the past two years they have attended the meetings and gone back, according to their own acknowledgment, worsted. No money has ever been made there and now the interested baseball men are thinking seriously of withdrawing entirely from the professional arena. It is a well known fact that Harry Quin, the present secretary of the club, will dispose of his interest as soon as he can and even now may have made all the necessary arrangements. It seems that the only games that draw in Milwaukee are the ones played on Saturday and Sunday. The rest of the days, the grand stand is empty and the bleachers are bare. In view of this fact it is proposed to see the franchise and the players to the best advantage.
>
> In Chicago are perhaps 50 semi-professional clubs composed of some very good players. The plan is to go there and secure some of the best players at a far lower salary than the present ones are receiving and form a club. A schedule will then be arranged so that games with different clubs can be played at Milwaukee on every Saturday and Sunday of the season. A.G. Spalding has also made the proposition to the Milwaukee people to bring his club and whatever other club is at Chicago at the time over to Milwaukee to play such Sundays as are embraced in Chicago's home schedule.

Finding a replacement for St. Joseph in the Western Association came within two weeks. On November 15 Kansas City withdrew from the American Association, ending its one-year stay, and within ten minutes joined the Western again. The day after K.C. was admitted, it was reported Toledo did not want in the American Association and thought of transferring to Des Moines. Toledo did, however, end up in the association. In December a special meeting was being discussed to admit St. Louis and Louisville to form a 10-club circuit. St. Paul and Minneapolis were in favor of the plan, being sure the American Association could not survive in the three-league war. The meeting was never held, as the association lived. Then in March Chris Von der Ahe of St. Louis offered to buy Sioux City for $7,500, to strengthen his St. Louis Browns. The Sioux City management decided not to sell, believing the players would be worth more in June if the club had to be sold. Thus the Western Association for 1890 lined up with Des Moines, Milwaukee, Minneapolis, St. Paul, Sioux City, Denver, Omaha and newly recruited Kansas City.

The war between the National League and Players' League intensified, and the Western, as well as all minor leagues, became a pawn. First Albert Spalding of the National League put forward a scheme of drafting players from the minors. It would put his National League and the American Association in Class A, the Western in Class B, and the International, New England, Atlantic and other minor leagues in Class C. Class A clubs could have the opportunity of taking players from Class B at a week's notice, and the Western could buy from Class C leagues with that money. Sam Morton immediately said that the Western Association would support the Brotherhood if the scheme was adopted. The plan fell through.

To protect themselves the minors began to adopt a law among themselves that was not embraced in the National Agreement: "Any player under reserve with a club, deserting the same, his name will be placed on the blacklist and thereafter he will not be employed by any of the minor league clubs part to the agreement."[47]

The National League then denied it would raid minor leagues, but Morton had "no doubt [the National League] will sign whatever players it needed to begin the season in open defiance of any agreement it might have with any other organization in existence."[48] Phelps, secretary of the National Board of Arbitration, then issued a notice to the minors desiring protection to make application, if they had not already. The Players' League then sent out circulars to form its own alliance. As it turned out, the Western had little trouble with either league and applied for admission to the National Agreement in March. The *Sporting Life* believed the Western was lucky.

> The Western Association is the only prominent baseball organization that has escaped injury in the general upheaval. Its circuit comprises well populated, conveniently located cities; its teams are strong and well balanced, and its clubs all fairly well off financially.... It is, in fact, the strongest minor league in the country, and presents many advantages not enjoyed by the American Association.[49]

After the near-disastrous year of 1889, everyone realized having a player-manager was a failure. The club determined Ezra Sutton would be released shortly after the season, and in November he was. The new manager was to be Charles E. Cushman. From Muskegon, Michigan, the 39-year-old manager started his playing career 17 years earlier in Philadelphia. In 1886 he served as an umpire and then assumed the management of the Charleston, South Carolina, club, where he finished third. In 1887 Cushman went to Toronto of the International League, where he won the pennant and stayed until after the '89 season. A fine handler of players, Cushman was also innovative.

> Cushman had considerable trouble with a pitcher who handled the ball in admirable style, but who would persist in stepping out of the box. To cure him he procured a rope, which was attached to

the man's right foot. This the manager held in his hand while he sat on the bench. Whenever the pitcher's foot was about to strike out for the rear, the rope would tighten and he be kept in the box.[50]

The Milwaukee club reserved its players after the 1889 season, but changes were made before the spring of 1890. First, Bobby Lowe was sold to Boston for $1,000. Even during the season, Manager Anson of Chicago was after Lowe, and the press was unhappy the club sold the popular player. Bill Krieg, a catcher who played part time in four years with the Union Association, American Association and National League, was signed in his place. The *Daily News and Daily Review* defended the club, citing Krieg, who played with St. Joseph in 1889, hit .326 to Lowe's .315. Milwaukee soon signed Fred Clausen, a Bay View pitcher.

Billy Earle was next to leave. Chicago had the rights to him and that club took him back in November. The Brewers then signed three of their reserved players in December— Davies, Jantzen and Poorman. The club also signed Patrick Welch, Albert Ike, John Thornton, Harry Howe and Tom Flannagan in December. Welch, a second baseman, came from the Texas League. Ike, also an infielder, came from Grand Rapids of the Michigan State League. Thornton was a pitcher, having pitched briefly in Washington the previous season. Howe had been with the Fayette, Iowa, club the previous year and "developed wonderful speed an accuracy."[51] Flannagan, another pitcher, had been with Sioux City in 1889. After the new year the Brewers signed Robert L. Westlake, a catcher from Springfield of the Tri-State League who had hit only .214 but had a .960 fielding average. Home, a pitcher, was also secured, but did not stay long. The club then lost its only player to the Brotherhood League, Jeremiah Hurley, who signed with Pittsburgh. Another reserved player, Frank Mills, went to Seattle of the Pacific League.

Management was having trouble with some of its reserved players. They could not get in touch with Morrissey, and when they did, he wanted too much money. Griffith and Alberts also wanted more money. Shoch, another reserved player, signed in February for a raise of $200 and a captainship. In March Alberts was finally signed, as were Morrissey, Philip Meech, a pitcher from Indiana, and Jumbo Keel, a catcher, with neither of the last two staying with Milwaukee. Clark Griffith was not as easy to sign. In late March he returned his contract, calling for a $200 raise, unsigned. He wanted $2,000 and threatened to jump to the Players' League. Philadelphia was reportedly interested in Griffith. Milwaukee was only willing to give $1,500, thinking he "overestimates his own worth."[52] By opening day Griffith had singed with the Brewers, having signed for $1,900.

A lengthy contract dispute arose when Milwaukee secured outfielder Robert Pettit. Pettit had been secured by Toronto in the middle of the 1889 season from Wilkes-Barre for $300 a month. Although he never signed a formal contract, Pettit was advanced money, played, and was reserved by Toronto after the season. Early in 1890 he signed with New Haven, still on Toronto's reserve list. Pettit contacted Cushman in March and said he would like to play in Milwaukee if his contract in New Haven was not binding. Cushman then secured Pettit's release from Toronto for $200 and offered him a contract. Pettit then said he would report to the Brewers only if they would match his New Haven contract. The case was put before the Board of Arbitration. In April Cushman received a telegram from that board stating it had decided in Milwaukee's favor. When the season began, Pettit was playing in New Haven. He could be blacklisted and New Haven fined $500. Cushman immediately sent a letter to President Young of the National League to clear the case. The Atlantic Association soon called a meeting to take action on the case, and it voted to leave the National Agreement if the case was lost. In May the Board of Arbitration stated Milwaukee had the sole rights to Pettit and he would be blacklisted if he did not report to the Brewers. Pettit requested the board reverse its decision. He claimed Toronto had failed to tender him a contract before April 1, as National Agreement rules required, so he was no longer under reserve. New Haven then asked Milwaukee what price Pettit's release would be. The price was too high for them. Pettit was ordered to report to Milwaukee and asked for advance money, which he received, and reported on June 5. The dispute cost Milwaukee $10 in telegrams.

The Western Association held a meeting in Omaha in February and Cushman, with a reputation as one of the best schedule makers in the country, teamed with Mulcahy, Rowe and Thompson to write a schedule. The Brewers received 12 Sunday dates, but neither Decoration Day or July 4. The Spalding ball was adopted as the official ball and umpires were to be paid $200 a month plus expenses. Cushman also pushed a rule through that set baseball tradition, when the Western adopted white uniforms for the home clubs and visitors a different color. "Now any stranger will be able to tell at a glance which club is in the field and which is at bat."[53] Milwaukee's home uniform was white flannel with blue trimming and a solid blue cap with a white button on top. The traveling uniform was a chocolate gray, with maroon trimmings, stockings, belt and necktie. The body of the cap was also of chocolate gray, the sides being built of five distinct ribs of cloth, gray and maroon alternating. The uniforms were purchased for $12.25 a piece from Spalding and Company of Chicago.

Admission to Milwaukee's Athletic Park would again be 25 cents and 50 cents for grandstand seats. The pavilion was removed and one grandstand was erected, seating capacity now being 6,500. Ladies were again admitted free on weekdays, but no beer or cigars were to be sold in the grandstand this year, except on Sundays. Cushman set up headquarters at Horwitz's Cigar Store at Second and Grand (West Wisconsin Avenue), and appointed William M. Becker (a railway ticket broker on Grand Avenue) to preside over the box office at Athletic Park, which was moved from Seventh to Eighth Street. Cushman was also said to have paid the club owners "a handsome price for fence and scorecard privileges."[54]

Charlie Cushman's players began to report in late March and practiced at the armory on Farwell Avenue. Cushman had problems finding an indoor site in which to practice. "The objection raised principally by the owners of eligible buildings is that the windows would get broken by the flying sphere. This is met by the assurance that the modern netting would be stretched on all sides and on top — placing the men in a cage, as it were, and protecting the windows completely."[55] Thus, an early edition of the batting cage was in use. Cushman had rules for his players when they arrived in Milwaukee. While at home every player had to report twice a day for practice in a uniform that was neat, clean and in good repair. No smoking was allowed in uniform. A curfew of 11:30 P.M. was set. The club dressing room was for members only and no passes to the grounds from a player would be honored. Players relieved from gate duty (a usual spot for injured players) and not in uniform were forbidden on the bench. Of course, all had to conduct themselves like gentlemen. Fines of $5 to $50 were assessed for breaking these rules. All players were to "abstain from excessive indulgence of spirituous liquors,"[56] the fine being $25 for the first offense, $50 for the second and $100 for the third, and any more meant suspension for the balance of the season.

The first practice game was held April 6 at Athletic Park, with 500 in the audience. The club split up, with the Never-been-Beatens beating the Stars 9 to 1. The Brewers then beat the local Commercials and Phoenix by big scores before defeating the Chicago Whitings, 16 to 1. The season was at hand and the *Chicago Times*, among others, believed the

Western Association teams to be evenly matched. With Omaha selling some of its stars, the other clubs strengthening, and the addition of the Kansas City franchise, an exciting pennant race was ahead.

The Brewers opened their 1890 Western season in Minneapolis, losing 13 to 5 on April 17, The opening day lineup was: Poorman — rf, Alberts — 3b, Shoch — ss, Morrissey — 1b, Krieg — lf, Jantzen — c, Welch — 2b, Silch — cf, Davies — p. Thornton relieved Davies, who took the loss before 2,500 spectators. The Brewers lost the next day, collecting only 3 hits, and then dropped the entire series the following afternoon. Both clubs then traveled to Milwaukee for three games. "There was a crowding and pushing at the park gate, a wild scramble for seats, the tooting of horns, yells of applause, shouts of derision, epithets of scorn"[57] at Milwaukee's home opener before 5,000, which Thornton won 8 to 7 on Sunday April 20. After Davies lost, Charles Heard, a new pitcher from Philadelphia, won the final game of the Minneapolis series. In this win Jantzen hit the first home run of the season for the Brewers at Athletic Park, "winning a pair of pantaloons offered by a tailor to the first man who made a continuous round of the bases."[58] To make room for Heard, Albert Ike was transferred to Toronto for good money. Des Moines then came to town and won two of three, followed by St. Paul, which lost two of three, with the Brewers scoring 23 runs on 20 hits in the last game.

On April 30 the Brewers acquired an old favorite, Abner Dalrymple. Dalrymple had started his climb to fame in Milwaukee in 1877 after being stranded in Janesville, needing a ride and a job. He signed with the West End Club for $10 a week and board. After winning the 1878 National League batting title with the Milwaukee Grays, he played in Chicago for eight years, averaging .295 for Cap Anson, hitting over .300 three times. He also led the National League in home runs in 1885 and runs scored in 1880. Dalrymple then went to Pittsburgh, not doing well, and then to Denver. A few days earlier Rowe offered Dalrymple for Clark Griffith, but Cushman declined and Dalrymple received his release.

The Brewers traveled to Des Moines, where Davies won and lost one, and Flannagan won. Traveling up to St. Paul, the team won two of three to even its record at 9 and 9. Back home, the Brewers had their first encounter with Denver. When Dalrymple came to the plate with his new club, he received an ovation. Griffith went on to win the game 8 to 1. The Brewers split the next two games. Harry Howe, Ed Silch and Fred Clausen were then released. Howe went to the Ottawa, Illinois, club, but was soon re-engaged by Milwaukee. Clausen went over to the local Phoenix, and Silch to Spokane Falls. Kansas City then came into Milwaukee, and the Cowboys won two of three. In a rain-shortened series Davies beat Omaha, and then Griffith and Thornton beat Sioux City, before Davies lost to end the three-game winning streak. Charles Heard, with a 1 and 2 record, was suspended indefinitely after he left the club complaining about the weather. "The idea of wearing a storm coat in May makes me tired."[59]

Around this time a rumor was about that St. Paul would disband before Decoration Day. The three directors had been spending money lavishly, but receipts were almost nothing, and the outlook was not favorable. In its last three games attendance did not amount to one guarantee, paid admissions to the last game being less than $6.14. If they did sell, the club would stay in the Western. When the players were not paid their May salaries, they threatened to strike. Secretary Roche then stated the club would not disband. The players had been paid through May 15 and would get paid again when they returned home. Finally on June 27 Thompson sold his St. Paul club to W.J. Bicket, J.M. Pattgiesen, James Starkee and Roche for $21,000. The new directors immediately signed some new players for the 13 and 33 club.

Meanwhile, the Brewers lost in K.C. on Decoration Day 11 to 1, but bounced back to win the next day 8 to 2 behind Thornton, who raised his record to 6 and 2. Thornton then lost in Denver in a one-game, rain-shortened series. Robert Pettit was now with the Brewers in right field, Poorman moving to center and Krieg behind the plate. Traveling into seventh-place Omaha's territory, the Brewers won all three, moving into third place. Morrissey was seventh in Western hitting, averaging .348. Dalrymple and Shoch were right behind, hitting .343 and .342. The team average was .254. In the pitching department, Thornton was 7 and 3, and Griffith 6 and 2. On June 12 in Sioux City, John Thornton won his eighth game, striking out four, walking one, and allowing no hits. Only two other Cornhuskers reached on errors.

SIOUX CITY		AB	R	H	E	MILWAUKEE		AB	R	H	E
Cline	rf	4	0	0	0	Poorman	cf	4	1	1	0
Strauss	c	4	0	0	0	Dalrymple	lf	4	1	1	0
Glenn	lf	4	0	0	0	Pettit	rf	3	1	1	0
Kappell	3b	3	0	0	0	Shoch	ss	4	0	1	0
Brosnan	2b	3	0	0	1	Morrissey	1b	4	0	0	2
Powell	1b	3	0	0	0	Alberts	3b	3	0	1	0
Hanrahan	ss	2	0	0	1	Krieg	c	2	0	1	1
Genins	cf	3	0	0	0	Welch	2b	3	0	0	0
Burdick	p	3	0	0	0	Thornton	p	3	1	1	0
		29	0	0	2			30	4	7	3

```
              1  2  3  4  5  6  7  8  9
Sioux City    0  0  0  0  0  0  0  0  0 — 0
Milwaukee     0  0  2  0  0  0  0  2  x — 4
```

Griffith and Thornton then beat Sioux City. Tom Flannagan got his pink slip to cut down expenses, then signed with Denver. Harry Howe was again gone, and soon Thornton's contract was doubled.

The Brewers' six-game winning streak was stopped in Des Moines, but a win there by Thornton (10 and 3), and four over Minneapolis, put the club in first place with a 27 and 16 record. The June 22 game, played in Milwaukee, which put the Brewers in first, became a double protest. In the fourth inning an argument ensued over a dropped fly resulting in a double play. The umpire, Hurst, forfeited the game to Minneapolis when Milwaukee failed to take the field on time. Cushman then told Sam Morton if his team left the park, he would not give Minneapolis one cent of money and would refund the money to the customers. Attendance was 6,391 and both managers agreed to play. But Hurst refused to officiate any further, stating the game was a forfeit. Otto Schomberg then umpired the rest of the game. Milwaukee protested that Hurst did not tell them it was a forfeit, only Morton. Minneapolis claimed a forfeit after the Brewers won 2 to 0. Hurst reported to the Western a 9 to 0 Minneapolis win. This controversy raged throughout the season.

After beating St. Paul at home two of three, Milwaukee acquired Billy Sowders, who had been 29 and 30 with Boston and Pittsburgh the last three years, for Charles Heard, who had been suspended for deserting the club earlier. The Brewers then won four from Des Moines. A curious incident happened during this series. After one of the games Gus Alberts' bat and bag went missing. "A ball player always thinks as much of his bat and case as a mother of her first born baby," and Gus had been hitting well the last few weeks. The bat was "located in the possession of Flannagan, the Des Moines first baseman," just before the train left the depot, and he "yielded up his booty." Flannagan's manager gave him "a severe roasting, but as the salaries are all behind on the team, didn't care to fine him."[60]

The Brewers had now won 17 of their last 20 games. In St. Paul, they lost three to the last-place Apostles. After losing to St. Paul in the morning on July 4, Thornton lost in Minneapolis in the afternoon, dropping Milwaukee into second place behind the Millers. The Brewers came back to win three games in three days from Minneapolis to regain first by .005 percentage point.

Kansas City came to Milwaukee and the Brewers took two of three. After Griffith lost to Sioux City to put his record at 14 and 4, Thornton beat the Cornhuskers to raise his to 15 and 6. Sowders then evened his record at 2 and 2 with a 6 to 2 victory. Throughout the game Sioux City had "yelled like maniacs, howled like wolves, cavorted like savages, snapped and snarled and showed their teeth like a pack of hungry curs after one bone, and heaped abuse upon the umpire that would have made a Cincinnati hoodlum blush for shame."[61] The Brewers then lost two out of three to Denver to drop into second again. Billy Sowders was released, his 2 and 3 record lower than expected. He signed with Omaha, which was in town, losing four to the Brewers. Milwaukee was back in first place.

Maybe it was only the sting of these defeats that caused the *Omaha Bee* to call for the Brewers' ouster from the Western Association, "as she has not the interest of the organization at heart." The *Bee* claimed Milwaukee refused to put up the guarantee money in the spring because it wanted to go to the American Association if Toledo failed. The *Milwaukee Sentinel* defended the Brewers, writing the management refused to put up money because in previous years the privileges they acquired "were recklessly disregarded by an incompetent secretary and a thoughtless president." The *Sentinel* went on, reporting Milwaukee never wanted in the association, and as to being kicked out of the Western, "without Milwaukee the [Western] Association could not live in its present status, and would degenerate to a third rate organization.... For Omaha to talk about kicking out Milwaukee is like the mayor of Kalamazoo talking about kicking out the President of the United States." The *Bee* wrote back, "The Brewers, when they are playing winning ball, are the most arrogant and assumptive in the whole circuit." The Milwaukee *Daily News and Daily Review* wrote, "Omaha should get a new team or get out of the Western Association. At their present gait they are a disgrace to their companion clubs. They can't play ball at all."[62]

The Brewers traveled to third-place K.C. and lost three of four to fall back into second place. On to Denver, losing two of three, the club still regained first place. Going into August the Western Association had a four-team race: Milwaukee (47–30), Minneapolis (47–32), Kansas City (45–31) and Denver (42–35). The Brewers then won three from Omaha, but lost two of three in Sioux City, Griffith winning his 20th game against only 7 losses. Milwaukee's other two pitchers also were going well, with Thornton 18 and 9 and Davies 8 and 8.

On August 9 Des Moines sold out to Lincoln, Nebraska. As far back as June, the club was hurting financially and had not paid its players for two months. A meeting was held with leading Des Moines businessmen to raise $5,000 to carry the club through the season. In July the players could not be paid. The club had lost an average of $40 a game, and was said to have quit. The club stayed in because its owner had not been paid according to stipulation. Kansas City refused to play Des Moines until it was officially declared in the Western Association. K.C. forfeited two games and was fined $300 when Des Moines stayed in. Finally Des Moines collapsed, having lost $6,000, and Lincoln took over its schedule and the club's 33 and 50 record. "Winning the pennant in 1888 practically killed baseball in Des Moines, as the people will not support a losing team after being so ably represented."[63] St. Paul was also having trouble, releasing four players to cut expenses and transferring its home games to other cities because of low attendance. Soon three-fifths of the Denver club was sold to a Denver syndicate. Rowe and Van Horn still owned the other two-fifths.

The Brewers greeted Lincoln into the Western Association by beating them 15 to 6 in Lincoln. The Brewers split the remaining two games there. Robert Westlake, the catcher signed by the Brewers early in 1890, played with Lincoln in this series. The Brewers then traveled to Minneapolis, where they split two with the Millers. Kansas City, meanwhile, slipped into first place. Milwaukee then swept a three-game home series over St. Paul to regain first place.

Charlie Cushman then leveled a blast at the fans. "It is absolutely sickening to think that after all the trouble we have taken and the expenses we have incurred to put a winning team in the field, we come home to play to empty benches."[64] Cushman claimed the attendance at the three St. Paul games did not meet the guarantee. Harry Quin claimed it cost from $250 to $300 to put on a game, and only $80 to $90 was brought in at the gate. If things did not pick up, he would be forced to leave the city. The *Journal* on August 22, 1890, sided with Cushman and Quin.

> The good people of Milwaukee are not taking the amount of interest they should in the winding up series of baseball games. Whatever may have been distasteful to them in the past, it is still a fact, patent to all, that the management has got together a club this season, of which Milwaukee or any other city might feel proud.... It would be a crying shame and lasting disgrace to Milwaukee should a lack of local patronage compel the directors as a matter of economy to let some of their most expensive [players] go. The pennant is now in sight and Milwaukee has a clear lead for it. Nothing but the most untoward circumstances can change this course of events, unless the people see fit, through lack of proper support, to kill off one of the most thorough-going sporting enterprises ever offered to the Milwaukee public.

Lincoln then came to Milwaukee and lost three to the Brewers. The Brewers then beat the St. Paul Apostles two of three, before splitting two with Minneapolis in a home-and-home series. The Western had a close pennant race going, but different papers showed different leaders. The *Milwaukee Sentinel* showed Milwaukee first, Minneapolis second, and Kansas City third — all within a game and one-half of the lead. The *Minneapolis Tribune* showed its home club in first, with Milwaukee in second and K.C. third. The *Kansas City Journal* had Minneapolis, K.C., Milwaukee. The *Denver Republican* put the Millers in first, Brewers in second and the Blues in third place. The problem was no official word from Secretary Roche and the disputed June 22 game.

The Brewers won five of their next six games at home, beating Sioux City twice and Denver three times. Kansas City was scheduled next. K.C. directors offered Milwaukee $400 a game to transfer the three games to Missouri, or take 75 percent of the receipts, whichever was to the Brewers' advantage. Kansas City was drawing big, but the Brewers did not accept, anticipating big crowds and wanting to play at home during the pennant race. It proved a failure, as crowds were not huge and the Cowboys won all three games. George Davies was released even though he won six in a row before losing to K.C. He left with a 14 and 9 record. To replace Davies, the club had signed James Renwick, a pitcher from Calumet, Michigan. Milwaukee then beat Omaha in six straight games, four at home and two in Nebraska.

In early September the St. Paul club was sold to C.P. Flattly, a general western passenger agent of the Duluth, South Shore & Atlantic Railway, for $3,000. The club had lost $5,000 and was about to default on salaries. Flattly immediately put up enough money to carry the club through the end of the season.

The Brewers traveled to Sioux City and lost two of three, killing their pennant hopes.

The Brewers then won two and tied one game in Denver before ending the season in Kansas City, losing two of three. When Secretary Roche gave the official 1890 final Western standings in October, he gave the disputed June 22 game to Minneapolis, costing Milwaukee second place.

Kansas City	78	39	.666	Sioux City	56	64	.466
Minneapolis	78	45	.634	Omaha	51	69	.425
Milwaukee	77	45	.631	Lincoln	47	73	.391*
Denver	57	63	.475	St. Paul	38	84	.311

*Des Moines had been 33 and 50 when dropped from the Western. Lincoln was 14 and 23.

Milwaukee had three complaints on the third-place finish. First, of course, the disputed game with Minneapolis. Second, Manager Cushman claimed the Brewers had two postponed games at Denver to play, with hopes of winning them both, but Rowe refused to play them, even though Milwaukee offered to waive the guarantee. Also, Minneapolis beat Sioux City on September 30 to take second place. Minneapolis' season was to end on September 29, meaning this game, the Brewers contended, was illegal.

After the regular season Milwaukee and Minneapolis set out to play some post-season exhibitions in Milwaukee. Soon Minneapolis demanded two games be played there. On October 3 less than 100 attended the first game in Minneapolis, the Brewers winning. Only 50 witnessed the next game, also in Minneapolis, Milwaukee winning again. Minneapolis then refused to come to Milwaukee, ending the series. Minneapolis ownership then changed, with A.H. Griffith purchasing a two-thirds interest in the club for $10,400, buying out Sam Morton and Fred Glade. The Brewers ended the season playing Adrian Anson's Chicago National League club, winning 4 of 5.

The Brewers' team batting average for the Western season had been .270, second to Kansas City's .275. Milwaukee's fielding was the best in the league, at a .932 average. Dalrymple was second in Western hitting with a .328 average. Pettit hit .308. Shoch came close to the coveted mark with a .294 average. Griffith won 25 games, losing only 11, while giving up 162 runs, 62 earned (1.82 earned runs per game). Thornton was 29 and 14, giving up 186 runs, 77 earned (1.82 earned runs per game). Renwick finished 2 and 1.

Financially the Western had mixed results. Minneapolis and Kansas City made big money, Minneapolis $27,000 and K.C. about $13,000. Denver made a little, as did Lincoln, according to some sources, others claiming losses of $2,000 to $3,000. Omaha lost $4,000 to $5,000, but made $8,000 to $9,000 selling its star players. St. Paul lost a lot, as did Sioux City, estimates being between $4,000 and $8,000. Milwaukee was a little ahead on the season according to the *Sentinel,* and about $6,000 by the *Evening Wisconsin* figures.

10

A Baseball War and Merger (1891)

The year 1891 proved to be an interesting season for baseball in Milwaukee. The interest actually started in early September of 1890 when one of the directors of the Brewers announced the club was for sale. Because of the low home attendance, the club was also considering selling some of its stars. In a few days it was learned Charles Cushman, manager of the club, had an option to buy the club for $6,000—$4,000 less than its previous year's price—and lease Athletic Park for $2,500. Cushman wanted to form a stock company of $15,000, at $15 a share. Within days, $6,100 was subscribed, with John A. Hinsey (a cable car owner) and Charles Pfister (son of the later tannery and hotel owner, Guido Pfister) having put themselves down for $1,000 each. It was reported that players Robert Pettit and Abner Dalrymple had taken $200 worth of stock. On September 10, 1890, the *Milwaukee Sentinel* told the real behind-the-scenes story to its readers.

> The fact of the matter is that the option [to buy] is simply a matter of form, as at least one of the present owners will be heavily interested in the stock company and may possibly have the largest individual share of stock.

This caused Charles Pfister to report he would only buy in if the old members were out. By September 21, $7,000 had been subscribed.

By late September the owners were becoming restless. The option to buy had been given on September 7, with the understanding that the new owners would take the club and pay all salaries, about $1,500. When the new owners did not take over by September 15, the present owners paid the players' salaries. Harry Quin and Robert Maguire were considering two possibilities. First, sell the players in demand and take their chances on getting a good club together for 1891. They had offers of $3,000 each for Thornton and Griffith from National League clubs, and believed Shoch and Pettit could be sold for $1,500 to $2,000. The other idea was to go into the American Association, if possible. Columbus had paid $10,000 to enter into that association two years earlier, which was thought to be a fair price. The second possibility seemed unlikely, as Quin had received a letter to attend the association meeting, but did not attend.

Meanwhile, subscriptions continued to come in. The Blatz Brewing Company subscribed $1,000. At a meeting at the Plankinton House on October 6, Cushman reported $10,000 had been subscribed. The owners of the club offered Cushman a lease on Athletic Park for two years at $2,500, or free if they were allowed to retain privileges such as beer, scorecards and advertising. The next night another meeting was held. J.C. Iverson reported that the new organization had been granted a two-week extension on the option to buy. At this meeting it was decided to accept the $6,000 price tag of the club, which some thought was still too high, on these terms: $3,000 in cash, $1,500 on January 1, 1891, and the balance before April 1, 1891.

By mid–October between $13,000 and $14,000 had been subscribed, with about 50 men in the company. The idea of getting the players interested in the company had been abandoned. On October 27 a temporary organization was formed, with Charles M. Kipp, the president, to arrange for the transfer of the stock company. On November 5 the old Milwaukee Baseball Company passed out of existence and on November 10 a permanent organization formed. Robert W. Maguire, from the old organization, was elected president. Zack Bartlett was elected vice president, A.W. Friese elected treasurer, and W.M. Becker took over as secretary. Maguire, Bartlett, William E. Furlong, H.E. Gillette and J.C. Iverson were the board of directors. Cushman was named manager of the team, to no one's surprise.

On August 19, 1890, the *Sentinel* wrote, "The annual story about Milwaukee going into the American Association next season has already been sprung." With the Players' League obviously dying in its first year, new leagues were being proposed. The *Milwaukee Journal* commented, "Baseball is like politics and gets many queer stories going about matters connected with it."[1]

The first plan reported was that the American Association, Western Association and National League would merge. After dividing into eastern and western divisions, a 142-game schedule independent of each other would be adopted. After the regular season, a 12- or if necessary 13-game play-off would be played to determine the world's championship. There would be no Sunday ball and 50-cent admission. The strongest players in each of the three associations would be signed. The eastern division would include New York, Boston, Philadelphia, Brooklyn, Washington, Cincinnati, Pittsburgh and Cleveland. The western would be Chicago, Milwaukee, Minneapolis, Indianapolis, Kansas City, Omaha, St. Louis and Detroit. Another plan would split the three leagues into a Western, Middle and Eastern league. Then from Philadelphia came a story that the Players' League would merge with the American Association. This merged league would have Sunday ball, 25-cent admission, and allow the selling of beer. The National League would get all the players who had jumped back in this plan. This league would consist of New York, Boston, Baltimore, Philadelphia, Chicago, St. Louis, Louisville and Milwaukee.

As most believed the American Association would survive, that is where most hopes rested. A.W. Thurman, president of the American Association, dampened spirits in January when he said Milwaukee would not be in his association. Still hopeful, John C. Iverson, Harry Gillette and Charles Cushman attended the American Association meeting in New York in January — "If by any deal or slip an American Association franchise should go begging, Milwaukee would be delighted to go in."[2] The American Association was eyeing Boston and Chicago, but the *New York Evening Telegram* believed it would do better to go with the non-league territories of Milwaukee and Washington. At the meeting Toledo, Rochester and Syracuse were bought out and the American Association was to enter Boston, Washington and Chicago. A rumor was about that Chicago's Sunday games would be played in Milwaukee. Iverson was very unhappy, telling a *New York Sun* reporter that if Chicago failed, which he thought it would, the American Association should not look to Milwaukee. Some thought Milwaukee still had a chance, as Albert Spalding was against another club in Chicago. The *Sporting News* of February 7, 1891, wrote, "It is the general opinion that the American Association has made a mistake. Chicago, if admitted, is sure to prove a losing venture, and Milwaukee is as much to be preferred over Toledo as a big, red Spitzenberg to a crab apple."

Trouble soon began between the American Association and the National League. Boston and Pittsburgh of the National League signed two A.A. Philadelphia players, whom the previous Philadelphia ownership had inadvertently failed to reserve. When the National Agreement's Board of Control turned over the players to the National League, the American Association unanimously resolved to withdraw from the National Agreement. The American Association also decided to place a franchise in Cincinnati, dropping its plans for Chicago. The American Association thus entered the 1891 season with this lineup:

Charlie Cushman — Milwaukee's very popular manager for a number of years.

Boston	St. Louis
Baltimore	Columbus
Philadelphia	Cincinnati
Washington	Louisville

Milwaukee directors were sure Minneapolis and Kansas City lobbied against their efforts to get into the American Association in order to keep the Western Association in tact. This baseball war would have many direct results on the Western Association and Milwaukee baseball.

What cities would represent the Western Association in 1891 was a big question mark. Sioux City had lost a lot of money, Lincoln was thought too small, and Denver was too far away. Feelers were sent out to Chicago and St. Louis. It was known Detroit and Grand Rapids wanted in. A circuit of Milwaukee, St. Paul, Minneapolis, Omaha, Kansas City, Grand Rapids, Detroit and Indianapolis would have a population of 1,230,000. A story was also out that Kansas City might replace Cincinnati in the National League. However, Davy Rowe of Lincoln believed only Sioux City would leave the Western Association. Both Peoria and Detroit wanted the Denver franchise. Toledo was also mentioned as a replacement.

Lincoln was attempting to get Sunday games allowed to help home attendance and ensure a spot in the Western. In November, L.C. Krauthoff of Kansas City was elected president of the Western Association, and he stated any city wanting in the Western would have to buy out an existing club. In late January it was reported Sioux City had withdrawn from the Western after losing about $10,000 the last two years. St. Paul and Minneapolis supported Grand Rapids as a replacement, but Sioux City refused to fall. A new organization brought a $3,000 certified check to the Western Association meeting in February to ensure the Sioux City franchise from being shut out.

The Western Association meeting, held in Chicago, promised to be exciting. Milwaukee was still hoping to go to the American Association. Henry Hack of Minneapolis said, "We [the Western] couldn't afford to let Milwaukee get away from us, for if we lost Milwaukee, we could be blocked from going any further east."[3] Everyone thought Sioux City, Denver and Lincoln would be dropped, and Toledo, Detroit and Indianapolis would be admitted. To everyone's surprise, no franchise changes were made. In fact, the offers of the three cities did not even come up for discussion. A 30 percent guarantee, or not less than $100, to visiting clubs was adopted, with the pooling of receipts on holidays. A $5,000 bond for each club was endorsed and passed. A rule requiring each club to carry at least eleven men at all times was also enacted.

The Western Association was in good condition for 1891. It was not only a part of the National Agreement, but on equal status with the two major leagues. Allan Thurman (American Association), L.C. Krauthoff (Western Association) and John I. Rogers (National League) sat on the National Board of Control. However, this board was soon broken up when the American Association withdrew. Krauthoff was sure the war would not affect the Western Association, as the American Association had assured the Western it would not tamper with its players. As we shall see, he was wrong.

With a strong team left from 1890, the Brewers looked like a prime contender for the pennant in 1891. Fred Clausen was signed immediately after the 1890 season, and Cushman reserved his players for the next season. On October 9 the club received a jolt. It was reported that one of the Brewers' aces, Jack Thornton, had signed with Philadelphia of the Players' League. The Brotherhood claimed Thornton had no contract with the Brewers, as under the terms of the National Agreement a player could not sign with a club before October 20. However, there was nothing about personal contracts. On September 5 Thornton had signed a personal contract with the president of the Milwaukee club for $1,800. Agreed time of the contract was January 1, 1891, to January 1, 1892. The *Sporting Life* claimed that if Milwaukee had Thornton under contract, Philadelphia would withdraw its claim. Milwaukee was not to get Thornton back. On December 26 he was traded by the Brewers to the Philadelphia Phillies of the National League for Tom Vickery and Bill Schriver. Vickery was a 23-year-old pitcher who had pitched for Cushman in Toronto in 1889 and went to the Phillies in 1890, winning 24 games. Schriver was a 24-year-old catcher who began his big league career in Brooklyn in 1886 and had played the last three years in Philadelphia.

The Brewers' next acquisition was John Grim, who had also played in Toronto, and had played all the positions with Rochester in 1890. Rochester tried to contest Grim's signing in Milwaukee, but because the American Association had dropped from the National Agreement, the Board of Control gave him to Milwaukee. Grim was reported to be the highest-salaried man on the Brewers. Within days, John Buckley was signed. A pitcher, Buckley had a 1 and 3 record with Buffalo of the Players' League in 1890. Soon Cushman signed Jim Brady, a catcher from Pittsburgh, and Sam Dungan, also a catcher from Oakland who had led the California League in hitting. With these two acquisitions, catchers August Jantzen and Robert Westlake were released, as was first baseman Tom Morrissey. To replace Morrissey, Cushman signed William J. Campion. Campion had played in the Atlantic League in 1890, but the 26-year-old first baseman had signed with Lebanon of the Pennsylvania League. President Nick Young of the National League said his contract there was not binding. An outfielder, Eddie Burke, was then signed. Burke had started in 1890 in Philadelphia, but had been traded to Pittsburgh for Billy Sunday in August, and released to Milwaukee for $400. The 23-year-old was another who had played for Cushman in Canada. In late February the Brewers bolstered their pitching by signing Fred C. Smith. Smith had pitched for Toledo the past two years and had won 19 games in the American Association in 1890. Three reserved players were also signed: Gus Alberts, Abner Dalrymple and George Shoch. Players released were Tommy Poorman, Patrick Welch, Bill Krieg and James Renwick. When George Davies signed, only Robert Pettit and Clark Griffith were left unsigned. Pettit was asking for $1,700 and the directors were only offering $1,350. Soon the directors split the difference and signed Pettit for $1,500.

Clark Griffith was a different story. Milwaukee dropped all negotiations with him very early because of his high salary demand. Then the *St. Louis Sporting Times* reported Griffith had signed with the St. Louis Browns at a salary $75 more than the Brewers had offered. Milwaukee reportedly offered him $2,000 and was willing to go up $200 or $300. Griffith would be the first Brewer loss in the association/league war.

The Brewers entered the 1891 season with 15 players: Clausen, Vickery, Buckley, Smith and Davies—pitchers; Brady, Dungan and Schriver—catchers; Campion, Grim, Shoch and Alberts—infielders, first to third; Burke, Pettit and Dalrymple—outfielders. The Brewers' salary list was said to be $22,000, which probably replaced Kansas City as the highest-salaried club in the Western Association.

Before the Western Association's playing season even began, the war with the American Association began to hit home. As seen, the Brewers lost Griffith to St. Louis. An association club offered Dalrymple $800 more than his Milwaukee contract, but Abner refused "for reason of self-preservation, if nothing else."[4] Later it was reported Pettit had signed with Louisville, but this turned out to be false. Pettit disclosed Baltimore also tried to sign him, but he asked for too much—$4,000, with $2,000 in advance. In retaliation for the signing of Griffith and these attempted signings, Cushman tried to sign Silver King, the St. Louis Browns pitcher. However, Pittsburgh of the National League signed King. In March Sioux City signed two Philadelphia American Association players who were under contract. The association retaliated by offering Killen, the Minneapolis pitcher, $1000 to break his contract. The A.A. also began flirting with St. Paul players. President Beck of St. Paul tried to prevent warfare by writing American Association President Kramer, telling him the Philadelphia players would be returned if they were under contract. Sioux City at first refused to let one of the players go, but within a week gave him up. The American Association continued the raids, signing players from Omaha, Kansas City and St. Paul.

Spring training for the Brewers started with the players reporting in late March. By April 2 all were in town except Buckley. The club soon left for Des Moines to play some exhibitions. Cushman originally wanted to go east and play exhibitions, but the trip would cost $3,800 and only Philadelphia responded to his request for games. The *Evening Wisconsin* pointed out that most other Western teams were going to Hot Springs or "some other balmy climate"[5] to practice, and the club should spend a little more money to get the players in shape. In Des Moines the Brewers beat the local club twice, then went on to beat Sioux City. The Milwaukees beat Chicago of the National League, 3 to 1, to end exhibition play.

The Brewers opened the 1891 Western schedule in Omaha with Vickery winning, 13 to 6. Every Brewer scored at least once, with Pettit collecting 3 hits and scoring 3 times. Milwaukee then dropped two straight before ending the Omaha series with another Vickery victory before 8,000 on a Sunday afternoon. After the series Jim Brady was released, as he was not needed. Traveling to Lincoln, Davies pitched a shutout before the Brewers lost three straight, dropping to seventh place. With its usual flair, the *Journal* wrote of the continued losses.

> Babylon has fallen, and the most sacred citadel of Jerusalem have been laid open to the coyote.... Like a holy bension it rested for a moment on turret and tower before sinking with a solemn thud into the mysterious depths in its daily wont to traverse in its tireless endeavor to accomplish Horace Greeley's advice and go West.[6]

In Denver Davies pitched his second shutout, winning 5 to 0; Smith then lost the next day, 27 to 8. On April 27 Campion drove in Shoch in the sixth inning for the game's only run, as Tom Vickery no-hit Denver, striking out three and walking three.

	DENVER						MILWAUKEE				
		AB	R	H	RBI	E			AB	R	H	RBI	E
McGlone	3b	3	0	0	0	1	Burke	cf	4	0	1	0	0
Tebeau	cf	4	0	0	0	0	Pettit	rf	4	0	2	0	0
McClellan	rf&ss	2	0	0	0	0	Shoch	ss	4	1	0	0	0
Curtis	lf	3	0	0	0	0	Dungan	lf	3	0	1	0	0
O'Brien	1b	3	0	0	0	0	Grim	2b	4	0	1	0	1
Werrick	2b	3	0	0	0	0	Campion	1b	4	0	2	1	0
White	ss	2	0	0	0	0	Schriver	c	3	0	0	0	0
Lohbeck	c	3	0	0	0	0	Vickery	p	4	0	1	0	0
Keefe	p	3	0	0	0	0	Alberts	3b	3	0	0	0	0
Kennedy	rf	2	0	0	0	0							
		28	0	0	0	1			33	1	8	1	1

```
               1 2 3 4 5 6 7 8 9
      Denver   0 0 0 0 0 0 0 0 0 — 0
      Milwaukee 0 0 0 0 0 1 0 0 x — 1
```

Davies was then defeated to end the series. After losing the first game in Kansas City, the Brewers beat the Cowboys three straight, including Davies' third shutout. The Brewers stood in fifth place, with an even 8 and 8 record.

The Brewers returned home to find changes in the front office. The Wisconsin Central Railroad moved to Chicago, necessitating Robert W. Maguire's resignation as president of the club. It was believed Lester C. Stadler (a physician with offices at 204 Grand) would be the best man available, but both he and Zack Bartlett (Oscar Z. Bartlett, a commerce merchant who owned Bartlett & Son) declined the position. On May 13 William E. Furlong (the old West End player who now was a lawyer in the legal department of the Northwestern Mutual Life Insurance Company) was elected president by the directors.

For the 1891 season, tickets were again available, costing $20 for the season and being transferable. The scorecard for this season was in pamphlet form, containing four pages with heavy covers. It was reported the scorecard (from Augustus W. Friese, club treasurer and owner of a downtown sporting goods store) "is a magnificently lithographed affair, and the finest publication of the kind ever issued in Milwaukee."[7] Friese also furnished the Brewer uniforms. The home uniforms were of pure white, with a dark blue collar to the shirt, and black socks. The traveling uniform was again gray. Director Gillette wanted the home uniforms to be orange and black, but his idea was dismissed "because it was feared that the players' lives would be endangered if an Irish crowd should gather at the park,"[8] joked the *Evening Wisconsin*.

On Tuesday, May 5, the Brewers opened at home before 1,600 fans; Davies lost to the Lincoln "Ancients" 12 to 8. Lincoln went on to win two of the next three. The *Journal* believed "stiffs from a cemetery could beat the Brewers."[9] To help out, Pettit was moved to second, Grim to catcher and Dungan into the field. Kansas City next came to the Beer City and the Brewers won three of four, the final game a 23 to 2 victory behind Davies. Manager Charlie Cushman was looking for pitching help and telegrammed Ed Cushman, who said he would report in 10 days. However, Ed Cushman soon said he did not want to report. It seemed he had signed with Rochester. Meanwhile, Cap Anson in Chicago offered the Brewers infielder Bill Dahlen and several hundred dollars for Schriver, but Cushman declined. Cushman released John Buckley and sent Fred Clausen to Hot Springs to recuperate for six to eight weeks. Looking for pitchers, Cushman signed John "Phenomenal" Smith, recently released by Pittsburgh. Smith could not report to Milwaukee, as some of the National League clubs refused to waive their claims to him. The *Jour-*

nal reminded the Brewers that "money is a magnet, gentlemen, and it talks with a great big M."[10]

Denver next visited Milwaukee and the home club took three straight. After beating Omaha two of three, the Brewers roared into second place behind Omaha. Then Minneapolis came to town and won three of four. The Brewers signed Howard Earl, recently released by the Millers, to play second base, putting Pettit back in right field. In a few days, Shoch resigned as captain and Pettit took his place.

Around this time, it was rumored St. Paul would sell out. A scheduled game in St. Paul with Denver on May 20 was attended by only nine spectators. The contest was postponed due to wet grounds and low attendance. Jay Anderson was attempting to buy the franchise in St. Paul, with plans of transferring it to Duluth. This St. Paul club entered Milwaukee and lost three of four, including a Decoration Day doubleheader sweep. The afternoon game of this twin bill, in which Vickery won his tenth game, drew more than 3,000. The Brewers then swept three from Sioux City to end the homestand. During this series Earl hurt this hand and was out for a few games. Campion blasted Cushman for criticizing his play. The first baseman said if it continued, he would ask for his release. On a sad note, Gus Alberts missed a number of games due to the death of a child.

Milwaukee next traveled into troubled St. Paul, a franchise having more trouble. Louisville of the American Association had just signed the Apostles crack shortstop, Fred Ely, for $2,000. Louisville also signed Jouett Meekin, a pitcher. To make matters worse, the Brewers swept the four-game series. Rumors were around of the team's transfer to Duluth. Traveling over to Minneapolis, the Brewers lost three of four to the Millers, dropping to third place.

More rumors were flying that players were deserting the Western Association. A report was in the newspapers that three Omaha players had signed with the American Association. Omaha was ready to take legal steps, but the report proved false. Then the *Chicago Tribune* reported that Tom Vickery and Bill Schriver had signed with Louisville. The Brewers denied the report, but confirmed an agent of the Baltimore Orioles approached Grim, who had turned the agent down. The American Association clubs claimed Western clubs were not paying the players and they could thus sign them. Western officials denied this, except for possibly the St. Paul club. It turned out an American Association agent was, in fact, attempting to sign Vickery, Grim and Shoch. Cushman had detectives follow the agent, Jimmy Macullar, a former Oriole. Though rumors persisted that the three players had deserted, Macullar eventually went home empty handed. Director Gillette later informed the public that Baltimore had offered Grim $1,000 in advance, and promised him a three-year contract for $3,500 a year. Vickery had been offered $700, $200 in advance. Shoch's offer was for $500, half in advance. While all these cloak and dagger negotiations were going on, the Brewers left Minneapolis, traveled to Sioux City and split two games, lifting the club to second place. Fred Clausen also returned, ready to play.

Reports circulated that St. Paul would either be transferred to Duluth, or switch teams with Lincoln by July 4. Even though in first place, Lincoln was losing money, averaging only 300 to 400 people a game. It was believed St. Paul would support a winning team. Elsewhere, on June 13 Denver was sold to local interests. Then on June 18, St. Paul was transferred to Duluth. At the time of the transfer, the Apostles' record was 17 and 34, in last place.

With four full days of rest, the Brewers opened in Denver, with Vickery winning his fifteenth. Vickery won again the next day, before Fred Smith lost to end the series. The Brewers went on to Kansas City, where they again won two of three. Milwaukee was reportedly trying to sell Dungan, as there was no place for him to play. The team then split four games in Nebraska, winning two from first-place Omaha, before losing to Lincoln twice.

The Brewers opened their second homestand on July 4 with a doubleheader. Before 2,100 in the morning game Vickery won number 20, beating Sioux City 8 to 7. The afternoon game drew 4,700, Davies losing. Vickery then lost his outing to end the series. Cushman succeeded in signing "Phenomenal" Smith, who had been released by Philadelphia. The Milwaukee manager also signed another pitcher, E.P. "Pink" Hawley, from Beaver Dam. However, Hawley never reported to the Brewers, instead pitching for Markesan. Fred Clausen was released.

A Lincoln player next caused problems for the Western Association. Harry Raymond, an infielder, had jumped to Louisville and then back to Lincoln. While at Louisville he had been placed on the blacklist. What was his status now? Milwaukee president William Furlong said he would protest any game in which the infielder played. However, Raymond was soon officially re-instated by National League president Nick Young. Some thought Raymond was a "stool pigeon"[11] for the Western to get some Louisville players to jump. Whatever Young's reasoning, he took abuse from the press, as the *Sporting Life* put it:

> N.E. Young
> Baseball to Suit Anybody
> Furnished Upon Application[12]

Minneapolis then came to Milwaukee and lost two in a rain-shortened series. After the series, Minneapolis sold its star shortstop, Bill Shugart, to Pittsburgh of the National League for $4,800. The Millers were followed into Milwaukee by the Duluth club. John "Phenomenal" Smith won his first game in a Milwaukee uniform, 3 to 1. Vickery won yet another game before Phenomenal lost his first.

With the homestand over, Furlong resigned as president of the Milwaukee club. Citing his rundown physical condition, Furlong planned on taking an extended trip to the Rocky Mountains. Harry E. Gillette, a well-known restaurant owner at 11 Grand Avenue (at the site that later became Gimbel's Department Store on Wisconsin Avenue), was appointed the third president of the year. The *Evening Wisconsin* reported he was "one of the most hustling directors the Milwaukee club has got. The next thing on earth he loves next to his wife is a baseball game."[13] According to the Milwaukee *Sporting News* correspondent, in Gillette "the qualities of an astute business man, a well posted base ball man and a vigorous hustler are all cominbed."[14]

Omaha now became the Western Association's troubled spot. On June 26 it was reported the franchise was about to be sold to a St. Paul syndicate for $16,500. Sioux City immediately offered to sell out for $5,000, and soon dropped the price to $3,000. Nothing happened at this time, as the Omaha price was too high and the Sioux City owners changed their minds. Then on July 13 it was reported Omaha Owner McCormack had turned his players and franchise over to the Western. Two days later it was reported the club was under new management, but several of its players and its manager, Dan Shannon, had jumped to Washington of the American Association. It was then announced the Omaha franchise was defunct and out of the Western Association. Plans were made to salvage the situation. One plan was to drop Sioux City, a club $2,000 in debt with player salaries not paid in full, and continue as a six-club circuit. Another plan was to take in Grand Rapids, Superior or Indianapolis. Grand Rapids men had offered to take over the franchise. Before the Western could meet, Omaha declared its intention to stay in the association, but some of their players had signed with other clubs in the meantime. It soon came out that McCormack and Shannon were in with the American Association on the demise of the franchise. Several players had been told by these two men to go to the American Association immediately after the club disbanded. Western Association President Krauthoff claimed some of the releases were dated July 1. It was also reported Shannon was getting paid by the American Association for his actions. "The theory is that the American Association failing of success in its attack on the Western Association through its players, who were asked to jump, centered upon Omaha as one of the Western Association's vital parts, and struck their blow which was expected would upset the whole association."[15]

The Western rallied quickly. President Young of the Board of Control advised all National Agreement clubs not to touch Omaha players. The eight Omaha players who had jumped to the American Association would be blacklisted and all the players with National Agreement clubs were ordered to return. Omaha would continue its schedule in the Western Association, with all forfeited games now called postponements. Seven Omaha players said they would return to the team. Western clubs supplied the other players, with Milwaukee giving Omaha Sam Dungan, costing the Brewers $200, as Kansas City had offered that amount for him. In addition, six other Western clubs put up $500 each to see Omaha through.

Throughout all this the Brewers were on a road trip, winning three from the Millers, losing three in Sioux City, and winning three in Duluth. Milwaukee returned home July 25 and beat Omaha 17 to 1, 20 to 7, and 17 to 2. The *Sentinel* wrote, "The reconstructed Omaha could not have held on to a victory if it had been sewed on to their uniforms."[16] Denver then came to the Cream City and Vickery won his 25th game in the first contest of the series. Denver forfeited the second game over a call by the umpire, giving Milwaukee first place over the sliding Omaha team. Davies then finished Denver off. At this point, Abner Dalrymple was leading the Western in batting. Lincoln came to Milwaukee and the Brewers won two of three. In the second Lincoln game, Shoch was badly spiked and would miss a few weeks. The incident escalated and the two managers became involved in a fistfight near the players bench. The crowd also thought the injury intentional and it took the police 20 minutes to clear the field before play could resume. In the third contest, Davies won his twentieth game. Kansas City then beat Milwaukee two of three.

Financial problems were again hitting the Western Association. The Lincoln franchise was up for sale. The club was offered to a West Superior man on the condition he would take over the back salaries, about $2,400. The offer was declined. Within days the Minneapolis club announced it would disband. The Minneapolis president said he would lose $4,000 to $5,000 if he stayed in the Western. Within a day, the club was purchased by a local syndicate for $5,000. Duluth was out about $2,000 and was on the verge of disbanding.

With the Western Association beginning to fall apart at the seams, Milwaukee directors said they would put up a $5,000 or a $10,000 bond to finish the season, if the other clubs would as well. No other club would, so Milwaukee decided to play out the Western schedule and take the first chance it could to join the American Association. It was reported the association in early July had offered Milwaukee the Louisville franchise, a club $6,000 in debt and ready to quit the American Association. However, the Milwaukee directors wanted to stay in the National Agreement at that time. When the *St. Louis Globe Democrat* reported Brewer officials were in St. Louis to discuss taking over the Louisville franchise, Gillette denied it, saying Milwaukee would go to the association only as "a last resort in order to save themselves."[17] In August the *Sporting News* reported Milwaukee directors were interested in purchasing the controlling interest in the Louisville club for 60 cents on the dollar and transfer the franchise to Milwaukee. The deal fell through. Meanwhile, the Brewers released Fred Smith, who had an 8 and 13 record. Davies and John Smith then beat Sioux City in Milwaukee before Vickery lost his decision.

The August 14 *Milwaukee Sentinel* reported Cincinnati of the American Association would transfer to Milwaukee. It had been rumored the Ohio club would transfer to Indianapolis, but the *Sentinel* told the reason why Milwaukee was chosen: "The Association recognizes that Milwaukee is the stronghold of the Western Association and the withdrawal of that club will destroy the Western Association and throw a number of good players upon the market."

The Louisville owners originally wished to transfer their club to Milwaukee, but wanted $8,000, which Milwaukee directors thought was too high. The Cincinnati franchise was property of the American Association, not of any individual or stock company, and had been losing money all year. Milwaukee club president Harry Gillette received the consent of five American Association clubs to receive Cincinnati on August 14, 1891.

Not everything went smoothly, however. At this point it was unknown if the Cincinnati or Louisville club would be transferred to Milwaukee. The *Journal* wrote Milwaukee would welcome either. It

Harry Vaughn would lead 1891 American Association Brewers with a .333 batting average.

was a case of "How happy could I be with either, were t'other dear charmer away."[18] The Brewers were to open in the American Association in St. Louis on August 15. The previous afternoon Manager Cushman had his club leave the field during the seventh inning of a game against Sioux City, forfeiting the game, to go to the train depot. Cushman then received a telegram from St. Louis owner Chris Von der Ahe reporting that Cincinnati would play in St. Louis. Von der Ahe was against the Milwaukee transfer. He owned the controlling stock in the Cincinnati franchise and was reluctant to surrender the city. Von der Ahe had put considerable expense in fixing up grounds in Cincinnati and was personally responsible for the five-year lease on the park. Von der Ahe did give in and the Brewers traveled to St. Louis.

The Cincinnati franchise had been sold to the Milwaukee men for $12,000, half in cash and the remainder payable in 30 days. Frank Bancroft, the Cincinnati manager, would come to Milwaukee and look after business affairs, while Cushman would handle the players. The Brewers would take John [Frank] Dwyer (p), Willard Mains (p), John Carney (1b), Harry Vaughn (c) and James Canavan (ss) from the Cincinnati team. The other Cincinnati players went to Washington or were released, except for Mike Kelly, who went back to Boston. Mains returned home to recover from injuries. The Brewers released John "Phenomenal" Smith and William Campion. Tom Vickery and Bill Schriver went to

Chicago of the National League, neither wanting to leave the National Agreement. George Shoch and George Davies were given bigger contracts too stay in Milwaukee. (The *Sporting News* reported after the season Davies would enter the office of Dr. Stadler of Milwaukee, also a Brewer baseball director, and study medicine at Wisconsin University.) Grim was offered $1,500 by Chicago, but declined.

The Western Association was gasping for air. Three Minneapolis players jumped to the American Association. At a meeting in Minneapolis on August 17, the Milwaukee franchise was declared forfeited and the players released from their contracts. This made them able to sign with any National Agreement club. Lincoln and Omaha merged to form a six-club Western Association. At this time the eight-club record for 1891 was: Milwaukee (59–37), Minneapolis (52–45), Omaha (46–40), Sioux City (50–46), Kansas City (50–47), Lincoln (45–47), Denver (38–56) and Duluth (39–61). On August 20 the Western dropped Minneapolis and Duluth, becoming a four-club circuit. Finally on September 17, the Western Association disbanded, and Sioux City was awarded the pennant.

The American Association had been formed in late 1881, and for its first season of 1882 consisted of Baltimore, Cincinnati, Louisville, Philadelphia, Pittsburgh and St. Louis. This new American Association had three outstanding features the old National League lacked: Sunday ball where allowed, 25-cent admission and the sale of alcoholic beverages in its parks. After one year of hostility with the National League, baseball peace came about, and the American Association added Columbus and New York to form an eight-club circuit. Except for the 1884 season, the year of the Union Association with the American Association expanding to 12 teams, the American Association remained an eight-club circuit. From 1884 through 1890 franchises were expelled and dropped, and there were defections. At the end of 1890 the American Association towns were Syracuse, Rochester, Philadelphia, Baltimore, Louisville, Columbus, St. Louis and Toledo. As we saw earlier in this chapter, the cities changed again for 1891. Milwaukee was officially enrolled in the American Association on August 17, 1891, with the following resolution:

> Resolved: That the application of Milwaukee for membership in the American Association, upon the terms and conditions named, this date, be and is hereby accepted with the express reservation that the Cincinnati Club be retained in full membership, the latter, however, to transfer its dates to Milwaukee for the residue of the present season. The Cincinnati Club is to retain full power in the American Association.[19]

In theory, the American Association now had nine members.

When Milwaukee entered the American Association, taking Cincinnati's record of 43 and 57, the team stood in sixth place, 4½ games behind Columbus, 25 games behind first-place Boston.

On the way to the Brewers' first game in the American Association, Abner Dalrymple had a run-in with the law in Chicago. The *Sporting News* reported the Brewer outfielder owed C.A. Weldenferrier, of the previous year's Brotherhood Association, $300, which Abner had borrowed and not paid back. A Chicago constable was waiting for Dalrymple at the depot and arrested him on a capias. "Dal" was held briefly until he settled the account. Milwaukee opened in the American Association on August 18, in St. Louis, before 2,000 fans.

St. Louis		AB	R	H	E	Milwaukee		AB	R	H	E
Hoy	cf	2	2	2	1	Burke	lf	6	1	2	0
Fuller	ss	3	0	1	1	Pettit	2b	5	0	0	0

		St. Louis						Milwaukee			
		AB	R	H	E			AB	R	H	E
McCarty	rf	4	0	1	0	Earl	rf	4	0	0	1
O'Neil	1b	4	0	0	0	Dalrymple	lf	4	0	0	0
Stivetts	p	4	0	0	0	Canavan	ss	4	2	1	0
Comiskey	1b	4	0	2	1	Carney	1b	3	1	1	0
Boyle	3b	4	0	0	0	Grim	c	4	2	0	0
Darling	c	3	0	0	2	Alberts	3b	4	0	0	0
Robinson	2b	3	0	0	1	Davies	p	2	1	0	0
		31	2	6	6			36	7	6	1

	1	2	3	4	5	6	7	8	9
St, Louis	1	0	0	0	0	0	0	1	0—2
Milwaukee	0	0	0	1	0	0	3	3	x—7

Two days later Dwyer beat the Louisville Colonels, 5 to 2, Dalrymple going 4-for-4 at the plate. The Brewers then signed Frank Killen, late of Minneapolis. After a rain-out in Louisville, the Brewers traveled to Boston. More than 3,700 fans saw Charles Buffington pitch a 3-hit, 8 to 0 win over the Brewers, with Shoch back in the lineup. The Brewers lost the remaining two in Boston.

President Harry Gillette of the Brewers now disclosed the Brewers were in financial trouble, with nearly $12,000 in debts. The club had made no money in the Western Association, and still had to pay the American Association $3,000. When the club entered the American Association, Gillette and Zach Bartlett had paid the first $3,000 themselves, thinking the local people would buy stock after the club was in the American Association. This had not happened. At a meeting on August 27 it was resolved that if anyone would assume the debt, the club would be his. If that did not happen, the stockholders would be assessed an extra 25 percent on their stock. At a meeting on August 29, Bartlett and Dr. L.C. Stadler decided to assume the debts of the club with Gillette. It was reported Charles Pfister, George Ziegler and Charles Kipp dropped out and donated their stock ($3,000 between Ziegler and Pfister, $500 from Kipp) to the club. Even though Gillette, Bartlett and Stadler would control the club, the directors would be kept for the present. The small stockholders (about 50 in all, holding from one-half of a share to five shares) would in effect be frozen out. These stockholders would lose the full amount of their stock. Gillette explained all association clubs were being assessed 10 percent to pay for the buying out of Rochester, Toledo and Syracuse earlier in the year. The directors announced season tickets for the Western Association games would be honored at American Association games. Approximately $4,000 was also contributed by Milwaukee citizens to help the club. The syndicate never took the club over and the stockholders were assessed the 25 percent.

The Brewers traveled to Washington and lost 4 to 3, before Davies won 5 to 1. Moving on to Baltimore, Dalrymple collected three hits, including two triples, and scored three runs in a 9 to 5 victory for Killen. The Brewers dropped the next two games to the Orioles. Charlie Cushman was looking for a pitcher, as Milwaukee traveled to Philadelphia and lost four of five to the Athletics. Pettit injured his leg in the first game and was sent home.

On Thursday, September 10, the Brewers opened at home, beating Washington 30 to 3, before 2,000. The Brewers collected 24 hits, as everyone except Alberts had at least two hits. Every Brewer scored, with Burke and Dalrymple scoring five times each. Dwyer and Davies finished off the sweep, with Dalrymple hitting for the cycle in the final game. After the series, Frank Bancroft resigned his position as administration manager of the Milwaukee club, forfeiting his last two weeks' salary. As his only job was selling tickets, he was quoted as saying he felt "like the fifth wheel of a wagon."[20]

Philadelphia came into Milwaukee for a series and Milwaukee won two of three with Pettit back in the field and the Sunday doubleheader drawing 6,751. The Orioles came next, with the Brewers winning two of three. Willard Mains, having returned, lost the lone game. Next, the Boston Reds split four games at Athletic Park, including a one-hitter by Killen. The Sunday game at Athletic Park had been attended by 7,500. However, the club found trouble with city officials. The building inspector gave notice such large crowds would not be allowed in the grandstand — more particularly on the roof — unless the structure was strengthened.

The Brewers were in sixth place, only two games behind Columbus, the team coming into town. After 28 games the Brewers were 14 and 14. Davies had a 5 and 5 record, Dwyer was 4 and 4 and Killen 5 and 4, with Mains 0 and 1. Dalrymple led the club with a .342 average and Shoch was hitting .326. Canavan was averaging .297 and Vaughn .292. Earl, Carney and Burke were respectable at .258, .240 and .233, but Grim was only at .202, Alberts at .150 and Captain Pettit at only .141. The team batting average was .260. The pitchers had given up 131 runs; the batters produced 170 runs. Before Columbus arrived, Cushman signed Thomas Letcher, a right fielder from Marinette, Wisconsin, and Jim Hughey, a pitcher from Green Bay. Howard Earl was released about a week later.

After winning 5 to 4, the Brewers beat the Buckeyes behind Davies 5 to 0 (a 5-hitter) and 12 to 1, behind Killen's 2-hitter, to take over fifth place. The Brewers then beat Louisville two of three. The team was scheduled to travel to Columbus to finish the season, but a transfer was arranged. The first game was played in Minneapolis in front of a good crowd, as Killen shut out the Buckeyes 5 to 0. Back in Milwaukee, Hughey ended the season by winning 8 to 4 before only 400 on a cold, rainy day.

The final American Association standings for 1891, with the Cincinnati and Milwaukee records combined, are:

Team	W	L	Pct.	Team	W	L	Pct.
Boston	93	42	.689	Milwaukee	64	72	.471*
St. Louis	85	51	.625	Columbus	61	76	.445
Baltimore	71	64	.526	Louisville	54	83	.394
Philadelphia	73	66	.525	Washington	44	91	.326

*Milwaukee's record was 21 and 15 in the American Association.

After the season the Brewers traveled to St. Louis, playing five exhibition games, losing four. These two teams traveled to Milwaukee, where the Browns won two of three, the last game in front of "about seventy five people [sitting] in the grandstand trying to keep themselves warm."[21]

The *Milwaukee Sentinel* estimated after the season that attendance at Athletic Park for the American Association games was 30,000. At 35 cents an average ticket, total receipts would have been $10,500. Of this amount, the Brewers collected 45 percent, or $4,725; the visitors the same, and 10 percent to the association to pay the debt from the Syracuse, Rochester, Toledo deal. Fortunately, Benjamin M. Weil, a local businessman in insurance and real estate, furnished money to help the financially distressed Brewers, saying he was not a fan but took pride in seeing Milwaukee enterprises prosper. (From a later judgment in the Milwaukee Superior Court, it is learned Weil lent Gillette $4,500, with J.C. Iverson and Zack Bartlett as securities, Gillette pledging $6,200 worth of stock to the two. When the money came due, Iverson and Bartlett had to pay it back, as Gillette had gone to Hot Springs, Arkansas, to dispose of some property there, forcing the two to obtain a judgment against Gillette.) In addition, the stockholders were assessed 50 percent to pay the players. In the later judgment in the Milwaukee Superior Court, it was reported $3,200 worth of stock was turned over to Gillette from some stockholders, who preferred giving up their stock to paying the assessment. The public was then addressed for help. The directors said the increase in salaries from the Western Association to the American Association was about $7,000. They had paid the initial $6,000 for the franchise and $4,000 more was needed in October to pay player salaries. The club needed an additional $7,000 to make it through to 1892. Money had been lost when the club was in the Western Association, as the club had paid out $5,000 more to Western clubs than it had received. In November Gillette announced all debts were paid and there was money in the treasury. He blasted the local breweries, for which the Brewers were named, for not contributing, saying only Pabst had given money to the club.

The end of the season did not stop the National League-American Association war. The association again announced its intentions of entering Chicago. Louisville was having financial troubles, but vowed to stay. At the Association meeting in Chicago in October, Chicago was awarded a franchise, with a capital stock of $50,000. Either Columbus or Milwaukee were slated to be dropped from the American Association. A ten- or twelve-club circuit was also discussed, with Kansas City, Buffalo and Minneapolis considered. The percentage system to visiting clubs was done away with, the home club to take all money brought in. Then in November it was reported the National League and American Association were considering a merger into a 12-club circuit. These first reports included Milwaukee being in the 12-club circuit, with Columbus and Louisville — a club sold to new owners in November for $6,359, the amount of the mortgage held against it — out of the new circuit. The National League denied the report and announced it would drop its long-standing 50-cent admission to a quarter.

The Milwaukee club continued as usual. By November Vaughn, Killen, Letcher, Hughey and Canavan had been signed. After the 1891 season Charlie Cushman had been rehired. As a manager, Charlie was in demand, having received offers from several other clubs. A little later the Brewers signed Bill Dahlen, Chicago's third baseman, for $3,000, including $500 in advance. This was said to be in retaliation for the earlier signings of Vickery and Schriver. In November William Furlong resigned as a director and Charles Polacheck was elected in his place. Gillette was also reported to be resigning to attend to his private business, but changed his mind. In early December president Harry Gillette did resign, selling his stock in the club for 65 cents on the dollar. The *Sentinel* gave another reason for his resignation: "Mr. Gillette's administration had been marked by a more active and liberal policy than ever prevailed during any other regime, but it has not been in all respects satisfactory to some of the officials who are more conservative and inclined to keep the strings as tightly drawn as possible upon the money bag."[22]

The *Sporting News* correspondent reported other directors believed Gillette was too extravagant upon paying $6,000 for the franchise to the American Association when it was well known Milwaukee could have entered the A.A. free of charge. The weekly paper later reported this was not the case. It was true in July the franchise was free for the taking, but at that time Milwaukee wanted to stay within the National Agreement. By the time the Milwaukee directors wanted to switch the franchise, the price was $4,000, and then raised to $6,000. Still, John C. Iverson, who took over as acting president of the club, was quoted in the *Sporting News* as saying Gillette "has proven grossly incompetent in every way."[23] The *Sentinel*, championing Bert Smith for the presidency, was very critical of the Brewer management: "Heretofore there have been a lot of fogies among the directors whose only thought was to keep their names and their actions in connection with the club out of print. Investments in baseball are perfectly legitimate, and, like other investments, are made for revenue only. In other cities the men most prominent in business and social circles are connected with baseball, and do not hesitate to have their names appear in that connection, and the sooner the Milwaukee people awaken to this fact the better it will be for them and the game. If any of them are ashamed of the connection let them get out, and make room for men with broader minds."[24]

The Brewers continued with player problems. After signing Ed Eiteljorge, a pitcher who pitched with Omaha and Washington in 1891, trouble began. It was then reported Davies signed with Cleveland, even though he had a contract with the Brewers through November 1, 1892. Cleveland gave him a salary of $2,800 and a bonus of $800. The Brewers were contemplating legal action to get back their $225 in advance money. Davies' claim was this was not advance money but an increase in salary for 1891, promised to him by Dr. Stadler. Charlie Cushman said there was no such provision in Davies' contract. George Washington Davies would play in Cleveland in 1892. Harry Vaughn then stated he was a free agent. He claimed he signed for $2,800 and $500 in advance, but the advance money had not been paid. The *Sporting Life* reported New York had been negotiating with Vaughn. Pittsburgh claimed to have signed Killen and Grim, but the Brewers denied the reports.

The Milwaukee Baseball Club had bigger problems, however. A local lawyer "had been instructed by Eastern men with plenty of capital to negotiate for a controlling interest in the Milwaukee Baseball Club."[25] The directors reported a controlling interest could be purchased for $25,000, provided the new owners would keep the club in Milwaukee. The Brewers believed it was an attempt by the American Association to get rid of Milwaukee, and the association would never pay $25,000. The directors based their price for a controlling interest "on the actual amount of money invested in the club"[26]: Stock—$17,000; American Association franchise—$6,000; extra association salaries—$5,000; paid to association—$1,000; advance money—$500; and extra assessments of stockholders—$3,000. The American Association would pay no more than $10,000 for the franchise. The *Sentinel* figured the Brewers could draw an attendance of 140,000 in 1892, for a gate income of $35,000, the home club and visitors each receiving $17,500. For the 50-cent grandstand section, estimating 65,000 seats would be sold in that section, another $16,250 could be made, with all this money going to the home club. The club would probably receive at least $17,500 on the road. Thus total receipts would be $51,250. With expenses of $42,000, a $9,000 profit would be made. The club would be foolish to sell.[27]

Talk of the merger of the National League and American Association continued, but the Milwaukee directors believed the association had the upper hand. President Zach Phelps of the American Association assured Charlie Cushman the American Association would stay intact. It was reported 51 percent of the Brewers' capital stock was held in trust by the association, "and under the circumstances it is utterly impossible to vote or drive them out."[28] Negotiations continued in December. It was reported American Association officials were split on a merger. Major obstacles were the number of teams in the new league and Sunday ball (it was reported four National League clubs were also in favor of Sunday ball). However, the *New York Herald* believed the 12-club league was a "sure go."[29] The Philadelphia owners stated if a majority of A.A. clubs were in favor of a merger they would "do all in their power to bring that end about."[30] The Boston Association owner wanted out, unwilling to put any more money into the franchise. Baltimore and Washington had made plans to leave by early December. Publicly, St. Louis owner Chris Von der Ahe—"the sly old rascal of base ball"—was against a merger, but "all the time has been watching for a chance to get in out of the rain."[31]

In Indianapolis, on December 15, 1891, an agreement to merge into a single 12-club league was entered into. Chicago of the American Association had been fighting against a merger. Iverson of Milwaukee was non-committal, but apparently "only too glad to let his club go if the league would reimburse the men he represented for their outlay,"[32] estimated at $13,000. The *Sporting News* of December 19 reported the agreement allowed Sunday ball and 25-cent admission in "cities demanding it." Columbus was bought out for an estimated $12,000. Philadelphia and Boston were bought out for a reported $27,000 and $43,000. Organizers in Chicago reportedly received the money (said to be $13,500) they had spent in their efforts to establish an American Association team there.

The Milwaukee owners were offered the $6,000 they had paid for the franchise. In the December 31, 1891, issue of the *Sentinel*, John Iverson related to the paper what had happened. He had talked with Chris Von der Ahe, and realized "Milwaukee's goose was cooked and that we would be ousted." Iverson told the newspaper Von der Ahe was "interested in the Louisville club to the extent of $3,000 or $4,000, and that amount he wanted to secure. If Milwaukee had owed him anything I have no doubt that we would have remained in the association. My opinion as regards the association magnates is unchanged. They are a lot of scalawags, and Von der Ahe is the worst one of them. If I were a fighting man there might have been a chance for a lively scrap at that meeting; as it was, however I was satisfied with fighting by using simple arguments. They were to no avail, however, and I finally took the $6,000. That was all I could get for the franchise."

Baltimore, Louisville, St. Louis and Washington were admitted to the National League to form the new 12-club circuit, "an enterprise of the grandest pith and moment ever conceived, as in the event of its not being a success, the future of baseball will be as knotty as the winkles of thought on the brow of Sir Edwin Arnold."[33]

It was felt Milwaukee did not receive enough money for the franchise. By being paid back only what had been paid for the franchise fee, not even enough money was received to cover the advance money given to players for 1892. It was believed Milwaukee was taken into the American Association as part of a scheme by some association owners that had begun in the early part of the season to force a merger with the National League. Milwaukee's departure was hoped to break up the Western Association, thus erasing a National League ally against the American Association. The Milwaukee transfer had also eliminated the Cincinnati A.A. franchise, which might have been a bone of contention in merger negotiations with the National League. It was also felt the money Milwaukee had paid to get into the association would help pay off the costs incurred in buying out the franchises of Toledo, Syracuse and Buffalo.

The new Chicago club in the American Association was also seen as only a lever against the National League in merger talks. However, the Chicago investors told Milwaukee's Iverson they were disgusted and indignant, as they had been induced under false pretenses to join the association. They claimed to have spent more than $17,000 on a park and grounds, and received only $12,000 to $13,000 for their franchise. A change in American Association by-laws decided upon back in September—which now required a simple majority instead of a two-thirds vote to dissolve the association—added to the thoughts the merger plans were in the works for some time. The *Sporting News* of December 26, 1891, asked, "Was a more deliberate piece of treachery or a more dishonorable freeze out ever known in the history of base ball in this country?"

Under the terms of the agreement, previously signed players of the dropped clubs could not be held to their contracts. Cushman believed the players should stay with Milwaukee because they had signed contracts with the Milwaukee Baseball Club, not the American Association. His opinion was wrong, as George Shoch was assigned to Washington, Ed Burke went to Cincinnati, Jim Canavan and John Grim went to Louisville, and Bill Dahlen went back to Chicago. According to a later report, the Milwaukee club did not get advance money back, at least not from Dahlen.

The Milwaukee club had played 36 games in the American Association, winning 21. Harry Vaughn led the team with a .333 average, George Shoch hit .315, and Abner Dalrymple ended with a .311 average. Jim Canavan led the Brewers with 33 runs scored, and Dalrymple scored 31, as did Ed Burke. Both Canavan and John Carney hit three home runs. The team had a .261 batting average, scoring 227 runs. Frank Killen was credited with 7 victories against 4 defeats, having a 1.68 ERA. The team had an earned run average of 2.50, giving up 156 total runs.

At the beginning of the Western Association season, the *Evening Wisconsin* had started a poll to find the most popular player on the Milwaukee club. Balloting continued throughout the season and on October 5, after nearly 65,000 votes were cast, Gus Alberts was the winner. Alberts was presented a medal of solid gold, 4½ inches long and 2 inches in width, weighing 774 grams. The medal had an eagle with its wings spread on a crossbar on top, with crossed bats below, and a figure of a ball player enclosed in a circular design on the bottom.

For now, Milwaukee had no baseball club.

11

Allotment and Bicycles Deaden Interest (1892–1893)

In October 1891 baseball men in Sioux City, Minneapolis, Kansas City and Lincoln reported they were in favor of reorganizing the Western Association. These four cities, along with Omaha, St. Paul, Duluth and Des Moines, were mentioned. Milwaukee was still in the American Association, but was informed the club would be welcome to the Western if it quit the American Association. Although publicly saying they thought the Brewers would be in the American Association, the Milwaukee directors kept an eye on the revival of the Western.

By December the Western appeared it would be without Milwaukee. After the Milwaukee franchise was bought out of the American Association, a new league was discussed. Proposed cities were Indianapolis, Columbus, Milwaukee, Detroit, Buffalo, St. Paul, Minneapolis, Omaha, Toledo, Kansas City and possibly Chicago. Just prior to Christmas a report came from Chicago that this proposed league, called the Central League, would consist of Columbus, Detroit, Milwaukee, St. Paul, Minneapolis, Omaha, Kansas City and Chicago. Players would be picked from the surplus in the National League–American Association merger. The *Evening Wisconsin* favored this Central League over the Western. Others were against it because some of the eastern cities were opposed to Sunday ball. Within a week the proposed Central League had changed to Indianapolis, Columbus, Milwaukee, Toledo, Rochester, Syracuse, Buffalo and Toronto. James A. Williams of Columbus, who proposed this circuit, cited all eight cities had populations over 100,000 and some over 200,000. From Kansas City, L.C. Krauthoff urged a Central League of Columbus, Indianapolis, Milwaukee, Minneapolis, St. Paul, Kansas City, Omaha, and Grand Rapids or Toledo. Milwaukee favored Williams' plan because of the proximity of the cities.

Meanwhile, another league was planned. From Philadelphia came a report the United Association of Baseball Clubs would be organized to take the place of the American Association. Franchises would be in Boston, Philadelphia, Columbus, Milwaukee, New York, Pittsburgh, Chicago and St. Louis. The United Association would have 15-cent admission with another dime in the grandstands. The report went so far as to say Philadelphia had players and grounds secured. Milwaukee directors knew nothing of the league, and the *Milwaukee Journal* thought the United Association had "the salty smell of the sea about it."[1]

President John W. Speas of Kansas City then called for a meeting on January 7 in Chicago to reorganize the Western. Before this meeting, which Milwaukee was invited to attend, the directors of the Brewers met at the Plankinton House and decided to form a new baseball club. John C. Iverson reported the expenses of the 1891 club were $44,917, of which $30,000 went to salaries. He believed expenses could be reduced to $28,695 — $12.980 for running expenses and $15,915 in salaries. A $7,000 profit could be had. On December 31 St. Paul was sold to John M. Bennett, head of a syndicate backed by $100,000. Reportedly Bennett favored a salary limit of $1,800 or $2,000 a month, and a Western Association of Kansas City, Omaha, St. Paul, Minneapolis, Milwaukee, Indianapolis, Detroit and Columbus. Iverson reported he was not sure of the new Western, as he did not want to enter a league with both St. Paul and Minneapolis, but would favor a consolidation of these two franchises. Columbus asked Milwaukee to stay out of the Western and join the proposed Central League.

John Iverson, Charles Polacheck and Robert Maguire went to the Western meeting in Chicago on January 7. Delegates from Kansas City, Minneapolis, St. Paul, Omaha and Columbus also attended, although Columbus was there to talk about the Central League. Nothing definite was set, but a Committee on Organization formed with Robert W. Maguire (Milwaukee), J.W. Speas (Kansas City) and Gus Schmelz (Columbus) on the committee.

On January 21 the Western met again and organized. By this time the Central League idea had folded. James Williams of Columbus was elected president, secretary and treasurer. The league consisted of Minneapolis, St. Paul, Kansas City, Omaha, Milwaukee, Indianapolis, Columbus and Toledo. The Western was to be a novel league. Williams would select eight teams of 12 players, as equal as possible, with the Committee on Organization to be the final judges. After the teams were balanced, they would be numbered and each manager would draw from a hat. The sale of players was abolished during the season. Only after the season could a player be sold, the amount realized would go to the Western, and then the league would furnish the club with an equal player. Sam Morton of Minneapolis called the new plan a "life-saver,"[2] as the Western could not afford another scramble for players and big salaries. The Western was responsible for player salaries, so every salary would be guaranteed. Contracts were for six months, with an option clause for one month at contract salaries for post-season exhibitions. This system "would do away with the fatal competition for players which helped wreck so many clubs."[3] A salary limit of $12,000 was put on each club, and with the league signing all players, it could not be violated. It was figured the cost of Western teams would be from $18,000 to $20,000, compared with $32,000 to $37,000 in 1891. Gate receipts were spit 45–45, with 10 percent going to the Western's sinking fund, which was thought would hit $25,000 by the end of the season. The Western also adopted a split season; the first from April through June, the second July through October. A playoff at the end of the season between the two winners would determine the champion. All games in the Western would be played to their entirety. A rained-out game of more than five innings would be played the next off day, as would games called due to darkness. "In this way the league will stop the foolish incident to a ball field when a team tries to hinder the playing of five innings to prevent it from being a game."[4] A new league rule provided players were no longer compelled to purchase their own uniforms, and clubs could not charge them 50 cents a day on the road. With these new ideas, it was predicted the Western would "claim the honor of having taken the first decisive steps toward putting the game on strictly business principles, and insuring to both owners and players a season without losses."[5]

Of course, to make this plan work the Western needed help. First, they needed the cooperation of the eastern leagues on the salary limits. Then a new National Agreement was needed. The National League proposed placing the minor leagues into Class A and B. Larger minor leagues, Class A, would contract and reserve players, and the National League would pay $750 for a player's release. Class A could draft from Class B for $375 a player. The price of the National Agreement would be $200 per club. The Western League, along with Cleveland, Cincinnati and Chicago of the National League, were against the plan. Finally, on March 1 a new National Agreement was completed. The National League would pay $1,000 to draft a man from the Western, and could only draft between October 1 and February 1. The Western would pay $500 to draft from other minor leagues. This protection cost the Western $150 a club, or $1,200.

On March 17, 1892, the Western again met in Chicago to pick the teams. Sixteen catchers, 28 pitchers, 9 first basemen, 12 second basemen, 12 third sackers, 8 shortstops and 27 outfielders were on the list. Many older veterans refused to go into the Western lottery, hoping the eastern associations—or the Western—would raise their salary limits. The list was whittled down to 96 players and equaled out. Bartlett picked for Milwaukee and received this team:

Catchers—Fred Lake and Bill Krieg. Lake had played briefly with Boston of the National League in 1891. Krieg, of course, had previously played for the Brewers.

Pitchers—Larry Twitchell, Harry Burrell and Henry Jones. Twitchell had wandered around the league since 1886 and played in 1891 in Omaha and Columbus. Burrell had a 4 and 2 record with the St. Louis Browns the previous year. Jones was a young and promising player from Erie of the New York-Pennsylvania League.

Infield—Howard Earl (1b), another former Brewer, and Frank Ward (2b), who had played in Minneapolis the year before. James "Chippy" McGarr (ss) was a 29-year-old veteran whose playing days went back to the Union Association. After playing with four American Association clubs in four years, he traveled to Boston of the National League in 1890 and then in 1891 played with Cleveland and Denver. Fred Roat (3b) started with Pittsburgh in 1890 and played in Lincoln the year previous to this.

Outfield—Ed Pabst, George Henry and Charles Hamburg. Hamburg led the Western in hitting in 1891 at St. Paul and Duluth.

Before the day was over, Cushman traded Ed Pabst to Columbus for pitcher Alex Ferson, another former Brewer of three years before, who had played in Buffalo in 1891. The *Journal* on May 7 would say of the 1892 team:

> There are no $10,000 beauties in the team, and nature has not strained herself to chisel their features into the shapes usually called handsome, but nevertheless they make a good appearance and will compare favorably with any of the other teams. They are a healthy, husky looking lot of fellows who seems to be satisfied to mind their own business and let the rest of the world look out for itself.

With a team in the Western League, the Brewer directors readied for the 1892 season. In October of 1891 Harry Gillette had announced he was negotiating for grounds just west of Thirteenth Street, between Fowler (St. Paul) and Clybourn. However, the club decided to again play at Athletic Park on Eighth and Chambers, and to enlarge its seating by 1,000. A stairway also would be built leading directly from Chambers Street to the grandstand. New dressing rooms for visiting players were constructed. The special police, groundskeepers and other employees were to be "dressed in a neat and tasty uniform"[6] for the new season. Four electric street cars that ran directly to the park were added that would accommodate twice as many people. To add to the beauty, groundskeeper Murphy planted flower beds near each of the player's benches. One sad note was the big shade tree in left field, where Abner Dalrymple and other left fielders had hidden from the sun, was scheduled to be cut down.

The board of directors met in February and decided to discontinue the sale of beer in the grandstand. Other vendors were also ordered not to sell while an inning was in progress. Another move, 100 years or so before it again became fashionable, was the setting aside a portion of the grandstand for smokers. A.W. Friese was again given the scorecard rights. Season tickets were put on sale for $25 for transferable tickets, and $20 for non-transferable tickets. The club was without a president. The *Sentinel* predicted George Ziegler would accept the position, and the *Evening Wisconsin* thought Robert Maguire should be president. The directors, however, wanted John C. Iverson and elected him president in April, even though he was in Mexico. Zack Bartlett was elected vice president, Augustus Friese secretary, with Charles Polacheck, Howard Clement and Samuel Wright the board of directors.

Charlie Cushman still had control of the team. After the lottery, Cushman had ordered all his players to report in St. Louis on March 28. He also reported he would only give the players $50 in advance money. Western League President Williams sent out a list of the extra players available if any clubs were interested. Cushman was looking for a catcher so he could move Krieg to the outfield and release Henry. Williams had two on his list, but they apparently did not suit Cushman. He was after McMahon, who had caught in St. Paul in 1891. The Brewers met in St. Louis and practiced at the St. Louis Browns' park. On paper the club looked strong. The *Sporting Life* figured Milwaukee to take first place in both parts of the split season. The *Chicago Herald* agreed that the Brewers were the strongest team in the Western for 1892.

On the exhibition field the Brewers did not look so strong. In the first exhibition game on April 2 against the Browns, Cushman played all twelve players and lost 9 to 1. On the next two days the Brewers lost 8 to 1 and 12 to 7. It was then on to Pittsburgh, where the Brewers lost to the Pirates 18 to 3. Cushman claimed the club had not practiced enough together, but would be ready for the regular season. To strengthen the club, Cushman wanted to sign Albert Maul, a pitcher, and John Burger, a catcher, both formerly of Pittsburgh. Williams denied him both, but assigned Milwaukee William Widner, a journeyman pitcher. Jones was released. Cushman was also offered pitcher Martin Duke, but refused him. Cushman wanted Con Murphy, a catcher. The Brewers ended the exhibitions by losing two to Louisville and Columbus. After the 0 and 8 exhibition record, Cushman and Iverson realized the team was weak. Iverson figured after the National League season began more players would be available to strengthen his club, which needed help at pitcher and catcher.

The Western was ready to open the 1892 lottery season in good shape. Milwaukee, of course, was owned by the directors previously named. Minneapolis was owned by Hy Hach and managed by Sam Morton. Speas and Krauthoff handled Kansas City. Rowe managed and partly owned Omaha. John T. Brush was the principal owner of Indianapolis. Gus Schmelz managed Columbus, while Williams owned the franchise. C.H. Morton managed Toledo. Only St. Paul looked weak, with John Bennett as its pilot. In March this city almost dropped out, going to Terre Haute, but A.M. Thompson put up a bond to stay in the Western. Frank Robinson, also owner of the Cleveland National League team, kept his eye on the St. Paul franchise in case it would falter and possibly move it to Fort Wayne.

The Brewers opened the 1892 season in Indianapolis on Saturday, April 16. Before 2,400 fans, Ferson beat the Hoosiers 5 to 4.

INDIANAPOLIS		R	H	PO	A	E	MILWAUKEE		R	H	PO	A	E
Letcher	rf	1	1	2	0	0	McGarr	ss	0	0	1	2	0
McQuaid	lf	1	1	2	1	1	Ward	2b	0	0	2	0	0
Maray	cf	0	1	1	0	1	Twitchell	rf	0	2	2	1	0
O'Brien	1b	0	1	9	0	0	Earl	1b	0	1	12	1	1
Carpenter	3b	0	0	2	3	0	Lake	c	2	1	5	0	0
Hengle	2b	1	0	2	2	1	Henry	cf	2	1	1	1	0

		INDIANAPOLIS							MILWAUKEE				
		R	*H*	*PO*	*A*	*E*			*R*	*H*	*PO*	*A*	*E*
Klugman	ss	0	0	4	1	1	Hamburg	rf	0	0	1	0	0
Quinn	c	0	1	4	3	0	Rost	3b	1	2	1	4	1
Madden	p	1	1	0	5	0	Ferson	p	0	0	1	7	0
		4	6	24	15	4			5	7	26	16	2

```
              1 2 3 4 5 6 7 8 9
Indianapolis  1 0 0 0 0 0 0 3 0 — 4
Milwaukee     0 2 0 3 0 0 0 0 x — 5
```

    The second game of the Indianapolis series was rained out. The Brewers then moved on to Columbus, where Burrell won 3 to 2, with the two other games being rained out. The umpire in this only Columbus game, Dan Corcoran, was fired after the game for drunkenness on the field. It was said his decisions were so bad "but for the interference of Columbus players he would have been hurt"[7] by the crowd. After the firing, Corcoran "went to a priest and took the total abstinence pledge."[8] He then talked to President Williams, who re-instated him. Milwaukee also talked to Williams about Con Murphy, but without success. Williams said Omaha was in need of a catcher and Murphy would probably go there.

    The Brewers traveled to Minnesota next, beating Minneapolis three straight — all played in cold, rainy weather — to run their record to 5 and 0. The Brewers traveled over to St. Paul, and after a rainout, Widner won the club's sixth straight before another rainout. In Kansas City Ferson lost to the Blues for the club's first loss, 8 to 3. The Brewers split the remaining two games. On to Omaha, but all three games were rained out.

    On Saturday, May 6, the Brewers played at home for the first time, with Ferson beating the Millers 8 to 0 on a four-hitter. Only 1,000 fans attended on a cold, clear day. On Sunday 3,500 to 4,000 saw Widner lose 10 to 9 to the Millers at Athletic Park. Burrell ended the series with a 20 to 8 win. St. Paul next came to town. After a rainout, Ferson won before a turnout of only 400. Roat, who had hurt his arm earlier in the season but returned, was out again and replaced on the roster by Krieg. Rain again prevented the final game. Omaha was in town next, beating Milwaukee two out of three, dropping the Brewers to second place, behind Columbus. Widner then beat Kansas City in Milwaukee; the final two games were rained out, as even on an open day the grounds were too wet to play on. Milwaukee then beat last-place Indianapolis three of four. Roat was back with the team, even though his arm was still sore.

    The Western League was beginning to have troubles. By mid–May it was found the Western did not have the competitive balance its directors sought. Through May 21 Columbus had played 19 and 5 ball, and Milwaukee was 12 and 6; no other club was close. Indianapolis had lost its first 8 games. Minneapolis was 5 and 12, St. Paul 5 and 11. Kansas City was the only other club over .500, just barely at 10 and 9. Another problem was the weather. Indianapolis alone had 19 rainouts by May 20. Milwaukee had 12 rainouts. Sunday ball was becoming sticky in some cities. Minneapolis was threatening to stop Sunday ball. On May 22 both the Columbus and Toledo teams were arrested in Toledo during the ninth inning of their game for violating the Sunday laws. The players were released on $1.50 bail and the managers posted $15. In June a jury found the clubs not guilty of the Sabbath laws, but Toledo would lose Sunday ball.

    The biggest problem, however, was in St. Paul. By early May it was rumored the club would transfer to Fort Wayne, although officials denied the reports. The club had lost $2,500 and had been carried by the Western since the beginning of the season. Fort Wayne was thought by many to be too small. Denver was suggested, but the distance seemed to hurt Denver. Terre Haute and Grand Rapids were also being considered. On May 25 St. Paul, with its 7 and 12 record, was transferred to Fort Wayne.

A player incident in May showed some of the problems and politics confronting the Western. On May 18 Brewer catcher Fred Lake quit the team, leaving for a semi-professional club in Boston that offered him more money. Milwaukee wanted James Donahue, a catcher who had played five years in the American Association, but he did not report right away. Brewer president John Iverson believed Columbus manager Gus Schmelz and owner James Williams were plotting to weaken second-place Milwaukee while helping their first-place team, which was in the Cream City at the time. James Williams, also president of the Western League, claimed Donahue was holding out for a higher salary. Milwaukee did not accept this explanation and threatened to quit the league and return its players if Donahue did not report immediately. He reported to Milwaukee on May 28. Another resignation involved Murphy, the groundskeeper, who went to Minneapolis.

On the ball field, first-place Columbus visited Milwaukee and helped their cause by winning two of three. The Brewers then traveled to Minneapolis, where they split a Decoration Day doubleheader with the Millers. Three more tries at games were rained out. Returning home, the Brewers had their twentieth postponement of the season. The Brewers then split two with the Hoosiers. After another postponement, the club split two games with Fort Wayne. The Brewers then beat the Toledo Black Pirates in two out of three contests.

On June 12 the Brewers were still behind Columbus with the same number of losses, 11. But Columbus had won 31 games to Milwaukee's 21. Cushman said that if the Brewers could win four of six games in the upcoming Columbus series, they would have a fighting chance. The Brewers had some strong hitting as they prepared for the series, with Roat leading the Western with a .389 batting average (in only 17 games), and Ward was third with a .336 average (24 games); Krieg was hitting .324 and Henry .305.

Columbus came to Milwaukee and Burrell opened the series, winning 6 to 3. Ferson then lost, and Widner lost after a rainout. The Brewers then prepared to travel to Columbus for their next series, but trouble started. A half-hour before the club was to leave, nine of the players went on strike for their salaries in advance to July 1. Brewer Vice President Bartlett at first threatened to suspend the men, but the Columbus games would be profitable, and he paid up. The revolt was said to have started because of the Pacific League's higher salaries. The club did travel to Columbus and lost two of three to almost assure Columbus the first-half pennant.

Milwaukee again ran head on with the Western League president on a player issue. Catcher Fred Lake, who had quit the club earlier and placed on the blacklist, asked the Western League to let him go to Kansas City. Western President Williams asked Milwaukee to reinstate Lake, but the Brewers refused to let him off the blacklist. Two days later Williams allowed Lake to go to K.C. Milwaukee directors demanded Williams' resignation, saying, "The captain of a schoolboy team would display more judgment in many cases than President Williams has shown."[9] Williams backed down a little, telling Kansas City to let Lake report, but not to play him without Milwaukee's consent. The Brewers refused to take Lake back or let the Blues use him.

The Western League was having more problems. In early June Louisville of the National League attempted to buy five players, two from Columbus and three from Kansas City, for $1,000 each. The Players' Committee refused to sell them. Some believed Milwaukee wanted out of the Western and had offered to buy Louisville for $30,000. The Brewer directors denied this report. Another report said the National League threatened that if the Western did not pay its dues by July 1, it would raid its players. The Western was rumored to be disbanding, but Williams said this was not true. He admitted the $1,200 due the National League had not been paid, but it would be. He said the bad weather conditions made it impossible to get all the money together. The lottery system of the Western was also under fire. Few expected the Western League to last much longer. The *Milwaukee Sentinel* offered this editorial on June 3, 1892:

> Every indication is offered that the millennium plan is on its last legs and will not outlast the first championship season of the Western League. President Gunnels of the Toledo club is threatening to throw up his franchise unless he gets two players, and Manager Morton of the Minneapolis team announces openly that if a good pitcher turns up he will sign him regardless of President Williams and his millennium plans.

The *Milwaukee Daily News* reported the average fan considered the allotment scheme "too much after the order of a hippodrome."[10]

The Brewers closed the first part of the split season by winning two of three in Toledo, losing two of three in Fort Wayne, and then winning two of three in Indianapolis. Milwaukee had only used three pitchers in the first half—Ferson (11 and 5), Burrell (7 and 8) and Widner (9 and 7). One game in Toledo had been forfeited to the Brewers. The official first-half results were:

Columbus	38	18	.679	Kansas City	25	27	.482
Milwaukee	28	19*	.596	Minneapolis	18	22	.450
Omaha	27	24	.529	Fort Wayne	19	27	.413
Toledo	23	22	.511	Indianapolis	11	30	.268

*Local newspaper accounts show the Brewers lost 20 games.

Amid rumors of disbanding and disenchantment within the league, the Western League opened its second half on July 2. One rumor had Columbus transferring to New Orleans if the Western folded. Unfortunately, like so many games in the first half, the Brewers playing at home were rained out in the opener. In four games with Indianapolis after that, the Brewers and the Hoosiers split.

Serious trouble developed and spread quickly through the Western. Milwaukee was from $2,800 to $3,500 out so far on the season, and "if any other city in the circuit is as good as even they are keeping remarkably quiet about it."[11] On July 5 Frank Robinson announced he was turning over his Fort Wayne franchise to the Western League. The club was on the road, due in Milwaukee, and it was placed under the wing of the Western. Fort Wayne arrived in Milwaukee on July 6 with only seven players and was forced to use its manager and the umpire to play the Brewers. As expected, Milwaukee won 18 to 9. That same night Minneapolis quit the Western. The club was three weeks behind in salaries and unable to continue. The *Milwaukee Sentinel* described the situation: "With no club in the Flour City and the erstwhile Fort Wayne about without a name; with rumor of an impending smashup at Columbus and not a bit of encouraging news from any other Western League city, the prospects are nothing if not decidedly gloomy."[12]

Milwaukee at first said it would stay "till the last dog is hung."[13] At a meeting of the directors on July 6, it was decided to turn the club over to a syndicate and go out of existence. The new syndicate would assume all liabilities and meet all outstanding obligations. There was no official word, but it was believed the new syndicate would include Zack Bartlett, John Iverson, Charles Polacheck and Samuel Wright.

This new syndicate never got a chance. The next day the club disbanded. "There wasn't enough left of the Western League to make a decent funeral,"[14] reported the *Sentinel*. The club divided the $18 in the treasury between the players. The *Daily News* put the blame on the Western president. "President Williams has been an abject and ignominious failure. His administration has been a blending of incompetency and favoritism and his acts, or lack of actions rather, have sent the Western League into a ragged and disorganized mob of otherwise good ball players."[15] One of the club's creditors, Mrs. Catherine Quin, attached the uniforms and other small effects of the club. Meanwhile, the Milwaukee players were being signed by other clubs. Ferson and Ward went to Baltimore. Roat (who had led the team in hitting with a .315 average) signed with Chicago. Burrell, Henry and Hamburg went to the Southern League. McGarr would end up in Rochester and Twitchell in Washington.

The Western League met in Chicago on July 8 and decided to continue with six clubs. Fort Wayne was transferred to Minneapolis. Columbus, Toledo, Kansas City, Omaha and Indianapolis would continue. Barnie, the new Minneapolis manager, blamed the old Minneapolis club and Milwaukee for the trouble since they refused to pay their guarantees and their share of the support money. He went on to say the National League could not sign the Milwaukee players because of the 10-day waiting period. Milwaukee did not attend the meeting, feeling the six-club circuit would not last one week. Within days, Western League President Williams ordered the former Milwaukee players to report to clubs as he assigned them, but the *Milwaukee Sentinel* thought this report ridiculous "in as much as most of the players have already been ensconced in comfortable berths, not only in the 12-club League, but in other cities, the orders from Columbus carry almost a tinge of the ludicrous."[16] The National League said it would keep the players it had taken because the Western had not paid the National Agreement money. The players refused the orders. Finally, on July 14, Columbus withdrew and the Western League folded.

On July 16 a benefit game was held for Charlie Cushman, the very good and almost forgotten manger of the Brewers. The two teams pitted against each other were the County Officials, including supervisors, aldermen and clerks, against the Newsmen. Nearly 200 attended at Athletic Park as the County won 26 to 8. About $150 was netted for Cushman. Cushman then left to become an umpire in the Eastern League.

Two more attempts were made to bring baseball back to Milwaukee in 1892. Harry Quin, still the owner of Athletic Park, tried to make arrangements with Chicago to play a game a week here. He offered each National League club a guarantee of $250 a game, and later upped the guarantee to $700 per club and 75 percent of the gate. The offer was refused. The second movement was made by the former popular infielder, Gus Alberts. The owners of the Oshkosh franchise of the Wisconsin-Michigan League wanted to sell the team and Alberts wanted to move it to Milwaukee. Oshkosh was about $500 out on the season, and with a salary list of only $800 a month, he believed it would go here. Alberts attempted to form a stock company but failed. Secretary Addis of the Wisconsin-Michigan League offered the Ishpening-Negaunee franchise to Milwaukee, but there was no interest. In September the *Sentinel* summed up the baseball situation in Milwaukee: "There are countless thousands who do not believe a professional ball team will ever play here again. Bicycling has taken the place of baseball beyond possibility of dislodgement."[17]

In the winter between 1890 and '91 a new craze hit the American scene: Indoor Baseball. The game was invented in 1887 and really caught on, especially in the East. It was basically baseball, except the pitcher stood 22 feet from home and threw a ball "as hard as an apple dumpling."[18] The batter hit with a bat resembling a billiard cue and ran bases 27 feet apart. A ball caught on a rebound off a wall was out. "Hustler Harry" Smith brought the plan to Milwaukee and soon an eight-club indoor league was formed. His idea was to play three games a week in different sections of the city. In the first game played, at the Farwell Avenue Battery Armory, the Social Circles beat the Batter Club 11 to 8 before 200 people. Numerous clubs were forming, some unable to find suitable halls to play in. Indoor baseball's life was very short in Milwaukee. By early December almost all interest was gone. The *Sentinel* sized up its failure. "The principal reason for the failure of the game was the total lack of attractiveness to the spectators. It affords plenty of fun to the players, but to outsiders it appears to be tiresome, and generally has the effect of driving people away from places where it is played."[19]

In the spring of 1891 amateur players again took to the fields. However, the city was ever expanding. "Corner lots are being built up so rapidly that the boys will have to get outside of the city limits in order to find a place to play ball this season."[20] Amateurs of all forms shaped the 1891 season, but again the semi-professionals took the lion's share of local baseball news. The Phoenix Club organized for the eleventh straight year, as did the Quicksteps for the same period. Unlike the Q's, the Phoenix was big stuff. After losing its first game on April 26 to Belle City, 21 to 3, the club dropped a 2 to 1 decision to Schiffler & Quentmeyer of Watertown, tarnishing their claim of the strongest club in the state. After a June game in Racine, the Phoenix claimed Racine refused to pay the guarantee and did not play there again. After losing in Sheboygan 1 to 0, the club beat Burlington and Waukesha. On July 4 the Phoenix again lost to Schiffler & Quentmeyer. The following day a 26 to 2 loss persuaded four Phoenix players to jump to Sheboygan. That club beat the Phoenix a week later. The only other excitement the Phoenix provided was later in July when the newly formed City League announced the Phoenix had been expelled for not playing a scheduled game. The Phoenix manager wondered how his club could be expelled when it was never in the City League.

Back in the spring of 1891 it was announced that there would be no City Commercial League that summer. In July four teams—Bay Views, Arctics, South Ends and Athletics—formed a City League, and opened July 19. Within four days the Arctics were out and the Greens were in. Admission was only 15 cents but no money was made. The games were well attended, "but many of the spectators look over the fences and pay nothing."[21] In October the Greens were champions of the league.

The Cream Citys again organized a team, opening on Sunday, May 3, at Athletic Park before 250, beating Bay View 8 to 7. The Cream Citys then lost to Green Bay of the Wisconsin State League 25 to 1, and to Schiffler & Quentmeyer 6 to 2. In late June they beat the S & Q team, but then lost to the Jefferson Blues on the Fourth of July weekend. In August the Cream Citys ended the year by losing to Schiffler & Quentmeyer 8 to 7 in eleven innings.

The 1892 season brought only one major club to local attention, James Morgan's Cream City Club. The club formed in late March with no big name players on its roster. The J.M.Cream Citys played their first game on May 22, beating Calumet 3 to 2. In June the club reorganized and soon lost in Watertown 7 to 3, before beating Waukesha 3 to 1 and Racine 20 to 4. Then on July 30 the club lost in Fort Atkinson 5 to 3, but won the next day 10 to 4. After the Western League folded, James Morgan's Cream City Club was the biggest baseball attraction in town. Moving into Athletic Park, the club beat the West Milwaukees on Wednesday, August 10, 5 to 2. That Sunday 200 attended as the Cream Citys beat the Athletics. The following Sunday 1,200 showed up at Athletic Park to see a female team from Denver beat the Cream Citys 12 to 10. Baseball interest then died at Athletic Park and Harry Quin said he would have a quarter-mile cinder track and a field for athletics put in at the park.

Other clubs of interest did form in 1892. The Greens in mid–March were the first to do so. In May Marquette College students organized a league consisting of the Whites, Reds, Blues and Browns. Another club to form was the Smith Club. The club consisted entirely of men with the surname Smith. The *Evening Wisconsin* and *Milwaukee Journal* played each other on June 30, the *Evening Wisconsin* men winning 20 to 19, clearing $75 for the Fresh Air Fund. The two teams again played on July 2, netting $76.25 for the Babies' Home. On Sunday, July 24, between 1,500 and 2,000 attended Athletic Park and witnessed Milwaukee's all-black Reds lose to Boston's all-black team, the Dips, 9 to 8. On August 6 the city's lawyers and doctors played before a good crowd at Athletic Park. The lawyers won 25 to 24, showing at least their hitting was equal to their professional abilities.

The Fourth of July was again the biggest day for amateur teams, many playing doubleheaders. Bay View lost two games in Reedsburg, 8 to 1 and 11 to 1. In Wausau, the Americans split their doubleheader, winning 10 to 7 before losing 15 to 6. The Greens lost to Oconomowoc 6 to 4 and 7 to 4. In Beaver Dam, the Crescents lost 11 to 8 and then won 7 to 6. And in Stoughton, the Athletics won two, 12 to 5 and 5 to 4.

The year 1893 showed the lowest interest in local baseball seen in the past two decades. A total of 261 local amateur clubs had made their way into the papers in 1892: only 102 made it in 1893. While amateur interest declined, professional baseball interest died. In January the Phoenix Athletic Club of St. Paul attempted to revive the old Northwestern League with clubs in St. Paul, Minneapolis, Grand Rapids, Milwaukee, Detroit, Indianapolis and two other cities. Unfortunately, the attempt failed. In April some Milwaukee capitalists made an effort to buy Louisville of the National League, a club having trouble finding grounds. Harry Quin telegraphed the Louisville directors, offering to buy the franchise for $10,000, but was informed the club was not for sale.

Another attempt to have professional ball played here came from Chicago. James Hart, now president of the Chicago National League club, in late 1892 attempted to push a bill through the National League to allow him to transfer one game of every home series to Milwaukee, as he thought the World's Fair in Chicago would hurt his attendance. In late December the *Sporting News* thought the plan was possible, of course, if Anson's Colts did not draw well at home. At it turned out, the World's Fair turned out to be a bonanza and other National League clubs wanted games transferred to Chicago. In May Gus Alberts attempted to get some National League clubs to come to Milwaukee on off-days to play exhibition games or play against his City League teams. Hart claimed with a sufficient guarantee, clubs would come. Quin also got into the act, trying to get one game a week in Milwaukee, and Hart helped by writing all National League clubs, saying that if the games in Milwaukee did not draw well he would have the remaining ones transferred to Chicago. William Barnie of Louisville killed these hopes by stating under no circumstance would the National League play in any non-league city.

Another idea was a new Western League. Charlie Cushman at first believed a strong circuit could be formed with the usual cities in past Western ventures. However, Harry Quin stated he would not lease Athletic Park to a minor league team, and it would be very hard to find someone to put money into a new park. In January Cushman said "Milwaukee is about the liveliest baseball corpse in existence today,"[22] but felt the Milwaukee people would not accept minor league ball, and it would be a waste of time to organize a minor league. The *Chicago Sporting Gazette* agreed, saying, "The Western League is obviously so dead that an electric battery couldn't resuscitate the corpse."[23]

Although Milwaukee was to have no professional baseball in 1893, a major rule change came about in the National League, which would eventually affect all of baseball. This was the moving back of the pitching distance from its 55-foot distance for the 1893 season. It was first proposed to put the pitcher back eight feet, but voted down, and 60 feet 6 inches was decided on. The pitcher had to face the batsman and have one foot in front of and in contact with a rubber plate 12 inches long and 4 inches wide. In addition the pitcher "shall not raise either foot unless in the act of delivering the ball, nor make more than one step in such delivery. He shall hold the ball before the delivery fairly in front of his body and in sight of the umpire."[24]

The longer distance was apparently done to boost offense, which was believed would help attendance. The *Sporting News'* New York correspondent was not certain the change would be all that effective. He believed the change would increase batting for perhaps a month. "The twirlers will not appear quite so near and consequently, not so awfully big to the diminutive batter, and the ball will appear as big as a house, so that the 'Spalding' trade mark may easily be read as the heretofore elusive sphere sails up to the plate." But he predicted the pitchers would adjust to the extra few feet and probably be "even more effective than before." He even thought the change in distance could even benefit some pitchers, as their curves would be "more abrupt, sharper" and harder to hit.[25] The aggregate National League batting average in 1892 had been .245. This jumped to .280 in 1893 and .309 in 1894.

A few of the other rule changes of the 1890s included the elimination of use of the flat bat — or the "board"[26]— a strike charged against the batter on a foul bunt (1894), and a foul tip caught by the catcher counting as a strike (1895). Foul balls were still not counted as a strike against the batter in this decade (the rule changed in 1901 in NL and 1903 in AL).

Gus Alberts, the popular former Brewer and owner of a tavern at 316 Chestnut (318 West Juneau Avenue), and some associates would not let baseball just die here. In March they formed a club called the Laurels, and made plans to form a City League. On March 31 this City League formed, composed of five teams: Laurels, James Morgan's Cream Citys, Athletics, Maple Leafs and South Milwaukees. The teams would play at Athletic Park and South Milwaukee Park on Sundays, with the odd team playing clubs in the interior of the state. A week later another meeting was held with Hugh E. Knoth of the Athletics elected president; William L. Fleischer of the Laurels, secretary; and Frank W. Ricker of the Cream Citys, treasurer. A constitution and by-laws were adopted, along with the 1892 National League rules; the City League staying away from the new 60' 6" pitching distance, as the *Journal* suggested. Admission was set at 15 cents and 25 cents in the grandstand, with ladies admitted free. A scorecard was also given with this admission.

The City League schedule was to open the 1893 season on May 14, and the five clubs took uniform colors in April. The South Milwaukees wore gray suits with black trimmings and stockings. The Athletics had maroon suits and stockings, while the James Morgan Cream City players wore cream-colored suits with black trim and stockings. The Maple Leafs wore navy blue suits with black stockings. The Laurels also had gray suits with blue trimmings and white stockings. The *Sentinel* predicted the league would be a success before it even started. "The various clubs of the City League represent different sections of the city and considerablelocal rivalry will be engendered. This spirit is already beginning to manifest itself, and as a result the games may be expected to create considerable enthusiasm."[27]

Because of the City League's co-operative plan — each player sharing profits at the end of the season — the *Daily News* also was optimistic: "The games will be full of spirit. Every player will be vested with a share of responsibility to make the enterprise a success. If good play is played, the audiences will be large. If the games are well attended, the players will be financially rewarded. While on the other hand, if fakes and snide ball are resorted to, their work and time will be wasted."[28]

The City League began with an exhibition on May 7 between the Laurels and Athletics at Athletic Park, with the Laurels victorious 5 to 2. Arthur Somers struck out 20 for the losers before a good-sized crowd on a chilly day. On opening day, May 14, 350 saw the Laurels again beat the Athletics 11 to 8 at Athletic Park. The South Milwaukee–James Morgan game was rained out.

The City League had players of some stature. Gus Alberts of the Laurels had played in Milwaukee before. Also with the Laurels, Ed Phillips, had played in Sheboygan and was captain of the 1892 Waukesha team. LeRoy Hensel had played with Lincoln of the Western League in 1890. The Laurels pitcher, Corcoran, had played in Green Bay. Charles Riley and Fred Heup of the James Morgan Cream Citys had played with previous Milwaukee clubs. Pat Sullivan of the Maple Leafs played for the 1884 Milwaukee Union Association club. Gus Krock, the pitcher who had pitched three years in the National League, was also with the Leafs. Tom Nagle and Ed Wallschlager had professional experience. Even with these talented players, the City League faltered. In June the South Milwaukees were dropped, with the Racine Maroons to be added. But Racine wanted an agreement that they play all their games in Racine, and never got in. Things were so bad that before one game at Athletic Park, a foot race, a 100-yard dash and other sports were presented to lure customers. By the end of June, the City League decided to play only one game a week. On July 2 only 100 attended the James Morgan–Maple Leaf game. Finally, on July 30, the James Morgans beat the Laurels for the City League championship, in addition to winning a side bet of $50.

What was the problem with baseball interest in Milwaukee? In a word, cycling. It was reported that not only Milwaukee but the entire country had gone crazy over bicycling. In early April the wheelmen, as cyclists were commonly known, converted National Park into a cycling track. Later that month, Harry Quin began to build a quarter-mile cycle track in Athletic Park so Milwaukee wheelmen could be represented in the National Cycling Association. The cyclists, however, preferred National Park, not wanting to be associated with a track used for various professional purposes. Most wheelmen were still amateurs in Milwaukee. When the bicyclists began to race at National Park, large crowds gathered. On Saturday, July 8, 2,500 attended. To help the sport here, Walter Sanger, a local cyclist, won the world's championship in England and told the London press "baseball has been quite eclipsed in the States by cycling, which is now all the rage."[29] He was correct. The sporting pages were almost all cycling, followed by horse racing, boxing and then baseball. Harry Quin was elected a member of the governing board of the National Cycling Association in July and put an additional $5,000 into the Athletic Park cycling facilities. Cycling became so big that in October, when Cincinnati and Cleveland of the National League agreed to play here on a date secured by the North Side Cycle club, they were told to forget it.

Although cycling clearly led the field, baseball was not completely dead. On July 17 at Athletic Park, 1,500 showed up for a charity game between the Chicago Board of Trade and the Milwaukee Chamber of Commerce. James Morgan's Cream City club was the biggest show in town, baseball speaking. With the City League dead, they played in Jefferson, Oconomowoc, Kenosha, Racine and Waukesha. On August 13 the James Morgans beat the Rose Royals Female Club from Denver at Athletic Park 12 to 10 in front of 500 fans. The Morgans ended the season by defeating the local Louis Vonier's Club 27 to 8, and the Columbias of Chicago 16 to 9, both at Athletic Park.

Baseball ended in Milwaukee for the 1893 season with the best show all year. Harry

Quin had arranged for Boston, the National League champions, to play an all-star team on October 1 at Athletic Park. Boston had such stars as Herman Long, one of the best shortstops in the 1890s; Bobby Lowe, the popular former Brewer; Tom McCarthy, a future Hall of Famer, in left field; and Billy Nash, a steady third baseman. Boston's pitcher was Madison's Charles "Kid" Nichols, another future Hall of Famer who would win 361 games in the National League. The All-Americans consisted of equally good players. William "Dummy" Hoy, a deaf man who played 14 seasons in the big leagues, played in center field; George Davis, possibly the best shortstop of the late 1890s, played at third base; George Shoch and Bill Dahlen, names from Milwaukee's past, also played in the infield. Joe Kelley of Baltimore, a .317 lifetime hitter and yet another future Hall of Famer, played right field. On a cold day, only 500 attended, as Nichols beat Kid Carsey of Philadelphia 10 to 1, with Charley Cushman and Bill Furlong umpiring the game. Two days later the All-Americans beat Boston 9 to 6 before only 123 at Athletic Park on a day with "an utter lack of warmth ... except when the players were obliged to run around to keep from freezing."[30] However, this extremely low turnout caused Quin to withdraw his standing offer of $10,000 for a National League franchise, as it was clear to him Milwaukee residents wanted 25-cent ball, and not the 50-cent and 75-cent prices of the National League.

Ideas and plans for a new league were all around. The *Journal* wrote this on baseball in Milwaukee:

> Our baseball past is a very dead one, and the man does not live, that is outside of Fred Wilkin's home for the insane, or similar institutions in the state, that would for one moment deem it necessary to exhume the corpse for autopsic consideration. It neither died by lightening, on a railroad crossing, nor with its boots on, but of a slow and cankerous ailment that brought with it thoughts of worms and dissolution.... It is dead, dead, dead, and its resurrection is a question of time — perhaps a long time.[31]

12

Picking Up the Pieces (1894–1896)

Times were right for a new minor league in 1894. The National League was a 12-club monopoly of major league ball and midwestern states had no solid minor league. A Western League did play in 1893, but it consisted only of Wichita, Topeka, Denver, Kansas City, Omaha and Pueblo. In early May Wichita and Topeka withdrew, and the league never amounted to much. In August 1893 it was learned the Western would be revived for 1894 with larger towns, Milwaukee included. In September John T. Brush, owner of the National League Cincinnati club, announced he was interested in putting a club from Indianapolis in the Western, which would bounce Denver, again thought too far west for the league.

Milwaukee was very interested in this revived Western League. Charles Cushman and Phil Lederer took the lead in October, obtaining a guarantee from ten local men to put up $5,000 each to start with. An informal meeting was held on October 19, with Cushman drawing up a statement on necessary expenses. Six days later Cushman, Otto Schomberg, Henry J. Killilea and Rudolph E. Giljohan went to Chicago for the Western meeting.

At the Pacific Hotel in Chicago, on October 25, the Western League took form. Fourteen clubs had made application, with Milwaukee, Kansas City, Indianapolis and Minneapolis made charter members. Charlie Cushman, John S. Barnes (Minneapolis) and James H. Manning (Kansas City) formed a committee to select the four remaining clubs. Cushman was in favor of admitting Toledo, Detroit, Columbus and Omaha to the openings, and shortly Toledo was admitted. Others talked of Sioux City or St. Paul instead of Omaha, and putting a club in St. Joseph instead of Detroit. Milwaukee representatives wanted only cities with a 100,000 population—Sioux City having only half that. Sioux City, "the little town where 40,000 would rather go without churches and hotels than not have a ball club,"[1] wanted in, and the team's backer, William H. Beck, was making a strong financial case. Citizens of the Iowa city got up a $1,500 bond to prove this. A drawn-out fight for the three remaining franchises was ahead.

The Western League committee wanted Detroit because of its rivalry with Milwaukee, in addition to a larger population. However, Fred Stearns of Detroit was thinking of buying out either Washington or Louisville of the National League, but their price was too high. Stearns then attempted to buy the Cleveland franchise, which was for sale, offering $45,000, but the deal fell through. The *Chicago Herald* reported Detroit, or any other city, did not stand a chance of getting into the National League because of the 10-year agreement signed in 1891, which stated if a club should fold, no club would replace it. Stearns still kept trying for the franchise. With Detroit up in the air, other cities were considered, including Cleveland. Charlie Cushman said that city wanted to stay in baseball but was tired of carrying the National League club. Columbus and Grand Rapids were talked of, with Grand Rapids in the lead because it was allowed Sunday ball. On November 18 it was reported Cleveland had been sold to a syndicate of local gentlemen, and Detroit appeared secured for the Western.

The Western League meeting was to be held later in November, and the Milwaukee men prepared an organization back home. The capital stock of the club was set at $4,000, divided equally among ten stockholders (R.E. Giljohan, Matthew R. Killilea, Charles Polacheck, Otto Schomberg, James Carrothers, Frederick Hall, Davis & Baird Omnibus line, Henry J. Wehr, Charles Cushman and Phil Lederer). On November 12, 1893, the Milwaukee Baseball Association met and elected Matthew Killilea as president. According to the 1897 *Men of Progress: Wisconsin*, Matthew Robert Killilea was born in the town of Poygan, Wisconsin (about 20 miles northwest of Oshkosh). He graduated from the University of Wisconsin in 1891. The following year Killelea was appointed assistant district attorney in Outagamie County by Leopold Hammel, but he could not serve, as he had not practiced law the required time. In 1894 Killilea was the Democratic nominee for the Wisconsin State Assembly from Milwaukee's 2nd and 4th Wards but was defeated. The *Men of Progress* biography informed its readers Matthew was a member of the Calumet and Bon Ami clubs, and a Knight of Pythias. He was Catholic and single. "He is a young man of fine, natural abilities, good attainments, and has a promising future before him." Otto Schomberg (a local man who played a while in the majors—after a career-ending injury he became a prominent lumber yard owner on West Bruce Street) was at first elected vice president, but shortly Charles Hellberg, a bookkeeper by profession, was named vice president. Schomberg had been slated to be the club's president, but declined, citing a busy business schedule. Philip Lederer (a local cigar store owner) was named secretary and treasurer. The board of directors were Polacheck (owner of a plumbing and gas fitting business), Giljohan (a tavern owner at 280 East Water—later address 332 North Water Street), Hellberg (a bookkeeper), Carrothers (proprietor of the Kirby House at East Water and North Mason Streets), Hall (city passenger and ticket agent for the Chicago, Northwestern Railroad) and Cushman (in the 1893 Milwaukee directory, Charles was listed as a clerk in the billiard hall of the Plankinton House; in the 1894 directory he is listed as manager of the Milwaukee Baseball Club—both directories give his residence as 666 Jackson [later address 1310 North Jackson Street]). The board also agreed to a year lease of Athletic Park, with a two-year option. Within the week articles of incorporation were filed in Madison.

On November 20 the Western League met in Indianapolis, with Cushman and Matt Killilea as Milwaukee's representatives. Grand Rapids, Sioux City and Detroit were admitted to the league. The Western officially consisted of Kansas City (population 192,000), Sioux City (54,000), Minneapolis (198,000) and Milwaukee (250,000) in the west; Indianapolis (115,000), Toledo (98,000), Detroit (215,000) and Grand Rapids (85,000) in the east. Omaha men had tried to get in, in lieu of Sioux City, at the last minute. They failed, as Omaha was not considered a good-paying town, the same as St. Paul and Lincoln. Columbus was asked not to join.

The Western adopted the National League constitution with a few changes. The most important clause prohibited the sale of players to outside clubs during the season. When more than one club wanted the services of a player, the dispute was to be settled by the Western League president. Gate receipts were to be divided 45–45, with the remaining 10 percent to go into a sinking fund. When this fund reached $8,000, the $1,000 forfeit bond of each club would be taken down. Sunday ball was permitted, where allowed. Admission was to be uniform in all cities: 25 cents general admission and 50 cents for reserved seating. No formal salary limit was established yet, but a list of $1,500 to $1,800 a month was expected to be the limit.

The last major issue at the meeting was the election of a president. Most believed L.C. Krauthoff of Kansas City or Ralph Stout of Omaha would get the position. The *Evening Wisconsin* urged that William Furlong of Milwaukee be elected to the position. The job went to Byron Bancroft Johnson, the 29-year-old editor of the *Cincinnati Commercial-Gazette*. D.A. Long told the *Sporting News* correspondent "Mr. Johnson, besides being an authority on base ball, is competent to fill the position to which we elected him. Our reason for having a president who resides in a city that is not in the league is to do away with any alleged partiality that may arise and making the other cities jealous, and they would of course kick, and claim that he was partial. By electing a president as we have done, you see we do away with that ill feeling."[2] The Western board of directors was to be George Van der Beck (Detroit), D.A. Long (Toledo), Beck (Sioux City) and Barnes (Minneapolis).

Matthew Killilea — Elected Brewer president in November 1893, and would be an important player in Western League to the American League story.

Ban Johnson immediately announced his intentions of joining the National Agreement. Most everyone was overjoyed with the revived Western. Charlie Cushman, who had received offers to manage in Brooklyn and Providence but turned them down to stay in Milwaukee, thought "there was never a brighter outlook for baseball in the west, not even in the past days of popularity."[3] The *Chicago Herald* wrote, "As a training school in developing young players [the Western League] is expected to exert a powerful influence upon the National League."[4] This same paper made it clear it thought of the Western only as a training school when it commented, "The Western League is but a kindergarten for the giant organization [the National League] and the league players who cast their fortunes with it will soon discover the truth of this assertion."[5] Some were loud in their criticism of the league for the selection of Ban Johnson, believing the presidency should have gone to a man from one of the Western League cities. However, the *Milwaukee Sentinel* of December 13, 1893, believed the choice was wise.

> It has been shown by experience, not only in this but in other leagues, that a president who lives in one of the league cities is always the target for criticisms of every city which thinks it has a grievance, and for this reason the president is kept constantly in hot water. Every city except his own is apt to accuse him of favoritism toward his home club and cannot be made to think otherwise, with the result that there is bickering as long as the season lasts and dissatisfaction after it has closed.

Cushman, again the Milwaukee manager, quickly began to assemble a team. First to sign was Carl McVey, a center fielder from St. Louis, who played in the old Western League and San Jose of the California League. Next Cushman signed John Luby for the outfield. Luby had played 1893 in New Orleans but had previously pitched for three years in Chicago, winning 39 while losing 36. Cushman wanted him for the field and would pitch him only in an emergency. Two days later Billy Clingman accepted terms. Clingman, a third baseman, had played in Memphis the previous year. Next Charlie Hastings, who pitched in Cleveland the previous year, signed.

Cushman had some failures in signing players. He laid claim in December to St. Louis's Arthur "Old Hoss" Twineham, but Twineham stayed in St. Louis. The Milwaukee manager then went after Frank Ward, the infielder who played in Milwaukee in 1892. He was under contract to Washington and Cushman could not get him loose. Cushman also tried to sign Will Hart, the old Brooklyn pitcher, but could not agree to terms. Ditto with Bill Moran, the St. Louis catcher. James Starring, a pitcher from New Mexico, wrote Cushman offering his services for $1,800. Cushman noted this was more than the average National League player made but tried him out, releasing him before the season started. By the end of the year the club had signed three more players: catchers William Roberts from the Hudson River League, Mike Johnson in his first professional year (having played 1893 with the University of Madison), and a left-handed shortstop, Robert Langsford, from New Orleans.

Trouble then appeared out of St. Louis. A story broke that Milwaukee, Minneapolis and Kansas City were combining to sign the most desirable players, especially from the disbanded Southern Association. The *Sporting News* called the triple alliance "the Dreibund."[6] President Johnson denied the story, saying "the story is ridiculous. There is no truth in it."[7] Johnson told the *Sporting News* it was apparent by looking over the lists of players from the Milwaukee and Minneapolis clubs this was not the case. Admitting Kansas City was made up of former Southern players, Johnson explained it was because K.C.'s manager wanted players he knew and who had played for him before. The trouble would come up again later.

After the first of the year Cushman again began signing players. By mid–January 1894 he had 15 signed. Along with the previous eight, he had signed George Cobb, a pitcher from Riverside of the Pacific League who had pitched in Baltimore in 1892. Also signed was Pete Lohman, a catcher from Los Angeles. Three signed players came from Altoona of the Pennsylvania League: Dan Shields, a second baseman who had hit .304 in Altoona the previous year; John Scheible, a pitcher who also had played in Cleveland; and George Carey, a first baseman who had hit .381. A shortstop from Macon, Sam Gillen (who had played three games for Pittsburgh in 1893) and J.J. Bate (a catcher in his first professional year from Youngstown, Ohio) rounded out the squad. In February, Cushman strengthened the club by adding Charlie Newman, an outfielder. Newman had played briefly with the Brewers in 1889. In '92 he had played with Chicago and New York of the National League but quit because of typhoid fever. Another acquisition was Frank Figgemeier, a pitcher who played the last year in St. Joseph. Another pitcher, Tom Williams, recently with Cleveland, was secured.

This team, minus Bates, Gillen and Starring, who were released before the season started, was dubbed the Blue Ribbons because of the great breweries located in Milwaukee. Cushman guaranteed "the boys will be given enough of the blue ribbon tonic to deserve the name."[8] Cushman went so far as to have little blue ribbons flutter on the club's road uniforms. "These are not to show that the members of the team belong to a total abstinence society, but that they come from the city that makes the best beer in the world."[9] The ribbons were the same in size and appearance as those given to the Pabst Brewing Company at the Columbian Exposition, and on today's bottles and cans. These ribbons were attached to a chocolate gray uniform with maroon trim. The home uniform was white with black trimming. Both uniforms were purchased from Spalding & Company of Chicago.

A few internal troubles hit the Western League late that winter. Both St. Paul and Fort Wayne made eager to get into the Western but were turned down by Johnson. In Grand Rapids president George Ellis had a dispute with the local gamblers, who blamed him for their places being closed. If he did surrender his franchise, Columbus or St. Paul would be considered. St. Paul made an offer, but Ellis worked out his problems. In February it was announced the Detroit franchise would be transferred to Fort Wayne. Earlier a rumor had developed that the Detroit franchise would drop out of the Western and St. Paul would take its place. These stories probably came out as a result of Van der Beck's difficulty securing grounds for a park in Detroit. The Detroit owner claimed the owners of the land wanted double the price for a site and he refused to pay it. Finally in March Van der Beck secured grounds and the threat was gone. Even Milwaukee made news. Two stockholders offered $6,000 for the franchise, but the others refused to sell. The present owners would have made about $3,000 on the deal, as the purchasers were willing to assume all their liabilities.

Ban Johnson — The force behind the Western and American leagues.

On March 14, 1894, the Western League met in Milwaukee at the Plankinton House, Milwaukee represented by manager Charles Cushman and president Matthew Killilea. A 126-game schedule was prepared by Cushman and accepted with little change, to start April 25 and end September 25. Milwaukee received seventeen Sunday home dates but did not receive Decoration Day, July 4 or Labor Day. The eight Western teams were to travel more than 75,000 miles, with Detroit logging the fewest miles (8,412) and Sioux City the most (10,783). Others traveled the following: Indianapolis (8,719), Toledo (8,934), Minneapolis (9,136), Grand Rapids (9,242), Milwaukee (10,009) and Kansas City (10,147). Each club was to make its own contract with railroads for travel. Milwaukee received permission to have Ladies Day on all weekday games, but the women had to have an escort. Only Kansas City and Detroit had any other form of Ladies Day, K.C. admitting the fairer sex free on Thursdays and Detroit on Fridays.

All were happy with the Western meeting except George Van der Beck of Detroit. He told the Detroit press he "got the double cross" and other owners "walked all over him."[10] These comments were the result of a hearing at the meeting over four players he had signed earlier. When the Western was organized, Van der Beck was in California and signed Fred Carroll, Billy George, Lohman and Cobb. Before he obtained their signatures on contracts, however, the Western League awarded Carroll and George to Grand Rapids and the other two to Milwaukee. Van der Beck said he had claimed the players as early as December 12. Grand Rapids retained their two players and Cushman kept Lohman, giving up Cobb, as he had enough pitching.

The Western almost had one last fatality. In mid–April the Indianapolis club almost had to disband. Owing to a misunderstanding, the Hoosier players were signed to six-month contracts, contrary to the provisions of the Western constitution, which permitted only five-month contracts. President Johnson would not permit the management to pay the April salaries and, of course, the players objected. Five days later Brush made the men sign new contracts, dated April 25, and the crisis ended.

Spring training began on April 6 with all the Milwaukee players being advanced $50 to meet in Cincinnati. The next day the team lost to Cincinnati, 5 to 3, to start exhibition play. Cushman's men lost to Cincinnati again the next day, 20 to 7. While in Cincinnati Bill Widner, the pitcher from the 1892 club, attached Milwaukee's share of the receipts, $123, for salary due from that year. The problem was that that club had gone out of existence and he was now dealing with a new club. Brewers President Killilea promised to look into it for Widner. The Milwaukees then traveled to Cleveland and beat the Spiders 7 to 2. The team then traveled to Pittsburgh and lost two of three to the Pirates. After losing four of six to National League teams, the Brewers—as the press began to call the team again, dropping Blue Ribbons—beat the Tiffin (Ohio) club, 17 to 3. The Brewers lost two more to Louisville before beating Jacksonville and Peoria. Going back to National League clubs, the Brewers lost, 6 to 1, to the St. Louis Browns on April 22. This was the last of the spring exhibitions as the games scheduled next in St. Joseph were cancelled because Cushman did not want any of his players injured. The Brewers' exhibition record was 5 and 7, beating only two league clubs, and all of their seven losses were to that circuit's teams. The exhibitions were costly, Cushman estimating the small crowds and bad weather (three rainouts, plus the St. Joseph games) had cost the club about $1,000.

The season was ready to begin, and despite the local paper's bright prospects, the *Minneapolis Tribune* picked Sioux City, Kansas City, Detroit and Grand Rapids to take the first four slots. Milwaukee and Indianapolis were predicted to fight it out for the cellar.

On Wednesday, April 25, the Brewers opened in Kansas City. Before 2,000 the Blues won, 12 to 3, Darby beating Hastings. The bad times began even before the game started. Milwaukee officials sent a good luck telegram to Cushman, but the Kansas City team received it by mistake.

Kansas City		R	H	PO	A	E	Milwaukee		R	H	PO	A	E
Ulrick	2b	3	2	2	2	1	Shields	2b	1	0	3	3	0
Daniels	rf	3	1	3	0	0	Clingman	3b	1	1	1	1	0
Hernon	lf	1	2	6	1	0	Newman	lf	1	1	2	0	0
Klusman	1b	1	3	7	0	0	Langsford	ss	0	1	1	5	0
Nicholi	cf	1	1	3	1	0	Luby	rf	0	0	1	0	0
Niles	3b	1	3	1	1	0	Carey	1b	0	1	13	2	1
Sharpe	ss	1	1	3	1	0	McVey	cf	0	0	2	0	1
Donahue	c	1	1	1	1	0	Lohman	c	0	1	3	3	0
Darby	p	0	1	1	3	0	Hastings	p	0	0	0	3	1
Figgemeier	p	0	0	1	3	0							
		12	15	27	10	1			3	5	27	20	3

```
                  1  2  3  4  5  6  7  8  9
Kansas City       1  0  5  0  0  4  0  2  0 — 12
Milwaukee         0  0  0  0  0  0  0  3  0 —  3
```

Immediately after the game Cushman released recently signed George Carisch, a pitcher from Alma, Wisconsin. Mike Johnson was also released. It was reported that both these players, "while fair men, are too young and unsteady to do good team work."[11] Kansas City's opening day crowd of 2,000 was the lowest of the Western towns that day. Toledo reported 6,000, Indianapolis 3,264, and Sioux City 3,000. After a rainout Hastings again lost to the Blues, 8 to 5. After leaving Kansas City the night of April 27, the Brewers ran into trouble with the law. Nolan, the business manager of the St. Joseph club, was attempting to recoup some of the lost money from the cancelled exhibition games with the Brewers in that city a week earlier. As the Missouri club had undergone considerable trouble and expense advertising the games, he thought Cushman should pay half the bill — $25. Nolan reported Cushman had answered in a very sarcastic manner, telling him he would not give any money. This "aroused the ire" of Nolan and his business associate Kneisley, and a warrant was sworn out for Cushman and the Milwaukee club. On the way to Sioux City the train the team was traveling on had to stop in Sioux City. The Sioux City managers and "a brace of constables" met the train at the Union Depot as it pulled in at 11:40 P.M. Accompanied by another officer, the constables boarded the train and awakened some of players to find out where Manager Cushman was. At first the players told the police that Cushman was not on the train, having gone ahead on business. This was not believed and all the players were awakened, hoping to find someone in authority. As even the captain of the team, John Luby, kept himself scarce, it was decided to seize "a big stack of uniforms in bags, hat and bat bags, masks and other stuff," taking it off to another car. The players pleaded their case in vain. Finally Cushman, "seeing that he was cornered," came forth and the writ was served on him. "He fumed and blustered and threatened but it did no good; as he refused to pay the damages asked for, the stuff was taken off the train," which pulled out for Sioux City.[12] I could find no disposition on the case (which was reportedly set for trial on May 10), but as the Brewers played the next day in Sioux City — apparently with their uniforms and equipment — one must assume some resolution came about. As stated, the Brewers went to Sioux City, where Scheible lost, 8 to 7. The other two games with the Braves were lost to rain.

Cushman realized his pitching was not as strong as it was thought as he traveled into Minneapolis. To strengthen this position he tried to obtain George Nichol and Addison Gumbert from Pittsburgh's overloaded staff. When these efforts failed, Cushman tried for Tom Colcolough, with the same results. On May 2 Hastings beat the Millers, 6 to 5, for the Brewers' first win. The following day Figgemeier gave the Millers their seventh defeat without a victory. Cushman thought Hastings and Figgemeier were the only pitchers worth keeping, and he released Tom Williams and John Scheible. Harry Clayton, a catcher recently released from Chicago, was then signed. The Brewers and Millers tied in the last game of the series.

On Saturday, May 5, the Brewers played their first home game, with 2,000 attending at Athletic Park to see Figgemeier lose to Minneapolis, 5 to 4, this being the Millers' first win. Incidentally, the directors had put Gus Alberts, the old favorite, in charge of the grounds at Athletic Park, and no one complained of his job. Cushman was still looking for pitching help and signed Johnson, whom Sioux City had just released. He could have used Luby but preferred to keep him in the outfield. Johnson immediately lost to the Millers, 8 to 7, on Sunday before only 2,100 fans. Johnson was soon released. Hastings lost the final game to put the Brewers in the cellar. Cushman then strengthened his pitching by signing George Stephens. Stephens had played in Milwaukee in 1888 and had just been released by Washington of the National League. Kansas City was in town, and Figgemeier lost before Luby went to the mound and won his first game to move the club out of last place. Sioux City was in town next and split two games before a rainout.

Milwaukee was hit by a stretch of cold and rain, and six straight games were lost to the weather. However, fans had baseball sidelights to read about during this period. First, John Luby and Cushman had a public disagreement over Luby's "failure to bat as he should have done when at bat" in the last Sioux City game. Cushman had wanted his team captain to punch for a single, but "Jack thought only of hitting the ball out to Whitefish Bay"[13] and struck out. Luby talked of quitting, and Cushman assured him if he did he would not play in the Western League. Within days the split was patched up. Then to help sagging attendance, the club announced beginning May 20 boys under 15 would be charged only 15 cents to attend games at Athletic Park. That same day the *Sentinel* attacked Toledo for exaggerating attendance figures. In a recent game Toledo had given the attendance as 11,600 when only 3,900 paid to get in. The paper wrote, "This is not a Brotherhood year [when attendance figures were reported higher for propaganda reasons] and Toledo should not forget to remember what was done with it when it didn't tell the truth at school. Eleven thousand and six hundred people? Are there that many in Toledo?"[14] Cushman also signed a new pitcher, Bill Whitrock, just released by Louisville.

Finally on May 24, after an eleven-day rest, Stephens beat Toledo in the only game played of the scheduled series. Grand Rapids then came in, and the Rustlers won two of three, the Sunday game drawing 4,000. Milwaukee was now in sixth place with a 6 and 10 record, but the rainouts put them many games behind other clubs. Grand Rapids, for example, had played 29 games. With the Brewers going badly, Luby was criticized by the press for being too easygoing and suggested that perhaps Clingman should replace him as captain. Cushman looked for help elsewhere. First he attempted to sign Sam Dungan from Chicago, but Detroit beat him. He again tried to obtain Frank Ward, still in Washington, with failing results. Cushman also decided to pitch Luby. Meanwhile, the Brewers "got the usual dose,"[15] losing three of four in Indianapolis.

The club returned home and beat the Hoosiers twice. The Indianapolis club had an old Milwaukee favorite, Abner Dalrymple, in center field and captaining the team. Things were not too rosy for the Brewers. As the *Sentinel* of June 3 wrote, "The Milwaukee baseball team is not a desirable organization to belong to in any capacity, from manager down to water carrier at the present time." This time it was Charlie Cushman's bad showing the directors were worried about. The paper claimed he was too severe on the players and criticized them too much in public. The players had lost their enthusiasm. Many thought Cushman would be replaced, "but Milwaukee likes Cushman and wants Cushman," the *Sentinel* wrote on June 4. The *Daily News* thought the Brewers were losing because "the players are flat-footed. They waddle when they should run, and they stand like wooden Indians while hot liners go whistling by them into the outfield."[16] Injuries were hurting the club; Langsford was hurt and Lohman, a catcher, went to shortstop. Then John Luby left the team, saying Cushman "uses his players like dogs."[17] (In the *Sporting News* of June 23, Luby denied saying this, being quoted in the St. Louis weekly, "Cushman has treated us like gentlemen and I for one never worked under a better man. I think the other members of the team will say the same thing.") Luby also cited an agreement he had with the management that if he pitched he would receive additional pay, which was not coming. Luby was suspended by President Killilea, but within days he was back when Killilea promised him the money.

The Brewers next traveled into Michigan, losing two of three to Grand Rapids and two to Detroit. With a 10 and 17 record Cushman made more changes. He signed Harry Howe, an infielder from Kansas City, and placed him at shortstop, moving Langsford to the outfield. Billy Devinney was tried at shortstop, but immediately ran into trouble with his attitude. The *Sporting News* wrote, "In the second Grand Rapids game here he couldn't get the ball within two yards of first base, but that was not what got the crowd mad. It was when Killen threw over Carrather's head that everyone got hot at Devinney. He smiled and seemed tickled to death because some one besides himself made errors. This proof that his heart was not in the right place was enough."[18] Devinney made three errors in his one game as a Brewer. Cushman signed Joe Walsh, late of the Sioux City Braves. Walsh had played in Milwaukee in 1886 and '88 as a shortstop but now went to second and Dan Shields was gone. Walsh also replaced John Luby as field captain. The *Sporting News*' Milwaukee correspondent spoke highly of Walsh: "What Joe Walsh don't know about captaining a ball team does not amount to much, if they do not keep up now there is an awful Jonah lurking around the Cream City bat bags."[19] The Brewers then returned home to play a Sunday game with Indianapolis, Luby losing 9 to 8. This one game was played in Milwaukee because Detroit had no Sunday ball. On Monday the Brewers returned to Detroit to finish the series and lost, 15 to 2. Frank Figgemeier was released to Peoria. The Brewers then fell apart, losing their next nine games before beating Minneapolis to end the road trip. During this trip John Luby and Harry Clayton were released, although Luby was soon re-engaged. Hastings was 2 and 8, the press suggesting he also be released and the club spend $1,500 or $2,000 to get two or three first-class players. Cushman tried to pry Bob Stafford, a utility man, from New York but without success.

About this time Sioux City was again in the news. Word was about that the Braves would transfer to another city because of low attendance. Van der Beck of Detroit thought Saginaw would be ideal. The *Evening Wisconsin* thought the dispatch "a fairy tale"[20] and suggested Van der Beck would probably like to trade teams with Sioux City, as his was playing so poorly. The reports continued for a while, some saying Watkins of Sioux City wanted to transfer, which was denied. One went so far as to report Bob Leadley, an old baseball manager from Detroit, wanted to transfer Sioux City's club to Saginaw and Bay City jointly, if the Western League did not object. Of course, it did.

The last-place Brewers returned to Milwaukee on June 26, and that day Charles Cushman resigned as manager. No one had been selected to replace him. Joe Walsh was temporarily in charge of the club. Sioux City was in town and took three of four games from the Brewers. Meanwhile, Cushman asked the club to reconsider accepting his resignation. He figured the team was only a few players away from winning; he thought he could get them from the tottering Southern League. Cushman stayed and made his moves. First he made an arrangement with Kansas City to get "Peck" Sharpe, the Blues shortstop. Both clubs were after Ollie Beard, and Cushman would let him go to K.C. for Sharpe. Then Jocko Fields, a catcher, and Fred Clarke, an outfielder, both from the Southern League, were signed. Carl McVey was released. Clarke jumped his Milwaukee contract, going to Louisville, where he started a Hall of Fame career as a player and manager. Milwaukee officials were not happy about losing Clarke. Earlier, Western League president Ban Johnson had telegraphed Killilea, telling him to leave the Southern League players alone. Then the clubs began to fold, and Louisville jumped on Clarke, whom Cushman had signed but was in limbo because of Johnson's telegram. John McCann from Savannah was signed in Clarke's place. Jimmy Long from Atlanta was also signed for the outfield. The home series ended with Kansas City winning three of four. The Sharpe deal fell through, and none of the other new players were yet with the team. After the deal fell through, Cushman tried to trade Hastings to Grand Rapids for Bobby Wheelock, a shortstop, but President Ellis of Grand Rapids was not interested.

It was around this time Howard & Mock secured the outside privilege to sell popcorn near the ball grounds. The firm hit upon a novel plan. "Hereafter in each package of popcorn will be enclosed a patent score card, so that in the future two luxuries may be enjoyed for the small sum of a nickel."[21]

The Brewers hit the road again. The first date was July 4 in Grand Rapids, where the teams split a doubleheader. On this Fourth of July, 1894, Sioux City held first place (41–14), followed by Toledo (33–23), Minneapolis (33–24), Kansas City (32–25), Grand Rapids

(25–35), Indianapolis (24–35), Detroit (23–34) and Milwaukee (14–35). Luby and Whitrock then lost to close the series.

Milwaukee traveled into Indianapolis and their Southern League players (Fields, McCann and Long) finally arrived. Robert Langsford was released to Omaha of the Western Association. Killilea also signed outfielder Bill Goodenough, second baseman, Wally Taylor and catcher Peter Bolen from the Southern League, which was disbanding. The Brewers then dropped all three to the Hoosiers. The Brewers were scheduled to come home for a July 13 exhibition with Brooklyn, but Killilea cancelled the game. He felt it was not good policy to have Western and National League clubs play in Milwaukee during the season. One other game was cancelled during the trip. On that Sunday the Brewers and the Hoosiers were to travel back to Milwaukee to play one game. A railroad strike was in progress, though, so the Brewers cancelled a trip to Toledo in order not to be stranded. Brewer officials announced the strike made it impossible to come back to Milwaukee. The *Journal* thought differently, noting the passenger trains were now running regularly. "To a man up a stump it looks as if the management feared that the receipts of the game would not pay the double transportation. At any rate, nobody is sorry that the team didn't come home and that it didn't play yesterday."[22]

Meanwhile, more changes were made. Charlie Hastings, with a 3 and 9 record, was traded to Kansas City for J.P. "Peck" Sharpe. Catcher William Roberts was released. Larry Twitchell, who had played in Milwaukee in 1892, was also signed from Louisville. The Brewers now had 17 players:

Lohman, Fields, Bolan—catchers
Stephens, Whitrock, Luby—pitchers
Carey (1b), Howe, Taylor, Sharpe (2b), Clingman (3b), Walsh (ss)—infielders
Newman, Goodenough, McCann, Long, Twitchell—outfielders

The team then lost in Toledo, won in Detroit, beat Indianapolis in Milwaukee in a Sunday game, and went back to Detroit and split two games. The Indianapolis game in Milwaukee cost the Brewers an extra $400. While en route from Detroit to Chicago, the train was wrecked at Lakeville and the team arrived in Chicago after the regular train for Milwaukee had left. Cushman telegraphed Killilea, who immediately chartered a special train over to the station to bring the team to Milwaukee.

The Brewers returned home and dropped two of three to the Millers. Again the club made changes. Patrick Bolan was released, according to the *Sentinel*, because "the products of local breweries and Kentucky stills were his friends, and when it came time for him to dress for [a] game he was a-waving like a flagstaff in a gale and wanted to shake hands with everyone he met."[23] The *Evening Wisconsin* reported he was injured crossing Chestnut [Juneau] Street near Third Street when he "accidentally collided with one of the Pabst beer wagons."[24] Bolan then skipped town, owing the club $100, but soon returned and was re-engaged. Kirtley Baker, a pitcher from the Southern League, was then signed and John Luby was released to Minneapolis. Charlie Newman and Harry Howe also got their pink slips. Gus Klopf, from the local Bay View club, signed on as a shortstop. Charles Campau was signed to take right field for McCann. Another pitcher, Charles Fraser, was signed after he was released from Minneapolis. Toledo then came to town and the "Swamp Angels" split four games with the Brewers. Grand Rapids then split two and tied one with Milwaukee, and Bill Whitrock, owner of a 4 and 14 record, was released when Baker arrived. George Rettger, a pitcher, was also signed and Fraser went back to Minneapolis. Larry Twitchell finally reported, took over as captain, and Charles Campau was released to Detroit. John McCann was also released. Certainly keeping track of who was a Brewer and who was no longer a Brewer is (and no doubt was) a bit difficult.

A few events of interest were occurring throughout the Western League. In late July the *Minneapolis Tribune* accused Minneapolis players of losing on the road "for the purpose of swelling gate receipts, thereby netting a larger profit for the owners of the team."[25] Everyone came to the players' defense and the matter was dropped. In Milwaukee it was learned that Buckenberger of Pittsburgh was looking at Western players for his National League club. He was impressed with Carey, Long and Taylor for the 1895 season. In another incident president Ban Johnson had to step in. Van der Beck of Detroit had tried to sign Kirtley Baker after Milwaukee had signed him. Johnson made Baker report to Milwaukee. Van der Beck also was after "Count" Campau and got him after Twitchell arrived in Milwaukee. On August 2 the Western League met in Minneapolis. Billy George, Fred Carroll and Pete Lohman were suspended for refusing to pay back advance money they had received from Detroit before the season. They, however, continued to play for their respective clubs. Lohman appeared to have settled the matter, claiming he signed an illegal contract with Detroit. Also numerous games were thrown out because of appeals. As President Johnson never released official standings, it is hard to find the actual standings of the Western clubs. Meanwhile, the Brewers continued their long homestand, winning 9 and losing 6 to put the club's record at 30 and 53, still in last place. Jocko Fields was then given his release.

George Rettger would pitch five full seasons and parts of two others in Milwaukee (Historic Photograph Collection/Milwaukee Public Library).

Just as it seemed the Brewers were getting their game together, it suddenly fell apart again. In Sioux City the team lost a doubleheader on August 18 but won two the next day, Baker winning both ends. Stephens lost the final game, 6 to 0, the Brewers getting only two hits. Then in Kansas City, the Brewers lost five games in three days. The Milwaukees then lost three of four in Minneapolis. The team slumped so sharply because of injuries. Long, Twitchell and Clingman were playing with sprained ankles. Sharpe injured his leg and was out for the season. Bolan was also injured and out. Rettger and Stephens were also hurt but playing. The *Daily News* commented the directors were also to blame. They would not let Cushman release or sign the players he wanted. "It is politics in sport — a new deal and a non-paying one."[26]

The Brewers returned home and split four with Grand Rapids. With Klopf hurt, Gus Alberts filled in for a game and the infield was forced to shift around. Toledo then came to the Cream City and lost two of three, one ending in a tie. The tie game caused turmoil. A doubleheader was scheduled for that Monday, but as there were only a few hundred fans in Athletic Park, Toledo stalled for rain. First Dennis Long, the Toledo manager, called for a different umpire. When his request was denied, he refused to play with the balls used in Athletic Park because they did not have an official stamp on them. Finally the morning game was called. On September 4, 1894, the *Sentinel* voiced its opinion:

The few spectators present were greatly disappointed and went away feeling anything but friendly toward baseball. A game should have been played if only three persons paid admissions. The public will begin to think pretty soon that magnates haven't the welfare of the game at heart, except when plenty of money comes in at the gate.

The final game, a 5 to 0 win for Stephens, was the club's first shutout of the season. Unfortunately, Lohman broke his finger and Bolan was forced to catch for the remainder of the season. This shutout also started a seven-game winning streak. First the Detroit Creams lost three games in two days. The Creams almost did not make it to Milwaukee to play this series, as their train wrecked in Illinois and they arrived one day late. Then Indianapolis dropped three before breaking Milwaukee's winning streak. During this streak the Brewers picked up a new third baseman, Pat Flaherty, formerly of Louisville. Clingman went to shortstop, Taylor to second, and Carey continued at first. The Brewer infield remained unchanged for the rest of the season.

Before traveling to Detroit, the Brewers played an exhibition with Brooklyn of the National League. The Bridegrooms had few stars but did have George Shoch, an old Milwaukee favorite, at second base. Somewhere between 3,000 and 5,000 attended Athletic Park to see "General Cushman's"[27] men tie the mighty National League club from the City of Churches, 6 to 6. In Detroit the Brewers won one, lost one, and tied one. The Brewers then traveled to Toledo, winning two of four. The Brewers finished the season beating Grand Rapids three times before losing two of three to Indianapolis.

The final standings of the 1894 Western League were as follows:

Sioux City	74	51	.592	Grand Rapids	62	64	.492
Toledo	67	55	.549	Indianapolis	59	66	.472
Kansas City	68	58	.540	Detroit	56	69	.448
Minneapolis	63	62	.501	Milwaukee	49	73	.402

These results are those released by Ban Johnson in mid–October. Other standings give slightly differing win/loss records for certain teams, but the positions of the teams are the same.

Western League president Ban Johnson reported in January 1895 that Milwaukee was the only club to lose money. However, club President Killilea stated his last-place Brewers finished about $800 ahead. These conflicting statements could be due to the Western League's sinking fund, which amounted to over $23,000, and all except $8,000 was divided among the clubs, giving each club an additional $2,000 profit in October. Killilea also claimed the Brewers' expenses were the highest in the Western, "as the best hotels were always patronized and the best railroad accommodations obtained."[28] Only Kansas City traveled as well, he claimed. First-place Sioux City made money, but its directors declined to say how much. That club sold five players to the National League and probably made a significant amount. Toledo made between $5,000 and $6,000 and sold six players to the National League in the draft. Kansas City made from $10,000 to $12,000. Minneapolis earned over $10,000 and expected to make $2,000 more selling players. Indianapolis made $5,000, a figure that could have been more. Their home attendance was good, but they lost about $1,500 in each Western city on the road. Grand Rapids made about $6,000, while Detroit made around $5,000. Kansas City led home attendance figures, followed in order by Minneapolis, Indianapolis, Milwaukee, Detroit, Grand Rapids, Toledo and Sioux City.

The Brewers had finished as one of the strongest clubs in the Western, winning 16, losing 7 and tying two in September. The three pitchers had come on very strong at the end. George Stephens won 21 on the season while also losing 21, Baker was 10 and 10, and

Rettger was 7 and 9. The Brewer batting was also very good; for that matter, the entire Western hit well. No fewer than 90 men in the Western hit .300 or better for the season. The Brewers had 14 men that hit this barrier who had played with them during the season. Those who finished the season in Milwaukee uniforms were Sharpe (.383); Twitchell (.382), who also won the Milwaukee gold medal "for being the best all-round player on the team;"[29] Cary (.364); Clingman (.333); Taylor (.328); Long (.324); Flaherty (.310); Goodenough (.306); and Walsh (.300). These high averages prompted the press to suggest the Western adopt a different ball than the lively Reach ball. Instead the Western kept the Reach ball, but the company put less rubber in it to deaden it for the next year. Eighteen ninety-four was now history, and the Western looked ahead to another profitable year.

The Western League held its annual meeting on October 3 in Chicago. The meeting, by constitution, should have been in the pennant-winning city, Sioux City, but the seven other owners did not want it there, and they had their way. This marked the end for Sioux City. As early as August it was thought Sioux City would be dropped because of its light attendance. At a later meeting Matt Killilea said Sioux City received more money as its share in one Sunday in Milwaukee than the Brewers did in Sioux City all season. Already in September, St. Paul was making an effort to take the spot. At the league meeting Sioux City was awarded the pennant, and the Western started taking steps to drop the franchise. According to its constitution the Western League only lived one year. The board of directors decided to disband the organization and then reorganize on a permanent basis. Under the reorganization, the Sioux City franchise would not be included. This ploy was not new. The American Association had tried the same idea in 1886 when it attempted to drop the New York Metropolitans. The Mets, however, went to court and won. The Sioux City officials recalled this and expected "a reasonable sum from the league for giving up their franchise,"[30] or they too would go to court. It was believed $2,000 would buy Sioux City out and the Braves would cause no trouble. Sioux City, however, applied for admission to another minor league, the Western Association, and dropped the matter.

Which city would take Sioux City's place was a mystery. It appeared St. Paul had the inside track, but no one was certain. James Hart of Chicago applied, but it was thought his chances were not good. Hart ran into trouble because he wanted to play his surplus National League players on the Western club and then buy them back. Without this privilege he would not join, so he was not accepted. Williams of Columbus applied and was thought to have a good chance. Nashville applied but was too far away to be considered. Duluth wanted in, "but the best burglar's outfit in existence couldn't get it in,"[31] as its population was too small. The best bet at that moment was St. Paul, but four different organizations from that city were applying. One applicant was Charles Comiskey, Ban Johnson's friend. Comiskey was still under contract in Cincinnati but felt he could get away. Robert J. Martin, secretary of the Minneapolis club, was another. The third was T.W. Flynn. Some, however, thought Flynn was only a front man for Barnes, the Minneapolis Millers owner, to block St. Paul from getting a franchise. The fourth candidate was Thomas Foley, a billiard room keeper in St. Paul.

At the second day of the Western meeting it was decided Sioux City would be dropped and a president elected. Ban Johnson had done a fine job. Only his choice of umpires could be brought up against him, but some still wanted him out. The *Evening Wisconsin* thought Harry Wright, now the chief of National League umpires, would be ideal as the Western president. Van der Beck of Detroit agreed. Wright's name was brought up, as was Jim Hart's, but Johnson was re-elected unanimously. The new Western board of directors was to be

Killilea, Manning from K.C., Ellis from Grand Rapids and Indianapolis owner W.F.C. Golt. The meeting adjourned until November 20.

A new force was to make matters interesting in the Western and in Milwaukee baseball. Back in September a new major league, the American Association, was in the planning stages. At first National and Western League men gave little substance to the rumors. Milwaukee was not mentioned in the new association, and thoughts were again on a National League franchise. As early as July it was rumored Milwaukee would get the Louisville franchise for $10,000. League officials and the press put no stock in the rumor, but it persisted. By mid-September it was thought Louisville and/or Cleveland might drop from the National League and Milwaukee and Indianapolis would get in. Other rumors had the league paring down from twelve clubs to eight. When Brooklyn played the exhibition in Milwaukee, Brooklyn Owner Byrne and Hart of Chicago were in town and said they would like to see Milwaukee take the Louisville franchise. William Barnie of Louisville even came to Milwaukee and talked to local baseball men. Louisville was up for sale, but there were no takers. A rumor in Milwaukee said that several wealthy residents would buy out the Western League club here (Killilea said he was offered $15,000 for the club in August but declined to say from whom), give Louisville $17,500 for its franchise and players, and join the National League. The *Sentinel* felt this idea had flaws. Louisville had finished the 1894 season in last place with a miserable 36 and 94 record. Even if the Colonels and Brewers combined, only a weak team could be formed. It would probably take $30,000 to $35,000 to get a team strong enough to be in the pennant race. A Louisville paper even reported the National League bought the Louisville franchise for $25,000 and would sell it to Milwaukee. Killilea called the Louisville talk nonsense, and the *Journal* pointed out the impossibility of the scheme. A unanimous vote would be required to oust Louisville against its will, and Louisville, of course, would vote to keep itself in.

Then the American Association changed plans and included Milwaukee in its circuit. Killilea said he knew nothing of the association, but he was in for a surprise. Harry Quin was after the American Association franchise and said he would begin to sign players after October 15, when the Brewers' lease on Athletic Park expired.

On October 18 the American Association met in Philadelphia to organize. A circuit of Philadelphia, New York, Brooklyn, Washington, Chicago, Pittsburgh, and Milwaukee was formed. The eighth franchise would be awarded to St. Louis, Detroit, Columbus or Buffalo. The association would have 25-cent admission and allow Sunday games. Gate receipts would be divided on a 45–45 split, with a general fund maintained at $25,000. As with other new leagues, this American Association would not break contracts but would not honor the reserve clause. F.R. Richter, editor of *Sporting Life*, was made chairman of the meeting until W.S. Kames of Philadelphia was elected president. The new association claimed to have more than enough money behind it, with each club supposedly putting up $25,000. Brooklyn was reportedly backed by a traction company. Al Buckenburger, A.K. Scrandett and W.A. Nimick backed Pittsburgh. Chicago was to be backed by Fred Pfeffer and a railway company, and possibly George Williams, "the oyster house man."[32]

National League and Western League people immediately came out against the new association. Nick Young, president of the National League, stated he did not want a baseball war, but would engage in one if necessary. The *Milwaukee Sentinel* of October 28, 1900, wrote:

> The new association starts out, if it starts, with one thing certainly assured. The press in every city except Milwaukee is united in denouncing it as a pirate organization, without baseball men of brains identified with it and without capital or principal.... If the new organization has the finan-

cial backing that it claims to have, it is very foolish not to allow the light of the sun to fall upon the men with the golden fleeces.

Ban Johnson wrote Matt Killilea, telling him to worry about the American Association, as it had no financial backing. But Harry Quin came to its defense: "The American Association is organized in opposition to no baseball organization. We are organized on the principle that allows any merchant to come into a city and open up a business and compete with other merchants." Quin went on to say the association would say little "and saw wood."[33] Players would be obtained from the Western and National leagues. He claimed the association had much better cities than the Western, citing Toledo and Grand Rapids.

Milwaukee Western League men looked at Quin's association motives differently. The Brewer directors thought they were paying too much rent at Athletic Park, still owned by Quin and Robert Maguire, and believed Quin saw his chance to make them pay his price by threatening a Milwaukee entry into the American Association. The owner of the Brewers did not come to any agreement on their option on the park before it expired on October 15, and now Quin was making his move. Quin wanted $3,000 for rent of Athletic Park and said, "Before we would have leased them the park for $2,999.99 we would have cut it up into lots."[34] Killilea doubted Quin would actually risk the high cost of the association. He issued this statement to the press:

> You can readily see how easy it was to get a franchise in the new organization when there weren't enough cities represented to take the eight franchises.... Mr. Quin is simply carrying his bluff for the rent he wants to desperate straits and I believe that he no more intends to put an American Association team in here than I do.[35]

Killilea said the Brewers would not have any more to do with Quin in a business way. It was first reported the club had engaged grounds on National Avenue, west of National Park, with construction to start in early spring. However, the club soon leased the Kipp property on Twelfth and Wright streets, the old Wright Street Park site. Athletic Park was the biggest park in the Western League, and Killilea planned to build a bigger one. The grounds were 550 x 360 feet, and four street car lines ran to the park. The new park would cost $6,000 to $8,000 and seat 6,000 in the grandstand, and two bleachers would sit 2,000 each, for a total capacity of 10,000.

On October 22, 1894, Harry Quin brought suit against the Western League club for $400 rent he claimed had been due on August 15. Killilea said the money was in a local bank and that he had intended to pay the rent but now would fight the matter on the grounds that Quin took possession of Athletic Park before the lease expired. Quin denied he took possession of the park until after October 15. In November Quin went to Superior Court to get his money and was awarded the full amount in December.

The National and Western leagues began to be concerned over the new association. Rumor, propaganda, blacklists, and talk of franchise shifts were the order of the times. James Hart of Chicago, looking out for himself, suggested the American Association should take Buffalo and Milwaukee as a nucleus and then combine with St. Louis, Louisville, Washington, Cleveland and Cincinnati, which he was sure the National League would drop in November. His idea was not well taken anywhere. Then on October 31 it was reported Buckenburger withdrew his support from the American Association Pittsburgh club, citing lack of suitable grounds. President Kames denied the report, calling it a "National League fake."[36]

The National League tried using the Western League in its moves against the American Association. First Hart attempted to get a franchise on the south side of Chicago into the Western to block the association from moving into that city. His stand on players killed his chances, though. However, Matt Killilea was in favor of putting a club in Chicago to reduce mileage. He noted that Toledo was not looked upon favorably by the other clubs, hinting that franchise could go to Chicago. Then George Williams, a Chicago association backer, suggested he would be interested in taking his club, along with St. Louis and St. Paul, into the Western and dropping Grand Rapids, Toledo and Sioux City. Killilea expressed his fondness for this idea, but saw problems in dropping Grand Rapids and Toledo, as it would cost money to buy them out. Others, such as the *Chicago Herald*, thought Columbus could be added and Minneapolis and St. Paul merged into one franchise. In the meantime, Quin denied a report Williams was out of the association and said the association would stay in Chicago and enter St. Louis and Detroit. Quin admitted Pittsburgh might not be in, but Van der Beck in Detroit said he would not join the association and would stay in the Western.

The Western League appeared to be in the middle of this new league-association war. The National League wanted to see the Western get into the good baseball cities before the American Association got a foothold. The National League was also thinking of dropping four franchises (St. Louis, Washington, Cleveland and Louisville) and giving the Western League the players it did not want, so they would not go to the association. The American Association was planning to go into at least two Western League cities. The National League then met on November 17, but did not drop any franchises, fearing the new association would get more good players if they were unable to place the players in the Western. To fight against the American Association, the National League suspended Bill Barnie, Fred Pfeffer and Al Buckenburger, three major association backers, from any league activities.

The Western League had to make its own moves. With the American Association deciding to enter St. Louis and Chicago, both still in the National League, the Western did not believe it could fight both leagues in both cities. But Killilea still favored going into Chicago, figuring this would kill the association. St. Paul was given a franchise in the Western Association, and it looked doubtful if that city would get into the Western League. Chicago was now thought the best possibility. The Western meeting started on November 20 in Chicago, with Ban Johnson immediately asking the National League for protection against the American Association, and giving his support to the National Agreement. The next order of business was a successor to Sioux City. The Western thought it best to dodge Chicago because of Jim Hart's words on drafting players for the National League, apparently believing Williams was connected with Hart in some way. St. Paul was admitted to the Western, with Charles Comiskey at the head. Most baseball goers in St. Paul thought Thomas Foley, who said he would put the Chicago star outfielder Walter Wilmot at the helm, should have gotten the franchise. However, the Western feared if Wilmot got control of the franchise, Hart would be able to control it. Comiskey was so sure he would get the franchise he already had engaged eight Sioux City players. John Brush originally said Comiskey would play for him in 1895 and not St. Paul, but Comiskey asked for his release and obtained it. The section of the constitution providing against the farming out of players was amended to a $50 fine per game. This was a direct slap at Brush, who used the Indianapolis club as a feeder to his National League club. It was also decided to play a shorter season, starting in May. The life of the Western League was set at ten years.

Meanwhile, the proposed American Association was having trouble. Buckenburger had claimed he had no ties with the National League since he was released in early September as the Pittsburgh manager and could join the new association. But in early December he surrendered, signing an affidavit claiming he had nothing to do with the American

Association, and the National League re-instated him. Barnie and Pfeffer also were reinstated. Before Christmas 1894, the American Association was "deader than a barrel of herrings,"[37] as Harry Quin put it. The *Sentinel* had mixed emotions on new leagues and the death of this proposed American Association, as it editorialized on December 23, 1894, "There is room for another major organization organized on the proper principles and it would be a good thing for baseball if one would spring into existence. But there is no room for American Associations."

The death of the American Association was by no means the end of the problems between the Brewers and Harry Quin, as we shall see.

✳ ✳ ✳

Milwaukee looked ahead to the next season with high hopes, but it was also apparent it would be with a new manager. First evidence Charlie Cushman was on the way out came in September when a Chicago paper reported Tom Loftus was offered the job but refused it. Killilea denied the report, carefully stating no "official representative of the club"[38] had any correspondence with Loftus. Cushman did attend the Western League meeting in October, reserving George Davies, Harry Truby and George Carisch, but failing to sign any of the three. Rumor was already out that Larry Twitchell was to replace Cushman, and in November Cushman resigned. Charlie apparently liked Milwaukee as much as Milwaukee liked him, as in the November 30, 1895, issue of the *Sporting News* it was reported he was in charge of the new billiard hall in connection with the Davidson hotel and theater in downtown Milwaukee. After a disappointing season umpiring in the Western League in 1895, Cushman returned to managing in the Southern League at Mobile to begin the 1896 season. Charlie was back umpiring in the Western in 1897 and claimed to have been offered the Minneapolis managing job after that year, but it was given to Gus Schmelz.

On December 5, 1894, Lawrence Grant Twitchell signed as the Brewer manager and captain. He was given full charge of the team, financially and in matters of engaging and releasing players. Twitchell was born in 1864 in Cleveland and started his baseball career twenty-two years later, pitching for the Zanesville (Ohio) club. He finished the season in Detroit of the National League and stayed there two more years, converting to the outfield. In 1889 Twitchell signed with Cleveland but jumped to the Players' League in 1890. In 1891 he started with Omaha of the Western Association and went to Columbus of the American Association when the Western folded. The year 1892 found Larry in Milwaukee, then joining Washington when the club disbanded. He spent 1893–94 in Louisville until returning to Milwaukee. In nine years in the big leagues, Twitchell hit .263 and had a 17–11 record as a pitcher.

Larry Twitchell said he would stick to about the same team that finished 1894, but needed help for Bolan at catcher, as Pete Lohman was gone, having signed with Grand Rapids. Twitchell also needed help in the infield as Billy Clingman had been drafted by Pittsburgh. By the end of January Twitchell had nine men under contract. Besides himself, he had Peter Bolan, George Carey, Wally Taylor, George Rettger, J.P. "Peck" Sharpe, and Kirtley Baker. His two new players were William Summers, a catcher who played the previous year in Toledo, and William Armstrong, a pitcher from Columbus who Brooklyn also had eyes on. Soon Gus Klopf was signed, and so was pitcher Jerry Eddinger, a semi-professional from Iowa. Four players from 1894 were not signed (Goodenough, Stephens, Long, and Flaherty), but no trouble was expected.

Trouble did come in early February. It was reported Carey had signed with Baltimore. Killilea said Baltimore had no claim to him, as the February 1 drafting date had passed. Twitchell conceded Carey had been drafted on January 28 (it had been reported in the *Milwaukee Journal* on January 29) and was Baltimore's property. The $500 for Carey was finally received in March to make it official. Twitchell, now looking for a first baseman, reported George Stephens, Bill Goodenough and Jimmy Long had signed. He wanted to sign Charlie Frank, an outfielder who played the last two years in St. Louis, but could not settle on terms. Frank went to Atlanta of the Southern League. It appeared the Brewers would be unable to sign Pat Flaherty, and Twitchell also looked for a new third baseman. He first sounded out Llewellyn Camp, the St. Paul third baseman, but could not get him as Comiskey wanted a pitcher in return. He tried to pry George Tebeau from Cleveland but could not. To help out behind the plate and in the outfield, Twitchell signed William Weaver, an outfielder who had spend seven years in Louisville before going to Pittsburgh late in the 1894 season, having just been released. Weaver would be forced into the field when Goodenough jumped his contract to play with Atlanta in April. Pat Flaherty was given his release in late March, and Twitchell signed Al McCauley, recently released by St. Paul, to play first base. To play third base he signed Oliver LaRett, who had played in the New York State League the previous year and hit .357. When spring training started in Milwaukee on April 1, the Brewers had 15 players under contract:

> Pitchers—Stephens, Eddinger, Rettger, Baker, Armstrong.
> Catchers—Bolan, Summers.
> Infielders—McCauley (1b), Sharpe (2b), LeRett (3b), Taylor (ss).
> Outfielders—Long, Weaver, Twitchell.
> Utility man—Klopf.

Three state players were on hand—George Lumsden, Claude Elliott and Johnny Diamond—all pitchers, but none stayed with the club.

Meanwhile, the battle over Athletic Park still raged. In early February 1895, the stockholders of the Brewers held a meeting to discuss the playing field situation. When they learned Harry Quin would not lower his price, they decided to build at Twelfth and Wright streets. Plans for the new park were drawn up by the architects Guettler & Riemschneider and accepted on February 4. The double-deck grandstand would seat 7,000, and 3,000 could sit on the bleachers. The style of the architecture would be Swiss, being 340 feet long on the Wright Street side and 500 feet on Eleventh Street, with a 12-foot fence surrounding the park. The whole structure would cost $8,000.

Then on February 23 the Brewers' new secretary, Theodore Engel, received notice from the Board of Public Works that the resolution passed, granting the club permission to occupy the grounds as Twelfth and Wright was illegal. The notice ordered the club to remove all erected fences and obstructions. The board was acting on an opinion from city attorney Charles H. Hamilton, who claimed it was illegal for the council to obstruct or close a public highway except upon a public petition or verdict of a jury. He further claimed it was incompetent for the council to grant a corporation a right or privilege in a highway for its exclusive benefit. The resolution also provided for the expenditure of money and was not countersigned by the comptroller. Work on the park had begun and all the necessary materials were already there. Engel was sure Harry Quin was behind the whole thing to get the Brewers to use his park. Engel said they would move to the south side if necessary. City Attorney Hamilton denied Quin put any pressure on him. He claimed he was presented with petitions protesting the closing of alleys and streets. When asked who presented them, Hamilton replied, "H.D. Quin, but it makes no difference who gave them to me, however, as the resolution was illegal and it was my duty to call the attention of the mayor to the fact." When asked if he was Quin's attorney, Hamilton said, "I have been his attorney at times ... but I am not (now) retained by Mr. Quin." Matthew Killilea accused Hamilton of being a friend and attorney of Quin and said he was "playing a very underhanded game." Killilea said, "I will give my stock to George Washington Scott before I will allow the team to play at Athletic Park." He said work at Wright Street would continue until an injunction was issued. The alley over which all the trouble occurred ran from Wright to Clarke, between Eleventh and Twelfth Streets. It was never really opened but existed on the plat of the property.[39]

One of only two photographs known of Milwaukee Park on West Lloyd Street, home of Brewers from 1895 until 1901 (courtesy of Milwaukee County Historical Society).

On February 26 the Brewers' directors met with Mayor John C. Koch, but he said he would take no action to help them. That same day one of the stockholders, Fred Gross, found a piece of property between Lloyd Street and North Avenue, bounded by 16th Street on the east and Roundy's subdivision on the west (a little past Seventeenth Street) that had never been platted and could be rented. The property was 844 feet by 410 feet and owned by Milwaukee lawyer Ephraim Mariner. The directors found Mariner and signed a five-year lease within one hour. Work began immediately. The new park would be centrally located and hundreds could walk to the park. For those further away, a half-dozen street car lines ran by or near it. The grounds were only ten minutes from downtown. The steel framework grandstand was to be on the Lloyd Street side, with the entrance at Lloyd and Sixteenth Street. This semi-circular grandstand held 3,500 to 4,000, and two semi-circular bleacher sections (giving the spectators a better view than the customary straight bleachers) held another 3,000, for a total capacity of the park of about 7,000. The fans would "not be called upon to rest their weary limbs upon benches. There will be the latest style of opera chairs, similar to those used in the grandstand in the Polo Grounds in New York."[40] The park was 640 feet long (compared to Athletic Park's 400) and 440 feet wide. From home plate to the fence would be 550 feet, and home runs over the fence were "out of the question."[41] John Piehl was appointed groundskeeper of the park. Initially called Sportsman's Park by some reporters, the park was officially named Milwaukee Park, with the name painted in bold letters along the rear of the grandstand.

On March 12 the Western League met in Milwaukee and adopted a schedule. The Western would open on May 1 and keep the 126-game schedule. Milwaukee again received no home holiday dates but opened at home and had 14 Sunday dates. One new rule was adopted, fining a manager $100 and the gate receipts if his team failed to take the field for a scheduled game. In player disputes George Van der Beck was again involved but won two of three this round. The Detroit owner, however, was having his troubles and was almost out of the Western League. In February Bob Glenalvin, his second baseman and manager in 1894, claimed Van der Beck owed him money on his '94 salary. Glenalvin also made the claim Van der Beck had each player sign two contracts, one going to president Ban Johnson of the Western League, the other for the actual salary, exceeding Johnson's salary limitations of $125 a month. If found guilty Van der Beck could be fined up to $1,000 or expelled. Johnson ordered him to pay Glenalvin $812.02 by March 1 or forfeit his franchise. Van der Beck did pay him but let it be known he was willing to sell. A stock company of Detroit citizens offered him $3,500 in March, but he wanted $5,000 and kept his franchise.

Larry Twitchell ordered his players to report in Milwaukee on April 1 and surprised everyone by deciding there would be no exhibition games played. He thought a bigger crowd could be had May 1 if the fans did not see the park or players before then. The *Daily News* thought this was a mistake. The paper believed the club should spend more money in spring but could see it had no intention "to tear up money on tours."[42] The club did decide, however, to advertise more. Colored lithographs were prepared, showing the portraits of all the members of the team. This lithograph was to be attached to the schedule and hung in glass at the hotels and various clubs. All cities within a radius of 100 miles were to be billed for games to perk up attendance. It was also announced Ladies Days would be abolished. The Brewers' uniforms would be cream with a grayish cast, and the cap would be the same color with brown stripes; the lettering on the shirt was in brown.

The players reported April 1, but as the new park was not completed, they reported to National Park. Their workouts only consisted of running and playing catch for the time. Management rented a flat for the out-of-town players at Eighth and Chestnut (Juneau Avenue). "Some of them are experts on the banjo and guitar, while others know how to sing, so that they will not be lacking for entertainment while keeping bachelor apartments."[43] On April 20 the club played its first practice game, with the Milwaukee Athletic Society, winning 24–6. A few more practices were played, with the team splitting into the Colts and Regulars. On April 28 a large crowd came into the new park to see these teams play. Two days before the season began, Jerry Eddinger was released.

Finally it was Wednesday, May 1, 1895. "The sun shone down from a light blue sky hot enough to take the coolness from the wind that came up over the lofty shore line from the bosom of the lake, and in no quarter was a single cloud visible."[44] The Milwaukee and Minneapolis players paraded around town in uniform, starting on the south side, and then to the courthouse, where Mayor Koch and other city officials paraded with them and a brass band. Sixteen carriages were in the parade. At the park Mayor Koch (who had never seen a baseball game and "did not understand the first principles of the game"[45]) gave a short speech to the 5,000 in attendance, including many city and government employees who were given half-day holidays. The Brewers started this lineup: Long—lf, Sharpe—2b, Twitchell—rf, Weaver—cf, McCauley—1b, Taylor—ss, LaRett—3b, Bolan—c, Baker—p. Unfortunately, the Brewers lost, 4 to 3. Stephens and Rettger then also lost to finish the first series.

St. Paul was next in, but they were rained out on Saturday. Twitchell realized LaRett could not make it at third and looked for help. He looked south to Chicago at Bill Everett or Asa Stewart, but Adrian Anson would not release either. Twitchell then looked to his own bench and found Klopf. Gus had played several years in the Western, California and Southern leagues before returning to his home in Milwaukee. Play resumed on Sunday at Milwaukee Park, and almost 8,000—the largest crowd ever to attend a baseball game in Milwaukee to date—saw Baker beat the Apostles, 2 to 0. St. Paul won the next day.

The Brewers then traveled to Minnesota, not taking LaRett and releasing William Summers. Rettger lost in St. Paul and rumor held that he was to be released. Killilea denied this, saying Rettger was "a hot weather"[46] pitcher and would come around. Over to Minneapolis, the Brewers split two with the Millers. A Sunday game was then scheduled in St. Paul, but the pastor of the Church of the Messiah obtained an injunction to prevent the contest. The mayor said he would not enforce the Sunday laws, and the game was played. About 2,500 saw Rettger win, 11 to 10. Back in Minneapolis the next day, Stephens won, 13 to 12.

The Brewers then returned for a short homestand, beating Kansas City two out of three. Oliver LaRett was given his release and went to Rockford. The Brewers then went to K.C. and dropped three to the Blues. The Brewers were playing with only 12 players—8 fielders and 4 pitchers—and if anyone would be injured, a pitcher would be forced to take over a position. Twitchell was trying to get Cleveland to farm Chippy McGarr to Milwaukee but did not succeed. The club traveled on to Toledo, winning two of three, and then into Indianapolis, where they dropped two more to the first-place Hoosiers. The Brewers then returned home for a single Sunday game, Baker beating St. Paul before 2,000 on a bitter cold day. The Milwaukees then traveled into Michigan, losing two of three in Grand Rapids and winning two in Detroit on Decoration Day. The Brewers were 12 and 15, and having trouble in the field. Taylor and McCauley were not playing up to form. McCauley did not cover much ground and was a weak hitter. Twitchell said the problem with the Brewers was their lack of hitting. One of the Brewer officials went east in search of players, but Twitchell warned all National League clubs were holding onto their extra men for a while to see how the pennant race developed.

The Brewers returned home May 31 and the team collected 27 hits in a 25 to 7 rout of St. Paul. Indianapolis was next in and Armstrong got his first start, beating the first-place club. The two clubs split the remaining two games. Detroit was to be next in, but the Tigers missed their train connection in Chicago because of a train wreck. The Brewers took the field at 3:30 p.m. and the game was forfeited to them. Detroit, of course, protested the forfeit, but it stood. The Tigers won the two games played. Toledo came in and injuries hit the club. First Bolan was out one game; then Sharpe, who was leading the club with a .327 average, hurt his hands. Twitchell went to second and Baker or Rettger went to right field until a new player, George Nicol, arrived from Indianapolis. During this series the Brewers sported new uniforms consisting of dark blue knickerbockers with white stockings, cap and belts. MILWAUKEE was printed in black letters on the shirt. Grand Rapids ended the homestand losing two games. Bolan managed to accomplish the impossible in the sixth inning of the second game, hitting a ball "so far over the left field fence that people in Williamsburg heard something drop, and took a line of thought of meteors and wondered if all stars were so small and round when they got through falling."[47]

The Brewers traveled into Minnesota and won half of the six games played in St. Paul and Minneapolis. Sharpe returned to the lineup, but Bolan was injured, as was Klopf. Twitchell went to third base, where he had no success. The Millers then came to Milwaukee and lost to Stephens, 8 to 6, as trouble on the field occurred. Perry Werden, the Minneapolis first baseman, was fined $50 and escorted from the field by two police officers. Umpire John Sheridan also fined two Millers $15 and $10, and Nicol $5, all for arguing extensively. The Brewers also won the two remaining games. St. Paul then came to the Cream City and won two of three. Klopf returned to the lineup in right field, but Bolan returned home to Memphis for the funeral of his eight-month-old child and was gone for the remainder of the homestand. Kansas City finished the homestand, losing two of three games, the last Sunday game drawing 7,000. Before the Brewers hit the road, William Armstrong was released.

The Western was having franchise and other problems. On June 25 Thomas Murphy, secretary of the Minneapolis club, was suspended indefinitely for throwing stones at an umpire on June 2 in Minneapolis. The Western League was unhappy with John Barnes and Murphy because of the way games were conducted in the Flour City and even thought of giving the franchise to some local businessmen, but they took no action yet. Across the river, St. Paul was also having troubles. In May a judge issued a permanent injunction against Sunday ball in the city. Comiskey thought of moving his franchise to Columbus, Ohio, which was thought to be a better city for the Western. On July 3, Toledo, which also lost Sunday ball, did transfer its franchise, but to Terre Haute, Indiana, after all the Western clubs voted in favor of the move. Dennis Long had complained of low attendance in Toledo and asked for permission to transfer. Detroit, Kansas City and Minneapolis at first objected because of the increased mileage, but some concessions were made to these clubs. The Swamp Angels had compiled a 23 and 29 record in Toledo.

The Brewers left for Kansas City, where they lost two of three. President Killilea headed south, where the Southern League was expected to expire, in search of players. He managed to sign Ollie Beard, Evansville's shortstop, and Robert Stafford, the first baseman of New Orleans. These players would become Milwaukee's property when and if the Southern League died. Unfortunately for the Brewers, the league lived the season. In July Killilea gave up his claim on Beard and let Grand Rapids have those rights. The Brewers traveled into Michigan and beat both Detroit and Grand Rapids two of three. Then on to the new kid in the league, Terre Haute, where Milwaukee again won two of three. The final game was on a Sunday, and the 1,700 attendance was about 500 fewer than the previous Sunday, blamed on the saloons being open that day and not the previous week. The road trip ended with the Brewers losing two of three in first-place Indianapolis.

Twitchell's men came home on July 18 in third place and immediately won nine in a row—four over Grand Rapids, three from Terre Haute, and two from Detroit. The team was hitting .286, with Sharpe at .349 and Twitchell and Weaver at .343. The only loss in the stretch did not count in the Western League standings. On July 26 eleventh-place Washington of the National League played the Brewers at Milwaukee Park before 1,000 spectators, beating Milwaukee, 8 to 0, in a rain-shortened, five-inning game. Twitchell pitched Johnny Diamond, who had refused to sign for $125 a month when the season started and still was not signed, against the Senators to save his three regular pitchers.

More difficulties plagued the Western League. Terre Haute was having poor home attendance. Owner Long now thought of transferring all his home games to other cities. The *Sentinel* gave Ban Johnson an opinion.

> The [Western] League should devise some plan whereby each city procuring a franchise furnishes a guarantee that it will go through the season and maintain a team properly. These changes from city to city do not help the interest of baseball. They have an effect of giving the impression that the league is not on sound financial basis. The Western League, however, is the best minor league in existence when it comes to finances, and the chance for it going under before the season closes is not worthy of consideration.[48]

On July 22 the Western board of directors met in Chicago and transferred John Barnes' and J.W. Flynn's interest in the Minneapolis club to Thomas Murphy. Murphy was also relieved of the suspension he suffered for the stone-throwing incident. It was reported Barnes received $7,000 for his interests. The Detroit forfeit from June 4 was also brought up, but no action was taken. Ban Johnson reported the Western had a $15,000 surplus in the treasury and expected it to reach $20,000 by season's end. The Western president told Milwaukee officials they added the most into the treasury, twice as much as some clubs.

The Brewers, after the winning streak, were playing 45 and 33 ball. First-place Indianapolis arrived in the Beer City and won all three, dropping the Brewers to fourth place. In the Twin Cities, the Brewers lost four to St. Paul and three to Minneapolis. The Brewers had now lost ten in a row, and their team batting average had dipped six points. It was decided to get new players. First, Pete Bolan was released. Paddy got drunk, was unable to catch the final Indianapolis game, and was fined $50. In St. Paul he continued to drink and was finally released, soon signing with Grand Rapids. Bill Schriver, who had played in Milwaukee in 1891 and jumped to Chicago when the club went to the American Association, had just been released by New York and signed to catch with the Brewers. Another catcher, Bill Moran, was also signed on loan from Chicago. Schriver, however, never appeared with Milwaukee. He could not sign with a minor league club until all the National League clubs waived claim to him, and St. Louis claimed him. Instead of joining St. Louis, Schriver joined Scranton of the Eastern League. The Brewers then bought Robert Stafford from New Orleans for $1,000 (Ban Johnson would later report this as $800, as would the *Sporting News*' New Orleans correspondent) and a $200 bonus to play first base, as McCauley was injured. Stafford had wanted his release as he was "afraid of being attacked with disease"[49] in New Orleans and was finally sold after he decided to return to his home in North Carolina. Pittsburgh then released Bill Niles, a third baseman, and Milwaukee wired him for terms, as did Detroit and Indianapolis. Cleveland of the National League also claimed him on waivers. In order to make sure Milwaukee got Niles, Connie Mack of Pittsburgh recalled his release and turned him over to the Brewers for the rest of the season. Washington also wanted Niles and claimed they had no chance to claim him. As he was on loan to Milwaukee, he was actually still a member of the Pirates. Jimmy Long and Al McCauley were released by the Brewers. Killilea tried to obtain Joshua Goar, a pitcher from Terre Haute, but Denny Long refused to part with him.

The Brewers, meanwhile, traveled to Kansas City and lost three more games. The clubs was now 45 and 46. On August 12 the Brewers returned home and beat K.C., 19 to 8. The team was now Klopf—lf, Weaver—c, Sharpe—2b, Twitchell—rf, Stafford—1b, Niles—3b, Taylor—ss, Nicol—cf, Baker, Rettger and Stephens—p, and Moran the extra man. The Blues and Brewers split the remaining two games. Minneapolis was next in and won two games. Bolan was back on the club now, signing a pledge "to keep away from John Barleycorn, brewery wagons and the like."[50] Bill Moran became sick and was returned to Chicago. Niles also injured his hand, returning Klopf to third and Weaver to the outfield. St. Paul came into town to end the home series and split two games. The Brewers' losing ways were hurting attendance, and fights on the field were becoming more commonplace. On August 14, 1895, the *Daily News* said of the situation, "If rowdy baseball is not checked at once decent patrons will stay away from the game and the police courts will eventually render the most important decisions on the day's mischief. When that stage shall have been reached goodbye professional baseball."

On the road again the Brewers beat the Tigers two of three in Detroit, returned home for a Sunday victory, and then went back to Detroit to lose two games. Then on to last-place Grand Rapids, the Milwaukee club won two of three. The Brewers made a very short stop at home on September 1 and 2, as Terre Haute had transferred its games to Milwaukee, and the Brewers dropped three games to the Hottentots. Niles was finally back at third base, but Stafford took ill, forcing Twitchell to first and Klopf into the outfield. The Brewers then traveled back to Indianapolis, losing four, to finish road play for the year.

The club returned home to finish the season, with Stephens losing to Minneapolis, 12 to 9. The next day Rettger won to break the nine-game losing streak, the *Sentinel* proclaiming "VICTORY! VICTORY! STRANGELY ENOUGH MILWAUKEE WINS A GAME."[51] The victory was before only 300 spectators at Milwaukee Park. Stephens ended the series with a loss, and Stafford was back at first base. But Kirtley Baker had an injured hand and was unable to pitch. He went home with a 14 and 24 record. To take his place Twitchell signed Claude Elliott, the pitcher from Portage (Wisconsin) who had tried out for the club in the spring; his record at Portage in 1895 had been 15 and 2, in addition to winning eleven games with other clubs during the season. Also signed was Burns of the local Northwestern Mutual Life Insurance Company of the Commercial League. Burns sat on the bench one game but never saw action with the Brewers. Elliott pitched his first game against Grand Rapids. In the eighth inning the score stood 9 to 9 when an argument ensued, and Grand Rapids forfeited. Rettger then won the only other game in this series, with Grand Rapids pitching Burns.

Robert Stafford wanted out of New Orleans and ended up playing in Milwaukee for 5 seasons.

Matt Killilea was again attempting to strengthen the club, but looking ahead to 1896. He signed Hyleman, a shortstop from Maysville, Kentucky, for the '96 season, but he never reported to Milwaukee. John LaFleur, Elliott's catcher from Portage, was also signed and caught the remainder of the season, resting Bolan. Indianapolis came into town and split two, then Terre Haute won two of three. When Terre Haute left the Brewers had a new third baseman, Fred Hartman. It was originally reported Killilea traded Hartman for Bill Niles and a bonus of cash. It was soon learned that Connie Mack, the Pittsburgh manager, notified Twitchell that Niles did in fact belong to Washington and he could not play in the Western. Niles was only to be loaned to Terre Haute, and Hartman was purchased for $1,000. Niles did not want to go with Terre Haute, so Gus Klopf was loaned in his place. Niles finished the season in Milwaukee. The season only consisted of three more games with Detroit, the Brewers winning one, the Tigers winning one, and the season finale a 6 to 6 tie.

The final Western League standings for 1895:

Indianapolis	78	43	.645	Detroit	59	66	.472
St. Paul	71	51	.582	Milwaukee	57	67	.460
Kansas City	73	53	.579	Terre Haute	55	72	.433
Minneapolis	65	58	.528	Grand Rapids	38	86	.306

Indianapolis led the Western from mid–May until the end. Other clubs wanted very much to do something to prevent John Brush from drawing players from his National League Cincinnati club to Indianapolis whenever he needed them. Even before the season had started, Brush had stocked Indianapolis with six players from the Cincinnati club. The *Sentinel*, having noted Cincinnati placed eighth in the National League, wrote an open letter to the Indianapolis owner.

Mr. Brush of Cincinnati. Will you please look your team over again and say whether you have not been mistaken by placing your Cincinnati team at Indianapolis and your Indianapolis team at Cincinnati?[52]

The *Journal* thought cheap management had hurt the Brewers as much as Brush's tactics had helped his Hoosiers. The other clubs "borrowed or bought men without difficulty, while Milwaukee stood back with its hands in its pockets, fondling the cash, and took whipping after whipping. The plethoric pocketbook, however, places the club in a healthful condition for next year, and if there is not a winning club in the field at the beginning of the season, the cause will be apparent."[53]

Financially the Western again did very well. Ban Johnson reported on average the clubs made one-third more money than they did in 1894, and all eight clubs made money. St. Paul made about $20,000, while Indianapolis and Detroit were ahead about $10,000. Even lowly Grand Rapids claimed to have made $3,500. Matthew Killilea reported Milwaukee made $11,000, with the *Journal* reporting a profit as high as $15,000. The Brewers spent $1,800 for players, the most in the Western. The Brewer management also had spent about $8,000 on putting up Milwaukee Park.

Unlike in 1894, this year the Brewers finished as one of the worst clubs in the Western. In September the club had a 6 and 13 record and had only been 8 and 18 in August. The Brewers had only managed to beat Detroit and Grand Rapids in the season series, tying with Toledo–Terre Haute. The Brewers won only four of seventeen games with the Hoosiers. Of the three full-time pitchers, only Rettger won more than he lost (21 and 18). Baker was 14 and 24 and Stephens 20 and 23. Elliott finished 2 and 1. Twitchell led the club in hitting at .343, with Weaver and Nicol close behind at .341. Klopf had hit .301 and Taylor .300. A total of 69 men hit .300 or better in the Western, and all clubs had a team average over .300, Milwaukee bringing up the rear with a .300 average. Indianapolis hit an amazing .354.

One note of interest after the season was a new idea of a winter California League by some of the Western leaders. This league was to play from October 15 to December 15 and consist primarily of Milwaukee, St. Paul, Minneapolis and Detroit players. Theodore Engel, the Brewers secretary, took eight of the Brewers, including LaFleur, Rettger, Sharpe, Taylor, Weaver, Niles, Twitchell and Nicol, to set up his team in San Jose. Back home the press believed it would be a failure because of the short season and foreign players to the area. The prediction was accurate. By mid–November the league folded due to mismanagement and low attendance — or wet weather, small diamonds and drunken players on the field, depending on whom you read in the papers. Engel returned home $3,400 poorer. His club had finished with a 9 and 9 record. Many of the players in the league were left stranded and broke, but Engel was given credit for paying his players' salaries in full, getting them all to Chicago, and then buying them all tickets to their respective homes.

✱ ✱ ✱

Interest in amateur baseball picked up amazingly in 1894 with the new Western League. Only a little over 100 clubs had organized in 1893, and this skyrocketed to a record 589 in 1894. However, no leagues formed and not much worthy of repeating actually occurred. The first game of the local season was played on April 8, with the Chicawees defeating the Brownies, 12 to 9. The following Sunday the bigger clubs started as the Leaders beat the

Whitings, 20 to 16, and the West Ends beat the Silver Cities in Wauwatosa. The James Morgans traveled the farthest that year, going to Manistee, Michigan, on July 1 and 2, winning both games. In September the Morgans beat Janesville to claim the amateur championship of the state. In September the Quicksteps beat the Leaders, 16 to 6, and claimed the city championship. This was disputed by the Zieglers, who based their own claim on their excellent record against the strong clubs of the city and state. Other local clubs claimed championships in 1894. The Starlights claimed the 17-year-old championship with a 22 to 2 record. The problem there was the Banners also claimed it with a 15 to 1 record, and they had beaten the Starlights on October 1. A challenge was set up for the championship and $25, but it never took place. The West End Juniors claimed the 9-year-old championship of Milwaukee. The Freedoms claimed the 13-year-old championship, and the Silver Springs called themselves the 15-year-old champs.

Again in 1895 local baseball interest was high. For this season two local leagues formed: the City League and the Commercial League. The idea of the City League began in November with Gus Alberts behind the movement. On December 2, the City League formed into an 8-club circuit. The west side of Milwaukee was represented by the James Morgans and Arenas; the east side by the George Zieglers; the south side by the Leaders, Quicksteps and Unions; and the north side by the Laurels and Black Diamonds. Colonel Gustav Pabst was elected president, but he soon was forced to quit and Harry D. Quin was elected to the position. Quin declined, so William Stone, proprietor of the Sherman House on 36th and National Avenue, became president. Athletic Park would be used along with proposed grounds in Bay View, Whitefish Bay and Soldier's Home Heights. Once Lloyd Street Park was built, it was used along with Athletic Park. The league divided costs 60 percent to the winner, 20 percent to the loser, with the remaining 20 percent to go to the league fund each game. Admission was 25 cents, and an extra 10 cents in the grandstand. To defray costs the City League planned a dance in April at the West Side Turner Hall, selling more than 100 tickets.

By March contracts were signed with players, but trouble began. That month the Quicksteps and Arenas dropped out, and it was decided to go with six clubs. Competition was also there when the Commercial League organized in February with four clubs of players employed in local business houses. The Commercial League consisted of the Milwaukee Athletic Society, Northwestern Mutual Life Insurance club, H.D. Quin's, and the Post Office Alerts. The Commercial League elected Alvin P. Kletzsch, secretary of the company that owned the Republican Hotel on Third and Kilbourn, its president and required a $10 forfeiture bond. The league wanted only amateur players, as a standard contract will show.

I _____ agree to play with _____ during the championship season of the Milwaukee Commercial League of Amateur Players, in the year ... without any money consideration.
_____,Player
Witnessed _____
_____ [54]

This contract had to be signed three days before the time of the game. Admission to these Commercial League contests would be 15 cents for adults, a dime for boys, and all ladies admitted free. This competition would not be head-to-head, as the City League played on Sundays and the Commercial League on Saturdays. A good many players belonged to both leagues, and the City League ordered its players out of the Commercial League so they would not be tired for their games. The Commercial League could only see this move as trying to weaken their league. The City League then softened this stand, saying only pitchers could not compete in the other league. Even with this move, the City League was not financially strong and eventually dropped the Unions and Leaders. Gus Alberts also quit the Laurels to go to Rockford of the Illinois-Iowa League, causing the City League to lose its most popular player. The remaining four clubs—Zieglers, Black Diamonds, Laurels and James Morgans—all put up a $25 forfeiture bond.

Both leagues started play the same week. The Commercial League began Saturday, May 11, with the Milwaukee Athletic Society beating the Post Office Alerts, and the Quins beating the Northwestern Mutuals at Athletic Park. The following day the City League opened with the Black Diamonds beating the James Morgans at Milwaukee Park, and the Zieglers defeating the Laurels at Athletic Park. After this opening week the Laurels changed their name to the H.G. Razalls, a blank book manufacturing company on North Water Street. The Black Diamonds jumped quickly into first place in the City League and held it until August, when the Razalls took over that position. The City League stayed in tact all season, with the Razalls winning the pennant in late September and all four clubs breaking out about even financially. The Commercial League, playing at National Park and Athletic Park, did not have such smooth sailing. Just after July 4, the last-place Post Office Alerts disbanded. The Bradley & Metcalf team replaced them for one game, losing, before the Skidmore & Friedlick's took over to finish the season. The Commercial League closed August 31 with the Athletic Society team ahead from start to finish. Hansell and Jahn of the Athletics led the league in hitting with .414 and .407 averages. The two leagues' finishes were as follows:

COMMERCIAL LEAGUE			CITY LEAGUE		
Milwaukee Athletic Society	12	5	H.G. Razalls	13	6
Northwestern Mutual Life	9	6	Black Diamonds	11	8
H.D. Quin's	10	10	James Morgan's	10	8
Skidmore & Friedlick's	3	13	George Ziegler's	4	16

After the season the Razalls played the James Morgans at Milwaukee Park for $100 a side, the Morgans winning, 16 to 7, with Will Riley pitching for the winners.

Other notes of interest in 1895 in local baseball include the Bloomer Baseball Club of Boston's victory over the Badgers, 13 to 8. Between 1,500 and 2,000 came to Milwaukee Park to see the eastern women win. The Badgers were one of the better amateur clubs but "didn't play hard and allowed the women to win!"[55] On July 4 the Quins traveled into Michigan and split two games with Escanaba. In June the Bay Views had traveled to Manistee and lost two games. Another club to take a trip was the White Diamonds, which traveled through the state, winning 7 and losing 6 to various clubs.

The City League continued on with its plans for a six-club circuit in 1896. Unfortunately, the Commercial League died. In November the Zieglers resigned from the City League in order to play outside clubs. The Quins from the old Commercial League applied for admission, as did the Skidmores and the Racine club, having said they could obtain special railroad rates to and from Milwaukee. The West End Club also applied, and league officials still pondered a six-club circuit, but most believed Racine would not be in, and the City League would consist of five clubs.

City League affairs were quiet until February. President Knouth stated the league consisted of the James Morgans, Razalls, and the new Otto Brothers, which apparently replaced the Black Diamonds. Knouth claimed the league was having trouble finding another club because several of the stronger clubs in the city were planning on playing out of the city on Saturdays for bigger gate receipts. Later that month the James Morgans announced their intention to drop out but stayed on for the time being. Finally the Quins replaced the Zieglers to become the fourth club of the circuit. In March things finally began to roll along. O.E. Remey, the sporting editor of the *Sentinel*, was elected president of the league on March 2. Four days later the Razalls decided to drop out and play entirely out of city games and were later replaced by the Skidmores. Then a new club, the C.H. Matthews club, replaced the James Morgans but actually consisted of the same players. A schedule of 24 games was drawn up, starting May 3. The four City League clubs were the C.H. Matthews, Quins, Otto Brothers and Skidmores, all new names in the league.

The City League opened May 3 with the Ottos beating the Matthews, 7 to 3, at Milwaukee Park, and the Quins defeating the Skidmores, 19 to 2, at Athletic Park. By June 1 the City League was going along fine, with the Otto Brothers and Quins tied for first place. The only setback was the canceling of Decoration Day games because of a city street car strike. Later in June the league abandoned Athletic Park, playing both games at Milwaukee Park due to the low attendance because of the strike, charging one admission to see both games. By the end of June the Matthews club was in first place, but trouble was around the corner. On July 1 the Skidmores dropped from the league, and the league continued with three clubs. For the rest of the season the Quins and Ottos battled for first place. On October 4 the regular season ended with the Quins and Ottos tied for first with 12 and 8 records. However, the Ottos claimed first place because the Quins had failed to show for a postponed game that morning. The following week a playoff game was played, and the two teams tied, 5 to 5. A week later the Ottos won, 9 to 8, for the championship. Hansell of the Quins led the City League in hitting with a .382 average. Riley of the Matthews was second with a .379 average. The final 1896 City League standings and team batting averages:

| Otto Brothers | 13 | 8 | .280 | C.H. Matthews | 9 | 12 | .258 |
| H.D. Quins | 12 | 9 | .308 | Skidmores | 1 | 6 | .259 |

The Razalls, which had dropped from the City League, did play outside clubs, but not with the frequency or success they hoped for. In May the Razalls went to Jefferson and won, 19 to 11. Returning in June they lost, 13 to 6. Later in June the Razalls traveled to Escanaba, Michigan, and lost, 17 to 4. The Fourth of July weekend found them in Manitowoc, Wisconsin, splitting two games. No more was heard of the Razalls that year.

✳ ✳ ✳

After the successful 1895 season the Western League looked toward 1896 with an eye on circuit changes. As early as July, Manager Watkins from Indianapolis thought out loud that Columbus and Omaha would replace Grand Rapids and Terre Haute, making St. Paul the smallest city in the circuit. In August his boss, John T. Brush, went on record as being opposed to Grand Rapids as a member of the Western. On September 1 a secret meeting of four Western clubs was held in Chicago, and it was decided to drop Long and his Terre Haute franchise from the league and replace it with Columbus. The *Toledo Commercial* and the *Milwaukee Sentinel* thought Toledo would get Terre Haute's place, and Columbus would replace Grand Rapids. Western League president Ban Johnson went on record in favor of Columbus for Terre Haute. Another rumor had Robert Leadley and Charlie Bennett taking the Detroit franchise from George Van der Beck. The two had a number of businessmen behind them, but Van der Beck said he would not sell out. He even said he was going to build a new park in Mt. Clemens in order to have Sunday ball.

In late September the Western met in Chicago, and it was recommended that Columbus take the Terre Haute franchise and Toledo replace Grand Rapids. Omaha had tried to get in but was considered "a frosty ball town."[56] Rockford also wanted a spot, thinking it was a good town as it had Sunday ball, which neither Toledo nor Columbus had. The Western reorganized for a period of five years, giving the six remaining franchises specific owners. John Goodnow, H.P. Watson and Marcus Haynes were awarded the Minneapolis franchise from Murphy at a cost of a reported $12,000 for the transfer. Detroit was owned by Van der Beck; Indianapolis by John Brush and W.F.G. Golt; St. Paul by Charles Comiskey; Milwaukee by Matthew Killilea; and Kansas City by John Manning. Ban Johnson was re-elected president, secretary and treasurer. Johnson, Golt and Killilea formed a committee to look into the two replacements and would report its findings at the November meeting.

Omaha still wanted in and even offered a $50,000 bond as good faith money. Denver wanted in as well, but the distance again killed any hopes. By the end of October it was all but settled that Toledo would be in the Western, with J.W. Gunnels, who owned the 1892 club there, as the owner. The Columbus Street Railway Company had offered to build a ballpark and offer a 10-year lease if the Western located there. With this Columbus was also assured a spot, with Tom Loftus the owner. The committee visited both cities and reported it would officially recommend them both. The committee was opposed to the third city, Omaha, because of the distance, although the western clubs in the league favored it.

The Western League met on November 20 and decided Grand Rapids and Terre Haute would be dropped. Terre Haute gave no fight, as they had already applied for admission to the Western Association. Dubuque, of the Western Association, had transferred to Omaha, so that city was also out of the Western League plans. Columbus and Toledo appeared to be shoo-ins. The problem facing the Western was that four groups were looking to place a club in Columbus. The following day the two cities were voted in. Dixon and Talbot, J.J. Shipperd, Bert Dasher and Tom Loftus had applied for the Columbus franchise. Four of the six Western clubs favored Loftus. Brush of Indianapolis wanted Dasher and Loftus to be partners. Goodnow of Minneapolis favored Shipperd. Tom Loftus was finally awarded the franchise and was to buy the Grand Rapids team from George Ellis. J.W. Gunnels was the only applicant for Toledo and was willing to pay $2,500, provided he could get the franchise for five years. The Western would only give Gunnels the franchise for one year because Toledo had no Sunday ball, and he left the meeting in disgust. The Western moved quickly and moved to transfer the Toledo franchise, along with the players, to Omaha. Thomas J. Hickey, president of the Western Association, said Omaha was in his association and would not go into the Western League. Even Matt Killilea admitted as much, saying Grand Rapids would probably be back in the Western League, and Toledo was still technically in the Western. Soon Manning from Kansas City came out in favor of Grand Rapids, as Omaha was not financially sound. Comiskey from St. Paul agreed. The Western League went to the National Board of Arbitration to see if it could get Omaha into its league and received a favorable ruling. However, the Western then decided against admitting the city. Two owners in favor of admitting the Nebraska city were Brush and Goodnow. The *Sporting Life* claimed they wanted Omaha because Brush controlled Indianapolis, Columbus and Minneapolis, and Omaha would give him half the Western. He could then control legislation of the league. Finally, on December 30, the Western League met in Milwaukee and awarded Grand Rapids a one-year franchise. George Ellis and Theodore Engel both wanted the franchise. Engel had disposed of his Milwaukee stock and was on his own. Ellis was asked if he wanted to take Engel as a partner but declined, and was awarded sole ownership.

Not all was settled, however. The Minneapolis and Indianapolis directors immediately filed a formal protest over Grand Rapids being admitted. They claimed it took a three-fourths vote to award a franchise, and Ellis received only five votes, while their two ballots were blank. Their protest was ignored for the moment. Ellis did not deposit the $1,000 bond until February. He would not put the money up until the ruling was changed so that he only had to take the players from the Toledo club he wanted and not all as originally required. He also brought up that three of the Terre Haute stars had been sold toward the end of the season and he wanted some sort of guarantee that he would be reimbursed for the money he put into the club if he lost it after one year.

The Western League now consisted of Milwaukee, Minneapolis, St. Paul, Detroit, Grand Rapids, Indianapolis, Columbus and Kansas City. New rules and new problems faced the league. The 10 percent fund was abandoned, and each club was to pay $1,000 to the secretary "and such sums as may be assessed for salaries for umpires and other expenses."[57] Another rule was passed that if a National League club drafted a man and later cut him, the player was again the property of the original Western club.

The Western's major problem was in Minneapolis. It was first reported the new owners had no money and might lose the franchise. This was denied in a report saying they had $30,000 in the treasury. Then Walter Wilmot was named the Millers' manager. Once again others thought Minneapolis was under the control of Jim Hart, of the Chicago National League Colts. Because of Wilmot's alleged National League ties, Brush's obvious ties (not only did he own Cincinnati, but he had stock in the New York Giants), and a *Detroit Free Press* story that suggested Cleveland and Pittsburgh were going to make farm clubs out of Grand Rapids and Columbus, the local press called the Western "a kindergarten"[58] for the National League. The press called for the Western directors to act. At the December meeting it was rumored a resolution would be introduced to bar any magnate who had an interest in a National League club, but it was not brought up. To add to all this intercourse, the *Cincinnati Times-Star* claimed Cleveland would let Tom Loftus have some of its young players for his Columbus team. Ban Johnson's old newspaper, the *Cincinnati Commercial-Gazette*, denied the *Times-Star* story. Goodnow looked at the situation differently, believing the Western League was combining against Minneapolis and Indianapolis to prevent them from strengthening their clubs.

On the local scene the first matter of importance was the question of the club's manager. Even before the season opened, it was not known if Larry Twitchell would be rehired. He had received two other offers and rightfully wanted to know. The problem was that half of the stockholders were not in favor of spending money on purchasing players when weak spots existed. The purchase of Stafford had convinced these stockholders to not keep Twitchell. The *Sentinel* urged that Twitchell be rehired, writing the club's large profits had been chiefly due to his management of financial affairs. Dissension grew worse and two or three stockholders reportedly wanted to sell out. After the season Twitchell was rehired for 1896, "given more liberty [to act] as he pleases in signing new men and releasing others."[59]

The troubles, however, got even worse after the Western meeting. Matthew Killilea was given sole ownership of the club, and if he wished to own the club, the other stockholders would be out in the cold. It was known Killilea wanted two or three of the 15 stockholders out, and by getting the franchise in his name he could let in only those he wanted. Some stockholders feared Killilea would team with Harry Quin and run the club. The *Sporting Life* of Philadelphia thought that would be a profitable idea. Killilea said he would call a meeting soon to discuss the situation. On November 4 the directors met and elected Fred Gross, owner of Fred C. Gross Meat Packers on South Muskego & West Canal Streets, to replace Theodore Engel as secretary of the club. Killilea was re-elected president and Charles Hellberg vice president. A board of control was elected that would have charge of the affairs of the club and matters of business. This board consisted of Killilea, Gross and Charles Polacheck. Beside these three, only Rudolph Giljohan was left from the original ten stockholders of the club. Giljohan would be a strange choice as a stockholder in today's baseball world. It appears a tavern on East Water Street had been previously used by Giljohan as a baseball pool room, an operation where the managers of the pools collected 10 percent of the tickets sold—"a hefty thing for the pool seller at the end of a lively day."[60] It appears the authorities frequently looked the other way, but in September 1886 and again in April 1890, pool rooms in Milwaukee were closed down, with Giljohan's being closed both times. In December the Brewers announced their headquarters would be at 343 Third Street (1131 North Third Street in the later address numbering system). The club had no official office in the past and "the better class of patrons charged that the club maintained headquarters in saloons only."[61]

Milwaukee management now had to assemble a team. Twitchell said he wanted a catcher to replace Pete Bolan, whom he wanted to release, as well as a shortstop and a pitcher. Within a week after the 1895 season, the Brewers signed two local pitchers, William Wolf and Will Riley. Both were from the James Morgan club, but Wolf had played the previous summer in Dubuque. Bolan was given to St. Paul, and Twitchell looked to Bill Schriver to replace him. But Killilea later reported all negotiations were off with Schriver, as he wanted too much—$300 a month. Paddy Bolan was having a tough time of it in Memphis. In February he was arrested for assault with intent to murder his ex-wife. He was found guilty and sentenced to 11 months and 27 days in jail but was told by the judge that his sentence would be suspended if he left town. The *Sporting Life* reported he took the first train out of Memphis.

The search for players went nationwide. The Brewers were after several players from the Virginia League, most notably Lehay, a shortstop, and E.F. Foster, a catcher. Neither came to Milwaukee. The club was interested in numerous players from the Southern League. From the ill-fated trip to California, Twitchell found five men, the most promising Bert Jones, a pitcher from Pueblo, who was signed in December. It was said Jones had "terrific speed" and "uses his head to good advantage."[62] In November Killilea informed President Jones of the Montgomery Southern League club he was going to draft Mike Kehoe and pay the required $500. Killilea had first offered Bolan in a trade, but Jones declined. Twitchell then signed Frank McPartlin, who had been 17 and 2 with Norfolk of the Virginia League, but he soon jumped and signed with Toronto. Smith, a pitcher from the New Orleans club recommended by Stafford, was also signed.

Next the Brewers went after George Speer and Fred Barnes, the catcher and pitcher of Lincoln of the Western Association. Speer was "undoubtedly the best catcher in the league ... unsurpassed as a thrower to bases and he uses his head at all times."[63] Barnes had won 35 games with Lincoln in 1895. First Engel went to Lincoln to sign the two but failed. The Lincoln franchise was then transferred to Cedar Rapids, and Twitchell went there to talk to manager Buck Ebright. It seemed the two players had no contract with Cedar Rapids for 1896, as there was a clause in their 1895 contracts to the effect that they could not be reserved by Lincoln (Cedar Rapids now). Ebright claimed they were reserved, however. Twitchell offered to buy the two for $990 but was turned down. Milwaukee then drafted them for $500 apiece. The Brewers had now spent $2,800 on players, which was more than most National League clubs had spent, according to the *Daily News*. But Speer was quoted as saying he did not want to come to Milwaukee. It was learned St. Paul, Kansas City, Columbus, and Indianapolis were after the two players, who were being tampered with. In January, Barnes, who had won 37 of 44 games in 1895, signed with Cedar Rapids, which was equivalent to his signing with Milwaukee, as they owned his contract. Speer still held out. The Brewers were offering him a $100 raise, but he wanted more. Killilea said of the situation, "It is possible that [Speer] may want a portion of the gross receipts, a section of the grandstand, or a four carat diamond as an inducement for him to play with Milwaukee next year. We have offered him a good salary and if he does not desire to accept that, he will not play ball at all."[64] As Milwaukee was sure they would acquire Speer, they decided not to sign Kehoe, who signed with Columbus.

The Brewers lost a few players too. Pittsburgh had called back Bill Niles and loaned him to Grand Rapids. Claude Elliott was released. John LaFleur was considered too small for a catcher and was released to sign with the Roanoke club of Virginia. Gus Klopf was given his release to manage in the Pacific Coast League.

In February the Brewers signed Bill Wetterer, a shortstop from Cincinnati's crack amateur Shamrocks team on Wally Taylor's recommendation. Indianapolis also wanted Wetterer, but Western League president Ban Johnson gave him to Milwaukee, saying he was a wonder. This caused John T. Brush to attack Johnson, claiming he signed Wetterer for Milwaukee. The *Cincinnati Commercial-Gazette* wrote of Brush:

> The trouble is that the Hoosier magnate laid plans to capture the minor circuit hook, line, bob and sinker. His scheme went awry and now he is crying like a schoolboy who is refused a second piece of pie. The whole thing reminds one of the wail of the shiftless farmer who fancies because his crops are poor that the hand of Providence is raised against him.[65]

Johnson claimed he only recommended Wetterer to the Brewers. Twitchell also signed John Nonamaker, a pitcher from Ohio, and Edward Mrzena,[66] reported to be the best shortstop in the Southern League. By mid–February, Twitchell announced he had also signed Rettger, Stafford, Taylor, Hartman, and Nicol. Baker wanted more money but was expected to sign for the same salary as 1895. Weaver was expected to take a cut. In early March, George Speer finally signed. Also March, Peck Sharpe was sold to Columbus for $350. To back Speer, Twitchell signed James Outcalt, who had caught with Toledo/Terre Haute in '95. Another player who did not make the club was George Stephens. Suffering from consumption, he was not well enough to play and died on August 5, 1896. Now all the players were signed except Weaver. The club offered Weaver $250 a month, but he wanted $300, which had been his 1895 pay. What Weaver wanted would put the club over the salary limit, a secret, but believed to be in the area of $2,400 a month. Weaver soon dropped his demand to $275 and was finally signed.

In March Twitchell made his final cuts and announced his club:

Catchers: George Speer and James Outcalt.
  Pitchers: Kirtley Baker, George Rettger, Fred Barnes, John Nonamaker, Bert Jones.
  Infielders: Robert Stafford (1b), Wally Taylor (2b), Fred Hartman (3b), Ed Mrzena (ss), Bill Wetterer (ss).
  Outfielders: Bill Weaver, George Nicol, Larry Twitchell.

The local press felt this club was 50 percent stronger than the previous year, but most others disagreed, pegging the club for fourth place.

The Brewers' strength, or any minor league club's strength, from year to year depended to a certain extent on the National League draft. The bigger minor leagues had succeeded in getting the draft price up to $1,000 per man for 1896, and it had excellent results. Only eleven Western League players had been drafted after the 1895 season, compared to twenty-one the year before. Milwaukee lost none, and the $1,000 price was cited. Minor league officials were sure this would help stabilize their leagues. The National League soon moved to change the drafting price back to $500 from Class A, and lower prices down the line. John Brush was instrumental in this move. The *Milwaukee Journal* thought the reduction would not hurt the Western because it would be in a class of its own. The National League met in February, and Ban Johnson went to discuss the draft. Johnson argued that any player having sufficient ability to play in the National League was worth $1,000 to the Western, as he was a star in that league and consequently a drawing card. He noted that the approximately 20 players drafted from his Western after the 1894 season had cost $10,000, equal to the 10 drafted at the higher price after 1895. Johnson made his point, but it was the wrong way. The league lowered its drafting prices to save itself money. It set the following draft prices for the league classifications: Class A—$500, B—$300, C—$200, D—$100, E—$75, and F—$50. The Western, in Class A, claimed it could not replace good players for near that price. To make matters worse, the National League told minor officials they had no right to say what class they desired to be placed in. The National Board made that decision based on the last government population census. The National League also inserted a clause that would stop any minor league club from negotiating or joining a league that the National League thought dangerous to the National Agreement. No minor leagues were happy, but that was how it stood. The minors started to do something, though. On March 16 the minors met in Washington, with the Western League, Western Association, New England League, Eastern League, Pennsylvania League, and Southern League represented. Ban Johnson was elected president and J.C. Morse of the New England League secretary. The talks were secret, but it was reported the minors had enough money to bolt the National Agreement if necessary. The *Cincinnati Commercial-Gazette* called the National League protection system blackmail. It warned, "The National League, under the guidance of such master hands as those of John T. Brush and Charles Byrne, is sowing the wind. Sooner or later it will reap the whirlwind."[67]

The Western League met again in early March in St. Paul and adopted its schedule for 1896. The 140-game schedule started on April 22. Milwaukee opened at home again, receiving 12 Sunday dates and Labor Day. On the new schedule the Brewers were to travel only 7,891 miles, or about 2,500 fewer than in 1895. "This will result in the savings of several dollars to the owners of the organization and a pleasure to the players, who are by no means in love with railroad traveling."[68] Some constitutional changes were made. No club could sell a player to a club outside the Western without the unanimous approval of the other clubs, and the 10 percent rule of Western club receipts was restored. The so-called farming system had a damper put on it. A constitution change read: "Any member joining a Western League club and coming from the National League or any other baseball organization must deliver to the secretary of the Western League his bona fide release before participating in a championship game. When a player who hereafter is drafted or sold to a National League club, being the property of the Western League, $200 must be deposited in the treasury of the league."[69] Matt Killilea and George Van der Beck of Detroit had suggested that the money made in the draft be divided among all eight clubs. They believed a star player was a benefit to the whole league. No one else agreed. However, this modified plan would stop the transferring of players back and forth. The *Detroit Free Press* offered a handsome silver cup valued between $400 and $500 to be contested for after the season by the first- and second-place clubs. The offer was accepted.

The Milwaukee players began to arrive in town in late March and practiced indoors because of the bad weather. Manager Twitchell was against going south for training and was quoted by a *Daily News* reporter, "No good. I prefer to train right here where I am to play. Those southern trips are a mistake. The players come back into a chilly, raw spring air to open the season, and it stiffens them up so that they are no good on earth."[70] According the Brewer president Matt Killilea, Twitchell did not believe in much more than running for conditioning for his players. Killilea was quoted in the March 14, 1896, *Sporting News*:

> Manager Twitchell has recently received letters from all of the men who have been signed by the Milwaukee team for next season. As a matter of course, they all report as being in magnificent condition and ready to play the game of their lives. Many of them started in doing gymnasium work and so notified Twitchell. He notified them at once to desist and not to take any other exercise than with indoor athletic apparatus. Twitchell says from his long experience he has learned that such method of training is positively injurious to a ball player. For boxing, wrestling or building up the system, general athletic apparatus is almost indispensable, but for a base ball player it stiffens the muscles. This is just the thing that should be avoided above all things. Every muscle in the body should be soft and supple, else in throwing, or in making a sudden stop in running, a man is likely to strain, or perhaps break a tendon in one of his limbs. Running is all the exercise a ball player needs in order to get into condition and therefore Twitchell holds that a corncob in each hand is superior to all the dumb bells in the world.

Thus spring training in 1896 consisted of the pitchers running from five to 10 miles and then getting a rubdown. The other players took part in short dashes the first few days, and then began hitting and fielding. A favorite pastime for the players was bowling.

The club's first outside practice, on April 5, drew 2,000 at Milwaukee Park. One week later the Brewers played the City League All-Stars at Milwaukee Park, giving the amateurs four outs, and still won, 16 to 2. Two exhibition games were played against the all-black Page Fence Giants from Adrian, Michigan, the two teams winning one game each. The last exhibition was against the local Razalls, the Brewers winning, 12 to 3.

The Western League season was about to open, and the Brewers had made a few improvements at Milwaukee Park. A new clubhouse was to be built behind center field, as the old one was too small and had no bathrooms. Other improvements were for the fans. The club built a place under the grandstand for cyclists to park their bicycles when they attended games. Also a carriage park was built outside of center field and the wall lowered to 2½ feet so fans could witness the games from their carriages. On opening day a crowd of between 2,500 and 3,000, including league president Ban Johnson, saw Milwaukee's new Mayor Rauschenberger make an address after the usual parade to the park. The Brewers' opening day lineup for 1896 was: Nicol—cf, Weaver—lf, Hartman—3b, Twitchell—rf, Stafford—1b, Taylor—2b, Wetterer—ss, Speer—c, Baker—p. St. Paul won the April 22 contest, 6 to 5. After a rainout Rettger beat the Apostles to even the series. The Brewers then beat Minneapolis two of three to end the first home series.

The club then traveled into Minnesota, losing two of three to both the Millers and the Apostles. Returning home, the club lost two of three to Kansas City and then again lost two of three to the Blues in K.C. The Brewers were 7 and 10, and Twitchell continued with the same lineup, occasionally substituting Mrzena and Outcalt in the outfield. Baker, Rettger and Barnes were doing the pitching. The club was just not hitting, and Twitchell was not playing well at all. The *Evening Wisconsin* suggested he take himself out of the lineup. Coming back home the Brewers lost to Grand Rapids on May 11 before only 400 people. Indianapolis was next in, and the Brewers finally began to turn things around by beating the Hoosiers twice, once on a forfeit after an argument, before losing the final game. The Brewers changed their mascot from a lad named Rollo to a bulldog and went on a tear. Milwaukee won eight in a row, including three over Columbus (where they picked up the nickname "Sons of Thirst"[71]), three over Grand Rapids and two from Detroit, before losing to the Tigers, 7 to 2, behind Fred Clausen, whom the Brewers had just signed. Clausen was a local player who pitched with the Brewers briefly in 1890 and '91. Since then he had pitched in Louisville and Chicago of the National League, winning 16 and losing 22. In 1895 he had pitched in the Southern League. The Brewers originally wanted Jim Hughey but could not pry him from Pittsburgh. Also from Pittsburgh, the Brewers almost secured pitcher Johnny Foreman, but he refused to consent. Twitchell had also replaced Barnes with Nonamaker in his pitching rotation during this streak. The only trouble on the home stretch was a streetcar strike in Milwaukee, which was keeping attendance down. Things looked good for the team as it left home with a 17 and 13 record, good for third place. Before leaving, Jim Outcalt was released, Twitchell figuring Mrzena could help Speer behind the plate.

The Brewers traveled to Indianapolis, where rumor was spreading the Hoosiers might go to the National League. The word was that the league wanted to trade Cleveland for Indianapolis, as Cleveland was drawing poorly at home. Killilea said he had not heard anything but would not be surprised if Brush were trying something. Another report had Indianapolis selling out to Omaha, as the Nebraska city had Sunday ball, which Indianapolis did not. Brush would neither deny nor confirm the report. Still another story claimed Brush was to buy the Des Moines franchise of the Western Association, a club in first place in that minor league. Meanwhile, the Brewers lost three and tied one with the Hoosiers. The Brewers then finished the road trip losing two of three in Omaha, losing four of five to last-place Grand Rapids, and beating Detroit once. During this stretch Wetterer took ill and would be out for the rest of the season. Mrzena took his place. The June 5 *Milwaukee Journal* believed Mrzena had shown he was "completely lost in the position," but Twitchell defended him six days later in the same newspaper, saying Mrzena was playing shortstop "in good fashion."

The Brewers returned home June 11 and beat St. Paul three of four to go back into third place. At this point Detroit was in first place, as they had been all season, but Indianapolis was only a half-game out of first. Detroit was the only Western club to have traveled to the south in the spring, some citing this for their fast start. The Brewers were only one win behind the Tigers. Barnes was back in the pitching rotation now, and Minneapolis took three of four from the Brewers. The Brewers left town for Minnesota with a 25–25 record, then lost eight in a row to the Twin City clubs. The press was now beginning to print rumors of a shake-up in the club. During the series Twitchell used Bert Jones in relief for the first time in the season (Jones had been in Colorado and was not instructed to report until now). On June 27, 1896, the *Milwaukee Journal* blasted the club for its losing ways.

> A professional baseball team that combines reprehensible management with the poorest kind of individual and collective playing deserves no consideration at the hands of lovers of the game. Milwaukee, whose generous patronage of the sport merits a first class team, is cursed with an aggregation that is imbecilic in every way.

The *Milwaukee Daily News* of June 16 was also critical.

> The Milwaukee public is becoming decidedly disgusted with the article of baseball being put up by the Milwaukee team, and unless someone who knows what to do takes some action to make the boys play ball, the crowds which have been making the directors of the club jingle the gladsome dollar in their breeches pocket will grow small by degrees and beautifully less until a deficit will be gnawing a hole in their bank account.

The Brewers returned home June 27 and beat Kansas City behind Rettger, 17 to 14. The following day Barnes again beat the Blues. Larry Twitchell announced after the game that he was resigning as manager as soon as another man could be found. Larry said publicly that the strain of the job was too much for his health. However, a *Journal* reporter later alleged Twitchell claimed that during the club's winning streak in May he was asked by a club director "when he expected to lose." Twitchell said he always expected to win and was told, "It was not policy, from a financial point of view, to be winning invariably, that [Twitchell] should lose a game occasionally in order to keep up interest in the sport." Twitchell was upset and decided "it was best to retire."[72] Twitchell denied the story, saying, "In the first place Milwaukee never won enough games to scare the directors and in the second place the directors are not men who would do such underhand work."[73] Secretary Gross also denied the story.

Robert Glenalvin replaced Larry Twitchell as manager and had a rocky time at the helm.

The day following Twitchell's resignation, Robert J. Glenalvin was named manager of the Brewers. Glenalvin had been born Rodney Dowling in Indianapolis 28 years earlier and had limited baseball experience. In 1890 he played second base for Chicago of the National League and again showed up in Chicago in 1893 for 16 games. In 1894 Glenalvin managed and played for Detroit and became involved in a contract dispute previously mentioned with Van der Beck. He started the 1896 season managing Portland of the Pacific Coast League until that league collapsed. Glenalvin would play second base in Milwaukee and move Taylor to shortstop. Twitchell remained in right field. The *Sentinel* did not agree with Glenalvin as a manager, believing Bill Weaver or John McCloskey, released recently by Louisville would have been better. The *Minneapolis Times* was extremely unkind to Glenalvin: "Milwaukee will never play winning ball as long as Glenalvin is manager. He isn't fit to manage any ball team. He is a disorganizer, a kicker, disliked by the public and hated by the players and as a player he himself has no license to be in this league."[74] Killilea vowed he would "X-ray the baseball world"[75] to find players to fill the weak spots. Twitchell had finished with a 27 and 33 record as the 1896 manager. The local press was rather unkind to him, writing he was lax with the men and did not practice or run them enough. In short, he was "too good natured with the men."[76] The *St. Paul Dispatch* was kinder.

> The criticisms of Larry Twitchell by the Milwaukee papers are ill-timed and in some respects contemptible. Larry Twitchell put Milwaukee in the game and kept her there for a considerable length

of time. They shouldered on him the responsibilities of captain and manager and required him to play ball in addition, and it is a wonder that he was able to go through it all without physical reaction. Twitchell is an educated man and a gentleman and considered above the owners of the Milwaukee team who inspire the reporters to write those uncalled for roasts.[77]

Glenalvin pitched Jones in his first start and lost to Kansas City, 12 to 8. Baker ended the series with a 14 to 6 win. Before leaving town, the Brewers met Louisville of the National League in an exhibition game at Milwaukee Park, losing 7 to 6 before only 600 fans.

After losing three of four over the Fourth of July weekend to third-place Kansas City, the Brewers returned to Milwaukee. Last-place Columbus was in town first, and the Cream City men won three of four. Glenalvin rested Speer in the series, catching Mrzena. Fred Clausen was released. In the past month Indianapolis had caught fire and was now in first place by a good margin, with St. Paul, Kansas City and Minneapolis in a close battle for second. Detroit had dropped to fifth, Milwaukee sixth, with Grand Rapids and Columbus way down in the cellar. The Hoosiers were next into Milwaukee, splitting a four-game series. The Tigers then came in, and the Brewers won three of four from them. In an exhibition game Nonamaker lost to Washington of the National League. Back to regular Western League play, the Brewers won three of four from the Grand Rapids Gold Bugs to end the homestand. The club was now 40 and 42 overall, and 13 and 9 under Glenalvin.

The Brewers hit the road, and the winning spirit died. First the club lost two of three to seventh-place Grand Rapids. Then they lost three in Detroit, followed by three of four to the last-place Columbus Senators. The Brewers picked up a new pitcher, George Borchers, who had seen limited action in the National League for two years, the latest with Louisville. After winning two of three in Indianapolis, Glenalvin signed John White, an outfielder from Burlington of the Western Association, and put Twitchell on the bench. Back home on August 7, the Brewers lost two of three to the Millers, then won three of four from the Apostles. While St. Paul was in town, word was out that Paddy Bolan was dying of consumption in Toledo. A benefit game was to be played in Toledo for him and Milwaukee players purchased 20 tickets. In addition, a contribution box was placed in the grandstand at Milwaukee Park for those who wished to help him out.

A new shortstop had been acquired when Minneapolis was in town, as Bob McHale was obtained in a trade for Kirtley Baker with the Millers. When the St. Paul Apostles left, Larry Twitchell was released to them as their center fielder and captain. Ed Mrzena and John Nonamaker were also released. The Brewers lineup was now Nicol—cf, Weaver—lf, Hartman—3b, White—rf, Stafford—1b, Glenalvin—2b, Speer—c, McHale—ss, Taylor—substitute; Barnes, Borchers, Jones, Rettger—pitchers. Kansas City helped conclude the homestand, the Blues losing two of three.

Milwaukee traveled into Minneapolis, losing six in a row to the Apostles and Millers. Charges were freely made by the *Minneapolis Times* that Milwaukee threw the ballgames. However, the *Evening Wisconsin* said this suggestion was nonsense and probably started with the earlier *Milwaukee Journal* story on Twitchell's resignation. The *Daily News* simply wrote "BREWERS ARE ROTTEN."[78] Minneapolis now led the Western League, with Indianapolis falling to second. St. Paul and Detroit stayed very close behind. The Brewers then lost two of three in Kansas City, the last on a forfeit as Glenalvin had his team leave the field at 5:14 p.m. to catch the 6:20 train. Western rules allowed only one hour before departure to leave a game. Taylor was now at shortstop and McHale out in center field. The *Sentinel* suggested Taylor go to second, McHale to shortstop and Glenalvin to the bench, as they were better players. Glenalvin did not take this advice.

The Brewers then came home and beat Columbus three straight. Glenalvin was having more trouble with the press. The *Journal* wrote, "He not only lacks the faculty of maintaining harmony in the team, but he is not covering second base as it should be covered."[79] Then Glenalvin had problems with his players. First it was George Borchers. Glenalvin released him, and Borchers claimed Glenalvin owed him money from when he pitched on Glenalvin's Portland team. Glenalvin claimed he owed Borchers nothing. "Finally Borchers took it out of the hide of the Brewers captain in the most approved style a la Marquis of Queensbury."[80] Then Nicol was fined $25 for intentionally striking out. Nicol said he did not, and became unhappy. He claimed Glenalvin was berating him while he was batting, saying he could not play ball and should be on some state semi-professional club. Nicol told the manager it was not the time nor place for that, and Glenalvin repeated it. Nicol was only playing because McHale was hurt. Meanwhile, the club lost two of three to Indianapolis. On September 3, Grand Rapids failed to appear in Milwaukee. The next day the scheduled game was not played, the Brewers instead playing in Sheboygan. Needless to say, the fans that showed up at Milwaukee Park were unhappy. After a rainout, the Brewers finally played Grand Rapids, winning a doubleheader. President Killilea could not be blamed for the shabby show, as he had departed for Europe and left secretary Fred Gross in charge of the club. The home schedule for the Brewers ended with Detroit splitting a Labor Day doubleheader before 3,500, and then beating Barnes, 9–6.

Milwaukee hit the road and lost the first seven games in Detroit and Indianapolis. Glenalvin finally benched himself, following the *Sentinel*'s idea, as McHale was fit to play again. As the club continued to lose, he went back into the lineup, putting McHale behind the plate. The Brewers finished out the season losing two of three in Columbus, winning two of three in Detroit, and winning the final two games in Grand Rapids. This last game had only 48 people in attendance. The final 1896 Western League standings were:

Minneapolis	89	47	.654	Kansas City	69	67	.507
Indianapolis	78	54	.591	Milwaukee	62	78	.443
Detroit	80	58	.580	Columbus	52	88	.371
St. Paul	73	63	.537	Grand Rapids	46	94	.329

After the season Minneapolis played Indianapolis for the Free Press Cup, the Millers winning three of five to take the cup. However, it was said the players violated the terms of the contest by dividing the receipts equally instead of the stipulated 60–40 percent division.

The Brewers had played terribly. They could only manage season series victories over Columbus (13–7) and Grand Rapids (12–8). The other clubs walked all over the Brewers: Detroit (9–11), Indianapolis (6–14), Kansas City (9–11), Minneapolis (5–15), St. Paul (8–12). The Brewers again hit well, batting .298, led by Weaver (.357), Nicol (.340), Stafford (.324), Glenalvin (.308), Hartman (.307) and McHale (.307). Fielding and pitching hurt the team. The fielding average of .928 ranked fifth in the Western, Taylor averaging .904 at short and Hartman .904 at third. Glenalvin only averaged .914 at second. In the pitching department, only Nonamaker was over .500 (3–1). Rettger was 22 and 23, Barnes 16 and 17, Jones 8 and 13, Baker 12 and 13, Clausen 1 and 6, Borchers 0 and 4, and Twitchell 0 and 1.

Western League president Ban Johnson told the *Sporting News* that every club in the league except Grand Rapids made money. He said Detroit made 35 percent more than it had two years previous. It was reported Minneapolis made $6,000 on the season. The *St. Paul Dispatch* claimed Detroit, Minneapolis, Indianapolis and Kansas City were the only clubs to draw well at home. The others made their money by going to these cities. One must wonder how the Brewers did financially. Although officials claimed after the season they broke even and would have made $20,000 if it were not for the streetcar strike, this is doubtful. Ten days before the season had ended it was rumored the club was for sale. Directors denied the statement, at that time stating the club would lose about $2,500. It was said Van der Beck had offered $8,500 for the club and Fred Gross offered to buy it for $8,000. It was further claimed a third offer of $9,000 from an unknown party — speculated to be "Deacon" Ellis from Grand Rapids — was made. All offers were refused. Even the *Sentinel* reported it would buy the club for $9,000. There were also rumors that ball players were interested in putting money into the club. Those rumored to be interested were Roger Connor of the St. Louis club, ex-Brewer Larry Twitchell and Connie Mack of Pittsburgh. The baseball club was apparently not worth as much as it had been earlier. In January of 1896, Killilea had stated that "one of the best known businessmen in Milwaukee"[81] offered him $12,000 for the club. Killilea replied the club was not for sale at any price. After three losing season in the Western League, the club had apparently depreciated in value. The *Daily News* on September 11, 1896, gave opinions on the past practices and future of the club.

> Milwaukee is one of the best towns in the whole country, and gives better support to the game than half of the big league places, and that, too, despite treatment which would have killed the game in many places. It is well known that the Milwaukee team has been a profitable piece of property. If it is to continue so, it is time to adopt a more liberal policy on the part of the stockholders of the team. They must become metropolitan in their views, and cease to be a Schwartzburg gang, and not try to run a professional team on a Pigville basis, or think to buy good players for a bag of peanuts.
>
> The continuance of the policy of the past means disaster to the club, and a long setback to the national game in the Cream City. The baseball enthusiasm of Wisconsin's metropolis has been bounced to the limit, and unless some disposition is shown to give something in return for the money, baseball in Milwaukee will next year fall as flat as a stiff hat that has been sat down upon by Chief Cole of the Kirby.... The warning has been given. The local press, unanimous in this direction, but faithfully reflects the public feeling among the patrons of the game, and next season Milwaukee will either have a ball game equal to its deserts or the game will be let severely alone.

13

The Mack Years (1897–1900)

After the Brewers' disappointing sixth-place finish in 1896, everyone agreed the club needed a new manager. Charles Cushman was the favorite of the local press. Others mentioned were Roger Connor (playing manager of the St. Louis Browns), Arthur Irwin (manager of the New York Giants) and David Foutz (manger of the Brooklyn Trolley Dodgers). Brewer president Matthew Killilea went to New York in August to negotiate with Foutz, offering him the manager's job on a percentage basis, but no deal was made. In September secretary Fred Gross was told by a third party (perhaps Ban Johnson) that Connie Mack was available. Born Cornelius Alexander McGillicuddy on February 22, 1862, he broke into the National League with Washington in 1886. Mack remained there as a catcher until 1890, when he caught for Buffalo of the Players' League. After the Brotherhood war, Mack played in Pittsburgh through the 1896 season, also managing the club from late in the 1894 season through 1896. In his eleven big league years Connie hit only .247, but was one of the finest defensive catchers of the era. As a manager his Pittsburgh clubs had recorded 149 wins and 134 losses. On September 21, 1896, Connie Mack was hired as the Brewer manager, signing a $3,000 contract — the highest ever given to a manager in Milwaukee.[1] The *Sporting Life* wrote of Mack's salary, "That is a pretty steep salary for even so strong a minor league and it is safe to assert that no other manager in the circuit will receive so much salary."[2]

Mack was given free rein of the team and began to build a club he believed would be a winner. He had twelve players reserved from the 1896 team: Stafford, White, Speer, Taylor, McHale, Barnes, Wetterer, Weaver, Rettger, Nicol, Hartman and Jones. His first loss was George Nicol, drafted by Philadelphia after the season. Mack quickly claimed Brownie Foreman, released by Pittsburgh; Snyder, an infielder from the Eastern League; Shaw, a pitcher from the New England League; James Bannon, released by Boston; and Bill Gallagher, released by Philadelphia. However, Mack could not sign any of these players. His first signing was John Taylor, who had pitched for Cambridge of the Virginia League. Taylor was reported to have "a very speedy delivery, good control of the ball and an abundance of stamina."[3] He was known as "Old Reliable" in the Virginia League. Milwaukee then lost Fred Hartman in the draft to St. Louis. At the Western League meeting in November, Connie Mack was busy. First James Hannivan, a shortstop, and Erving Waldron, an outfielder, were purchased from Pawtucket of the New England League for $700. The Brewer manager then purchased the contract of J.E. Johnstone from St. Paul for $250, but Johnstone was shortly released, have been called "a breeder of discord."[4] Also purchased was Arthur Clarkson, brother of Hall of Famer John Clarkson, from Baltimore for the same price. Then Tom Delahanty and Tom O'Brien were purchased from the Pittsburgh farm club in Toronto for $500 each. Bert Meyers, a third baseman, was bought from St. Louis in lieu of the draft money for Hartman. L.W. Lippert, an outfielder from Fall River of the New England League, was purchased for $300. O'Brien was soon lost to Baltimore, however, as he had not been waived. Before the year ended, John Newkirk, a pitcher from the Oil City (Pennsylvania) club, was signed. Mack now had the contracts of 18 players and claimed the rights to a few more.

The Western League had had an exciting fall and early winter. Immediately after the 1896 season closed, Indianapolis and Minneapolis petitioned the National Board of Arbitration to withdraw from the Western League. The problem went back to the admission of Grand Rapids, which the two clubs protested at the time. Of course, John T. Brush had a plan. He wanted the players of Milwaukee, Detroit, St. Paul, Kansas City, Grand Rapids and Columbus transferred to the National League and then returned to these cities, but the franchises given new owners. Brush pegged Harry D. Quin as the Milwaukee magnate. Western League owners were apprehensive as Brush, along with National League president Nick Young, Brooklyn owner Charles Byrne, and Boston owner Arthur Soden, sat on the Board of Arbitration. The day after the petition was filed, Ban Johnson and George Van der Beck came to Milwaukee, registered at the Republican House under assumed names, and talked over the situation. From there Matthew Killilea and Johnson appear to have gone to Chicago to talk with Jim Hart about the petition. On October 6 the Indianapolis-Minneapolis petition was turned down by the Board of Arbitration, as that body had no jurisdiction. Brush again failed to get the upper hand in the Western League. Matt Killilea was becoming more respected in baseball circles, and in its February 27, 1897, issue the *Sporting News* commented he "is now looked up to as the legal advisor of the Western League magnates."

With this victory some advocated kicking Indianapolis and Minneapolis out of the Western League and replacing them with Toledo and Des Moines, Sioux City or Omaha. If the Western lost National Agreement protection, these advocates were sure most players would stay in the minor league. Van der Beck was at the head of this group. Of course, with John Brush on the National Board of Arbitration, he would know in advance what the National League would do with Western League protection. It was reported the Western would use the $15,000-plus in its treasury to fight the case in court if they lost their protection. It was pointed out the Western League could not kick the two clubs out because of the five-year clause in the constitution. The six other Western club owners held a secret meeting in Chicago on October 19 with Ban Johnson present. Although they would not discuss with the press what transpired, it was believed the owners talked of putting a franchise in Chicago.

With the Western League's annual meeting approaching, transferring of clubs was again discussed. Chicago appeared not to be acceptable. Grand Rapids was given little chance of staying, and Toledo was the first to negotiate for a franchise. Some thought Brush wanted to buy the Cleveland franchise and transfer Indianapolis into the National League, but no serious moves took place in that direction. In addition to Toledo, Omaha and Des Moines expressed interest in joining the Western. Some Western owners, including Matthew Killilea, favored Omaha as it would break up the long trip to Kansas City. Brush was in favor of transferring Grand Rapids to Toledo, but George Ellis said he would rather stay in Grand Rapids than transfer to that city. The Western meeting was to be held November 12 in Chicago, and Minneapolis was making waves. First, Marcus P. Haynes, one of the other three Minneapolis directors, said he would attend the Western meeting instead of Goodnow with the proxies of his fellow directors. Goodnow had claimed he would fight the 10 percent fund, saying Indianapolis, for example, had paid about $1,800 and Grand Rapids only $22. After the season any surplus was divided equally among the clubs. Goodnow countered Haynes by buying H.P. Watson's quarter share and owning half the club. Haynes publicly said he foresaw no problems with Goodnow at the upcoming meeting.

A young Connie Mack, as he was pictured in the *Milwaukee Sentinel* prior to opening day 1897.

Goodnow attended the Chicago meeting and immediately teamed with Brush in wanting Omaha to replace Columbus, but Omaha made no application. Toledo and Des Moines, however, did. The Western League decided to make no changes, with Grand Rapids and Columbus given four-year franchises to match the rest of the Western. Johnson was re-elected president for four years and the 10 percent fund remained, although changed so that at the end of the season each club would be charged for one-eighth of the expenses and the balance would revert to the clubs as they contributed, no longer in equal shares. Remarkably, Goodnow deserted Brush and voted with the majority at the meeting. The only major rule of the meeting passed was in regard to the salary limit. According to statistics, Milwaukee and Columbus had paid the highest salaries in the Western, and a limit of $2,200 was recommended. All clubs except Kansas City and Minneapolis favored this. Finally a salary limit of $2,400 a month was passed, with a penalty of $500 to be assessed to clubs that exceeded it. The *Detroit News*, however, thought this only a bluff and said no one really expected to live up to the limit. Later a report came out of Indianapolis saying the Hoosiers were probably the only club in the league keeping to the limit. "A look at the payroll of the Milwaukee club would be interesting, and President Killilea, who was a strong advocate of the policy, would probably have a hard time to explain the figures. Men like Esper [who would be lost by the Brewers], Clarkson, Weaver and Meyers are not in the game for their health."[5] The Western League meeting closed with each club receiving $2,000 from the treasury surplus.

While the Western meeting was in progress, the National League passed a resolution that stated no member of the National League could be eligible to membership on the National Board of Arbitration if he had interests in any minor league club. This, of course, was aimed at John T. Brush. However, Brush claimed to have no financial interest in Indianapolis, saying he originally had $1,000 worth of stock in the club but had quickly lost it, and on the reorganization, $500 worth of stock had been allotted to him but he never received it. According to Brush this was the extent of his dealings with the club. Ban Johnson claimed to have a document signed by Brush to receive Indianapolis' money from the 10 percent fund, with Brush listed as president of the club. The National League pretended to believe Brush and re-elected him to the Board. The *Daily News* gave this opinion on the situation:

> This means that John T. Brush again holds his power in the National League. Still worse, it means that his sly scheme to give the board of arbitration almost unlimited power has carried. It means that the minor leagues are practically at the mercy of the board of arbitration, which is under the control of Brush. It was the most signal victory yet won by the Cincinnati baseball boss and

is a tremendous step upward in his march to autocratic power at the head of the baseball world.[6]

Within days after the Western meeting George Ellis stunned the baseball world by selling his Grand Rapids club to Robert Leadley and Robert Glenalvin. The *Grand Rapids Democrat* reported the club sold for $4,000 in cash and included players, park and franchise — for a $2,000 profit. Glenalvin would manage the club. It was believed, however, that Ellis only sold an interest to the two so they could assume the active management of Grand Rapids and give him an opportunity to devote his time to the Newark club, which had been very profitable the previous season. Rumors were also about that Brush was behind the sale to again try to control the Western League.

The Milwaukee management made no such big changes. Matthew Killilea announced after the 1896 season he would not accept the club presidency again, but he reconsidered, and at the November 30 meeting he and Fred Gross were re-elected. Charles Polacheck and Charles Hellberg were also appointed directors. Rudolph Giljohan, Theodore Engel and James Murphy sold their stock to the first-mentioned four and dropped from the club. The scorecard privilege, always given to local people in the past, was given to Harry Stevens of New York for $2,000. Stevens' scorecard was 36 pages, containing half-tones of the players in addition to "interesting gossip."[7] In June Stevens began printing some scorecards in German, and "this unique departure made a hit with the spectators."[8] Twenty-five cents would still get one into the ballpark, but grandstand seats were 50 cents. A book of 50 season tickets could be bought for $20, or 70 for $26.25.

After New Year's Day 1897, Connie Mack continued his search for players. First he claimed Charles Reilly, a veteran third baseman recently secured by Washington of the National League and assigned to the Brewers by Manager Schmelz. Claim to Reilly was relinquished when Washington found they needed him. In February Wally Taylor ended his three-year association with the Brewers when he along with John White was sold to Toronto of the Eastern League. On February 8 Mack reported he had Delahanty, Clarkson, Hannivan, Newkirk, John Taylor and Lippert signed. He sent contracts out to Jones, Barnes, Weaver, McHale, Stafford, Speer and Waldron. Rettger and Meyers had their contracts. Wetterer wrote Mack saying he would not be able to play before June 1 because of "a lucrative business that will occupy his entire attention until that date."[9] Mack said if Wetterer wanted to play he had better be ready by April.

Later in February Mack purchased Charles Esper, a pitcher from Baltimore, for $1,000. Esper had pitched in the major leagues since 1890, winning 97 and losing 89. A Pittsburgh paper wrote, "The opinion among the local fans over the purchase of Esper's release by Milwaukee is that Connie Mack not only strengthened his own team, but did an act of kindness to Pittsburgh, a club he still holds in high regard."[10] Esper had always been a stumbling block to the Pittsburgh team. In March Chris Van der Ahe of St. Louis asserted Esper was his, as he had claimed him. National League president Nick Young said all clubs waived Esper as of February 16, and put him on his formal list. Indeed, when Baltimore received the Brewers' money for the pitcher, that club said he had cleared waivers. On March 12 Esper signed with St. Louis. It turned out Esper had gone to Baltimore to object to his being transferred to a minor league and Manager Hanlon told him he could "make it all right"[11] with the Brewers. The *Pittsburgh News* related that the National League met earlier and it was decided to help Van der Ahe's club out. The signing of Esper (and Minneapolis' loss of pitcher Bill Hutchinson to the Browns) showed the National League was helping. Milwaukee management was outraged, but Killilea thought it would be useless to go to the

National Board of Arbitration, as now Young said the Browns had not waived him. Milwaukee, of course, got its money back.

This was not Milwaukee's first problem with waivers and drafting. As a matter of fact the entire Western League was having trouble in this area. The *Indianapolis News* noticed a change in the attitude toward farming. In 1896 only Minneapolis and Indianapolis were for it. This year the paper claimed Detroit was looking toward Philadelphia for young players. Milwaukee was taking Pittsburgh's, and Kansas City drew on both Boston and New York. St. Paul had a lease on Chicago talent. Columbus expected to get some Cleveland players. Grand Rapids had several Louisville players. Of course, Indianapolis drew from Cincinnati. The Milwaukee press and Mack denied this story, saying the Indianapolis paper was just defending Watkins, but one could see the trend. Furthermore, the Western was drafting very frequently from the lower classes; more than any other league, and Detroit more than any other club. John T. Brush gave an insight into drafting when he stated, "It costs too much to buy stars, and the majority of clubs won't sell theirs. The cheapest and best way to secure stars is to develop them yourself. A team can afford to nurse a promising player for two or three years in order to develop him into a star."[12] When Philadelphia drafted George Nicol, the club promised to return him to Milwaukee if he was not needed, but he was released to Detroit. Philadelphia had in fact drafted seven of the fifteen minor league players, presumably mostly for the Tigers. The *Philadelphia Press* wrote that Van der Beck's having Philadelphia draft for him could backfire as "some of the Western League clubs may have friends in the big leagues who can enforce it [the waiver rule] this time."[13] Milwaukee said it would prefer charges against Van der Beck unless Nicol was returned to them. In February the National Board of Arbitration awarded Nicol to Milwaukee after Reach of Philadelphia testified he drafted Nicol for Detroit at the request of Van der Beck. At the Western League meeting in March, Killilea preferred charges against Van der Beck for his complicity in the Nicol deal. It came out that Van der Beck advanced Nicol $100 even before he was drafted. The Detroit owner was fined $100 in the case. The *Daily News* foresaw the death of independent minor league clubs some 50 years before it happened.

> Unless something is done to check the abuse of the drafting system, the Western League will find itself in a state of hopeless anarchy at the end of another season.... Carried to its logical result, it will compel every minor league club to have an alliance with a big league organization, which will obligingly draft all its valuable players at the end of each season, and return them when the danger of being robbed is past.[14]

This was not the only irregularity the Detroit owner was involved in. Van der Beck had been signing players from other minor leagues without properly drafting them. In December he signed Harry Steinfeldt from Galveston because his name was spelled wrong on the reserve list. In January Ban Johnson awarded Frank Hahn to St. Paul from Detroit because of irregularities, although the National Board of Arbitration would award him back to Detroit in April. The Detroit owner then signed a Mobile player without the consent of management, and the board awarded the player back to Mobile, which sold him to Columbus.

Mack, who had purchased stock and owned one-fifth of the Brewers, began to sign more players. Waldron and Jones signed in February. In March Barnes, Weaver, Speer, Rettger and Nicol signed. Also in March Mack signed Eddie Lewee, an infielder from the Buffalo club. On March 16 Hannivan was traded to Brooklyn for Tom Daly, a second baseman. Daly had been in the National League since 1887, first as a catcher and then shifting to second base, and had just come off a .281 season. He soon cleared waivers and signed April 1. On April 3 Bob McHale was traded to Pittsburgh for outfielder Joe Wright. Wright had played most of 1896 in Memphis, appearing in 15 games with the Pirates. McHale was unsigned and had said he might stay in California to play in a new league.

Going into spring training the Brewers had only three unsigned players. First baseman Stafford had written to the club announcing he was retiring to run his store in North Carolina. Wetterer still had not been heard from since his last statement. Bert Meyers was a different story. Immediately after his purchase, he said he was unhappy, as he had been promised he would stay in St. Louis, where he made a reported $1,500. The *Sporting Life* predicted in February that he would not sign with the Brewers and Hartman would be returned. Mack said he doubted this, but Meyers returned his contract in March unsigned. Meyers said he wanted the same money he made in St. Louis and would not even accept any advance money, as that would be like signing. Mack believed the Washington club was attempting to influence Meyers not to sign in Milwaukee. Reportedly, Milwaukee offered Meyers $1,250, but he insisted on $1,500. As spring training approached, Meyers remained unsigned and the *Washington Post* claimed he would play with the Senators. When spring training opened, Meyers was working out with Washington.

The Western League met in Detroit in March and held its spring meeting. The most important issue was the Van der Beck cases with drafting of players. Word also came out that the Eastern and Western leagues were thinking of combining forces. The *Daily News* of March 15, 1897, editorialized what it thought the minors should do.

> It is time that the proposed combination of the leading minor leagues for protection against the big league be taken up and pushed. It should receive the cordial support of all the sporting writers, and the projection kept before the sporting public until something is accomplished. One of the principal reforms which would come about would be the doing away with the drafting of players by major league clubs for the purpose of selling them back at a higher price. This would be accomplished by an agreement on the part of the minor leagues not to buy back drafted players at more than the drafted price. Then there are numerous petty impositions practiced by the big league magnates on the smaller leagues which could be greatly curtailed by the minor leagues standing together and resisting all aggressions.

The Western also was pushing to be represented on the National Board of Arbitration. The schedule was drawn up, starting April 22. The Brewers received two holiday home games: Memorial Day and July 4. In the 1897 schedule Detroit would travel the most— 10,512 miles—followed by Milwaukee with 9,813. The other teams were scheduled to travel as follows: Kansas City, 9,316 miles; Indianapolis, 9,191; Columbus, 9,062; Minneapolis, 8,534; St. Paul, 8,377; and Grand Rapids, 7,906. Detroit, St. Paul, Indianapolis and Grand Rapids had no Sunday ball. The *Detroit Free Press* felt the schedule dates were intentionally unfair to Van der Beck and his Detroit team. "Detroit was generously given all the Mondays possible and has the privilege of playing on Thanksgiving Day, Christmas and News Year's at home. It is also given dates which are semi-holidays in other states where the birthdays of famous men are celebrated. Georgia's, Oklahoma's, North Dakota's and Key West's fete days are remembered by giving Detroit home games. The celebration of the ascension of the Shah of Persia was overlooked in some unmistakable way."[15] It was felt this unfair treatment was because of Van der Beck's player dealings mentioned above. The *Sporting News* in its March 20, 1897, edition, editorialized, "The fundamental principle of a base ball league is that the interests of the parties to it are mutual. It is a partnership dependent for its permanency upon the prosperity of all its club members…. In revenging themselves upon President Van Derbeck, the dominant faction hurt their own pockets. It was a pretty price to pay for a petty proceeding."

A new Western League policy required the players to purchase their own uniforms.

The Brewers' home uniforms were white trimmed with light blue, with caps and stockings of the same color. The traveling uniforms were gray with light blue trim.

As spring approached, the annual predictions were made. Connie Mack thought Indianapolis and St. Paul had two of the stronger teams in the Western League, Kansas City was a fast team, and Grand Rapids and Columbus had improved teams. Mack doubted if Minneapolis would be strong and said Detroit was weaker than it had been in '96. Mack figured the Brewers would be up in the standings. He said his club was fast, with some heavy hitting, and had the best pitching in the Western. The *Sentinel* picked Indianapolis for the pennant with St. Paul, Kansas City and Milwaukee to fight for second. Most of the papers representing Western League cities agreed. The *Journal* wrote an article on spring baseball reporting.

> Do not place too much confidence in the published accounts of the training trips of the different teams now in the south and you will not be astonished at their playing when the season opens. A majority of the correspondents who accompany their respective teams on these spring tours regard a "jolly" as the proper thing and discover championship timber in players who are discarded as worthless when the real campaign begins. Glowing reports will now be coming in daily from the south, but they should be taken with a few grains of salt.[16]

Tom Daly played two seasons in Milwaukee and would captain the 1898 team.

The exhibition season started in St. Louis, with the players reporting April 1. On Sunday, April 4, the first game was played, with the Brewers losing to the St. Louis Browns 12 to 1. Not all Mack's players had reported yet, including the entire first-team infield, and Connie had to make do with what he had. The next day "an uninteresting audience of vacant seats and the empty condition of the cash box where gate receipts are taken in"[17] caused cancellation of the game. To shore up his infield Mack signed Frank Houseman, who had played in New Orleans the previous year, hitting .302, to take third until Meyers reported. In Louisville the Brewers lost two games. Finally on April 8 Meyers accepted Milwaukee's terms, reportedly $350 a month, and was on his way to meet the club. The Brewers then played in Dayton, winning 5 to 3, and returned to Milwaukee. Back in the Beer City the Brewers beat the Racines, the Otto Brothers of the City League, University of Wisconsin nine, Jackson club of the Michigan League and the Page Fence Giants. Six other exhibitions were rained or snowed out. Nothing had been heard from Robert Stafford as of yet, and Bill Wetterer had indeed retired from professional ball, playing with an amateur team in Cincinnati instead while making barrels for his father, who was a cooper. On the day before the season started, Stafford finally signed with Milwaukee.

The 1897 Western League season opened on April 22 with the Brewers at home against the Minneapolis Millers. After the usual parade and festivities, 3,163 attended Milwaukee Park at 16th and Lloyd and saw Barnes lose to the Millers, 8 to 6.

		Kansas City						Milwaukee				
		R	H	PO	A	E			R	H	PO	A	E
Ulrick	2b	3	2	2	2	1	Shields	2b	1	0	3	3	0
Daniels	rf	3	1	3	0	0	Clingman	3b	1	1	1	1	0
Hernon	lf	1	2	6	1	0	Newman	lf	1	1	2	0	0
Klusman	1b	1	3	7	0	0	Langsford	ss	0	1	1	5	0
Nicholi	cf	1	1	3	1	0	Luby	rf	0	0	1	0	0
Niles	3b	1	3	1	1	0	Carey	1b	0	1	13	2	1
Sharpe	ss	1	1	3	1	0	McVey	cf	0	0	2	0	1
Donahue	c	1	1	1	1	0	Lohman	c	0	1	3	3	0
Darby	p	0	1	1	3	0	Hastings	p	0	0	0	3	1
Figgemeier	p	0	0	1	3	0							
		12	15	27	10	1			3	5	27	20	3

```
                    1 2 3 4 5 6 7 8 9
        Kansas City 1 0 5 0 0 4 0 2 0 — 12
        Milwaukee   0 0 0 0 0 0 0 3 0 — 3
```

Milwaukee bounced back in the second game, winning 15 to 3, with Weaver — whom Mack had just named captain — collecting four hits and scoring four runs. Rettger dropped the final game before 9,600; the game was protested by Mack on an improper ruling by the umpire, when a thrown ball hit the umpire on a steal of second, which in those days required the runners to return to their bases. St. Paul then came to town and won two of three, even though Mack had his infield intact now, with Stafford at first, Daly second, Delahanty short and Meyers third. L.W. Lippert was released, having played three games and committing five errors with seven chances. Wright went to right field and Weaver to left. John Newkirk was also released, Mack figuring he needed a little more experience.

The Brewers traveled into Minnesota, losing three of four in St. Paul (one on a forfeit when Meyers refused to leave a game when ejected by the umpire) and then splitting four in Minneapolis. The Brewers returned home with a lowly 5 and 9 record (Jones having four of those wins), but money in the pocket. Crowds were good so far; opening day in St. Paul drew 4,753, or $590 to Brewer management. Clarkson was recuperating from a severe cold and had been out of the lineup. Eddie Lewee took over as the regular shortstop and would soon become a local favorite. "Hardly a day passes that he don't make some seemingly miraculous play. The crowds go wild over him and women smother him with flowers."[18] Tom Delahanty was released, going to Kansas City. Erving Waldron was also loaned to St. Joseph of the Western Association. More than 6,000 passed through the Milwaukee Park turnstiles on Sunday, May 9, and saw Barnes beat Kansas City 6 to 4. Rettger, Jones and Taylor then completed the sweep over the Blues, to climb the Brewers back to .500. Before hitting the road again, Mack purchased William "Adonis" Terry from Chicago, the estimated price tag being from $600 to $1,000. The 32-year-old Terry had been in the big leagues since 1884, winning 197 and losing 196, including two no-hit games. It was reported he picked up his nickname "principally because he is far above the average player in the matter of handsome appearance."[19]

Milwaukee then traveled to Kansas City, winning three of four, with Mack catching in one of his infrequent appearances (called "McGillicuddy" in the box scores of the *Milwaukee Sentinel*). The Brewers were credited also with one less loss, as Ban Johnson awarded the earlier protest to them. Coming back home the club continued its winning ways, beating the Tigers two of three, Columbus two, Indianapolis Hoosiers three of four, and Grand Rapids Bobolinks four straight. Clarkson was back with the club, and Terry and Jones were pitching great, with 5 and 0, and 9 and 1 records, respectively. At the gate the club was breaking all previous attendance records and it was said the Brewers had taken in enough already to meet expenses for the year. The directors were even thinking of enlarging the seating capacity, as at the last Sunday game one thousand people were turned away, with more than 10,000 in the park. The *Journal* asked for at least one special streetcar to run to the park from Wisconsin Avenue to help fans get to the park easier and quicker.

The Brewers traveled into fourth-place Columbus and dropped four straight to the Senators. The team dropped to fourth with a Sunday loss to Detroit in Milwaukee. George Rettger, who had been with Milwaukee since July of 1894, was released on loan to Columbus. He had an even 2 and 2 record for the Brewers in '97. On to Indianapolis, Barnes broke the five-game losing streak with a 7 to 6 win, but Clarkson and Terry lost the next two games. The Brewers then traveled into Michigan splitting a four-game series in Grand Rapids and losing three of four in Detroit. The Brewers' record now was 27 and 23, having lost 12 of their last 16 games. Mack's pitching staff was in rough shape. Barnes (5 and 6 record) had a split finger on his pitching hand, Clarkson (2 and 5) had been hit in the ankle with a line drive. Terry (5 and 3) had a cold. Taylor was only 1 and 3. Only Jones was pitching well, boasting an 11 and 4 record. Speer's catching was also off because of bruised fingers. In a distant fourth place, with the fifth-place Tigers closing in, Mack made some changes. To shore up his pitching he signed Bill Reidy, released by Grand Rapids the previous week, and released Arthur Clarkson. Wright was not playing up to par in the outfield so Harry Blake, a four-year National League veteran, was secured from Cleveland on loan. It was reported Milwaukee would give Cleveland the first claim to Bert Jones for the deal, but Mack immediately denied this. It later came out that Jones was indeed the property of Cleveland, and they even suspended him in October when it was found he was playing unauthorized ball in New Mexico. The *Milwaukee Journal* reported the Brewers were to get the use of Blake, and then get Lou Criger, the Cleveland catcher, in 1898 and $2,000. Jones was a hot item. Before the season even started Mack was offered $1,000 for the pitcher from a National League club. Then in late May Brooklyn offered cash and George Shoch for him. Mack said he would only trade Rettger for Shoch, and nothing happened. Another player in demand was George Nicol, whom Pittsburgh wanted and had offered $1,000 and another player for. Mack was hoping to turn things around with the new players he had acquired.

The Brewers returned home June 19 and Reidy won his first start, against St. Paul, 4 to 1. St. Paul won the next two before Reidy won again. The Cream City men finished the homestand by winning nine in a row over Minneapolis and Kansas City. The Brewers won these ten straight behind Taylor, Terry and Reidy. Mack had rested Jones, who was injured, and only used Barnes in the final game.

During this 1897 season an interesting duel between management and a local entrepreneur took place. Charles Prochazka (listed in the 1897 city directory as a shoemaker, residence of 762 Eighteenth Street, later renumbered 2154 North Eighteenth Street) erected a 37-foot-high grandstand outside the left field wall, seating 100 people. "The management did not seem to have a just appreciation of the desire of the boys to see the game without squandering a quarter each time."[20] Prochazka let them see the game for 10 cents. The building inspector condemned the structure as not being strong enough. But Prochazka continued. The Brewers then put up some tall poles and had canvas put up. Prochazka decided to put his stand on wheels. The club then erected a fence of slats to shut off the view of the "Butcher's"[21] stand. Prochazka then moved his stand 30 yards down the line to frustrate management. The papers never reported the final outcome of this battle.

But thrifty Milwaukeeans had other ways to see a game free. The *Journal* wrote, "The freckle faced, tow-haired youngsters ... with short trousers jauntily supported by the relics of suspenders (would have) their eyes firmly glued to kindly crevices and peepholes and spasmodic moans attested to sundry base hits or glaring errors." The scene around Milwaukee Park must have been almost comic on occasion as the *Journal* continued: "Step ladders, painter's ladders, ladders whose construction from nondescript pieces of lumber had taxed to the utmost the constructive genius of their makers, and ladders that had seen property were thrown at all possible angles."[22] Of course, others just clung to the top of the fence.

The Brewers then hit the road, winning three and tying one in Kansas City. The 13-game win streak was broken in St. Paul, with Reidy losing his first game, after five wins. Terry and Barnes won the remaining two games. The trip ended with a two-game split in Minneapolis. After winning 16 of their last 18 games, the Brewers were still in fourth place, with a 44 and 27 record, but only a half-game behind Columbus and 3 games behind first-place St. Paul. Indianapolis occupied second place.

William "Adonis" Terry was a handsome player, who would have an unusual "home only" clause in his contract for 1898 (Transcendental Graphics).

The Brewers again opened a home series on July 13, winning two of three from sixth-place Grand Rapids, and one from the seventh-place Millers. Indianapolis then won two of three. The Sunday game was a 15-inning 4 to 3 Brewer victory—the longest game in the Western League that year and the longest in Milwaukee since 1887, witnessed by 6,000. Mack's pitching staff again took a hit. His ace, Bert Jones, had not pitched since June 16—more than a month—and now Terry had to leave for Brooklyn to see his very ill 8-year-old son. Mack's other pitchers kept going strong, however, as the team beat Detroit four straight to take third place. Second-place Columbus then came into Milwaukee and shut out the Brewers 4 to 0, Taylor losing. Taylor was also lost to Mack in the game, as he suffered a severe shoulder injury and was forced to return home. The Brewers won the remaining three games.

Mack's men had a record of 55 and 31, but he felt he needed to strengthen the team. Pete Dowling, a lefty pitcher, was secured on loan from Louisville. He had started the season in Paducah, Kentucky, and was then 1 and 2 in the National League. Joe Wright was released, his .267 average considered too weak. The Brewers ended July in third place and ready to move up. Stafford was leading the club in hitting with a .382 average, and Weaver was at .350, Lewee .315, Daly .303, Meyers .291, Speer .284, Blake .274 and Nicol .255. Bert

Jones, still out, led the pitching staff with his 11 and 4 record. Terry was 11 and 5, Barnes 11 and 7, Reidy 9 and 3, and Taylor 8 and 5.

After beating Minneapolis in a single home game, the Brewers split four with Detroit and won two of three in Grand Rapids. With a shot at first place, Milwaukee traveled into Indianapolis but dropped all three games. Then the Brewers dropped further out of contention, losing three straight to second-place Columbus, extending their losing streak to seven games and dropping into fourth place. On August 11 Mack's men returned home to face Kansas City. Meyers had an injured finger and Mack tried out John Imig, a local boy who had played in the Michigan League until it folded, at third base. Imig played well for a few games, but did not wish to play professional ball. Milwaukee beat K.C. in their one game and then swept three from Grand Rapids. Interest in the Brewers was very high, "not only among the few rabid base ball cranks, but in all parts of the city, among all classes of people. And this interest is not altogether confined to the city, for a large number of country towns in the state, some many miles from Milwaukee, contain cranks none the less enthusiastic than those of the city itself, even if they have never seen a professional game."[23] Mack took advantage of this interest with a short barnstorming trip, playing exhibitions in Hartford, Fond du Lac and Waupon (all in Wisconsin). During this time Mack secured Elmer Smith from Bay City of the Michigan League to play third base. The Brewers the split four games with the Columbus Senators, the last two a Sunday doubleheader at Milwaukee Park drawing a record 12,000.[24] Indianapolis finished the homestand winning all three from the local club. The Brewers had lost 12 of their last 18, partly because injuries had plagued the team. Of course, Meyers was out. Jones and Taylor had been lost for the season. Then Smith was hurt, forcing Stafford to third and Mack to first. When Nicol became ill, Smith went back to third and Stafford to right.

On the road again the Brewers won two of three in Columbus with Smith, Nicol and Stafford back at their regular positions. A loss and a tie in Indianapolis followed. Back home against Grand Rapids, Stafford was forced to go to second base when Daly became ill, but the Brewers won all three games. With Meyers back at third base, the Brewers split four with Detroit. Then came another single win over Kansas City. With Meyers back, Elmer Smith was released, even though he was hitting .356 and fielding better than Meyers. John Pappalau, a pitcher released by Grand Rapids to cut expenses, was signed. Pappalau was owed $70 from the Furniture City club, and when he put in a claim for the money after the season, he found the Grand Rapids owner had fined him the entire amount and he would not be reimbursed.

The Brewers ended the season winning two of three in St. Paul; beating the Millers three straight in Milwaukee, with Terry pitching four-hit and one-hit shutouts; sweeping two in Kansas City; and winning two of three from St. Paul and two from Minneapolis at home. One other note of interest was that in the second-to-last game of the season, the Brewers played a new first baseman. Although the name Jim Corbett means little today, it meant enough then to draw 2,500 to Milwaukee Park on a cold Monday afternoon in late September. Corbett was an ex-heavyweight boxing champion and was barnstorming the country, playing first base and making good money. His share in this game was one-third of the gate, or about $250. He was said to be a good ball player too, having gone 2-for-5 with the game-winning hit in the ninth inning. The Brewers finished 1897 where they had been most of the year, in fourth place.

| Indianapolis | 98 | 37 | .726 | Detroit | 70 | 66 | .515 |
| Columbus | 89 | 47 | .654 | Minneapolis | 43 | 95 | .312 |

St. Paul	86	51	.628	Kansas City	40	99	.298
Milwaukee	85	51	.625	Grand Rapids	35	100	.259

In the Free Press Cup Series Indianapolis won 3 of 5, but both teams were anxious to return and decided to stop play. Receipts were split and the players received about $75 a man.

Despite finishing fourth, the Brewers played good, exciting ball. Four regulars hit over .300: Weaver. 343, Stafford .348, Daly .333, and Lewee .325. Other batting averages of regulars included Blake .293, Speer .289, Meyers .282 and Nicol .259. Even Mack hit .288, playing in 24 games. Blake, who had been in Milwaukee on loan, went back to Cleveland when the Western season ended. Stafford led the team in home runs with 8, and Daly had 46 stolen bases. Terry led the pitching staff with a 22 and 6 record, Barnes was 19 and 17, Reidy 16 and 9, Jones 11 and 3, Taylor 9 and 6, Dowling 4 and 3, Pappalau 2 and 1, Rettger 2 and 2, and Clarkson 2 and 5. The Brewers finished second in fielding in the Western League for 1897, although overall the infield fielded lower than the average. Shortstop Lewee and left fielder Weaver were first in their positions defensively, Stafford was sixth at first base, Daly and Meyers seventh at second and third. Speer, Nicol and Blake nailed down fourths at their positions.[25]

Financially, the Brewers were doing well. They led the Western League in attendance (estimated to be 160,000 at home and 120,000 on the road) and it was reported in September the club would make about $20,000, although at the later Western meeting they claimed only a $5,000 profit. The *Journal* attempted to tabulate the Brewers' true financial situation. Figuring the average home game receipts were about $700, and the visitors received 12½ cents per ticket (the home club got the benefits of the extra grandstand sales) and the 10 percent fund to the Western League, the *Journal* figured the Brewers' share of the gate at about $400 per game. With 71 home games the table was drawn up.

Total Home Receipts	$31,600
Total Receipts Abroad	7,200
Returned Money for 10 percent Fund	3,000
Total Taken In	41,800
Total Expenses	19,700
Net Profit	$22,100[26]

The rest of the Western did not fare as well. Indianapolis was the only other club to make money, about $3,000. St. Paul, Columbus and Detroit broke even. Kansas City lost $10,000 (another source said $22,000); Grand Rapids and Minneapolis were the bad spots of the Western. In August Glenalvin had sold his interests to Leadley and got out of the game, calling Grand Rapids "a dead rabbit town."[27] Neither Grand Rapids nor Minneapolis had paid their players since September 1, and the Western was forced to take control of the clubs and pay $900 to the Grand Rapids players and $1,900 to the Miller players. It was at first reported four players from the Bobolinks were sold to St. Louis to meet the liabilities of the club, but Leadley denied the story. On the season Grand Rapids lost $5,000 and Minneapolis $12,000. The 10 percent fund also caused some trouble. In Minneapolis Goodnow had resigned as president and declined to add his share to the partnership, so the club fell behind in payments. Haynes and Saulpaugh then put themselves in Ban Johnson's hands. It was reported that Milwaukee had paid more than $4,000 to the fund and got $3,000 back. Columbus and Detroit paid in $1,600 and collected $400. Kansas City put in $1,400 and received $200. Minneapolis and Grand Rapids were forced to put in an extra $300 in back pay at the meeting. Milwaukee was solid financially, but the rest of the Western was faltering.

✳ ✳ ✳

After the 1897 season the Western League was close to falling apart. Grand Rapids and Minneapolis were in the hands of the Western. Columbus had low attendance and looked like it would be dropped. Rumors were around before the season ended that Grand Rapids would either consolidate with Toledo or go to Denver. Neither was considered a good idea. Next, word was out Des Moines and Omaha would succeed Grand Rapids and Columbus for 1898. The *Sentinel* wrote, "Omaha couldn't support a circus with three rings more than a week and Des Moines is staggering like a drunken sailor under a Western Association team."[28] Still, most believed Omaha and Toledo would be in the Western League. Then in mid–September it was learned Buffalo might succeed Grand Rapids. Seven Western League magnates were in favor of the move. Only Kansas City opposed this move, thinking the trip too far. Buffalo, at present in the Eastern League, had Sunday ball and good crowds. Leadley, however, wanted $7,000 for his franchise, which Buffalo thought too much, and the excitement cooled. The *Daily News* doubted that Buffalo would join the Western. The Eastern League was on a par with the Western, and easterners considered their ball better. It was doubtful if they would support a Western club there. It was also thought the long trips would cause financial trouble. The *Sporting News* wrote "Buffalo may be a member of the Western League when airships furnish quicker and cheaper transportation than we now enjoy."[29] The *Buffalo Express* pointed out several Western League magnates wanted to close out, causing the Buffalo owners to think twice. The *Toledo Blade*, however, was probably the closest when it wrote Buffalo was just testing the market to get into the National League, in place of Cleveland.

The Western League met in Chicago on October 7 to discuss the franchise situation. It was revealed that John Goodnow had mortgaged his half interest in the Minneapolis club to the Pennsylvania & Ohio Coal Company. The mortgage having been foreclosed, the company wanted to retain interest in the club. The club, however, was sold to a six-man syndicate headed by Marcus Haynes. Haynes was later offered $18,000 for the club and refused. It was also reported Grand Rapids was sold to R.D. Harrison of Des Moines for $5,000, but because Leadley had forfeited the franchise, the sale could not stand. No disposition was made on any other franchise. The Western met again on October 21 and seven cities applied for the Grand Rapids franchise. The Western magnates placed the disposal of the franchise in league President Johnson's hands. Johnson would accept the best proposition made, and then the league would take a formal vote.

Johnson wanted to put the franchise in Chicago, thinking it would be a good business decision, but it was up to the Western owners. Jim Hart of Chicago said he knew nothing of a proposed club. Meanwhile, Fred Pfeffer, the ex-ball player, and J.D.W. King, who had earlier been granted the scorecard privilege for the entire Western League, applied for the open franchise, wanting to move it to Omaha. Then George Ellis said he wanted to buy the Grand Rapids franchise back. Des Moines also made an offer. In all there were five applicants for the franchise. It was reported Frick of Des Moines would rather be in the Western "than own real estate in Chicago or a Milwaukee brewery, but his chances for admission within the charmed circle are as remote as hot weather in the Klondike."[30]

On December 18 the Western League met again to decide what to do with the Grand Rapids franchise. "One by one the applicants were led before the magnates like lambs to the slaughter."[31] The Western wanted $2,500 for the franchise, thought too high by most, as five players had been sold to liquate the debt owed the league. Most thought $1,000 was about right. A. Edwin Antisdel of Grand Rapids had the best offer. He had a $10,000 stock company and proposed to build a park outside of Grand Rapids to assure Sunday ball. "Without Sunday games we would not risk counterfeit money in a ball team in Grand Rapids,"[32] he was quoted as saying. Although Pfeffer and King did not attend, others represented Omaha, including James McKee, who had organized the Milwaukee club in 1884. McKee was offered the franchise but found the Western's conditions too stiff. He was asked to put up a $10,000 bond and assume the debt of $1,800 of the Grand Rapids club. McKee also pointed out he would have to buy new players and get new grounds. It would cost him $10,000 to get a club into running order. Milwaukee, Columbus and St. Paul favored Omaha, as did Ban Johnson, but the others wanted the Furniture City, and nothing was decided.

The next day the price of the franchise was dropped to $2,000, and a formula was set up to supply the club with players. The formula was similar to the one to be used many years later when the major leagues expanded in the second half of the twentieth century. Each owner would sell four players to the new company for a sum to be determined by an arbitration committee. With these 28 players a good team could be had for $3,000 to $5,000. The plan did not draw favor, though. Again no action was taken. A committee was then selected to investigate the financial status of all applicants, and the price of the franchise lowered to $1,495. Finally in late January R.E. Schuman and M.J. O'Brien, Chicago real estate men, bought the franchise and placed it in Omaha, which had a population of about 250,000 in the metropolis and neighboring cities. At the February meeting the new owners were granted a three-year franchise. However, Schuman soon gained full control of the franchise and O'Brien was threatening to sue for the one-third gate receipts he claimed were his.

At the second October Western League meeting, the magnates could obviously see the problems facing them, so they turned to their biggest man (mentally and physically) for help. They gave Ban Johnson unheard of powers. As already stated, they placed the disposal of the Grand Rapids franchise in his hands. They also empowered their president to discipline players or managers found guilty of "conduct detrimental to the welfare of the game," this covering "a multitude of sins ranging from drunkenness and rowdyism on the part of player to the use of profane language by spectators."[33] A salary limit of $2,000 a month and $200 per player was enacted with a $500 fine for each offense. To ensure this new limit, Johnson was given the authority to sign all reserved players for the eight clubs, the managers preparing the contracts and Johnson sending them out. The *Daily News* was leery of the salary limit: "Whether the rule will be adhered to is an open question. The league has not had startling success in enforcing similar regulations in the past."[34] Johnson added a clause in some players' contracts that money would be withheld from their contract until the end of the season to ensure they did not drink. Johnson also received authority to examine the books of the clubs at any time. To go with all these powers, he was also put in charge of railroad transportation for the entire league. As always, he retained his power of hiring umpires. The National League adopted the double umpire system, but Johnson said the Western would not, as it would raise expenses nearly $5,000.

It was reported Connie Mack had offers from three National League clubs for the next year. He was reported to be "$2,000 richer than he would have been if he had remained in the big league last season"[35]—no doubt due to his part ownership in the club—and signed with the Brewers immediately after the 1897 season ended. Mack began attempting to improve the Brewers for the coming season. Mack had the nucleus of his club returning, losing Harry Blake and Pete Dowling to the National League clubs that had loaned them to Milwaukee. Bert Jones was also gone, having departed for Cleveland in the Blake deal for somewhere between $1,500 and $2,000. On the final day of the season it was announced Eddie Lewee and Bob Stafford would be sold to Louisville for $1,500. Mack figured he would lose them in the draft anyway. Fred Barnes was then drafted by Brooklyn. Rettger and Waldron, who had been loaned out during the season, were back on the Brewers reserved list. To help his pitching Mack claimed William Wolf, the local pitcher who had a 24 and 7 record with Sheboygan in 1897. Mack began to claim almost every player in sight. By December he had 30 players either reserved or claimed, causing Kid Speer to say the club would be obliged to enlarge the dressing room to accommodate them all. By February Connie had an incredible 55 players on his lists. A story was about that one of the semi-professional ball players in Chicago had disappeared and his mother was on the lookout for him. She was told "if anyone knew anything concerning her son it would be Connie Mack, as he has signed, claimed or reserved about all the players in the country." The mother addressed a letter to Connie asking for information about her "wandering boy."[36] On a more serious note, some of the state papers were complaining about this practice, stating so many state players were being claimed that it had the effect of delaying the organizing of several clubs and prevented some players from getting jobs.

These high numbers were almost a necessity because of the drafting and farming procedures of the day. The storm was brewing and Milwaukee was no angel. Shortly after Stafford and Lewee were sold, it was reported they had been placed with Louisville to protect them from the draft and they would be back in Milwaukee in 1898. Club president Matthew Killilea denied this, and the Louisville president only would say the two would be back with Milwaukee if they could not make it in the National League. By February Mack was including both in his infield plans and Killilea admitted they would return. As it turned out Mack found out Indianapolis wanted the two and Cincinnati of the National League was going to draft them. Mack wired President Pullman of Louisville and had him draft the two and then return them. In March the two were officially released back to Milwaukee and shortly after signed. Fred Barnes also came back when Brooklyn mysteriously dropped claim to him in late October.

Other Western League clubs were having troubles, however. Columbus lost six players, and Detroit and St. Paul lost four in the draft. Indianapolis reported it might drop from the league, fearing the club might lose all the good players from the championship team. Indianapolis did lose six players. Ban Johnson did point out that while the other seven clubs reserved their entire starting teams, Indianapolis reserved only eight players; practically the entire starting team had been transferred to Cincinnati for protection from the draft. The *Sporting Life* also caught this act with a bit of sarcasm, stating, "Indianapolis has fewer players reserved than any Western League club, and Cincinnati has the most in the big league. Nothing strange about either reserve list."[37] The *Evening Wisconsin* wrote all this drafting was a "case of killing the goose that laid the gold egg."[38]

What the Western wanted was a rule that a player would be able to stay two years in a Class A minor league (Western, Eastern and Atlantic leagues) before the big league could draft him; only two players to be drafted from any one club; the drafting price to be raised from $500 to $1,000 a player; a shorter drafting period; and a provision that a drafted player who is cut and sent back to the minors be paid at a minor league scale, not what he received in the National League. Thomas J. Hickey, president of the Western Association, a Class B minor league, also suggested only players from Class A be drafted into the National League, giving young players a chance to graduate degree by degree to the big league. Ban Johnson described the problem.

> Fierce competition among National League clubs has spurned the magnates onto desperate extravagance in the matter of drafting players. Nets are thrown out to all sides for desirable young material. The player who shows some promise, despite the fact he is often of less than one year's experience in a minor league, is grabbed up, given a brief trial, found wanting and then is turned adrift, or worse still, is farmed out to some minor league team.[39]

The minors petitioned the National Board of Arbitration in November, and the board suggested to the National League that a player should spend at least two seasons in the minors prior to being drafted. The board, however, did not recommend any of the other grievances. On the suggestion of John T. Brush, an amendment was recommended that would give National League clubs permission to loan a player to a minor league with the understanding he could be recalled on 30 days notice. Brush was a big man in National League circles, owning the controlling interest in Cincinnati, $25,000 in the New York Giants, a considerable amount of the Pittsburgh franchise, all of Indianapolis of the Western League, and was the mentor of Chris Von der Ahe and his St. Louis club, according to the *Brooklyn Eagle*. The *Milwaukee Sentinel* of December 20, 1897, thought Brush's clause "contains enough Websterian dynamite sufficient to wreck the Western League or any other minor baseball organization owing allegiance to the National League." In short, a National League owner could send a pitcher to his farm club for a crucial series that could decide a pennant and then call him back. Ban Johnson was against farming, but admitted some Western League clubs were doing it regularly. The *Sentinel* looked bleakly into the future through the past.

> A great many minor league magnates either cannot or do not care to see the rocks toward which they are drifting by building up the system of borrowed players from the National League, although the baseball trail is strewn with the wrecks caused by their short sighted policy in placing themselves under the thumbs of the men who control the National League destinies.[40]

In late January the Western and Eastern leagues met and discussed the situation. After agreeing on a salary limit of $2,000 a month ($2,250 if a club had a player-manager), they decided to petition the National League not to adopt Brush's 30-day clause. The *Journal* thought the two minors should combine. "From the obedient, docile and servile off springs they might become a haughty, wayward and mischief making youngster that would prove too much for the old man."[41] An amusing note came from National League sources after this meeting. Some league owners were complaining about minor league players being sold to National League clubs to protect them from the draft! Jim Hart even accused Johnson of "jobbing"[42] the official averages of certain players so they would not be drafted. At the National League meeting in March, all the minor leagues' proposals were turned down.

Meanwhile, the Milwaukee club had held its annual meeting, re-electing its officials. The directors of the club were now Matt Killilea, Charles Hellberg, Charles Polacheck, Fred Gross and Christian Gross. A dividend "of ample proportions"[43] was also declared. The scorecard deal with J.D.W. King died, and Theodore Engel was given the privilege at Milwaukee Park for $2,000. Fridays were declared Ladies Day at the park.

Connie Mack was sorting through all the names he had and building a team. In December he purchased George Shoch, who had played in Milwaukee from 1889 through '91, from St. Louis for $800. Shoch had played the previous two seasons in Brooklyn, but a deal was effected after the season whereby Shoch was traded to St. Louis and then Mack was able to arrange with the St. Louis owner, Chris von der Ahe, to have George transferred to Milwaukee. In February Mack began signing his players. First to sign was Tom Daly. Next signed was Adolphus Vollendorf, a pitcher from Manitowoc, Wisconsin, whom Mack had claimed in July of 1897 from the Jackson club of the Michigan League. Soon

George Speer, George Nicol, Frank LaPorte, a catcher from the Pennsylvania State League, and Alexander Langervine, a catcher from Smithbridge, Massachusetts, were signed. Wolf and John Taylor were then signed. By the end of March, Waldron, Weaver, Pappalau, Barnes, Lewee, Stafford and John Riah, a catcher from Manitowac, Wisconsin, were also signed. Langervine, Wolf and LaPorte were farmed to lower minor leagues. Indianapolis accused Mack of burying two other young players, Ed Dalrymple and Beecher, who had been claimed from Mansfield of the Interstate League and later released back. Indianapolis had wanted the two and thought Mack had claimed them so they would not go to the Hoosiers.

Ban Johnson was finding it difficult to sign many players. Many were balking because of the new salary limit. It was even said some Western League players had formed a union to fight the limit. These players were opposed to Johnson handling all contracts because if there would be any trouble, the management would not be held responsible. Mack pointed out that without the salary limit, the clubs would only be able to sign ten players per club instead of 13 to 15. Another problem in signing players was the Western League's policy of no advance money. Milwaukee was having troubles signing Shoch, Rettger, Terry, Reidy and Meyers. Terry said the salary offered him was too low, and he was thinking of retiring. He soon decided to sign, however he said he would not go south with the team, but stay in Milwaukee and attend to his business. Terry's contract had an unusual clause in it, requiring him only to pitch in home games so he could stay in Milwaukee and look after his billiard hall in the Plankinton House while the Brewers were on the road. Rettger was sent a $160 a month contract and he said he would retire before he played for that. It turned out Rettger wanted the reserve clause out of his contract. When denied, he finally signed. Going into spring training the Brewers still had Shoch, Reidy and Meyers unsigned. Killilea was worried that if a war started with Spain, as the Spanish-American War was about to erupt, some of the players might enlist. Mack eased him by saying "they would prefer $200 a month to hard tack and $13 per month."[44]

The Western League held its spring meeting and abolished the Free Press Cup Series. The schedule was written up beginning on April 20 and closing September 20. Milwaukee's only holiday date was Memorial Day. The Brewers were scheduled to travel 9,975 miles, and the entire Western League 74,404. Cost to the circuit would be $11,160 for travel. Ban Johnson's annual salary was raised $500, to $3,500.

Spring training for the Brewers began in Louisville on April 1, although some players had started practice with Mack in Milwaukee a few weeks earlier. Mack's first act was to name Tom Daly captain of the team. Although Mack's team was almost fully assembled on paper, key players were missing in Louisville. Terry, as mentioned, stayed in Milwaukee. Shoch, Reidy and Meyers were unsigned. Stafford was detained in North Carolina with business complications. On April 3 the Brewers played the Louisville Colonels in their first exhibition, losing 11 to 8. Mack had Rettger and Barnes pitching, Speer catching, himself at first base, Daly at second, Lewee at short, Riah at third, Weaver, Nicol and Waldron in the field. Connie would not play during the regular season, only wearing a uniform when on the coaching lines. The weather was bad in Louisville and five games had to be cancelled. On to St. Louis, Mack put Barnes at third and pitched Taylor, Rettger and Vollendorf. Again the Brewers lost, 5 to 4. The club then lost three more to the Browns, Mack keeping Barnes at third, himself at first, and using all his pitchers.

The first of Milwaukee's three holdouts to come to terms was Bill Reidy. It had been reported a Western Association club had wanted to purchase him and Mack considered it, to buy a National League pitcher, but the price was too small. Reidy did, however, join the club in St. Louis. Shoch was still asking for as much money as he would have received in St. Louis. Bert Meyers wanted more as well, but he also wanted out. The contract Johnson sent him called for a $75 a month cut in pay, and Meyers said he would not play in the Western League for that kind of money. The *Sentinel* thought the price was right, as Meyers had "swallowed too much of the product of Breweryville ... and was out of condition."[45] Meyers wrote Mack, saying Washington of the National League wanted to buy his release. Mack said he would only take a third baseman in exchange. Mack also said he was thinking of trading Meyers to a Western Association club so "the joke would be on the other side."[46] When Meyers ordered a Milwaukee uniform in early April, Killilea announced he would probably play with the Brewers. Meyers was practicing with Washington, however, and it was reported the Senators were tampering with him. President Wagner of Washington soon offered to purchase the third baseman for $1,000, but Mack wanted $2,500. After the *Chicago Tribune* reported Meyers would play for Washington, Killilea formally protested to National League president Nick Young. The Louisville club sympathized with Milwaukee and offered Joe Dolan to the Brewers. Mack refused, noting Dolan had hit only .210 and had a weak arm. Just prior to the season's opening, Meyers offered Mack $500 for his release but was refused again. Mack said he would not try to sign Meyers any longer, but let him sit.

The Brewers continued spring exhibitions by traveling to Dayton, but had both games rained out. The club traveled over to Mansfield, Stafford joining them there, and split two games. The final two exhibitions were against Canton, the Milwaukees winning both. Mack was ready for the season, saying all his players were in top shape. His team consisted of Barnes, Daly, Lewee, Nicol, Pappalau, Reidy, Rettger, Riah, Speer, Stafford, Taylor, Terry, Vollendorf, Waldron and Weaver. Shoch and Meyers were still unsigned as the season began.

The Brewers looked strong with the addition of Waldron and Riah, but the loss of Jones and Meyers remaining unsigned hurt. Mack still believed the club would be in the race all season. Indianapolis was again the team to beat. The Hoosiers lost some key players, but always had Cincinnati of the National League to draw from. The *Sporting Life* also alleged the Hoosiers had four players over the salary limit. The *Kansas City Star* editorialized:

> It would not be surprising to see John T. take his whole Cincinnati team down to Indiana or visa versa some day when there is an off day in one place and a hard game in the other. How long President Johnson and the Western League managers propose to stand this pirate's methods is the Question that is bothering the lovers of fairness in Fandom.[47]

The *Detroit Free Press* even found out that Johnson did not sign the Indianapolis players by special agreement because "of the mixing up of Indianapolis affairs with Cincinnati."[48] As for the rest of the league, the St. Paul team looked very dangerous. Columbus looked a little weaker than the previous year. Minneapolis was "as full of new faces as a plum pudding is of currants, and may be a dark horse."[49] Kansas City, now a Pittsburgh farm team, looked better than 1897. Detroit would not be strong and Omaha was looked upon to take the cellar.

The Brewers opened on April 21 in Columbus with John Taylor losing 8 to 2. Besides Taylor, Mack's lineup had Weaver, Nicol and Waldron left to right field; Stafford, Daly, Lewee and Barnes, first to third, and Speer behind the plate. Reidy lost the remaining two contests in Columbus. The lack of spring practice was showing on the team, especially on the mound. Shoch accepted terms and it was hoped he would shore things up in the infield. Barnes, however, continued on at third in Indianapolis, as Milwaukee dropped three of four, falling into the cellar. The Brewers' first road trip was a disaster. The team hit only .246. Riah had went 3 for 3, Nicol was at .345 and Speer at .300, but Lewee was only batting .110 and Waldron .185. The fielding was even worse. Stafford, Lewee, Barnes and Nicol each had four errors in those seven games. The team had a total of 23 errors. Vollendorf, Reidy and Rettger had come down with sore arms. John Pappalau, who had lost his only decision, was released, joining Toronto of the Eastern League.

The Brewers opened their first homestand losing to Columbus 8 to 7 behind Terry, but won the remaining three games of the series with Shoch at third base. The club then went to Detroit and won two of three. Barnes took the loss and was apparently having trouble adjusting back to pitching. In his first start, against Columbus in the home series, he had pitched poorly, but Reidy eventually won the game. In Detroit he only faced two batters, walking them both. Milwaukee's men then returned home, only to drop four to the Hoosiers. The Brewers' record was only 6 and 12, and on May 11 the *Sentinel* ran this want ad: "Wanted — A first baseman and two outfielders who can hit a balloon." But the club's main problem was pitching. Adolphus Vollendorf was forced to leave the club because of his sore arm, and was loaned to New Haven of the Connecticut State League. As mentioned, Barnes (0 and 1) was having trouble. Reidy (2 and 4) had a sore arm. Terry (0 and 1) was not in condition, and it was reported in the *Sporting News* Mack suspended him for not being in shape, but lifted the suspension in late June. Only Rettger (1 and 1) and Taylor (3 and 4) were healthy. After splitting a four-game series with the Tigers, the club remained six games under .500.

The Cream City men continued this long homestand, winning two of three from St. Paul. The team then got hot, beating Omaha and Kansas City four games each to run the winning steak to nine games, and their record to 18 and 15. For the May 27 game with K.C., President Killilea said he would tender the entire receipts to Mrs. Lydia Ely to help her raise the amount needed to send a 253,000-pound Soldier's Monument to New York. One thousand dollars was expected to be turned over, but low attendance resulted in only $167.28. Injuries then caught up with the Brewers. Weaver was injured, causing Barnes to play left field for a game. Then Shoch split a finger and Barnes went to third, with Riah going to left. The Brewers still managed to win two of four from the Millers to end the homestand.

The Milwaukee club traveled into Minnesota, winning two of three in Minneapolis and three in St. Paul, with Weaver back in left but Shoch still out. Then in Kansas City the Brewers lost three of four to the Blues. This was followed by Mack's men losing three of four games to the last-place Omaha Babes. After winning two against Columbus, the Brewers ended the road trip losing three in Indianapolis, that team now being called the Indians in some papers. During this road trip the Brewers ended their association with Bert Meyers by selling him to Washington for $1,000. Philadelphia had also been after Meyers, offering a pitcher and infielder in exchange. As Meyers was hitting only .182 for Washington after a few weeks, the Senators wanted to give him back, but Mack did not want him — only the $1,000 Washington had not sent yet. Milwaukee was finally paid in August after Matthew Killilea went to the National Board of Artitration.

Having lost ten straight to Indianapolis, the Brewers beat the Hoosiers four times to open the homestand. Barnes was forced into center field when Nicol was injured in the first game. Taylor then shut out Columbus on a 2-hitter before Rettger won and lost to the Senators. This homestand ended with Terry beating Detroit 9 to 3. The teams then went to Detroit for the Fourth of July week, the Tigers winning three of five. At the halfway mark the Brewers were 38 and 31, in fifth place, only a game behind Columbus. St. Paul was one game in first place over Indianapolis, and Kansas City was also knocking on the door. Detroit, Omaha and Minneapolis were way out of contention.

As a matter of fact, Omaha was out of the Western League. On July 8 the Western met and President Schuman transferred his interest in the Omaha club to W.T. Van Brunt, who transferred the club to St. Joseph, Missouri. St. Joe had been in the Western Association, which had folded in late June. President Hickey of the disbanded association immediately went to Chicago to start the wheels turning to buy the Omaha club, which had already lost $10,000. Van Brunt was president of the St. Joseph Street Railway Company, and figured the 85,000 population of St. Joseph would support a Western League club. The Western League paid the Omaha players the money due them, about $1,500. The Western technically took over the franchise, but Van Brunt assumed the liabilities incurred by the club. Omaha exited the Western League with a 22 and 39 record. The Western League also nearly lost Columbus, but Tom Loftus decided to remain in Columbus for the balance of the season, and then move to Denver in 1899. A Columbus source reported Loftus would transfer to Dubuque, but he did not. Loftus did, however, think of transferring all home games to other cities, but it was believed this was only to influence the attendance in Columbus.

The Brewers opened the second half of the Western season at home on July 9, losing to St. Paul 2 to 1. The club that day signed a new infielder, Jimmy Burke, from the Peoria club. Mack was claiming numerous players from the disbanded Western Association, causing the *Indianapolis News* to state "judging from the reports sent out from league headquarters Mack has a mortgage on every player that ever played in the Western Association...."[50] The next day Milwaukee won a Sunday doubleheader from the Saints before 5,500, but then dropped the final game of the set. The new St. Joseph club then came in and lost all three to the Brewers. The Minneapolis Millers were next to Milwaukee Park and the Brewers won four of five, with Burke at third base. The homestand ended with Kansas City losing two of three, as Shoch went back to third. The Brewers were now in third place, having won 12 of their last 14 games. They were winning on good pitching for the most part, as Taylor had 17 wins and 7 losses, Rettger was 14 and 9, and Terry 8 and 2. No Brewer was hitting over .300, Weaver leading the club at .294. Daly was at a respectable .283, but the rest of the regulars were under .270, with Lewee at .237 and Speer at only .228.

On the road the Milwaukee aggregation lost two of three in Kansas City and again in St. Joseph. Traveling into St. Paul Mack picked up a southpaw pitcher, Charles McDonald, who had been released by St. Joseph. The *St. Paul Pioneer* now questioned if Milwaukee could possibly be within the salary limit with 15 men on its roster. The Brewers beat the Saints three of four, and then the Millers were beaten three straight. Charles McDonald and Jimmy Burke (hitting only .150 in six games) were loaned to Minneapolis when the Brewers left, most figuring because the Millers now had contenders to play and Mack was trying to help the Millers help him.

Back home the Brewers lost two of three to Columbus, now nicknamed the Wanderers, as the club was transferring games to other Western League cities as often as possible. Mack's men won exhibitions against the all–Negro Chicago Unions and Milwaukee Athletic Club on the following three off days. John Riah, who had played in only 12 games, hitting .238, was then loaned to Sheboygan (Wisconsin) for the balance of the season. In fourth place, but within striking distance, the Brewers split two with first-place Indianapolis on August 11 and 12. The team then swept three sets from Detroit and St. Joseph to climb into second place behind Kansas City. A split with St. Paul kept the club in the runner-up spot. Next in was first-place K.C. Nicol had been injured and Barnes was in center field, so Mack picked up Clarence Beaumont from Waupon (Wisconsin) to play in left field, moving Weaver to center. Mack had claimed Beaumont — later to be nicknamed Ginger, but now referred to as Butch — earlier in the winter when he played for Beloit College. Alexander Smith, a catcher signed to rest Speer, was also obtained on loan from Brooklyn of the National League. On August 23 Rettger beat the Blues 5 to 3 in a 5-inning rain-shortened game to tie the two clubs for first place with 63 and 45 records. Beaumont was the hero of the game with two hits in two at-bats while scoring two runs, in addition to making a phenomenal catch to save the game. The next day Rettger won again, as the Brewers remained tied for first, but now with Indianapolis. Beaumont was the hero again in the third game with a home run, but Milwaukee dropped into second as Indianapolis won a doubleheader. On August 26 Reidy shut out Minneapolis and the Brewers had sole possession of first place. Details of the game were the headline of the *Sentinel*, with a front page picture of a player holding a pennant. The Brewers then won two of three from the Millers, but dropped into second by .0001 of a percentage point. Alexander Smith then went back to Brooklyn, having hit .217 in 12 games, and Charles McDonald was recalled from Minneapolis.

Clarence Beaumont would hit .354 in the latter part of 1898 for the Brewers; he later went to Pittsburgh in a "shady transaction."

The Brewers traveled into Detroit and split four games, but retained first place. The club then went to Indianapolis for the big showdown. But the showdown almost did not start. W.F.C. Golt, the Indianapolis president, was feuding with Ban Johnson and was threatening to resign from the Western immediately. The problem started when Manager Bob Allen of the Hoosiers took the Milwaukee, St. Paul & Chicago Railway from St. Paul to Chicago, instead of the Wisconsin Central, with which the Western League had its arrangements. When Johnson heard this he requested Indianapolis be taken off the special rates, adding Allen disclosed the lower rates the Western received from Wisconsin Central — the additional expense for the trip being $250. Allen denied this. Golt said he would remain at home and play exhibitions with National League teams if he did not get the lower rates back. Disaster was avoided when Johnson and Golt settled their differences. With Clarence Beaumont out the whole series with an injury, the Brewers dropped all three games and fell into third place. In St. Paul Beaumont returned and the team split two and then lost one in Minneapolis. All hopes were then lost as Kansas City beat Milwaukee three straight in the Blues home park. The Brewers finished at home sweeping a three-game series from St. Joseph — this series having been transferred from St. Joe to Milwaukee by Ban Johnson a short time previous. Kansas City and Indianapolis see-sawed through the final week, with the Blues beating the Hoosiers in the final game of the season to take their first Western League flag. Incredibly, some local fans, apparently supported by the *Journal*, were accusing Mack of "jockeying" the games so that Kansas City would win the pennant over Indianapolis. It was claimed the Brewers looked bad the last road trip of the season, especially in Kansas City, forgetting or choosing to ignore the club also lost three in Indianapolis. The *Journal* also pointed out Mack was not anxious to win, leaving Reidy behind and taking Barnes, who was "no equal"[51] to Reidy. Charles Comiskey from the St. Paul club commented on the talk, "This is all rot, pure and simple."[52] Said the *Milwaukee Journal*, "Whether Milwaukee lost the pennant purposely or whether it was one of those accidents that can never be accounted for, is a mystery that will never be explained, but it is a fact, nevertheless, that the fans hate such mysteries and that a team will get better patronage if the end of the season is not clouded by any dark and unexplainable happenings."[53]

The final 1898 Western League standings:

Kansas City	88	51	.633	St. Joseph	42	93	.311*
Indianapolis	84	50	.627	Columbus	73	60	.549
Milwaukee	82	57	.590	Detroit	50	87	.365
St. Paul	81	58	.583	Minneapolis	48	92	.343

*Omaha was 22 and 39, St. Joseph 20 and 54

Indianapolis disputed Kansas City's claim to first place, basing this on four disputed games. One game was an early Kansas City game against the Minneapolis Millers, played as a doubleheader to make up a postponed game. A league rule forbade the playing of two games for one admission in the first series between clubs. Golt of Indianapolis claimed this K.C. win was thus illegal. A game was also in dispute between the Blues and Detroit, which Golt thought should go to the Tigers. And finally, there was the matter of a doubleheader called off in St. Joseph. The St. Joe officials refused to play the games on account of wet grounds, but Golt claimed the field was in good condition. To counteract this, James Manning of Kansas City said he would file a protest of two Indianapolis wins in May, in which Manning claimed Indianapolis violated a league rule that no former player from the National League could return to the club owning him short of one year. On October 11 the Western League turned down the Indianapolis protests, making Kansas City the official pennant winner.

The Brewers had played well and had their highest finish in the Western League. Beaumont led the club in hitting with a .354 average (in 24 games). The full-season players' averages included: Daly .288, Weaver .282, Shoch .278, Stafford .269, Nicol .263, Waldron .259, Speer .228 and Lewee .218. Daly led the team in runs scored with 111, and Stafford hit 10 home runs. The team hit .269, fourth in the league, but led the Western in fielding with a .944 average. Taylor led the pitchers with a 28 and 13 record, and Rettger was 24 and 12. Terry was 11 and 3, Barnes 7 and 9, Reidy 10 and 19, while McDonald won his only decision and Pappalau lost his sole decision.[54]

The Western League clubs split evenly on financial matters. In July the *Washington Post* had written "Kansas City and Milwaukee are the only cities in the Western League that are financially located at the junction of Velvet Avenue and Easy Boulevard."[55] At the time a Kansas City paper figured the club would make about $10,000. The close pennant race changed that. The top four clubs in the Western "reaped the rich harvest."[56] The exact figures were not made public, but the *Sentinel* figured Kansas City made about $25,000, Milwaukee $20,000 (on about 150,000 admissions to Milwaukee Park; another report gave Milwaukee's home attendance as 160,000, and 120,000 on the road), Indianapolis $8,000, and St. Paul $6,000. On the other side of the ledger Detroit lost about $2,000, Minneapolis $4,000, Columbus $6,000 and St. Joseph $12,000. Other reports were even higher, although the *Sporting News* also gave Milwaukee's profit as $20,000. Both attendance, especially early in the season, and profits were hurt by the Spanish-American War, which began in April. However, Ban Johnson said Western League attendance was as large as that in the National League on a per-game basis. Except for a few weak entries, the Western League was very solid.

✻ ✻ ✻

Connie Mack's relationship with the local press continued to degenerate following the 1898 season. On the final day of the season it was announced Tom Daly and John Taylor had been sold. Daly went to Brooklyn for $800 and Bill Hallman. Hallman was an eleven-year National League veteran second baseman who had had four straight .300-plus years from 1893 to '96, but was on the decline. Mack was even quoted as saying he was not counting on the veteran to play second base. Taylor was sold to Chicago for $2,000. Both deals had been made a few weeks earlier, but not made public until the close of the season. Both players immediately joined their new clubs, Daly hitting .329 in the remaining 23 games and Taylor winning five games without a loss for the Colts. A week later it was announced Clarence Beaumont and Ervin Waldron were sold to Louisville. The fans and the press, especially the *Journal*, now began to question Mack and what his plans were for 1899, with four of his starters gone before the draft even had started. Matthew Killilea (re-elected as the club president in October, with Charles Hellberg as vice president and Fred Gross the treasurer) came to his manager's defense, saying the club had received word that Baltimore was going to draft Waldron and Cincinnati would take Beaumont. Some thought it was a "phony deal"[57] with Louisville — similar to the case of Lewee and Stafford the previous year — and the two would be back in Milwaukee in 1899.

Mack, at least publicly, showed no pressure from the criticism. He announced John Riah would not be back with the club, as he could not make it in the Western. Mack did recall Jimmy Burke and Adolphus Vollendorf to the Brewers, but Burke was soon drafted by Cleveland. Mack began negotiations with Chauncy Fisher, the St. Joseph ace pitcher, but Baltimore drafted him. Later in October Burke was returned to Milwaukee, having hit only .105 in 13 games for the Spiders. Bill "Adonis" Terry retired from baseball to attend to his billiard parlor and work at Milwaukee's downtown Plankinton House as a clerk, where he would "hand out keys with the same grace that formerly marked his delivery of the ball when he wore the spangles."[58] Terry would later umpire in the National League in addition to opening and running for years a popular bowling alley. In December Mack traded Clarence Beaumont to Pittsburgh of the National League for Billy Gray and Will Hart. This move of getting Beaumont back from Louisville and trading him showed how "almost any old shady transaction goes in baseball."[59] Louisville sent Beaumont back to Milwaukee on the pretense they did not need him, but in reality Milwaukee had protected him from being drafted by Pittsburgh and Mack now received two players for him. Gray, a third baseman, had hit only .229 for the Pirates, and Hart had won only five of fourteen decisions on the mound. Later that month Louisville also transferred Erving Waldron back to the Brewers. Immediately after the first of the year, Mack, reported to be down with typhoid fever at his home back east, announced Bill Hallman had signed and would be the Brewer captain. It was also reported Fred Barnes had been sold, three months prior, to Baltimore. In February 1899, Milwaukee signed another ex-National Leaguer, Cy Swaim, who had pitched two losing seasons in Washington prior to being released after the 1898 campaign with a 13 and 22 two-year record. Later that month Barnes was bought back by Mack.

In February Mack began signing his players. Connie had trouble with only a few players this year. George Rettger wanted a raise, as his contract called for the same amount, but he signed with little ado later. Vollendorf was also kicking, but signed before April 1. Before this date Mack had also signed Barnes, Gray, Hallman, Hart, Lewee, McDonald, Nicol (who had wintered in Milwaukee and managed the billiard room at the Davidson Hotel), Reidy, Speer, Stafford, Swaim, Waldron and Weaver. Milwaukee had signed its players so easily the *Detroit Free Press* wrote some were not aware there was a salary limit in the Western League. Only Kansas City was doing as well signing players. The Brewers sold Jimmy Burke to Rochester of the Eastern League for $300. George Shoch again wanted more money, but was at the limit. He did sign before the season started. Mack had again claimed more than 50 players, the *St. Paul Dispatch* writing, "Connie Mack of Milwaukee has 52 men on his claim list. He has two ball players, Speer and Weaver."[60] Many of these on the claim list were college boys, "but he can remember the names of only 29"[61] the *Sentinel* reported. None were expected to sign yet, but some no doubt would when the college season ended.

The Western League circuit plans for 1899 were going full swing, even before the '98 season closed. There were persistent rumors that Indianapolis would take Cleveland's place in the National League. John Brush claimed the Western League was only given protection for one year at a time by the National Agreement, so the league could take Indianapolis if it chose. The deal hung mainly on whether Indianapolis could get Sunday ball. It was believed that the Cleveland club would transfer to St. Louis, and the St. Louis club to Indianapolis. Even Frank Robison of Cleveland admitted the deal was in the works. Western League backers believed if the National League entered Indianapolis, the Western should go into Chicago. Others disagreed. Matt Killilea of Milwaukee thought it would be "suicidal"[62] because the Western would lose its protection. The *Evening Wisconsin* pointed out that if the protection was lost, the National League would sign some good players, but the Western could sign the released players of the league. The Western could also notify all players that if they jumped, they would be banned from the Western. The *Sporting News* doubted if placing a franchise in Chicago would work, noting Chicago was in a Western years back and failed because of low attendance.

> How long would an out club, dependent for its patronage upon the drawing ability of Detroit, Columbus, Milwaukee and other Western League cities with their $2,000 a month teams, live in the western metropolis, which wants the bet regardless of price? The Western League will be under National protection in 1899 or some of the club owners will be paupers in 1900.[63]

At the Western League meeting in October, Golt of Indianapolis was fined $150 for the railroad incident of that summer; he threatened to withdraw, but did not. Although the Western again talked of entering Chicago, their attention was quickly focused on three eastern cities.

Columbus and St. Joseph were the Western League's trouble spots, and it was felt they had to go. Ban Johnson favored admitting Buffalo, a club losing money in the Eastern League, or Toronto. James Franklin of Buffalo said he would accept a Western League franchise on two conditions: that it be given to him gratis and another be given to Toronto. The *Evening Wisconsin* liked the Toronto idea, thinking the two Eastern League cities added to the six strong Western League cities would form the strongest minor league ever formed and press the National League for honors. Toronto's only drawback was no Sunday ball.

Franklin said he would apply, but probably would not join the Western if Kansas City was in it because of the distance. At the October meeting Buffalo did apply, along with Rockford, Toledo and Denver. Buffalo was not admitted, however, as Franklin wanted the St. Joseph franchise free and the players to go with it. As it turned out, the stumbling block was that Milwaukee, Kansas City and St. Paul owned the St. Joe franchise jointly. Each of these clubs had $400 in the St. Joseph club, and by selling the players they could get their money back. No action on franchises was taken at all, but Buffalo was still considered by the Western magnates, and a committee of four was established to study all applicants.

The Western had plans for its sick Columbus franchise. Killilea suggested each club owner pay $500 toward purchasing Toronto and turn it over to Tom Loftus gratis. Four clubs agreed, Indianapolis being one of the clubs against the proposal. Loftus, however, wanted to move his Columbus club to Denver. He said he would charge 40 cents to the bleachers and 65 cents in the grandstand. He also said he would probably guarantee $150 to visiting clubs to compensate for the distance. Indianapolis was also against this, and any transfer needed a unanimous vote. Loftus then decided not to abandon Columbus "unless he has strong assurance that he will profit by it."[64] In late November the Western decided to purchase the territorial rights to Toronto from Arthur Irwin. Irwin, however, wanted $6,000 for the rights.

Buffalo, meanwhile, agreed to terms with the Western League. Franklin would get the St. Joseph franchise and players, and then release Dan Daub, the ace pitcher, to Kansas City for $400. On December 2, 1898, Buffalo was admitted to the Western League. With Buffalo gone from the Eastern League, Irwin dropped his price on Toronto to $3,000, still twice as much as Loftus was willing to pay. The National League now entered the picture. The *Cleveland Press* reported the National League might drop Cleveland and the Western League might enter that city. Word was soon out that both Cleveland and Louisville would be dropped, and the Western would pick both of them up. The *Sentinel* of December 17, 1898, reported of the situation:

> While the National League magnates are preparing to slice each other's weazen and the Eastern, Atlantic and New England Leagues are in a state of insurrection, the Western League is really the only baseball organization that is intact and in a position to bag the persimmons whenever the squabbling magnates shake the tree in their efforts to dislodge Cleveland and Louisville from the league branches.

It was reported some National League clubs were in great financial difficulty. Louisville was $38,000 in debt. Baltimore was "financially crippled."[65] Washington lost $50,000 in four years and Brooklyn $75,000 since it entered the league. Ned Hanlon said the league would drop to eight clubs, but it would cost too much. Washington, for example, wanted $100,000 to drop out.

None other than John T. Brush offered the Western League a spot on the National Board of Arbitration. The catch was the Western would have to dissolve its organization, and then Milwaukee, Kansas City, St. Paul, Buffalo, Indianapolis and Detroit would join up with Louisville and Cleveland or Washington to form a new league. With this "tempting bait" the Western League would become "the servile tail of the National League dog."[66] Not surprisingly, Golt was in favor of Brush's new league, but the other Western League owners "dodged the poison arrow."[67] The Western was ready to move Columbus to Cleveland if the league dropped that city, although some owners—Killilea for one—preferred Louisville because it had Sunday ball.

The whole issue hinged on a court case in St. Louis. The National League wanted to get rid of Chris Von der Ahe of St. Louis because he could not operate a successful franchise with his funds. If successful, the league would move Cleveland to St. Louis. Von der Ahe lost and his St. Louis club went on the auction block. The plan was to have Robison of Cleveland buy St. Louis, reportedly with the backing of Brush. Then Tom Loftus got into the act. Loftus had lost any hope of going into Toronto as that franchise had stayed in the Eastern League. The Western owners had taken up Killilea's idea of loaning Loftus $500 apiece, but the Columbus owner stalled to see if Toronto would be excluded from the Eastern League, as he would then get the territory free. Loftus now decided to bid on the St. Louis franchise, along with Charles Comiskey. Some believed Loftus was trying to buy St. Louis for Robison, and then move his Western club to Cleveland. The National League moved quickly to block Loftus. It took the position that when Sportsman's Park and the St. Louis franchise would be auctioned off, the baseball franchise would die and the National League would

A cartoon in *Milwaukee Sentinel* of March 7, 1899, depicting the number of players on whom Connie Mack had claims.

not have to allow the new owners into their organization. Robison then dropped from the bidding. Many thought the league's position illegal. To be on the safe side, the Board of Arbitration suggested St. Louis be suspended for failure to pay a minor league club for players. The National League, afraid of the law, decided to wait until after the auction to take action, but resolved St. Louis' new owner would not be entitled to automatic admission. The league also adjourned its scheduled meeting in March to see what Loftus would do at the auction. At the March 14 auction, R.A. Gruner purchased the franchise for $33,000. Loftus did not bid. Within days Gruner sold out to Edward Becker, supposedly to enable Cleveland to transfer to St. Louis. In reality Frank Robison was now the owner of both St. Louis and Cleveland, owning 51 percent of the St. Louis club. However, the National League made no franchise moves and Loftus was stuck in Columbus.

During all this commotion the Western League almost had troubles in Indianapolis and Detroit. First the Indianapolis Board of Public Works ordered a street to be opened through the ballpark. The directors said the expense of leasing and equipping a new park would not be warranted by the income and would drop out of baseball. Most thought the threat a bluff, as two years before the owners of the Hoosiers were thinking of moving to a more satisfactory location. In February the city decided not to cut a street through the Hoosiers' park. In Detroit Van der Beck apparently wanted out of the Western and offered to buy Louisville for $50,000, but could not swing a deal. Comiskey also had wanted to buy the Minneapolis franchise and combine his St. Paul franchise with the Millers to form one club. With Marcus Haynes having died in December, it was thought Comiskey might make the purchase, but Saulbaugh would not allow it.

With the Western League positioned in Buffalo, Columbus, Detroit, Indianapolis, St.

Paul, Milwaukee, Minneapolis and Kansas City, a 126-game schedule was written up in March, starting April 27 and closing September 11. Only Indianapolis was against the shorter schedule, as its players were signed to Cincinnati National League contracts, which called for a six-month salary, the *Sentinel* claimed. The Western League drew this praise from the *Sporting News* in its January 14, 1899, issue:

> The Western League is the most important and substantial minor organization base ball has ever known. Its affairs are ably and conservatively conducted by President Johnson, who devotes his time to his official duties exclusively. Every club is well financed and each team will be handled in 1899 by a first class manager with major league experience.

Spring training began on April 1 with the players reporting to Milwaukee. Unfortunately, Milwaukee Park was two inches deep in snow and practice there was delayed a week. All Western teams were staying home this spring, the owners claiming they could not afford to pay $1,500 to $2,000 to go south. The cost to train at home was only $600 to $700. Mack's team had its first exhibition game on April 11 in Madison, with the Giants winning 13 to 10 over the University nine. The Giants? Connie Mack had decided because his players were the biggest in the Western League — Swaim, for example, was 6' 4"— he would rename his club the Giants. A Chicago paper reported the Milwaukee management objected to the local breweries getting free advertising and decided to change the name. Mack denied this. The local press at first used the nickname, but rather quickly went back to calling the team the Brewers, as the fans did not take to Giants. The club's uniforms for 1899 were to be white flannel with dark blue trim at home, and gray flannel with the same trim while on the road. Hats, stockings and belts were also dark blue. The team played three more games in Madison, winning all by lopsided scores. Speer did not make the trip, causing Mack to be rather unhappy with the little catcher and forcing him to use Riah temporarily. The Giants/Brewers then traveled home, playing a few games among themselves by splitting into the Veterans and Colts. Back to outside competition, the Milwaukee club beat the University of Michigan team twice before beating Alonzo Stagg's Chicago Varsity team. The Jefferson, Wisconsin, team lost to Milwaukee, and the all–Negro Chicago Unions lost three of four to the Brewers to finish spring exhibitions.

During these home exhibitions Kid Speer strained a ligament in his throwing arm and was forced out of the lineup for a few weeks. Speer's early training might seem different when compared to today's players. He used the punching bag to reduce his weight and then boxed with Western League umpire Joe Cantillon; the two managed to get in considerable work. Long walks were also part of the program. Mack turned to the versatile Fred Barnes to go behind the plate until a replacement could be found for the injured Speer. Mack immediately purchased Pat Crisham, a rookie catcher, from Brooklyn for $500 to fill the gap. Crisham, however, refused to report to Milwaukee, even after Mack offered to raise his salary $50 a month. Crisham was claimed by Baltimore, where he reported. Mack was forced to put Speer back into his lineup. Because Speer's arm suddenly got better, rumor was about the Kid was being punished for not being in shape when he reported.

Before opening day Mack analyzed the Western League teams. He figured his own boys to finish high, as his pitching was some of the best in the league, the infield good, and Speer had no superior in the circuit. St. Paul had improved very much. Indianapolis was as good, if not better, than it was in 1898. Mack figured defending champion Kansas City had better hitting this year. Minneapolis had picked up some good hitters and Detroit had improved. Columbus again would be strong and Buffalo would be this year's dark horse.

On April 27 a large crowd attended Milwaukee Park, but rain ended the contest in the fourth inning. The following day the opener was played, Milwaukee beating Minneapolis 4 to 1. The Brewers' lineup was Waldron (rf), Nicol (cf), Barnes (lf), Gray (3b), Stafford (1b), Hallman (2b), Shoch (ss), Speer (c) and Rettger (p). Prior to the game Mack announced he cut Eddie Lewee from the club. Swaim lost and Vollendorf won to end the Millers series. St. Paul then came in and took two from the Brewers. The Brewers then returned the trip to the Twin Cities, leaving McDonald and Vollendorf behind. In Minneapolis the club split four, and then lost two of three in St. Paul to drop the Brewers into the cellar.

The Brewers returned home on May 11 to beat Kansas City three of four. Charles McDonald, unused by Mack, was loaned to the New Haven club. The two teams then traveled to K.C., Mack leaving Swaim at home and taking Vollendorf. The Blues again lost three of four to the Foam Blowers, as the Kansas City players referred to the victors. Coming back to Milwaukee, the Brewers lost two of three to Detroit. Cy Swaim was released, having lost all five games he pitched in. Within days Mack purchased Danny Friend from Kansas City for $500 to replace Swaim. Meanwhile, Indianapolis lost three straight in Milwaukee Park. Buffalo was next in, and by winning the opener on May 26, 8 to 6, the Brewers went into first place with a 16 and 11 record. The Brewers then beat the Bisons twice more to sweep the series in front of big crowds. The homestand ended with Columbus winning two of three from the Brewers. Adolphus Vollendorf was loaned to Rockford of the Western Association, as he was not seeing much action with Milwaukee, compiling a 2 and 1 record. In mid–June the Western Association folded and Vollendorf went on loan to New Haven. The Brewers' surge from last to first was accomplished by good hitting and defense. They led the Western in hitting with a .287 average, Weaver the highest at .386. The team was second in runs scored with 163. Milwaukee was also tied with Columbus for the honors in fielding.

Bert Husting — A college pitcher who had success in Milwaukee, then was involved in a contract dispute with the aborted American Association and American League. He would later be a U.S. District Attorney in Milwaukee.

On June 1 the Brewers traveled to Buffalo for the first time and dropped three to fall into third place. On Sunday the club was to play in Detroit, but the Wayne County sheriff refused to allow the game. Hart won the following day to put the Brewers in a tie for first place with Minneapolis. On to Indianapolis, the Hoosiers won three straight, one a no-hitter for Doc Newton, to drop the Brewers down to sixth in the tight Western race with a 20 and 19 record. Hart split a finger and was out for over a week. Rettger and Reidy pitched every other day — with Friend breaking the rotation once with his first victory — as the Brewers lost two of three in Columbus and then split four in St. Paul. Friend was not in the rotation because he had been arrested in Columbus for stabbing a hack driver. Mack suspended and fined him all the salary due him. Friend's case was soon dismissed for lack of prosecution and he was re-instated to the team after signing a temperance clause.

Returning home, Mack used a new pitcher, Bert Husting. Husting had played semi-professional ball with the Mayville team, the Kewannees, and then in Fond du Lac (all in central Wisconsin), doing splendid work. He then attended the University of Wisconsin and played on the varsity team; he also played halfback for the football team. Husting had signed with Mack in the winter, with the stipulation he would come to the Brewers after school in June. Husting beat the Millers, but Reidy and Rettger lost. Then in Minneapolis the Brewers lost three of five to the Millers and Saints. The Brewers' hitting was simply terrible and Mack released second baseman Bill Hallman in late June for his lack of hitting, as he was batting only .209. Fred Barnes took his place in the field. The press also wanted Stafford's head, as his hitting had fallen off. The Brewers' next nine games were against Kansas City, with Milwaukee winning only three. The *Sporting Life* correspondent, H.H. Cohn, hinted of something sinister in his July 1, 1899, column:

> Commencing with June 1 and ending June 24 inclusive, 19 games have been played, of these 13 were lost and seven of them were shut-outs. Is not that the worst you have ever heard? And to what is this to be ascribed? To nothing but weak hitting. This is said to be due, according to rumor, to various causes. Which is the correct or real cause I care not to investigate or go further into the matter, as that is the business of the management, and the sooner they get at the bottom of it the better for them. The attendance has fallen off 50 per cent, and is going to fall off more yet, unless the change comes soon, and it is to be hoped that the management has discernment enough to see that for themselves.

It was now July 4 and Minneapolis led the Western League with a 36 and 25 record; Indianapolis was second with a record of 33 and 26, followed by Columbus (32 and 27), Detroit (30 and 29), St. Paul (29 and 31), Milwaukee (29 and 34), Kansas City (28 and 34) and Buffalo (24 and 35). The *Sentinel* was attacking the Brewer management for not changing faces as the team continued to lose games. Mack had brought in one new face, Charles Chech, a pitcher from the University of Wisconsin who could also play the infield. As the Buffalo Bisons took two of three from the Brewers, Mack made some more changes. First he purchased Harry Smith, a catcher from Wilkes-Barre, Pennsylvania, of the Atlantic League for $800. Mack then sold Danny Friend to Minneapolis for $350. Friend had a 2 and 5 record with Milwaukee. Smith, however, was ill and never reported. The press suspected Louisville, which was looking for a young catcher, of tampering with him. It was soon found, however, that Louisville offered to purchase Smith's release, but he thought he was too ill to play anywhere. Meanwhile, the Brewers took two of three from Columbus and split two with Indianapolis. Mack then secured the services of George "Texas" Brady, late of the Austin club, who played center field in two games before getting his release. The homestand ended with the Tigers taking three from the Brewers. The Milwaukee club was in need of some hitting. Waldron and Weaver were hitting well, at .333 and .324, but Stafford and Speer were under .240. Gray was at .282, Shoch .274, Barnes and Nicol in the .260s. Nicol's play had fallen off and it was thought a new center fielder should be secured. The same situation was seen at second base, where Barnes played hard, but just was out of position.

The Western League had a new franchise on July 17. Tom Loftus finally gave in to the small crowds in Columbus and transferred to Grand Rapids. Grand Rapids, in the Interstate League, transferred to the Ohio city. Columbus transferred with a record of 36 and 35.

The Brewers traveled east to Detroit to split two games with the Tigers. There was then a single-game loss in Indianapolis. On to Grand Rapids, the Brewers won two of three and picked up two new players. Richardson, a catcher and second baseman, was secured from Austin of the Texas League. Bill Congolton was secured from Hamilton of the Canadian League to play center field. The Brewers then went to Buffalo, where they swept a doubleheader and lost a Sunday game. After this July 30 game, the players of both clubs were taken to the police station and charged with violation of Sunday laws. President Franklin put $200 up for each player, although it was not necessary for the Brewer players to stay in town. This was the fourth time the Buffalo players and visitors had been arrested for playing on Sunday; the three previous times they were acquitted by juries the following week. This game was no exception. Arrests were also made for playing on Sunday during the year in Detroit and Indianapolis.

The Brewers then returned home with another new face. Rooney Viox, a second baseman, had been purchased from Kansas City. He had hit .291 with the Blues, but was playing in Reading because of a salary dispute with Manning. Richardson was loaned to Hamilton by Mack to make room. Milwaukee took two of three from St. Paul, and then lost three to Minneapolis. Mack continued changing faces, releasing Will Hart and signing Melville Smith, an infielder from Purdue University, who also had played with some of the best semi-professional teams in Ohio. Hart was 6 and 15 when released. The Brewers then returned the trip to Minnesota, splitting six games.

After a series of exhibitions around the state with local teams, the Brewers returned home for their final homestand. Melville Smith finally arrived, played one game at first base, and went back to college. The team lost three of four to first-place Indianapolis and two of three to Detroit, causing the *St. Paul Dispatch* to comment "that a few old weeds in Connie Mack's garden have gone to seed and should be thrown over the back fence."[68] Mack purchased Charles Atherton from Washington for $400 to play second base. Atherton had hit only .248 in 65 games with the Senators at third base. After Milwaukee won two of three from Grand Rapids, George Shoch was released, many believed to cut expenses. Buffalo was next in and Mack found himself temporarily without a shortstop. Shoch was gone and Viox was injured, so Mack signed Ed Holly of the Manistee (Michigan) club to fill in for one game. Milwaukee won that day but lost a doubleheader to the Bisons the next day with Viox at shortstop.

Milwaukee went traveling for the final two weeks of the season, playing 15 games in eleven days, including six doubleheaders. In Detroit Gray came up with a lame shoulder and Barnes finished the year at third. The Tigers lost three of five to the Brewers. In Grand Rapids Milwaukee won two of three. In the first game Waldron became ill in the seventh inning. Speer went to right field and Connie Mack went behind the plate, playing in his first game since 1897. The Brewers then lost three in Buffalo and split four in Indianapolis to finish the 1899 season. Indianapolis clinched its third Western League championship in the league's six-year history with the two wins over the Brewers.

Indianapolis	75	47	.615	St. Paul	57	69	.452
Minneapolis	76	50	.603	Milwaukee	56	68	.452
Detroit	64	61	.512	Kansas City	53	70	.431
Grand Rapids	63	62	.504	Buffalo	53	70	.431

The Brewers had their worst finish by far in three years. Although Reidy (17 and 13), Husting (19 and 8) and Rettger (15 and 14; George also won a suit of clothes from the Hirsch-Silverstone Company as the most popular player in Milwaukee for the year) finished with winning records, the other pitchers were way off. Swaim had been 0 and 5, Hart 6 and 14, Friend 2 and 5, and Chech 4 and 9. The team's hitting improved at the end to a .297 average, third in the Western. Waldron led with a .332 norm, followed by Weaver at .329, Atherton .324, Congolton .297, Shoch .285, Speer .276, Gray .272, Viox .246, Nicol .243, Barnes .242 and Stafford .238. The club was first in fielding with a .940 average. Mack defended himself by saying, "Yet in spite of the fact that they [the Brewers] have been playing rotten ball the greater part of the season, money would not buy players who could put up a better game."[69] Secretary Gross thought Milwaukee's poor showing was just bad luck. The press and fans clamored for new faces again after the disastrous season. The *Sporting News* correspondent from Milwaukee wrote this after the 1899 season:

> This is too good a baseball town to be represented by such a team and if Mr. Quinn can put in a winner here he is sure to find it a paying investment. It looks as though the present team were run for revenue and revenue only. Of course, base ball is a business; still the public want something in return for their money and the moment the directors of the club make it evident to the public that they are in it for the coin regardless of the position of the team then that is the time the public sours on them. When the team here was handled by Mr. Quinn, he spared no expense to strengthen a weak spot and the people appreciated the fact that he was doing his best to give them a good team and they gave it their support. The popular idea is that the Brewers are run on a very cheap basis.[70]

Ban Johnson said attendance had fallen off in the Western, although only Buffalo appeared to lose money. Kansas City was said to have made $4,000 to $6,000 with a last-place team. Detroit profits were about $4,500. Others were not recorded. The *Sporting Life* Western League editor was not optimistic about the future of the league. Citing some of the teams in larger cities, including Milwaukee, did not make a good run at the pennant, the paper wrote on November 11, 1899, "Under such disappointing conditions in four of the largest cities of the league it was only natural that the season should prove a financial disappointment also. It is claimed that none of the clubs lost money. While this may be true, it is quite certain not more than three out of the eight clubs can show more than a very mediocre profit on the season and in four of the cities—Milwaukee, Buffalo, St. Paul and Grand Rapids—the outlook for next season is anything but reassuring. Only skillful and conservative handling saved the League from shipwreck this season." However, the Western was now getting ready for a big step in 1900.

✳ ✳ ✳

While Connie Mack's Brewers continued to prosper, the local ball players kept up their usual existence. The first efforts to reorganize the City League for 1897 began in January of that year, with the league to consist of the Quin, Matthews, Otto and Racine clubs. In February it was decided to expand, adding Sheboygan and Kenosha or Manitowac. Sheboygan, however, soon joined the Northern Wisconsin League and Manitowac became part of the Wisconsin State League. The *Evening Wisconsin* urged the City League to take in Waukesha, Kenosha and Racine, along with three local clubs, stating, "It is a well known fact that six local clubs forming the City League cannot make money as the people here do not appreciate amateur ball to any great extent."[71] As March rolled in, only Racine was counted in the league. Later that month Racine dropped out and it looked doubtful the league would organize, as only one park in Milwaukee was suitable for play. To organize the league for play, the Razalls replaced the Quins and the Phoenix club recruited. On April 1, 1897, the City League clubs (Razalls, Matthews, Ottos, Phoenix) elected Frank Ricker, owner of a saloon at 9th and Walnut, as president, Henry Otto as treasurer, and A.J. Somor secretary. Milwaukee Park was rented from the Brewers for $5 a Sunday when the Western League club was on the road. It was decided to play only seven innings "as long games are considered too great a tax upon the players who get but little training and preparation for the severe work!"[72] The City League opened play Sunday, May 16, with the Razalls beating the Ottos and the Matthews club beating the Phoenix at Milwaukee Park. In between playing out-of-town clubs, the league finished a very short schedule five months later, with the Razalls taking first place with a 4 and 2 record. Will Rily of the Matthews club led the hitters with a .440 average in the eight games he played.

Another league to form in 1897 was the Junior League, consisting of the Standards, Palmers, Bay Views and Crescents. Unfortunately, no final standings are available for this league. A third was the Third Ward Baseball League, consisting of the Red Caps, Ivy Boys, Louisville Stars and Union Athletics. Another interesting feature was the resumption of the Police-Fire baseball game. Before 4,000 at Milwaukee Park, the fire eaters burned the crime fighters 43 to 2. The $3,500 netted by the game was given to Chief Janssen for entertainment of the visiting chiefs of police at their convention the next spring.

The year 1898 was not a good one in local baseball circles. Although many amateur clubs continued to play all over the city, organized leagues fell on hard times. The City League opened the season with four clubs—the Razalls, Matthews, White Diamonds and Phoenix. William Sasson was the president this year. A schedule was drawn up, with each club playing 15 games, starting April 24 and ending in October, and the double umpire system was adopted. The City League opened on schedule with the White Diamonds beating the Razalls 22 to 10 on the south side, and the Matthews defeating the Phoenix 14 to 6. By late May the league was going to pieces. Two reasons were cited. The first was a loss of a large number of players in the league. The White Diamonds, for example, lost seven players. Second was the failure of the games on the south side. Large crowds witnessed the games, but with no fences or other facilities, they saw the game for nothing. In June the Skidmores replaced the Matthews, but then the Razalls dropped out and the league folded, with the Phoenix club claiming the championship.

One club to make it in 1898 was the Milwaukee Athletic Club. Although playing only match games as clubs did in the 1860s and '70s, the M.A.C. had control of Milwaukee Park when the Brewers were away and built a clubhouse for its members at the park with 40 lockers and a shower. M.A.C. beat such clubs as the East Side High School, St. John's Military Academy, Kenosha, Concordia College and Chicago Athletic Association. In the team's loss to the Brewers, the *Daily News* was not impressed with the Milwaukee Athletic Club. On August 11, 1898, the paper wrote M.A.C. "appeared to have glass arms and they gave a peachy exhibition of how not to throw to the bases." One other club, the Seniors, claimed the 18-year-old championship by a victory over the Lake Parks 9 to 8 in September.

Amateur ball was still very popular in 1899, but only the City League had organized play. On April 11 the City League organized with three clubs—the Razalls, Skidmores and Phoenix clubs. The Pabst club was the candidate for the fourth team. A week later the league was reorganized with the Munzingers and South Milwaukees joining the Razalls and Skidmores. The South Milwaukees were chosen as they had enclosed grounds and were allowed to play all their games at home, giving the visiting clubs a guarantee for each game. The other grounds for the City League were those at Milwaukee Park when the Brewers were not at home. Playing on Sundays, the league opened on May 7 with the Munzingers defeating the Skidmores 8 to 3. The Munzingers dominated the season, winning their first five games, and finished in September with an 8 and 1 record. The Skidmores and South Milwaukees were 5 and 5, and the Razalls only 1 and 8. Munch of the Munzingers led the City League with a .500 batting average, followed by Kern of the South Milwaukees at .476. In all, seven players hit over .400. Again the City League made no money and its future was dim. Talk was an Inter-City League would be formed for 1900, with six to eight clubs from Milwaukee, Racine, Port Washington and Sheboygan in it. Nothing organized in 1900, and organized amateur baseball died in the city for a while.

* * *

The Western League's future was changed drastically by events that took place in the fall of 1899. As early as May, dispatches out of New York reported a new American Association was being organized quietly and could include at least three Western League cities, among them Milwaukee. Brewer president Matthew Killilea stated he had no intention of leaving the Western League, but it was discovered the association was going to place a second club in Milwaukee. The new association was approaching Harry D. Quin, who still owned Athletic Park at 8th and Chambers. The *Sentinel* thought at this time a new club would meet "with a hard frost from the public."[73] Quin quickly denied he wanted to re-enter baseball. The plan for the American Association came out of St. Louis and was being promoted principally by Chris Von der Ahe, who had just lost his National League franchise, George Schaefer, a St. Louis promoter, and Albert Spink of the *St. Louis Dispatch*. In August a secret meeting was held in Chicago, and Schaefer claimed sixteen clubs applied.

On September 17 the American Association promoters met in Chicago. Ten cities were represented. Among those present were Cap Anson (Chicago), Von der Ahe (St. Louis), Mike Scanlon (Washington), Frank Buckley (New York), Frank Hough (Philadelphia), and Harry Quin and Charles S. Havenor (Milwaukee). (Havenor was owner of the Davidson Hotel, and the alderman of Milwaukee's 4th Ward, at that time running from the Milwaukee River west to 13th Street and the Menomonee River north to Kilbourn Avenue. It was also reported in the *Sporting Life* that Robert W. Maguire, now the auditor of the Sante Fe Railroad, would be a silent partner in the club.) Representatives from Detroit, Baltimore, Cleveland and Louisville were unidentified. Ban Johnson was reportedly offered the presidency at $10,000 a year, but refused. Anson also declined the job. Harry Quin was elected temporary president. The platform of the new association would be "honest competition, no syndicate baseball, no reserve rule, to respect all contracts and popular prices."[74] This, of course, was the platform of all new leagues since 1882 that had tried to fight the National League. The following day the association meeting adjourned with no concrete plans, but announced clubs would be in St. Louis, Chicago, Milwaukee and Detroit or Buffalo in the west; New York, Washington, Philadelphia and Baltimore or Boston in the east. The association's actual strength was not known, but Schaefer did control the park in St. Louis and Milwaukee's Quin had Athletic Park. New York, Philadelphia and Washington claimed to have parks. If Baltimore was admitted, John McGraw and Wilbert Robinson were to head the club. Stallings would reportedly head Detroit.

Opinions differed on the American Association. John T. Brush said no city in the country could support two clubs. Connie Mack thought the time was right for a new major league, but did not think Milwaukee could support two teams. Matthew Killilea agreed, but did not think much of the American Association idea. The *Evening Wisconsin* agreed with Mack, believing two clubs would not last half a season "unless they had a barrel of money to drop."[75] Havenor was quoted in the *Sporting News* as saying, "We will have no opposition at Milwaukee next year. The Western League team will simply withdraw and place us in possession of the field."⁷⁶ The alderman told the local press how the Milwaukee club would be run.

> We are not out to fight the Western or any other baseball organization. We are in this as a business proposition and there is no money in fighting. We will have a baseball team in Milwaukee and we will endeavor to make it a good one.... We are not in it for health nor for glory, but for money. We have health and we do not wish glory. We have seen what the public thinks of baseball players who are willing to work on small salaries. If any person thinks that good pitchers, for instance, can be secured for $85 or $100 a month, it is a mistake. We expect to get the best available men and we expect to pay enough for them to make it an inducement for them to play the best kind of ball for us. For my part, the business will be run just as I run my business. I have no fight with the tailor up street, nor the tailor down street, but I am trying to build up my business in a legitimate way. That is what we will do with baseball.⁷⁷

Havenor said he was willing put $10,000 in the new club.

Frank Hough, sporting editor of the *Philadelphia Inquirer* and secretary of the association, claimed the association was backed in most cities by capitalists who had anywhere from $200,000 to $300,000 — more than most National League magnates could boast of. It was reported St. Louis breweries were backing Van der Ahe, and the Schoenhofer Brewing Company was backing Anson in Chicago. National and Western league owners claimed not to be concerned over the American Association, but the *St. Louis Republic* disagreed.

> Whatever the meeting amounts to, it is going to create considerable of a stir in baseball circles and is likely to cause the National League a good deal of worrying. That baseball has not been conducted properly by the National League is admitted by all the minor league magnates. The National League magnates have lost sight of the sport. The decadence of the National League has had a direct effect upon the minor leagues, and these organizations are ripe for rebellion. The draft rule has been heavy upon them. They have reaped no advantage, but have been forced to aid the big league all the time. If the new organization is formed along lines which further the best interests of the sport of playing, they are ready and willing to listen. They are even predisposed to favor such principles, but they are not ready to lose money. They have had hard enough times making the Western League a success to take any chances.⁷⁸

James Hart of Chicago stated the National League would probably stay at twelve clubs to stop the association from taking any dropped cities and getting players, showing the league was indeed concerned. When Quin announced three prominent Detroit businessmen put up a $10,000 bond to join the association, Van der Beck became concerned. The press reported the citizens of Detroit did not like Van der Beck's "public be d—d attitude,"⁷⁹ and would take to the association. Publicly Van der Beck said he took no stock in the new club, doubting if any Detroit men were in it, but sold three of his better players and word was out he was about to give up the fight.

Ban Johnson saw the American Association challenge to the National League in a different light. He again called for a higher draft price for his players. John Brush turned around on drafting, saying he agreed and a player should stay in the minors to mature. Johnson saw the National League would be willing to make concessions to his Western to stop the challenge, so he went ahead and asked Jim Hart for permission to move into Chicago. Hart thought a Western club in Chicago might stop the association there, so he gave his consent to Johnson.

Ban Johnson made the next move at the Western meeting on October 11, 1899, in Chicago. The Western League changed its name to the American League by a unanimous vote. Matt Killilea initially voted against this, but when he saw he stood alone, he went with the name change. The *Sporting Life* of October 21, 1899, wrote, "This shrewd and unexpected move is designed to deprive the proposed new rival American Association of the benefits of a traditional title, without infringing upon the League's rights in the matter: to remove the ex-Western League from its hampering sectional basis, and to place it in position to become national known." However, Milwaukee's correspondent to the *Sporting Life*, H.H. Cohen, thought "what the magnates intend to gain by this move it is hard to see, and in my opinion they lay themselves open to the criticism of the public, who may charge them with attempting to steal the new League's title. However, in adopting this name they in no way injured that organization."[80] The new American League decided to go back to a 140-game schedule and petition the National League for a change to a $1,000 draft price and a minimum of two years for a player in a minor league. Nothing was set on a circuit change, but word was out Tom Loftus would transfer his Grand Rapids club to Chicago, and Charles Comiskey would shift his St. Paul club to Cleveland or Toronto. Both Grand Rapids and St. Paul were poor drawing cards. Comiskey received only $7.79 back from the Western fund and Loftus' share was only $19. Before making any moves, the American League was waiting for the National League to drop some clubs, as they were expected to do.

Outwardly the American Association showed little worry. Harry Quin said the Western League changing names meant the public now knew the two leagues were afraid of his association. He said the new American Association would have $120,000 in the treasury before the season started, and the western section would consist of Detroit, Milwaukee, St. Louis and Chicago. Adrian Anson, who Quin said was "the heart and soul of the new association,"[81] claimed to have Bill Lange as his captain, plus a pitcher and catcher signed. In an interview in the *Sporting News* of October 21, 1899, Quin said his association would not try to outdo the National League in salaries, but would pay "good, fair wages." He did say his association could pay much better salaries than the Western or Eastern leagues, "but we will not start a war of prices, as that would be the most foolish move imaginable." Locally, Quin said that in Milwaukee Troop A First Cavalry, which had been using Athletic Park as a drill ground, would be asked to vacate in order for the new club to move in. It was also reported Quin was negotiating with Hughey Jennings of Baltimore to manage here. In the East, Scanlon reported Washington was in fine shape. Tom O'Rourke, a New York boxing promoter, took over the New York franchise. Boston supposedly had grounds secured, but backers would not be named. As little news of the new association came out and Quin stopped talking, Killilea said it had died. But it had not.

Meanwhile, the American League was having trouble in Chicago. Ban Johnson said he had not given up all hope of entering the Windy City with National League permission. Jim Hart wanted the Americans to play in his park on the west side when his club was on the road, but Johnson wanted to locate on the south side. The American League president said that if at all possible his league would enter Chicago, meaning another baseball war. Then it was reported Tom Loftus would accept the Chicago National League management and move his Grand Rapids club to Chicago under George Tebeau. Johnson announced the American League would enter Chicago and Charles Comiskey would head the franchise, fearing Loftus might turn it into a National League farm for his Colts. Johnson took the position that there was nothing in the National Agreement stopping him; he said it only covered two clubs in the same league. Hart disagreed. In Indianapolis on November 25, William Watkins, former manager of the Hoosiers, purchased that club for between $10,000 and $15,000 from John T. Brush and a few minor stockholders. Indianapolis had been in turmoil for a while. After the close of the 1899 season, it was reported Golt was asked to retire by Brush and let Watkins take over, although Golt denied it at the time. Then in October the club lost its grounds to the local street railway company.

When Watkins did take over — most believed with Brush's backing — he leased new grounds. Louisville also wanted in the American League. E.P. Rucker of the city wanted to buy Grand Rapids and transfer it. Another report said Minneapolis would be dropped from the American League and Louisville added. Even though Minneapolis had led the old Western in attendance, with St. Paul gone it was now isolated from the rest of the league.

The American Association was not dead, planning to invade at least five National League cities, and the National League was still having internal problems. Barney Dreyfuss of Louisville sold fourteen players to Pittsburgh for $25,000, using the money to buy enough stock in the Pirates to get him elected president of that club. Louisville was left for dead. On December 15 the National League met. Not wanting to have a war with the American League, it upped the draft price to $1,000 a player and made some other concessions. No decision on circuit reduction was made, although a committee was formed to study it. The American Association offered to buy the Baltimore and Washington franchises and players from the league for $80,000. The National League, of course, was not interested. On Christmas Eve the *Chicago Tribune* reported the National League was trying to sell its four weak franchises to minor leagues. Baltimore and Washington were offered to the Eastern League, Louisville and Cleveland to the Western. (The National League still carefully referred to the American League as the Western League, apparently to give it a minor sound.) As a concession to the minors they would not be asked to pay cash for the franchises, but were offered on a percentage plan. Few thought the American League would accept.

Indeed the American League did not accept. Instead, the American League further prepared for a war. At a meeting in Chicago on New Year's Eve it was reported a majority of American League owners decided to break from the National Agreement. It was reported the Americans would go into Chicago and St. Louis in the West, and Boston and Philadelphia in the East. New York was also considered. The proposed circuit would be Chicago, St. Louis, Milwaukee, Detroit, Boston, Philadelphia, Buffalo, and New York or Baltimore. The Americans went so far as to stay with the Reach ball (they had earlier decided to use Spalding's ball), apparently as a slap to the Chicago club. Ban Johnson denied his league had any intention of leaving the National Agreement. Jim Hart thought it only a bluff and said he would welcome a war with the Americans to settle the situation. The *Chicago Chronicle* reported the National League and American Association were thinking of forming a new National Agreement and leaving out the American League, but this story was doubtful. Anson did, however, hint that Andrew Freedman, owner of the New York Giants, would let his association have Manhattan Field, which the National League club owned. Freedman was after other league owners to help support his club and believed this threat would bring them around.

The American Association had been quiet of late. But in late January, it made news when it was announced a group of capitalists had subscribed $20,000 in Baltimore to form an association club, with John McGraw at the helm. It had also secured the grounds of the National League Orioles for $3,500. All was not rosy, however. Anson said that unless the association entered New York, he would not put money in a club. On January 30 the American Association met in Philadelphia and admitted seven clubs: Boston, Philadelphia, Baltimore, Chicago, Detroit, Milwaukee and St. Louis. Providence was given the open spot days later. On February 2 Boston, Baltimore, Milwaukee, Detroit, Chicago and St. Louis signed the American Association agreement, each furnishing a $1,200 bond. Philadelphia could not find backers, with two groups having declined. Providence had decided not to join, instead staying in the Eastern League. Within days, however, Philadelphia did sign the agreement. All the clubs claimed to have at least $20,000 in backing as well as grounds or an option on grounds. Quin said of his association, "We are not seeking cheap notoriety nor are we bluffing. Our new association will be run on business lines and we will try our level best to purify baseball of the evils that have been fostered by the National League. All we ask is a fair deal from the press and the public and in return we will endeavor to keep faith and give them their money's worth."[82]

The National League took steps to stop the association's headway. It announced it would start a minor league farm system, calling it the American Association, with clubs in Chicago, St. Louis, Philadelphia and Boston, charging 25 cents admission. The purpose was to have a counter attraction in town whenever the association played. Secretary Gross of Milwaukee thought the National League's farm system would really hurt the American Association. The league could afford to lose about $20,000 on each club, but the association could not afford to lose any money. The National League also announced it planned to challenge the American Association on the use of the name, saying it had bought the rights to that name in the 1891 merger with the old American Association. Baltimore then filed an injunction to prevent the association from using Union Park. The American Association countered to some extent by changing its name to the New American Association. On February 13 the association met in Chicago and formally organized with Chicago, St. Louis, Milwaukee, Boston, Philadelphia, Baltimore and Louisville as members. Adrian Anson was elected permanent president, Quin claiming he positively declared he would not accept any office. The New American Association policy was to be no reserve rule, no salary limits, an equal division of gate receipts, and a varying admission fee. Citing alleged internal fighting, the *Chicago Times-Herald* reported "evidences are up that the league will never see daylight despite the grandiloquent proclamation of the promoters."[83] Two days later, the association died for all practical purposes. The Philadelphia promoters backed out, as they could not secure adequate grounds. Anson and McGraw had agreed if Philadelphia did not post its money, they too would drop out. A few days later Philadelphia decided to deposit the money. The delegates from five association cities called for Anson to call a meeting or they would oust him, but Anson declined and the New American Association died.

The *Daily News* took a very sober view of the National Agreement, or trust baseball, and the American Association.

> The quality of ball provided by the teams in the trust has gradually fallen off season by season, until last year not four cities in the twenty comprising the two more important associations [National and Western] were witnessing games that were even up to amateur standard. The world of fans fretted and fumed under the parsimonious methods of the magnates who were running the game for the money there was in it and regardless of the quality of game provided; but patrons were obliged to accept the game as it was laid before them or do without. In this predicament they reluctantly continued to spend their money in support of the trust. The American Association project, however, has revealed to the trust managers that the public is against them; that its sympathies will be with any organization that promises to relieve them from the clutch of the trust. Therefore, fail or succeed, the American Association has fulfilled a mission.[84]

With the American Association threat gone, Jim Hart would not let the American League enter any part of Chicago. Ban Johnson said Hart had promised him in October his league could enter Chicago and he would. The American League had been asked to go into Chicago during the association threat to stop that new league. "It was a case of acting hastily, for that invitation is the pinion which is now impelling the steel shaft of the American League,"[85] the *Sentinel* wrote. Hart said it was a free country, but Johnson would be violating the National Agreement. Cleveland then entered the picture. The American

League had issued an ultimatum to Tom Loftus, requesting him to give up his Grand Rapids franchise because of his ties with the Chicago club. Loftus agreed, and the American League bought him out. The Americans entered Cleveland with Charles Somers, a wealthy coal dealer, and J.C. Kilfoyle as the owners; the team was made up of the Grand Rapids players of 1899. Frank Robison was determined not to lease his grounds in Cleveland to Somers if the Americans entered Chicago. Somers purchased other grounds.

The National League prepared for war. It bought out four franchises—Louisville, Cleveland, Baltimore and Washington—to again become an eight-team circuit. The 12-club league still existed legally for two more years. John Brush said the National League controlled all properties of these cities "that have asked not to be included in the schedule for two years."[86] Reports then were about that the National League would make an American Association farm league consisting of Cleveland, Detroit, Chicago and Milwaukee to fight the American League. It was soon reported this association would expand to eight clubs, but Johnson called it a bluff. Comiskey went ahead and filed articles of incorporation for the Chicago club with a capital stock of $30,000.

The key to ending the baseball war was made in Cleveland. The Cleveland team was so bad they transferred all their home games out of town in July, as nearly all other National League clubs refused to travel there because of low attendance. According to a *Sporting Life* article on July 1, 1899, gate receipts averaged under $25 a day. Cleveland ended the 1899 season with a 20 and 134 record. Robison wanted $15,000 for the Cleveland park, but the Americans were only willing to pay $10,000. In late March Johnson reached agreement with Robison, and Charles Somers paid $10,000 for a five-year lease on the park. Johnson also gave Hart the right to select two American League players, which he did in August. War was avoided as Johnson also promised not to encroach any longer on National League territory, adopt a non-conflicting schedule when possible, and not to make use of the name Chicago in advertising Comiskey's team.

The American League had one other internal change. George Van der Beck was forced to put his Detroit club on the market. He was going through a divorce and the ball park, franchise and players were ordered seized and sold by the courts to pay for alimony and attorneys fees in January. An auction was ordered, but Van der Beck received a stay. It came out in court that Frank Navin had offered him $12,000. James Burns had offered $20,000 for the franchise in September, but Van der Beck wanted $50,000. Navin wanted to put Detroit in the American Association, which was still alive at the time. In February Mrs. Van der Beck became owner of the club, paying $9,500 at the auction. George appealed his case to the Michigan Supreme Court and complied with a court order to post $9,000 bond of payment of his alimony. It was thought he might get the club back. Ban Johnson said unless things were straightened out soon, the Detroit franchise would be forfeited and placed in Louisville. James Burns and George Stallings purchased the franchise from Mrs. Van der Beck for $12,000, paying Van der Beck $2,500 for his equity.

The American League, which put the American Eagle on its passes and letterheads, had the following franchises and owners for 1900: Buffalo (James Franklin), Indianapolis (William Watkins), Cleveland (Charles Somers and John C. Kilfoyle), Detroit (James Burns and George Stallings), Chicago (Charles Comiskey), Milwaukee (Matthew Killilea), Minneapolis (Clarence Saulpaugh) and Kansas City (James Manning). The American League had a total population base of about 4,000,000: Milwaukee—300,000; Chicago—2,000,000; Detroit—300,000; Cleveland—350,000; Buffalo—400,000; Indianapolis—200,000; Kansas City—250,000; Minneapolis (including St. Paul)—350,000.

The Milwaukee Brewers held their annual meeting on November 28, 1899, re-electing their officers and rehiring Connie Mack. Instead of declaring a dividend, the money was kept in the treasury to purchase new players. Mack immediately began to revamp the Brewers. Right after the 1899 season, Ed Holly from Manistee, Hemphill from the Canadian League and William Conroy, a shortstop from Cortland of the New York League, were secured. Bill Reidy was sold to Brooklyn for $1,000. Rooney Viox was released. Jimmy Burke was reacquired from Rochester, where he had played in 1899, but was quickly drafted by St. Louis. Later in October Charles Atherton and Kid Speer were traded to Buffalo for Jim Garry, an outfielder, and Cy Diggins, a catcher, in separate deals. In November, Milwaukee secured Fred Raymer, a second baseman who had played with Kansas City in 1899 until he retired in July to accept a government job in Topeka. Conroy and Harry Smith, who had been ill all of 1899, were signed in November. Erving Waldron was selected by Louisville during the drafting period, but soon was returned, as was Jimmy Burke from St. Louis.

In January, Mack claimed five players from the New York State League (Conroy also had previously been taken from this league). This almost ruined the league. This practice of claiming so many players was condemned by the *Sporting News* with a vigorous editorial, reading in part:

> If a player refuses to accept the terms offered him he is virtually blacklisted by other Western League (now American) clubs and must look elsewhere for an engagement. No club should be allowed this extraordinary privilege without restrictions. If, at the expiration of three days, an agreement as to salary is not arrived at with the player, who is offered less than the limit—$200 a month—other clubs should have the right to do business with him. If the claiming club's offer of $200 a month is refused, then no injustice is done the player in keeping him on the claim list. This prospective property in a player is something not recognized by the clubs in other leagues.[87]

Of the five players only two, Bill Hallman and Bill Gilbert, were in the Brewers' plans. These two were technically purchased from Louisville, which had drafted the two in the fall. Killilea denied Mack had actually claimed the players, but there appeared to be ample evidence that he had. Some believed, however, the New York State League had the Brewers covering the players to protect them from the draft. The *Daily News*, acknowledging that the American Association was still alive, commented, "If this is the kind of team the American League people think of placing in opposition ... local patrons will hardly support it."[88] Mack then purchased Willie Clark, a first baseman, from Pittsburgh. Again from Pittsburgh, Mack purchased Pete Dowling, a pitcher who had been 13 and 17 with the Pirates in 1899. Bill Congolton was sold to Wheeling. A week later Mack obtained Tully Sparks, also from Pittsburgh, who had an 8 and 6 record the previous season.

Mack had sent out contracts, but they were slow coming back. With the American Association still threatening, players were waiting to see what happened. One member of the team said he had been offered a $200 increase to sign right away but refused. Once the association died, things changed. Fred Barnes, for example, was not even offered a contract, released to the Rome club of the New York State League, and eventually became a free agent. The contracts sent to Nicol, Weaver, Gray and Stafford had large pay cuts in them, and Mack did not expect these players to sign. By the end of the first week of March, all Mack's pitchers were signed: Rettger, Sparks, McDonald, Reidy (back from Brooklyn) and Dowling. Bert Husting and Charlie Chech again went to college and would not be expected until June.

On March 2 Mack continued securing new players by obtaining George Yeager. He had caught sparingly in Boston from 1896–1899 before being farmed to Worcester. Also secured was George Wheeler, a pitcher who had won 21 and lost 20 in four years in Philadelphia, but had pitched with the Rome club in 1899. Later in March Henry Reitz, a 32-year-old National League veteran second baseman, was purchased from Pittsburgh, reportedly for $500 and the privilege to take Harry Smith after the season or $500 to reacquire Reitz. He had played only 34 games in 1899 due to an injury, but held a .292 bating average in seven National League seasons. Then John Anderson and Dave Fultz were purchased from Brooklyn for $800 each. Anderson, an outfielder, was a prize catch. In six National League seasons the 26-year-old had a .298 average. Fultz, who had played only two years and 78 games in the National League, claimed Brooklyn illegally sold him. The second baseman claimed to have no reserve in his contract, having been illegally sold to Brooklyn in 1899, meaning that club could not trade him. Killilea denied this. It was learned Fultz wanted more money, but his contract called for more than he was making in the National League. Fultz signed later in April for Milwaukee's price. Anderson also signed in April after initially balking because of a $75 a month cut in pay. Cy Diggins and Bob Stafford were released to Cleveland in accordance with an American League agreement that all the clubs would give Cleveland some players to bolster the new club.

The Brewers of 1900 began spring training in Richmond, Indiana, on April 1. Mack had a large number of players still on his club — twenty-three. After a week of practice his team beat Springfield, lost to Dayton and beat Dayton. Mack then cut the roster by releasing Billy Gray, Bill Gilbert, George Nicol, and William Weaver. The latter two had been with the Brewers since 1895, the longest continuing service with the club. The team played a few more exhibition games before the season was to begin. Mack's club was down to size and consisted of only three players who had played with the Brewers in 1899 — Rettger, Reidy and Waldron. The team was Dowling, Rettger, Sparks, Reidy, Wheeler and McDonald — pitchers; Clark — first base; Fultz, Raymer and Reitz — second base; Conroy — shortstop; Burke — third base; Smith and Yeager — catchers; Anderson, Garry, Hallman and Waldron — outfielders. Mack said he had spent more than $5,000 on players that spring, and it is very doubtful he was within the American League $200-per-man salary limit with all his ex–National Leaguers.

The American League met on April 12 and wrote up a 140-game schedule, beginning on April 19. Many felt this was too soon, but it stood. Ban Johnson's salary was raised $1,000 for the fine work he had done that winter. It was thought the American League on the whole would be as strong as the 12-club National League circuit of 1899 had been. Milwaukee and Minneapolis were the strongest of the circuit, locals believed, and of course, Cincinnati would help out Indianapolis.

With bad weather in Chicago, the Brewers' American League opener was postponed two days. It was proposed to transfer the opener to Milwaukee, but Johnson insisted the game be played in Chicago. On Saturday, April 21, 1900, before 4,500 in Chicago's new south side stadium, the Brewers won 5 to 4 in ten innings.

MILWAUKEE		AB	R	H	E	CHICAGO		AB	R	H	E
Waldron	rf	5	0	0	0	Hoy	cf	3	1	0	0
Garry	cf	4	0	1	0	McFarland	rf	5	0	2	0
Fultz	2b	5	1	1	0	Lally	lf	4	1	3	0
Anderson	lf	5	0	2	0	Hartman	3b	5	1	2	1
Clark	1b	5	1	1	0	Shuggart	ss	5	0	1	1
Conroy	ss	4	0	2	0	Fadden	2b	3	0	0	1
Smith	c	4	1	2	0	Isbel	1b	3	0	1	1
Burke	3b	4	1	2	0	Sugden	c	4	0	2	1
Dowling	p	4	1	2	0	Katel	p	5	1	1	0
		40	5	13	0			37	4	12	5

	1	2	3	4	5	6	7	8	9	10	
Milwaukee	0	0	1	0	0	0	2	1	0	1	— 5
Chicago	0	0	1	0	0	0	3	0	0	0	— 4

The White Stockings won the remaining game, as Reitz took over at second base. Then in Kansas City the Brewers won two of three. The team came home on April 27 and beat Chicago 6 to 2 before 4,000, to put the Brewers in first place. After Reidy won the next day before 2,400, Dowling lost in front of 13,903 fans, the largest crowd ever at Milwaukee Park. Mack was exchanging Smith and Yeager behind the plate, and released Bill Hallman, Fred Raymer and Charles McDonald to Sioux City of the new Western League. Rettger won the final game of the series. A new feature at the ballpark this year was a man who sent announcements through the grandstand and bleachers, informing the crowds of changes in the lineups. Kansas City ended this homestand, losing two of three. Reitz and Clark were injured and Mack was forced to use Yeager at first and Fultz at second for a while.

Milwaukee then traveled to Minneapolis and swept a three-game series. The Brewers then traveled east, losing two of three in Cleveland and winning three of four in Buffalo. The team had dropped to second place, a half-game behind Indianapolis, with a 15 and 7 record. Reitz had hit .450 in seven games before a spiking. Playing full time, Anderson was hitting .356, Garry .344, Fultz .338, Conroy .311, Waldron .294, Burke .279, and Clark only .217. Smith and Yeager, splitting the catching duties were hitting .209 and .346.

Back in Milwaukee for a Sunday game, Wheeler lost before 10,000, and then the teams split in Indianapolis. Willie Clark broke his ankle and was out for the season, Yeager going to first base. The trip ended in Detroit, the Tigers winning three of four.

The Brewers returned home on May 27 and split four with the Millers, having reacquired Cy Diggins to play first. Cleveland then also split four games with the Brewers. Mack secured Tommy Dowd from Chicago of the American League for $800 to play left field and placed Anderson at first. George Wheeler, with a 5 and 5 record, was released. Henry Reitz, who had not played for some time, went home to San Francisco for his wife's funeral, joined the California League and was suspended by the American League. Detroit and Indianapolis were next into Milwaukee, both splitting four games. The road trip ended with Milwaukee taking three of four from Buffalo. Dowling, who led the club with nine victories, had hurt his shoulder, but Bert Husting, now out of school, filled his spot. Conroy was also injured, and a player from Marquette College named O'Rourke filled his spot for one game. After two months the Brewers were in third place with a 28 and 21 record. Yeager led the club with a .403 average in 21 games. Playing full time, Anderson was at .344 and Fultz at .321. Waldron was hitting .285, Garry .260 and Burke .258. Conroy and Smith were down at .236. Diggins, filling in at first base, was at .295 in 12 games. Before leaving home the Brewers traded Charlie Chech, also back from school, to Cleveland for Louis Bierbauer. The 34-year-old second baseman had played 13 years in the big leagues, hitting 267.

Milwaukee traveled to Chicago, shifting Fultz to short, and lost three to the White Stockings. Then in Minneapolis the Brewers lost two of three, dropping to fourth place. The Brewers returned home and beat K.C. three of four, with Dowling back in the rotation, and the Brewers returning to the third spot. The Millers were next in, and Mack secured a new outfielder, Fred Ketchum, who had started the season with the Wilkes-Barre club of the Atlantic League until that league's collapse and was now on loan from Pittsburgh. In the first game Milwaukee was declared the winner on a forfeit because of a fight, but the decision was later reversed. The Brewers did win the remaining two games. Before hitting the road, George Yeager, who was hitting .387, was released. He had been injured and was slow recovering. Mack offered him full pay for the rest of the year if he signed for 1901, but Yeager declined.

In Kansas City the Brewers won four straight to extend their winning streak to six games. Milwaukee was in second place, only two games behind Chicago. On July 5 the Brewers played Chicago at Milwaukee Park. On the evening of July 8 the Brewers were five games out, having lost three straight to the White Stockings. On this brief homestand the Brewers lost two players. First Jim Garry was released to Buffalo, as his hitting was weak (.271 average). Ketchum went to center field to replace him. Then Bert Husting was suspended. Husting explained he had no written contract with the club, offering to start at $150 a month, as he had no spring practice. It was understood if he did good work he would get a $25 raise. After being 4 and 1, he wanted more money, but was refused it and left the team. He was then suspended.

The Brewers traveled to Cleveland next. Mack had been alternating Diggins and Smith behind the plate and now decided to rest Bierbauer, putting Conroy at second and Fultz at shortstop. The club split two with the Cleveland Lake Shores. In Indianapolis the Brewers won two of three prior to a Sunday game back in Milwaukee. Injuries plagued the team. With Clark out for the season, Anderson went to first, but he now had a split finger. Burke had an injured shoulder and Diggins went to third base and then to first, with Conroy moving to third. In Detroit this makeshift lineup lost two of three to the Tigers, and again in Buffalo lost two of three. After three months the Brewers were still in second place with a 44 and 37 record. Diggins, in 30 games, was hitting .336, and Ketchum, in 18 games, was at .333. The regulars were Anderson at .323, Fultz .305, Waldron .281, Burke .266, Smith .252, Dowd .247, Conroy .224 and Bierbauer 218.

The club returned home July 23 and lost four straight to the Buffalo Bisons. To strengthen his pitching, Mack acquired George "Rube" Waddell. Rube had left Pittsburgh and was suspended the same day Husting also had been. Mack had received an O.K. to sign Waddell from the Pirate management. Within a week the suspended Husting would sign with Pittsburgh, but Mack denied it was an exchange, although it turned out the contracts of both players had a recall clause in them. Waddell was a character. The *Sporting Life* wrote of him, "You are liable to hear of him tending bar some day while the game is going on and the club manager is looking high and low for him. They say that Fred Clarke had Rube on the card one day and wanted to pitch him; yet the silly lout was running around an Indian show just outside of the grounds and cutting up monkey shines, forgetful of the fact that he had a duty to perform."[89] Later in August, with the club on the road and Waddell home — with permission — he helped a farmer in Pewaukee fight a barn fire and badly burned a hand. He told a reporter, "I'm a peach at a fire. There is nothing I like better than to fight fires."[90] Different as he was, he was a great pitcher. He would go on to win 193 games in 13 big league years, and post a lifetime 2.16 earned run average, sixth best in history. In 1946 the southpaw would be elected to the Baseball Hall of Fame. The Pittsburgh organization was glad Waddell went to Milwaukee, thinking Connie Mack could handle him. An exchange claimed Mack signed Waddell for $250 a month, $50 over the American League's salary limit.

After the four losses to Buffalo, Reidy broke the string with a victory over Cleveland. Then on July 28, before 2,500 at Milwaukee Park, Pete Dowling no-hit the Lake Shores, walking two and striking out four.

MILWAUKEE		AB	R	H	E	CLEVELAND		AB	R	H	E
Conroy	2b&ss	4	0	0	0	Pickering	cf	4	0	0	0

MILWAUKEE		AB	R	H	E	CLEVELAND		AB	R	H	E
Waldron	rf	4	0	0	0	Frisbie	rf	3	0	0	0
Dowd	cf	4	1	2	0	Genius	lf	3	0	0	0
Anderson	lf	4	0	0	0	LaChance	1b	3	0	0	1
Fultz	ss	4	1	2	0	Flood	2b	2	0	0	0
Ketchum	cf	4	1	2	0	Sullivan	3b	3	0	0	1
Burke	3b	1	0	0	0	Shea	ss	2	0	0	1
Diggins	c	3	1	1	0	Chrisham	c	3	0	0	0
Dowling	p	3	0	1	0	Hoffer	p	3	0	0	0
Bierbauer	2b	2	1	1	0						
		33	5	9	0			26	0	0	0

```
                        1 2 3 4 5 6 7 8 9
           Milwaukee    0 0 0 0 2 0 1 2 x — 5
           Cleveland    0 0 0 0 0 0 0 0 0 — 0
```

The next day Waddell won 4 to 0, on a two-hitter. The Brewers then lost two of three to Detroit and won two of three from the Hoosiers to end the homestand in third place.

The Cream City men then traveled to Minneapolis and split four with the Flour City men. Mack lost Louis Bierbauer to Buffalo in a complicated deal. The Bisons had lost Atherton and Hallman, so Milwaukee sold Bierbauer — hitting only .203 — to the Bisons. The Brewers were to get Bill Gilbert from Syracuse to replace Bierbauer. However, Gilbert refused to leave Syracuse and was suspended. Meanwhile, the Brewers returned home and took three from Kansas City, playing Conroy at second and Fultz at short. Anderson went to left field, as Dowd was injured, and Diggins played first. To bolster his ailing club Mack signed Ed Abbaticchio, recently released by Minneapolis, for second base, and reacquired Bill Hallman from Sioux City. Tom Dowd was released. The homestand ended with Chicago winning two and tying one.

On August 18 the Brewers dropped two to the White Stockings by 1 to 0 scores. The next day Waddell pitched both games of the doubleheader, winning the first game 3 to 2 in 17 innings, and winning the second in 5 innings, 1 to 0, on a one-hitter. Milwaukee then traveled to Kansas City in fourth place with a 57 and 50 record and lost two of three but climbed to third.

The club returned home and caught fire, beating Minneapolis three straight in a short homestand. Before traveling east Mack obtained Harry Spies, a catcher, from Cleveland. Cy Diggins, who had done a fine job filling in, hitting .275, was released. The Brewers won three more in Detroit, followed by three of four in Indianapolis. Before going on, Rube Waddell was called back to Pittsburgh, having had a 10 and 3 record with Milwaukee. The Brewers ended their final road trip winning two of three in Cleveland and dropping two in Buffalo.

The Brewers returned home to finish the season on September 7. The team took two of three from Buffalo, three from Detroit, two from Indianapolis, and split four with Cleveland to end the season on September 18. The Brewers had won 20 of their last 27 games to finish the highest they had in the Western/American League.

Chicago	82	53	.607	Kansas City	69	71	.493
Milwaukee	79	59	.572	Cleveland	64	73	.467
Indianapolis	71	64	.526	Buffalo	61	78	.439
Detroit	71	68	.511	Minneapolis	54	85	.388

The Brewers' downfall had been Chicago (losing 12 of 18) and lowly Buffalo (9 and

11). The Brewers won every other matchup. Reidy led the pitchers with a 19 and 8 record. Sparks was 17 and 12, Waddell 10 and 3, Dowling 16 and 19, Rettger 7 and 11, Husting 4 and 1, and Wheeler 3 and 3. Anderson led the club in hitting with a .309 average and the league with 50 stolen bases. Spies hit .317 in his short time in Milwaukee. Fultz hit .298, Waldron .293, Smith .269, Burke .245, Conroy .234, Ketchum .231, Hallman .219 and Abbaticchio .200.

Brewer president Matthew Killilea would not give the financial results of the club, saying, "The public is no more interested in that than it is in the day's sales of one of the large dry good houses ... the public doesn't care so long as we give them good baseball."[91] Connie Mack did declare, however, the attendance at Milwaukee Park was about 130,000. The local press estimated the club made about $8,000 on the year. Most likely all the American League clubs, with the possible exception of Minneapolis, profited in 1900. Ban Johnson said American League attendance was up about 28 percent, but expenses were up too. The American League was on solid ground and now began to prepare for the final step in its evolution.

14

The Final Step (1901)

The American League's final step to independence from the National League had numerous courses to guide it. One was the lack of good, solid leadership in the National League. Its president, Nick Young, was just the opposite of Ban Johnson, having little control over league affairs. The November 10, 1900, *Sporting News* commented: "How different have been the methods of the major league magnates. The president of the National League is vested by its Constitution with powers which he does not dare to exercise. The club owners, instead of being held to strict account under the terms of the partnership, have been allowed to do as they please, regardless of base ball law, either through fear or favoritism." After citing some examples, the paper finished by writing, "The more one studies the methods under which the National and American Leagues are conducted, the easier it is to account for the decadence of the former and the advancement of the latter in popular favor."

The problem of rowdiness and continuing arguments by managers and players with umpires was a constant in the press. Calling for an end to rowdyism, the *Sporting News* of October 6, 1900, called for "the elimination of the evil, that has paralyzed its popularity, and made it unprofitable in many of the cities of the National League." In this same issue of the St. Louis weekly, H.G. Merrill, the Wilkes-Barre correspondent, headed his column, ROWDYISM THE GAME'S GREATEST HANDICAP, while the paper's Kansas City correspondent commented "the advancement made by the American League in 1900 in the matter of discipline of players, the elimination of rowdy ball players and snappy play makes it a formidable rival of the major body."

The time was right for a new major league. The *Sporting News* of October 13, 1900, wrote:

> The National League cannot maintain its monopoly on professional base ball much longer. It is only a question of a year or two when it will have to share the field with a friendly or a hostile organization. Rivalry is conductive to the game's good.... The National League can only protect its circuit from invasion by assenting to the expansion of the American League, along the lines of the old American circuit. With the best cities in the country on its circuit the National League has nothing to fear from a friendly rival.

Three other factors in the American League's status we will explore in greater depth: the Players' Association, a new American Association, and the American League's urge to push east.

In June 1900 players met in New York to plan a formation of a players union. Talk of the players forming was nothing new. The Players' League of 1890 has been discussed. Again in 1897 talk of the players organizing surfaced. The *Cincinnati Commercial-Tribune* had then reported the players believed "they are being made slaves of by the magnates, but realize that under the present state of affairs they are helpless."[1] A longer season at less pay and trades without consent were the players' major grievances. Connie Mack said the brotherhood would be a "frost," and Charles Comiskey said any player joining "is not sane."[2] Both these men had played with the Players' League in 1890, but were on the other side of the fence now. In July 1900 Charles Zimmer, Pittsburgh's catcher, Hugh Jennings of Brooklyn and Fred Clarke of Pittsburgh were elected president, secretary and treasurer of the union. Players of the American and Eastern leagues were taken into the association, with thoughts that later a few other minor league players "will be granted the privilege of the order."[3] Jennings soon claimed every National League player was in the Player's Association. The players stressed "the organization is not to be unfriendly to the league magnates. Their only purpose in getting together is to be able to place their claims before the magnates in a more forcible manner."[4] The union's first concerns were an improved players contract, and ending the practice of farming out players to the minor leagues. We will see how the Player's Association factored more into the events.

In August the American League owners met in Chicago and decided to petition the National League to give up the drafting of American League players. This was looked on as a declaration of independence, and the first stop toward major league status. Word also came from the meeting that the American League was thinking of expanding into St. Louis, Cincinnati and two eastern cities. Minneapolis was a sure bet to lose its American League franchise. The club received no local support. Toward the end of the 1900 season the Millers were transferring games out to eastern cities and laying off players to cut expenses. President Clarence Saulpaugh claimed to have just cleared expenses, but that is doubtful. On two weekday games in Minneapolis in July, Detroit claimed only 300 attended and its share was $33.75. The Tigers' hotel bill was $25 a day. According to Ban Johnson, Minneapolis drew only 71,000, or less than half of the Brewers' attendance. By the American League meeting in October, it was a known fact the league wanted to drop Minneapolis and Kansas City and move into Baltimore and Washington. James Manning of Kansas City was, as expected, against the eastern movement. Saulpaugh realized he had to move. William Watkins of Indianapolis was also against this, as the move would make Indianapolis the smallest city in the circuit. Talk was Colonel John Rogers of the Philadelphia Phillies would allow the American League into that city, and Indianapolis would be the likely city to be dropped. Watkins went on record as saying the present American League was as strong as any proposed to him. A committee of Johnson, Manning, Somers and Comiskey was formed to study any moves.

The last factor was the re-organization of the National Association. With the players and the American League causing trouble, the time was again right to try to form. In September the National Association met in Baltimore with six cities represented: Baltimore, Philadelphia, Chicago, Milwaukee, Boston and St. Louis. Harry D. Quin again backed Milwaukee, while Charles Havenor and Milwaukeean Joseph O'Brien backed Chicago. Still another Milwaukeean, August H. Koch — listed in the 1902 City of Milwaukee directory as "speculator"— backed Philadelphia. It was reported Detroit and Washington would probably fill out the circuit. The Chicago correspondent of the *Sporting News* had these thoughts on the new league: "Starting a league on the capital shown by the Milwaukee crowd is suspicious business. I always think of messenger boys who grab a place in a line at a theater box office and hold the place hoping to sell out when I think of these fellows trying to organize on newspaper publicity."[5]

So far the National Association was again only a paper league, but it threatened both the National League and American League. If the Americans could enter Washington and Baltimore, it could be a death blow to the National Association. The American League moved quickly against both leagues. At its October meeting farming was abolished. No club would be allowed to use a player that had not received his unconditional release. Johnson then looked toward the Player's Association. He announced the American League would adopt a new form of contract with a three-year reserve clause. He further acknowledged the association and said he would grant its demands, the major ones being no suspension for more than ten days, clubs to pay doctor bills of injured players, no trades without consent, plus the three-year reservation. The *Sentinel* explained the American League's situation.

> It is true that the American League has decided that henceforth it will be a major league, but that does not make it so and the circuit it has named does not make it so. It is working hand in glove with the National League, for the protection of the National League and for its own good as there can be no doubt; if the National Association comes into existence, that the American League will be less important than ever.[6]

The National League also made up a war plan. In this plan the American League would enter Boston, Philadelphia, Baltimore, St. Louis and Washington, stay in Chicago, Milwaukee and Cleveland, and share grounds in some cities. This would provide continuous baseball in cities where the National Association would be. The National League also thought of going back to 12 clubs.

Ban Johnson did not want to join with any league. When Johnson failed to pay the National Agreement dues, Nick Young sent out a special bulletin reminding all minors it was expiring. Johnson still held out, but said he would welcome a new National Agreement that would give his league equal footing with the National League. By the end of October Johnson announced the American League would go into Baltimore, Washington and Philadelphia. It was not decided what cities would be dropped, although Kansas City and Minneapolis were certain. Indianapolis or Buffalo would probably be the other. James Manning had decided to go to Washington, and it was reported Philadelphia had sufficient financial backing, rumor being Connie Mack would head the organization. Word then came out that John McGraw and Wilbert Robinson would head the Baltimore club. This move by the American League left the National Association on shaky ground, as these two were big names in their plans. By December the National Association idea had died.

With the National Association gone, Ban Johnson set out on his plans for major league status. It would be a hard road to travel. A writer for the *Sporting News* doubted if the American League with its smaller cities could seriously challenge the National League. He believed these cities could not bring in enough money to pay big salaries. Although no war had been declared yet, the lines were drawn. Nick Young denied there would be a war. In early November he made this statement:

> We are not going to have any baseball fight. The American League will be on exactly the same footing as the National League. Fights cost money. The brotherhood contest in 1890 cost them $1,500,000. The Association fight in 1892 cost it $1,000,000. The National League is too strong to be fought.... At the end of the season the winners of the two pennants will contest for the championship of the United States. That is the whole baseball story for 1901.[7]

Later that month Young made an even stronger statement, saying, "We are willing to recognize the American Leagues on an equality with us.... I hope to see the American League a success and the National League will do all it can to make it a success."[8] He said Johnson was the only one talking of war. The American League's five-year agreement ran out on November 20, but was extended 30 days. At a secret meeting of the American League, the Baltimore franchise was given to McGraw and it was decided Indianapolis would be dropped in favor of Philadelphia. In December McGraw signed a 10-year contract with the Americans. In Philadelphia all the backers were not known, but one was—Connie Mack. As early as October it was rumored Mack would go to Philadelphia, although both he and Matthew Killilea denied it. On November 4 the Milwaukee Baseball Club filed an amendment to its articles of incorporation, increasing the capital stock to $25,000. The principal stockholders were Matthew Killilea, Fred Gross and Connie Mack, each holding an equal amount of stock. In late November Killilea was saying he would not stand in Mack's way if he wanted to own part of the Philadelphia franchise. Mack said he was working under the assumption he would remain in Milwaukee, although he had not talked to anyone in the Brewers organization. He did, however, admit he had talked to Philadelphia people. In December the *Sporting News* reported Mack was setting up in Philadelphia. Later that month a Philadelphia paper confirmed he would be an owner in the club, having sold his stock in the Brewers. Connie Mack was lost to Milwaukee and would manage in Philadelphia for 50 years, by far the longest tenure of any major league manager. He would place first 9 times and last 17 times. He holds all-time managerial records for games managed, games won and games lost, and was inducted in the Baseball Hall of Fame in 1937.

At this point the Player's Association again entered the picture. Ban Johnson met with the association and told them he would accept their demands. The next day the players' attorney met with the National League, presented the players' ideas, including a few new ones, which were turned down. The association told its players to wait and not sign with either league.

The National League then moved against the American League. Rogers of the Phillies changed his position, saying he would not consent to the American League entering Philadelphia, calling the American League "carpetbaggers."[9] At the National League meeting in December, the St. Paul, Minneapolis and Kansas City territories were awarded to the Western League. This move strengthened that minor league and prevented Johnson's American League from re-entering those cities. Then a new league, under National Agreement protection, was formed. It was composed of Boston, New York, Philadelphia, Washington, Buffalo, Louisville, Indianapolis and Milwaukee. National League sources also reported John McGraw would abandon the Americans and go to New York. The American League countered quickly. Ban Johnson said if McGraw was really leaving, he would transfer Baltimore to Boston. In reality, Johnson was thinking of going into Boston anyway. Then a Western Association, under the patronage of the American League, was formed to fight the Western League. Most believed this minor was only a bluff, and in fact, never met again, as the Interstate League formed under the National Agreement to kill it. After the first of the year, the National Agreement's American Association moved its Buffalo franchise to St. Louis. It was also announced Harry D. Quin and Charles Havenor would head Milwaukee, and Watkins would be at the head of the Indianapolis franchise. This meant the American League had lost Indianapolis to fall back on. An Indianapolis dispatch claimed the National League was backing the American Association and "there would be no lack of money to keep the association afloat, at least till the American League is killed off."[10] It was said John Brush had guaranteed them $20,000. Ban Johnson said this association was "nothing but wind."[11] The pro-National League *Sporting Life* wrote on December 22, 1900:

> The American Leaguers are finding expansion to major league proportions a very much harder proposition than they anticipated, as well-laid plans are going awry and now obstacles constantly arise to confound them. Many hurdles have been placed in their path—and more are to come. Not the least of their difficulties will ensue from the hostile attitude of the National League, which has cleverly put the seceding American League upon the defensive—a position that might have been

avoided had there been more expediency and diplomacy, less bullheadedness and less talk of force; which should always be the last, not the first, resort.

War was near, and Johnson took emergency steps. All American clubs reportedly put 51 percent of their stock in a trust, with their president holding it. No owner could dispose of his holdings without Johnson's permission. Each club also had a price set on it so if it wanted to sell out, the franchise could be bought by the league. Burns of Detroit, however, later denied Johnson had these privileges, but it had been considered. Johnson then announced the American League would enter Boston and had secured grounds. The *Milwaukee Daily News* thought "baseball is getting like the final betting stage in a stud poker game."[12]

The war was now on. The National League charged that it had a contract with the American League that the Americans would forfeit $5,000 if a single game was played in Chicago without National Agreement protection. Johnson said the contract was not worth the paper it was written on. Again the National League changed American Association franchises, moving Philadelphia to Detroit and New York to Baltimore. August Koch, with his secretary Joseph O'Brien, now owned the Detroit franchise. The National League allowed the association the privilege to reserve five men, giving it a sort of higher-than-ever minor league status. It was thought the National League would turn over its surplus players to bolster the association. Johnson called the American Association "a big joke,"[13] but heads turned in Milwaukee when Quin signed Bert Husting to a $1,200 contract (another source gave $1,500), who had an agreement to come back to the Brewers. Quin also incorporated a club with $30,000 in $1,000 shares. The officers were Quin, president; Henry J. Bauman, vice president; and Havenor, secretary and treasurer.

The American League met on January 28 and admitted Washington, Baltimore, Philadelphia and Boston to its ranks; Indianapolis, Kansas City, Buffalo and Minneapolis were dropped. A ten-year agreement was set up and 51 percent of each franchise was reportedly given to the league with first option of purchasing a club. The American League also promised Franklin of Buffalo it would not sign any of his players if he went to another league; he did, joining the Eastern League. The Baltimore franchise was granted to a new corporation headed by Sidney Franks. Connie Mack was awarded Philadelphia, and Charles Somers headed Boston. James Manning received Washington. Somers was the big money man in the American League. When Washington was taken in, it was about $15,000 of his money that paid for the preliminary work on the grounds. Mack received about $25,000 of his money when he invaded Philadelphia. Somers also spent about $65,000 to start Boston's franchise and his "bank account helped pay salaries and other incidentals"[14] in Cleveland. The *Sporting Life* changed its tune, now writing, "The American League has the advantage of brains and ability in its membership, nerve and experience in its leaders, and a fine circuit geographically and numerically."[15]

The American League met with the Player's Association in late January 1901. The American League agreed to the union's demands for a contract that would not bind a player for a period longer than five years, and a clause "providing that no player shall be traded, farmed or sold to any other club, except with his consent."[16] In early February the Player's Association advised its members who played in the American League they were able to sign for 1901 in that league only, but "all such members are advised to send their contracts to the association attorney for inspection before signing."[17] If a player did not finish with an AL club in 1900, he was not to sign for 1901. No member was to sign a contract in the National League, Eastern League or American Association until further instruction. The

National League agreed to meet with the union later in February, but players were still deserting to the American League, causing the NL owners to insist the union could not control its members. On February 26 the union met with the National League magnates. The players presented their conditions and an agreement was made, the NL making concessions to them. Charles Zimmer issued this statement: "As president of the Protective Association of Base Ball Players, as its authorized representative, I hereby agree, in return for concessions granted by the National League and American Association of Professional Base Ball Clubs, this 26th day of February 1901, that all National League and Eastern League players who may sign American League contracts will be suspended pending action by the Player's' Protective Association as a body."[18] The union's lawyer, Harry Taylor, soon sent out a letter that cleared up this suspension issue. He wrote, "We simply agreed to suspend any National man who signed with the American, pending action on his case by our Association as a body. You can see that this does not bind us as a body not to immediately remove any such suspension or not to take any action we see fit as a body. We stand, as we always have, in favor of no league and no set of players as against any other."[19]

Meanwhile, the American Association was still around. To go with his one player, Harry Quin signed a manager, Walter Wilmot, late of Minneapolis. The *Daily News* did not think much of Quin's choice, writing, "In his day Walter Wilmot was a good player, but that day is long past. In addition to this he has never made very many friends here, and how he will be received here is a question."[20] Quin also circulated a story that the Brewers would be transferred to St. Louis, which Matt Killilea denied. However, the *Sporting News* of February 2, 1901, included a special correspondence from Detroit that the American League had left open the possibility of transferring the Milwaukee franchise to St. Louis, if the National League persisted in a war. It was reported Matt Killilea was "ready for the shift and had secured an option on the Von der Ahe grounds through St. Louis capitalists." The National League denied any connection with the American Association, but held the leases on all their parks. Killilea challenged Quin to play three Sunday games with his team for $1,000 each, half going to charity, winner taking the rest, if his club organized. Quin said as the Brewers were outlaws, he could not. This brought a blast from the *Sporting News*, noting twice in the past two years Quin tried to fight the National Agreement himself. The paper wrote Quin had only himself and August Koch on his mind "first, last and all the time since he started out to break into baseball, via any old route."[21] Late in January the *Chicago Tribune* wrote, "There are signs of irritation in the National League's vermiform appendix ... and indications of serious complications, which may result fatally unless an operation is performed."[22] The American Association did not receive the financial support it believed it would from the National League and died in late February.

Nothing was in the way now, and war between the National and American leagues was declared. Ban Johnson made this statement: "We were forced into this trouble by the National League in protection of ourselves and in order to save the American League. We will strike earnestly to eliminate those evils brought upon base ball by selfish or unscrupulous men, and to lift the game back to the same high plane it once occupied and save it from falling into the hands of unscrupulous people. And we will win."[23]

With a baseball war on, the signing of players became an interesting feature. Several of the 1900 Brewers were lost immediately after the season. John Anderson and Dave Fultz were slated to go back to Brooklyn, as Mack had only secured them for one year of service. Fred Gross explained in March what had happened with the two players. Anderson and Fultz had been sold to Milwaukee for $1,500 in March of 1900, with a clause that Brooklyn could recall the two before October 1. A few days before the option of recalling the men expired, Brooklyn management returned to Milwaukee the check for $1,500 and asked for the two players' return. Matt Killilea asked for an extension of the agreement to cover 1901, with Brooklyn keeping the $1,500. Brooklyn refused, perhaps believing Milwaukee would pay more for the two, as both had good years in 1900. As it turned out, the war between the American and National leagues flared up and the American League did not honor the National League reserves. Anderson would remain with Milwaukee, and Fultz would play for Connie Mack in Philadelphia. Thus Brooklyn kept the $1,500, but lost the two players. The loss of Fultz was not lamented by all, as the *Sporting News*' Milwaukee correspondent reported, "He is a good ball player, but Milwaukee is a Sunday town and Fultz don't play Sunday ball, and a player in the infield must be in the game regularly to have good teamwork, especially when the local attendance is largest on Sunday."[24] Fred Ketchum and Harry Smith were back with Pittsburgh, as they had been on loan to Milwaukee. Wid Conroy was drafted by Cincinnati, but Killilea contested the drafting, as he had spent only one year in a Class A minor league. Of course, the upcoming baseball war would stop drafting and loaning policies between the two leagues.

With Connie Mack going to Philadelphia, the Brewers were left without a manager. Even before Milwaukee officials would admit Mack was leaving, a report from Chicago said Hugh Duffy would manage in the Beer City. In early December the *Boston Herald* reported Duffy had a good offer to come to Milwaukee and wanted to, but it was unknown if Arthur Soden, the Boston National League owner, would let him go, being afraid to bolster the American League. Once the war was in full swing, Mack went to Boston to work on Duffy. Duffy said he had not signed with Milwaukee because the Player's Association was advising its members not to sign yet. In late January Duffy signed to manage the Brewers for $3,000.[25] Immediately the American Association, in its dying days, offered Duffy $1,000 more, but he refused. It was also reported Connie Mack's stock in the Brewers was sold to Duffy. Soden then threatened to sue for breach of contract, as Duffy was reserved to Boston, but American League lawyers said his suit would have no chance of holding up and it was never actually filed. Hugh Duffy had been born in Cranston, Rhode Island, 34 years earlier. His big league career began in 1888 with Chicago. In 1890 he jumped to the Player's League and then went to Boston of the old American Association. Since 1892 he had played in Boston with the Beaneaters. Duffy was a first-class hitting outfielder. After hitting .282 in 1888 and .295 in 1889, he never hit below .300 until 1898—hitting .298 that year. In 1894 he had hit .440, an average that has not been topped since. Hugh had also topped the National League in home runs in 1894 and 1897. In 1900 the new Brewer manager had hit .304. In 1945 Hugh Duffy would be enshrined in the Baseball Hall of Fame.

Killilea and Duffy now began to assemble a team. Wid Conroy had been signed the previous year to a two-year contract, and Bill Hallman was signed immediately after the 1900 season. In late January Jimmy Burke and Erving Waldron were signed. Next to sign was second baseman Billy Gilbert, who had played the 1900 season in Syracuse. Joe Connor was then signed. Connor, a catcher and brother of future Hall of Famer Roger, had played briefly with Boston in 1900, but had been drafted by New York. Duffy also signed another backstop, Bill Maloney, from the Attleboro, Massachusetts, club. By the end of February the Brewers signed John Anderson, Fred Raymer and Pete Dowling—Anderson reportedly for $2,200.

In early March the Brewers made their first major catch in the jumping players war when they signed Virgil "Ned" Garvin. Garvin had pitched the last two years in Chicago, winning 19 and losing 31. He had been traded to New York that winter and the Giants immediately offered him $200 more, but he turned them down. Jim Hart of Chicago claimed Garvin accepted $50 in advance money, so he had jumped his contract. Garvin claimed Hart only loaned it to him, and soon repaid the debt. A major reason Garvin signed in Milwaukee was Matt Killilea got him a job that winter with the F.C. Gross Packing Company and it "struck a tender spot in Virgil's heart."[26] The packing company happened to be owned by Brewers co-owner Fred Gross. The tall twirler apparently had a quick temper and a lot of pride in his home state. An article in the January 26, 1901, *Sporting News* reported he was arrested in Chicago for allegedly knocking a man down, and when "the complainant was prostrate, the aforesaid Garvin placed a beer glass over his face and stamped upon it, as the cook cuts crullers from the dough." As can be expected the two men had differing accounts of what led up to this. Matt Daly, also "a ball player by profession," said he "simply advised Garvin to stop taking the stuff that makes him think he is a great base ball pitcher and go back to the ranch in Texas." Garvin insisted Daly "cast dispersions upon his birthplace, the Lone Star State ... and insinuated that it would have been a great boon to humanity if the Galveston disaster had extended as far north as the Oklahoma line," giving him "sufficient provocation to make his mark" on Daly. Virgil concluded, "That riled mah hot southern blood, suh, an' Ah defended th' honah of mah state. Any gentleman would ah done th' same, suh, under the circumstances." Garvin would get into more trouble with the law during the season. The *Sporting Life* reported on August 10, he was arrested in Milwaukee for firing two shots from a revolver at one James Harrison, a black man working as a "bootblack." According to the October 19, 1901, *Sporting Life,* Garvin was freed after paying a $50 fine and costs.

Garvin was Milwaukee's only major catch in the war. Unfortunately, other American League clubs were doing much better. Clark Griffith jumped to Chicago and Cy Young went to Boston. At this time it was reported about 30 National Leaguers had joined the Americans, and Milwaukee surely was not doing as well as most. Ban Johnson decided not to announce which players the American League was signing to force the National League to offer higher prices. The National League fought back, offering big salaries for players to jump to their side. Another scheme leaked out that Soden and Conaut of the Boston Beaneaters had made a cash offer of $15,000 to Somers to withdraw from the American League and turn his park over to them. The Boston National Leaguers also promised Somers a franchise in the National League for 1902. Somers turned them down.

Matt Killilea signed Burt Husting on March 6 to a two-year contract for $250 a month, but complications arose. Husting had signed with Quin's American Association club, but contended there was nothing in his contract to bind him to Quin when the association died. Husting did, however, offer Quin $200 for his release. Quin refused him. Later that month Quin assigned Husting's contract to Boston of the National League for $500 and said he would go to court to prevent Husting from playing for the Brewers. But Husting was a Brewer. The Brewers lost Harry Spies during this period, as he signed with Los Angeles. To replace the lost catcher, Tom Leahy was signed. Leahy had played sparingly in the National League a few years previous, but had spent the last year with Providence of the Eastern League. Tully Sparks and Bill Reidy also signed to fill out the team. George Rettger, not in the Brewers' plans, was released after seven years with the club, going to Kansas City of the Western League. Fred Raymer jumped his contract and signed with Chicago of the National League, claiming the Brewers had not lived up to their part of the contract owed him money. The Brewers claimed Raymer owed the club $85 in advance money and would sue him and Chicago president Jim Hart. Secretary Gross of the Brewers was still trying to improve the team and made Jesse Burke, the hard-hitting St. Louis outfielder, a $3,200 contract offer.

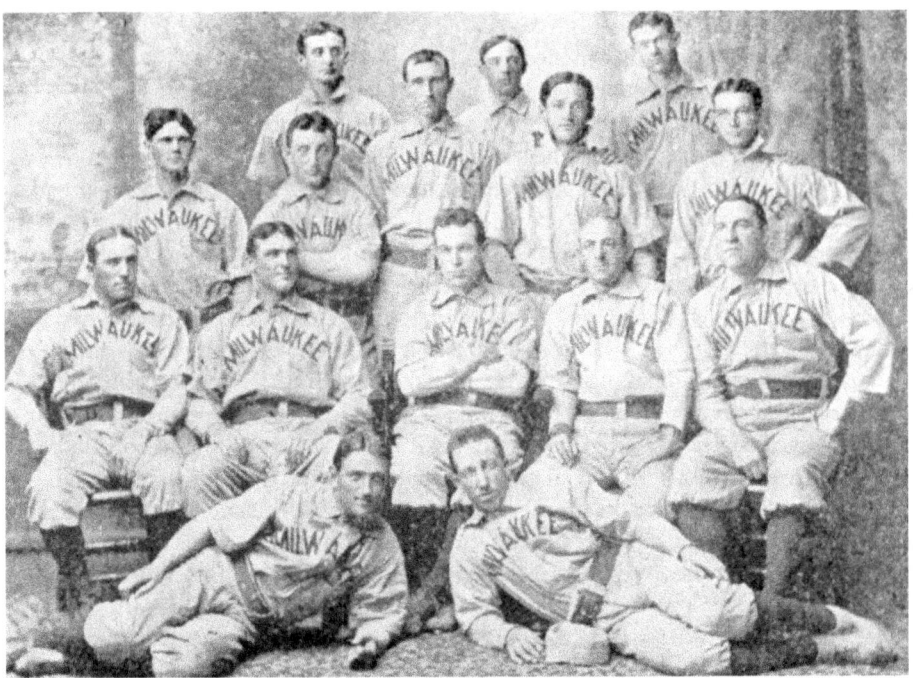

1901 Brewers team photograph. *Back row, left to right:* Bill Reidy, Wid Conroy, Joe Connor. *Second row:* Bill Maloney, Tom Leahy, Ned Garvin, Bert Husting, Tully Sparks. *Seated:* Jimmy Burke, John Anderson, Manager Hugh Duffy, Billy Gilbert, Pink Hawley. *Front:* Bill Hallman, Irving Waldron.

Burke signed with the Cardinals for $3,400. Gross did, however, sign Bill Friel to replace Raymer in the infield. The last Brewer to be signed before the season started was Emerson "Pink" Hawley. Pink had pitched nine years in the National League, winning 160 and losing 165. He was in the twilight of his career and wanted a two-year contract at $3,000 a year, plus a no-cut clause. Gross would meet his price, but would not go with the no-cut clause. Hawley went back home to Beaver Dam, Wisconsin. He soon signed a two-year contract at $3,000, plus a clause if he was injured he would still be paid.

Milwaukee had 17 players under contract, three over the American League limit: Dowling, Garvin, Husting, Sparks, Reidy and Hawley — pitchers; Connor, Maloney and Leahy — catchers; Anderson, Gilbert, Conroy, Burke and Friel — infielders; Hallman, Waldron and Duffy — outfielders. The Brewers salary list was estimated at $24,000. Others were estimated at: Philadelphia, $35,000; Boston, $33,000; Chicago, $32,000; Detroit and Cleveland, $25,000; Washington, $24,000; Baltimore, $20,000. Hugh Duffy thought the Brewers would do well in the 1901 season. He told a *Journal* reporter, "We certainly are going to have a crackerjack of a team this season. Our pitching staff is strong, and our infield can't be beat by any other team in the league. And the outfield will be there with the goods when the time comes."[27] Others disagreed. Odds were made that Chicago would win the pennant, favored 13 to 5. Baltimore was at 3 to 1; Detroit, Boston and Philadelphia 5 to 1; Cleveland, Milwaukee and Washington at 15 to 1.

The American League met in March for final preparations. Matt Killilea had a bad case of bronchitis and missed the meeting, as he went to Arizona, not returning until the end of May. Fred Gross and Hugh Duffy attended the Philadelphia meeting. It was thought the American League would try to avoid conflicts in scheduling with the National League, but when the 140-game schedule appeared, there were 56 conflicting dates. While the National League charged its basic 50-cent admission, the Americans stuck to 25 cents for the bleachers, 50 cents for the grandstand and 75 cents for the box seats. The older circuit charged 25 cents more for the grandstand and boxes than the Americans. Visiting clubs in the American League received 12½ cents per paid admission, all extra revenue from box seats and grandstands staying with the home club. The Americans also stayed with the Reach ball. They further decided to go to court on contract jumpers. The American League was set for its first major league season.

The Brewers began spring training in St. Louis on April 1. The players were slow reporting, with the first exhibition game played on April 7, the Brewers losing to Chicago 2 to 1. Duffy then moved his team to Excelsior Springs, Missouri, because National League agents were tinkering with his players in St. Louis. Both Burke and Husting's salaries were reportedly increased $500 not to jump to the National League, although Duffy and Gross denied this. The Brewers lost two more to the White Stockings before Ban Johnson stopped the games, saying with the Brewers out of condition, the games were not fair. It was believed Johnson did not want the Brewers to look too bad, as it could hurt attendance once the season started. The games were not profitable either, taking in only $221 in paid admissions. The Brewers then returned to Milwaukee and beat the Milwaukee Medical College and Cream City clubs. Duffy's players were to wear white uniforms with dark blue trim, white caps and blue stockings. The club's visiting suits were gray with blue trim, blue caps and blue stockings. The *Evening Wisconsin* interviewed several fans regarding the team, one Joe Holland giving this statement: "Why, every German and Mick in the town will be out rooting for the Brewers this season. The team is strong and the pitching staff great."[28]

The American League's first major league year started April 24, 1901, but the Brewers were rained out in Detroit. So on April 25 the Brewers met the Tigers. The *Sentinel* of April 26 reported on the game: "Milwaukee lost its opening game ... because its pitchers had not been trained to endure nine innings, and second, because the crowd which overflowed the field nearly to the diamond, closed in on the left foul line during the last innings and prevented Hallman, in the left garden, either from catching three flies that went down there, each of which was counted as a two-bagger by reason of going over his head, or making them singles." What had happened was a record Detroit crowd of about 9,000 overflowed the park and watched the Brewers take a 13 to 4 lead going into the ninth. These three hits and some errors helped the Tigers score ten runs and win 14 to 13. The *Sentinel* told its readers after the game, "The great throng rushed out on the diamond and Dillon was hoisted on the shoulders of six men, and surrounded by the shouting thousands, carried about the grounds until he begged to be put down."

DETROIT		AB	R	H	E	MILWAUKEE		AB	R	H	E
Casey	3b	6	3	2	0	Waldron	rf	5	1	0	0
Barrett	cf	5	1	1	0	Gilbert	2b	6	1	3	0
Gleason	2b	6	1	3	1	Hallman	lf	5	1	0	1
Holmes	rf	6	3	2	1	Anderson	1b	4	1	2	0
Dillon	1b	6	3	4	1	Conroy	ss	5	4	4	1
Eberfield	ss	4	1	2	3	Duffy	cf	4	2	1	0
Nance	lf	5	0	1	1	Burke	3b	5	2	3	2
Buelow	c	4	1	1	0	Leahy	c	4	1	1	0
Miller	p	0	0	0	0	Hawley	p	3	0	1	0
Frisk	p	5	1	3	0	Dowling	p	1	0	1	0
Husting	p	0	0	0	0						
		47	14	19	7			42	13	16	4

Detroit	0	0	0	2	1	0	0	1	10 —	14
Milwaukee	0	2	5	0	0	0	3	3	0 —	13

The next day the Tigers scored two in the ninth to beat Garvin 6 to 5. After the third loss, 13 to 9, the April 28 *Sentinel* headline read, BREWERS AMONG THE ALSO RANS. The same pattern continued in the final Detroit game, as the Tigers scored four in the ninth to win 12 to 11. Then on to Cleveland and the pattern continued, as the Blues scored three in the eighth to beat Hawley 4 to 3. Finally, after five losses, Garvin held an 8 to 6 lead to earn the Brewers' first win of 1901. The two teams split the remaining two games.

Even though the Brewers started terribly, the American League fared better. In the first weekend it was claimed the American League outdrew the National League by twice as many patrons. After the usual parade, "Pink" Hawley lost the home opener to Chicago 11 to 3 before 4,000 on Friday, May 3. The frustration showed on the field. Burke, the club's captain, was ejected in the second inning; Maloney, the catcher, was ejected by umpire Connolly in the fifth. After losing again to the White Stockings the next day, the Brewers finally broke it open, scoring 21 runs and collecting 25 hits. Gilbert and Hallman each had 5 hits. Hawley lost the final game of the series. Before Detroit came into town Duffy, changed the starting time of home games from 3:30 to 3:45, as businessmen claimed they could not leave their offices early enough to see the games. The change did little good for the team, as the Brewers lost two of three to the Tigers, Duffy being ejected for the first time as the Brewer skipper in the last game. The Brewers' record was only 4 and 11, and the *Sentinel* called for the club to spend some money to obtain better players. Chicago's Charles Comiskey offered a trade: Dutch Hartman and Frank Shugart, his third baseman and shortstop, for Burke and Conroy. Duffy was not interested. The Brewers then got hot, sweeping four from Cleveland, to put the club in sixth place. The White Stockings cooled them off, sweeping four in Chicago, Duffy being ejected by Umpire Connolly in one of the games and fined in the next game.

Ban Johnson was coming down hard on the league's managers. On May 11 Clark Griffith of Chicago was suspended for five days for an incident with the umpire. John McGraw also drew a suspension from Johnson. McGraw's Orioles were next into Milwaukee, but because of bad weather only one game could be played, Reidy winning 6 to 3. Friel went to the outfield to replace Duffy, and Gilbert was elevated to the leadoff spot. Philadelphia was next in and took three of four. Then Washington lost two of three and Boston split four. In personnel changes, Pete Dowling, with a 1 and 4 record, was released to Cleveland. Bill Friel was loaned to Oshkosh of the Wisconsin State League. Connor replaced Leahy as Duffy's starting catcher, and Waldron went back to the leadoff spot.

On June 7 the Brewers opened in Boston and lost four straight. The Brewers then lost two of three in Philadelphia to drop back into the cellar. Traveling up to Baltimore, the Brewers lost three of four. Duffy was alternating Maloney and Connor behind the plate, and released Tom Leahy to the Philadelphia Athletics, as he could not stop base runners. Bill Friel was called back, as Gilbert was suspended for five days for spiking Umpire Mannassau. The Brewers then split four in Washington. The club began to travel west, Garvin winning in Cleveland, but then the team lost three in Detroit, the final games on shutouts.

The local press was coming down hard on Irv Waldron. The *Sentinel* wrote, "He uses absolutely no judgment after he reaches first base, and on the bases he is frequently like a chicken with its head removed."[29] The paper also wrote he was bad in the outfield, especially on balls behind him. To shore up his outfield, Duffy signed Phil Geier, released from Philadelphia. On June 30 the Brewers returned to Milwaukee Park and Pete Dowling came back to haunt them, winning 7 to 0 on a no-hitter. Cleveland also won the remaining two games. The Tigers then won two of three to end the homestand with the Brewers deep in the cellar.

Milwaukee traveled to Cleveland, splitting two with the Blues. Before returning home Duffy signed John "Jiggs" Donahue. Jiggs had caught for Minneapolis of the Western League and claimed to have not had a contract with that team, but the Western suspended him for jumping his contract. Duffy planned to use him at first base and move Anderson to the outfield. After Reidy beat Cleveland 2 to 0, Duffy released Erv Waldron, hitting .283, to Washington. Jimmy Burke was released to the Chicago White Stockings. Commenting on Burke, the *Chicago News* wrote, "The unsympathetic Milwaukee bleacherites are responsible for Burke's release, as they kept nagging the young man so persistently that he finally asked Manager Duffy to release him. The ex-Brewer is rated as a good ball player, but this year he started badly and the fans have embarrassed him to such an extent that he has not been playing the game that he is capable of."[30] Burke hit only .203 for the Brewers. Jimmy would stay in the big leagues until 1905, but never live up to expectations. Duffy tried to get Fred Hartman from Comiskey, but the Old Roman would not let the third baseman go. Hugh Duffy's team was now: Maloney and Connor—catchers, Donahue—first base, Gilbert—second base, Conroy—shortstop, Geier and Friel—third base, Anderson, Hallman and himself in the outfield. Sparks, Husting, Garvin, Reidy and Hawley were his pitchers.

Meanwhile, the Brewers had lost five of six to the White Stockings. The season was now almost three months old, and at this halfway point the club was 23 and 46. Duffy had appointed Conroy captain to replace Burke, a move the *Sporting Life* called "a well deserved recognition."[31] Donahue was hitting .375 in his short time in Milwaukee. Duffy and Anderson were at .328 and .320. Hallman was hitting .284, Gilbert .281, Conroy .251, Geier .240, Connor .233, Friel .231 and Maloney .210. Under the headline, NEW PLAYERS DEMANDED, the *Sentinel* wrote on July 13, "That Milwaukee should be represented by such a battered aggregation of ball players is a disgrace to the city and the circuit around which the team travels.... Milwaukee patrons are tired of attending poor exhibitions of baseball, and demand that some beneficial changes be made at an early date in the team, even at the expenditure of a considerable sum of money."

Returning home on July 17 the Brewers lost two of three to Connie Mack's Athletics. Duffy signed George Hogriever from the Indianapolis club that had just disbanded to play center field. The Brewers then lost three of four to Baltimore. While in Milwaukee, a reporter from the *Baltimore News* wrote this description of Milwaukee Park:

> The city has been in first class minor ranks for some time, and the stands, while in good condition, are old fashioned. The grandstand is hexagonal in shape, and the first row of benches is as high off the grounds as the second story of a house. There are 12 rows of benches, with solid wood backs and arm rests, that remind one of a good, old fashioned Quaker meeting house. The press box is above the center and is very commodious. Something unique was a small third story above the press box. Here the policemen gather, "far from the maddening crowd." That would take them about a week to get down "to the front" in case of a disturbance in the bleachers, unless a parachute was at home. This does not matter to the easy going German officers of the law, however, and they say, when the "coppers" get to rooting "or fair," their comments on the ability of the Irish players is something wonderful.[32]

Manager Duffy was becoming frustrated. He was quoted in the *Sporting Life* of August 3, 1901, "If this thing keeps up I will be fit for a luny farm. I don't mind losing games when we are not hitting the ball and play the game, but to go in and outbat the other fellows as we have done in this series and lose the games by rank errors is enough to drive a man to drink." With his club faltering badly, Duffy made some changes. Phil Geier, after hitting only .179, was released. So was Joe Connor, who was finding the American League too fast for him. Jiggs Donahue went from first base to behind the plate. Within a short time, the *Sentinel* was reporting Donahue "is one of the best, if not the best, young catchers in the American or any other league...."³³ Donahue, by the way, was one of those rare left-handed catchers in baseball. John Anderson went back to first base. These changes helped Milwaukee split four games with Boston.

Jimmy Burke — nagged by Milwaukee bleacherites until he asked for his release.

July ended with the Brewers taking three of four from the Washington Senators. Chicago had a comfortable lead over Boston. Baltimore, Detroit, Washington, Philadelphia, Cleveland and Milwaukee filled out the standings. The Brewers were in the cellar for good reason. Their .260 batting average was on the bottom of the heap, as was their 336 runs scored. Only two teams could top the Brewers' 186 errors, and no second baseman could match Gilbert's 29 errors. Donahue (.342), Duffy (.323) and Anderson (.321) were hitting well, but no other player was over .275.

The war with the National League was still going strong. The big weapons were offers and counteroffers to players. William Watkins, now an agent for John Brush, offered Wyatt Lee, a Washington pitcher, $3,500 to sign with Cincinnati for 1902 but was turned down. Watkins also talked to Roxy Miller, Detroit's star twirler. Others talked to by National League agents were Cleveland's Earl Moore and Erv Beck, Patton of Washington and Ed Plank of Philadelphia. The Nationals, however, failed to sign any of these players. A gap started to build between Ban Johnson and John McGraw, as the American League czar claimed the Baltimore manager was working for the National League. McGraw quickly denied this.

The Brewers kept playing, and losing. On August 2 ex-Brewer Pete Dowling pitched a one-hitter to lead Cleveland to a 7 to 0 victory. The Blues also won the next day. The Brewers then snapped to, beating Detroit three of four to finish the homestand. In the final game Duffy's newest player, Ed Bruyette, an infielder from the Aurora club, was forced into action when Duffy was ejected by Umpire Manassau. Only days before the *Sentinel* had commented on the umpire, "Why Manassau is retained on the American League staff of umpires by President Johnson is causing comment all around the circuit. He has always been incompetent and has no control over the players, while he is indecision personified during the progress of a game."³⁴

On August 7 the *Daily News* said of the arbitrator, "His sheer incompetence and complete inability to preside over a diamond contest has nauseated all who watched him work." But on August 3 Duffy had told the *Evening Wisconsin* he believed Ban Johnson was right backing his umpires. "I have changed my mind since [entering the American League] and now take off my hat to the officials of the American League." The umpire followed the club to Cleveland where Milwaukee lost 5 to 4. In an argument with him in the ninth inning, Duffy "handed Manassau an expression of his regard in the way of a right hand jab on the jaw."[35] The Milwaukee manager was fined $50 and suspended for 10 days. Conroy and Friel were fined $10 for pushing the arbiter. The American League had only four umpires, which the *Sentinel* rated thusly: Manassau and Jack Haskell "hopelessly incompetent," Jack Sheridan "fair" and Joe Cantillion "good."[36] Warren Hart of Baltimore was then suspended indefinitely for striking Haskell on August 6. Later that month two Chicago players were arrested for an attack on Haskell in Washington. Frank Shugart, one of the two, was suspended. Joe McGinnity of Baltimore was expelled for "expectorating in Umpire Connolly's face,"[37] but was later re-instated. Ban Johnson claimed Clark Griffith, John McGraw and Hugh Duffy were the troublemakers of his league. However, Griffith believed Johnson was the trouble, saying his umpires were incompetent. The *Boston Globe*, however, praised the umpires.

> The American umpires run the game the best and seem to hold the players in check, while the [National] League umpires are often forced to eat humble pie. Johnson's umpires have explicit confidence that their boss will back them up, while the league officials are never sure of their ground.[38]

Word was around the league, however, that the umpires "knowing that Johnson will back them absolutely in anything they do, are getting too domineering for any use. It is claimed that they run players to the bench and out of grounds on no pretexts at all, and that some of the rows have been the result of decisions so hideous that no excuse could be made for them. Johnson, of course, stands grimly by the guns, and says he will back up his umpires to a finish."[39] Meanwhile, the Brewers lost all three in Cleveland, as Bruyette went out to center field to replace Duffy. Milwaukee then won two of three in Detroit, but then lost four in Philly and three in Boston. The team then split two in Washington and two again in Baltimore.

The Brewers returned home to start the final month of the season, but Duffy stayed back east in an attempt to sign some National League players for 1902. Bill Reidy became the acting manager. The homestand started with the Brewers winning two of three from the Philadelphia Athletics. Pink Hawley, with his 4 and 14 record, was released from the club. Three new players were signed to help the Brewers finish 1901. Outfielder Davy Jones and pitcher Claude Elliott from Rockford of the Three I League were signed. Jones, the batting champion of the Three I League, reported when that league's season ended, but Elliott injured himself in the final game of the Three I season and was unable to pitch. The third player was George Bone, a shortstop from New Haven of the Connecticut League who signed for $300 a month. Duffy said he had failed to sign any big National League players because they wanted $3,500 to $4,000 to sign when the same players only wanted $2,000 to $2,500 a few weeks before. The players realized the war between the American and National leagues was going to continue and that they could make money out of the war. The homestand continued, meanwhile, the Brewers defeating Baltimore three of four. The team then split two with Boston, lost two of three to Washington and lost two of three to Chicago to end the final homestand, Duffy using a local 20-year-old George McBride at shortstop. The former City League player had played that year with Fargo in the Dakota League. McBride would play 15 more years in the big leagues, mostly with Washington, hitting only .218 in 1,659 games.

On September 13, the day before President William McKinley died of a gunshot wound he received in Buffalo eight days earlier, the Brewers opened their final road series. After losing two of three in the Windy City, Duffy released George Hogriever, hitting only .235, putting Davy Jones in the outfield, and also using a Chicago amateur, Lou Gertenrich, in two games. Then on to Washington, the Brewers split a doubleheader with the Senators, now playing Bone at shortstop. On September 19 all baseball was suspended as the dead president was buried. Over to Baltimore the Brewers lost two doubleheaders to the Orioles. The season ended with the Brewers losing two of three to the Athletics in Philadelphia and three straight in Boston, Duffy using a player called Fred King [his real name was John Albert Butler, a student at Fordham playing under an alias] to catch the final game of the season.

Not surprisingly, the Brewers ended the season where they had been most of the season.

Chicago	83	53	.610	Baltimore	68	65	.511
Boston	79	57	.581	Washington	61	73	.455
Detroit	74	61	.548	Cleveland	55	82	.401
Philadelphia	74	62	.544	Milwaukee	48	89	.350

The Brewers' lowly record was indeed truly deserved. The *Daily News* on September 30, 1901, wrote the Brewers played "the very rottenest ball ever dished up by a major league organization." Their batting average of .261 was the lowest in the league by eight points. Their run total of 641 was also the lowest. In the field the team's 393 errors was topped by only two other teams. Their pitching staff gave up 832 runs. Individually, John Anderson had a fine year. In addition to having a .330 batting average, Honest John had 190 hits (second in the American League), 46 doubles (second), 99 RBIs (third), 8 home runs (fourth) and 274 total bases (third). Napoleon Lajoie of Philadelphia led all these categories, plus a few others. Jiggs Donahue hit .283 in 37 games with the Brewers and George Bone .302 in his 12 games. Hugh Duffy hit .302 in 79 games. Other averages included Maloney .293, Gilbert .270, Friel .266, Conroy .256, Hallman .246, Bruyette .183 and Jones .173. No pitcher on the staff won more games than he lost. Beside Dowling (1 and 4) and Hawley (7 and 14), who had been released before the season was completed, the pitchers' records were Husting (10 and 15), Garvin (7 and 20), Reidy (16 and 20) and Sparks (7 and 16). In season series, the Brewers managed to beat only one team, the Washington Senators, winning 10 on the year and losing 8. Against the other teams in the American League they were 9 and 11 versus Cleveland, 7 and 12 against Baltimore, 7 and 13 with Detroit, 6 and 14 against Philadelphia, 5 and 15 against Boston, and a miserable 4 and 16 against Charles Comiskey's Chicago White Stockings.

Head on with the National League, Ban Johnson's American League did not do poorly at all. Ernest Lanigan gave the following attendance figures in the *Sporting News* of October 19, 1901.

NATIONAL LEAGUE		AMERICAN LEAGUE	
Chicago	205,071	Chicago	354,350
Boston	146,502	Boston	289,440
Pittsburgh	251,955	Detroit	259,430
Philadelphia	234,937	Philadelphia	206,329
New York	297,650	Baltimore	141,952
Brooklyn	198,200	Washington	161,661
Cincinnati	205,728	Cleveland	131,380
St. Louis	379,988	Milwaukee	139,034
	1,920,031		1,683,584[40]

Lanigan had earlier reported the biggest crowd in Milwaukee was a May 26 game against the Philadelphia Athletics, drawing 10,000. In all, only eight games drew more than 5,000 people. On 15 dates attendance dropped below the 1,000 mark and the last home date of the season—a doubleheader against Chicago—drew only 200.[41]

Financially the American League was a great success. Ban Johnson claimed only Milwaukee had lost money. This, however, is doubtful. As early as August 1 the *Sentinel* claimed Cleveland had lost $10,000. By the end of that month the claim was $15,000 in the hole. Robison of St. Louis thought Cleveland probably lost at least $20,000. It was estimated Boston cleared about $35,000; Chicago, $30,000; Philadelphia, $15,000; Washington, $10,000 to $14,000; and Baltimore, $5,000, although Ban Johnson later said the Orioles did not make money. Detroit's true financial results are not known. At first it was said the club made about $30,000, but it was determined that its financial picture was a mess. Johnson found the Tigers' gross receipts were $61,000, but the books showed the club still lost $6,000 to $7,000.

John Anderson—The Brewers' 1901 offensive star (Transcendental Graphics).

How the Brewers did financially is in question. In late August Matthew Killilea was reported as saying the club would earn from $10,000 to $15,000 for the season. However, after the season the *Sentinel* wrote: "That the season of 1901 has not been of pecuniary benefit to the Milwaukee magnates there is little room for doubt, and the fact that the team lost so consistently from start to finish inclines one to the belief that the bank accounts of the owners of the franchise suffered to the extent of about $5,000."[42] In the beginning of the season, Harry Quin believed the Brewers would have a total expense of about $30,175. B.F. Wright in the October 5, 1901, *Sporting News* figured that after the 10 percent American League fund deduction and money given to visiting teams, the Brewers took in about $25,850 at Milwaukee Park and $24,975 on the road (having a road attendance of over 222,000), thus totaling $50,825—a little more than Cleveland and not much below Washington and Baltimore. Wright could not understand how Milwaukee lost money, thinking possibly the statement was "to reconcile the Milwaukee fans to the transfer of the club to St. Louis." However, in the October 12, 1901, issue of the *Sporting News,* Frank Patterson pointed out some cities' attendance reports "were at times very much exaggerated." This included Milwaukee's, which were "padded very considerable." Patterson also believed Wright underestimated salaries in the American League. He reported the Brewers' salary list "was hardly below $40,000."

As far back as February of 1901 rumor was about that the Brewers would transfer to St. Louis. On February 25, the *Sentinel* wrote if the Brewers did not transfer before the 1901 season, they probably would by 1902. According to a later *Sporting News* report, the American League picked Milwaukee over St. Louis "for sentimental reasons." Killilea had "declined to accede to the request of President Johnson, Charlie Comiskey and other prominent in the American League" to transfer his team to St. Louis "with protestations of civic pride."[43] The talk died until June when the American League magnates met in Chicago and said they would enter St. Louis and/or New York in 1902, dropping Milwaukee and/or Cleveland. Later there was talk of the American League going into Pittsburgh but doubted by most, as the Pennsylvania city was not allowed Sunday ball. In late July Matt Killilea conferred with Charles Comiskey and Ban Johnson and reported the American League plan was to transfer the Washington franchise to New York and Cleveland to St. Louis. Killilea said he would "personally vouch for the retention of this city [Milwaukee] in the circuit."[44] He told the public he had just turned down a $30,000 offer for his franchise from St. Louis people.

> The club and franchise is not for sale at any price, as we are satisfied that in years to come the Milwaukee team will be a money maker. The patronage here has always been liberal, and while this season the team has not been playing up to its usual form, the attendance has been larger than we expected under the conditions existing. Milwaukee will continue to be in the American League during the life of its franchise, which has nine years to run after this season, and it will be the aim of the owners of the club to place the best team in the field that money commands. We are making every effort to strengthen the weak spots, and hope before the present season ends to merit the support that Milwaukee people have been giving us.[45]

Others, including Jim Manning of Washington, insisted Milwaukee would go to St. Louis.

Meanwhile, talk of peace between the two major leagues was heard. Even a rumor that the two leagues would merge into a 10-club circuit was about. Both sides denied these stories. In August a story broke that Ban Johnson had received an option on the stock from the St. Louis National League owners and he had given Killilea a chance to take up the option. Privately, Johnson was admitting Milwaukee would be transferred to St. Louis, and stated "the players at present with the Milwaukee club are popular in St. Louis and they, with a materially strengthened team, would undoubtedly be well supported there."[46] The *Sentinel* believed the Brewers would go to St. Louis, and Baltimore would transfer to Providence, as New York's National League owner Andrew Freedman was too strong in baseball and political circles to crack. It appeared nothing was to come of the story, but something was definitely brewing in St. Louis. Johnson said the American League would enter St. Louis, but at this point declined to say what city would be dropped. The *Daily News* was sure it would not be Milwaukee because of Matthew Killilea. "He has been one of the staunchest supporters of the American League, and he did as much if not more than any one person to place Ban Johnson in the comfortable berth he has today. Mr. Killilea is high in the councils of the American League and if he cares to have one of its teams here next season his wishes will be respected."[47]

In late August Killilea again turned down an offer for his club. "An authentic source" said some National League ball players "who are in the possession of wealth accumulated during a long term of service"[48] composed a syndicate that offered Killilea $42,000 for the Brewers. Names were not announced, but it was believed Bid McPhee, Jake Beckley and Frank Bancroft, all associated with Cincinnati, formed the syndicate. They wanted to move the club to St. Louis, but concentrated on the Cleveland franchise when turned down here.

By mid–September reliable sources were claiming the Brewers would be transferred to St. Louis and the team would be composed of the best Milwaukee players and some of the best St. Louis National League players. Henry Killilea, now the directing head of the Brewers, as his brother Matthew was ill, denied this. A St. Louis dispatch reported, however, that Killilea had secured nine players from the National League Cardinals to play with St. Louis in the American League in 1902. Matt Killilea told the Milwaukee press he wanted to retire from baseball and would not run the St. Louis club if the Brewers moved there. He also said he had received an offer of $30,000 for the franchise from St. Louis men. Then in late September Philadelphia sources claimed Ban Johnson had reportedly made a deal where the Milwaukee owners would receive $25,000 for 40 percent of the stock they held from a St. Louis brewer, and Matt Killilea would be made president of the club after the transfer to St. Louis. In early October Henry Killilea went to St. Louis, reportedly to negotiate the disposal of the franchise. The Milwaukee owners were reportedly opposed to the move, but liberal inducements were offered them. Killilea returned shortly and St. Louis dispatches reported the Brewers would transfer, and Jim McAleer would manage the club. Ban Johnson also reported the transfer. Milwaukee officials, however, denied this. McAleer did come to Milwaukee to talk to Henry Killilea and Fred Gross. The *Sentinel* wrote, "You pays your money and takes your choice"[49] on who was telling the truth. The *Evening Wisconsin* was sure the Brewers would transfer and gave reasons.

> It is an impossibility for Milwaukee to spend as much money in getting a team together and putting up the salaries requisite to get gilt-edged players and put a team in the field like Chicago, Philadelphia and Boston, and unless the Milwaukee fans are content to travel along as the tail-enders of the American League for another season, the best thing that can be done in the interests of the sport locally will be to quit and get into a class where Milwaukee will be able to hold its own in place of simply serving as the means to fatten the averages and standings of the other teams.[50]

However, there were people who thought Milwaukee could survive in the American League. The Milwaukee correspondent to the *Sporting Life* wrote on September 28, 1901:

> The statement that Milwaukee cannot afford to support a team of equal caliber with Washington and Detroit is absurd. If the Milwaukee magnates engage high-salaried players, and the team makes a favorable showing—that is, winning half of their games—the patronage they will receive will surprise those who are now deriding the ability of Milwaukee for supporting first-class exhibitions of base ball.... Milwaukee will not support a tail-end team or a mediocre aggregation of ball players. It demands the best, and when that is provided there is no limit to the extent of the patronage.... Milwaukee is a better ball town than Baltimore, Cleveland or Washington, and as good as Detroit, and if these cities can afford to secure leading talent for their respective teams for 1901, then the management of the Milwaukee Club can surely take a similar risk.

The evidence was mounting that Milwaukee was on the way out of the American League. On October 10 it was reported Hugh Duffy resigned as manager of the Brewers, wanting to go back to Boston, but this was denied. The following day Ban Johnson announced he had signed five players from the Cardinals to play for the new St. Louis club. Killilea, however, still denied any move was in the works. These continuing reports and denials led the Milwaukee *Sporting News* correspondent to write these were only "one of the thousand little and big things which prove how much confidence may be placed in the announcements of the base ball magnates these days. They have adopted a policy of denying and claiming everything, so that when a piece of news that is authentic is dug up, it must be supported by oaths and pledges, or it looks like the stuff that is being piped by the guess artists of the major league cities."[51] Back in St. Louis dispatches reported Gussie Busch, Zach Tinker and George Heckel would back the club, and they wanted Matt Killilea for president. The group went so far as to name the team players, including eight Brewers. Others in the American League favored the transfer. Manning and McGraw, for example, believed that St. Louis would pay visiting clubs $5,000 more during the season than the clubs could get in Milwaukee. On October 13, 1901, the *Sentinel* attacked Ban Johnson and his cronies:

> American League magnates are exhibiting a selfish streak of well developed proportions this fall in making an attempt to deprive Milwaukee of its franchise. For years this city was the backbone

of the league, supplying Johnson and his associates with the sinews of war even when the team representing Milwaukee was not considered a factor in the championship race. Now that the American League has expanded into a simon pure organization, and simply because the Brewers graced the tail end of the processions ... and did not attract the people to the ball grounds as they had in preceding seasons, the other magnates now say 'T'ell with Milwaukee.'

The Milwaukee owners did not give in that easily. They set a price tag of $60,000 for the franchise, a figure they believed too high for acceptance. They were right. Ban Johnson said, "There is not a club in the country that is worth $60,000 today in these troublesome times of baseball."[52] Back in St. Louis, Zach Tinker backed out. It was reported Tinker was willing to put $25,000 into the St. Louis club for half interest, but was told he would need more to have even a 40 percent interest. Tinker wanted control of the club, but the Milwaukee owners wanted to retain that. It was said an imposition of a special tax of $2,000 by the St. Louis city council deterred Killilea and Gross from trying to run the club with St. Louis interests. Failing to get controlling interest, Tinker dropped out.

The Milwaukee press believed the deal was off and the Brewers would stay. Ban Johnson said otherwise. He called Milwaukee a "one day town,"[53] saying they only drew good crowds on Sunday. Johnson stated the Brewers would go to St. Louis and there would be no local money in the club, the capital would be furnished by the American League, and the franchise the league's "common possession until such time as a proper man could be found to relieve it of the holds and take personal charge."[54]

The St. Louis-Milwaukee mess was not clearing up. Bill Reidy and three other Brewers stated they would ask for an increase in salary if the club was transferred, as their contracts with the Brewers did not require them to play in St. Louis. Ned Garvin said he was dissatisfied with the situation and was going to jump to the National League. Billy Gilbert said the same. Wid Conroy did, jumping to Pittsburgh.

The American League could not find grounds in St. Louis. Charles Comiskey said the American League "does not want to buy the city, simply a slice thereof, but the figures asked are out of reason." Finally, old Sportsman's Park was secured.

On December 2, the American League met in Chicago and re-elected Ban Johnson as president. Fred Gross was at the meeting, but as Matthew Killilea had been detained by the trains, Milwaukee was not dropped. Killilea told newsmen, "The owners of the Milwaukee club are opposed to the transfer to St. Louis and the American League cannot make a change without the consent of the owners."[55] Word was around, however, that he wanted $48,000 for the franchise. The next day, after a session that lasted past 11:00 in the evening, the long-awaited transfer was completed. Matthew Killilea purchased the majority interest of his brother Henry, who did not want Matt in baseball because of his failing health, and transferred the club to St. Louis. Matthew Killilea was president and principal owner of the St. Louis franchise. Jim McAleer was named manager. The *Milwaukee Journal* was not kind, saying, "It is a very clever trick of the American League bunch in keeping Killilea ... on their staff with ground awaiting them in Milwaukee in case St. Louis should go to the bead."[56] The *Daily News*, bitter over the transfer, wrote Killilea and Gross "have pink tea in their veins instead of sporting blood"[57] for not taking a chance on Milwaukee. The *Sentinel*, however, said of the transfer on Dec. 6, 1901:

> The owners of the Milwaukee club removed their team to St. Louis as a business proposition. They expected to sell out, but the absence of capitalists in the Mound City to shoulder the burden made it necessary for them to carry the load themselves, and it is possible that they may make their independent fortunes as a result of the move. The Killileas and F.C. Gross stated that Milwaukee could not adequately support the expensive team they had secured; so they had to leave the city.

Because of his health, Matt Killilea spent the winter in Texas and left George Munson, who had been secretary to Chris von der Ahe of the old St Louis Browns, to run the club in his absence. Some, the *Daily News* and the *Chicago American* included, doubted if Killilea was really behind the club because of his health, thinking Johnson and Comiskey were looking after the finances of the club. In January Matthew Killilea sold out to a St. Louis syndicate for a reported $40,000, and along with brother Henry bought into the American League Boston club. Matthew Killilea died July 27, 1902, of tuberculosis.

The Brewers of 1901 went in different directions. Hugh Duffy

Cartoon from *Milwaukee Sentinel* showing Matt Killilea taking his team from Milwaukee to St. Louis.

would remain in Milwaukee and manage a minor league club in the Western League. Wid Conroy signed with Pittsburgh. John Anderson, Bill Friel, Jiggs Donahue, Davy Jones, Bill Maloney and Bill Reidy transferred with the club to St. Louis. Tully Sparks pitched the 1902 season with the New York Giants. Bert Husting pitched with Boston and Philadelphia of the American League. [Husting also had an interesting local legacy. Born in Mayville, Wisconsin, Berthold Juneau Husting — middle named after his grandfather, Solomon Juneau, founder of Milwaukee — became a lawyer after his baseball career. From 1933 to 1944 he served as U.S. District Attorney in Milwaukee, commuting to his office in Milwaukee from Mayville because he never liked big city life. He practiced law in his hometown until his death in 1948.] Ned Garvin ended up with the White Stockings and Billy Gilbert with Baltimore. George McBride, George Bone, Ed Bruyette and Bill Hallman dropped back into the minors.

* * *

The Brewers' transfer from Milwaukee to St. Louis was in some ways a matter of timing, as well as necessary in the America League's war strategy. Matthew Killilea was reported in September as saying, "If there was no war, then Milwaukee would be sure to remain in the American League. You must fight the devil with fire, and the American League must go into the National League's territory to wage a successful war. Before peace is declared the American League will doubtless be in New York and St. Louis."[58] The 1900 census showed St. Louis' population to be 575,238 — the fourth-largest city in the United States, with more than twice as many people as Milwaukee's 285,315. The attendance figures reported above from the *Sporting News* of October 19, 1901, show the St. Louis National League team had the highest major league attendance for the 1901 season.

Ban Johnson's dream of transferring Baltimore to New York was accomplished in 1903. From 1903 to 1954 the American League of Boston, Philadelphia, New York, Washington, Detroit, Cleveland, Chicago and St. Louis remained unchanged. In 1954 the St. Louis Browns were transferred to Baltimore.

Could Milwaukee have flourished in the American League and avoided the fate of the St. Louis Browns? So many factors entered into what happened and what might have happened that nothing can be certain. And in any event, history cannot be changed. But it is fun to look back and wonder, What if?

Appendix I

Results of Cream City Match Games with Top Clubs

1866
May 30	Cream City	48	Capitol City of Madison	15
June 28	Cream City	23	Julian of Dubuque	15
June 29	Cream City	14	Forest City of Rockford	13
June 30	Bloomington	23	Cream City	20
August 22	Forest City of Rockford	24	Cream City	10
August 23	Cream City	44	Capitol City of Madison	15
November 8	Cream City	29	Whitewater	11

1867
June 19	Beloit Olympians	43	Cream City	25
July 4	Atlantics of Chicago	48	Cream City	45
July 28	Atlantics of Chicago	71	Cream City	20
September 5	Cream City	32	Capitol City of Madison	13
September 6	Cream City	44	Whitewater	19

1868
June 22	Brooklyn Atlantics	67	Cream City	13
July 4	Garden City of Chicago	52	Cream City	20
August 2	Cream City	41	Capitol City of Madison	15
August 7	Unions of Morrisana	43	Cream City	16
August 17	Cream City	45	Racine College	16
August 27	Cream City	45	Capitol City of Madison	18
October 9	Cream City	20	Atlantics of Chicago	17
October 22	Cream City	67	Muscles of Randolph	16

1869
July 5	Cream City	34	Athletics of Chicago	20
July 30	Cincinnati Red Stockings	85	Cream City	7
September 11	Janesville Mutuals	55	Cream City	46

1870
May 28	Chicago White Stockings	71	Cream City	19
July 4	Cream City	36	Athletics of Chicago	26
July 18	Athletics of Chicago	32	Cream City	21
July 19	Amateurs of Chicago	35	Cream City	22
July 27	Harvards of Boston	41	Cream City	13
August 1	Cream City	26	Occidentals of Quincy	11
August 2	Cream City	53	Occidentals of Quincy	24
August 18	Cream City	64	Janesville Mutuals	20
August 22	Racine College	33	Cream City	27
August 30*	Janesville Mutuals	19	Cream City	17
September 2	Forest City of Rockford	53	Cream City	4
September 6	Centrals of Elkhorn	33	Cream City	25

*Championship game forfeited to Cream City; played a picked nine in an exhibition game.

Appendix II

Results of West End Games with Top Clubs, 1876–1877

Opponents include amateur and professional clubs.

1876

Date	Team	Score	Opponent	Score
May 26	West End	14	Evanston College of Illinois	5
May 30	West End	22	Alerts of Milwaukee	15
June 10	West End	11	Evanston College of Illinois	5
June 14	Racine College	11	West End	4
June 21	Chicago White Stockings	11	West End	1
June 29	West End (Forfeit)	9	Racine College	0
June 30	Athletics of Philadelphia	14	West End	4
July 5	West End	10	Fairbanks of Chicago	6
July 7	Hartford Dark Blues	17	West End	2
July 10	Pacific Slope of San Francisco	8	West End	4
July 12	West End	12	Pacific Slope of SF	3
July 15	West End	14	Clippers of Winona, Minnesota	4
July 17	West End	7	St. Paul Red Caps	0
July 22	West End	9	Alerts of Milwaukee	7
July 29	West End	10	Fairbanks of Chicago	7
August 4	Amateurs of Oshkosh	18	West End	14
August 12	Fairbanks of Chicago	5	West End	2
August 15	West End	20	Janesville Mutuals	4
August 24	West End	11	Janesville Mutuals	9
August 26	West End	9	St. Paul Red Caps	5
August 29	West End	18	St. Paul Red Caps	3
August 31	West End	12	Freeport Red Stockings	10
Sept. 2	West End	7	Detroit Aetnas	3
Sept. 8	West End	7	Fairbanks of Chicago	5
Sept. 14	West End	24	Janesville Mutuals	2
Sept. 15	West End	5	Detroit Aetnas	1
Sept. 16	West End	5	Detroit Aetnas	2
Sept. 18	Detroit Aetnas	18	West End	0
Sept. 19	West End	19	Alerts of Milwaukee	11
Sept. 21	West End	21	Alerts of Milwaukee	9
Sept. 23	Athletics of Racine	6	West End	5
Sept. 28	Chicago White Stockings	10	West End	7
Sept. 30	West End	25	Liberty of Chicago	1
Oct. 2	West End	24	Athletics of Racine	9
Oct. 3	West End	28	Chicago West Ends	7
Oct. 12	St. Louis Brown Stockings	17	West End	5
Oct. 21	Chicago White Stockings	11	West End	10

1877

Date	Team	Score	Opponent	Score
May 5	West End	8	Fairbanks of Chicago	5
May 8	West End	4	Syracuse Stars	4
May 9	Syracuse Stars	8	West End	0
May 12	Janesville Mutuals	4	West End	3
May 15	Janesville Mutuals	13	West End	1
May 18	St. Louis Brown Stockings	13	West End	10
May 23	West End	12	Fairbanks of Chicago	7
May 25	Fairbanks of Chicago	9	West End	8
May 30	Minneapolis Blue Stockings	13	West End	11
June 1	West End	4	Minneapolis Blue Stockings	1
June 2	St. Paul Red Caps	1	West End	0
June 6	Cincinnati Red Stockings	7	West End	5
June 15	West End	3	Racine	0
June 16	West End	22	Evanston College	1
June 18	Memphis Reds	4	West End	0
June 19	West End	2	Memphis Reds	1
June 20	West End	3	St. Paul Red Caps	1
June 22	West End	4	St. Paul Red Caps	0
June 23	West End	8	Racine	2
June 26	West End	7	Minneapolis Blue Stockings	0
June 27	West End	2	Chicago White Stockings	2
June 29	Racine	10	West End	4
June 30	West End	16	Minneapolis Blue Stockings	2
July 4	West End	7	Janesville Mutuals	0
July 7	West End	6	Janesville Mutuals	1
July 12	Chicago White Stockings	16	West End	2
July 18	West End	10	Syracuse Stars	8
July 20	Indianapolis Blues	1	West End	0
July 24	West End	3	Manchester	2
July 25	Chicago White Stockings	5	West End	1
July 27	West End	6	Hartford Dark Blues	1
Aug. 2	West End	2	Manchester	0
Aug. 4	Janesville Mutuals	3	West End	2
Aug. 7	Janesville Mutuals (Forfeit)	9	West End	0
Aug. 8	Cincinnati Red Stockings	1	West End	0
Aug. 9	Louisville Grays	6	West End	1
Aug. 10	Louisville Grays	8	West End	4
Aug. 11	West End	5	Indianapolis Blues	2
Aug. 16	St. Louis Browns	10	West End	4
Aug. 18	Janesville Mutuals	4	West End	3
Aug. 23	Alleghany of Pittsburgh	3	West End	2
Aug. 25	West End	8	Alleghany of Pittsburgh	4
Aug. 28	Alleghany of Pittsburgh	1	West End	0
Aug. 31	West End	13	Janesville Mutuals	1
Sept. 1	West End	16	Janesville Mutuals	2
Sept. 6	West End	6	Janesville Mutuals	0
Sept. 8	West End	8	Springfield Reds	4
Sept. 10	West End	10	Springfield Reds	4
Sept. 13	West End	7	Janesville Mutuals	3
Sept. 14	West End	6	Janesville Mutuals	3
Sept. 18	West End	4	Syracuse Stars	3
Sept. 20	West End	18	Syracuse Stars	3
Sept. 21	Alleghany of Pittsburgh	7	West End	5
Sept. 26	West End	11	Cass of Detroit	1
Sept. 27	London Tescumsehs	11	West End	8
Sept. 28	West End	11	London Tescumsehs	1
Oct. 1	West End	3	Buffalos of Buffalo	2
Oct. 2	West End	3	Buffalos of Buffalo	0
Oct. 6	West End	7	Indianapolis Blues	7
Oct. 24	Chicago White Stockings	7	West End	5
Oct. 25	West End	6	Chicago White Stockings	1

Appendix III
Batting and Pitching Statistics

The following are the batting and pitching statistics of major league players of Milwaukee teams.

1878 — National League
1891 — American Association
1884 — Union Association
1901 — American League

HITTERS	Year	G	AB	H	2B	3B	HR	R	RBI	SB	BB	AVG	POS
ALBERTS, Gus	1891	12	41	4	0	0	0	6	2	1	7	.098	12–3b
ANDERSON, John	1901	138	576	190	46	7	8	90	99	35	21	.330	125–1b; 13-of
BEHEL, Steve	1884	9	33	8	1	0	0	5	—	—	3	.242	9–of
BENNETT, Charlie	1878	49	184	45	9	0	1	16	12	—	10	.245	35-c; 20-of
BIGNALL, George	1884	4	9	2	0	0	0	4	—	—	1	.222	4-c
BLISS, Frank	1878	2	8	1	0	0	0	1	0	—	0	.125	1–3b; 1-c
BONE, George	1901	12	43	13	2	0	0	6	6	0	4	.302	12-ss
BROUGHTON, Cal	1884	11	39	12	5	0	0	5	—	—	0	.308	7-c; 5-of
BRUYETTE, Ed	1901	26	82	15	3	0	0	7	4	1	12	.183	21–of; 2b-3; 1-ss; 1–3b
BURKE, Ed	1891	35	144	34	9	0	2	31	21	7	12	.236	35–of
BURKE, Jimmy	1901	64	233	48	8	0	0	24	26	6	17	.206	64–3b
CANAVAN, Jim	1891	35	142	38	2	4	3	33	21	7	16	.268	24–2b; ss-11
CARNEY, John	1891	31	110	33	5	2	3	22	23	5	13	.300	31–1b
CONNOR, Joe	1901	38	102	28	3	1	1	10	9	4	6	.275	30-c; 1–2b; 1–3b; 1-of
CONROY, Wid	1901	131	503	129	20	6	5	74	64	21	36	.256	118-ss; 12–3b
CREAMER, George	1878	50	193	41	7	3	0	30	15	—	5	.212	2–2b; 17-of; 6–3b
DALRYMPLE, Abner	1878	61	271	96	10	4	0	52	15	—	6	.354	61-of
	1891	32	135	42	7	5	1	31	22	6	7	.311	32–of
DONAHUE, Jiggs	1901	37	107	34	5	4	0	10	16	4	10	.318	19-c; 13–1b
DUFFY, Hugh	1901	79	285	86	15	9	2	40	45	12	16	.302	77–of
EARL, Howard	1891	31	129	32	5	2	1	21	17	3	5	.248	30–of; 1b-2
ELLICK, Joe	1878	3	13	2	0	0	0	2	1	—	0	.154	2-c; 1-1b; 1-p
FALCH, Anton	1884	5	18	2	0	0	0	0	—	0	0	.111	3–of; 2-c
FOLEY, Bill	1878	56	229	62	8	5	0	33	22	—	7	.271	53–3b; 7-c
FRIEL, Bill	1901	106	376	100	13	7	4	51	35	15	23	.266	61–3b; 29-of; 9–2b; 6-ss
GEIER, Phil	1901	11	39	7	1	1	0	4	1	4	5	.179	8–of; 3–3b
GERTENRICH, Lou	1901	2	3	1	0	0	0	1	0	0	0	.333	1-of
GILBERT, Billy	1901	127	492	133	14	7	0	77	43	19	31	.270	127–2b
GOLDEN, Mike	1878	55	214	44	6	3	0	16	20	—	3	.206	39–of; 22-p; 1–1b
GOODMAN, Jacob	1878	60	252	62	4	3	1	28	27	—	7	.246	60–1b
GRIFFIN, Tom	1884	11	41	9	2	0	0	5	—	0	3	.220	11–1b
GRIM, John	1891	29	119	28	5	1	1	14	14	1	2	.235	16-c; 10–3b; 3–2b
HALLMAN, Bill	1901	139	549	135	26	6	2	70	47	12	41	.246	139–of
HOGAN, Eddie	1884	11	37	3	1	0	0	6	—	0	7	.081	11-of

312

Batting and Pitching Statistics

HITTERS	Year	G	AB	H	2B	3B	HR	R	RBI	SB	BB	AVG	POS
HOGRIEVER, George	1901	54	221	52	10	2	0	25	16	7	30	.235	54-of
HOLBERT, Bill	1878	45	173	32	2	0	0	10	12	—	3	.185	30-of; 21-c
JENNINGS, Alfred	1878	1	2	0	0	0	0	0	0	—	1	.000	1-c
JONES, Davy	1901	14	52	9	0	0	3	12	5	4	11	.173	14-of
KING, Fred (John Butler)	1901	1	3	0	0	0	0	0	0	0	1	.000	1-c
KNOWDELL, Jacob	1878	4	14	3	1	0	0	2	2	—	0	.214	2-c; 1-of; 1-ss
LEAHY, Tom	1901	33	99	24	6	2	0	18	10	3	11	.242	28-c; 2-of; 1-2b
LETCHER, Tom	1891	6	21	4	1	0	0	3	2	1	0	.190	6-of
MALONEY, Bill	1901	86	290	85	3	4	0	42	22	11	7	.293	72-c; 8-of
McBRIDE, George	1901	3	12	2	0	0	0	0	0	0	1	.167	3-ss
MORGAN, Daniel	1878	14	56	11	0	0	0	2	5	—	3	.196	13-of; 3-3b; 1-2b
MORRISSEY, Tom	1884	12	47	8	2	0	0	3	—	0	0	.170	12-3b
MYERS, Al	1884	12	46	15	6	0	0	6	—	0	0	.326	12-2b
PETERS, John	1878	55	246	76	6	1	0	33	22	—	5	.309	34-2b; 22-ss
PETTIT, Bob	1891	21	80	14	4	0	1	10	5	2	7	.175	9-2b; 7-of; 6-3b
REDMOND, Bill (Real name Bill Redmon)	1878	48	187	43	8	0	0	16	21	—	8	.230	39-ss; 7-of; 3-3b; 1-c
SEXTON, Tom	1884	12	47	11	2	0	0	9	—	0	4	.234	12-ss
SHOCH, George	1891	34	127	40	7	1	1	29	16	12	18	.315	25-ss; 9-3b
VAUGHN, Harry	1891	25	99	33	7	0	0	13	9	1	4	.333	20-c; 4-1b; 1-of
WALDRON, Irving	1901	62	266	79	8	6	0	48	29	12	16	.297	62-of

PITCHERS	Year	G	IP	H	R	ER	ERA	BB	SO	W	L	Pct.
BALDWIN, Charles	1884	2	17	7	5	5	2.65	1	21	1	1	.500
CUSHMAN, Ed	1884	4	36	10	4	4	1.00	3	47	4	0	1.000
DAVIES, George	1891	12	102	94	48	30	2.65	35	61	7	5	.583
DOWLING, Pete	1901	10	49	71	49	31	5.62	14	25	1	4	.200
DWYER, JOHN [Frank]	1891	10	86	92	41	21	2.20	21	27	6	4	.600
ELLICK, Joe	1878	1	3	1	1	1	3.00	1	0	0	1	.000
GARVIN, Ned	1901	37	257	258	155	99	3.46	90	122	7	20	.259
GOLDEN, Mike	1878	22	161	217	171	74	4.14	33	52	3	13	.188
HAWLEY, Pink	1901	26	182	228	133	93	4.59	41	50	7	14	.333
HUGHEY, Jim	1891	2	15	18	6	5	3.00	3	9	1	0	1.000
HUSTING, Bert	1901	34	217	234	151	103	4.27	95	67	10	15	.400
KILLEN, Frank	1891	11	96	73	42	18	1.68	51	38	7	4	.636
MAINS, Willard	1891	2	10	14	19	12	10.80	10	2	0	2	.000
PORTER, Henry	1884	6	51	32	25	17	3.00	9	71	3	3	.500
REIDY, Bill	1901	37	301	364	183	141	4.21	62	50	16	20	.444
SPARKS, Tully	1901	29	210	228	157	82	3.51	93	62	7	16	.304
WEAVER, Sam	1878	45	383	371	214	83	1.95	21	95	12	31	.279

Appendix IV

Players on Milwaukee's Minor League Teams, 1884–1900

The following is a list of the year, name of league, manager, record and place of finish of the team that season, followed by a list of all the players who played on Milwaukee's minor league teams from 1884 through 1900. For a handful of players, it has thus far proven impossible to determine a first name.

Year	League	Manager	Record	Place
1884	Northwestern League	James McKee Tom Loftus	53–34	1st Place when league disbanded
1885	Western League	Tom Loftus	22–13	League disbanded, no final standings
1886	Northwestern League	Ted Sullivan	35–41	5th Place
1887	Northwestern League	Jim Hart	78–43	2nd Place
1888	Western Association	Jim Hart	61–63	5th Place
1889	Western Association	Ezra Sutton	59–63	5th Place
1890	Western Association	Charles Cushman	77–45	3rd Place
1891	Western Association	Charles Cushman	59–37	1st Place when team quit to join American Association
1892	Western League	Charles Cushman	28–19	2nd Place
1894	Western League	Charles Cushman	50–74	8th Place
1895	Western League	Larry Twitchell	57–67	6th Place
1896	Western League	Larry Twitchell Robert Glenalvin	62–78	6th Place
1897	Western League	Connie Mack	85–51	4th Place
1898	Western League	Connie Mack	82–57	3rd Place
1899	Western League	Connie Mack	56–68	6th Place
1900	American League	Connie Mack	79–59	2nd Place

ABBATICCHIO, Ed 1900
ALBERTS, Gus 1889–91; 94
ALEXANDER, Daniel 1889
ALMIN, Charles 1886
ALVORD, Bill 1885
ANDERSON, John 1900
ANDERSON, Varney 1887
ARMSTRONG, William 1895
ARUNDEL, Harry 1884
ARUNDEL, John 1885; 86
ATHERTON, Charles 1899
BAKER, Kirtley 1894–96
BALDWIN, Charles "Lady" 1884; 85
BANNING, James 1886
BARNES, Fred 1896–99
BEAUMONT, Clarence 1898
BEHEL, Steve 1884; 85; 86

BIERBAUER, Louis 1900
BIGNALL, George 1884
BISHOP, George 1886; 87
BLAKE, Harry 1897
BOLAN, Patrick 1894–95
BORCHERS, George 1896
BRADY, Jim 1891
BRADY, George "Texas" 1899
BROUGHON, Cal 1884; 87
BROWN, Joe 1885
BRYNAN, Charlie 1889
BUCKLEY, John 1891
BURKE, Eddie 1891
BURKE, Jimmy 1898; 1900
BURNETT, Hercules 1887
BURNS, 1895
BURNS, Dick 1885
BURRELL, Harry 1892

CAMPAU, Charles (Count) 1894
CAMPION, William J. 1891
CAREY, George 1894
CARLSON, George 1894
CHECH, Charlie 1899
CLARK, 1889
CLARK, Willie 1900
CLARKSON, Arthur 1897
CLAUSEN, Fred 1890; 91; 96
CLAYTON, Harry 1894
CLAYTON, Zach 1884
CLINGMAN, Billy 1894
COLGAN, William 1886
CONGOLTON, Bill 1899
CONROY, Wid 1900
CORBETT, Jim 1897
CROSSLEY, William 1888–89

CUSICK, Andy 1888
CUSICK, John 1886
DAILY, Hugh 1886
DALRYMPLE, Abner 1890–91
DALY, Tom 1897–98
DAVIES, George 1889–90; 91
DAVIN, David J. 1888
DEALY, Pat 1884
DELANEY, T.F. 1884
DELHANTY, Tom 1897
DEVINNEY, Billy 1894
DIGGINS, Bill (Cy) 1900
DONAHUE, James 1892
DOUGHERTY, T. 1886
DOWD, Tommy 1900
DOWLING, Pete 1897; 1900
DOYLE, 1889
DUNGAN, Sam 1891
DUNN, Steve 1884
EARLE, Billy 1889
ELLIOTT, Claude 1895
EMMERKE, Robert 1889
FALCH, Anton 1884; 85
FASS, Fred 1886
FERSON, Alex 1888; 92
FIELDS, John "Jocko" 1894
FIGGEMEIER, Frank 1894
FISHER, Albert 1888
FITZSIMMONS, O.K. 1887
FLAHERTY, Pat 1894
FLANNAGAN, Tom 1890
FORSTER, Tom 1885; 86–88
FRASER, Charles 1894
FREEMAN, Julius 1889
FRIEND, Danny 1899
FULLER, William 1888–89
FULTZ, Dave 1900
GARRY, Jim 1900
GILBERT, Bill 1900
GLENALVIN, Robert 1896
GOODENOUGH, Bill 1894
GORMAN, Jack 1885
GRABE, 1886
GRAY, Billy 1899
GRIFFIN, Tom 1884
GRIFFITH, Clark 1888–90
GRIM, John 1891
HALLMAN, Bill H. 1900
HALLMAN, William W. 1899
HAMBURG, Charley 1892
HARPER, Joe 1886
HART, Robert 1887
HART, Will 1899
HARTMAN, Fred 1895–96
HASSAMAER, Bill 1889
HASTINGS, Charlie 1894
HAWES, Bill 1888
HEARD, Charles 1890

HENDRICKS, John "Kid" 1886
HENRY, George 1892
HERR, Joe 1889
HEUP, Henry 1888
HIMMELSTEIN, Phillip 1884
HINES, Harry 1887
HOGAN, Ed 1884
HOLLY, Ed 1899
HOLMES, W. 1886
HORNER, Jack 1888
HOWE, Harry H. 1890
HOWE, Harry 1894
HUGHEY, Jim 1891
HULL, Arthur 1887
HURLEY, Jeremiah 1889
HUSTING, Bert 1899; 1900
IKE, Albert 1890
IMIG, John 1897
ISAACSON, Charles 1886
JANTZEN, August 1889–90
JOHNSON, James 1894
JOHNSON, Mike 1894
JONES, Bert 1896–97
KEAS, Ed 1889
KELLEY, William 1886
KETCHUM, Fred 1900
KILLEN, Frank 1891
KIRBY, John 1889
KLOPF, Gus 1894–95
KLUSMAN, William 1889
KNOUFF, Ed 1899
KRIEG, Bill 1890; 92
KROCK, Gus 1886; 89
LaFLEUR, John 1895
LAKE, Fred 1892
LANGSFORD, Robert 1894
LaRETT, Oliver 1895
LAVIN, John 1886
LEE, Tommy 1885
LETCHER, Tom 1891
LEWEE, Eddie 1897–98
LIPPERT, Louis "Gus" 1897
LOEHRBECK, Joe 1889
LOFTUS, Tom 1884
LOHMAN, Pete 1894
LONG, Jimmy 1894–95
LOWE, Robert 1888–89
LUBY, John 1894
MACK, Connie 1897; 99
MAPPIS, George 1885
MASKREY, Leach 1887–88
MASRAN, Joe 1886
McALEER, James 1888
McCABE, John 1888
McCANN, John 1894
McCAULEY, Al "Pop" 1895
McCULLOM, T. 1889

McCULLUM, Thomas 1886
McDERMOTT, Mike 1884
McDERMOTT, Tom 1884
McDONALD, Charles 1898–1900
McGARR, Jim "Chippy" 1892
McGINLEY, Dennis 1884
McGINNIS, George 1887
McHALE, Bob 1896
McQUAIDE, 1886
McSORLEY, John 1885
McVEY, Carl 1894
McVEY, George 1889
MEYERS, Bert 1897
MILLS, Frank 1887; 87–89
MORAN, Bill 1895
MORRIS, Peter 1884
MORRISON, Michael 1889
MORRISEY, Tom 1884; 87; 89–90
MOYNAHAN, Mike 1884
MRZENA, Ed 1896
MURPHY, 1889
MURPHY, Will 1884
MYERS, Al 1884
NELSON, 1889
NEWKIRK, John 1897
NEWMAN, Charlie 1894
NICOL, George 1895–96
NILES, Bill 1895
NONAMAKER, John 1896
O'BRIEN, Billy 1886
O'DONNELL, 1889
O'DONNELL, William 1886
O'ROURKE, 1900
OUTCALT, James 1896
PAPALAU, John 1897–98
PETTEE, Pat 1888
PETTIT, Robert 1890–91
PHELAN, Dick 1886
PICKETT, John 1886
POORMAN, Tommy 1889–90
POPE, Arthur 1886
PORTER, Henry 1884
PRINDIVILLE, 1886
PURVIS, James 1884
QUITZOW, 1889
RAYMER, Fred 1900
RECCIUS, Frank 1887
REIDY, Bill 1897–1900
REITZ, Henry 1900
RENWICK, James 1890
RETTGER, George 1894–97; 98–1900
RIAH, John 1898
RICHARDSON, 1899
RILEY, Charles 1889
ROAT, Fred 1892

ROBERTS, 1884
ROBERTS, William 1884
ROUSSEY, Elmer 1887
SAY, Louis 1886
SCHEIBLE, John 1894
SCHIERZ, 1884
SCHILDKNECHT, Luke 1898
SCHOENECK, Lewis 1885
SCHOMBERG, Otto 1884
SCHRIVER, Bill 1891
SEXTON, Tom 1884; 86
SHARPE, James Peck 1894–95
SHENKLE, Bill 1887–89
SHIELDS, Dan 1894
SHOCH, George 1889–91; 98–99
SHREVE, Leven 1886
SILCH, Ed 1889–90
SLOCCUM, 1886
SMITH, Alexander 1898
SMITH, Elmer 1897
SMITH, Fred 1891
SMITH, Harry 1900
SMITH, Henry 1887
SMITH, John (Phenomenal) 1891
SMITH, Melville 1899
SOWDERS, Billy 1890
SPARKS, Tully 1900
SPEER, George (Kid) 1896–99
SPIES, Harry 1900
STAFFORD, Robert 1895–99
STELLBERGER, William 1887
STEPHENS, George 1888; 94–95
STEVENS, Benny 1887
STOCKWELL, Len 1885
STRAUB, Joe 1884
STRAUSS, Joe 1887–88
STRUCK, John 1888
SULLIVAN, Pat 1886
SULLIVAN, Ted 1886
SUMMERS, William 1895
SUTTON, Erza 1889
SWAIM, Cy 1899
SWEENY, 1886
SYLVESTER, Lou 1887
TAYLOR, John 1897–98
TAYLOR, Wally 1894–96
TERRY, William "Adonis" 1897–98
THORNTON, John 1890
TOOLE, 1884
TWITCHELL, Larry 1892; 94–96
VICKERY, Tom 1891
VIOX, Roony 1890
VOLLENDORF, Adolphus 1899
WADDELL, Rube 1900
WALDRON, Erving 1897; 98–1900
WALSH, Joe 1886; 88; 94
WARD, Frank "Piggy" 1892
WARNER, Edward H. 1888
WEAVER, William "Buck" 1895–99
WELCH, Patrick J. 1890
WELLS, Frank 1889
WESSLING, 1886
WESTLAKE, Robert 1890
WETTERER, Bill 1896
WHEELER, George 1900
WHITE, John 1896
WHITROCK, Bill 1894
WIDNER, Bill 1892
WILLIAMS, 1886
WILLIAMS, Owen 1887
WILLIAMS, Tom 1894
WILSON, Bert 1888
WINKLEMAN, George 1888
WISSING, 1886
WRIGHT, Joe 1897
YEAGER, George 1900
YOUNG, Doug 1886

Appendix V

Amateur Clubs Organized in Milwaukee, 1860–1899

Abend Post—1895
Abenshines—1894
Abeles, Mahler & Co.—1890
Academy of Music Nine—1885
Academy Stock Co.—1899
Academys—1871; 75; 77; 85; 94
Ackerman Shoe Co.—1897–98
Acme Opera Co.—1884
Acmes—1877; 85–94; 97
Acorns—1891
Actives—1866–70; 75–76; 84–85; 88; 90–91; 97
Actors—1898
Adams (F.F.) Nine—1895–96; 99
Adams Express Drivers—1889; 91
Adams Tobacco Co.—1888
Adler (Davis) & Sons—1881; 83, 85–87; 90–91; 94–95; 97–98
Admirals—1895; 98–99
Adonis Co.—1884
Aetna Social Circles—1898
Aetnas—1877; 83–85; 87–88; 92; 98
Agitators—1876
Aggressors—1891
Akron Oil Co.—1895
Alamatics—1898
Alaska Blues—1884
Albernales—1899
Alcoynes—1896
Ald. Blackwell 9—1884
Ald. Kurtz 9—1888
Ald. Schneider 9—1888
Alerts—1867–71; 75–76; 78, 81, 84–85; 88–91
Alert Juniors—1890
Alkalines—1895
All Amateurs—1898
All American's—1889
All Saints Cathedral—1889; 94–95
All Stars—1895
All Universities—1897–98
Alleghanies—1878; 85–86; 97
Allis (E.P.) & Co.—1885; 95; 98–99
Alma Centers—1894
Alps—1897
Amateurs—1870; 77; 85; 89
Amazons—1895; 99
American Beauties—1899

American Boys—1892
American Candy Co—1897
American Eagles—1884–87; 95; 98
American Express—1884; 87; 91
American Fine Arts—1897
American Juniors—1892–95; 98
American Orioles—1894
American Stars—1888–89; 94–95; 99
American Vinegar Works—1888–90
Americans—1884; 92; 94; 96–98
Amethysts—1888
Amicitias—1898
Amitys—1888–89
Anchors—1888; 90–91; 94; 96–97
Anchor Juniors—1897
Andreas—1895; 97
Antaractics—1890–91; 95; 99
Antiques—1891
Apaches—1899
Apache Athletics—1899
Apel (H.C.) Co.—1895
Apollos—1894; 97
Apple Blossoms—1895
Arcadies—1894–95
Arcanas—1891
Archers—1883; 97
Arenas—1891–94; 97–98
Arlie Lathams—1890
Arlington—1894
Armory Boys—1895
Aromatics—1884
Aromatic Bowling Club—1884
Arrows—1883; 90; 95
Artic Juniors—1888
Artics—1867; 77–78; 81–86; 88–91; 95; 97–98
Artoes—1895
Ashlands—1889
Ash Leaves—1888
Astors—1895
Athletics—1869; 73; 75–77; 83–99
Athletic Juniors—1892; 95
Athletic Parks—1888
Athletic Socials—1894
Atkins, Ogden & Co.—1884
Atlantics—1867–69; 84–85; 88; 91; 94–95

Atlas Milling Co.—1899
Atlases—1899
Auburn Socials—1894
Aucklands—1876–79
Auer Rifles—1894; 96
Avenues—1886–87; 92; 97
Axehandlers—1892
Babbitt's Shop—1890
Babcocks (J.)—1884
Bach & Fitzgerald—1884
Bachelors—1887; 96
Bacon's—1895; 97
Badger Bedding Co.—1890
Badger Boys—1866; 75; 90–99
Badger Juniors—1897–98
Badger Oil Co.—1895
Badger State Juniors—1895
Badger States—1866–67; 91
Badger Wheelmen Shindiggers—1895
Badgers—1869–70; 84–99
Bahrs—1897
Bailey (Wl.) Nine—1897
Balaklaves—1897
Baldauff (Geo.) Nine—1891
Ball & Goodrich—1881–83
Balleaters—1898
Baltics—1884–85
Baltimore Juniors—1897
Bandanas—1888
Bank Clerks—1894
Bankers—1892
Banners—1894–96; 99
Banner Stars—1897
Barbers—1888; 92; 95–96; 98
Barber's Union—1897
Bark (F.H.) Nine—1897
Barling & Wambold—1892
Barney Hard Knocks—1876–77; 85
Barneys Gladiators—1888
Barrells—1888
Barretts—1899
Bartlett (L.) & Son—1897
Bartz (Paddy) 9—1899
Battery A First Light Artillery—1894
Battery Boys—1896; 98
Baumbach (Chahles) Co.—1885; 90–91; 95; 97
Bay Cities—1899

Bayleys—1885; 98
Bay States—1895
Bay Views—1884–95; 97–98
Bay View Amateurs—1888
Bay View Blues—1886
Bay View Browns—1886
Bay View Clippers—1887
Bay View Juniors—1885; 92–93
Bay View Lakeshore—1896
Bay View Mickies—1898
Bay View Nationals—1892
Bay View Pickups—1888
Bay View Stars—1886–87; 91–92; 94
Bay View Unions—1886
Bay View Welcomes—1891
Bay View Whites—1886; 91–94; 97
Beacons—1897
Beals, Torrey & Co.—1884; 95; 98–99
Bears—1884; 86
Beauties—1897
Bechtner's (Paul)—1888–90
Beck (C.A.)—1888
Beck & Paul—1894
Beckers—1896–97
Becker (WI.) Leather Co.—1895; 99
Bee Hives—1894
Beer Keys—1894
Bell Boys—1885
Belle Views—1888; 90–91; 94–95
Bellevues—1894
Belvidere Boys—1888
Belvideres—1887–89; 93; 99
Benedict (H.) & Co.—1887
Benedicts—1891
Benevolent Societies—1890
Bengals—1881
Ben Hurs—1896–97
Benson & Rixon—1894
Benton, Waldron & Co.—1888
Benz Juniors—1891
Berger Bedding Co.—1888–89; 91; 99
Bernitts—1897
Bethlehem School—1890
Bethlehem YMS—1895; 99
Biersdorph (WI.)—1890
Big Fours—1898
Big Joes—1898
Big Scorchers—1894
Bijou Opera Bouffe Co.—1894
Bijous—1894–95
Billy Ryans—1892
Binner Engraving Co.—1892
Birge & Smith—1884
Blacks—1894
Blackbirds—1895
Black Rays—1896
Black Clouds—1890; 96
Black Diamonds—1891–98
Blackhawks—1891; 94–95
Black Hills—1898
Black Jacks—1895
Black Pearls—1894
Black Ravens—1895

Black Rocks—1895
Black Scrubs—1894
Blacksmiths—1895
Black Stars—1896–97
Black Walnuts—1892
Blaine & Logan Co.—1884
Blatz Brewery Co.—1894; 98–99
Blatzs—1897
Block's Colts—1898
Bloomers—1896
Blue Banners—1899
Blue Bells—1890–91; 95–98
Blue Birds—1892
Blue Bloomers—1895
Blue Boys—1885–86; 94; 96
Blue Caps—1877; 90; 97
Blue Chippers—1896
Blue Clippers—1894
Blue Clouds—1894
Blue Flags—1894
Blue Jeans—1898
Blue Lights—1895
Blue Lillies—1895
Blue Mounds—1888; 96–97
Blue Mountain Boys—1894–95; 99
Blue Ribbon Boys—1894–95; 98
Blue Ribbon Juniors—1894
Blue Rockets—1894
Blue Rocks—1899
Blue Roses—1895
Blue Stars—1884; 91; 93–99
Blue Stockings—1870; 90; 98
Blue Violets—1895
Blue Waves—1895
Blue Whiskers—1890
Blue Willows—1888
Blues—1883–89; 91–92; 94–96
Bluffers—1892; 95
Bluffs—1889
Blue's Indians—1896
Board of Public Works—1897
Board of Trades—1898
Boland Club—1894
Bolan's Stars—1895
Bon Tons—1891
Bon Ton Juniors—1892
Boodiers—1888
Boss Boys—1887; 94
Bosworth & Sons—1882; 85–85
Boulevards—1892; 94
Boundry, Peckham & Co.—1883
Bourgeois—1894
Bowling Greens—1888
Boys of '94—1895
Bradley & Metcalf Co. 1884; 86–88; 94–95; 97; 90
Bradstreets—1899
Bradys—1898
Brand Stove Co.—1885; 95
Bresslers—1883
Brewers—1894; 95
Brewery Boys—1895
Brickbacks—1898
Bricks—1897
Brickyards—1888; 92; 99
Bridge Tenders—1895; 97
Bridgets—1896

Bright Garnets—1895
Bright Lights—1890
Bright Stars—1886; 90; 94–95; 97; 99
Brilliants—1898
Broadways—1886
Broadway Juniors—1896
Brodessen Manufacturing Co.—1895
Brookfields—1891
Brookhavens—1895
Broommakers—1888
Brown & Harper Brothers—1890; 94
Brownies—1894–96; 98–99
Brown Stockings—1875
Browns—1883–86; 88; 92; 95–97; 99
Bub & Kipp's—1890
Bubble Blowers—1893
Bucks—1898
Buds—1895
Budweisers—1894
Buff's (F.J.)—1884
Buffalos—1888
Bullet Stoppers—1888–98
Bulls—1884; 86
Bully Boys—1891; 94
Bunker Hill Boys—1896
Burk's Graybeards—1899
Burnetts—1897
Burnhams—1896
Burrells—1898
Butcher's Soups—1898
Buttercups—1895
Butterfingers—1870
Butterflies—1894
C.C.C.'s—1888
C..L.C.'s—1898
C.W.'s—1892
Cadet Light Infantry—1888
Cadets—1884–85; 92
Caddotts—1889
California Quartettes—1894
Callahans—1892
Calumet Juniors—1894; 97–98
Calumets—1884–88; 90–92; 94–95; 97–99
Cameos—1899
Camp (A.K.) & Co.—1896
Campbell Laundry Co.—1888
Camp Douglas—1893
Campers—1894
Canadas—1898
Canar Colts—1896
Canners—1898
Cannon Balls—1889
Can Rushers—1895; 97–99
Capitols—1894
Capitol Cinches—1895
Carbonic Acid Gases—1898
Carltons—1899
Carnations—1894; 97
Carnivals—1898–99
Carpeles, Schram & Co.—1884
Carpenter & Underwood—
Carpenters Conclave—1887–88
Carroll & Keough—1894

Cashmeres—1898
Casinos—1892; 94
Castiles—1895; 99
Castles—1895
Catalpas—1892; 99
Cataracts—1894-95
Cathedral Athletics—1885
Cathedral Council YMI—1896
Cathedral Institute 9—1894
Cawteles—1899
Cedars—1898
Centennials—1876; 79; 90; 92
Centers—1894-95; 98
Center Street Cowboys—1884
Centrals—1885; 94-95; 98-99
Central National Bank—1894
Central Stars—1899
Centuries—1894
Chain Belts—1899
Chamber of Commerce Club—1889-94; 97-98
Champion Unions—1884
Champions 1884; 88; 92; 97
Chapman (T.A.) Co.—1883; 88-91; 94; 96; 99
Chapman Guards—1890
Chapman Juniors—1888
Charter Oaks—1884
Chase Valley Glass Blowers—1882
Chemicals—1884-86; 88
Chemungs—1898
Cherokees—1883-84
Cherry Blossoms—1896
Cherry Stars—1888
Chestnuts—1894
Chestnut Street Bells—1894
Chicago Boys—1895
Chicago, Milwaukee & St. Paul Railroad—1884; 87-89; 94-95
Chicago & Northwestern Railroad—1894; 99
Chicawees—1894
Chinesse—1888
Chippewas—1875
Christainson's (Geo.)—1894
Cities—1894-95
City Bluffs—1895; 99
City Engineers—1890
City Halls—1897-99
City Socials—1897-98
City Social Juniors—1897-98
City Sports—1894
City Treasurers—1899
Clancy's Sluggers—1892
Clarks—1897
Clark Stones—1896
Classens—18985
Clay Pipe Juniors—1895
Clement Musicals—1897
Clermonts—18893-94
Cleveland & Hendrich Co.—1884
Cleveland Juniors—1888
Clevelands—1889
Climax—1888; 95
Clingstones—1888
Clinton Boys—1894-96
Clintons—1883; 95-99

Clipper Musical Society 1892
Clippers—1876-77; 82-83; 85-86; 90; 92; 99
Clothing Co.—1886
Central Station Policemen 1895-96
Clover Boys—1895
Clover Leafs—1897-98
Clovers—1891
Club Houses—1885
Club House Sandwiches—1897
Cnife Zangs—1895
Coal Heavers—1888; 91
Cohen Clothing Co.—1888; 89
Cohn Bros.—1899
Colby (C.I.) Co.—1884
Cold Springs—1884-85; 88; 90-91; 93; 97
Cold Spring Juniors—1898
Collegians—1890
Collingbourne (T.B.) Co.—1884; 88
Colonels—1895
Colored Lads—1895
Colts—1891; 96
Columbia Boys—1895-97
Columbias—1891; 94-96
Colvilles—1888-89
Comets—1877; 83-85; 88; 90; 92; 95; 97-99
Comical Youngsters—1898
Comicals—1877-79; 83
Commerce Club—1890
Commercials—1890
Commission Boys—1887
Commission House—1894
Commonwealers—1894
Company A—1897
Company F—1897-99
Company F Juniors—1898
Company G—1897
Company H—1894; 97
Compounders—1891
Concordia College—1883-85; 88-89
Concordia Fire Insurance Co.—1888; 94-95
Concordia YMCA—1894
Coney's (N.E.)—1895
Connie Macks—1897
Conquerors—1895
Conrads—1895
Convents—1892
Conways—1887
Coogan & Co.—1884-85
Coorsen (Frank) Co.—1891
Cop Dodgers—1898
Corbetts—1898
Corbitt & Skidmore Co.—1888
Cordials—1884
Corduroy Octoroons—1896
Clouds—1891
Corkers—1894; 97
Corks—1895
Comets—1888; 90; 95
Cornhuskers—1894
Counter Jumpers—1888
Country Boys—1899

County Asylums—1899
County Hospitals—1897
Court House Club—1890; 94-95; 99
Cowboys—1887; 99
Cow Bunkers—1896
Cowslips—1897
Coxies—1894; 97
Cracker Jacks—1896-99
Crap Shooters—18895
Crazy Men—1895
Cream City Athletics—1897
Cream City Blues—1894
Cream City Boys—18895
Cream City Brewery Co.—1894; 98
Cream City Club—1865-70; 75; 78; 81-89; 91; 94-98
Cream City Hat Co.—1898
Cream City Juniors—1867; 90; 92; 94-97
Cream Citys—1889-90; 92
Creek Waters—1888
Creoles—1895
Crescent Outing Club—1897
Crescents—1888-89; 92; 94-99
Crickets—1888; 90; 96
Crombie, Miller & Co.—1891
Crombie, Smith & Co.—1887-88; 90
Cross Church YMCA—1896
Crownleafs—1889
Crystal Stars—1894
Crystal Juniors—1892
Crystals—1892; 94; 98
Cubans—1898-99
Cuban Social Circles—1899
Cuban Stars—1899
Cudahy Bladders—1898
Cudahy Bros.—1890; 92; 94; 99
Cudahy Dewdrops—1899
Cudahy Juniors—1899
Cudahy Regulars—1899
Cudahy Shamrocks—1897
Cudahy Victors—1899
Cudahys—1896-098
Curriers—1884
Cushman Juniors—1894
Cushmans—1894
Custers—1897
Cutters—1894
Cycling Club—1897
Cyclones—1885; 88; 90-91; 95; 99
D & M's—1886
D.M.O. Stars—1892
D.M.V. Juniors—1885
D.M.V. Stars—1892
Dahlman (Y.A.) & Co.—1890
Daily News Club—1891; 94; 96-99
Daily News Juniors—1898-99
Daily Review—1888
Daiseys—1885; 88; 90; 94-95
Daisey Boys—1895
Daisey Fields—1892; 94
Dandelions—1895
Dandies—1895
Dantys—1888

Davidson Theater Club—1898
Davis Roller Co.—1895
Davis Omnibus Co.—1887
Day & Lebner—1892
Daytons—1897
Debonas—1898
Debrozzo's (Sam)—1897
Deckers—1895
Dees—1893
Defenders—1897
Defiance Club—1890-91
Dells—1895
Delorme & Axentin's—1884
Demons—1899
Depots—1898
Derprowns—1888
Dessengers—1888
Detroit, Grand Haven & Milwaukee Fling & Pere Marquette Anchor Boat Lines—1894
Deutcher Mannervereins—1886
Dewey & Davis Co.—1890; 94
Dewdrops—1883-85; 88-95
Dextors—1883-84; 94
Diamond Hills—1895
Diamond Juniors—1894
Diamond Kings—1885; 96
Diamond Reserves—1896
Diamond Stars—1890
Diamonds—1884-90; 92; 94
Dime Museum Club—1887
Dingwalls—1890
Directors—1891
Districts—1892
Dobbs—1896
Doc Reed's Invincibles—1891
Doctors—1888; 90; 92; 95; 97
Dohman (F.) Co. 1895
Domestics—1895
Donahues—1898
Donavan House Club—1885
Double Stars—1894; 96
Doyn & Kalvelages—1888
Drake House Club—1882
Dreadnaughts—1883-85; 88-89; 91; 95
Druggists—1888; 90; 95; 97-98
Drugstores—1884
Dudes—1884
Duffers—1891-92; 95
Dukes—1890; 95
Dummers—1890
Dunlaps—1890
Dunns—1898
Durands—1890; 97
Dusold Bros.—1887-88
Du Sachast Uck Mit Circles—1897
Dutcher Iron Works—1896
Dwarfs—1890; 92
Dwyers—1884
E.S.H.'s—1897
Eagles—1885; 88; 90-01; 94; 99
Earls—1899
Early Stars—1894; 96
East Americans 1898
East Ends—1888; 90; 94-99

East End Juniors—1895; 98-99
East Maines—1898
East Milwaukees—1884-85; 89; 93
East Side Active Turners—1884
East Side Badgers—1899
East Side Barbers—1886; 88-90; 94; 97
East Side Brownies—1897
East Side High School—1894-98
East Side Juniors—1898-99
East Side Lawyers—1895
East Side Music House—1895
East Side Standards—1896
East Side Victors—1892
East Side Visitors—1892
East Side Welcomes—1894
East Sides—1884; 98
East Stars—1898
Easterns—1884-85
Eastern Excelsiors—1884
Eastern Pickups—1884
Easy Monies—1895
Ebenies—1898
Echos—1888; 94; 99
Eckfords—1870
Eclectrics—1892
Eclipse—1883; 86; 88; 91; 94-95; 97-99
Eclipse Juniors—1895-96
Eclipse Socials—1897
Edison Boys—1894
Effertz—1888
Eighth District School—1894-95; 97
Eighth Streets—1885
Eighth Wards—1890; 94
Eighth Ward Juniors—1895; 97
Eighteenth Ward Bladders—1898
Elbs—1895; 98
Eldorados—1888
Electricans—1895
Electrics—1888-89; 91-92
Electric Lights—1896
Electric Sparks—1895
Elects—1890
Elerts—1890
Eleventh District School—1894-95
Eleventh Street Hobos—1895
Eliens—1899
Elities—1892; 95-99
Elite Juniors—1898-99
Elks—1888; 95-99
Elm Groves—1894
Elms—1892; 98-99
Elmwoods—1884
Elkines—1899
Elpines—1899
Elroys—1893
Emblems—1890; 95
Emeralds—1877; 88; 90-91; 95-98
Emerald Social Circle—1890
Emil Meyer Night Hawks—1894
Empires—1896; 99
Empty Leads—1885

Energetics—1894
Engineers—1888; 92
Enoles—1895
Ensigns—1899
Erbachs—1895; 97
Eries—1892-93; 95-96
Espenhein & Bartel's—1885; 88
Etnas—1886
Euchres—1889-90
Eurekas—1869; 85-86; 88; 92; 94; 97; 99
Evangelines—1887
Evening News—1895
Evening Wisconsins—1883-84; 86; 88-89; 92; 94-97
Everglades—1895
Evergreens—1884-85; 88-92; 94; 98
Everits—1898
Excelsiors—1860; 67-71; 75-77; 81-85; 87-89; 91; 97-99
Ex-chamions—1885
Exports—1897
Expositions—1883; 95
Exposition Roller Rinks—1898
Eyelights—1898
F.A.L.'s—1890
F.L.P.'s—1888; 95
F.L.S.'s—1890
F.L.T.'s—1896
F.S.T.'s—1895
F.T.L.'s—1888
F.X.T.'s—1888
Failures—1895
Fairbanks—1870; 83-86; 88
Fair Boys—1877; 85
Fair Oaks—1898
Fairplays—1885
Fairports—1897
Famous Yorks—1895
Farmers—1888; 97
Farwell Avenues—1897
Farwells—1885; 88-89; 91; 94-94
Fast Boys—1884
Fastnachts—1897
Fast Steps—1884
Fat Men—1876-77; 88; 91; 94; 97
Favorites—1884; 88; 91. 95
Favors—1894
Fay Templeton Opera Club—1884
Fearless Jupiters—1885
Federals—1894-95
Fennimores—1894
Ferdinand Conradts—1897
Fernekes—1881; 88
Fern Leafs—1884
Fernwoods—1894; 97
Fesslers (Wl.)—1899
Feverts—1895
Fielders—1897; 99
Fields—1894
Fifer Stover Co.—1895
Fifteenth District School—1890
Fifth Avenues—1895
Fifth District School—1891; 95-97
Fifth Wards—1888; 94; 96-97

Fifth Ward Juniors—1895
Filer & Stowell's—1892
Finnis (R.J.) Club—1886
Fire Department 1895–97
Fire Insurance Co. 1898
First Avenues—1895
First Light Battery Co.—1888; 95
First Nationals—1888
First National Bank—1892; 94; 97–99
First Street Sluggers—1899
First Ward Hustlers—1887
First Ward Juniors—1888; 94; 97
First Ward Stars—1885
Flashback (D.) & Sons—1883; 85
Fischer & Dover Co. 1899
Fischer & Sons—1884
Fisher's Colts—1898
Fitzsimmons—1898
Flasch Bros.—1898
Flats—1897
Flavors—1897
Fleck (Henry) Club—1894; 97
Fleck (R.) Club—1892
Flies—1895
Flint (J.G.) Co.—1884; 95; 99
Florals—1896–97
Floridas—1895–96
Flowers—1888
Flowery Shirts—1888
Fly Catchers—1898
Flying Dutchmen—1870; 85
Flying Squadrons—1898
Foam Blowers—1899
Fontella Pleasure Club—1897
Forest Cities—1875
Forrestals—1895
Fortunes—1884–85; 87–88; 94
Foth's (J.)—1888
Four Leaf Clovers—1891; 98
Four M's—1885
Fourth District School—1889; 91–92; 97
Fourth Wards—1873; 97
Fourth Ward Stars—1888
Foxes—1891
Fox Hounds—1896
Fox & May—1894–95
Frankforts—1895
Frankfurth (Wl.) Co.—1885–91; 99
Franklin Juniors—1898
Franklin Pleasure Club—1888
Franklin Social Club—1895
Franklin Streets—1887
Franklins—1878; 82; 88–89; 92–95; 97
Franzen's—1898
Fraugh-o-Bulauges—1899
Free Cubans—1898
Freedoms—1894; 98–99
Freedom Social Circle—1890
Free Lancers—1885
Free Lunches—1888
Freie Presse Club—1881
Freight Agents—1899
Freitag (Wl.) Club—1897
French Airs—1888

Friese (A.W.) Club—1890–92
Friedman (Charles) Co.—1883
Friend Bros.—1885–87; 90; 94–97; 99
Friendly Boys—1888
Friendships—1890; 95–96
Frochback & Biersack's—1887–88
Fuller & Warren—1891; 94–95; 98–99
Furnaufers—1896
G.A.R.'s—1890
Galenas—1894
Galena Stars—1899
Galleys—1895
Galvanizers—1896
Gardens—1898
Garden Cities—1869
Gardners—1884
Garfield Avenues—1885
Garfield Heights—1896
Garfields—1894–95
Garigans—1895
Garlands—1899
Garnedos—1892; 94–95; 97–98
Garnets—1898
Garnstoes—1894
Gauers—1894
Gaugers—1887; 91
Genderium Cycle Club—1897
Genesees—1897; 99
Gerhardt's (Fred)—1896
German-English Academy—1892; 96
German M.E. Church—1897
German Saloonkeepers—1899
Germanias—1883; 85; 90–92; 95; 98
Germania Bowling Club—1893
Gems—1894; 96
George Hills—1894; 97–98
George Washingtons—1894; 97–98
Geuder & Paeschke Co.—1897
Giants—1889–92; 96; 98
Gibbaroons—1888
Gilettes—1898
Gimbels Bros.—1888–89; 94–95; 99
Ginderman & Hverson—1895
Gladitors—1892; 94; 96–98
Gleason's (J.M.)—1894
Glenwoods—1894; 99
Globes—1891; 93; 95
Globe Tailoring Co.—1895
Gocornes—1899
Godfrey & Sons—1897
Goebel's (Peter)—1894
Goelz (J.G.) Club—1899
Gold Dusts—1898
Gold Leaves—1894; 97; 99
Golden Eagles—1881; 84–95; 97
Golden Edges—1895
Golden Medals—1890
Golden Rays—1898
Golden Reds—1896
Golden Rods—1896
Golden Stars—1884; 86; 88–89; 91; 95–96; 98

Golden Wreaths—1894
Goldens—1894; 98
Goldsmith & Co.—1888
Goll & Frank Co.—1884; 87
Goodman's (W.E.)—1886; 89
Gophers—1899
Gordons—1895–97
Gorgons—1897
Gottschalk's—1895
Goyors—1899
Grade (Henry) & Co.—1892
Graf (Wl.) & Co.—1887; 92
Gram (Edmund) Co.—1898
Grand Avenue House Club—1885
Grand Opera House Club—1885–86
Grand Unions—1891
Granite House Club—1899
Grants—1890; 95
Grasshoppers—1895
Gray Beards—1899
Gray Eagles—1891
Gray Oak Juniors—1899
Gray Oaks—1888; 90–94; 96–99
Gray Stones—1890
Gray Woods—1888
Grays—1885–86; 88–90; 92; 98
Greens—1883–85; 87–93; 95
Green Bays—1894; 99
Green Diamonds—1895–97; 99
Green Diamond Juniors—1898
Green Elms—18982; 94; 97
Green Leaves—1881–83; 85–86; 88–91; 94–98
Green Mountain Boys—1895; 97–98
Green Oaks—1892
Green Ripons—1898
Green Slades—1885
Green Stars—1894–95
Green Valleys—1894; 96
Green Valley Juniors—1896
Greene & Button Co.—1882; 85; 90–91
Greenfields—1884–87; 89–92; 95; 98–99
Greenfield Pleasure Club—1890
Greenhills—1890; 94
Greenwoods—1897
Greese Box Club—1888
Greeve Lithographing Co.—1894; 97–99
Gregons—1899
Greshams—1898
Grizzlies—1888
Grizzly Juniors—1894
Gross (I.) Club—1895
Gross (P.A.) & Co.—1892
Grove Street Boys—1894
Grove Street Everglades—1885
Grove Street Sluggers—1885
Groves—1897
Growlers—1884–85; 88–89; 94–95
Gruhl Sash & Door Co.—1895
Guards—1897
Guenters—1898

Guasban & Kehrein Co.—1886
Gugler Lithography Co.—1884–85; 87; 89; 94–95; 97
Guides—1886
Gully Boys—1897
Gumz & Co.—1899
Haerter's (Fred)—1899
Hagemeisters—1894
Hales Corners—1885; 95
Half Moons—1895
Hallihooks—1894
Halsey Bros.—1894–95
Hamilton & Bros.—1883–84
Hampdens—1892
Hanford Oil Co.—1889–90
Hansen's Empire Fur Factory—1884; 87
Hanswirths—1899
Happy Cal Wagners—1898
Happy Hollows—1894–95; 98
Happy Howlers—1892
Happy Lees—1888
Hard Hitters—1896
Hard Knocks—1898
Hard Times—1894–95
Hard Wood Finishers—1898
Hardly Ables—1894
Harlands—1889
Harmonies—1888
Harmonie Society Club—1888
Harney Boys—1894
Harolds—1881; 83; 87–88; 90–91
Harper Bros.—1888
Harper & Sons—1884; 92
Harris Club—1892
Harrisons—1889
Hartfords—1892; 98
Harvesters—1882
Harveys—1894–95
Haver Boys—1894
Haverhills—1895
Hawkeyes—1898
Hawthornes—1891
Haymakers—1869; 83
Haymarkets—1897
Hayseeds—1896; 98
Haystacks—1895
Haywards—1892
Hazel Boys—1876
Health Department Club—1895
Heavy Weights–1894
Hecedahs—1889
Heiler & Aaron C.—1890–91
Heimann Co.—1881–84; 87; 91–92; 95; 97; 99
Heinn Specialty Club—1898
Hellen's Red—1888
Heller Juniors—1895
Helming & Palmer Co.—1883; 85
Hemlocks—1895–96; 99
Henni Couts—1899
Henry Boys—1894
Henschel Manufacturing Co.—1895
Hereos—1892; 95; 97
Herman Co.—1891; 94; 97
Heyer (A.J.) Club—1897
Heyer (George) Co.—1892

Hiawathas—1895
Hibernias—1890; 94; 97
Hickeys—1890
Hickories (Frank)—1894
Hickory Juniors—1892
Hickory Leafs—1888
Hickorys—1888–89; 92–92; 95
Hi-Hi's—1899
Highland Juniors—1898
Highlands—1897–99
High Stars—1894
Hiles (George) Club—1895
Hills—1897
Hillsides—1884; 93; 96; 98
Hiltons—1894
Hinz Club—1888
Hobos—1894–95; 97–99
Hobsons—1898–99
Hobson Juniors—1899
Hoegers—1885
Hoff's Boys—1894
Hoffman, Billings & Co.—1883; 94–97; 99
Hoffman College—1897; 99
Hogans—1898
Hollyhocks—1884–85; 88–89; 94
Holsteins—1889
Holy Cross Church—1899
Holy Names—1896; 98
Holy Name Juniors—1896
Holy Rosary Juniors—1896
Holy Roses—1890
Holyokes—1879
Home Boys—1899
Home Plates—1895
Home Runs—1885; 98
Homers—1896
Honeydews—1896
Hoodoos—1895
HooHoos—1895; 97
Hopkins—1897
Hopper's—1893
Hop Waus—1888
Horilon House Club—1896
Horribles—1889
Hot Foots—1898
House's Broommakers—1885
Houstons—1878
Houtkamp & Cannon—1887
Howard Juniors—1894
Howlers—1884–85; 88–89; 94; 96
Howling Bulls—1894
Hubs—1895; 98
Hugs—1896
Humboldts—1894; 96–97
Humboldt Boys—1875; 88; 90–91; 93
Humboldt Juniors—1895
Humboldt Reds—1894
Humboldt School—1894; 98
Humbugs—1894
Hummelstein's (F.)—1890; 99
Hummers—1890; 97–98
Hurons—1895
Hurricanes—1890
Hustlers—1893–94
Ideals—1884; 90
Illinois Steel Co.—1896; 99

Immanuel YMS—1899
Imperial Juniors—1891
Imperial Social Club—1894
Imperials—1886; 88–91; 94
Independence Club—1867; 97–98
Independents—1894; 97
Independent Cycle Club—1897
Indians—1896; 98–99
Industrial School—1889
Infants—1894–95
Ingelsides—1898
Inky Dinkys—1894
Inmans—1867
Insurance Boys—1894
Insurrerables—1882
Insurgents—1891
Internationals—1892
Invincibles—1883; 92
Ionas—1894
Irish Boys—1882; 98
Irish Saloonkeepers—1899
Ironclads—1890; 94
Ironhands—1875
Iron Moulders—1895
Iron Oaks—1895
Iron Range Club—1889
Ironsides—1895
Iroquois—1888; 96–99
Iroquois Colts—1896
Iroquois Indians—1897
Irvings—1870; 75
Ishpemings—1890
Island Sash & Door Co.—1888
Italian Boys—1869
Ivanhoes—1885; 99
Iverson (J.C.) Co.—1886; 88; 95
Iverson Social Club—1895
Ivory Juniors—1895
Ivys—1889–92; 97–98
Ivy Boys—1896–98
Ivy Leafs—1886–88; 92; 94
J.F.F.'s—1885
J.I.C.'s—1891
Jackets—1885
Jacksons—1897–99
Jaints—1888
James Boys—1890; 94
James Morgans—1882–86; 88–89; 94–95
James Morgan Cream Citys—1892–95
Jamie Nugents—1892
Jansen's (F.W.)—1888–89
Jay Goulds—1884–87
Jenner (J.E.) Co.—1897; 99
Jim Ludingtons—1877
Jobbers—1895
Joe-Joe Rushers—1896
Johnny Wards—1894
Johnson's (Y.W.)—1888
Johnson Boys—1895
Johnson Bros. Bakery—1881; 96
Johnson Electrical Co.—1897–98
Johnson Soap Co.—1897
Johnston Boys—1895
Johnston Colts—1897; 99
Joliets—1894; 90–91

Jolly Boys—1894
Jolly Jumping Jays—1899
Jolly Muffers—1884
Jolly Nine—1891; 97
Jolly Pathfinders—1890
Jonas—1894
Jones Islands—1895-96
Journals—1891-92; 94-96; 98
Joys—1888; 91-92
Jubilets—1884
Jugglers—1885
Jug Waters—1884
Julius Mantlas—1884
Jumbos—1883
Juneaus—1867-70; 88; 95
Juneau Athletics—1896
Juniors—1882; 85; 90; 92; 97-98
Junior Americans—1892
Junior Athletics—1897
Junior Boys—1894
Junior Milwaukees—1882
Junior Pathfinders—1895
Junior Pffeuger & Kuehmsted's—1895
Junior Turners—1884
Jupiters—1888; 90; 92
Juveniles—1885; 89-90; 92; 95-96; 99
Kahn (I.R.) Club—1895
Kaife Zangs—1896
Kalamazoo Knitting Co.—1899
Kalamazoos—1887
Kalt's (James)—1888
Kanard's Colts—1895
Kanders (Sidney)—1892
Kanas Citys—1895
Kants—1898
Kanucks—1896
Katz (J.) Co.—1891; 97
Katzer's—1891
Kaufman's (A.)—1899
Kaziskowski's—1897
Kelly (P.L.) Club—1895
Kellys—1894
Keough's (Ed)—1894
Kern's (J.B.A.)—1892; 97
Key Wests—1893-96
Keystone Juniors—1888; 92; 95; 99
Keystones—1870; 84-89; 91; 94-99
Kickapoos—1888; 96
Kickers—1886; 89; 91; 94-95; 98
Kid McCoys—1898
Kidders—1895
Kiels—1889; 99
Kilbourns—1888; 95; 98-99
Kimmerlain & Kuenzil's—1895
Kindergartens—1891
Kindling (Louis) Co.—1892
King, Lawton & Fowle Co.—1884-85; 88; 94
Kings of the Diamond—1894
Kingstons—1894; 99
Kinnickinnics—1883-85; 94-95; 97-98
Kinnickinnic Seniors—1894
Kipp Bros.—1884-85; 87-89; 91

Kirbys—1894
Kirby House Club—1894-96
Kiemets—1896
Kissingers—1897
Kitts—1888
Klass' (John)—1894
Klein Painters—1895
Klett Boys—1895
Klondike Miners—1898
Klondikes—1897-98
Kluckler's (Frank)—1895
Knaubels—1891
Knauber Lithographing Co.—1894; 97; 99
Knickerbockers—1894; 98-99
Knights of Pythias—1892
Knights of the Quill—1870
Knights Templars—1894
Knockabouts—1897
Knockers—1894; 97
Knousts—1888
Koch & Loeber's—1894
Korky Juniors—1899
Krause Boys—1894
Krueger's Colts—1899
Krumholtz Bros.—1899
Kuffenkamm's (Chris)—1894
Kuhn's (Julius)—1894
Kummel's (Edward)—1884
Kunnkel's (Bill)—1897
Kurtz's (August)—1894; 97
Kuryer Polskis—1897
Lackawannas—1883-84
Lafayettes—1897
Lake Michigans—1888
Lake Parks—1895; 97-99
Lakeshore Boys—1885
Lakeshore Browns—1889
Lakeshore Firemen—1888
Lakeshore Juniors—1898
Lakeshores—1883-86; 88-93; 95-96; 98
Lakeside Pinions—1889
Lakesides—1876; 82; 86-87; 89; 91-92; 94-95; 97; 99
Lakeviews—1886; 88; 94-95; 98
Lalonias—1894
Lancasters—1898
Landauer & Co.—1881; 84; 87-89; 91; 94-95; 98
Laphams—1895; 98-99
Lappen's (F.H.)—1891
Lasters—1888
Later Stars—1897
Laurel Juniors—1895
Laurels—1893-97; 98
LaVioletas—1899
Lawyers—1892
Layton & Co.—1895; 98
Layton Parks—1890; 95
Laytons—1886; 91; 94-96
Leaders—1885-86; 88-94; 96-98
Leagues—1898-99
League Juniors—1890-91; 94; 96
Leans—1876; 88; 91; 94; 97
Leatherswipes—1891
Lederer's Cigar Dudes—1888
Leffor Boys—1898

Lefties—1898
Lehighs—1886
Lehigh House Club—1888
Lehigh Valleys—1883
Lemanski's (J.)—1899
Leroys—1898
Letz (John) Co.—1891
Libertys—1888; 94-95; 97-98
Liberty Bells—1894
Liberty Boys—1894-95; 97
Liederkrans—1888
Liedersdorfs—1895
Liesonfelds—1897
Light Oaks—1888
Lightening Messenger Boys—1898
Lilacs—1883; 88; 93; 95; 97-98
Lillies—1885
Lilliputians—1894; 97
Lincolns—1891-94; 96-99
Lincoln Juniors—1895
Lions—1894
Lippert Plumbing Co.—1895-96
Lisbons—1888; 94-95
Little Badgers—1895
Little Dandys—1894
Little Drops—1894
Little Dutchs—1897
Little Gems—1897-99
Little Juniors—1892
Little Marquettes—1894-96
Little Plumbers—1896
Little Rocks—1888-89; 92; 95; 97; 99
Little Sports—1894; 96
Little Stars—1895
Little Tycons—1887
Live Oaks—1877-79; 82-84; 86
Lively Blues—1896
Lively Jumpers—1895
Living Oaks—1891
Lizards—1899
Lloyd Street Hobos—1899
Local Fifteens—1886
Local Insurance Men—1897
Local—1891
Lochmalers—1897
Logans—1895
Lone Stars—1870; 74-77; 84; 87-91; 94; 98
Long Greens—1899
Lotus Club—1888-89
Louievards—1892
Louisville Stars—1896-97
Lowells—1884
Lower Third Street Club—1888
Loyals—1891; 97
Lufinski Juniors—1896
Lunch Grabbers—1894
Lunch Takers—1894
Lund's (John)—1895
Lurexs—1899
Lutheran Stars—1894
Lyons—1894
Lyrics—1897-98
M.E.R. & L.B.B.'s—1899
M.H. & Co.—1891
Machalinski Barbers—1895

Mack's (H.S.)—1884; 90
Madisons—1895; 97
Maecthle Boys—1895
Magaras—1890
Magies—1891
Magnets—1888–89; 96
Maid of Belleville Opera Club—1886
Mail Carriers—1896
Maines—1898-98
Maine Juniors—1898
Majestics—1891
Malleable Iron Works—1891
Mames—1899
Manasses—1891
Mandans—1896
Manhattans—1896-98
Manilas—1898
Manila Bombarders—1898
Maples—1894-96
Maple Groves—1888
Maple Leafs—1876–88; 91; 93–97
Marble Boys—1896
Marine Insurance Co.—1888
Mariners—1888
Marines—1889; 92–93
Mark Twains—1884
Market Clippers—1890
Market Street Clippers—1893
Market Squares—1899
Markham Academy—1878
Maroons—1886–87; 92
Marquette Alumni—1894; 96
Marquette Blues—1890; 92
Marquette Browns—1892
Marquette College—1884–85; 89–99
Marquette Juniors—1886; 89–92; 94–97; 99
Marquette Minions—1890
Marquette Minors—1885
Marquette Reds—1892
Marquette Seniors—1893; 95
Marquette Volunteers—1890
Marquette Willows—1889
Marquette Whites—1892
Marr & Richards Co.—1890; 95
Mascots—1888; 90; 95; 97–98
Masons—1892; 95
Master Plumbers—1895
Matthews Bros. Furnture Co.—1883; 87
Matthews (C.H.)—1896–98
Maustons—1889
Maybelieves—1891
Maybells—1888
Mayer Boot & Shoe Co.—1895
Mayer (F.) Co.—1895; 97–99
Mayfields—1891; 93–96; 98
Maynards—1890
Mayor (Charles) Co.—1894
Mayvilles—1896
Maywoods—1888
McCaigne Juniors—1896
McDonalds—1894
McDonald College—1897
Meadows—1885; 88–93; 96–97
Meadow Boys—1890; 94–95; 97

Meicke & Co.—1890
Meineckes—1884–85; 88; 91; 95
Meinecke Factory—1895
Meinecke Toy Co.—1895
Melsebach (A.D.) Co.-1897
Mendel & Smith Co.—1888; 94–95
Menemonees—1884; 88; 90; 94
Menomonee Centers—1895
Menomonee Views—1894
Menz Club—1899
Merchandise Brokers—1885; 87–88; 94
Merchant Mills—1885
Merchants—1882–83
Merchants Exchange Bank—1892
Mercuries—1895–96
Mercury Cycle Club—1899
Mercury Flyers—1899
Meredians—1894
Mermaids—1888
Merrilliners—1894
Merrill Parks—1894; 96; 98–99
Merrill Park Juniors—1895; 97
Merrill Park Sluggers—1888
Merrimacs—1869; 85–86; 88; 92–95; 97–99
Merrins—1894
Merry Makers—1891
Merry Ramblers—1888
Merry Six—1885
Meteors—1891–92
Meter Department Club—1894
Metropolitans—1885–87; 96
Mets—1888
Meyer & Co.—1888
Meyer's Business College—1894
Michigan Beefers—1894
Midway Boys—1894; 96–97
Mikados—1888
Miller Box Factory—1896
Miller Brewery Co.—1894; 96–98
Miller (H.C.) & Co. 1898
Miller Printing Office—1887
Millers—1892; 96–97
Miltons—1890
Milwaukees—1860–61; 79–83; 85; 89
Milwaukee Academy Club—1898
Milwaukee Athletic Club—1898
Milwaukee Athletic Society—1894-98
Milwaukee Bag Co.—1899
Milwaukee Boiler Co.—1895
Milwaukee Box Co.—1888; 99
Milwaukee Boys—1869; 75; 86; 94
Milwaukee Brickmakers—1893
Milwaukee Bridge & Irons Co.—1897
Milwaukee Cement Works—1898
Milwaukee Chair Factory—1888; 94–96
Milwaukee Gas Light Co.—1894
Milwaukee Harvester Co.—1893
Milwaukee High School—1881–87; 90–92
Milwaukee Juniors—1888–89

Milwaukee Juveniles—1889
Milwaukee Law Class—1895
Milwaukee Lithographing Co.—1887–89; 91; 94; 99
Milwaukee Manufacturing Co.—1897
Milwaukee Mattress Co.—1883
Milwaukee Mechanics Insurance Co.—1888–90; 93–95; 99
Milwaukee Medical College—1895; 97–98
Milwaukee Merchants Insurance Co.—1888; 93–94; 99
Milwaukee Mirror & Art Glass Co.—1891
Milwaukee Musical Circles—1890
Milwaukee & Northern Railroad—1887; 89
Milwaukee Parlor Furniture Co.—1891–92
Milwaukee Road—1899
Milwaukee Sash & Door Co.—1886
Milwaukee Sports—1888
Milwaukee Stove Works—1885
Milwaukee Temples—1888
Milwaukee Wheelmen—1895
Milwaukee Wholesale Grocers—1894
Milwaukee Worsted Mill Club—1894
Minatures—1895
Minerals—1888; 90; 94–95; 98–99
Miners—1890
Minneshahas—1894
Minnesotas—1898
Minors—1891
Missing Links—1885
Mitchell Bank Club—1892
Mitchell Heights—1888
Mitchell Street Tailors—1891
Mixups—1898
Mock Traegers—1894
Mocks, Jonas Co.—1883–84
Model Boys—1894–95; 98
Models—1890–91; 99
Modocs—1875; 94
Mohawks—1885; 89; 97–98
Mohawk Browns—1889
Mohecans—1894
Molly Maguires—1876
Monarchs—1884; 88; 91–92; 94–99
Monarch Juniors—1892; 97–98
Monches Fan Tans—1895–96
Monchow's (Robert)—1895
Moners—1897
Monitors—1867–71; 75; 82–92; 94–99
Monograms—1882; 98–99
Monons—1897
Monroes—1891–92; 95
Monroe Juniors—1892
Moonlights—1884–85; 88–90; 92; 94; 97
Moonshines—1888

Morawetz & Bros.—1884; 90
Morning Glories—1896–97
Morning Stars—1890; 94–97; 99
Mossoits—1897
Motive Powers—1889
Mountain Boys—1891; 94; 96
Mountain Springs—1895
Mount Olives—1896
Mt. Vernons—1894–95
Mud Hens—1897
Muellers—1896
Mueller Bros.—1897
Mueller & Ihlhardt Co.—1888
Muench Boys—1894–95
Muenzingers (C.H.)—1897–99
Muffers—1891–92
Muffins—1867
Muldoons—1898
Muncys—1894; 99
Murphys—1895
Murray's Additions—1888
Mushrooms—1886
Muskego Avenues—1896
Mutual Pleasures—1889
Mutuals—1869–70; 73–77; 82–85; 89; 95
Myer's (J.W.)—1887
Myer's Parks—1888
Myrtles—1894; 96
Myrtle Leafs—1891–94
Mystics—1877; 84–86; 88; 90–92; 94–99
Nailers—1892
Nashvilles—1898
National Avenues—1884
National Drilling Co.—1895
National Exchange Bank Club—1894; 99
National Flags—1897–98
National School Jrs.—1895
National Whites—1885
Nationalities—1895
Nationals—1867–70; 77; 82; 84–92; 94–98
Navals—1898
Navigators—1889
Navys—1899
Navy Blues—1883–84; 88; 92–93
Navy Juniors—1894–96
Nazereth Church—1896
Netzler Co.—1883
Neublings—1891
Never Rests—1884
Never Showups—1899
Never Sweets—1885; 90
Never Wins—1888
Nevil Boys—1896
Nevitts—1896
New Atlantics—1895–96
Newburghs—1894
New Coelin Boys—1896
New Green Leaves—1895
Newhall House Mutuals—1881
Newports—1882; 94
News—1898
Newsboys—1888
Newspaper Men—1895
Newspaper Terrors—1884

New Yorks—1894
Niagaras—1890–91; 94–99
Niagara Wheelmen—1898
Niedecken's—1887–88; 99
Night Hawks—1883
Night Messengers—1897
Night Naws—1896
Night Owls—1899
Night Ramblers—1894
Nine Arrows—1899
Nine Balls—1899
Nine Bells—1894–96; 98–99
Nine Bows—1899
Nine Diamonds—1894
Nine Knights—1895
Nine Pins—1883; 85; 96
Nine Pints—1894
Nine Points—1886
Nine Rodees—1892
Nine Spots—1896
Nine Stars—1894
Nineteenth Centuries—1894
Nineteenth Wards—1897
Ninety Fives—1895
Ninety Sixes—1896
Ninth District School—1897–98
Nobodys—1895
Nolan's Colts—1898
Nonames—1888; 95
Nonparells—1868–69; 93–99
Nonparrell Juniors—1895–96
Normal School—1896–99
Normal School Juniors—1895; 97
North Avenues 1895; 97
North Avenue Juniors—1897–98
North Avenue Stars—1898–99
North End Juniors—1894
North Ends—1884–85; 90; 92–98
Northern Clippers—1884
Northern Lights—1887–88
Northern Oil Co.—1894
Northern Stars—1895–96
Northerns—1889
Northfields—1888; 94
North Greenfields—1889; 94; 96–97; 99
North Juniors—1897
North Lakes—1895
North Lights—1892; 94; 96; 98
North Milwaukees—1883–84; 87–88; 90; 97–99
North Milwaukee Boys—1897
North Milwaukee Cycling Club—1897
North Pipes—1890
North Points—1890
North Stars—1894–99
North Streets—1888
Northside Barbers—1888
Northside Businessmen—1895
Northside Corkers—1899
Northside—Cycling Club—1895; 97–98
Northside Juniors—1895; 97
Northside Pleasures—1891; 96
Northside Stars—1899
Northside Turners—1876
Northsides—1887–88

Northwestern Juniors—1895; 97
Northwestern Malleable Iron Foundry—1894–95; 97
Northwestern Mutual Life Insurance Co.—1883–85; 90–91; 95–99
Northwestern National Insurance Co.—1899
Northwestern Oil Co.—1894
Northwestern Sleigh Co.—1883; 94
Northwestern Stars—1895
Northwestern Straw Works—1888
Northwesterns—1888; 90; 94–95; 98
Nyacks—1894; 96–97
Oak Creeks—1890–91
Oak Dales—1890
Oaken Buckets—1894
Oakland Boys—1892–94; 96–97; 99
Oakleaves—1877; 83–86; 88–92; 97
Oakleys—1884
Oaks—1895
Oats—1895
Oberlins—1898
Obermann's (J.)—1886
Odds—1885
Odells—1894–95
O'Donnells—1897
Ogdens—1885; 90–91
Ogden Avenues—1894
Ogemas—1884
O.K.'s—1890–91; 99
Old Crowe—1891
Old Glories—1884; 97
Old Ironsides—1884; 97
Old Kentuckys—1894
Old Staggs—1896
Old Timers—1885
Oliafleeces—1894
Olive Leaves—1894–98
Olives—1896–97; 99
Olympias—1889; 97; 99
Olympics—1894; 96–97
Olympic Bowling Club—1886
Onbyies—1898
Oneidas—1898
Operas—1885
Orchards—1895; 99
Oregons—1894; 99
Orientals—1871
Orients—1898
Originals—1894
Original Badgers—1895
Orioles—1893–95; 97–99
Orivas—1894
Ormonds—1893
Ornstines—1898
Otto Bros.—1896–9
Otto's (John)—1892
Our Boys—1877; 83–86; 88
Owls—1888; 91
Oxfords—1875; 95
Oxygens—1898
Pabsts—1897–99

Pacifics—1869; 84–86; 88; 91; 94; 96
Painters—1893; 95; 98
Palace Laundry—1890
Palaces—1888
Palmer House Club—1885
Palmers—1884; 95; 97
Palmettics—1896
Panner & Co.—1889
Park Hotels—1898
Pastimes—1879; 82–83; 98
Pathfinders—1888
Patriots—1898
Patton's (James)—1886; 88; 97
Peach & Rabbits—1895
Peach Gang—1897
Peanuts—1894
Peanut Pickers—1894
Pearls—1890; 94–96
Pearsons—1897
Pearson's Woodbines—1888
Peck's Bad Boys—1884
Peerless Club—1894; 96–97
Penner's (H.)—1888; 91
Penwipers—1896
People's Theater—1887
Pepper Boys—1894
Perigos—1895
Peterson & Sons—1894–96
Pfister & Vogel Club—1891
Pfister Bell Boys—1896
Pfister Colts—1897
Pfisters—1892; 96–97; 99
Pfuggradt Candy Co.—1897–98
Phatoms—1889
Philadelphia Clothing House—1888
Phipps Bros.—1894
Phoenix—1881–92; 94–99
Phoenix Bowling Club—1892
Physicians—1888
Picketts—1883–88; 90–91; 94
Pickups—1884–86; 90–92; 94–95; 97
Pigsvilles—1886
Pilgrims—1896; 98–99
Pilots—1877; 96
Pine Leafs—1882; 95
Pinkies—1898
Pinkles—1897
Pink Stars—1896
Pintche Bowling Club—1884
Pioneer Fire Proof Co.—1892
Pio Nono College—1891; 94; 96; 98
Pio Nono College Juniors—1896
Pirates—1894; 98–99
Plain Talks—1888
Planets—1884–91; 94–95
Planet Juniors—1897
Plankinton House Reds—1890
Plankinton Juniors—1894
Plankinton Packing Co.—1896
Plankinton Porters—1885; 87
Plankintons—1886; 92–94; 96
Plasters—1894
Plate Workers—1888
Playfairs—1893

Pleasures—1896; 98
Plow Boys—1890–91
Plug Hats—1898
Plumb (L.H.) Co.—1884–85; 88
Plumbers—1895
Plutes—1894
Plymouths—1883
Polschech's (C.H.)—1884
Polar Stars—1898
Policemen—1895; 97
Polish Euchres—1884; 89
Pollack, Spitz & Landauer Co.—1885
Pollak & Strauss Co.—1885
Populars—1892; 98
Popular Leafs—1884
Popwscups—1896
Porkers—1896
Porto Ricans—1899
Posson's (P.E.)—1895
Post Offices—1894–96
Post Office Alerts—1895
Postals—1895; 97–99
Postal Telegraphers—1897
Praire Boys—1876; 94–95
Pratts' Ponies—1898
Pratt's Rivals—1898
Prescotts—1896–99
Press Club—1886; 96
Printers—1893
Pritzlaff Co.—1884–85; 87–89; 91; 95; 99
Private Drivers—1883
Privateers—1889
Privates—1888
Professors—1891
Progressives—1897
Prospect Avenues—1897
Prospects—1895; 97
Pueblos—1895–96; 98
Puleffers—1898
Pumpi Lules—1888
Pumpmakers—1888
Puritans—1887; 97–98
Push Club—1892
P.V.'s—1883–84
Quakers—1896
Queen Cities—1895
Queens—1889
Quicksteps—1881–97; 99
Quiets—1894
Quilldrivers—1882
Quinceys—1892–97; 99
Quins—1895–99
Raasch's Hereos—1897
Rabbits—1897
Racines—1884
Racine Streets—1887
Rackets—1894
Racoluts—1896
Rags—1884
Rainbows—1895; 98
Rainmakers—1896
Raleighs—1899
Ramien Bros.—1891
Ramrods—1888
Rathke Bros. & Kortsch Co.—1898

Rattlers—1888
Razall Juniors—1896
Razalls (H.G.)—1895–99
Razoos—1896
Razzle Dazzles—1899
Reachers—1894–95
Real Estate Men—1892
Records—1892; 94–96
Recreation Bowling Club—1891
Rectifiers—1887
Red Beasts—1895
Red Boys—1898
Red Caps—1881–83; 85; 90; 95–97
Red Cedars—1894; 96
Red Clovers—1890; 95; 98
Red Collars—1895
Red Crosses—1894
Red Diamonds—1896–97
Red Hearts—1884–85; 88; 92
Red Hot Liners—1897
Red Howlers—1893
Red Lights—1891; 95
Red Moons—1892
Red Mounts—1891
Red Nlags—1891
Red Nobs—1896
Red Oaks—1887–91; 93–95; 98–99
Red Oak Juniors—1895–96
Red Rockets—1895
Red Rocks—1895–96; 99
Red Roses—1895–98
Red Rubies—1895
Red Stars—1883; 91; 94–99
Red Stockings—1879; 82–82; 98
Red Tops—1892
Red, White and Blues—1892; 95–99
Redmonds—1891
Reds—1883–85; 90; 92–95; 97
Register of Deeds Office—1899
Regulars—1885; 97; 99
Regulations—18984
Regulators—1882–84; 86–88; 91–95
Regulator Juniors—1895
Regulator Reserves—1885
Reindeers—1884; 95
Reliables—1898
Reliance Club—1884–85
Reliants—1885
Representatives—1897
Republican House Cub—1896; 98
Reservoir Boys—1888; 95
Resolutes—1869–70; 73; 77; 85; 88; 96
Retinners—1896
Retzlaffs (F.)—1888
Revenges—1891
Revenus—1892
Reveres—1887
Reviews—1887
Rice & Friedman's—1888
Rice's Big Burlesques Club—1884
Rice's (Sam)—1892
Rich Boys—1890; 94

Richards—1890
Richeliens—1892
Rich's Success Club—1890
Ricker's (Frank)—1897
Ricker, Cromble & McLaren Co.
 —1883–85
Rickersons—1897
Ricketsons—1894–95
Riffles—1894
Righties—1898
Rio Stars—1896
Rival Furnishings—1888
Rival Juniors—1895
Rivals—1885; 88–89; 94–98
Riverside Printing Co.—1894
Riverside Rowing Club—1890
Riversides—1875; 85; 87–88; 92–
 92; 94; 96–97
Rivulets—1890
Roanokes—1869; 79; 95
Roche (John) Juniors—1894
Rochesters—1883
Rockenbach's (Jacob)—1897
Rockets—1894–95; 98
Rockfords—1894
Rocklands—1895
Rocky Mountain Boys—1891; 99
Rodt's—1886–88
Roetke's (Willie)—1895
Rogers—1897
Roldfinger's (Wl.)—1898
Roll Turners—1899
Rollers—1892
Rolling Mills—1875; 83
Rolling Mils Carpenters—1896
Rolling Mills Machinists—1896
Romatka Bros.—1899
Rose Hills—1888; 94
Rose Leaf Pleasure Club—1899
Rose Royal Female Club—1893
Rosebuds—1885; 94–96
Roth Manufacturing Co.—1888
Rough & Readies—1895; 97
Rough Riders—1899
Round House Blues—1894
Roundy & Peckman & Co.—
 1883–84; 86; 94
Rovers—1891
Royal Adelphias—1887–88
Royal Boys—1897
Royal Juniors—1897
Royal Socials—1897–98
Royals—1890; 94; 96–99
Rubies—1894–95
Rudolph Bros.—1898
Ruehl's (G.)—1898
Rustics—1899
Ruith's (N.)—1899
Rundle & Spence Co.—1883–84;
 90–91
Rurals—1888; 90
Rush Avenues—1895
Rushers—1889
Rusk Guards—1890
Sabayers—1891
Sacred Heart College—1890
Sad Lights—1890
Sad Sights—1890

Safetys—1890
Sailor Boys—1895; 99
St. Anthony's—1899
St. Boniface's—1891
St. Charles Hotel Club—1896
St. Francis Club—1891; 97; 99
St. Francis Juniors—1896
St. Francis Seminary—1883; 92;
 96
St. Francis YMS—1891
St. Gall's—1895
St. James Club—1894–95; 99
St. John's Cathedral—1889; 94–
 95; 97
St. John's School—1896; 99
St. John's YMI—1896
St. Joseph Church—1895–96; 99
St. Joseph School—1897
St. Luke's Choir—1897
St. Mark's—1898
St. Mary's School—1896–97
St. Patrick School—1895
St. Patrick's YMI—1896
St. Paul's Choir—1889; 91–92;
 94–95; 99
St. Paul Railroad—1883–84; 89;
 94; 96; 99
St. Peter's Church—1899
St. Stanislaus—1899
Sally—1895
Sampsons—1898–99
Sam's Indians—1897
Sand Artists—1885
Sanders—1895
Sandrock's (L.)—1897
Sanger & Sons—1894
Sanrals—1895
Sapbans—1898
Sardines—1899
Sast Stars—1898
Satillites—1888
Saulman's—1885
Savers—1894
Scalpers—1885; 97–99
Scarlets—1890
Schafskopfs—1892
Scheftel's—1894
Schick's—1886
Schiller's (Fred)—1894
Schlehlem's (Matthew)—1895
Schlitz Boys—1898
Schlitz Brewers—1894
Schlitz Globes—1897; 99
Schlitz Palm Gardens—1899
Schlitz Park Opera Co.—1892;
 95–97
Schlitz Park Tragedians—1887
Schlitz Park Ushers—1884
Schmidt's (Eli)—1899
Schmidt's (J.E.)—1899
Schoegel's (G.C.)—1895; 98
Schoemecher's (F.)—1890
School Boys—1888
School Sections—1888
Schultzes—1895
Schuster's (George)—1894; 97
Schwechia's (Joe)—1899
Scorchers—1894–94

Scots—1895
Scrantons—1896
Scrapeaters—1895
Scrapers—1894
Scrap Irons—1895
Scribes 1897–98
Scrubs—1889; 99
S.D.'s—1894
Searchlights—1894
Sea Shores—1894
Second Avenue Jollys—1897
Second District School—1890;
 95–97
Second Wards—1890; 99
Second Ward Stars—1887
Secrets—1889–92; 94
Secret Sons of Rest—1895; 97
Seebotes—1895
SeeSees—1898
Segnitz & Co.—1884
Seifert & Schoeffel Lithography
 Co.—1888
Senators—1897–99
Seniors—1897–99
Sentinels—1876–77; 83–84; 86;
 90; 94; 98
Serlings—1888
Seventeenth Streeters—1896
Seventh District School—1892;
 96
Seventh Wards—1891; 94; 96
Seymours—1899
Shadbolt & Boyd Co.—1882–85;
 87–89; 96
Shadows—1888; 91
Shakespeares—1889
Shakman (L.A.) Co.—1896–99
Shamrocks—1883–84; 86–88; 90–
 99
Sharks—1899
Sharp Corners—1887; 89–90
Sharps—1897
Sharpshooters—1898
Shaughnesseys—1895
Shavers—1884
Sheboygans—1884
Sheffels & Co.—1895
Shepherd Juniors—1898
Shepherd Kings—1894
Sheridan Guards—1886–87; 89–
 90
Sheridan Rifles—1895
Sheridans—1895
Shiners—1886
Shingle Splitters—1890
Shining Stars—1895–97
Shipolks—1890
Shoe Flies—1870
Shoemakers—1894
Shooting Stars—1894–95
Shorties—1896–99
Siefert's Groves—1898
Siegler's (Frank)—1892
Signal Lights—1889
Silver Boys—1895
Silver Citys—1894–97; 99
Silver City Juniors—1895
Silver Clouds—1891–92

Silver Clowns—1884
Silver Kings—1888
Silver Leaves—1889
Silver Meadows—1895–96
Silver Rocks—1884; 96
Silver Rods—1895
Silver Springs—1888; 90–92; 94–95; 98
Silver Stars—1888–91; 93–94; 96–99
Silver Stones—1886–88; 94
Silver Tips—1893- 96
Singer Manufacturing Co.—1890–91; 94–98
Sitting Blues—1891
Sitting Bulls—1898
Sivyer & Betz Starlights—1895
Six Brothers—1899
Sixteenth District Club—1890–92
Sixteenth District School—1896
Sixteenth Streeters—1897
Sixth Avenues—1877; 94
Sixth District School—1885; 92; 94; 98
Sixth District School No.2—1896
Sixth District Union School—1891
Sixth Graders—1897
Sixth Ward Corkers—1897
Skaters—1895
Skeffington Juniors—1896
Skidmore & Friedlick's—1894–99
Skidmore & Hendrickson's—1892
Skidmore Juniors—1895; 99
Skippers—1884
Skittles Bowling Club—1891
Skobis Manufacturing Co.—1895
Skylights—1895; 97
Skyrockets—1892
Skyscrapers—1899
Slashers—1899
Sleepyeyes—1898
Sliders—1898
Sluggers—1890; 94–95
Small Boys—1898
Smiths—1892
Smith (C.J.) & Co.—1896; 98
Smith (Wallace) Club—1897; 99
Smith, Mendel & Co.—1884
Smith & Stoughton's—1894
Sneakers—1894
Snowballs—1897–98
Soapiness—1891–92; 94–95
Sociables—1888
Social Friends—1888
Sod Cutters—1894
Sokol Drum Corps—1894–97
Solicitors—1897
Solider Boys—1895–98
Solomon Juneaus—1869
Sioux—1895; 99
South Bays—1894–96; 98
South Boys—1894–96
South Ends—1876; 83–86; 91–96; 99
South Foundry Club—1895; 98

South Milwaukees—1891–99
South Milwaukee Crescents—1897
South Milwaukee Helms—1896
South Milwaukee Juniors—1893; 99
South Milwaukee Nonparells—1896
South Milwaukee Stars—1894
South Milwaukee Victors—1897
South Milwaukee Welcomes—1895–96
South Paws—1895
South Points—1894–96
South Side Boys—1896
South Side Businessmen—1895
South Side Club Swingers—1888
South Side Cycle Club—1897
South Side Dumb Bell Lifters—1888
South Side Fatties—1887
South Side Grays—1891
South Side High School—1894–99
South Side High School Juniors—1894
South Side Juniors—1892; 95; 97
South Side Leans—1887
South Side Saloonkeepers—1895
South Side Station Policemen—1895
South Side Sports—1896
South Side Turners—1876
South Side Victors—1895
Southern Stars—1894
Spalding Juniors—1894–95; 97
Spaldings—1888–94; 96; 99
Spaniards—1898
Sparkling Diamonds—1894
Sparkling Springs—1894
Spence (G.A.)—1888
Spence & Lyon's—1883
Spencerians—1896–97
Spencerian Business College—1870; 89; 92–92; 97; 99
Spencers—1883; 91; 93
Spheres—1891
Spinnefergifters—1898–99
Spirits—1896–97
Sports—1888; 96
Sports of Omaha—1891
Spring Brooks—1879
Spring Chickens—1888
Spring Cities—1898
Springfields—1885–86; 94–96
Squash Diggers—1894
Squibs—1895
S.S.S.'s—1896
Stamm & Wartmann's—1892
Standard Juniors—1897
Standard Oil Co.—1892; 94–95; 97
Standard Paper Co.—1884; 97; 95
Standard Printing Co.—1891–98
Standards—1885; 87–98
Star Athletics—1895; 99
Star Bobs—1890
Star Boys—1884–85; 88; 90–95

Star Pointers—1899
Star Social Circle club—1887; 90
Stark Bros.—1891
Starlights—1876; 84–89; 91–92; 94–99
Starlight Juniors—1892; 94
Stars—1867–70; 75; 78–79; 82; 84–99
Stars and Stripes—1898
State Street Boys—1894
Steamheaters—1889
Steffens—1889
Steinback's—1894
Steinel Broommakers—1885
Steinmetzer's—1885; 88
Stephenson's (J.)—1892
Sterlings—1893; 94; 96–98
Stermann & Hayden's—1897
Stern (H.) Co.—1884; 98
Stickems—1870
Stillwaters—1888
Stockyards—1890
Stonewalls—1895
Storm Hill & Co.—1876
Stove Molders—1888
Stowalls—1890; 98
Straw & Ellsworth & Co.—1887; 95; 95; 97–98
Street (W.H.) Co.—1897
Striffers—1895
Strusys—1896
Stumpf & Langfoff Co.—1898
Stusseys—1896
Submarines—1898
Success Club—1889
Sueldohn & Seefeld's—1888; 96
Summer Boys—1870
Sunbeams—1891–92; 94
Sunday Mornings—1886
Sunflowers—1889
Sunlights—1890; 95–96
Sunlight Juniors—1896
Sunnysides—1884
Sunsets—1894
Superbas—1891
Superior Juniors—1892; 94–96
Superior Social Circles—1894
Superiors—1883–84; 90–92; 94–97; 99
Swackten (Henry) Club—1895
Swain & Tate's—1888; 90
Sweaters—1895; 98
Sweet (N.H.) Co.—1897
Swifts—1888
Swiftrunners—1887
Swimmers—1895
Switchmen—1891
Sycamores—1898
Sylvans—1889
Tacklers—1888
Tacomas—1898
Tallyhoes—1889
Tame Cats—1899
Tankers—1899
Tanner (A.F.) & Co.—1894
Tanners—1892; 94
Tannez Furniture Co.—1891
Taylor's (Charles)—1895

Tecetis—1898
Tecumshes—1895
Telegrams—1895
Telegraph Boys—1882
Telegraph Messengers—1888
Telegraphers—1887; 90
Temple Pratts—1898
Tenth District School—1894; 96–97; 99
Tenth Warders—1890
Teutonias—1867
Teutonia Stars—1895–99
Three Brothers—1894
Three C's—1888
Third District School—1885; 88–89; 95
Third Ward Clippers—1890
Third Ward Juniors—1894
Third Ward Mayflowers—1894
Third Ward Tarries—1888
Third Ward White Caps—1889
Thirteenth District School—1891; 94–96; 99
Thirteenth Wards—1890
Third Ward Skates—1895
Thirty-Sixth Streets—1896
Thistles—1890
Thomas Brass Works—1890
Thompson Opera Co.—1885
Thorns—1897
Thorntons—1891
Thorps—1889; 97
Timilies—1892
Tin Plates—1884
Tippecanoes—1888; 96
Tiptops—1888
Tired Boys—1895
Tobadings—1897
Toledos—1882
Tomboys—1895
Tom Dooleys—1894
Tony Lamers—1888
Toothpicks—1888; 90
Tornados—1885; 95
Torpedo Boat Destroyers—1898
Torpedoes—1892; 98
Tory Hills—1891–92; 95; 97
Tory Hill Rubbernecks—1895
Town of Lakes—1895; 97
Town of Milwaukees—1896
Train Dispatchers—1884
Trainers—1897
Treasury Department Club—1898
Tree Tops—1895
Trentonia Stars—1895
Triangles—1897–98
Trifles—1894–95
Trilbies—1895; 98
Trilby Bunters—1896
Trinity Boys—1890; 96
Trinnitas—1892
Triumphs—1890; 95
Trojans—1899
Trostel (Albert) & Sons—1895–96; 98
Trotts—1893
Troys—1892; 94–95

Troys Stearn Laundry Co.—1888
Tryanchles—1897
Tumblers—1890
Tures—1899
Turn Verein Humboldts—1895
Turn Verein Milwaukees—1899
Turn Verein Voraerts—1896–97
Turnovers—1897–98
Tuttis Old Settlers—1899
T.V.B.'s—1897
T.V.J.'s—1898
T.V.M.'s—1895; 97; 99
Twelfth District School—1895–96; 98
Twelfth Wards—1898
Twelfth Ward Juniors—1897
Twentieth District Schoo—1898l
Twenty-first Wards—1897
Twenty-ninth Street Boys—1899
Twilights—1894–95
Twilers—1895
T.Y.A.'s—1896
Type Foundry—1885
Typewriters—1890
Ucans—1888
Ueberall Bros.—1897
Unanklagbarens—1882
Uncle Sam's Stampstickers—1882
Underwriters—1897
Unions—1867–68; 75; 83–86; 90; 92–96
Union Athletics—1897
Union Boys—1884–85; 94–96; 98
Union Cigarmakers—1897
Union Depots—1884; 91; 95–99
Union Eagles—1899
Union School—1895; 98
Union Stars—1897
Uniques—1896
Uniteds—1894
United Social Circle—1893
United Stars—1894
Universalists—1896
Universals—1890–91
Unknowns—1877; 81; 83–84; 88; 90; 95
Upper Storyities—1870
Upper Third Streets—1888
Uprights—1895
Up-To-Dates—1898
Us Boys—1890
U.S. Eagles—1890
U.S. Express Club—1884; 95
Utopias—1899
Valleys—1891–92; 94–95
Van Normans—1895
Verdts—1894
Vernons—1894–95; 97–99
Viaducts—1895
Victorias—1883
Vicotos—1898
Victors—1888; 90–99
Victor Juniors—1891–92
Vigilants—1894
Vikings—1896–98
Vilters—1895
Violets—1891; 94–96
Virginias—1895

Vogt & Killian's—1895
Volunteers—1889–91; 94; 96; 98–99
Vonier's (Louis)—1893–94
Voodoos—1896
Vorwaert's Turners—1890; 95
Vouchers—1889
Vulcans—1894
Wadham Oil & Grease Co.—1891; 99
Wagners—1895
Wagon Makers—1899
Wagon Tongues—1892
Waldo & Co.—1888
Walk Fasts—1888
Walker Conclaves—1887–88; 90
Walker Streets—1897–98
Walkers—1887; 92
Wallschlaggers—1895
Walnuts—1888
Walnut Hills—1894
Walnut Stars—1899
Wambertas—1895
Wanderers—1888
Wansers Flinsterers—1896
Ward & Dooley's—1892
Warders—1886
Warren Avenues—1897
Warren Avenue Bullet Stoppers—1898
Warren Avenue Sports—1898
Warren Boys—1894
Warriors—1896
Wartburg Juniors—1899
Washburns—1897
Washington (P.A.) Co.—1894
Washington Avenues—1895
Washington Juniors—1895
Washingtons—1867; 91; 95–96
Water Department Club—1890; 94–96; 98–99
Water Lillies—1888
Watt's Its—1887
Waubecks—1898
Wauwatosa Alerts—1892
Wauwatosa Blues—1892
Wauwatosa Grays—1892
Wauwatosa Hayseeds—1899
Wauwatosa High School—1896–97
Wauwatosa Juniors—1895
Wauwatosa Men—1894
Wauwatosa Monarchs—1898
Wauwatosa Reds—1899
Wauwatosas—1889; 94–96; 98–99
Waverlys—1888
Wavers—1884
Wa-Wa-Sakes—1897
Wayland Academy—1898
Waysides—1898
Weapons—1890
Websters—1895
Weden & Co.—1898
Wehr (Henry) Co.—1888; 94
Weigel Bedding Co.—1889–89; 99
Weiman & Muench Markels—1899

Weiss (Charles) Co.—1890
Welcomes—1882-89; 91-96; 98-99
Welcome Juniors—1896
Welgens—1891
Wellauer (Jacob) & Co.—1884-85
Wellingtons—1895
Weltons—1888
Wenzel's (Otto)—1894
Wergell's (A.)—1888
Wergins—1891
West Fielders—1899
West Green Leaves—1895
West Juniors—1894
West Milwaukees—1884-85; 88-95; 98
West Milwaukee Car Department Club—1894
West Milwaukee Juniors—1894
West Milwaukee Shops—1888; 94; 97; 99
West Points—1898-99
West Sides—1888; 91-92; 97; 99
West Side Actives—1876
West Side Alerts—1895
West Side Athletics—1895
West Side Badgers—1899
West Side Bankers—1898
West Side Barbers—1888; 90; 94-95; 97-98
West Side Blues—1888
West Side Cycling Club—1897
West Side Fatzers—1899
West Side High School—1895-98
West Side Juniors—1893; 99
West Side Lawyers—1895
West Side Music House—1895
West Side Pickets—1888
West Side Pleasures—1882
West Side Police Station—1896
West Side Rifles—1895; 97; 99
West Side Rivals—1898
West Side Standards—1891
West Side Tailors—1894-95
West Side Turners—1894-95
West Water Street Commission—1883-84
West (H.H.) Co.—1890; 92; 94
Western Boys—1873; 75-76; 93
Western Milwaukees—1885
Western Rapids—1888
Western Railway—1883
Western Stars—1885-86; 91-94; 97; 99
Western Unions—1876; 84; 86; 88-90; 94-95; 97-98
Westerns—1881-86; 88; 90; 94; 96; 98
Wests—1896
West Ends—1875-78; 83; 85-86; 88-90; 93-99
West End Juniors—1895-97; 99
Wetzler Shops—1883
White Caps—1882; 95-96; 99
White Clouds—1888; 94-96
White Clovers—1895-96
White Diamonds—1891-99

White Diamond Juniors—1894; 96-97; 99
White Eagles—1894-95
Whitefish Bays—1897
White Flyers—1899
White Globes—1896
White Hills—1885
White Leafs—1895
White Lilacs—1895; 98-99
White Lillies—1894-95; 97
White Metals—1899
White Oaks—1888-92; 94-98
White Oak Juniors—1894; 97
White Pearls—1894-95
White Rocks—1888; 94
White Roses—1894; 97
White Starlights—1895
White Stars—1895-97; 99
White Stockings—1869-70; 75; 85; 90
White Valleys—1895
White Wings—1888
Whites—1883-88; 91; 94
Whalebacks—1898
Whalebones—1895
Whales—1886
Whirlwinds—1896
Whiskers—1892
Whitcombs—1897
Whiting Grays—1899
Whitings—1884-85; 88; 90-94; 97
Whitneys—1893
Whittakers—1890
Wholesale Grocers—1883
Whoppers—1892
Wide Awakes—1876; 85-86; 88; 92; 95
Wiener Upholstering Co.—1895
Wiener's (E.)—1894; 97
Wild Cats—1899
Wild Dogs—1899
Wild Roses—1895-96; 99
Wilkens—1891
Williams—1894
Willows—1883; 85-89; 92-95; 97-98
Wilmann Bros. Lithograph Co.—1892
Wilmonts—1897
Winchesters—1895
Windlakes—1899
Windsors—1894-95
Winfields—1894
Winnebagoes—1884
Wisconsin Centrals—1883; 87-88; 95-99
Wisconsin Juniors—1893-95; 99
Wisconsin Marbeable Iron Works Co.—1891
Wisconsin Marine Bank Club—1892
Wisconsin Marine Fire Insurance Co.—1888
Wisconsin National Bank—1894-95
Wisconsin Newsboys—1888
Wisconsin Planning Co.—1886

Wisconsin Semi-Centennials—1898
Wisconsin Telephone Co.—1894
Wisconsin Temples—1888; 90
Wisconsins—1860; 76-78; 93-97
Wizards—1894; 97
Wolf's—1885-86
Wolleager Manufacturing Co.—1895
Wolverines—1898
Wood Choppers—1896
Wood Engravers—1890
Wooden Indians—1894
Woodoos—1895
Worries—1896
Would-bes—1895
Would-be-Sports—1898
Wringers—1898
Wyandottes—1888; 90
Wynns—1893
X-Rays—1899
YMCA Club—1888; 91; 95
YMCA Juniors—1888; 91; 95; 97
Yahoos—1897
Yales—1894; 96-97; 99
Yale Juniors—1897
Yankee Boats—1897
Yankee Champions—1875; 77
Yellow Astors—1895
Yellow Kids—1897
Yellow Mountain Boys—1897
Yellow Stars—1893; 99
Yellow Stones—1895-96
Yellow Willows—1894
Yewdale's (J.)—1888-89
Yorks—1894-96
Young (Benjamin) Co.—1891; 97
Young Additions—1891
Young Admirals—1899
Young Alerts—1884; 89-90
Young Alleghanies—1885
Young Americans—1884-86; 88; 91; 94-99
Young Arctics—1895
Young Athletics—1890; 96
Young Badgers—1895-97; 99
Young Banners—1896
Young Bay Views—1890; 97-98
Young Beavers—1895
Young Bostons—1892; 99
Young Brewers—1895-96
Young Bulldogs—1896
Young Butterflies—1896
Young Calumets—1899
Young Chicagos—1896
Young Clevelands—1899
Young Clippers—1885
Young Colts—1895-96
Young Comets—1895
Young Commanders—1896
Young Cowboys—1896
Young Coxeys—1894
Young Cream Cities—1885; 94-95
Young Cubans—1897-98
Young Cudahys—1899
Young Cyclones—1895
Young Dalsys—1899

Young Defenders—1899
Young Detroits—1895–96
Young Deweys—1898
Young Diamonds—1884
Young Eagles—1894–95
Young Eclipse—1894–95; 99
Young Elearts—1895
Young Emeralds—1895; 97; 99
Young Excelsiors—1884; 88
Young Fairbanks—1888
Young Farwells—1895–96
Young Fauntleroys—1899
Young Fernwoods—1897
Young Fielders—1899
Young Frolics—1899
Young Glenwoods—1894–95
Young Glories—1898–99
Young Golden Eagles—1884
Young Grand Rapids—1894
Young Greenfields—1894–99
Young Greenleaves—1896
Young Greshams—1898
Young Haymarkets—1899
Young Headers—1894
Young Hobos—1898–99
Young Hollands—1895
Young Hopkins—1896
Young Hummers—1899
Young Hunters—1895
Young Hurons—1897–99
Young Hustlers—1899
Young Ikes—1897
Young Imperials—1895
Young Ivys—1892; 95; 99
Young Jacksons—1897
Young Journals—1899
Young Juniors—1895; 98–99
Young Keystones—1896
Young Klondikes—1898
Young Knights Templars—1894
Young Ladies—1889
Young Lake News—1899
Young Lake Shores—1883; 94
Young Lake Views—1899
Young Laytons—1895; 99
Young Leaders—1885; 94–97; 99
Young Liberty Boys—1894–95
Young Lincolns—1894; 98
Young Madisons—1895–96
Young Maines—1898
Young Maple Leafs—1879; 82–83; 88; 93

Young Married Men—1894
Young Marquettes—1899
Young Mascottes—1888
Young McKinleys—1898
Young Men—1899
Young Menominees—1896
Young Mens Bowling Club—1886
Young Merchants—1887
Young Merrills—1894
Young Merrill Park Stars—1899
Young Merrimacs—1895
Young Michigans—1898–99
Young Milwaukees—1882–83; 85; 91–92; 95; 97–99
Young Milwaukee Whites—1892
Young Minerals—1895; 99
Young Monitors—1883; 90; 96
Young Morgans—1885
Young Morning Glories—1896
Young Mutuals—1891
Young Nationals—1895–96
Young Nonpareils—1895
Young Northern Lights—1899
Young Northwesterns—1897
Young Oakland Boys—1894
Young Oakleaves—1888; 95
Young Oaks—1895
Young Pabsts—1894
Young Phoenix—1882–83; 85; 88; 92
Young Pierres—1891
Young Plumbers—1896
Young Premiers—1891
Young Pueblos—1896
Young Quickfeet—1896
Young Quicksteps—1883–84; 88; 95
Young Quincys—1892; 95
Young Regulars—1899
Young Regulators—1886
Young Reliables—1891
Young Reserves—1885
Young Review Boys—1888
Young Rifles—1894
Young Roses—1898
Young Royals—1899
Young Saddery Co. 1894; 99
Young Sailors—1895
Young St. Pauls—1895–96
Young Senators—1898
Young Springfields—1896
Young Standards—1894

Young Starlights—1889
Young Stars—1885; 88; 91; 93–99
Young Starters—1897
Young Starlings—1894
Young Sunflowers—1894
Young Superiors—1895
Young Tigers—1897
Young Torys—1895
Young Troys—1897; 99
Young Turfs—1899
Young Valentines—1896
Young Victors—1894–95; 97
Young Violets—1895–96; 99
Young Washingtons—1895; 99
Young Welcomes—1894; 96–97; 99
Young West Ends—1884
Young West Side Juniors—1899
Young White Diamonds—1895; 98
Young Willows—1894
Young Winchesters—1896
Young Wisconsins—1895–97; 99
Young Zieglers—1896
Yukans—1888
Yukeers—1894
Zellusky's—1895
Zeas—1898
Zehriauts—1899
Zeniths—1884
Zeocolus—1899
Zieglers—1881; 83; 87; 91–92; 94–95; 97–98
Zimmerman Bros.—1884
Zimmerman Juniors—1895
Zimmerman (Rud) Club—1898
Zion Juniors—1896
Zion Seniors—1896
Zion's Church YMCA—1896; 99
Zoehriants—1896
Zouave Drum Corps—1894
Zozo Opera Co.—1886
Zwelsackers—1894
Young Shamrocks—1883; 88–89; 97
Young Signals—1895–96
Young Singles—1895
Young Slowfeet—1896
Young South Boys—1896
Young Spaldings—1895–96
Young Spaniards—1898
Young Sports—1896–98

Chapter Notes

Chapter 1

1. *Daily Milwaukee News*, December 20, 1859.
2. *Milwaukee Sentinel*, April 6, 1860.
3. *Milwaukee Sentinel*, May 16, 1860.
4. *Milwaukee Sentinel* May 17, 1860.
5. *Milwaukee Sentinel* April 20, 1860.
6. *Milwaukee Sentinel* June 8, 1860.
7. *Milwaukee Sentinel* May 7, 1860.
8. *Milwaukee Sentinel* June 20, 1860.
9. *Daily Milwaukee News* September 2, 1860.
10. Seymour R. Church, *Base Ball: The History, Statistics and Romance of the American National Game* (Princeton: Pyne Press, 1974), page 6. Reprints of 1902 edition.
11. David Nemec, *The Rules of Baseball: An Anecdotal Look at the Rules of Baseball and How They Came to Be* (New York: Lyons & Burford, 1994), page 27. Nemec writes the umpire was required to warn the pitcher "an unspecified number of times" about pitches out of the strike zone; so more than three balls actually walked a batter.
12. *Daily Milwaukee News* April 11, 1860.
13. *Milwaukee Sentinel* July 3, 1860.
14. *Milwaukee Sentinel* June 20, 1861.
15. *New York Times* July 12, 1858.
16. *Milwaukee Sentinel* August 14, 1865.
17. *Daily Milwaukee News* April 24, 1860.

Chapter 2

1. *Milwaukee Sentinel* August 11, 1865.
2. *Daily Milwaukee News* September 21, 1865.
3. *Milwaukee Sentinel* October 7, 1865.
4. *Milwaukee Sentinel* November 8, 1865.
5. *Daily Milwaukee News* November 9, 1865.
6. *Daily Milwaukee News* November 9, 1865.
7. *Milwaukee Sentinel* March 12, 1866.
8. *Daily Milwaukee News* May 13, 1866.
9. *Daily Milwaukee News* May 27, 1866.
10. *Daily Milwaukee News* May 26, 27, 1866.
11. *Daily Milwaukee News* May 30, 1866.
12. *Daily Milwaukee News* May 31, 1866.
13. Often player names were spelled differently in different newspapers, and even in the same paper from issue to issue. Archibald McFadyen's (a clerk who lived on Milwaukee's near south side) name was also spelled McFadyn and McFayden. Redington and Kelly were also spelled Reddington and Kelley.
14. *Milwaukee Sentinel* June 4, 1866 and *Daily Milwaukee News* June 19, 1866.
15. *Daily Milwaukee News* June 24, 1866.
16. *Milwaukee Sentinel* June 26, 1866.
17. *Milwaukee Sentinel* June 29, 1866.
18. *Milwaukee Sentinel* June 29, 1866.
19. *Milwaukee Sentinel* June 30, 1866.
20. The information and quotes on this tournament in these two paragraphs are from *Milwaukee Sentinel* of July 2, 1866.
21. *Daily Milwaukee News* August 10, 1866.
22. *Milwaukee Sentinel* August 23, 1866.
23. *Daily Milwaukee News* November 10, 1866.
24. *Milwaukee Sentinel* July 20, 1866.
25. *Milwaukee Sentinel* June 27, 1867.
26. *Milwaukee Sentinel* July 18, 1867.
27. *Milwaukee Sentinel* May 6, 1867.
28. *Milwaukee Sentinel* June 21, 1867.
29. *Milwaukee Sentinel* July 3, 1867.
30. *Milwaukee Sentinel* July 6, 1867.
31. *Milwaukee Sentinel* July 12, 1867.
32. *Milwaukee Sentinel* August 17,1867.
33. *Milwaukee Sentinel* July 29, 1867.
34. Information on Beloit tournament based on articles in *Milwaukee Sentinel* of August 2, 5, 20, 1867, and September 4, 1867.
35. *Milwaukee Sentinel* September 9, 1867.
36. *Milwaukee Sentinel* September 25, 1867.
37. *Milwaukee Sentinel* April 29, 1868.
38. *Milwaukee Sentinel* April 29, 1868.
39. *Daily Milwaukee News* May 27, 1868.
40. *Milwaukee Sentinel* June 23, 1868.
41. *Milwaukee Sentinel* June 23, 1868.
42. *Milwaukee Sentinel* July 3, 1868.
43. *Milwaukee Sentinel* September 1, 1868.
44. *Daily Milwaukee News* July 10, 1868.
45. Harold Seymour, *Baseball: The Early Years* (New York: Oxford University Press, 1960), page 44.
46. *Milwaukee Sentinel* August 8, 1868.
47. *Daily Milwaukee News* August 25, 1868.
48. *Milwaukee Sentinel* April 11, 1867.
49. *Milwaukee Sentinel* October 27, 1868.
50. *Milwaukee Sentinel* July 30, 1868.

Chapter 3

1. *Milwaukee Sentinel* April 15, 1869.
2. *Milwaukee Sentinel* June 17, 1869.
3. Account of incident taken from *Milwaukee Sentinel* and *Daily Milwaukee News* of June 19, 1869.
4. *Milwaukee Sentinel* July 27, 1869.
5. This is Harry Wright's official record for 1869. Darryl Brock in his article, "The 1869 Red Stockings" (SABR, *The Perfect Game*, 1998, pages 89–94) gives an interesting account for the conflicting number of wins

often cited, and makes a case for an official record of 60 wins.
6. Stephen D. Guschov, *The Red Stockings of Cincinnati: Base Ball's First All-Professional Team*, McFarland & Company, Inc., 1998, page 27.
7. *Daily Milwaukee News* July 31, 1869.
8. The *Cincinnati Gazette* of July 31, 1869, reported two or three thousand persons attended.
9. *Milwaukee Sentinel* September 7, 1869.
10. *Milwaukee Sentinel* August 7, 1869.
11. *Daily Milwaukee News* June 30, 1869.
12. *Milwaukee Sentinel* July 19, 1869.
13. *Daily Milwaukee News* August 26, 1869.
14. *Milwaukee Sentinel* August 27, 1869.
15. *Milwaukee Sentinel* August 30, 1869.
16. *Daily Milwaukee News* September 12, 1869.
17. *Milwaukee Sentinel* September 17, 1869.
18. *Milwaukee Sentinel* January 27, 1870.
19. *Milwaukee Sentinel* March 5, 1870.
20. *Daily Milwaukee News* May 29, 1870.
21. *Milwaukee Sentinel* May 31, 1870.
22. *Milwaukee Sentinel* June 1, 1870.
23. *Milwaukee Sentinel* July 4, 1870.
24. *Milwaukee Sentinel* July 6, 1870.
25. *Milwaukee Sentinel* March 30, 1868.
26. *Milwaukee Sentinel* July 16, 1870.
27. *Milwaukee Sentinel* July 19, 1870; *Daily Milwaukee News*, July 20, 1870, gave the score as 38 to 21.
28. *Daily Milwaukee News* July 21, 1870.
29. *Daily Milwaukee News* July 21, 1870.
30. *Milwaukee Sentinel* July 26, 1870.
31. *Milwaukee Sentinel* August 31, 1870.
32. *Milwaukee Sentinel* September 2, 1870.
33. *Milwaukee Sentinel* September 3, 1870.
34. *Milwaukee Sentinel* November 24, 1870.
35. *Milwaukee Sentinel* March 11, 1870.
36. *Milwaukee Sentinel* March 21, 1870.
37. *Milwaukee Sentinel* June 20, 1870.
38. *Milwaukee Journal* June 26, 1897.
39. *Milwaukee Sentinel* July 2, 1870.
40. *Milwaukee Sentinel* July 8, 1872.
41. *Milwaukee Sentinel* March 27, 1871.
42. *Milwaukee Sentinel* March 27, 1871.
43. *Milwaukee Sentinel* July 6, 1871.
44. *Milwaukee Sentinel* August 10, 1871.
45. *Milwaukee Sentinel* May 22, 1872.
46. *Milwaukee Sentinel* August 21, 1874.

Chapter 4

1. *Milwaukee Sentinel* May 18, 1875.
2. *Daily Milwaukee News* August 4, 1875.
3. *Milwaukee Sentinel* September 28, 1875.
4. *Daily Milwaukee News* August 7, 1875.
5. These incidents were found in the *Daily Milwaukee News*, May 30, July 3, 27, August 5, 1875; and *Milwaukee Sentinel* of July 1, 7, 19, 21, 25, October 18, 1875.
6. *Milwaukee Sentinel* May 29, 1876. From much higher attendance estimates in the newspapers during the season, it appears there was much room for standing.
7. *Milwaukee Sentinel* August 26, 1876.
8. *Milwaukee Sentinel* July 8, 1876.
9. *Milwaukee Sentinel* May 15 and July 13, 1876.
10. *Milwaukee Sentinel* May 29, June 1, 12, 1876.
11. Game information and quotes from *Milwaukee Sentinel* and *Daily Milwaukee News*, May 31, 1876.
12. *Milwaukee Sentinel* July 1, 1876.
13. *Milwaukee Sentinel* July 11, 1876.
14. *Daily Milwaukee News* May 31, 1876.
15. *Milwaukee Sentinel* July 17, 1876.
16. *Milwaukee Sentinel* July 18, 1876.
17. *Milwaukee Sentinel* July 24, 1876.
18. Neil W. MacDonald, *The League That Lasted* (Jefferson, NC: McFarland, 2004), pages 154,159.
19. *Evening Wisconsin* September 9, 1876.
20. *Beadle's Dime Base Ball Player*, 1878, page 65.
21. *Milwaukee Sentinel* October 5, 1876.
22. *Daily Milwaukee News* July 11, 1876.
23. *Milwaukee Sentinel* July 15, 1876.
24. *Milwaukee Sentinel* July 15, 1876.
25. *Milwaukee Sentinel* August 14, 1876.
26. *Evening Wisconsin* August 30, 1876.
27. *Milwaukee Sentinel* August 30, 1876.
28. These alleged betting incidents are reported in the *Milwaukee Sentinel* of August 11, September 16, 19, 20, 1876, and the *Daily Milwaukee News* of June 30, September 20, 1876.
29. *Milwaukee Sentinel* May 31, 1876.
30. *Daily Milwaukee News* June 25, 1876.
31. *Daily Milwaukee News* July 7, 1876.
32. *Milwaukee Sentinel* July 12, 1876.
33. *Milwaukee Sentinel* August 7, 1876.
34. See the August 11, 1876, edition of the *Daily Milwaukee News* for a complete copy of this constitution.
35. *Milwaukee Sentinel* September 16, 1876.
36. *Milwaukee Sentinel* July 25, 1876.
37. *Milwaukee Sentinel* July 12, 1877.
38. These incidents were reported in the *Milwaukee Sentinel* of April 22, June 10, August 2, 1876, and May 24, 25, 1877.
39. *Milwaukee Sentinel* April 17, 1877.
40. *Milwaukee Sentinel* August 25, 1877.
41. Details of these two meetings found in *Milwaukee Sentinel* and *Daily Milwaukee News* of March 13 and 15, 1877.
42. *Milwaukee Sentinel* March 28, 1877.
43. *Daily Milwaukee News* May 10, 1877.
44. *Daily Milwaukee News* May 11, 1877.
45. *Milwaukee Sentinel* April 3, 1877.
46. Information on this lawsuit found in *Daily Milwaukee News*, April 19, 1877, and *Milwaukee Sentinel*, May 14, 1877.
47. Both quotes from *Sporting News*, November 10, 1888.
48. *Milwaukee Sentinel* August 29, 1877.
49. *Milwaukee Sentinel* May 10, 1877.
50. *Milwaukee Sentinel* May 14, 1877.
51. *Milwaukee Sentinel* February 13, 1885.
52. *Milwaukee Sentinel* June 21, 1877.
53. *Milwaukee Sentinel* June 23, 1877.
54. It is now known Billy Redmond is William T. Redmon; however, as his name was spelled with the ending "d" in all accounts of the time, I have kept this form in this book.
55. *Milwaukee Sentinel* July 6, 1877.
56. *Milwaukee Sentinel* May 9, 1877.
57. *Milwaukee Sentinel* May 14, 1877.
58. *Milwaukee Sentinel* June 28, 1877.
59. *Milwaukee Sentinel* August 6, 1877.
60. *Milwaukee Sentinel* August 9, 1877.
61. *Milwaukee Sentinel* August 20, 1877.

62. *Milwaukee Sentinel* August 24, 1877.
63. *Milwaukee Sentinel* August 27, 1877.
64. *Milwaukee Sentinel* August 29, 1877.
65. *Milwaukee Sentinel* November 13, 1877.

Chapter 5

1. David Quentin Voigt, *American Baseball: From Gentleman's Sport to the Commissioner System* (Norman: University of Oklahoma Press, 1966), page 76.
2. William A. Cook, *The Louisville Grays Scandal of 1877* (Jefferson, NC: McFarland, 2005), page 135.
3. *Milwaukee Sentinel* December 1, 1877.
4. 1876 National League Constitution, Article V, Section 2.
5. *New York Clipper* December 15, 1877.
6. *Milwaukee Sentinel* December 1, 1877.
7. *Milwaukee Sentinel* January 14, 1878.
8. *Milwaukee Sentinel* April 8 and 13, 1878.
9. *Milwaukee Sentinel* January 18, 1878.
10. *Milwaukee Sentinel* April 15, 1878.
11. Voigt, *American Baseball*, page 79.
12. Voigt, *American Baseball*, page 77.
13. *Milwaukee Sentinel* April 10, 1878.
14. *Milwaukee Sentinel* June 19, 1878.
15. *Milwaukee Sentinel* July 2, 1878.
16. *Milwaukee Sentinel* June 24, 1878.
17. *Milwaukee Sentinel* April 15, 1878.
18. *Milwaukee Sentinel* March 29, 1878.
19. *Milwaukee Sentinel* July 22, 1878.
20. *Milwaukee Sentinel* July 11 and 13, 1878.
21. Complete rules found in *Milwaukee* Sentinel, April 6, 1878.
22. *New York Clipper* April 6, 1878.
23. *Milwaukee Sentinel* March 22, 1878.
24. *New York Clipper* February 9, 1878.
25. *Milwaukee Sentinel* April 6, 1878.
26. *Sporting News* January 20, 1894.
27. *Milwaukee Sentinel* April 6, 1878.
28. *Milwaukee Sentinel* April 6 1878.
29. *Milwaukee Sentinel* March 26, 1878.
30. *Milwaukee Sentinel* April 25, 1878.
31. *Milwaukee Sentinel* March 28, 1878.
32. *Milwaukee Sentinel* April 10, 1878.
33. *Milwaukee Sentinel* March 16, 1878.
34. *New York Clipper* March 23, 1878.
35. *Milwaukee Sentinel* March 28, 1878.
36. *Evening Wisconsin* April 13, 1878.
37. *Daily Milwaukee News* April 13, 1878.
38. Summarized from *Beadle's Dime Base-Ball Player*, 1878.
39. *Milwaukee Sentinel* May 17 and June 4, 1878.
40. All rules and quotes in this section, except for that of the changing of the home club batting first, which was found in the *Milwaukee Sentinel* of December 10, 1877, are from the 1878 *Beadle's Dime Base-Ball Player*.
41. *Milwaukee Sentinel* May 4, 1878.
42. Quotes from both Cincinnati newspapers found in *Milwaukee Sentinel* of May 4, 1878.
43. *Milwaukee Sentinel* May 10, 1878. Some newspapers (such as the *Milwaukee Sentinel, Indianapolis Journal,* and *Boston Globe*—all of May 10, 1878) credited Weaver with a no-hitter, while others (*Indianapolis News* and *Daily Milwaukee News*—both of May 10, 1878) show he pitched a one-hitter. The *New York Clipper* ran two stories and two box scores on the same page of the May 16, 1878, edition one crediting Weaver with a no-hitter and one with a one-hitter! No major league official records of today credit Sam Weaver with a no-hitter.
44. *Milwaukee Sentinel* May 15, 1878.
45. *Milwaukee Sentinel* May 18, 1878.
46. *Milwaukee Sentinel* May 17, 1878.
47. *Milwaukee Sentinel* May 17, 1878.
48. *Milwaukee Sentinel* May 22, 1878.
49. *Milwaukee Sentinel* May 27, 1878.
50. The *Milwaukee Sentinel* box score of June 7 credited Morgan for this relief pitching appearance. The *Daily Milwaukee News* of June 7 listed Joe Ellick. *Total Baseball* credits Ellick with one game pitched in 1878, Morgan with none.
51. *Milwaukee Sentinel* June 5, 1878.
52. *Milwaukee Sentinel* August 19, 1878.
53. *Milwaukee Sentinel* June 17, 1878.
54. *Milwaukee Sentinel* June 19, 1878.
55. *Milwaukee Sentinel* June 20, 1878.
56. *Milwaukee Sentinel* June 21, 1878.
57. *Milwaukee Sentinel* Aug 21, 1878.
58. *Milwaukee Sentinel* July 17, 1878.
59. *Milwaukee Sentinel* August 22, 1878.
60. *St. Louis Globe-Democrat* September 1, 1878.
61. *Milwaukee Sentinel* August 12, 1878.
62. *Milwaukee Sentinel* August 12, 1878.
63. *Milwaukee Sentinel* Sept 2, 1878.
64. *Evening Wisconsin* August 16, 1878.
65. *Milwaukee Sentinel* November 16, 1878.
66. *New York Clipper* December 14, 1878.
67. *New York Clipper* December 14, 1878.
68. Voigt, *American Baseball*, Voigt, page 76.
69. Dalrymple was credited as the National League batting leader at the time with a .356 average. Much later in the twentieth century tie games were counted in statistics and Dalrymple's average fell to .354 and Paul Hines of Providence went to .358. The Sixth Edition of *Total Baseball* (pages 627 and 1921. lists Dalrymple as the batting champion.

Chapter 6

1. *Milwaukee Sentinel* December 17, 1878.
2. *Evening Wisconsin* February 27, 1879.
3. *Daily Milwaukee News* March 8, 1879.
4. *Evening Wisconsin* February 27, 1879.
5. *Evening Wisconsin* March 25, 1879.
6. *New York Clipper* November 25, 1882.
7. *Sporting News* January 2, 1894.
8. *Milwaukee Sentinel* May 1, 1878.
9. *Milwaukee Sentinel* July 4, 1878.
10. *Daily Milwaukee News* May 5, 1878.
11. *Milwaukee Sentinel* July 23, 1878.
12. *Milwaukee Sentinel* May 26, 1879.
13. *Daily Milwaukee News* July 6, 1879.
14. *Milwaukee Sentinel*, July 14, 1879.
15. *Evening Wisconsin* May 12, 1879.
16. *Daily Milwaukee News* July 15, 1879.
17. *Milwaukee Sentinel* May 22, 1880.
18. *Milwaukee Sentinel* June 9, 1880.
19. *Milwaukee Sentinel* June 6, 1880.
20. *Milwaukee Sentinel* June 9, 1880.
21. *Daily Milwaukee News* May 30, 1880.
22. *Milwaukee Sentinel* July 24, 1880.

23. *Milwaukee Sentinel* May 9, 1877.
24. *Evening Wisconsin* August 5, 1876.
25. *Milwaukee Sentinel* June 6, 1881.
26. *Milwaukee Sentinel* July 26, 1881.
27. *Daily Republican & News* August 1, 1881.
28. *Milwaukee Sentinel* August 14, 1881.
29. *Milwaukee Sentinel* October 2, 1881.
30. *Milwaukee Sentinel* May 2, 1882.
31. *Milwaukee Sentinel* May 31, 1882.
32. *Milwaukee Sentinel* June 19, 1882.
33. *Milwaukee Sentinel* June 26, 1882.
34. *Milwaukee Sentinel* June 8, 1882.
35. *Milwaukee Sentinel* July 31, 1882.
36. *Milwaukee Sentinel* June 23, 1882.
37. *Milwaukee Sentinel* October 22, 1882.
38. *Milwaukee Sentinel* June 18, 1882.
39. *Milwaukee Sentinel* August 21, 1882.
40. *Milwaukee Sentinel* July 9, 1882.
41. *Milwaukee Sentinel* July 23, 1882.
42. *Evening Wisconsin* June 27, 1882.
43. *Evening Wisconsin* June 27, 1882.
44. *Milwaukee Sentinel* July 28, 1882.
45. Seymour, *Baseball, Early Years*, page 136.
46. *Milwaukee Sentinel* July 16, 1882.
47. *Milwaukee Sentinel* October 29, 1882.
48. *Milwaukee Sentinel* March 19, 1883.
49. *Milwaukee Sentinel* April 9, 1883.
50. *Milwaukee Sentinel* March 5, 1883.
51. *Milwaukee Sentinel* July 28, 1883.
52. *Milwaukee Sentinel* April 30, 1883.
53. *Milwaukee Sentinel* July 2, 1883.
54. *Milwaukee Sentinel* July 2, 1883.
55. *Milwaukee Sentinel* August 20, 1883.
56. *Milwaukee Sentinel* August 9, 1883.
57. *Milwaukee Sentinel* July 22, 1883.
58. *Milwaukee Sentinel* May 18, 1883.
59. *Milwaukee Sentinel* April 30, 1883.
60. *Milwaukee Sentinel* May 28, 1883.
61. *Evening Wisconsin* May 31, 1883.
62. *Milwaukee Sentinel* June 1, 1883.
63. *Milwaukee Sentinel* June 25, 1883.
64. *Milwaukee Sentinel* July 2, 1883.
65. *Milwaukee Sentinel* July 15, 1883.
66. *Milwaukee Sentinel* July 16, 1883.
67. *Milwaukee Sentinel* July 9, 1883.
68. *Milwaukee Sentinel* August 6, 1883.
69. *Milwaukee Sentinel* July 29, 1883.
70. *Milwaukee Sentinel* August 26, 1883.
71. *Evening Wisconsin* September 3, 1883.
72. *Milwaukee Sentinel* September 3, 1883.
73. *Milwaukee Sentinel* August 27, 1883.
74. *Milwaukee Sentinel* September 24, 1883.
75. *Milwaukee Sentinel* September 24, 1883.
76. *Milwaukee Sentinel* October 11, 1883.

Chapter 7

1. *Milwaukee Sentinel* September 2, 1883.
2. *Evening Wisconsin* March 3, 1884.
3. *Milwaukee Sentinel* January 21, 1884.
4. *Milwaukee Sentinel* January 28, 1884.
5. *Milwaukee Journal* March 18, 1884.
6. *Milwaukee Journal* March 18, 1884.
7. *Milwaukee Journal* March 18, 1884.
8. *Milwaukee Sentinel* March 10, 1884.
9. *Milwaukee Sentinel* September 17, 1883.
10. *Milwaukee Sentinel* February 25, 1884.
11. In March 2, 1895, issue of the *Sporting News*, Milwaukee's correspondent remembered that when the grounds were enclosed, they were only 270 by 320 feet.
12. *Milwaukee Sentinel* July 5, 1884.
13. *Milwaukee Sentinel* July 7, 1884.
14. *Milwaukee Sentinel* June 13, 1884.
15. *Evening Wisconsin* June 20, 1884.
16. *Milwaukee Sentinel* May 26, 1884.
17. *Milwaukee Sentinel* May 31, 1884.
18. *Milwaukee Journal* May 31, 1884.
19. *Milwaukee Sentinel* May 23, 1884.
20. *Milwaukee Journal* June 3, 1884.
21. *Milwaukee Sentinel* June 5, 1884.
22. *Milwaukee Sentinel* June 7, 1884.
23. *Milwaukee Sentinel* June 8, 1884.
24. *Milwaukee Sentinel* June 12, 1884.
25. *Milwaukee Sentinel* June 13, 1884.
26. *Milwaukee Sentinel* June 15, 1884.
27. *Evening Wisconsin* May 28, 1884.
28. *Milwaukee Sentinel* June 15, 1884.
29. *Evening Wisconsin* June 11, 1884.
30. *Milwaukee Sentinel* June 21, 1884.
31. *Milwaukee Sentinel* June 22, 1884.
32. *Milwaukee Sentinel* July 1, 1884.
33. *Milwaukee Sentinel* July 4, 1884.
34. *Milwaukee Sentinel* May 9, 1884.
35. *Milwaukee Journal* June 19, 1884.
36. *Milwaukee Sentinel* July 11, 1884.
37. *Milwaukee Sentinel* July 22, 1884.
38. *Milwaukee Sentinel* July 23, 1884.
39. *Milwaukee Sentinel* August 5, 1884.
40. *Evening Wisconsin* August 15, 1884.
41. *New York Times* September 13, 1883.
42. *New York Times* November 14, 1883.
43. *New York Times* December 10, 1883.
44. *New York Times* December 17, 1883.
45. *New York Times* March 18, 1884.
46. *New York Times* July 2, 1884.
47. *Milwaukee Sentinel* March 3, 1884.
48. *Milwaukee Sentinel* September 9, 1884.
49. Both quotes from *Mirror of America* in *Milwaukee Sentinel*, September 22, 1884.
50. *Milwaukee Sentinel* September 28, 1884.
51. *Milwaukee Sentinel* October 5, 1884.
52. *Milwaukee Sentinel* October 12, 1884.
53. With so many franchise shifts and teams disbanding, the season totals of the Union Association are confusing and mean little. In addition, first-place St. Louis' season record of 94 and 19, winning its first 20 games, made for no meaningful pennant race.
54. *Milwaukee Sentinel* November 10, 1884.
55. *Milwaukee Sentinel* November 26, 1884.
56. *Milwaukee Sentinel* January 12, 1885.

Chapter 8

1. *Milwaukee Sentinel* February 5, 1885.
2. *Milwaukee Sentinel* February 2, 1885.
3. *Milwaukee Sentinel* February 23, 1885.
4. *Milwaukee Sentinel* April 7, 1885.
5. *Milwaukee Sentinel* May 18, 1885.
6. The *Milwaukee Sentinel* of March 4, 1885, gave expenditures of $36,190 (not broken down), which would be a loss of $963.40.

7. *Milwaukee Sentinel* April 6, 1885.
8. *Milwaukee Sentinel* April 27, 1885.
9. *Milwaukee Sentinel* May 14, 1885.
10. *Milwaukee Sentinel* April 23, 1885.
11. *Milwaukee Sentinel* April 27, 1885.
12. *Milwaukee Sentinel* April 27, 1885.
13. *Milwaukee Journal* May 6, 1885.
14. *Milwaukee Sentinel* June 15, 1885.
15. *Milwaukee Sentinel* June 5, 1885.
16. *Milwaukee Sentinel* June 10, 1884.
17. *Milwaukee Sentinel* May 30, 1884.
18. *Milwaukee Sentinel* June 29, 1885.
19. *Milwaukee Sentinel* August 17, 1885.
20. *Milwaukee Sentinel* August 16, 1885.
21. *Milwaukee Sentinel* August 29, 1885.
22. *Milwaukee Sentinel* September 6, 1885.
23. *Evening Wisconsin* September 29, 1885.
24. *Evening Wisconsin* October 12, 1885.
25. *Milwaukee Sentinel* February 13, 1886.
26. *Milwaukee Sentinel* February 15, 1886.
27. *Milwaukee Sentinel* April 12, 1886.
28. *Milwaukee Sentinel* March 17, 1886.
29. *Milwaukee Sentinel* March 8, 1886.
30. *Milwaukee Sentinel* March 27, 1886.
31. *Milwaukee Sentinel* June 14, 1886.
32. *Milwaukee Sentinel* June 21, 1886.
33. *Evening Wisconsin* June 21, 1886.
34. *Milwaukee Journal* June 29, 1886.
35. *Milwaukee Sentinel* July 19, 1886.
36. *Evening Wisconsin* July 6, 1886.
37. *Evening Wisconsin* August 2, 1886.
38. *Milwaukee Sentinel* August 23, 1886.
39. *Milwaukee Sentinel* August 24, 1886.
40. *Milwaukee Sentinel* August 26, 1886.
41. *Evening Wisconsin* August 2, 1886.
42. *Milwaukee Sentinel* September 6, 1886.
43. *Milwaukee Sentinel* September 27, 1886.
44. *Milwaukee Sentinel*, April 26, 1886. However, the *Evening Wisconsin* of June 28, 1886, complained "more useless scorecards were never before dispensed," as batting orders and positions always seemed to be wrong.
45. *Sporting News* October 11, 1886.
46. *Milwaukee Sentinel* December 27, 1886.
47. *Milwaukee Sentinel* April 17, 1887.
48. *Milwaukee Sentinel* February 3, 1887.
49. *Evening Wisconsin* May 3, 1887.
50. *Milwaukee Sentinel* March 28, 1887.
51. *Milwaukee Daily Review* May 14, 1887.
52. *Milwaukee Sentinel* May 4, 1887.
53. *Evening Wisconsin* June 27, 1887.
54. *Evening Wisconsin* July 11, 1887.
55. *Evening Wisconsin* September 1, 1887.
56. *Milwaukee Sentinel* April 29, 1887.
57. *Milwaukee Daily Review* September 6, 1887.
58. *Milwaukee Sentinel* September 5, 1887.
59. *Milwaukee Daily Review* September 10, 1887.

Chapter 9

1. *Milwaukee Sentinel* September 28, 1887.
2. *Milwaukee Sentinel* January 24, 1888.
3. *Milwaukee Sentinel* December 5, 1887.
4. *Evening Wisconsin* April 14, 1888.
5. The $25,000 price was reported in *Milwaukee Sentinel*, February 15, 1888. The *Evening Wisconsin* of February 29, 1888, reported the grounds had cost $21,000 and the *Daily Review* of February 15, 1888, reported the cost at $26,000.
6. *Milwaukee Sentinel* March 26, 1888.
7. *Daily Review* February 15, 1888.
8. *Evening Wisconsin* April 27, 1888.
9. *Milwaukee Journal* April 30, 1888.
10. *Milwaukee Journal* May 3, 1888.
11. *Milwaukee Sentinel* May 21, 1888.
12. *Evening Wisconsin* June 12, 1888.
13. *Milwaukee Sentinel* June 25, 1888.
14. *Milwaukee Sentinel* July 2, 1888.
15. *Evening Wisconsin* July 23, 1888.
16. *Milwaukee Sentinel* August 18, 1888.
17. *Milwaukee Sentinel* September 8 and 9, 1888.
18. *Milwaukee Sentinel* September 15, 1888.
19. *Milwaukee Sentinel* October 10, Nov 1888.
20. *Milwaukee Sentinel* October 1, 1888.
21. *Evening Wisconsin* December 6, 1888.
22. *Evening Wisconsin* October 25, 1888.
23. *Milwaukee Sentinel* August 27, 1888.
24. *Milwaukee Sentinel* November 19, 1888.
25. *Milwaukee Sentinel* December 10, 1888.
26. *Milwaukee Sentinel* February 25, 1889.
27. *Milwaukee Journal* May 9, 1889.
28. *Milwaukee Sentinel* May 9, 1889.
29. *Milwaukee Sentinel* June 3, 1889.
30. *Milwaukee Sentinel* June 8, 1889.
31. *Milwaukee Sentinel* June 12, 1889.
32. *Milwaukee Sentinel* July 22, 1889.
33. *Milwaukee Sentinel* July 26, 1889.
34. *Milwaukee Daily News* August 2, 1889.
35. *Sporting News* July 27, 1889.
36. *Milwaukee Sentinel* August 12, 1889.
37. *Milwaukee Sentinel* August 8, 1889.
38. *Milwaukee Sentinel* Sept 3, 1889.
39. *Evening Wisconsin* of September 23, 1889, reported Denver was ahead $11,000; only $7,500 clear, as $1,800 was paid out for releases and over $1,000 for other purposes.
40. *Milwaukee Sentinel* September 23, 1889.
41. *Evening Wisconsin* August 3, 1889.
42. *Milwaukee Sentinel* May 20, 1889.
43. *Milwaukee Sentinel* September 11, 1889.
44. *Milwaukee Sentinel* March 2, 1890.
45. *Milwaukee Daily News* October 25, 1889.
46. *Evening Wisconsin* April 28, 1890.
47. *Milwaukee Sentinel* January 13, 1890.
48. *Milwaukee Sentinel* February 8, 1890.
49. *Evening Wisconsin* January 16, 1890.
50. *Milwaukee Sentinel* February 24, 1890.
51. *Sporting News* March 1, 1890.
52. *Milwaukee Sentinel* March 31, 1890.
53. *Milwaukee Sentinel* February 17, 1890.
54. *Sporting News* March 1, 1890.
55. *Milwaukee Daily News* March 11, 1890.
56. *Evening Wisconsin* April 7, 1890.
57. *Milwaukee Sentinel* April 21, 1890.
58. *Sporting News* May 3, 1890.
59. *Evening Wisconsin* May 12, 1890.
60. *Sporting News* July 12, 1890.
61. *Milwaukee Sentinel* July 14, 1890.
62. Quotes on exchange between *Omaha Bee* and Milwaukee papers found in *Milwaukee Sentinel* and *Daily News* of July 22, 1890.
63. *Milwaukee Sentinel* June 21, 1890.
64. *Milwaukee Sentinel* August 22, 1890.

Chapter 10

1. *Milwaukee Journal* August 20, 1890.
2. *Sporting News* January 17, 1891.
3. *Milwaukee Sentinel* February 2, 1891.
4. *Milwaukee Sentinel* March 6, 1891.
5. *Evening Wisconsin* March 9, 1891.
6. *Milwaukee Journal* April 23, 1891.
7. *Sporting News* May 16, 1891.
8. *Evening Wisconsin* February 28, 1891.
9. *Milwaukee Journal* May 8, 1891.
10. *Milwaukee Journal* May 25, 1891.
11. *Evening Wisconsin* July 7, 1891.
12. *Evening Wisconsin* July 13, 1891.
13. *Evening Wisconsin* April 2, 1891.
14. *Sporting News* July 25, 1891.
15. *Milwaukee Sentinel* July 18, 1891.
16. *Milwaukee Sentinel* July 26, 1891.
17. *Milwaukee Daily News* August 6, 1891.
18. *Milwaukee Journal* August 18, 1891.
19. *Sporting News* August 22, 1891.
20. *Sporting News* September 19, 1891.
21. *Sporting News* October 17, 1891.
22. *Milwaukee Sentinel* December 3, 1891.
23. *Sporting News* December 19, 1891.
24. *Milwaukee Sentinel* December 6, 1891.
25. *Milwaukee Sentinel* December 6, 1891.
26. *Milwaukee Sentinel* December 6, 1891.
27. The *Milwaukee Sentinel* of December 31, 1891, reported the actual expenses of the club in 1891 to be $44,917, of which about $30,000 was paid to the players.
28. *Sporting News* December 12, 1891.
29. *Sporting News* December 12, 1891.
30. *Sporting News* December 12, 1891.
31. *Sporting News* December 12, 1891.
32. *Milwaukee Sentinel* December 16, 1891.
33. *Sporting News* December 19, 1891.

Chapter 11

1. *Milwaukee Journal* December 31, 1891.
2. *Milwaukee Daily News* March, 25, 1892.
3. *Milwaukee Sentinel* January 11, 1892.
4. *Evening Wisconsin* January 22, 1892.
5. *Milwaukee Sentinel* January 22, 18892.
6. *Milwaukee Journal* March 24, 1892.
7. *Milwaukee Sentinel* April 20, 1892.
8. *Milwaukee Sentinel* April 23, 1892.
9. *Milwaukee Sentinel* June 22, 1892.
10. *Milwaukee Daily News* June 1, 1892.
11. *Milwaukee Sentinel* July 3, 1892.
12. *Milwaukee Sentinel* July 7, 1892.
13. *Milwaukee Sentinel* July 7, 1892.
14. *Milwaukee Sentinel* July 8, 1892.
15. *Milwaukee Daily News* July 7 1892.
16. *Milwaukee Sentinel* July 12, 1892.
17. *Milwaukee Sentinel* September 23, 1892.
18. *Milwaukee Sentinel* November 8, 1890.
19. *Milwaukee Sentinel* December 7, 1890.
20. *Milwaukee Sentinel* April 25, 1891.
21. *Milwaukee Sentinel* August 7, 1891.
22. *Evening Wisconsin* January 21, 1893.
23. *Milwaukee Journal* April 6, 1893.
24. *New York Times* March 8, 1893.
25. *Sporting News* March 11, 1893.
26. *Sporting News* March 11, 1893.
27. *Milwaukee Sentinel* May 7, 1893.
28. *Milwaukee Daily News* April 17, 1893.
29. *Milwaukee Sentinel* July 13, 1893.
30. *Sporting News* October 7, 1893.
31. *Milwaukee Journal* October 20, 1893.

Chapter 12

1. *Milwaukee Sentinel* October 26, 1893.
2. *Sporting News* November 25, 1893.
3. *Milwaukee Sentinel* October 26, 1893.
4. *Milwaukee Journal* October 30, 1893.
5. *Milwaukee Daily News* December 26, 1893.
6. *Sporting News* December 16, 1893.
7. *Sporting News* December 16, 1893.
8. *Milwaukee Sentinel* February 24, 1894.
9. *Milwaukee Sentinel* April 1, 1894.
10. *Milwaukee Sentinel* March 19, 1894.
11. *Milwaukee Sentinel* April 26, 1894.
12. Incident details and all quotes found in *Sporting News* of May 5, 1894.
13. *Milwaukee Sentinel* May 18 and 20, 1894.
14. *Milwaukee Sentinel* May 20, 1894.
15. *Milwaukee Sentinel* June 3, 1894.
16. *Milwaukee Daily News* June 4, 1894.
17. *Milwaukee Sentinel* June 5, 1894.
18. *Sporting News* June 16, 1894.
19. *Sporting News* June 16, 1894.
20. *Evening Wisconsin* June 7, 1894.
21. *Milwaukee Journal* July 5, 1894.
22. *Milwaukee Journal* July 9, 1894.
23. *Milwaukee Sentinel* July 21, 1894.
24. *Evening Wisconsin* July 20, 1894.
25. *Milwaukee Sentinel* July 22, 1894.
26. *Milwaukee Daily News* August 28, 18894.
27. *Milwaukee Sentinel* September 12, 1894.
28. *Milwaukee Sentinel* September 26, 1894.
29. *Milwaukee Sentinel* September 2, 1894.
30. *Evening Wisconsin* October 6, 1894.
31. *Milwaukee Sentinel* October 31, 1894.
32. *Evening Wisconsin* September 24, 1894.
33. *Milwaukee Sentinel* October 21, 1894.
34. *Milwaukee Sentinel* October 21, 1894.
35. *Milwaukee Sentinel* October 19, 1894.
36. *Milwaukee Sentinel* October 25, 1894.
37. *Milwaukee Sentinel* December 16, 1894.
38. *Milwaukee Journal* September 10, 1894.
39. The exchange between the Brewers and City Attorney Hamilton taken from *Milwaukee Sentinel* of Feb. 24 and 25, 1895.
40. *Evening Wisconsin* March 2, 1895.
41. *Milwaukee Sentinel* February 27, 1895.
42. *Milwaukee Daily News* March 4, 1895.
43. *Milwaukee Daily News* April 3, 1895.
44. *Milwaukee Sentinel* May 2, 1895.
45. *Sporting News* May 4, 1895.
46. *Milwaukee Sentinel* May 10, 1895.
47. *Milwaukee Sentinel* June 14, 1895.
48. *Milwaukee Sentinel* July 21, 1895.
49. *Sporting News* August 24, 1895.
50. *Milwaukee Sentinel* August 19, 1895.
51. *Milwaukee Sentinel* September 10, 1895.
52. *Milwaukee Sentinel* September 17, 1895.
53. *Milwaukee Journal* September 1895.
54. *Milwaukee Journal* March 9, 1895.

55. *Milwaukee Sentinel* June 17, 1895.
56. *Milwaukee Sentinel* September 28, 1895.
57. *Milwaukee Sentinel* November 21, 1895.
58. *Evening Wisconsin* November 9, 1895.
59. *Sporting News* November 30, 1895.
60. *Milwaukee Sentinel* April 28, 1890.
61. *Milwaukee Sentinel* December 9, 1895.
62. *Sporting News* January 25, 1896.
63. *Sporting News* October 19, 1895.
64. *Milwaukee Journal* January 25, 1896.
65. *Evening Wisconsin* February 27, 1896.
66. The January 4, 1896, *Evening Wisconsin* spelled the name McZena in its biography of the players; however, by May the paper was spelling the name Mrzena.
67. *Milwaukee Journal* March 20, 1896.
68. *Milwaukee Journal* March 5, 1896.
69. *Sporting News* March 4, 1896.
70. *Milwaukee Daily News* March 5, 1896.
71. *Sporting News* June 6, 1896.
72. *Milwaukee Journal* August 12, 1896.
73. *Evening Wisconsin* August 14, 1896.
74. *Sporting News* September 12, 1896.
75. *Milwaukee Sentinel* June 29, 1896.
76. *Evening Wisconsin* June 25, 1896.
77. *Milwaukee Daily News* August 20, 1896.
78. *Milwaukee Daily News* August 20, 1896.
79. *Milwaukee Journal* August 24, 1896.
80. *Milwaukee Sentinel* August 31, 1896.
81. *Milwaukee Sentinel* January 11, 1896.

Chapter 13

1. The *Milwaukee Journal* reported on September 22, 1896, Mack signed for $3,000. On January 30, 1897, the same paper reported he was receiving $2,500. The *Milwaukee Daily News* reported on January 20, 1897, Mack received $1,500 for his services.
2. *Milwaukee Journal* January 30, 1897.
3. *Sporting News* January 2, 1897.
4. *Sporting News* November 28, 1896.
5. *Sporting News* March 13, 1897.
6. *Milwaukee Daily News* November 13, 1896.
7. *Evening Wisconsin* March 16, 1897.
8. *Milwaukee Sentinel* June 28, 1897.
9. *Milwaukee Sentinel* February 18, 1897.
10. *Milwaukee Sentinel* February 241897.
11. *Milwaukee Sentinel* March 13, 1897.
12. *Milwaukee Journal* March 25, 1897.
13. *Milwaukee Sentinel* January 9, 1897.
14. *Milwaukee Daily News* January 13, 1897.
15. *Sporting News* March 20, 1897.
16. *Milwaukee Journal* March 24, 1897.
17. *Milwaukee Sentinel* April 6, 1897.
18. *Sporting News* July 3, 1897.
19. *Sporting News* December 17, 1898.
20. *Evening Wisconsin* June 5, 1897.
21. *Evening Wisconsin* July 26, 1897.
22. *Milwaukee Journal* July 24, 1897.
23. *Sporting News* August 28, 1897.
24. Attendance figures must always be looked at with some skepticism. On September 4, 1897, the *Sporting News* quoted an exchange: "There is no town in the league where the attendance reports are padded like they are at Milwaukee. A crowd of 12,000 causes the report to be sent out: 'Attendance 7,000. Managers say the paid receipts and the reports vary in numbers to the extent of thousands."

25. Batting records taken from official Western League release. Some pitching and defense records taken from local newspaper articles, which differ from official Western League results in some cases. However, Western League statistics did not break down win/loss records or fielding records of the men who played for two teams, making Milwaukee totals unidentifiable.
26. *Milwaukee Journal* September 2, 1897.
27. *Evening Wisconsin* August 7, 1897.
28. *Milwaukee Sentinel* August 31, 1897.
29. *Milwaukee Journal* September 18,1897.
30. *Milwaukee Sentinel* December 19, 1897.
31. *Milwaukee Sentinel* December 19, 1897.
32. *Milwaukee Sentinel* December 19, 1897.
33. *Milwaukee Sentinel* October 22, 1897.
34. *Milwaukee Daily News* October 23, 1897.
35. *Sporting News* October 23, 1897.
36. *Sporting News* February 26, 1898.
37. *Milwaukee Journal* December 8, 1897.
38. *Evening Wisconsin* October 4, 1897.
39. *Milwaukee Sentinel* November 1, 1897.
40. *Milwaukee Sentinel* December 12, 1897.
41. *Milwaukee Journal* January 10, 1898.
42. *Milwaukee Sentinel* February 3, 1898.
43. *Milwaukee Sentinel* November 30, 1898.
44. *Milwaukee Daily News* March 11, 1898.
45. *Milwaukee Sentinel* December 13 1897.
46. *Evening Wisconsin* March 23, 1898.
47. *Evening Wisconsin* June 3, 1898.
48. *Milwaukee Journal* March 28, 1898.
49. *Milwaukee Sentinel* April 17, 1898.
50. *Evening Wisconsin* July 16, 1898.
51. *Milwaukee Journal* September 22, 1898.
52. *Sporting News* October 15, 1898.
53. *Milwaukee Journal* September 22, 1898.
54. Different papers gave differing totals, these taken from the October 29, 1898, *Sporting News*. One of the reasons for these differing totals could be explained in the Sunday games Clarence Beaumont played in. The *Milwaukee Journal* of September 19, 1898, stated, "Because of parental objections to Sunday ball games, Beaumont finds it necessary to choose a nom de plume for each of the Sunday games in which he participates. Weaver was given the honor yesterday." This Sunday the Brewers played a doubleheader, and Weaver is listed as the left fielder in both games.
55. *Milwaukee Sentinel* July 15, 1898.
56. *Milwaukee Sentinel* September 24, 1898.
57. *Sporting News* October 8, 1898.
58. *Sporting News* October 15, 1898.
59. *Sporting News* December 10, 1898.
60. *Sporting News* March 25, 1899.
61. *Milwaukee Sentinel* March 5, 1899.
62. *Milwaukee Journal* July 29, 1898.
63. *Milwaukee Journal* August 10, 1898.
64. *Milwaukee Sentinel* November 13, 1898.
65. *Milwaukee Sentinel* December 17, 1898.
66. *Milwaukee Sentinel* December 17, 1898.
67. *Milwaukee Sentinel* December 30, 1898.
68. *Milwaukee Sentinel* August 25, 1899.
69. *Milwaukee Daily News*, August 24, 1899.
70. *Sporting News* September 30, 1899.
71. *Evening Wisconsin* February 17, 1897.
72. *Milwaukee Sentinel* April 2, 1897.
73. *Milwaukee Sentinel* May 12, 1899.
74. *Milwaukee Sentinel* September 18, 1899.

75. *Evening Wisconsin* September 21, 1899.
76. *Sporting News* September 23, 1899.
77. *Milwaukee Journal* September 19, 1899.
78. *Milwaukee Sentinel* September 23, 1899.
79. *Milwaukee Sentinel* October 1, 1899.
80. *Sporting Life* October 28, 1899.
81. *Milwaukee Sentinel* October 3, 1899.
82. *Milwaukee Journal* January 30 1900.
83. *Milwaukee Sentinel* February 15, 1900.
84. *Milwaukee Daily News* February 13, 1900.
85. *Milwaukee Sentinel* March 9, 1900.
86. *Evening Wisconsin* March 23, 1900.
87. *Milwaukee Daily News* October 2, 1899.
88. *Milwaukee Daily News* January 15, 1900.
89. *Milwaukee Sentinel* August 6, 1900.
90. *Milwaukee Sentinel* August 22, 1900.
91. *Milwaukee Sentinel* September 28, 1900.

Chapter 14

1. *Milwaukee Sentinel* April 19, 1897.
2. *Milwaukee Sentinel* May 4, 1897.
3. *Sporting News* August 4, 1900.
4. *Sporting News*, August 4, 1900.
5. *Sporting News* October 6, 1900.
6. *Milwaukee Sentinel* November 15, 1900.
7. *Milwaukee Journal* November 13, 1900.
8. *Milwaukee Journal* November 23, 1900.
9. *Evening Wisconsin* December 6, 1901.
10. *Evening Wisconsin* January 25, 1901.
11. *Milwaukee Sentinel* January 9, 1901.
12. *Milwaukee Daily News* January 18, 1901.
13. *Milwaukee Sentinel* January 23, 1901.
14. *Milwaukee Sentinel* November 17, 1901.
15. *Evening Wisconsin* February 5, 1901.
16. *Sporting News* February 2, 1901.
17. *Sporting News* February 9, 1901.
18. *Sporting News* March 2, 1901.
19. *Sporting News* March 9, 1901.
20. *Milwaukee Daily News* February 8, 1901.
21. *Sporting News* March 2, 1901.
22. *Evening Wisconsin* February 28, 1901.
23. *Sporting News* February 16, 1901.
24. *Sporting News* October 27, 1900.
25. An article in the *Sporting Life* of March 9, 1901, reported Duffy's salary as player/manager to be $3,500 to $4,000.
26. *Evening Wisconsin* March 7, 1901.
27. *Milwaukee Journal* March 30, 1901.
28. *Evening Wisconsin* April 2, 1901.
29. *Milwaukee Sentinel* June 24, 1901.
30. *Milwaukee Sentinel* July 11, 1901.
31. *Sporting Life* July 27, 1901.
32. *Evening Wisconsin* July 27, 1901.
33. *Milwaukee Sentinel* July 23, 1901.
34. *Milwaukee Sentinel* August 3, 1901.
35. *Milwaukee Sentinel* August 8, 1901.
36. *Milwaukee Sentinel*, August 9, 1901.
37. *Milwaukee Sentinel* August 29, 1901.
38. *Milwaukee Sentinel* September 2, 1901.
39. *Milwaukee Journal* August 9, 1901.
40. The *Milwaukee Sentinel* of October 13, 1901, reported different attendance figures. In the *Sentinel* chart Milwaukee had the lowest total — 136,275; Cleveland showing a total of 142,664. All other cities also had different totals. The *Milwaukee Daily News* of October 16 had still differing numbers, these from the Associated Press. Milwaukee's home attendance was reported as 132,381, the lowest in the American League.
41. *Sporting News* September 28, 1901.
42. *Milwaukee Sentinel* September 30, 1901.
43. *Sporting News* September 21, 1901.
44. *Milwaukee Sentinel* August 1, 1901.
45. *Milwaukee Sentinel* July 30, 1901.
46. *Sporting News* August 24, 1901.
47. *Milwaukee Daily News* June 22, 1901.
48. *Milwaukee Sentinel* August 30, 1901.
49. *Milwaukee Sentinel* October 11, 1901.
50. *Evening Wisconsin* September 16, 1901.
51. *Sporting News* October 19, 1901.
52. *Milwaukee Sentinel* October 22, 1901.
53. *Milwaukee Sentinel* November 8, 1901.
54. *Sporting News* December 7, 1901.
55. *Milwaukee Journal* December 3, 1901.
56. *Milwaukee Journal* December 4, 1901.
57. *Milwaukee Daily News* December 6, 1901.
58. *Sporting Life* September 28, 1901.

Bibliography

Books

Brock, Darryl. *The Perfect Game,* "The 1869 Red Stockings." Cleveland: SABR, 1998.

Church, Seymour R. *Base Ball: The History, Statistics and Romance of the American National Game*. Princeton: Pyne Press, 1974. Reprint of 1902 edition.

Cook, William A. *The Louisville Grays Scandal of 1877*. Jefferson, NC: McFarland, 2005.

Guschov, Stephen D. *The Red Stockings of Cincinnati: Base Ball's First All-Professional Team*. Jefferson, NC: McFarland, 1998.

MacDonald, Neil W. *The League That Lasted*. Jefferson, NC: McFarland, 2004.

Nemec, David. *The Rules of Baseball: An Anecdotal Look at the Rules of Baseball and How They Came to Be*. New York: Lyons & Burford, 1994.

Seymour, Harold. *Baseball: The Early Years*. New York: Oxford University Press, 1960.

Thorn, John and Peter Palmer eds. *Total Baseball*. New York: Sport Classic Books, 2004.

Voigt, David Quentin. *American Baseball: From Gentleman's Sport to the Commissioner System*. Norman: University of Oklahoma Press, 1966.

Newspapers and Sporting Journals

Beadle's Dime Base-Ball Player 1878
Daily Milwaukee News 1859–1880
Evening Wisconsin 1876–1901
Milwaukee Daily News 1889–1901
Milwaukee Daily Republican & News 1881–1882
Milwaukee Daily Review 1887–1889
Milwaukee Journal 1882–1901
Milwaukee Sentinel 1859–1901 (This newspaper had variations on this title throughout the nineteenth century, but is filed under *Milwaukee Sentinel* in library holdings.)
New York Clipper 1877–1878, 1882
New York Times 1858, 1883–1884
Sporting Life 1899–1901
Sporting News 1886–1901

Index

Abbaticchio, Ed 286, 287
Abert, Byron 17
Abert, George 17
Abert, H.W. 17
Academy Baseball Club 34
Active Baseball Club of Chicago 31
Active Baseball Club of Milwaukee 14, 25, 34, 44, 45
Active Baseball Club of Racine 26
Adams, G.W. 5
Addis, M.P. 164
admission prices to games 7, 21, 24, 28, 36, 44, 46, 49, 54, 55, 72, 78, 79, 89, 94, 97, 112, 121, 128, 133, 136, 141, 144, 149, 156, 162, 164, 169, 180, 186, 194, 200, 202, 206, 212, 230, 247, 265, 268, 280, 297; fans not paying 252–253
advertising games 36–37, 55, 89, 97, 224
Alberts, Gus 153–154, 158, 168, 170, 171, 178, 181, 191, 199, 201, 202–203, 211, 215, 230, 231
Alert Baseball Club 14, 31, 32, 34, 36, 39, 41, 43–44, 74
Alert Baseball Club of Burlington 26
Alert Baseball Park 44
Alexander, Daniel 158, 159
Alford, Billy 116, 117, 118
Allen, C.B. 3, 4
Allen, Richard 8, 14, 17, 23
Allen, Robert 264
Allen, Rufus, Jr. 46, 70
Almin, Charles 124
Alonzo Stagg's Chicago Varsity Baseball Club 270
Amateur Club of Chicago 28
American Association 92, 106, 110, 111, 116, 121–122, 140–141, 167, 176–179, 181, 183, 185–190, 192; placing club in Milwaukee 130–131, 140–141, 151, 155, 165, 172, 175, 176, 183–184, 217
American Association (proposed) (1895) 218–221; (1900) 276–281, 282; (1901) 291–293, 294, 295
American League (1900) 277–281, 282, 283, 286–287, 288–289; (1901) 289–292, 296–297, 298, 301–303; Eagle on letterhead 281; evolution in major league 288–293; 1902 attendance 302,

349; and 1902 franchise moves 303–304
Anderson, John 283, 284–285, 287, 293–294, 296, 299, 300, 302, 303, 307
Anderson, Varney 132, 137, 142
Andrews, David 85
Andrus, Fred 41, 46, 47, 50, 54, 57, 59
Anson, Adrian "Cap" 71, 109, 168, 180, 224, 276, 277, 278, 279, 280
Antisdel, A. Edwin 256–257
Arctic Baseball Club 14, 76–77, 78–80, 85, 86, 87–91, 118–119, 120, 200
Arenas Baseball Club 230
Armstrong, William 221, 222, 225
Arundel, Harry 104
Arundel, John Tug 114, 117, 118, 127, 128
Atherton, Charles 273, 282, 286
Athletic Baseball Club of Chicago 24, 25, 27–28, 74
Athletic Baseball Club of Kenosha 21
Athletic Baseball Club of Milwaukee 25, 26, 37, 44, 45, 49; (1890s) 164, 200, 202–203
Athletic Baseball Park (Farwell Ave.) 72, 75, 77, 79, 84, 86
Athletic Park (Seventh and Chambers) 143–146, 159, 162, 163, 165, 169, 175, 187, 194, 199–203, 206, 211, 215, 218, 219, 222, 223, 230, 231, 276, 278, 337
Atlantic Baseball Club 1, 34, 35, 43
Atlantic Baseball Club of Brooklyn 18–19, 29, 57
Atlantic Baseball Club of Chicago 11, 14, 15, 21
Atlantic (Junior) Baseball Club 17, 21
Atlantic League 167, 258, 284
Auckland Baseball Club 45, 74, 75
Auer, Louis 92

Badger Baseball Club 231
Badger State Club of Milwaukee 14
Bailey, George 132, 144
Baker, Kirtley 214, 215, 216, 221, 222, 224, 227, 228, 229, 236, 238, 241, 242

Baldwin, Charles 94, 99, 114, 116, 117, 118
Baldwin, Clarence "Kid" 109, 112, 113, 114
Baltes, Franklyn 3
Baltimore American Association Club 181
Baltimore American League Club 289–290, 292, 296, 302, 303, 304
Baltimore National League Club 247, 268, 279–281
Bancroft, Frank 184, 186–187, 304
Banner Baseball Club 230
Banning, James 125
Bannon, James 244
Barclay, H. 3
Barnes, Fred 235–236, 239, 241, 242, 244, 247, 248, 252, 255, 258, 260, 261, 262, 264, 265, 266–267, 270, 271–273, 282
Barnes, John 131, 205, 207, 217, 226
Barnes, Roscoe 30, 32, 39
Barnie, William 199, 201, 218, 220, 221
Bartlett, Oscar Z. "Zack" 176, 180, 186, 187, 194, 195, 197, 198
baseball grounds in Milwaukee (misc.) 14, 32, 35, 50, 76, 78, 84, 86, 87, 135, 164, 202, 230
baseball players drinking 11, 41, 69–70, 104, 115, 126, 131, 146, 154, 169, 214, 227, 229, 257, 261, 271
Bate, J.J. 208
Bauman, Henry J. 292
Bay City Northwestern League Club 92, 99, 104
Bay View Baseball Club 118–121, 127, 128–129, 135–136, 161, 163, 165, 200, 201, 231, 275
Bay View Baseball Park 129, 135, 136, 161, 162, 163
Bay View Cricket Club 75
Beadles Dime Base Ball Player 21, 41, 61
Beard, Ollie 213, 226
Beatty (local player) 163
Beaumont, Clarence "Ginger" 264, 265, 266
Beaver Dam Baseball Club 43, 201
Beck, Erv 300

343

Index

Beck, William 4, 5, 8, 9
Beck, William H. 205, 207
Becker, Edward 269
Becker, W.M. 176
Becker, Washington 122
Becker, William A. 169
Beckley, Jake 304
Beecher (1898 player from Mansfield) 260
Behel, Steve 93, 94, 101, 103–104, 107, 109, 114, 115, 117, 127, 128
Belle City Baseball Club of Racine 200
Beloit Baseball Club 89
Beloit Olympians 15, 16
Belvidre Baseball Club of Illinois 16
Bennett, Charlie 46–47, 54, 56, 57, 62, 64, 65, 66, 70, 72–73, 83, 232–233
Bennett Park (Detroit) 57
Bentley, H. 8
Berger, John 195
Berlin, Wisconsin, Baseball Club 118, 120, 121
Berner, Lorenz 78, 80
bicycling 75–76, 199, 203, 238
Bierbauer, Louis 284, 286
Bigler (local player) 129
Bignall, George 104, 108, 114
billiards 7
Bishop, George 125, 137
black baseball teams and players 74, 88, 97, 102, 103, 119, 120, 164, 201, 238, 250, 263, 270
Black Diamond Baseball Club 230–231
Blake, Harry 252, 255, 257
Blatz Brewing Company 175
Bliss, Frank 37, 39, 46, 48, 65
Blonde and Brunette Baseball Club 121
Bloomers Baseball Club of Boston 231
Bloomington (Illinois) Baseball Club 11, 12
Boardman, M.A. 17, 23
Bolan, Patrick "Paddy" 214, 215–216, 221, 222, 224, 225, 227, 235, 241
Bond, Tommy 71, 102–103
Bone, George 301, 302, 307
Borchers, George 241, 242
Boston American League Club 290, 291, 292, 295, 296, 302, 303
Boston Dips 201
Boston Harvard Baseball Club 28
Boston National League Club 53, 55, 58, 59, 66, 68, 70, 204, 295; game for yellow fever sufferers 67; plays cricket match 67
Bosworth, F.J. 3
Bower City (Janesville) Baseball Club 18
Bradburg, George 62
Bradley, George 57, 58

Bradley & Metcalf Baseball Club 231
Bradley Brothers (architects) 96
Brady, George "Texas" 272
Brady, Jim 178, 179
Bray, Martin 17, 43
Brewers, nickname first used 148
Brimer, Alfred 26
Brooklyn National League Club 216, 218, 258, 268, 283, 294
Brosius, F. 113
Broughton, Cal 94, 101, 107, 110, 132, 134, 139, 142
Brown, Grant 102
Brown, J.B. 8, 9
Brown, Joe 115, 116, 117, 118, 121
Brush, John T. 195, 205, 220, 228–229, 232, 234, 236, 237, 239, 245–247, 248, 259, 261, 267, 268, 276, 278–279, 281, 291, 300
Bruyette, Ed 300, 301, 302, 307
Bryden, James A. 8, 9, 14, 119
Brynan, Charles 156, 157
Buckenburger, Al 218, 220–221
Buckley, Frank 276
Buckley, John 178, 180
Buffalo (N.Y.) baseball clubs 67, 70; arrests for Sunday game 272–273; National League 118, 121; (1898) proposed Western League 256; (1899) 267–268, 270, 271, 273, 274; (1900) 281, 286, 290, 292
Burdick, Morgan L. 3
Burke, Eddie 178, 191
Burke, James 93, 94
Burke, Jesse 295–296
Burke, Jimmy 263, 266, 267, 282, 283, 287, 294, 296, 297, 298, 299
Burlington Baseball Club 200
Burner (Arctic player) 88
Burnett, Hercules 132, 133, 134
Burns (1895 player from Milwaukee) 228
Burns, Dick 114, 117, 129
Burns, James 281
Burrell, Harry 194, 198, 199
Busch, Gussie 305
Butler, John Albert 302; see also King, Fred
Byrne, Charles 218, 237, 245
Byron (manager of Des Moines club) 135

California League 229, 284
Calumet Baseball Club 200
Cambria Whites 85, 120
Camp, Llewellyn 222
Camp Randall (Madison) 10
Camp Reno 11, 12, 14, 17, 19; see also Cream City Park
Camp Scott 8, 9–10, 11, 25
Campau, Charlie 214, 215
Campion, William J. 178, 181, 184
Canavan, James 184, 188, 191
Cantillon, Joe 270, 301

Capitol City Club (Madison) 10, 12, 13, 16, 17, 18, 19–20, 21, 23
Carbine, John 41, 46
Carey, A.L. 144
Carey, George 208, 215, 216, 217, 221, 222
Carisch, George 210, 221
Carney, John 184, 191
Carroll, Fred 209, 215
Carrothers, James 206
Cary, William 77, 85
Casey, Eugene 136, 162
Cass Baseball Club of Detroit 52
Catholic cemetery 95
Caverno, C. 5
Cedar Rapids Western Association Club 235–236
Central Baseball League 192, 193
Chamber of Commerce Baseball Club 164
Chandler, E.H. 14, 46
Chandler, Harry 37, 41, 42, 46, 47, 59, 119
Chandler, R. 5, 9, 11, 15, 17, 35
Chapman, John 18, 54, 57, 59, 64, 67, 68, 69, 72
Chapman (T.A.) store 73
charity and benefit games 43, 44, 160, 163, 201, 203, 241, 262
Chech, Charles 272, 273, 282, 284
Chelsea League Alliance Club 48
Chicago Acmes 120
Chicago Alaska Blues 90
Chicago American Association franchise 188, 190
Chicago American League Club (1900) 277, 278–281, 283, 286; (1901) 290, 296, 302, 303
Chicago and Northwestern Railroad 15, 206
Chicago Athletic Association 275
Chicago Base Ball Club (1860) 5; (1865) 8
Chicago Blues 88, 98, 120
Chicago Brown Stockings 88
Chicago Chamber of Commerce Baseball Club 45
Chicago Columbias 203
Chicago Crooks Baseball Club 74
Chicago Dreadnaughts 74, 80, 90, 119
Chicago Fairbanks League Alliance Club 48, 49
Chicago Gordons Baseball Club 97, 103, 104, 119
Chicago Greens 87
Chicago National League Club 36, 37–38, 39, 41, 50, 53, 58, 65, 199, 201, 234, 278
Chicago Picketts 88
Chicago, plans for Western League franchise 217, 219–220, 245, 256, 267, 277, 278
Chicago Reds 121
Chicago Star Baseball Club 87
Chicago Union Baseball Club 89, 263, 270
Chicago Uniques 74

Chicago Western Association Club 140, 142, 148, 150, 152
Chicago White Stockings (1870) 27, 29
Chicago Whitings 133, 160, 162, 169
Chicago World's Fair 201
Cincinnati American Association Club 184, 187, 190
Cincinnati Red Stockings 24–25, 26, 29, 32, 333
Cincinnati Red Stockings (National League) 41, 49, 53, 59, 62, 63, 66, 70, 118, 121, 174, 258, 261, 270, 283
Cincinnati Shamrocks 236
City Baseball League 120, 135–136, 160, 164, 200, 201, 202–203, 230–232, 238, 274–275, 301
Clark (1889 player from Ohio) 154, 155
Clark, Willie 282, 283, 284
Clarke, F. (pioneer player) 3
Clarke, Fred 213, 289
Clarkson, Arthur 244, 247, 251, 252, 255
Clarkson, John 133
Clausen, Fred 168, 170, 178, 180, 181, 182, 239, 241, 242
Clayton, Henry 211, 213
Clayton, Zach 87, 95, 99, 100, 102, 119, 129, 136, 162
Clement, Howard 195
Cleveland American League Club 279, 280–281, 283, 286, 290, 296, 302, 303, 304
Cleveland National League Club 189, 234, 239, 252, 255, 256, 267, 268–269
Cleveland Western League club 112, 116
Clingman, Billy 207, 212, 216, 217, 221
Clough (local pitcher) 123
Coate, Cap. 3
Cobb, George 208, 209
Cohn, H.H. 272, 278
Colcolough, Tom 211
Cold Spring Driving Park 80, 85, 86, 87, 90, 95, 118, 133, 135
Cole, S.H. 37
Colgan, William 126, 127
College League 78
Collins, Dennis 29
Columbus Western League Club (1892) 195, 196, 197–199; (1896) 232–234, 236, 242; (1897) 245–246, 249, 254, 255; (1898) 258, 261, 263, 265; (1899) 267–268, 272
Comiskey, Charles 99, 217, 220, 226, 233, 265, 269, 270, 278, 281, 289, 298, 303–304, 307
Commercial League 164, 230–232
Concordia College 275
Congolton, Bill 272, 273, 282
Conley, P. 119

Conner, Roger 243, 244
Conney, J. 17
Connor, Joe 294, 296, 299, 300
Connors, Joe 102
Conroy, William "Wid" 282, 283, 284, 287, 294, 296, 298, 299, 301, 302, 306, 307
Coons, Wilber 70, 72
Corbett, Jim 254
Corcoran (local player) 203
Corcoran, Cornelius 85
Corcoran, Dan 196
corruption in baseball 19, 33, 42–43, 53, 101, 118, 215, 240, 241, 264–265; *see also* gambling
Cotterell, J.P.C. 3, 5
Crandall, Robert 62
Crawford (1886 player from Iowa State League) 123
Cream Cities reserve team (1884) 98–99
Cream City Baseball Club 8, 9–33, 119; paid for playing 11, 21, 27, 28; state champions 13, 16, 21, 29, 30, 32, 33; uniforms 11, 28
Cream City Baseball League 136
Cream City Juniors 14, 16, 17, 20, 21
Cream City Park 19, 21, 23, 24, 26, 27, 28, 29, 30, 31, 32, 33, 35
Cream City (2nd Nine) Baseball Club 14, 17, 18, 19
Cream Citys Baseball Club (1889–1891) 163–164, 165, 200
Creamer, George 52, 54, 57, 58, 70, 72, 73
cricket 7, 10, 55, 67, 75
Cricket League Alliance Club 48
Criger, Lou 252
Crisham, Pat 270
Crossley, William C. 148, 152, 153, 154, 155
Cummings, Candy 47
Cushman, Charles 167, 169, 173, 174, 175–176, 178, 180, 181, 184, 188, 189, 191, 195, 199, 201, 204, 205–206, 207–209, 211–213, 215, 221, 244
Cushman, Edgar 94, 99, 100, 101, 102, 107, 110, 114, 122, 137, 142, 180; pitches no hitter 108
Cusick, Andy 142, 147, 149
Cusick, John 124, 125
Dahlen, Bill 180, 188, 191 204
Daily, Hugh 126, 127
Dalrymple, Abner 47, 49, 54, 57, 58, 60, 62, 64, 65, 71, 73, 83, 108, 109, 170, 174, 175, 178, 179, 183, 185, 186, 191, 194, 212, 335

Dalrymple, Ed 260
Daly, Matt 295; *see also* Garvin, Virgil
Daly, Tom 248, 250, 251, 255, 259, 260, 261, 265, 266
Daly, William 85
Darling, Enouch 3

Dasher, Bert 233
Daub, Dan 268
Davenport (Iowa) Baseball Club 67
Davenport Western Association Club 147, 148–150, 152
Davidson Hotel 221, 267, 276
Davies, George 155, 168, 170, 173, 178, 185, 189, 221
Davin, David J. 142, 16
Davis & Baird Omnibus Line 206
Dealy, Pat 93, 95, 99
Deffert, H. 132
Delafield Baseball Club 34
Delahanty, Tom 244, 247, 251
Delaney, Bill 88
Delany, Thomas 80, 87, 88, 95, 99, 119, 120, 136
Denver, attempts at Western League franchise 233, 256, 263, 267–268
Denver Western Association Club (1889) 152, 159; (1890) 166, 173, 174; (1891) 177, 185
Des Moines Northwestern League 131, 139
Des Moines Western Association Club (1888) 140, 142–143, 145, 148–150; (1889) 152, 154, 158, 159; (1890) 166, 172; (1896) 239; (1898) 256
Detroit Aetnas 42, 43
Detroit American League Club 281, 286, 296, 297, 302, 303
Detroit Baseball Club (1866) 11, 12; (1879) 74
Detroit Free Press Cup 238, 242, 255, 260
Detroit, Grand Haven & Milwaukee Railroad 98
Detroit National League Club 121
Detroit Western League Club (1894) 205, 206, 209, 216; (1895) 224, 226, 228, 229; (1896) 233, 234, 239, 242; (1897) 245, 248, 249, 254, 255; (1898) 258, 261, 265; (1899) 269, 270, 273, 274
Devinney, Billy 212
Diamond, Johnny 222, 226
Diamond Baseball Club of Waukesha 17, 31, 32, 33
Diggins, Cy 282, 283, 284, 286
Dixon and Berry Co. 73
Dixon and Talbot 233
Dodsworth, William 20, 119
Dolan, Joe 260
Donahue, James 197
Donahue, John "Jiggs" 299, 300, 302, 307
Dougherty, T. 124, 127
Dousman, Talbot 3
Dowd, Tommy 284, 286
Dowling, Pete 253, 255, 257, 282, 283, 284, 287, 294, 296, 298–299, 300, 302; pitches no-hitter 285–286

Doyle (1889 player from Boston) 156, 157
Drake House 78
Drew (local Arctic player) 89
Drew, Thomas 87, 88, 129
Dreyfuss, Barney 279
Driscoll, Dan 85
Driscoll, Denny 102
Driving Park (Beloit) 16
Duane (1886 player from Dubuque) 124
Dubuque County Agricultural Society 8
Duffy, Hugh 294, 296, 298, 299, 302, 305, 307; problems with umpires 300–301
Duke, Martin 195
Duluth Northwestern League Club (1886–1887) 123, 127, 131, 138
Duluth Western Association Club 181, 183, 185
Dungan, Sam 178, 181–182, 183, 212
Dunlap, R.W. 17
Dunn, J.T. 17
Dunn, Steve 93, 94, 101, 102
Durand, E.T. 72
Duvbeck (1886 player from St. Joseph) 124
Dwyer, John Francis 184

Earl, Howard 181, 187, 194
Earle, Billy 159, 168
East Side High School 275
Eastern League 237, 256, 258–259, 266, 268, 269, 278, 279, 289, 292
Eau Claire Baseball Club 120
Eau Claire Northwestern League Club (1886–1887) 123, 124, 131, 138, 139
Ebbitts (local Arctic player) 89
Ebright, Buck 235–236
Eckford Baseball Club of Milwaukee 30
Eckford Baseball Club of Racine 26
Eddinger, Jerry 221, 224
Edgerton, E.W. 3
Edwards, Noah 40–41
Eimermann's Park 35
Eiteljorge, Ed 189
Elgin (Illinois) Baseball Club 90
Elkhorn Centrals Baseball Club 30
Ellick, Joe 48, 54, 57, 64, 65, 70, 73, 335
Elliot, T.B. 5
Elliott, Claude 222, 228, 229, 236, 301
Ellis, George 208–209, 218, 233–234, 243, 245, 247, 256
Elmore, E. 37
Ely, Lydia 262
Emmerke, Robert 157, 158
Engel, Theodore 222, 229, 234, 235, 247, 259
Escanaba (Michigan) Baseball Club 2, 312, 332

Esper, Charles 246, 247
Evanston College Baseball team 38–39
Evansville Baseball Club 102, 103, 104
Evening Wisconsin Baseball Club 44, 45, 201
Everett, Bill 224
Everett Baseball Club of Oshkosh 18
Ewing, John M. 37
Excelsior Base Ball Club (1860) 5, 6; (1867) 14; (1870) 32; (1875) 34
Excelsior Base Ball Club of Chicago 11, 12, 15
Excelsior Baseball Club of Waukesha 26

Fair Grounds on Spring Street 4, 5
Fairbanks Baseball Club 75
Fairbanks Baseball Club of Chicago 41, 44
Falch, Anton 89, 94, 95, 99, 101, 108, 114, 117, 118
Falk, F. 113
Fall River League Alliance Club 48
Farrell (Wet End player) 41, 46
Farwell Avenue Armory 200
Fashion Race Course (New York) 7
Fass, Fred 125, 126, 129, 163
Ferguson, Robert 18, 71
Ferson, Alex 142, 145, 194, 198, 199
Fields, John "Jocko" 213–214, 215
Figgemeier, Frank 208, 213
Fisher, Albert 148, 149
Fisher, Chauncy 266
Fisher, William Cherokee 41, 42, 46, 48
Fitzsimmons, O.K. 137, 138
Flaherty, Pat 216, 217, 221, 222
Flannagan, Tom 168, 171
Flattly, C.P. 173
Fleischer, William L. 202
Flint, Silver 66
Flynn, T.W. 217, 226
Foley, Bill 54, 57, 58, 65, 69, 73
Foley, Thomas 217, 220
Foreman, Johnny "Brownie" 239, 244
Forest City Club of Cleveland 67
Forest City Club of Rockford 11, 12, 13, 23, 25, 29–30, 32
forfeit games 23–24, 29, 33, 39, 51, 79, 80, 84, 127, 147, 149, 150, 159, 171, 172, 183, 184, 198, 225, 226, 228, 239, 241, 242, 251, 284
Forster, Tom 109, 114, 117, 118, 127, 132, 133, 134, 139, 142, 148
Fort Atkinson Baseball Club 200
Fort Wayne club (1884 Northwestern League) 93, 98, 99, 104
Fort Wayne Western Association Club 197, 198, 199
Foster, E.F. 235

Foutz, David 244
Francis (local Arctic player) 89
Frank, Charlie 222
Franklin, James 267–268, 273, 281, 292
Franks, Sidney 292
Fraser, Charles 214
Freedman, Andrew 279, 304
Freedom Baseball Club 230
Freeman, Julius 154, 155
Friel, Bill 296, 298, 299, 301, 302, 307
Friend, Danny 271, 272, 273
Friese, Augustus W. 176, 180, 194, 195
Fuller, William 142, 147, 152, 153, 154, 155, 156
Fultz, Dave 283, 287, 293–294
Furcell (local Arctic player) 89
Furlong, Morgan 8, 9
Furlong, William E. "Billy" 40, 41, 46, 47, 59, 60, 101, 120, 176, 178, 182, 188, 204, 207

Gallagher, Bill 244
gambling on baseball games 42–43, 51, 90, 162; *see also* corruption; pool rooms
Garden City Baseball Club of Chicago 19
Gardner, A. 129
Garry, Jim 282, 283, 285
Garvin, Virgil "Ned" 294–295, 296, 299, 302, 306, 307; *see also* Daly, Matt
Gastfield, Ed 125
Gault, Edward 37, 41, 59
Geier, Phil 298, 299, 300
George, Billy 209, 215
Gertenrich, Lou 302
Gilbert, Billy 282, 283, 286, 294, 296, 298, 299, 300, 302, 306, 307
Giljohan, Rudolph 163, 205–206, 235, 247
Gillen, Dam 208
Gillette, Harry E. 176, 180, 181, 182, 183–184, 186, 187–188, 194
girls baseball teams 102, 121, 163, 200, 203, 231
Glenalvin, Robert 223–224, 240–242, 247, 255; forfeits game 241
Goar, Joshua 227
Golden, Michael 58, 59, 64, 65, 73
Golden Eagles 120, 121
Golt, W.F.C. 218, 233, 264, 265, 267, 268, 278
Goodenough, Bill 214, 217, 221–222
Gooding, W.E. 141, 148, 149
Goodman, Jacob 54, 57, 58, 65, 66, 69, 70, 73
Goodnow, John 233, 234, 245–246, 255, 256
Goodrich Steamboat Line 15, 31
Gorman, Jack 109, 114, 117, 118
Grabe (1886 local player) 125
Grand Rapids club (1884 North-

Index

western League) 92–93, 99, 103, 105
Grand Rapids Western League Club (1894) 205, 206, 208, 209, 212, 216; (1895) 220, 226, 228, 229; (1896) 232–234, 242; (1897) 245–247, 249, 254–257; (1899) 272, 273, 274, 278–279, 281
Gransberry, George L. 4
Gray, Billy 266, 267, 271, 273, 282, 283
Gray, Charles F. & Co. 21
Green, D.C. 17
Green Bay Baseball Club 89–90, 98, 118, 119, 200
Greens Baseball Club 118, 119, 121, 161, 163, 200, 201
Griffin, H.T. 17
Griffin, Tom 93, 94, 114
Griffith, Clark 147, 148, 151, 152, 153, 154, 168, 170, 174, 175, 178–179, 295, 301
Grim, John 178, 181, 185, 189, 191
Gross, Christian 259
Gross, Emil 115
Gross, Fred 223, 235, 240, 242, 243, 244, 247, 259, 266, 274, 280, 291, 293, 295–296, 305–306
Gross (F.C.) Meat Packing Co. 295
Gruner, R.A. 269
Guettler & Riemschneider (architects) 222
Gumbert, Addison 211
Gunnels, J.W. 233

Hach, Hy 195
Hack, Henry 177
Hagerty, John 85, 118, 120, 121, 129, 136
Hahn, Frank 248
Hair-Rakers of Kinnickinnick Baseball Club 34
Hall, Frederick 206
Hallman, Bill 266, 267, 271, 272, 282, 283, 284, 286, 287, 294, 296, 299, 302, 307
Halloway, A. 119, 165
Hamburg, Charles 194, 199
Hamilton, Charles H. 222–223
Hamilton Baseball Club of Canadian League 272, 273
Hammel, Leopold 206
Hanlon, Ned 247, 268
Hannivan, James 244, 247, 248
Hanrahan, John 87, 88, 129, 162
Hansell (local baseball player) 231, 232
Hansen, L.A. 132
Harbridge, Bill 114
Harmon, James 102
Harper, Joe 120, 123, 124, 125, 126
Harrington, W.R. 131
Harrison, James 295
Harrison, R.D. 256
Hart, James A. 131–134, 135–139, 140–142, 146, 148, 150, 151, 154,
201, 217, 218, 219–220, 234, 245, 256, 259, 277, 278, 279–281, 295
Hart, Robert 132, 133, 134, 135
Hart, Warren 301
Hart, Will 208, 266, 267, 271, 273
Hartford Dark Blues 37, 40, 50, 53
Hartford, Wisconsin, Baseball Club 120, 129
Hartman, Fred 228, 236, 238, 241, 242, 244, 249, 298, 299
Haskell, Jack 301
Hassamaer, Bill 155
Hastings, Charlie 207, 213, 214
Hathaway, J.L. 3, 5
Havenor, Charles S 276–277, 289, 291, 292
Hawes, William 148, 152, 153
Hawley, Emerson "Pink" 182, 296, 299, 301, 302
Hay, Sam 41
Hayden, H.R. 10, 17, 18
Haynes, Marcus 233, 245–246, 255, 256, 269
Heard, Charles 170, 171
Heckel, George 305
Heimann, (M.) & Company 77, 78, 80, 86, 119
Hellberg, Charles 206, 235, 247, 259, 266
Hemphill (1900 player from Canadian League) 282
Hempsted, N.H. 5
Hendricks, John "Kid" 125
Henry, George 194, 195, 197, 199
Henry, Louis 99
Hensel, LeRoy 203
Herr, Joe 153, 154, 155, 156, 157
Heup, Henry 146, 147, 203
Hewitt, C.P. 5
Hickey, Thomas J. 233, 258, 263
Hill, A.W. 70
Hill, F.H. 5
Hill, F.J. 3
Himmerstein, Phillip 89, 95, 99, 119, 129, 163
Hines, Harry 133, 134
Hines, Paul 71, 335
Hinsey, John A. 143, 175
Hirsch-Silverstone Co. 273
Hobdy (local player) 129, 163
Hoffer, Andrew 17
Hogan, Ed 93, 101, 103–104, 107, 114, 132
Hogriever, George 299, 302
Holbert, Billy 52, 54, 57, 58, 62, 64, 65, 66, 69, 70, 72, 73, 83
Holister, C.G. 15
Holland, Joe 297
Holly, Ed 273, 282
Holmes, W. 124, 125
Home (1890 player) 168
Homes, Thomas 3
Hooker, D.G. 5
Hooley, Joseph 17, 35, 37, 38, 39, 120
Horner, Jack 142, 146, 148
horse racing 7, 32
Horwitz's Cigar Store 169
Hosmer, George 3
Hosmer, Henry 3
Hough, Frank 276–277
Houseman, Frank 250
Howard, Samuel 8
Howard & Mock (vendors) 213
Howe, Harry 168, 170, 171, 212, 214
Hoy, Charles "Dummy" 204
Hughey, Jim 187, 188, 239
Hulbert, William A. 54
Hull, Arthur 132, 134, 135
Hurley, Jeremiah 155, 156, 159, 168
Husting, Bert 271–272, 273, 282, 284, 285, 287, 292, 295, 296, 297, 299, 302, 307
Hyleman (player from Kentucky) 228

Ike, Albert 168, 170
Imig, John 254
Independence Baseball Club 14
Indianapolis American League Club (1900) 278, 281, 283, 286, 289, 290, 292
Indianapolis Blues 48, 51, 54, 59, 62, 66, 68, 69, 70
Indianapolis Western League club (1885) 111, 117; (1892) 195, 198, 199; (1894) 205, 209, 216; (1895) 220, 228–229; (1896) 233–234, 236, 239, 242; (1897) 245–246, 249, 254, 255; (1898) 258, 260, 261, 262, 264, 265, 267; (1899) 268, 269–270, 273
indoor baseball 199–200
Inter-City League 275–276
International Baseball Association 53, 54, 67, 167
Interstate League 260, 272, 291
Irwin, Arthur 244, 268
Isaacson, Charles 124
Iverson, John C. 92, 101, 103, 113, 114, 175, 176, 187, 188, 190, 192–193, 195, 197, 198

Jackson, A. (Cream City player) 9, 10
Jackson (Michigan) Baseball Club 250
Jaffrey (local player) 163
Jahn (local baseball player) 231
James, Charles 3
Janesville Base Ball Club 4, 5
Janesville Mutuals 26, 29, 40, 41–42, 43, 44, 46, 48, 49, 51–52, 73, 74, 81, 230
Janssen, John 275
Jantzen, August 159, 168, 170, 178
Jefferson (Wisconsin) baseball clubs 200, 232, 270
Jenkins, James 8, 9
Jenning, R.L. 70
Jennings, Al 65
Jennings, Hughey 278, 289
Jennings, W. 26
Joannes, F.K. 89, 90

Johnson (1894 pitcher from Sioux City) 211
Johnson, Ban 207–209, 213, 215, 216, 217, 219, 220, 224, 226, 232, 233, 236, 237, 238, 242, 245, 246, 248, 255, 256–257, 258–259, 260, 261, 264, 267, 270, 276, 277, 278–281, 283, 289, 290–293, 297, 298, 300, 301, 303–304, 305–307; granted extraordinary powers 257, 292
Johnson, Mike 208, 210
Johnstone, J.E. 244
Jones, Bert 235, 236, 239, 241, 242, 244, 247, 248, 252, 253, 254, 255, 257–258, 261
Jones, Davy 301, 302, 307
Jones, Henry 194, 195
Julian Baseball Club of Dubuque 11
Juneau, Solomon 3, 144, 307
Juneau Baseball Club 14, 17, 19, 25
Junior Baseball League 275

Kaine, John L. 68
Kames, W.S. 218
Kansas City American League Club 281, 286, 289, 290, 292
Kansas City Western Association Club (1888) 140–143, 148, 150, 151–152; (1890) 167, 172, 173, 174; (1891) 177, 185
Kansas City Western League Club (1885) 111, 116; (1892) 195, 197–199; (1894) 205, 208, 209, 216; (1895) 228; (1896) 234, 236, 242; (1897) 245, 249, 255; (1898) 261, 264, 262; (1899) 268, 270, 273, 274
Kaukauna Baseball Club 163
Keas, Ed 153–155
Keefe, J.C. 45
Keel, Jumbo 168
Kehoe, Mike 235, 236
Keissler, Hugo 164
Kelley, William 125, 127
Kelly, G.P. 9, 10, 11
Kelly, Mike 71, 184
Kenosha Baseball Club 274, 275
Keokuk Western League club 112, 116
Kern (local amateur player) 275
Kershaw (local baseball player) 59, 120
Kershaw, C.J. 70
Ketchum, Fred 284, 285, 287, 294
Keyes, James 85
Keyes, W. 129, 163
Kilfoyle, J.C. 281
Killen, Frank 186, 188, 189, 191
Killilea, Henry J. 205, 304–305, 306, 307
Killilea, Matthew R. 206, 209, 210, 212, 213–214, 216, 217, 218, 219–220, 221, 223, 226, 233, 234–235, 237–238, 239, 240, 242, 243, 244, 245, 246, 247, 258, 259, 262, 266, 267, 276, 277, 281, 287, 291, 293–295, 296, 303–307
King, Fred 302; see also Butler, John Albert
King, J.D.W. 256–257, 259
King, Rufus 3, 4, 5
King, Silver 179
Kipp, Benjamin A. 92, 113, 123, 128, 131
Kipp, Charles M. 92, 111–112, 113, 114, 123, 128, 131, 160, 176, 186
Kipp, G.W. 113
Kirby, John 155, 158
Kirby, Oak 116
Kirby, Welcome 96, 105, 113, 120
Kirby House 17, 23, 104, 113
Klein, Kleiner 77
Kletzsch, Alvin P. 230
Klocksin, William 96
Klopf, Gus 165, 214, 215, 216, 222, 224, 227, 228, 229, 236
Klusman, William 153, 154
Knab, David 17
Kneeland, James 70
Knight, Joe 102
Knoth, Hugh E. 202
Knouff, Ed 157, 159
Knuth (local baseball organizer) 231
Knowdell, Jacob 65, 73, 74
Koch, August A. 289, 292, 293
Koch, Edward V. & Co. 144
Koch, John C. 223, 224
Krauthoff, L.C. 177–178, 183, 192, 195, 207
Krieg, Bill 168, 170, 171, 178, 194, 195, 196, 197
Krock, Gus 126, 129, 130, 141, 142, 159, 165, 203

LaCrosse Northwestern League 131, 139
Ladies' days 20–21, 46, 98, 99, 117, 124, 133, 144, 169, 202, 209, 224, 230, 259
Lady Elgin Steamship 6
LaFleur, John 228, 229, 236
LaJoie, Napoleon 302
Lake, Fred 194, 197
Lake Mills Baseball Club 120, 125, 129
Lake Mills Leader 125
Lander, F.C. 132
Langervine, Alexander 260
Langsford, Robert 208, 212, 214
Lanigan, Ernest 302–303
LaPorte, Frank 260
LaRett, Oliver 222, 224, 225
Larkin, Martin 8, 9, 10, 11, 12, 14, 15, 23–24
Laurels Baseball Club 202–203, 230–231
Lavin, John 125
Lawe (Cream City pitcher) 16
Lawler, Joe 40, 41, 46, 47, 48
Lawrence (Phillip) Shooting Gallery 7
Lay, Edward T. 43

Leach, O. Gilbert 8, 9
Leaders Baseball Club 230, 231
Leadley, Bob 213, 232, 247, 255, 256
League Alliance 48, 51, 52, 67, 82
Leahy, Tom 295, 296, 298
Lederer, Phil 144, 205–206
Ledyard, G.C. 3, 5
Lee, Johnny 88
Lee, Thomas 79, 87–90, 114, 118
Lee, Willie 85
Lee, Wyatt 300
Lehay (shortstop from Virginia League) 235
Letcher, Thomas 187, 188
Lewee, Eddie 248, 251, 255, 258, 260, 261, 265, 266, 267, 271
Ley, J. 119
Lincoln, Neb. Western Association franchise 140, 147; (1890) 172, 174; (1891) 177, 182, 183, 185; (1895) 235–236
Lippert, L.W. 244, 247, 251
Lloyd Street Park see Milwaukee Park (Sixteenth and Lloyd)
Loehrbeck, Joe 157, 158
Loftus, Tom 93, 99, 102, 103, 107, 108, 113, 114, 117, 131, 221, 233, 234, 263, 268, 269, 272, 278, 281
Lohman, Pete 208, 209, 212, 215–216, 221
London Tescumsehs 52
Lone Star Baseball Club of Milwaukee 35
Lone Star Baseball Club of New Orleans 28–29
Long, Dennis 207, 215, 226, 227, 232
Long, Jimmy 213–214, 215, 216, 221–222, 224, 227
Longmore, W. (player on Star club) 26
Lotz (1884 Terre Haute player) 102
Louisville American Association Club 140, 181, 182, 183–184, 188, 190
Louisville National League clubs 53, 57, 197, 205, 218, 241, 258, 261, 266, 268, 269, 272, 279, 281
Love, W. (player on Star club) 26
Lowe, Bobby 142, 148, 150, 152, 153, 154, 168, 204
Lowell (Mass.) Baseball Club 48, 67
Luby, John 207, 211–213, 214
Lucas, Henry V. 106–107, 109–110, 111, 112, 152
Ludington (James) Baseball Club 45
Lumsden, George 222
Lunt, Fred 155, 157
Lutz, Nicholas 96

Mack, Connie 227, 228, 243, 244, 247, 250, 251, 252, 254, 255,

257–258, 259, 260–261, 266, 270–274, 276, 282, 283–285, 287, 289, 290–291, 292, 294; accused of losing games 264–265
Macullar, Jimmy 181
Maguire, Robert W. 150, 165, 175–176, 180, 193, 195, 276
Main, Willard 184
Malone, Ferguson 70
Maloney, Bill 294, 296, 299, 302, 307
Manchester (New Hampshire) Club 50, 67
Manistee baseball clubs 163, 164, 231, 273
Manitowac baseball clubs 79, 232, 274
Mannassau, Alfred 298, 300–301
Manning, James 205, 218, 233, 265, 273, 281, 289, 290, 292, 304
Maple Leafs Baseball Club 44, 45, 73, 75, 76, 78, 80, 84, 86–91, 94, 107, 118–119, 124, 129–130, 136, 161, 162, 164, 202
Mappis, George 114
Mariner, Ephraim 143, 223
Marinette Baseball Club 162
Markham Academy Baseball team 38
Marquette College 201, 284
Martin, Robert J. 217
mascots 101–102, 134, 135, 239
Maskrey, Leach 132, 133, 134, 139, 142, 148, 152
Masran, Joe 124
Mathias, Johan 17
Matthews, C.H. Baseball Club 232, 274–275
Matthews Brothers Furniture Co. 86
Maul, Albert 195
McAleer, Jim 146, 148, 150, 151, 152, 153, 305, 306
McBride, George 301, 307
McCabe, John 148, 152, 153
McCall (1886 player) 124
McCann, John 213–214
McCauley, Al 222, 224, 225, 227
McClosky, John 240
McCormack (local Arctic player) 89
McCormick, J.S. 152, 158, 166, 182
McCullom, T. 156, 157
McCullum, Tom 124
McDermott, Michael 93, 100
McDermott, Tom 93, 100
McDonald, Charles 263, 264, 265, 267, 271, 282, 283, 284
McDonald, Hugh 37, 41, 46, 47
McDonald, Jim 132, 133
McFadyen, Archie 9, 10, 11, 12, 14, 15, 16, 23, 24, 27–28, 29, 82, 119
McFadyen, N. 11
McGarr, James "Chippy" 194, 199, 225

McGeoch, Peter 122, 143
McGinley, Dennis 93, 94, 100, 102
McGinnis, George "Jumbo" 137, 138
McGinnity, Joe 301
McGraw, Dick 129
McGraw, John 276, 279, 280, 290, 298, 300, 301
McHale, Bob 241, 242, 244, 247, 248–249
McIver, Felix 129, 136
McKee, James F. 92–93, 97, 99–103, 132, 257
McKelvey, Russell 70, 72
McKim, A.N. 112
McKinley, William 301–302
McKnight, Denny 113
McNabb, Edgar 157
McPartlin, Frank 235
McPhee, Bid 304
McQuaide (1886 player from Quincy) 124, 125
McSorley, John 109, 114, 117, 118
McVey, Carl 207, 213
McVey, George 153–154
Meadows, B.C. 37
Meech, Philip 168
Meister, John 114
Memphis Reds 48
Meyers, Bert 244, 247, 249, 250, 251, 254, 255, 260, 261, 262
Middleman, A. 16, 17, 119
Millard, Fred C. 43
Miller, Roxy 300
Mills, Everett 47
Mills, Frank 125, 135, 142, 146, 148, 152–155, 168
Milwaukee: population 1, 21, 83, 111, 160, 206, 281, 308
Milwaukee Athletic Society 99, 224, 230, 231, 263, 275
Milwaukee Base Ball Club (1860–61) 4, 5, 6, 8; (1879) 73, 74; (1880) 75; (1882) 79
Milwaukee Baseball Club (1885 amateur) 121; see also Quicksteps
Milwaukee Baseball Club (Northwestern League 1886–1887) 123–128, 130–135, 136–139; uniforms 133
Milwaukee Baseball Club (proposed American Association) (1895) 218–221; (1900) 276–280; (1901) 291–292, 293
Milwaukee Baseball Club (proposed National Association) 289
Milwaukee Baseball Club (Western Association 1888–1891) 140–150, 151–158, 165–174, 175, 178–184, 191; rules for players 169; uniforms 154, 155–160, 169, 180
Milwaukee Baseball Park (Sixteenth and Lloyd) 223, 224, 228, 230, 231, 238, 250, 252–253, 259, 265, 270, 274,

275, 284, 287, 298, 299; see also Prochazka, Charles
Milwaukee Baseball Park (Tenth and Clybourn) 52, 55, 59, 63, 70, 73, 74, 86
Milwaukee Brewers (American Association 1891) 183–191
Milwaukee Brewers (American League) (1900) 281–287; (1901) 290, 295–303; uniforms 297; transfer to St. Louis 293, 303–307
Milwaukee Brewers (Western League) (1892) 192–199; (1894) 205, 208–217; (1895) 223–229; (1896) 233–243; (1897) 244–255; (1898) 257–266; (1899) 267–268, 270–274; uniforms 208, 224, 225, 249–250, 270; use of Blue Ribbons nickname 208, 209; use of Giants nickname 270
Milwaukee Chamber of Commerce Baseball Club 44, 45
Milwaukee County Historical Society 3
Milwaukee Cricket Club 55, 67
Milwaukee Gardens 78
Milwaukee Grays (National League 1878) 53–60, 62–68–71, 82; rules of conduct 56–57; rumored moved to St. Louis 68–69; uniforms 62, 69–70
Milwaukee Grays (Northwestern League 1884) 92, 97, 99–105, 106–107; uniforms 99
Milwaukee Grays (Union Association) 106–109; expenses of club 113–114
Milwaukee Grays (Western League 1885) 111–115; uniforms 115
Milwaukee High School Baseball Club 77, 78, 79, 86
Milwaukee Journal Baseball Club 201
Milwaukee Medical College Club 297
Milwaukee military reunion 75
Milwaukee Reds 201
Milwaukee, St. Paul & Chicago Railway 264
Milwaukee Sentinel: interested purchasing Brewers 243
Milwaukee Sentinel Baseball Club 44, 45
Milwaukee Whites 118, 119, 121
Minneapolis American League Club 279, 281, 283, 286, 289, 290, 292
Minneapolis Blue Stockings 48, 49, 50
Minneapolis Northwestern League Club (1884) 92–93, 98, 99, 105; (1886–87) 123, 131
Minneapolis Times: claims Brewers throw games 241; unkind to of Glenalvin 240

Minneapolis Western Association Club (1888) 140, 141, 142–143, 148, 149; (1889) 152, 159; (1890) 167, 171, 174; (1891) 177, 182, 183, 185
Minneapolis Western League Club (1892) 195, 196, 199; (1894) 205, 208, 209, 215, 216; (1895) 220, 226, 228; (1896) 233–234, 242; (1897) 245, 249, 254, 255; (1898) 256, 261, 263, 265; (1899) 270, 273
Mitchell, T.L. 9
Mitchell Heights 95
Monitor Baseball Club 14, 17, 25, 32, 34
Moore, E.M. 9
Moore, Earl 300
Moore, Richard M. 129
Moran, Bill 208, 227
Moran, Dennis 85
Moran, E. 17
Morgan, Daniel "Pidge" 47, 49, 50, 54, 64, 335
Morgan (James) Club 81, 120, 121, 200, 202–203, 230–232, 235
Moriarity (local player) 163
Morris, Peter 87, 88, 95, 99, 119
Morrison, Mike 159
Morrissey, John 99
Morrissey, Tom 93, 99, 100, 101, 104, 105, 114, 119, 132, 134, 135, 139, 142, 153–154, 157, 168, 170, 178
Morse, J.C. 237
Morton, Samuel 92, 130, 131, 135, 140, 148, 150, 152, 154, 158, 166, 171, 174, 193, 195
Morton (George) cigar store 54
Moynahan (Davenport player) 70
Moynahan, Mike 102, 104, 107
Mrzena, Edward 236, 238, 239, 241, 339
Muffin Baseball Club 14
Munch (local amateur player) 275
Munson, George 307
Munzinger Baseball Club 275
Murphy (1889 player from Chicago) 156
Murphy (Athletic Park groundskeeper) 194, 197
Murphy, Con 195, 196
Murphy, James 247
Murphy, Thomas 226, 233
Murphy, Will 98, 99, 104
Muscles of Randolph 21
Musgrove, Frank 129
Muskegon club (1884 Northwestern League) 92–93, 99, 105
Mutual Baseball Club of Milwaukee (1873) 33, 44
Myers, Al 107, 109, 114

Nagle, Tom 203
Nash, James 153
Nashville Western League 112

National Association (proposed 1901 league) 289–290
National Association of Base Ball Players 4, 5, 6, 11, 15, 18, 21, 29
National Association of Professional Baseball Players 31–32, 33
National Board of Arbitration 113, 141, 151, 167, 168–169, 233, 245, 246–247, 248, 249, 259, 262, 268, 269
National Cycling Association 203
National League 53–54, 67, 68, 70–71, 79, 106, 109–111, 116, 121, 130, 158, 167, 176–177, 188–190, 193, 198–199, 205, 218–220, 234, 237, 239, 245–247, 258–259, 266, 267–269, 277–281, 288–293, 295–296, 300, 301; local attempts to join 72, 82–83, 118, 121–123, 201, 204, 207, 216, 218; 1901 attendance 302
National Military Asylum 24
National Park 90, 136, 164, 203, 219, 224, 231
Nationals Baseball Club 135–136
Navin, Frank 281
Neff, J.W. 54
Nelson (1889 player from Southern League) 156
New England League 167, 237
New Haven Baseball Club 168–169, 262, 271
New York Metropolitans 83; American Association club 217
New York State League 282
Newhall House 13
Newkirk, John 244, 247, 251
Newman, Charlie 155, 208, 214
Nicholas, Charles "Kid" 204
Nicol, George 211, 225, 227, 229, 236, 238, 241, 242, 244, 248, 252, 254, 255, 260, 261, 262, 264, 265, 267, 271, 272, 273, 282, 283
Niles, Bill 227, 228, 229, 236
Nimick, W.A. 218
Nolan, Edward "The Only" 50, 59, 64, 66
Nonamaker, John 236, 239, 241, 242
Nonparallel Baseball Club 21
Norris, Charles 17, 45, 46
North, Charles 102
Northern Wisconsin League 274
Northrop, H.M. 68
Northwestern Baseball League (1882) 84; (1884) 92, 94, 97, 99, 104–105; (1886) 123–128; (1887) 130–135, 136–139, 140; 1893 attempt revival 201
Northwestern Mutual Life Insurance Company 120–121, 164, 180, 228, 230, 231
Nunnemacher, Robert 82

Oak Creek Baseball Club 35, 162
Oak Creek Pioneer Baseball Club 32
Oberly (local pitcher) 162
O'Brien, Billy 127
O'Brien, Joseph 289, 292
O'Brien, M.J. 257
O'Brien, Tom 244
Occidental Baseball Club of Quincy, Ill. 29, 31
O'Connors, Hugh 85
Oconomowoc Baseball Club 201
Oconomowoc Brown Stockings 74
Oconto Clippers 162
O'Donnell (1889 player from Minneapolis) 155
O'Donnell, William 124, 126
Old Settler's Club 3
Oliver, Edwin 37, 120
Omaha Bee 172
Omaha Western Association Club (1888) 140, 142, 148, 150; (1889) 151, 155, 159; (1890) 166, 174; (1891) 181, 182–183, 185
Omaha Western League club (1885) 112, 116; (1892) 195, 198, 199; (1896 attempt) 233, 239; (1898) 256, 257, 261, 263
O'Rourke (1900 player from Marquette College) 284
O'Rourke, Jim 71
O'Rourke, Tom 278
Oshkosh Amateur Club 37, 41, 43, 162
Oshkosh Club of Wisconsin-Michigan League 199
Oshkosh Northwestern League Club 123, 125, 129, 131, 138, 139
Otto, Henry 274
Otto Brothers Baseball Club 231–232, 250, 274–275
Outcalf, James 236, 238, 239
Oxford Baseball Club 34, 35

Pabor, Charles 20
Pabst, Ed 194
Pabst, Gustav 230
Pabst Brewing Company 188, 208, 275
Pacific Baseball Club 25
Pacific Coast League 240
Pacific Slope Champions of San Francisco 41
Page Fence Giants 238, 250
Palmer Potter Club of Chicago 28
Pappalau, John 254, 255, 260, 261, 262, 265
Parker, Frank 87, 129, 163, 165
Parker, J.E. 162
Parks, J. 129
Pastime Baseball Club of Milwaukee 73
Patterson, Frank 303
Patterson, James 3
Pearce, Dickey 18
Peavy, James F. 158
Pennsylvania & Ohio Coal Co. 256

Pennsylvania League 237
Peoria Baseball Club 67
Peoria Northwestern League Club 92, 99, 104
Peters, John 57, 58, 59, 62, 64, 70, 73
Pettee, Pat 142, 146, 148
Pettit, Robert 168–169, 171, 174, 175, 178, 179, 181, 186
Pettit, W.B. 54, 68
Pewaukee Baseball Club 34, 36
Pfeffer, Fred 218, 220, 221, 256–257
Pfister, Chares 114, 175, 186
Phelan, Dick 113, 114, 127
Philadelphia American League Club 289, 290–291, 292, 296, 302, 303
Philadelphia Athletics 40, 47, 48
Philadelphia Phillies 134, 248
Philips, Ed 203
Phillips, E. 17
Phillips, Harry 54
Phillips, Harry K. Cigar and Tobacco store 49, 54
Phoenix Baseball Club 76–77, 78, 80–81, 84, 157, 161, 162–163, 165, 169, 200, 274–275
Pickett, John 123, 124
Piehl, John 223
Pierson, Jno. 5
Pittsburgh Alleghany Club 52
Pittsburgh National League club 227, 234, 236, 247, 248, 261, 279, 282, 284, 285
Planets Baseball Club 120, 163
Plank, Ed 300
Plankinton House 24, 31, 45, 54, 99, 110, 114, 122, 175, 192, 206, 209, 260, 266
Plankinton House Reds 164
Players' League 165–166, 167, 168, 176, 178, 289, 290
players' unions 260, 288–289, 290, 291, 292, 294
Players' Western League 166
Plummer (local player) 13
Polacheck, Charles 188, 193, 195, 198, 206, 235, 247, 259
Police-Fire games 164, 275
pool rooms 235; see also gambling
Poorman, Tommy 152, 153, 154, 168, 170, 171, 178
Pope, Arthur 125, 126
Portage Phoenix Baseball Club 85
Porter, Henry 104, 107, 108, 109, 113, 000
Post Office Alerts 230, 231
Pratt, Tom 18
press area at baseball parks 86
Prestiss, W.A. 5
Princiville (1886 player from Chicago) 126
prize fighting 7, 87
Prochazka, Charles 252
professionalism in baseball 21, 27, 29, 33, 40, 89

Providence Club (National League) 54, 59, 121
Purcell (Milwaukee Whites player) 119
Purdue University 273
Purvis, James 93, 95, 99

Quentas Park 14
Quicksteps Baseball Club 77, 78, 81, 84–86, 88, 89, 104, 118, 120, 121, 129, 136, 200, 230; see also Milwaukee Baseball Club (1885 amateur)
Quin, Catherine 199
Quin, Harry D. 82, 83, 84, 92, 103, 112, 113, 114, 117, 118, 121, 122, 123, 127, 128, 130–131, 135, 150, 154, 165–166, 173, 175, 199, 200, 201, 203–204, 218–220, 221, 222–223, 230, 235, 245, 274, 276–278, 280, 289, 291–292, 293, 295, 303
Quin (H.D.) Baseball Club 230, 231–232, 274
Quincy, Illinois club (1884 Northwestern League) 93, 99, 105
quiot club 7
Quistow (1889 player from Chicago) 156

Racine Athletic Baseball Club 43
Racine Baseball Club 124, 164, 165, 200, 231, 250, 274
Racine College Baseball team 20, 25, 29, 34, 39, 60, 74, 77, 78, 121, 136, 162, 163
Racine Maroons 203
Racine Western Baseball Club 34
railroad strikes, accidents, mishaps 214, 216, 225
Rauschenberger, William 238
Raymer, Fred 282, 283, 284, 294, 295
Raymond, Harry 182
Razalls (H.G.) Baseball Club 231, 232, 238, 274–275
Reach, Alfred J. 248
Reach baseball 217, 279, 297
Reading (Pa.) Baseball Club 273
Reccius, Frank 132, 133, 134
Red Stockings Baseball Club (Milwaukee) 77
Redington, George 10, 11, 12, 14, 15, 16, 19, 23
Redmond, Billy 48, 54, 57, 73, 334
Reedsburg Baseball Club 201
Regulators Baseball Club 135–136
Reidy, Bill 252, 255, 260–261, 262, 265, 267, 271, 273, 282, 283, 287, 295, 296, 299, 301, 302, 306, 307
Reilly, Charles 247
Reltz, Henry 283, 284
Remey, O.E. 231
Remson, John 70

Renwick, James 173, 174, 178
Republican Hotel 230, 245
reserve teams of 1884 94, 98–99, 100, 107
reserving and drafting of players 68, 112, 132, 141, 167, 193, 206, 216, 220, 222, 228–229, 234, 237–238, 247–249, 257–259, 260, 263, 266, 277, 278, 279, 280, 282, 283, 289–290, 292–294
Rettger, George 214–215, 216, 221, 222, 224–225, 227, 229, 236, 241, 242, 244, 247, 248, 252, 255, 258, 260, 261, 262, 265, 267, 271, 273, 282, 283, 287, 295
Riah, John 260, 261, 262, 263, 266
Rice, J. 88
Rice, Thurman "True" 79–80, 81, 87, 88, 89–91
Richardson (1899 player from Austin, Texas) 272, 273
Richter, F.R. 218
Ricker, Frank 202, 274
Rickerson, R. 9, 15
Riley, Charles 155, 156, 203
Riley, Will 231, 235, 275
Rindfleisch, Paul C. 43
Riordon (local player) 9
Roat, Fred 194, 196, 197, 199
Roberts (1884 Northwestern player from Philadelphia) 95, 99, 101, 104
Roberts, William 208, 214
Robinson, Wilbert 276, 290
Robison, Frank 267, 269, 281
Roche, M.J. 131, 135, 166, 170, 173, 174
Rochester International League Club 151, 178, 180
Rockford baseball tournament 11, 12
Rockford Western Association Club 271
Rogers, Charles D. 37
Rogers, John 289, 291
Rogers, Louis 37
Rogers, William P. 35, 37, 46, 49, 54, 55, 56, 57, 66, 68–70
roller skate baseball game 116
Rolling Mills of Bay View Baseball Club 34
Rose Royals Female Club of Denver 203
Roundtree, George H. 164
Roussey, Elmer 134, 137, 138
Rowan, Jack 85
rowdyism and related problems 28, 35, 44–45, 96, 98, 115, 127, 133, 172, 183, 225, 226, 227, 242, 257, 284, 288, 298, 301
Rowe, Davy 47, 48, 50, 152, 154, 158, 170, 173, 177, 195
Rowe, Jack 47
Rucker, E.P. 279
rules of baseball (1860s) 4, 6,

333; (1870s) 61; (1880s) 76; (1890s) 201–202
Rust, J.J. 92, 105

Saginaw Northwestern League Club 92, 99, 105
St. Bonifactus Catholic Church 144
St. John's Academy of Delafield 164, 275
St. Joseph baseball clubs 124, 210–211
St. Joseph Street Railway Co. 263
St. Joseph Western Association Club 152, 158, 159, 166, 167, 251
St. Joseph Western League Club (1898) 263, 265, 267, 268
St. Louis Browns 41, 49, 53, 179
St. Louis National League Club 267, 268–269, 304, 308
St. Louis Western Association Club 140, 142, 146–147
St. Paul club (1884 Northwestern League) 92–93, 99, 109
St. Paul Northwestern League Club (1886–1887) 123, 126, 131, 139
St. Paul Red Caps 36, 40, 41, 42, 48
St. Paul Western Association Club (1888) 140, 142, 145, 148, 150; (1889) 151, 159; (1890) 167, 170, 172–174; (1891) 177, 181
St. Paul Western League Club (1885) 111–112; (1892) 195, 196–197; (1895) 217, 220, 226, 228, 229; (1896) 232, 233, 236, 241, 242; (1897) 245, 249, 255; (1898) 258, 261, 265; (1899) 268, 270, 273, 274, 278
salary limits 130, 154, 155, 192–194, 206, 224, 236, 246, 257, 259, 260, 261, 263, 267, 280, 283, 285
San Jose California League club 229
Sanderson Baseball Club 72
Sands, H. (early Milwaukee player) 3
Sanger, Walter 203
Sasson, William 275
Saulpaugh, C.H. 255, 269, 281, 289
Say, Louis 126, 128
Scanlon, Mike 276, 278
Schaefer, George 276
Scheible, John 211
Schieldt's A.C. hall 138
Schierz, R.W. 77, 89, 93, 94, 99, 119
Schiffler & Quentmeyer of Watertown 200
Schlidknecht, Luke 152, 154
Schloegel, Tony 136, 160, 161
Schmelz, Gus 193, 195, 197, 221, 247
Schnure, Adam 17

Schoeneck, Lewis 109, 114, 117, 118, 119
Schoenhofer Brewing Co. 277
Schomberg, Otto 80, 87, 88, 95, 99, 119, 163, 165, 171, 205–206
Schriver, Bill 178, 180, 181, 184–185, 188, 227, 235
Schuman, R.E. 257, 263
Schwind, Frank 91, 119
scorecards 117, 133, 144, 161, 180, 194, 202, 213, 247, 256, 259, 337
Scrandett, A.K. 218
Seery, M.H. 17
Seniors Baseball Club 275
Sexton, J. 3, 5
Sexton, Pete 136, 163
Sexton, Tom 87, 93, 101, 104, 107, 109, 114, 123, 124, 125, 126
Shannon, Dan 182–183
Sharpe, James "Peck" 213–214, 215, 217, 221, 222, 224, 225, 227, 229, 236
Shaw (pitcher in New England League) 244
Shea, Jack 85
Sheboygan Baseball Club 163, 164, 165, 200, 263, 274
Sheboygan Red Jackets 31
Shenkle, William 132, 137, 139, 142, 146, 147, 148, 152, 153, 154, 155, 156, 157
Sheridan, Jack 301
Sheridan, John 225
Sherman House 230
Shields, Dan 208, 211
Shipperd, J.J. 233
Shoch, George 157, 158, 168, 174, 175, 178, 181, 183, 185, 186, 191, 204, 216, 252, 259, 260, 261, 262, 265, 267, 271, 273
Shortell (1886 player from Chicago) 125
Shreve, Leven 127, 128
Shugart, Frank 298, 301
Silch, Ed 125, 158, 170
Silver Spring Baseball Club 230
Silverstone Baseball Club 129, 135–136
Simonds, C.W. Chan 37, 60
Simonds, Charles 26, 31, 35
Sioux City Western Association Club (1888) 140, 147, 149, 150; (1889) 152, 157–158, 159; (1890) 166, 174; (1891) 177, 179, 182, 185
Sioux City Western League Club (1894) 205, 206, 209, 211, 213, 216, 217, 220; (1900) 284
Sivyer, William 3
Skidmore & Friedlick Baseball Club 231, 232, 275
Sloccum (1886 player) 125, 126
Smith (pitcher from New Orleans) 235
Smith, Alexander 264
Smith, Bert 188
Smith, Charley 18

Smith, Clarence 10, 11, 15, 16, 23, 29
Smith, Elmer 254
Smith, Frank 8, 9, 10, 11, 13, 17
Smith, Fred C. 178, 184
Smith, Harry 272, 282, 283, 287, 294
Smith, Henry 132, 134, 137, 141
Smith, "Hustler Harry" 199
Smith, John "Phenomenal" 180, 182, 184
Smith, Melville 273
Smith Baseball Club 201
Smythe, R.K. 17
Snyder (player in Eastern League) 244
Soden, Arthur 54, 245, 294
Soldier's monument on Grand Avenue 262
Somers & Meagan Co. 144
Somers, Arthur 203
Somers, Charles 281, 289, 292, 295
Somor, A.J. 274
South End Baseball Club 200
South Milwaukee Baseball Club 202–203, 275
Southern League 127, 130, 208, 213, 214, 226, 235, 237
Sowders, Billy 171, 172
Spalding, Albert 12, 29, 32, 39, 41, 47, 50, 71, 82–83, 123, 131–132, 140, 158, 166, 167, 176
Spalding (A.G.) and Brothers of Chicago uniforms 62, 84, 169, 208; baseballs 131, 135, 279
Spanish-American War 260, 266
Sparks, Tully 282, 283, 287, 295, 296, 299, 302, 307
Spear, Giles 70
Speas, John W. 192–193, 195
Speer, George "Kid" 235–236, 238, 241, 244, 247, 248, 252, 255, 260, 261, 265, 266, 270, 271, 272, 282
Spies, Harry 286, 287, 295
Spink, Alfred 276
Sportsman's Park (Milwaukee) 223
spring training 59–60, 99, 115, 124, 133, 144–145, 153–154, 169, 179, 195, 210, 224, 238, 239, 250, 260, 261, 270, 283, 297
Springfield (Mass.) Baseball Club 64, 67
Stadler, Lester C. 180, 185, 186, 189
Stafford, Robert 213, 226, 227, 234, 236, 238, 241, 242, 244, 247, 249, 250–251, 254, 255, 258, 260, 261, 265, 266, 267, 271, 272, 273, 282, 283
Stallings, George 276, 281
Stapleton, William 43
Star Baseball Club 14, 21, 25, 26, 27, 30–31, 32, 34
Starlight Baseball Club 230
Starring, James 208
Start, Joe 18, 71

Stearns, Fred 205
Steele, C. 3
Steever, J.G. 17
Steinfeldt, Harry 248
Stellberger, William 132, 133, 134
Stephens, George 145, 148, 211, 216, 221–222, 227, 229, 236
Stevens, Benny 135
Stevens, Harry 247
Stewart, Asa 224
Stillwater Northwestern League Club 92–93, 99, 104
Stockwell, Len 115, 117, 118
Stollenwerk, Anton 129
Stone, Percy 37, 41, 59
Stone, William 230
Straub, Joe 89, 93, 101–105, 119
Strauss, Joe 132, 134, 135, 138, 142, 145, 148, 152, 171
street car companies 11, 19, 24, 44, 95, 97, 105, 122, 143–144, 194, 219, 223, 233, 252, 278; strike 232, 239
Struck, John 142, 147
Sullivan (Amherst College catcher) 102
Sullivan, Denny 87, 88
Sullivan, John 70, 72
Sullivan, Pat 87, 102, 124, 125, 126, 136, 162, 203
Sullivan, Ted 21, 26, 39, 111, 113, 116, 123–128, 130–131
Summers, William 221, 222, 224
Sunday baseball 35, 53, 73, 74, 93, 102, 105, 112, 116, 119, 121, 123, 142, 144, 152, 163, 176, 187, 189, 190, 196, 206, 213, 225, 226, 233, 239, 249, 252, 257, 267, 271, 272–273, 294, 304
Sutton, Erza 151, 153–154, 157, 167
Swaim, Cy 266–267, 270, 271, 273
Sweeney, James 127, 129, 136, 165
Sweet, George O. 9, 10, 11
Swinburne (local player) 129
Sylvester, Lous 137
Syracuse Eastern League Club 286
Syracuse Stars 48, 49, 76

Taintor, W. 35
Tanner, Albert F. 92, 113, 114
Taylor, Billy 126
Taylor, Harry 293
Taylor, John 244, 247, 253, 254, 255, 260, 261, 265, 266
Taylor, Wally 214, 215–216, 217, 221, 222, 224, 227, 229, 236, 238, 240, 241, 244, 247
Tebeau, George 222, 278
Terre Haute Northwestern League Club 92, 99, 104
Terre Haute Western League Club 226, 228, 232–234
Terry, William "Adonis" 251, 252, 253, 255, 260, 261, 262, 265, 266; pitch only at home in contract 260
Teutonia Baseball Club 14
Theirs (West End player) 40

Third Ward Baseball League 275
Thornton, John 168, 170, 174, 175, 178; pitches no-hitter 171
Three-I League 301
Tiffany, George C. 3
Timlin (local umpire) 90
Tinker, T.C. 17
Tinker, Zach 305–306
Tisdale, W.G. 5
Tobey, C.H.M. 70
Toledo Western League club (1885) 111, 116; (1892) 195, 196, 197, 199; (1894) 205, 209, 212, 215, 216; (1895) 220, 226, 233–234
Toole, James 95, 99
Toronto Baseball Club 168; proposed Western League franchise 267–268, 269
Trapshuh, C. 17
Travers, Frank 37
Troop A First Cavalry of Milwaukee 278
Troy (National League) Baseball Club 79
Truby, Harry 221
Tunis & Company 21
Turner, W.J. 47, 60
Twineham, Arthur 208
Twitchell, Larry 194, 199, 214, 217, 221–222, 224–225, 227, 229, 234, 235–236, 238–241, 242, 243; asked to lose games 240

umpires 76, 89, 118, 135, 142, 152, 169, 196, 251, 257, 275; National League 60–61, 62, 65, 66, 257; American League 300–301
Union Association 94, 105–110, 111, 336
Union Baseball Club 14, 34, 129, 230, 231
Union Club of Morrisana, New York 20
United Association of Baseball Clubs 192
United States Department of Treasury 21
University of Michigan Baseball Club 270
University of Wisconsin 78, 133, 206, 250, 271–272

Van Brunt, W.T. 263
Vance, David 70
Van der Beck, George 207, 209, 213, 215, 217, 220, 223–224, 233, 237, 243, 245, 249, 269, 277, 281
Van Dyke, Douglas 26, 35, 120
Van Haltren, George 132
Vanvalkenburg, F. 5
Vaughn, Harry 184, 188, 189, 191
Vickery, Tom 178, 181, 184–185, 188, pitches no-hitter 179–180
Vieau, Paul 3
Viox, Rooney 272, 273, 282

Virginia League 235
Vogel (H.W.) of Watertown 165
Voigt, David Quentin 55
Vollendorf, Adolphus 259, 261, 262, 266, 267
Von der Ahe, Chris 122, 140, 147, 153, 167, 184, 189–190, 247, 259, 268–269, 271, 276, 277, 293
Vose, Hamilton 40, 41, 46

Waco Texas League Club 157
Waddell, George "Rube" 285–286, 287; burns hands in Pewaukee 285
wages of non-baseball workers 56, 142
Waldo, Robert 26, 35, 40
Waldron, Erving 244, 247, 248, 251, 258, 260, 261, 265, 266, 267, 271, 273, 282, 283, 287, 294, 296, 298, 299
Wallschlager, Ed 203
Walsh, J.W. 126
Walsh, Joe 148, 152, 153, 212–213, 217
Walthers, George 144, 159
Ward, Frank 194, 197, 199, 208, 212
Ward, John Montgomery 71, 166
Warner, Edward 142, 148
Washington American League Club 289–290, 292, 296, 302, 303, 304
Washington Nationals 14, 15, 67
Washington Senators (National League) 226, 227, 228, 241, 249, 261, 262, 268, 279, 281
Watertown Baseball Club 200
Watkins, William 113, 131, 213, 232, 278–279, 281, 289, 291, 300
Watson, H.P. 233, 245
Waukesha Baseball Club 200
Waukesha White Stockings 74
Wausau Baseball Club 201
Weaver, Sam 47, 50, 51, 54, 57, 60, 62, 63, 65, 69, 70, 71, 72–73, 83; pitches no-hitter 335
Weaver, William 222, 224, 227, 229, 236, 238, 240, 241, 242, 244, 247, 248, 251, 255, 260, 261, 262, 265, 267, 273, 282, 283
Wehr, Henry J. 206
Weil, Benjamin 187
Welch, Patrick 168, 178
Welcome Baseball Club 81, 118–119, 120, 129, 135–136, 160–162
Weldenferrie, C.A. 185
Welles, E. Clinton 15, 17, 23
Wells, Frank 152–154, 155
Werden, Perry 225
Wescott, W.S. 16
Wessling (local player) 125
West, F.K. 37
West, H.H. 5, 8, 9, 10, 35
West End Baseball Club amateur

club 35–36; professional club 36–52, 57, 76; uniforms 52
West End Juniors 230
West End Park (28th and Wells) 36, 37, 44, 45, 49
West End Park (34th and State) 48–49
West Milwaukee Baseball Club 200
West Milwaukee Shops Club 164
West Side Turner Hall 91, 230
Western Association (1888) 140–142, 145–150; (1889) 151–152, 154–155, 159; (1890) 165–167, 169–174; (1891) 176–179, 181–185, 188; (1896) 233, 237; (1898) 256, 261, 263; (1899) 271; (1901) 291
Western Baseball Club 34
Western League (1885) 111–117; (proposed 1887) 130; (1892) 192–194, 195–199; (1893) 201, 205; (1894) 205–209, 213, 215, 216–217; (1895) 217–220, 223, 226; (1896) 232–234, 237, 242–243; (1897) 245, 248–249, 255; (1898) 256–257, 258–259, 260, 263, 265–266; (1899) 267–270, 274, 276, 277; (1901) 291, 299
Western Star (Janesville) Baseball Club 18
Western Union 96
Westlake, Robert L. 168, 173, 178
Wetterer, Bill 236, 238, 239, 244, 247, 249, 250
Whaling, J.A. 17
Wheeler, George 282–283, 284, 287
Wheelock, Bobby 153, 213
Whitcomb, (Cream City player) 9
White, Jim "Deacon" 63

White, John 241, 244, 247
White, Will 63–64
White Diamonds Baseball Club 275
Whitefish Bay Railroad Company 143
Whitewater Baseball Club 13, 16, 18, 165
Whitmore (President of Quincy Baseball Club) 105
Whitney, Art 109, 114
Whitrock, Bill 212, 214
Wide Awakes of Menomonee Falls 26, 30
Widner, William 195, 198, 210
Wiesner, Mrs. Edward 3
Williams (1886 player) 125, 126
Williams, George 218, 220
Williams, James A. 194–196, 197–199, 217
Williams, Owen 132, 134, 142
Williams, Tom 208, 211
Wilmington Union Association Club 107
Wilmot, Walter 220, 234, 293
Wilson, Bert 148, 152
Winkleman, George 148, 152, 153
Winona Baseball Club (1884) 105
Winona Clippers 41
Winters (pitcher from Kalamazoo) 102
Wisconsin Base Ball Club 4
Wisconsin Central Railroad 117, 130, 133, 150, 180, 264
Wisconsin-Michigan League 199
Wisconsin State Agricultural Society 31, 133
Wisconsin State Baseball Association 16, 17–18, 23, 25, 30, 120, 128, 164
Wisconsin State Baseball Tournament 16

Wisconsin State Fair grounds 31
Wisconsin State League 200, 274, 298
Wise (local player) 162, 163
Wissing (local player) 127
Wolf, William 235, 258, 260
Wood, James 9, 14, 15, 17, 23, 28
Wright, B.F. 303
Wright, George 20, 24, 71
Wright, Harry 24, 53, 58, 67, 71, 102, 217
Wright, Joe 248–249, 251, 252, 253
Wright, Samuel 195, 198
Wright Street Park 95–97, 98, 107, 117, 120, 123, 127, 128, 131, 133, 143–144, 160, 162, 219, 222, 336

Yaeger, George 282, 283, 284
Yankee Champion Baseball Club 34
Yewdales Baseball Club 164
Yohn, C.G. 48
Young, Cy 295
Young, Douglas 87, 88, 119, 120, 126, 129, 136, 162, 163
Young, Nicholas E. 54, 118, 157, 168, 178, 182, 183, 218, 245, 247, 261, 288, 290
Young America Cricket Club 75
Young Chicago Baseball Club 34
Young Ladies Baseball Club of Chicago 163
Young Maple Leafs 74

Zettlein, George 18
Ziegler, George 92, 98, 113, 114, 186, 195
Ziegler Baseball Club 230–232
Zimmer, Charles 289, 293

www.ingramcontent.com/pod-product-compliance
Lightning Source LLC
Chambersburg PA
CBHW081536300426
44116CB00015B/2654